THE BRAINSTEM BRAINWAVES OF *ATMAN-BRAHMAN*

THE BRAINSTEM BRAINWAVES OF *ATMAN-BRAHMAN*

The Synthesis of Science and Spirituality

(In Two Volumes)

(Volume 2)

Sutapas Bhattacharya

GYAN

ISBN : 978-81-212-1221-2 (Set)

ISBN : 978-81-212-1283-0 (Vol. 2)
Price : Set (₹ 1850)
Price : Set (₹ 1850) Price : Volume 2 (₹ 925)

First Published, 2015

Published by

Gyan Publishing House
23, Main Ansari Road, Darya Ganj
New Delhi-110002
Ph. : 23242060, 23261060
Fax : 011-23285914
E-mail: books@gyanbooks.com
Website : www.gyanbooks.com

Laser Typesetting : Gyan Prints (AB-II), Delhi
Printed at : G. Print Process, Delhi

Cataloging in Publication Data—DK
Courtesy: D.K. Agencies (P) Ltd. <docinfo@dkagencies.com>

Bhattacharya, Sutapas, 1964-
The brainstem brainwaves of Atman-Brahman : the synthesis of science and spirituality / Sutapas Bhattacharya.
2 v. cm.
Includes bibliographical references and index.
ISBN 9788121212212

1. Âtman. 2. Brahman. 3. Science and spiritualism.
I. Title.

DDC 201.65 23

Contents

VOLUME 2

Part Two

THE ONE TRUE ONTOLOGY

Part Three

MY PATH TO THE LIGHT

Part Two

The One True Ontology

9

Advaita Vedanta as the Universal Spirituality and *Sanatana Dharma* as the True Ontology

Ekam sat vipra bahudha vadanti [Rig Veda 1.164.46]
(That which exists is One, sages call it by various names)

Universalisation of *Sanatana Dharma* by Ramakrishna as 'Unity of Faiths'

Projection of Deities onto the Light of Godhead

We find in the above testimony from 1932 of mathematical physicist and mystic, J.H.M. Whiteman, descriptions of Enlightenment familiar not only to those versed in perennial mystical philosophy but also to those who have read the popular books describing the Near-Death Experiences (NDEs) of ordinary people which proliferated especially in the 1990s. Michael Grosso states correctly that, although many Western "NDErs" report visions of 'Christ', (i.e., imagined forms of Jesus[N1]); often they actually see a Pure Light without form. The 'Christ-form' is usually projected onto this Pure Light[1]. The word *projection* is extremely apt in this regard as the physical correlates of such projection presumably involve superimposition of brainwaves. We have already encountered the Vedantic concept of mutual superimposition (*adhyasa*) with the Inner Light of Pure Consciousness in the construction of the world of sense-perceptions.

In a recent book about spiritual healing, Diane Goldner writes that surrender is essential to healing, the constant giving over of one's self to the Divine Light or God. Healing is a return to the Divine Light within us[2]. This Western notion of 'Surrender' is closely related to the Yogic 'letting go' which Carl Jung felt that Westerners were too afraid of so that Yoga was an inappropriate practise for them. This 'letting go' is releasing the grip of the ego mind with which we are all so familiar that we can hardly contemplate its disappearance. Yet the French call the sexual orgasm *petit mort* ('little death') as there is a phenomenological recognition here that orgasm involves a loosening of the ego boundaries or even a momentary ego dissolution experience which is similar to the ego dissolution of Nature mystics which occurs in the normal waking state. People can 'pass out' during an intense orgasm. John White states that the yogic death experience is literally *ecstatic* as the etymology of this word derives from *ex* (out of) and *stasis* (static condition). Ecstasy, he says, is the ancient term for the out-of-body experience or Astral Projection, the (Shamanic) flight of the soul[3].

Indeed, the famous positive descriptions of the *Atman-Brahman* (the impersonal Deeper Self that is within us all yet is also one with the macrocosmic Godhead) is that it is *Satchitananda*; Pure Being (*Sat*), Pure Consciousness (*cit* or *chit*), and Divine Bliss (*ananda*). This Bliss which, as we shall see, naïve Materialists try to reduce to merely opiate release, etc., in the brain, refers, not to simple heightened pleasure but to the release and freedom from worldly attachments (limitations, desires, anxieties, fears etc.) that comes with the loss of individuated existence and participation in the Divine. In this eternal (atemporal) Oneness (*nirguna Brahman*), Death has no meaning, for that which is Unborn and Uncreated (the Divine) is beyond the flux of creation and dissolution. Merrell-Wolff refers to the impersonal Divine Consciousness as the flow of the joy-giving force-field and recognises that, as in Vedanta, the Bliss aspect has to do with freedom from worldly attachment[4]. His description of the Plenum/Void, as we have seen, also parallels Vedantic knowledge.

My Retreat-to-the-Brainstem interpretation of Enlightenment accounts for such a sense of freedom from 'worldly attachments'. The individuated (egoic) consciousness withdraws from the cerebral cortex (dissipating and reconstituting in subtler form in deeper structures). This involves withdrawal from the neural network patterns that constitute our personal habits and world-modelling structures that 'clothe' the 'naked' core ego; hence the myth that we 'go naked before God'. The ego is 'stripped' of attachments constituting the so-called 'sheaths' (*kosa*) which surround the basic ego like layers of an onion. Deikman's notion of 'De-automatisation' of habitual modes of perception may be of some relevance here[5]. But such 'De-automatisation' wherein each percept seems as if it is being perceived for the very first time is more relevant to meditative practises which do not empty the mind of content. The Path to Enlightenment, *Raja Yoga*, involves the 'purification of Consciousness' or removal of objective superimpositions by suspending perceptions and other cognitive activity. Grosso's clarification of supposed experiences of Jesus by Western NDErs indoctrinated into Christian culture actually confirms the partial validity of the Constructivist thesis that mystical experiences are culturally-indoctrinated. However, the Constructivists argue that all mystical experiences are merely imaginary or hallucinations whereas the projection of the Jesus-image onto the Pure Light again underlines the universality and centrality of the Divine Light as the common, underlying universal core of all mystical traditions.

In Hindu philosophy, the form projected by the mind onto the Light or Godhead is known as the *Ishta Devata*, the Chosen Deity. Contrary to the patriarchal mythology of Christianity and Islam, any image, not only anthropomorphic ones, can perform this function of representing the Godhead. Thus the Brahmins of Bengal often worship the Goddess Durga or the

Vaisnavite (Vishnu-related) *avatar* (incarnation) Krishna. The Nondual Tantric Kashmir Saivism (Siva worship) is associated primarily with the Kashmiri Brahman Abhinavagupta. In O/OM I told of how a few days before I identified the physical correlate of the Inner Divine Light, I had a numinous experience with rays of sunlight shimmering on my ceiling as I lay half-asleep one morning. As I was mesmerised by the light shimmering above me, my Inner Voice said to me ,"Howsoever you shall conceive Me, in that form shall I appear".[N2] The philosophically trained mystic can withdraw his mental projections and describe things as they actually are. The great "god-intoxicated" Bengali mystic of the 19th Century *c.e.*, Ramakrishna attained the title Great Swan (*Paramahamsa*) as he became adept at floating in the Glory of the Divine Light. This metaphor of floating like a swan (or a lotus) resembles Whiteman's 1932 description quoted at the end of the previous chapter of the 'soul' being held aloft as if in the air. Ramakrishna meditated upon the major icons of the world's great religions and found that these icons were all symbols which, in a yogic master like himself, quickly triggered deepest *samadhi* (meditative absorption) filled with the Divine Light of Pure Consciousness.

The religious icons were but mythological symbols which various cultures had projected upon this Divinity within, just as 'Hinduism' allows people to represent the Divine in all manner of images according to local traditions and customs. Coming from Bengal, famous for its Tantric tradition emphasising the feminine *Shakti* energy aspect of the Divine, Ramakrishna himself worshipped Durga, the Bengali form of the Cult of the Great Mother, celebrated in the famous Durga Puja festivals of Bengal.[N3] The reader may recognise that the effect of the icons upon the yogic master Ramakrishna resembles the dream of the Dance of Siva experienced by Wolfgang Pauli in Bombay as an 'archetypal image' of the underlying archetype constituted of rhythmic patterns of (subtle energetic) activity. Although Odajnyk[N4] stressed that Jung understood archetypes as the primordial patterns of manifestation, Jung's concept of archetypes started off as Kantian *a priori* structures or inherited patterns of collective, racial memory. Jung's concept developed later into the mythological motifs of his so-called 'Collective Unconscious' before developing further into notions of a Psychoid Realm (resembling the *Akasa*) and the equivalence of archetypes with karmic impressions (*samskara*). The major religious icons upon which Ramakrishna meditated thus correspond to such mythological motifs or collective, cultural images representing deeper structures in the human psyche.

Ramakrishna's Doctrine of the Unity of Faiths as Universalisation of Traditional Hindu Inclusivism

This led Ramakrishna to pronounce his doctrine of the Unity of Faiths, the underlying common Truth which is the goal of all spiritual paths. Indeed, whilst this concept of the common Truth to which various spiritual paths lead is very recent in Western European and Middle Eastern theological debate, Ramakrishna's 19th Century doctrine which preceded contemporary Western notions was following the age old Brahmanic "Hindu" doctrine of the *Sanatana Dharma* (the Eternal Truth). I disapprove of the use of "Faiths" as yogic mysticism is based on phenomenological evidence, not the blind faith of Semitic religions. All the various spiritual viewpoints in India's panoply of cults and pantheon of deities were merely different expressions of the one underlying Divine Reality. The various philosophical schools in India argued with each other over details but they realised that they were all attempting to describe the same Ultimate Reality. Thus one finds variants of the famous saying that there are as many Hindu gods as there are Hindus as each person conceives or imagines God in his own way (e.g., the old claim that there are 300 million Hindu deities). The famous historical Unity in Diversity or the 'Idea of India' as a unity is a reflection of this *Inclusivism* (and *Pluralism*) of the 'Hindu' tradition. This understanding of the elite Brahmanical 'Great Tradition' reflected the famous Vedic saying that *Truth is One* though sages call it by many names.

In the 1660s Francois Bernier, became physician to the Mohammedan zealot Mughal Aurangzeb who had killed his half-brother, the mystically-inclined prince Dara Shukoh, and usurped the Peacock Throne. The latter had commissioned a Persian translation of the Upanishads. As with the later British Indologists, Bernier sought the 'real India'; Hindu India, behind the façade of Muslim conquered Northern India. Thus Bernier exchanged lessons in Western medicine and metaphysics to a court official, with whom he became intimate friends, for knowledge of Brahmanic philosophy. It was the Brahman pandit of Dara Shukoh who provided Bernier with the Persian translation of the Upanishads which Bernier brought back to Paris. This Persian translation was later translated into French (the *Oupnekhat*) making the translator Anquetil Duperron famous[6]. Bernier noted that, unlike most Christian clergymen, the Brahman pundits did not claim that their laws applied to everyone or that Christianity was false. The Brahmans said that there were many paths to heaven and they could not comprehend (the bigoted) Christian claims that Christianity was the one true path for the whole world whereas Hinduism was only fable and invention[7].

Not only did the Brahmanical tradition absorb the countless local traditions of the Indian subcontinent where each village has its own deity, under its unifying umbrella. We have seen that, in contrast to the religious bigotry of the Middle East and the West, Hindu India had for millennia been a land free from religious persecution and sectarian violence. The early French Indologists even named the Indian Tradition 'Tolerationism'[8]. India has provided sanctuary for religious communities fleeing persecution elsewhere for at least two and a half thousand years. Members of the Judean elite who were exiled to Babylon by Nebuchadnazzer came to India's Malabar Coast where they were allowed to practise freely. Many Jewish writers have sung the praises of India as the land where Jews have been allowed to live and prosper without persecution or discrimination by the majority community for 2,700 years. When in the 4th Century *c.e.* the Sassanid Emperor of Persia began a persecution of Christians, a number of Bishops and clergy fled to the tolerant Hindu Rajas on the West coast of India[9]. Faced with Mohammedan persecution, followers of the native Zoroastrian tradition found sanctuary and economic success in India where they are known as the Parsees. In more recent years India has become the sanctuary for the native Buddhist Tibetans fleeing the brutal occupation of their homeland by the Communist Chinese imperialists.

Buddhism, which for a thousand years after Asoka was pre-eminent in India, is viewed as but an unorthodox form of the *Sanatana Dharma*. I have mentioned the peaceful Brahmanism versus Buddhism debates of Buddha and Sankara (who lived about 1400 years apart). Pratima Bowes says that Sankara's *Advaita Vedanta* was itself heavily influenced by the Yogacara school of Mahayana Buddhism[10]. Aurobindo Ghose wrote that Sankara had synthesised positive aspects of Buddhism with Brahmanism thus doing away with the Buddhist's *raison d'être*. Merrell-Wolff argued, along similar lines to my own Bigger, Deeper Picture view in O/OM, in favour of the criterion of *more comprehensive insight*. The more comprehensive insight of one mystic is capable of revealing the lesser insight of another mystic to have only partial validity within limits. He says that Aurobindo's more comprehensive insights show the partial validity of William James[11]. Merrell-Wolff, like Michael Whiteman, understood Buddhism as being a partial view relative to the more comprehensive Nondual Brahmanism.

This reflects the deeper, more comprehensive insight of the later Mahayana (Greater Vehicle) Buddhists correcting some of the limitations of original Buddhism. The Kashmiri Saivites attacked Sankara's *Maya* doctrine of Creation as tacit dualism as they knew that Sankara's *Brahman* was the Vedantins' term equivalent to their Supreme Siva. The famous *Yoga Sutras* of Patanjali, the greatest yogic texts in the Hindu tradition, are not understandable without knowledge of Buddhism[12]; Whiteman notes that they utilise a Buddhist-hybrid Sanskrit. The *Sankhya* metaphysics, with its Spirit/Nature dualism which is usually projected by scholars onto the *Yoga Sutras*, only appeared 600 years after the *Yoga Sutras*[13]. Vivekananda asserted that Mahayana Buddhism was 'crypto-Brahmanism'[14]. As stated, Mahayana (Greater Vehicle) Buddhists corrected some of the limitations of original Buddhism. The most developed form of Tibetan Tantric Buddhism, *Dzogschen* (implying 'Super-completeness'[15]), has both an Inner Light and a Universal Ground Consciousness. These are essentially the same as the Vedantic *Atman* and *Brahman* (which Siddharta Gautama supposedly denied) but using new names for these old insights.

We have seen that the Dalai Lama has stated that he liked Fred Travis's Junction Point model of the Pure Consciousness as the background state of the cerebral cortex. This ties in, says the Dalai Lama with Buddhist knowledge of the Clear Light[16]. Herbert Guenther, an expert on Buddhism has stated that *Sunyata* is the *background field behind perception* (*emphasis mine* {*e.m.*})[17]. This again fits my RAS-brainwave correlation as these activating brainwaves generate the background field for the entire brain, including the cerebral cortex. Of course, having identified the physical process correlated directly with the Inner Light with a brain process which fits perfectly both Hindu and Buddhist knowledge of the Inner Light (*see Appendix*), such questions of underlying commonality are now beyond dispute for the impartial enquirer who is guided only by the facts rather than dogma.

However, in his so-called 'neurophenomenological' brain dynamics model[18, 19], repeated by his protégé Evan Thompson as the centrepiece of his

Mind in Life[20], Varela and Thompson ignored Buddhist knowledge using only Husserl's phenomenology. Even then, Husserl's clear distinction of the Flow of the Absolute Consciousness (or Stream of Consciousness) from the ego is ignored so that Husserl's disclosures may appear to conform to their preconceived, vague Emergent Materialist view of Mind (supposedly) appearing in living cell-like 'autopoietic' systems[N5 21]. Varela and Thompson reduce the Stream to the continuous dynamic nature of egoic mentation when both Husserl and Buddhists insist that, unlike the egoic mind, the Stream of Consciousness is unceasing. As Buddhists and Hindus know, it continues even in seemingly unconscious states, primarily that of Deep Sleep (as of course do the activating brainstem brainwaves of the RAS). In *Buddhism and Science* it is reported that the Dalai Lama has stated that, unlike the Waking and the Dreaming states, the (mind) moments of the Clear Light do not start and stop cyclically but are unceasing[22].

The appearance of the god-intoxicated mystic Ramakrishna created a sensation in 19th Century Calcutta, capital of the British-occupied India until 1911. Ramakrishna's presence was central to the Hindu Revival at a time when educated Bengali Hindus were becoming Westernised and denouncing their own indigenous culture during the so-called Bengal Renaissance which laid the foundations of modern India's elite national culture. In 1893, Ramakrishna's apostle Vivekananda became the *cause célèbre* of the World Parliament of Religions held at the Chicago World Fair. The Anglican Church refused to participate in the 1893 World Parliament on the grounds that it implied an unacceptable equality of faiths[23]. Not that Vedanta is actually a 'Faith' but a philosophy. However, the liberal New Englanders associated with the American Transcendentalists such as Emerson and Thoreau (themselves inspired by Brahmanism) made Vivekananda a celebrity in their circles and he was even offered Chairs at Harvard and Columbia Universities (an amazing thing for a non-white in those days).[N6] We have seen in Chapter 8 that Vivekananda had a profound effect on William James and this association influenced deeply James seminal work *Varieties of Religious Experience*.

Doniger's Freudian Disciples Project Personal Sexual Hang-ups onto Hindu 'Other'

Kripal Projects Catholic Paedophilia onto Ramakrishna and Presents Vedantic Yoga as Vows

We saw in Chapter 7 that the so-called 'Queen of Hinduism Studies' in the USA, Wendy Doniger (*a.k.a.* W. Doniger O'Flaherty) has made her name by peddling racy books full of sexual content given her Freudian misrepresentations of Hinduism. We saw that distinguished Sanskrit scholars have mocked her inaccurate and very misleading translations of Hindu texts. Under Doniger's guidance at Chicago University, Jeffrey Kripal undertook his PhD on Ramakrishna. Kripal spent time at the Ramakrishna Mission in West Bengal but did not let them see his manuscript prior to publication. Kripal's Ph.D. research was presented in a book entitled *Kali's Child.* This book won the First Book Award from the American Academy of Religion (AAR), an organisation in which Doniger and her colleagues hold powerful positions.

None of the AAR committee who glorified Kripal's book was fluent in Bengali. This success landed Kripal a position at Harvard followed by a prestigious Chair at Rice University[24]. Kripal is also associated with the (New Age) Esalen Institute. In his anti-Perennialist conclusions to *The Presence of Light*, Kapstein states, "Ramakrishna's disciples, as we know, took great care to clean up his act"[25]. The reference given here is to Kripal's *Kali's Child*. The influential *Encyclopedia Britannica* even listed Kripal's book as the top choice for further reading about Ramakrishna[26].

The Ramakrishna Mission's Swami Tyagananda and other Bengali scholars who had extensive discussions with Kripal are certain that Kripal simply doesn't know the Bengali language even though he claims to have read the Bengali documents he cited. When spoken to in Bengali about Bengali culture, Kripal did not understand and could not respond. Coming from the Bengali *bhadralok* intelligentsia myself, having been brought up with pictures of Ramakrishna, his wife and Vivekananda in our sitting room and my mother's bedroom, this Freudian distortion of Ramakrishna 'hits home'. Tyagananda stated[27]:

> *Kripal's conclusions come via faulty translations, a wilful distortion and manipulation of sources, combined with a remarkable ignorance of Bengali culture. ...Kripal's ignorance of Bengali culture jumps right off the page. ... [Furthermore,] it's painfully clear that he also has little knowledge of Sanskrit.*

As Pandita Indrani Rampersad states, Kripal asserts that his 'sexy, seedy and strange' interpretation of Tantra is authentic. Kripal mistranslated Bengali words such as those for *lap, head* and *touching softly* to the English, 'genitals, phallus and sodomy', respectively to present Ramakrishna as a homosexual paedophile rather than a true mystic. Tyagananda stated that Kripal may be at his most laughable when he writes that Ramakrishna's practice of Vedanta consisted of taking the monastic vows and eating rice[28].

I noted in Chapter 3 in regard to Enlightenment and the Innate Capacity argument that, from a scientific perspective using EEG studies, etc., Enlightenment resembles a Near-Death state. I pointed out that medical doctors had difficulty detecting a heartbeat in Ramakrishna when absorbed in deepest *Samadhi*[29]. Anyone familiar with the story of Ramakrishna knows that other monks, jealous of his meditative prowess would beat his unresponsive body when he was so absorbed in Brahman realisation! Huston Smith, who has experienced Enlightenment himself using drugs, wrote scathingly of *Kali's Child* in the *Harvard Divinity Bulletin* calling Kripal's work *'colonialism updated'*{*e.m.*}[30]. In fact, Kripal's is an extreme example of the neo-colonial Orientalism prevalent in supposedly 'Postmodern' Western academia.

Kripal responded with the facile argument that his critics were homophobes! In fact, using Kripal's own statements, a Professor Sil has analysed Kripal's psychosexual history. Kripal trained at a Catholic seminary where he was 'forced to explore the interfaces between sexuality and spirituality and felt 'more than tortured by [his] own psychosexual pathologies. Kripal wrote that he felt that Christian bridal mysticism was unholy given its apparent homoeroticism.; His own 'religious life was quite literally killing [him]'. As

Pandita Rampersad states in *Invading the Sacred: An Analysis of Hinduism Studies in the USA*, it is quite common for Western scholars to play out their private lives through their "scholarship" (*inverted commas mine*) about 'others'. Sarah Caldwell won the prestigious Robert Stoller Award for her writings on the Hindu Goddess. On the basis of a purported quote from one native, Caldwell claimed to have 'proved' that homosexual encounters are rampant in Kerala. This seems to be another case of autobiographical, self-projecting works posing as scholarship of an alien culture on the other side of the world which, in the past, could not respond. Paul Courtright admitted candidly that there was no evidence for his (lurid) claims about Hindu deity Ganesa as a symbol of castration etc. But he proceeded to pronounce his Freudian flights of fancy as valid, scholarly interpretations. Western Humanities academia, steeped in Gadamerian Hermeneutic ideology which claims that texts can be read and reinterpreted in any way, cannot prevent such 'hermeneutic' methodology becoming just arbitrary readings driven by the academic's own psychoses[31].

American Academics Divert Attention from Exposés by Demonising Hindus as Psychopathological 'Terrorists' etc.

Freudian Caldwell supported Kripal's work on Ramakrishna claiming that all complaints from Hindus were signs of psychological disorders within the Hindu community. In a racist manner she recommended 'psychoanalysing' Hindu society to uncover its 'pathologies'[32]. Rampersad writes that Aurobindo was not the only Indian intellectual who found Psychoanalysis to be infantile. Indian psychoanalyst Sudhir Kakar wrote of the deep gulf between Psychoanalysis with its inherent disdain for the mystical tradition and the Indian tradition[33]. We are told that Doniger's mother was Viennese[34], presumably from the same Jewish background as Freud. When Indians turned the tables and started 'psychoanalysing' the white Freudian scholars of Hinduism, the US academic establishment denounced them as 'attackers'. Labels such as 'Hindu Fundamentalists', 'Fascists' and even 'Terrorists' (*see below*) have been thrown by US academics at Hindus who have exposed their false scholarship in a Public Relations (PR) effort by the academics aimed at distracting attention from their own racist misrepresentations of Hinduism.

Christian fundamentalists utilise Courtright's fictional depictions of Hindu symbolism in order to demonise Hindus. But when in 2003 the Hindu Students Council at the University of Louisiana asked people to sign an on-line petition against Courtright's misrepresentations of Hinduism, spreading Hinduphobia, amongst 7,000 signatures there were about 20 petitioners who added threatening comments. This was seized upon by Courtright and his academic supporters to depict themselves cynically as the victims. Seizing upon the September 11th 2001 events, Hindu critics were even labelled 'Terrorists' as if a few on-line remarks protesting misrepresentation were equivalent to the Twin Towers attacks! Such diversionary tactics are commonplace in the Western media which demonises victims of Western Neo-Colonialist aggression who dare to 'fight back' such as the Palestinian native resistance to Zionist occupation. When has one ever heard the mainstream US media pointing out that the September 11th attacks were mainly undertaken by Saudi

Arabian citizens who stated that the primary reason behind these suicide attacks was the Zionist occupation of Palestine. Saddam Hussein and Iran had nothing to do with them! In fact, as I pointed out to Indrani Rampersad and Antonio de Nicolas in regard to *Invading the Sacred*, they had let the Freudians off far too lightly by not recognising that Freud's Psychoanalysis is a fraud with no evidential basis whatsoever and is only taken seriously by morons too stupid to understand simple scientific facts. To be fair, they did cite the views of Berkeley psychologist Professor John Kihlstrom who said that, scientifically, Freud is dead:

> *Freud's cultural influence [on the West] is based, at least implicitly, on the premise that his theory is scientifically valid. But from a scientific point of view, classical Freudian psychoanalysis is dead as both a theory of mind and a mode of therapy (Crews, 1998; Macmillan, 1996). No empirical evidence supports any proposition of psychoanalytic theory,* ...
>
> — John F. Kihlstrom[35]

Debunking the Fraudulent 'Psychoanalysis' of Sigmund Freud and the 'Postmodern' Charlatans of France

In his award-winning BBC TV series *The Century of the Self*, Adam Curtis told of how Freud's dubious ideas came to be popularised in the USA through the influence of Freud's nephew Edward Bernays (the father of PR). It was Bernays, drawing upon the idea of wish-fulfilment, who began the new style of advertising products, not on their intrinsic merits but by playing on the subconscious wishes of the public, associating the product with a sexy image, etc., that gave rise to Consumerism. Curtis stressed that the influence of Freudian thought grew due to its *titillating emphasis on Sex rather than its scientific credibility*. In fact Vedanta postulated wish-fulfilment as one of the many causes of dreams over a millennium before Freud who claimed absurdly that it was a universal characteristic of all dreams[36]. We saw in Chapter 7 that ancient philosophies and modern thinkers such as Carus and von Hartmann (both influenced by Vedanta[37]) had discussed subconscious processes before self-aggrandising Freud supposedly 'discovered' the so-called 'Unconscious Mind'. The book *Memory: The Key to Consciousness* was published by the US National Academy of Sciences in 2005 giving the latest scientific research and understanding of memory. It stated that "there is *no scientific evidence whatsoever to support the key Freudian notion of unconscious Repression of memories*" {*e.m.*}[38]. Stanislaw Grof has demonstrated how many of Freud's ideas are in fact projections of Newtonian mechanics onto the mind and, in keeping with outdated Classical Mechanics' views, the Freudian analyst is conceived as an impartial observer who does not interfere in the observations[39].

Psychologist Robert May points out that those who elevate Freud to almost godlike 'original genius' status are generally ignorant of the fact that, consciously or unconsciously, Freud secularised Jewish mysticism in his 'Psychoanalysis' omitting the supernatural elements. This was shown by David Bakan in his 1958 *Freud and the Jewish Mystical Tradition*[40]. In fact Kihlstrom's comments about our every thought and deed being driven by repressed *sexual* and *aggressive urges* ties Freud in with Jewish Mysticism. Jewish neurologist Rhawn Joseph in his *Neurotheology* lists the bloodthirsty, genocidal, *sexually aggressive* {*e.m.*}, petty, jealous and temperamental misdeeds of the Jewish Yahweh which certainly do not resemble the compassionate behaviour expected of a Spirit-like being. He associates Yahweh with mystical awakening of the Amygdala which is intimately involved in controlling Fear and Aggression. The Amygdala may well be a neurological correlate of mystical experiences of the primitive tribal war gods such as Yahweh and Wotan (*see Note 4*) which are invoked when the tribe is faced with danger to arouse aggressive bloodlust amongst the tribe[41]. Michael Persinger in his *Neuropsychology of God Beliefs* also links the Amygdala to aggressive Yahweh-like gods[42]. Carl Jung wrote that Freud replaced one jealous god Yahweh with a new jealous god Sexuality[43].

As Kihlstrom stated, Freud's theories were misleading and incorrect even when he published them[44]. In his 1973 book *Soul Murder* Morton Schatzman investigated the facts of the Schreber case which Freud had interpreted as an example of his nonsensical "Oedipus Complex". Schatzman found that Schreber's father had possessed 'disclipinary devices' for torture revealing that the truth of the matter was *real child abuse* {*e.m.*} and not unconscious fantasy as Freud had portrayed things. In the 1980s works like Masson's *Assault on the Truth* and Peck's *The People of the Lie* continued to undermine the superstitions of the Freud cult[45]. V.W. Odajnyk writes that Freud's obsession with the primal incest archetype led to dogmatic rigidity[46]. Freud even asked Jung to promise never to abandon the sexual theory, the foundation of Psychoanalysis and that Freud even asserted that "we must make a dogma of it"[47]. Freud referred to his disillusioned followers Adler and Jung as "heretics"[48]. Thus Freud, like Marx and Husserl, recapitulates Judaic archetypes such as messianic utopianism, dogmatic adherence to the creed and so on in his preachings.

Both Husserl and Sartre mocked Freud's use of the term 'Unconscious' for processes not involved in attention. Husserl called it nonsense to talk of an unconscious content that would only subsequently become conscious. Consciousness is necessarily Consciousness in each of its phases. The primal consciousness is not something inferred to on the basis of reasoning, it is rather something that can be seen, (i.e., experienced) as a constituting phase in (phenomenological) reflection. Sartre saw correctly that Freud's "unconscious thought" was a contradiction in terms[49]. The thesis that our thoughts gush from an impersonal unconscious and 'personalise' themselves by becoming conscious puts off the problem of existence, (i.e., the ontological problem of Consciousness)[50]. Sartre and Husserl did not clarify, as did Merrell-Wolff that nonegoic, nondual consciousness having no self/object distinction is still aware and not 'unconscious' (i.e., insentient)[51].

Schwartz and Begley point out that, as late as the 1980s, research published in the *Canadian Journal of Psychiatry* ascribed Phantom Limb syndrome in amputees to Freudian wish-fulfilment! Advances in neurosciences are undermining such absurd Freudian superstitions as the authors demonstrate in regard to Foot Fetishism. The somatosensory maps of the feet in the human brain are adjacent to the maps of the genitals with some overlap. These maps are not static but constantly shifting and some crossover presumably underlies the sexual sensations aroused in Foot Fetishism. Such biological explanation as with similar understandings of Phantom Limbs undermines the *absurd Freudian myths associated with sexual deviations* {*e.m.*}[52].

In *Archetype Revisited* Oxford medical professor and psychiatrist Anthony Stevens notes that frustration of archetypal intent (instinctual potentials requiring fulfilment in life) can occur at any stage in life, not just in childhood. Thus Freud was wrong to locate all the origins of adult psychological problems in infancy. Indeed, Steven's own researches into Rites of Passage and attaining 'Manhood', etc., indicate that adolescence is more important than infancy given modern society's frequent failure to let children attain 'manhood'. Stevens also points out that most dreams are of threatening situations and not Freud's wish-fulfilment. Modern dream research involving REM studies, etc., show that dreams in which predatory animals pursue you are common and such REM dreams help prepare young mammals including *homo sapiens*, descended from apes, for the threats it might face in its life-world. They have nothing whatsoever to do with castration as Freudians suggest moronically[53].

The British National Health Service sends therapists to train at Mindfields College run by psychologists Joe Griffin and Ivan Tyrrell who rubbish both Freud's ideas and his legacy and they argue that the 'therapy' of Freud and the Psychoanalysts actually makes patients worse! In his highly acclaimed book *The Origin of Dreams* Griffin had reported on years of recording in great detail his own dreams using an alarm clock to wake himself up at intervals. Contrary to Freud's view of all dreams as distortions of repressed infantile wishes with an ultimate sexual basis, Griffin's research showed that anything emotionally arousing can become the subject of dreams. Griffin and Tyrrell state that Freudian therapy by dredging up emotional history undid the highly effective stress control done by our dreaming which lowers emotional arousal. Most sane people don't remember their dreams. People undertaking Psychoanalysis appear to get madder and madder. They assert that the most valuable thing that Freud did was to draw the attention of the West to unconscious processes well-known in the ancient world[54]. However, we saw that Freud was not the first to do this although his titillating mythology reached a broader audience; the pseudo-intellectual literati and the gullible masses obsessed with all the references to sex! Griffin and Tyrrell refer to *Freud's messianic ambition and paranoia* leading to unrealistic models and *Freud's propaganda campaign for his bizarre ideas* (note also the role of Bernays). Freud, they say, effectively muddied the waters of Psychiatry and Psychotherapy for the rest of the 20th Century. *Psychoanalytic theories were never scientifically tested* by Freud or his followers (*only asserted as true*) and had their roots in just 6 case histories which were all that Freud ever published, and all were disastrous from the point of view of the patients (being misdiagnosed and mistreated by Freud). Yet, Griffin and Tyrrell add, literature, media and the entertainment industry don't seem to realise that Freud and Jung have little relevance to modern psychotherapeutic practice {*e.m.*}[55]

I have always perceived Psychoanalysis as something for neurotic, angst-ridden Jewish Americans living in a Woody Allen style New York. In one of the early episodes of The Sopranos, on hearing that her son is getting therapy, Tony Soprano's mother tells him that therapy is just a scam run by the Jews. Presumably Wendy Doniger's Viennese mother was from a similar background to Freud where such bizarre Kabbalistic superstitions about the mind were believed the gullible. I myself recovered from a nervous breakdown back in 1993, faced with the brazen 'jobs for the friends' corruption of the promotion process in the scientific publishing industry, without any therapy whatsoever but by getting a grip on myself.

Surveying the academic literature, psychologist David Wulff says that it is highly doubtful that mystical absorption is simply a regression to infantile pre-egoic states of awareness (as Freud claimed)[56]. In fact, Jordens' essay[57] on Jung's concept of Libido and the Vedantic *Prana/Atman* identity is one of many pieces of strong evidence supporting my RAS brainwave/Inner Light of Pure Consciousness correlation. The Freudian concept of a sexual libido or sexual energy is just nonsense from a scientific perspective as energy is, in itself, just neutral energy; it activates or energises things. The adjective *sexual* can apply to certain brain centres activated or aroused with extra energy, *not to the activating energy itself*. Jung's conception of Libido as a general psychological energy therefore makes sense. The RAS brainwaves generated by the brainstem Reticular Formation underlie all gross brainwave activity. They constitute the Reticular *Activating* System arousing the entire brain and selectively activating specific centres etc. Such scientific facts are totally inconsistent with Freud's sexual libido nonsense and its supposed sublimation but are consistent with Jung's notion of a general energy underlying egoic activity.

I have found that Freudianism is especially popular with what in Britain we call the "chattering classes", the pseudo-intellectual middle class literati who are well versed in novels, art, sociological and (if they are Left-leaning) Marxian 'theory' but generally ignorant of real science. The sex-obsessed Freudian mythology continues to exert a hold over the thinking of many in the UK's pseudo-intellectual intelligentsia, especially literary critics. As we have seen, the sort of scholarship passing as 'Philosophy' in much of the Humanities is actually just glorified Literary Criticism hence the use of fancy names like 'Hermeneutics' to make it appear to be more profound. The absurd assumption, as we have seen in regard to US Freudian scholars of Hinduism, is that the anything-goes 'poetic license' used in interpreting poetry and fiction is applicable to interpreting spiritual and philosophical texts. This charlatan-like approach allows you to make up anything and say it is a valid interpretation of the text. In 2006, the British literary reviewer Craig Brown concluded a rather obsequious review in the *Daily Mail* newspaper of a new book on Freud. Brown concluded suggesting that perhaps Freud will be remembered as the 'ocean' rather than the whale, implying metaphorically the vastness and depth of Freud's supposed 'genius'.

But Freudianism survives to this day in that bastion of pseudo-intellectual, poseur-*penseur* ponces pretending to be profound *philosophes,* France. Note that in the USA the word 'ponce' refers to one who tries to fake intelligence, class, and culture. Gallic gobbledegook knows no bounds nor any shame in its pretention, a pseudo-intellectual version of Gallic gastronomy with a worshipping public who make celebrities out of dubious 'philosophers' such as Bernard Henri Levi (born Sephardic Jew Beni Saf in Algeria) known as BHL. In the spring of 2010 Michel Onfray's book *Twilight of an Idol: The Freudian Fabrication* finally brought to the French the facts on Freud. Freudianism was exposed as the last untouchable religion revered by "stars and footballers". Onfray revealed that Freud was a fraud, a charlatan, homophobe and a perverted misogynist obsessed with sexual abuse. Freud's claim to have cured 18 patients was shown to have been fabricated. Freud kept lying about his supposed successes. As expected there was a backlash from those with vested interests. French 'national treasure' BHL came out in defence of Freud as he has come out in defence of fellow Zionist Jew, the IMF Chief Dominique Strauss Kahn (or DSK) after the sexual assault allegations in a New York City hotel. BHL was the same 'authoritative thinker' who earlier in 2010 had made a worldwide laughing stock of himself after he based his critique of Immanuel Kant (calling Kant 'raving mad' and a 'fake') on the work of Jean-Baptiste Botul and his school known as Botulism! In spite of this obviously concocted name, BHL had not realised that Jean-Baptiste Botul was in fact the fictional, satirical creation of a literary journalist Frederick Pages.

In the late 1990s physicist Alan Sokal had managed to fool the pretentious Postmodern literary journal *Social Text* with a fake paper posing as a 'transformative hermeneutics of Quantum Gravity'. This hoax was followed up with the book *Fashionable Nonsense: Postmodern intellectuals' abuse of science* exposing the pretentious guff spewed out by the likes of Freudian French hero Jacques Lacan[58]. A similar book *Higher Superstitions: The Academic Left and its Quarrels with Science* published in 1994 had brought to attention the gobbledegook posing as serious analysis of Science by Humanities academics. These academics came primarily from US University English departments inspired by another Sephardic Jew turned 'Rabbinical' text-obsessed zealot of 'deconstruction', Jacques Derrida. Derrida and his Kabbalistic disciples revel in rejecting the modern Western philosophical expectation for clarity of presentation. Rather than 'picking the bones' of Jane Austen or Hermann Melville in the mausoleum of English Literature, they crept out believing that they were equipped with the requirements to make grandiose pronouncements on grand philosophical questions relating to the truth claims of Natural Science[59]. This gives license to 'Lit-Crit' charlatanism, disguising Deconstructionist doggerel in convoluted, jargon-laden gibberish with pretensions of profundity that inflates the inferiority-complex ridden egos of professors of English posing as philosophers. Engrossed in the thought of another France-based Jew, the Talmudic commentator Emmanuel Levinas and the German Nazi Heidegger, Derrida made preposterous claims to undermine Graeco-Western (and also Indian) Monistic metaphysics in favour of tribal Judaic, Theistic Dualism using his obfuscatory, textual twaddle. Such Kabbalistic obsession with texts, scripture or supposedly holy books is based on literalist misapprehensions of the mystical meaning of the creative power of God's 'Word'.

Postmodern Humanities hermeneutic 'scholars' are not only obsessed with Gadamer and Derrida, but also Michel Foucault and his overzealous interpretation of all 'Discourse' being imbued with 'Power Relations'. In January 2005 the (Jewish-owned) *New York Times* published an unusual article in its Art section by its art critic Edward Rothstein. It was entitled 'Connections: The Scholar who Irked Hindu Puritans'. As with a similar article in the *Washington Post*, Rothstein almost completely paraphrased the pro-Doniger views presented by a Martin Marty posted on the Belief.net website a few weeks earlier. Doniger and her ex-student academics were portrayed as the victims of 'threats and attacks'. Her opponents were portrayed as 'irrational fundamentalists' and 'Hindu puritans'. Slanderously, Rothstein conflated Doniger's scholarly critics with completely unrelated sectarian violence in India. Through such demonisation tactics, associating Hindu critics falsely with violence, the central arguments about mistranslations, misrepresentations and poor quality scholarship were overlooked. As part of the subtle propaganda, a 50 year old photo of Doniger was used in the article to present her subliminally as a fragile white woman juxtaposed to 'violent' (dark-skinned) Hindu fundamentalists[60]. This resembles the subtle pandering to racist stereotypes, noted by Arab commentators, in the use of a blonde spokeswoman (of Eastern European origin) to defend publicly the 2008 Zionist massacre of dispossessed Palestinian natives still held 'imprisoned' within the giant refugee camp on the Gaza strip.

Ramakrishna's Unity of Faiths becomes Huxley's Perennial Philosophy

In the 1940s at the Ramakrishna Mission in New York, Swami Nikhilananda and Margaret Woodrow Wilson (daughter of Woodrow Wilson[N7]) translated the Bengali *Kathamrita* (Words of Nectar) into the famous *The Gospel of Sri Ramakrishna* which the famous scholar of world mythology, Joseph Campbell, helped to edit[61]. The grandson of Darwin's champion Thomas H. Huxley and brother of Nobel laureate Andrew F. Huxley, who developed the Hodgkin-Huxley or 'action potential' model of nerve conduction; Aldous Huxley was a co-publisher of *Vedanta and the West* in California from the 1930s. Huxley became a member of the California Ramakrishna Mission under Swami Prabhavananda. The latter was later to throw Huxley out due to Huxley's use of LSD and mescaline to expedite Enlightenment to experience for himself the Ultimate Reality which Huxley realised is variously called Godhead, Ground, *Brahman* or Clear Light of the Void[62].

While he was a member, Huxley wrote the influential *The Perennial Philosophy* showing the commonalities underlying the world's esoteric spiritual traditions. Comparative Religion academic Richard King criticizes Huxley's method in *The Perennial Philosophy* claiming that Huxley used Vedanticised Buddhism[63]. But King is hidebound ideologically to his 'Postmodern' Gadamerian relativism which claims, on false grounds, that there is no culture-free universal knowledge, including that of Natural Science! Given his Relativist bias and lack of appreciation of the veracity of perennial mystical phenomenology, I doubt that King would comprehend the 'more comprehensive insight' argument of actual mystic Merrell-Wolff. This accounts for superficial differences in conclusions. In his otherwise critical article *The*

Cult of Ken Wilber, Michel Bauwens claims absurdly that Ken Wilber has produced a 'masterly synthesis' of Nondual Hinduism and Buddhism[64]. Such false claims misappropriate Indian knowledge gleaned from thousands of years of collective yogic tradition and the likes of Aurobindo's 'Integral Yoga' and make this knowledge appear to be the 'intellectual property' of some hyped-up Western individual. Some Western scholars, including anti-Eurocentric J.J. Clarke, point to the fact that Huxley's choice of title is an anglicisation of the great German mathematician and philosopher Gottfried Leibniz's term *philosophia perennis*. It is true that Huxley referred explicitly to Leibniz but Clarke overlooks the background to Huxley's book in the Ramakrishna Mission and its doctrine of the 'Unity of Faiths'. I would thus interpret Huxley's use of 'Perennial Philosophy' as a modern re-interpretation of the Ancient Indian concept of *Sanatana Dharma*, which is also the Sanskrit name for the Indian spiritual tradition which foreigners call Hinduism.

The phrase 'Unity of Faiths' is grossly misleading for as we have seen, yogic spirituality is not based on blind 'faith' in dogma as with Semitic 'religions'. I shall not use *Perennial Philosophy* as this notion leads many ignorant believers in monotheistic faiths to the unfounded conclusion that, as all great spiritual traditions contain elements of the Perennial Philosophy this means that they can cling on to their superstitious myths which bear no actual relationship to true Universal Spirituality. The Semitic Religions all share these common core doctrines (actually derived from Zoroaster[N8]). (1) That their own religion (or their own sect) is the 'One True Faith' and therefore other religions are 'false'. (2) Creation *ex nihilo* by an anthropomorphic Creator God. (3) Bodily resurrection of only the 'true believers' on (4) a Day of Last Judgement when the 'world' will end (such Apocalypticism involves projection of the mystical 'End of Time', the ceasing of the Light creating Temporality, onto tribal history and then onto global history). (5) The (material bodies of the resurrected) 'true believer' community will go to a 'heaven' (imagined as being like material existence) and the Non-believers will go to a 'Hell' modelled on the Greek Hades, itself modelled on the volcanic caverns of Sicily (although some Jewish myths of the Afterlife may not conform to this simplified scheme). All of these are untenable myths not worthy of serious philosophical discussion.

In spite of the mystical meanings of St Paul and the writers of the four orthodox Gospels, it seems clear from historical studies that Paul and other early Christians were actually awaiting the 'Second Coming', the 'Kingdom of Heaven on Earth', etc., as actual historical events which would occur in the First Century *c.e.* Thus, although the likes of Whiteman point to the mystical meanings of the Bible, it would be misleading to say that the early Christians were not concerned with the materialistic, historical superstitions regarding the coming Apocalypse. The life of Jesus (both the allegorical myths and even the rare facts) has little to do with serious spiritual philosophy which would remain the same regardless as to whether or not Jesus actually existed. Obviously, *contra* the infantile propaganda of Christian missionaries, if one took the notion of 'idolatry' seriously, worshipping images of the historical man Jesus is more idolatrous than the 'Hindu' worship of mythical images utilised to symbolise the 'ineffable'. The Muslims forbid imagery of Mohammed so as not to confuse the man with the message. Even the Gospels, understood as mystical allegories, are neither unique nor original and they certainly do not constitute sophisticated conceptual 'Philosophy' in the Indo-European sense. The early success of the Christian religion was more to do with its Socialistic ethics and its schemes providing charitable welfare for the poorer members of the Christian community. The later success, as we have seen was due to its politically convenient adoption by Constantine and the *forced conversion* of the peoples of the Roman Empire, Holy Roman Empire and of Native Americans by the Iberian Conquistadors.

The letters attributed to St Paul contain more than 50 references to the Greek term *pistis* rendered in English as 'faith'. As Whiteman notes, Paul's original meaning was clearly not a simple belief in a dogmatically asserted creed (as with the later Nicene Creed), rather it was an orientation of the mind towards the Good or to live a mystical life[65]. The Vedanticised 'neo-Christian' text *A Course in Miracles* argued along similar lines that, rather than a naive 'faith', Jesus was calling for an altered perception of ourselves to see that we are never separate from God[66]. The whole thrust of Church Christianity (or 'Churchianity' as Vivekananda called it) is to deny the validity of other traditions and claim its dogmatic superstitions, its vulgar Materialistic misreading of mystical allegories, as the sole Truth! We have seen that the Church suppressed Gnosticism as heretical as it denied the need for clergymen is intermediaries between God and humans. The mainstream *exoteric* doctrines of all religions are very far removed from Huxley's *esoteric*, mystically-based Perennial Philosophy which has in the main been suppressed by the Semitic religions.

Huxley stressed the capacity of humans to attain union with the Ultimate Reality or the impersonal Godhead and such unitary Monism of course contradicts the theistic Dualism of Judaism, Christianity and Islam for whom such non-theistic union is heretical. Furthermore, we have seen that the Judaic god Yahweh is not the personification of Divine Light but the apotheosis of animal fear, sexual aggression and rage instincts associated with the amygdala. The problems with the use of *Perennial Philosophy* are also related to the inability of the likes of Huxley and other Perennialist scholars of Mysticism to explicate clearly this so-called 'philosophy' in detail. Huxley himself presented the Hindu *Advaita Vedanta* as the nearest particular view to the underlying essential truth. Although the likes of Schrödinger, Emerson, Huston Smith and even A.N. Whitehead have lauded *Advaita Vedanta* , sometimes even as the greatest metaphysical system known to humankind, I would view *Advaita Vedanta* as strong in regard to certain aspects of phenomenological philosophy but weak in regard to the ontology of Creation. But the *Advaita* philosophy also contains unsubstantiated speculations regarding the supposed transmigration of a *jiva* (individual soul) which cannot stand up to any serious intellectual scrutiny in this scientific age. Furthermore, alongside *Advaita Vedanta,* the traditional Perennialists have placed the rather vague Emanationism of Plotinus. We saw that Huston Smith, based on psychedelic drug or 'entheogen'-induced personal experience of enlightenment, claimed that Plotinus and the Vedantins were like mere hack reporters simply reporting the events[67]. I will demonstrate the general superiority of Brahmanic metaphysics over that of Plotinus in the next chapter.

Furthermore, there is a tendency amongst Western Rationalists and Westernised Neo-Hindus to emphasise the highly rationalistic Sankara with his *mayavada* (Doctrine of Maya) which denies that Brahman actually transforms even though the *Brahmasutras* (summaries of the Upanishads) clearly stressed *Brahmaparinama* (transformation of Brahman)[68]. Sankara's *mayavada* is a classic case of what de Quincey called 'Promissory Idealism'. Matter is supposed to arise from an ultimate Spirit/Consciousness which has no trace of materiality in it[69]. As Pratima Bowes pointed out in her critique of Sankara, the Upanishads do not deny the real existence of the phenomenal world of the senses[70]. Of course there is some truth in the interpretation of *maya* (the creative power of the Absolute) as a sort of illusion; we have seen parallels in Arthur Eddington's ontology (matter is insubstantial) and in Philo Judaeus's separation of God's subjective essence from matter. But there is a greater truth and clearer understanding in the Doctrine of Vibration of the Tantric Kashmir Saivites which accepts the transformation of the Absolute. The Nondual Kashmir Saivites such as Abhinavagupta correctly pointed out the tacit Dualism in Sankara's rationalistic arguments[71]. We have seen that the Tantric view ties in with the modern scientific understanding of Matter as the phenomenal appearances created by the underlying waveforms created by vibratory activity or 'energy'. Such notions were already present in inchoate form in the Upanishadic doctrine of *panch bhuta* with *Akasa* (Space as subtle matter characterised by Vibration) as the first created element which 'densifies' progressively into solid matter.

The sort of ideas presented by the Hellenized Jew Philo led to the later explicit dualism of Spirit and Nature in Christianity based largely on infantile anthropomorphic arguments about God's supposed (king-like) 'sovereignty'. The 5th Century *c.e.* Alexander of Lycopolis praised Christian ethics but recognised that Christian writers were incapable of precise philosophical thought[72]. After rising to monopolistic power in the Roman Empire, the totalitarian Christians burnt the tracts of the great Neoplatonist Porphyry. Porphyry's strategy had been to expose to the educated that the Christian texts were full of inconsistencies, exaggerations, impossibilities, fabrications and falsehoods. Porphyry attacked the foundations of Christian faith such as its claims to uniqueness and its claim to hold the monopoly on Truth and Salvation. He also mocked the ignorant and vulgar Christian doctrines that the true believer's material body survives until the End of Time when it will be resurrected from the grave and the belief in an Earthly paradise[73]. Clearly, in cultures dominated by superstitious Christianity and Islam, even where mystics have attained mystical union and related states, they have not been able to champion their insights publicly or debate these issues with philosophers well-versed in such mystical knowledge as has been the case in India.

Furthermore, as we have seen, even in mystically uninhibited India, Siddharta Gautama, the so-called 'Buddha', not only denied a Ground of all Being but also put forward the *Anatta* doctrine which, taken at face value, denies the Inner Light as well! As McEvilley noted, some Buddhist texts mistake Living-in-the-moment for enlightenment[74]. Siddharta Gautama ridiculed the Upanishadic notion of 'union with Brahman' even though similar criticisms could be directed at attaining Nirvana. He also claimed that the Vedic teachings of the Brahmans were ridiculous, mere words, vain and empty[75]. Thus Siddharta and his cult followers were not 'Sanatanists' like the Brahmans but Sectarians, incapable or unwilling to recognise the truths in other paths. Even today we find countless ignorant Buddhist spokesmen deriding Brahmanism on doctrinaire grounds. Buddhists have also been criticised for the concept of *nibbana* which suggests extinction rather than maintenance of lucidity via a 'naked ego' to experience *prajnaghana* (the dense luminous Wisdom Consciousness aspect of the Inner Light). Similar erroneous views in the West are associated with the misleading term 'Divine Darkness' of Dionysius the Areopagite (St Denis), the NeoPlatonic Father of Christian Mysticism.

The over-valuation of the doctrine of Ineffability has also contributed to the confusion in Buddhism and in other traditions. Ineffability is stressed in *Tao-te ching*, the first work to ascribe a metaphysical meaning to the word *Tao*. It dates from the 3rd or 4th Century *b.c.e.* although ascribed to the somewhat earlier Lao-tzu. The Formless and Eternal *Tao* is in essence Nonbeing[76]. Taoists strive to become one with the *Tao*. Chuang-tzu wrote of the Celestial Light shining forth allowing us to realise our True Selves and realise the Absolute[77]. The Taoist *Ch'i* is said to be the Life Energy, the Cosmic Spirit that or Primordial Energy that enlivens all things[78]. Thus, as with Fritjof Capra in his *The Tao of Physics*[79], Taoism stresses the Energetic aspect of the Ultimate and, mired in ineffability (perhaps due to Chinese language) says nothing of Consciousness. Although the Taoist texts don't seem to mention it, Western interpreters elaborate on the fact that *Ch'i* as experienced is in fact a Psycho-Physical energy.

We saw that the Pan-Experientialism of James, like the Pantheism of Spinoza is merely Nature Mysticism and remains ignorant of the Transcendental. Furthermore, many Western scholars interested in Perennial Mysticism can appreciate the common core of Mysticism as a fact of human psychology but cannot appreciate how such psychological or phenomenological insights could lead to grand metaphysical claims about cosmology or Creation. Thus, as we saw above, Jung misinterpreted naively the grand metaphysical claims of Gnostics relating to Divinity and Matter and he dismissed Indian Philosophy as 'pre-Kantian'. Thus it is totally erroneous to adhere to the facile New Age style 'anything goes' approach to Perennial Philosophy whereby any mystical myth, be it about Reincarnation or Ineffability has been accepted uncritically by New Agers who are concerned that they should not offend others by questioning the validity of their unsubstantiated beliefs.

Western Theists' Public and Secret Fears of Indian Spiritual Hegemony and the Coming New Age

In November 2011, the Vatican's exorcist Gabriele Amorth denounced Yoga (and Harry Potter) as the "work of the devil"[80]. In February 2014 the UN Committee on the Rights of the Child denounced the Vatican's cover-up of the massive-scale child abuse by Catholic priests. [N9] Exorcist 'Gabby' wasn't so 'gabby' (talkative) when faced with the truly diabolical deeds of his own secretive brotherhood of 'San Pedro' to make sure it is '*sans* paedos'! In regard to placing an emphasis on testing and evidence, the Semitic Faiths with their unquestioning dogmatic beliefs in the uniquely true status of their own mythologies, do not really stand a chance of survival given proper scientific scrutiny of true Spirituality. The ever-widening spread of modern secular education combined with the new scientific understanding of Spirituality will start eradicating religious superstitions which have survived because spiritual phenomena remained 'mysteries'. The Western-protected feudal House of Saud, founded by the barbaric Ibn Saud, dishes out its ill-begotten Petro-Dollars, funding indoctrination of poor peasants into the reactionary medieval mindset of the Wahhabi bigots. This helped create the Taliban and *Al Qaeda* but Saudi oil wealth will not last forever. The Pakistani Taliban, which the Pakistani military intelligence service (the ISI) helped to create, is now at war with the Pakistani failed-state and many younger urban middle classes questioning the theocracy of the 'Islamic state'. Even Christian scholar Robert Beckford stated that, if Christianity was not open to modern lines of enquiry then it could become extinct[81]. As indicated above, this is not self-aggrandising Neo-Hindu Nondualist bluster but the logical consequence of analysis of the perennial and universal spiritual knowledge. I do not accept popular polytheistic and monotheistic Hinduism as anything more than superficial mythology, appealing to uneducated peasants who are incapable of understanding philosophical thought.

J.J. Clarke in his *Oriental Enlightenment*, a copy of which he gave me as a token of appreciation, tells of the Neo-Vedantins Aldous Huxley, Christopher Isherwood and Gerald Heard living in California in the 1930s and 1940s:

> *In their magazine Vedanta and the West they advocated what Huxley called, with self-conscious reference to the scientific method, 'The minimum working hypothesis' according to which the idea of Brahman, the ground of being, was claimed to rest, 'not on blind authority, but upon empirical work which any enquirer may repeat... and confirm for himself'. The Vedantist world view was not only superior to the Judaeo-Christian tradition because 'it does not contradict the findings of science', but was actually supported by recent developments in science which suggested that 'the physical world' is a construction of the human mind... a basic unity which our animal senses break up into a manifold' (Isherwood 1945...)*
>
> — J.J. Clarke[82]

In this book Clarke also tells us that the interest in Buddhism in 18th and 19th Century Europe was not so much a 'flight from Reason' as some see it but rather the Victorian era excitement over the 'discovery' of Buddhism resulted from the belief that Buddhism represented, in contrast with superstitious Christianity, a religion compatible with Science[83]. Buddhophile Edwin Arnold's[N10] epic poem *The Light of Asia* (1879) had phenomenal success over thirty years selling nearly one million copies. Ironically its success coincided with the British imperial zenith and Christian missionary triumphalism[84]. One should note that William Wilberforce had seen the Christianisation of India as a greater priority than the Abolition of Slavery[85]. The Christian clergy saw *Light of Asia* as a threat and W.C. Wilkinson called Arnold "the Antichrist" and American Theologian Samuel Kellogg wrote a refutation entitled *The Light of Asia and the Light of the World* to combat the Buddhist menace[86].

Clarke also tells us that, prior to Stalin's terror against all religions, attempts were made at an accommodation between Buddhism and Bolshevism on the basis of the belief that Buddhism was essentially atheistic and scientific in outlook[87]. Ironically, the Third Reich was also into Buddhism sending an expedition to Tibet in 1939 seeking occult knowledge pre-empting the contemporary Shangri-La image of Tibet in the West. Harvard Divinity scholar Harvey Cox viewed Buddhism as an especially dangerous challenge to Christian faith. In the face of such threats from the East, Pope John-Paul II reiterated the (supposed) *uniqueness* and *exclusivity* of Christian revelation and the historical mission of Jesus {*e.m.*}[88]. The arch-proponent of Constructivism in Comparative Religion, the Head of Judaic Studies at Harvard, Stephen Katz has been accused of using false arguments denying Perennialist universal spirituality and mystical union as such denials sit comfortably with Judaism which does not refer to mystical union[89]. In fact, as Robert Forman shows, Katz's anti-Perennialist arguments are vacuous[90]. In spite of Western Buddhophile perceptions, Clarke himself notes, the common core truth underlying the world's spiritual traditions was most closely identified with Indian Vedanta (*Advaita Vedanta*) by Aldous Huxley in his influential *The Perennial Philosophy* (1946) [91]. As with the Bolshevik scientific materialists, Buddhism appeals to the spiritually and philosophically naive, especially those Westerners holding a Shangri-La image of Tibet. We saw that the true transcendental 'Light of Asia' was found in the hymns of the *Rig Veda* written at least one thousand years before the time of Buddha.

The 2003 book *Buddhism and Science*: *Breaking New Ground*, edited by Physics graduate turned Buddhist scholar (and translator for the Dalai Lama in meetings with scientists) B. Alan Wallace, whose studies were partly sponsored by Rajiv Malhotra's Infinity Foundation. It contains a chapter by the aforementioned Frenchman Michel Bitbol, who is into Nagarjuna's *Madhyamaka* and who suppressed the fact that Schrödinger's Idealism was derived from his Vedantism (Brahmanism)[92]. This mish-mash of extremely diverse viewpoints shows no indication whatsoever of any coming together of Buddhism and Science. Indeed, as stated previously, the chapter by the Dalai Lama actually contains some phenomenological knowledge of the Clear Light from the highest Buddhist *Vajrayana* tradition (about the Clear Light being a continuous series of moments[93]) which provides strong support for my own activating brainwaves from the brainstem correlation! As stated elsewhere, the *Dzogschen* Buddhism advocated by the Dalai Lama differs greatly from the original Buddhism propounded by Siddharta Gautama. Such Tantric Tibetan Buddhism with its Inner Light and Consciousness as the Ground views may be viewed as a form of 'crypto-Brahmanism' as Vivekananda asserted of all Mahayana Buddhism.

We saw above in regard to Kripal's misrepresentations of Ramakrishna's Vedantic practises that such Freudian scholars also justify their false scholarship by appealing to Hans Georg Gadamer's so-called 'Hermeneutics'. This says essentially that the scholar can make up any interpretation of a text. Whilst this approach may be appropriate in regard to Poetry and Literary

Criticism of novels, this 'anything goes' approach is not acceptable in regard to true Philosophy (*Philosophia*) which aims to bring us closer to the (Light of) Truth. Gadamer's ontological views were based on Heidegger's inchoate speculation (which Heidegger himself later rejected) regarding *Dasein*. Such Existentialist readings of Heidegger's unfinished work *Being and Time*, as we have seen, reject the possibility of humans transcending their sensory life-world. As Pandita Rampersad stated above, Gadamer's Hermeneutics just gives an excuse to allow supposed scholars to project their personal psychological hang-ups onto other traditions. I would say that it allows charlatans to pretend to be doing serious scholarship!

We can thus dismiss the Gadamerian, ideological objections of spiritually naive Religion scholar Richard King. King says that Nagarjuna's *Madhyamaka* undermines the supposedly self-aggrandising claim of Hindu Nationalists that *Vedanta* constitutes Universal Spirituality[94]. The well-known branch of Mahayana Buddhism known as the Middle Way (*Madhyamaka*), steeped in the, seemingly nihilistic, negative discourse of the Indian Buddhist Nagarjuna rejects a Ground of all Being (although Dallmayr claims that Nagarjuna did not actually reject the notion of *Brahman*[95]). This can only be due to dogmatic adherence to Nagarjuna's teachings which, if actually based on his own realisations, imply that he did not attain the deepest and most ultimate realisations. Buddhist scholar and practitioner Herbert Guenther tells us that Nagarjuna was a Logical Reductionist who thought in static terms and failed to gain a holistic understanding of lived reality[96]. Guenther adds[97]:

> *The much vaunted Madhyamaka philosophy, particularly in its Prasangika version is the ultimate in reductionism, and its manifestation as dogmatic intolerance in Tibetan history is well known. This system has much in common with the now-defunct Western school of logical positivism and its anemic revival, "analytical" philosophy. For this reason, the Madhyamaka system has attracted the attention of academics who, because of their tacit presuppositions, unwittingly paint a one-sided picture of Buddhist thought.*

See also the quote from Chinese Buddhist patriarch Tsung-Mi in Chapter 13 which derides Nagarjuna's negative discourse as pseudo-profound verbiage appealing to those who have not actually experienced *Sunyata*. King does however point out correctly that the Zen Buddhism of D.T. Suzuki popularised in the West (along with Alan Watts) was in fact atypical of actual Zen as it was a Vedanticised presentation[98].

In 2000, I heard that the Indian Union Minister of Education in the NDA coalition government, Maharaj Krishen Kaw, had written a little book called *The Science of Spirituality* calling for a scientific understanding of Spirituality, or a Science of Consciousness[99]. I sent him material about my book. He then read it and was impressed, emailed me saying that I should visit him if I came to Delhi. In fact, another ex-Union Minister in India, the ex-Regent of Kashmir Dr Karan Singh, a minister under Indira Gandhi, is well known for his interest in such Science-Spirituality integration and is a regular on the Western New Age events circuit. *The Times of India* reported on a conference in India in which Singh claimed that it was he, when a minister, had started government backing for scientific studies of Yoga and Consciousness. Singh, like most Western New Agers, seems to peddle the same old vague parallels and uncontroversial, feel-good Unity of Faith stuff lacking any real substance. He asked for a copy of my book after I emailed him with information. Thus, as I told people in my 2001 S&MN seminar entitled "The Rise of the East and the Globalisation of Indian Metaphysics", the 'New Age' is not something that the self-aggrandising American New Agers will bring about. By 'New Age' I mean an overthrow of the dominant Physicalist-Materialist metaphysics in favour of the core Indian Metaphysics based on the Primacy of Consciousness, Transcendentalism and paranormal phenomena. Such a dramatic shift going totally against the fundamentals of Western culture requires 'hard power'.

Just as the rise of Natural Sciences in Renaissance Italy was possible, against the resistance of the Church, due to the patronage of the new class of bourgeois Capitalists[N11] who gained economically and militarily from the new scientific inventions, so the New Age will come about through the rise of India and to a lesser extent China, where relaxations on Buddhism are underway. The Chinese Communists view Buddhism as indigenous and a counter to the alien Christianity whereas Indian Buddhism became largely syncretised with the indigenous Taoism. The 1900 Boxer Uprising was directed against Christian Missionaries who were becoming laws unto themselves during the European and Japanese 'Scramble for Concessions' in China. Europeans and Christians were protected from local authority jurisdiction by Western 'Gunboat Diplomacy'. Many Chinese converted to Christianity as this allowed them to escape punishment for crimes[100]. The Russians are concerned by US Evangelists peddling NeoLiberal economics, anti-abortion views, etc., in Russia as with the Evangelical inculcation of homophobia etc., in Kenya. As Malhotra and Neelakandan state in *Breaking India* Christian Missionary activity is closely tied to the politico-economic interests of the USA and Europe and thus acts against the national interest of India[101].

In the 19th Century Christian Missionaries were usually cheerleaders for Colonialism. Indian Christian proselytiser (linked to US and UK Evangelist groups) Vishal Mangalwadi regurgitates the self-justifying lies invented by the British colonial parasites that, due to Hindu superstitions, India had been mired in abject poverty for millennia, before the altruistic British Christians came to the rescue. For instance, Mangalwadi makes out that Indians did not know how to build irrigation canals before the British came when in fact, one of Mangalwadi's Evangelist heroes, Charles Trevelyan, had written of the remarkable ancient irrigation schemes of the Hindus still functioning in South India. British invasions of Indian states, followed by the British looting Indian treasuries, de-industrialisation and creation of famines through extortionate 'bloodsucking' of the peasantry had led to many of the old Hindu irrigation schemes falling into ruin. Mangalwadi even writes[102]:

The Herculean efforts to free India from her poverty were Christian efforts,... ...Philip Mason's popular book, The Men Who Ruled India, identifies that [Christian Evangelist] Sir Richard Temple ... as a man of tremendous vision and ceaseless action,...

In fact Richard Temple, acting for Benjamin Disraeli's hand-picked henchman Viceroy Lytton, forced Indian victims of the 1877 famine inflicted upon them by British 'Let-them-starve' policies, to travel for miles to do hard labour for smaller rations (including flour diluted with dirt) than Nazis gave to their Death Camp inmates in Buchenwald (not all Nazi Death Camps used gas chambers)[103]. As a conquered nation, India must pay tribute, stated Disraeli whilst the Marquis of Salisbury, India Secretary in 1875 had written that "India must be bled"[104]. The British covered-up the 94 per cent mortality rates in such 'Death Camps'. Simultaneously, Disraeli's regime forced India to export record amounts of food-grains to provide Food Security to the British and lowering prices for other Westerners. Contrary to the Malthusian myths (Malthus himself worked for the East India Co. at Hailebury) still peddled by many British, 19th Century India had a much lower population density than Britain. India as a whole always produced enough food for its population, even during famines, whereas it was Britain that did not grow enough for its population. By 1900 one quarter of Britain's wheat came from India even though in 1901 the *Lancet* (the prestigious medical journal) estimated that British policies had led to the death from starvation of 19 million Indians in Western India during the 1890s. In 1877, whilst millions of Indians starved, Lytton, organised the biggest feast in human history in Delhi to celebrate Disraeli's gesture of giving Victoria Saxe-Coburg the grand title 'Empress of India'. The Christian British even passed an Anti-Charitable Donations Act (1877) to stop private donors trying to help starving Indians[105].

In the East where yogic traditions have been sustained for millennia there is a far greater understanding and acceptance of the Primacy of Consciousness and the political establishment will want to promote the knowledge indigenous traditions against the pseudo-universalist mythologies of Western Materialist Science. Heisenberg wrote in *Physics and Philosophy*[106]:

> *...a certain relationship between philosophical ideas in the tradition of the Far East and the philosophical substance of quantum theory. It may be easier to adapt oneself to the quantum-theoretical concept of reality when one has not gone through the naive materialistic way of thinking that still prevailed in Europe in the first decades of this century.*

The True Underlying Ontology or the *Sanatana Dharma* (Eternal Truth)

Perennial Phenomenology and Arrogant Western Academia's Ethnocentric Epistemological Evasion of the Ontological Primacy of Consciousness

I argued, in my *The Oneness/Otherness Mystery*, that the fact that elements of the Perennial Philosophy could be found in all great spiritual traditions did not justify the dogmatic claims of these religions as, in fact, elements of the Perennial Philosophy can be discerned through the analysis of all systems of human thought, including Quantum Theory and General Relativity as all systems of human thought reflect the common, underlying structures of human cognition and conceptualisation. We saw in Chapter 4 that Denis Gabor and Karl Pribram both recognised that the formalism of Quantum Mechanics (QM) reflected the structure of perception and Pribram has even modelled perception using such Holonomic Quantum Field Neurodynamics[107]. In a sense, the Perennial Philosophy is a Perennial Phenomenology indicating the common structure of perceptual world construction common to all humanity. In fact, Husserl claimed to go beyond 'Psychology' in his 'Phenomenology' to the structures of Consciousness common to all human mental processes. This was a sort of culmination of a Kantian philosophical programme based on Kant's notion of such *a priori* or innate structures of human cognition through which all our cognitions are organised. However, this limitation of mystical insight to the deep structures of human cognition is a rather facile stance shying away from the grand metaphysical and cosmological significance of the perennial wisdom.

We have seen that Husserl's colleague Eugen Fink began in the 1930s to realise, though only in speculative thought, the ancient yogic knowledge that the fundamental forms of our perceptual time and space are established by the continuous underlying flow of the Absolute Consciousness (actually the Inner Light)[108]. This flow of the Inner Light constitutes the yogic Time/Space Matrix of Perception[109]. In contrast to Heidegger, who assumed that Husserl's programme was the final say in regard to deep questions of ego constitution, Fink also began to realise that Husserl had only touched the surface. Deeper forms of phenomenological reduction were necessary in order to progress beyond Husserl's superficial analysis of object perception in Waking consciousness to deeper levels of constitution of the human 'life-world'. Fink recognised that such a retreat into the depths of human consciousness would involve a sort of 'unhumanisation' in the sense of leaving behind the world-concepts or structures associated with human sensory perception of the external reality which constitutes the normal human 'life-world'[110]. By 'life-world' is meant the 'life' of the ego consciousness. We have seen that Husserl and Fink unwittingly touched upon the ancient Vedantic *Prana/Atman* Identity, calling the Flow of Absolute Consciousness the 'Life Stream'[111].

As I indicated in Chapter One, Fink's notion of 'unhumanisation' corresponds to my 'Retreat to the brainstem' interpretation of Enlightenment[112]. *Raja Yoga* or the yogic path to Enlightenment and mystical union involves deactivating the processes of sensory perception and normal mentation. This also corresponds to the yogic *withdrawal from worldly attachments*. The Vedantic tradition describes the onion-like layers or 'sheaths' (*kosa*) surrounding the innermost core (which is the *Atman* or the Pure Consciousness) through which the yogi must pass. World-renunciation expedites the sensory deprivation releasing our mind from habituated models of our external environs. Lucidity is attained in deeper states of consciousness by dissolution of the normal ego from its habitual networks constituting our current personality and stabilising new subtilised forms of ego or 'vehicles of Consciousness' in deeper brain structures. Thereby the normal Wakeful perception processes associated primarily with the cerebral cortex are left behind. The individuated consciousness of the yogi thus leaves the uniquely human structures of the neocortex and retreats towards the brainstem which in evolutionary terms is a very primitive structure not associated only with humans. The moment-by-moment wave-flow of the Inner Light not only constitutes subjective temporality but as it flows outwards through the cerebral cortex, it also appears to underlie the human perception of spatiality. The cerebral cortex includes the brain maps of body surfaces which are involved in our internal modelling of the body and its sensory world.

The activation of this world-modelling must be closely connected to our perception of our normal visual field or world of distinct object surfaces which appears to have 3D depth due to perspective. Note that spatiality is associated primarily with the discrete, extensive forms of our visual field. Conscious experiences due to tactile stimuli appear in our world-modelling as associated with specific body parts and smells, tastes and sounds appear to be localised in the nose, mouth and ears. But, as with moods other generic feelings, these experiences are more diffuse and less-defined spatially. Perceptual illusions hint at some of the underlying rules of perceptual object formation and we can be fooled into misplacing the actual location of stimuli. Our thoughts are not strictly part of our spatially-perceived world although they appear to us as being localised inside our heads and linked to our speech function. Thoughts are clearly sequenced temporally but, in themselves, are 'nonspatial'. We experience them as if occurring in our heads but cannot really localise them; if, for example, they arise in speech-related centres we cannot tell as the brain does not have maps of itself. Phenomenologically it seems as if thoughts reflect the entry into our attentional field (or ego) of non-sensory relational patterns abstracted from perceptual information associated with speech. We saw in Chapter 5 that more recent Cognitive Science suggests that, in evolutionary terms, conceptualisation 'piggybacks' on pre-existing structures of perception.

Our mundane perception of Cause-and-Effect (Space-Time Causality) follows from the sequential perception of the succession of temporal moments and from our perceptual abstraction and construction of discrete spatial forms. This masks the underlying interconnectedness of all phenomena where everything is being caused holistically by the influences from the rest of the universe. Through leaving the cortex behind, the yogi's awareness thus transcends normal 3D space, spatial causality and can apprehend nonlocal interconnectedness of phenomena. Thus the yogi in Enlightenment deactivates the cerebral brain structures normally activated in human mental activity and retreats into the depths towards the brainstem or the *Light at the Centre*, leaving behind the normal human 'world of experience'. Due to the deactivation of the brain centres, Enlightenment can resemble processes of dying or falling into a coma-like Near Death state which can also result in experiences of the Inner Light, psychic phenomena, 'omniscient' Gnosis etc.

Eventually, the final lucid vehicle of individuated consciousness (the purified and translucent 'naked ego'), the *anandamayakosa* or Bliss Sheath, stripped of all habitual forms is stabilised in the Light of Pure Consciousness (with all sensory and conceptual 'impurities' or superimpositions withdrawn) and momentarily dissolves and reconstitutes in this Light. By such means, anthropic limitations are transcended and *direct, unmediated apprehension of Reality as it is in itself* is attained. I have already indicated that it is becoming increasingly apparent that the only actually existent process or 'physical force' is Electromagnetism, the macroscopic manifestation of the subatomic realm described by QM; Gravity and the nuclear forces being epiphenomenal manifestations of this one underlying unitary process. Thus as my physical correlate of the Light of Pure Consciousness is the primary flow of electric energy through the brain, there is no incompatibility with the scientific picture here in regard to electromagnetic energy being the unitary Ground-stuff of the so-called 'physical universe' (which we have seen is only a human conception). The big difference is that concerning the Ontological Status of Consciousness.

As scientific theories of the universe and of matter are also, to some extent, reflections of human mental processes then they share a common basis with the phenomenology of the structures of human cognition. I have already hinted that intellectual insights such as formal logical or mathematical structures are associated phenomenologically with discrimination of the subtle, dynamic fringe processes which surround normal attention. These fringe processes are constituted of, as James stressed, actually existent relations or nexus of polarities that distinguishes concepts from one another rather similar to Jacques Derrida's opaque notion of the '*Différance*' (related to Kabbalistic Word Association experiences[113]). We have seen that Western Philosophy of Mathematics and Physics both face contradictions faced with the invention of non-Euclidean geometries which transcend our (normal) structure of perception. This has led to rejection of Kant's simplistic notion of *a priori* human concepts of Space and Time. This confusion originates from ignorance of transcendental realisations. LSD subjects well-versed in Mathematics can actually realise non-Euclidean space-time geometries in altered states of Consciousness[114].

The orthodox scientific establishment ignores or ridicules any attempt to question its own metaphysical assumptions or foundations, i.e., the hypotheses of knowledge acquisition (epistemology) and the assumptions of what ultimately exists (ontology) upon which Science is grounded.[N12] The Physicalist-Materialist metaphysics and other less explicit metaphysical assumptions are taken for granted by most scientists as self-evident or well-tested and proven. Often a naïve appeal is made to the authority of the scientific establishment or to the names of historical figures who had supposedly disproved contradictory views held by superstitious idiots of the past. However even the most immediate fact of our existence, our Consciousness, remains totally unexplained by Physicalist science which claims falsely that it provides a comprehensive picture capable of accommodating all aspects of Reality. We find this comment in the *International Dictionary of Psychology*:

> *[C] onsciousness is a fascinating but elusive phenomenon: it is impossible to specify what it is, what it does, or why it evolved. Nothing worth reading has been written about it.*
>
> — N.S. Sutherland[115]

In fact Sutherland's view, although extremely apt in regard to Western science, is Eurocentric in that he either is oblivious of Eastern yogic knowledge of the various States of Consciousness or he has simply dismissed this knowledge arrogantly as unworthy of interest as he is unable to understand it. His statement implies that Consciousness *must have evolved* but this is based on an assumption that *egoic consciousness is the only form of Consciousness*. This is of course one element of the *tacit metaphysics* assumed by Physicalist science.

Pure Consciousness in itself, the formless Ground of phenomena, is not a product of material evolution. We have seen various Western thinkers such as Jean Petitot, Arthur Eddington and Richard Jones distinguish the Substance of Reality from the law-like phenomena or dynamic structure described by Physics. This resembles the Hellenistic notion associated with Philo Judaeus distinguishing between God's (subjective) essence (*ousia*) and his powers (*energeia*). Science only describes regular patterns of energetic activity manifesting as matter and evolving into ever-more complex forms. However, Western science and almost all major Western thinkers refuse to accept the existence of Pure Nondual Consciousness (devoid of objective content) and Transcendental (Space-Time Causality transcending) consciousness as their minds remain trapped in their cultural conditioning. Note that Pure Consciousness lacks superimposed objective content as found in the normal dualistic subject-object mode to which Brentano's Intentionality refers. The fact that careful yogic discrimination reveals Pure Consciousness to contain, in a non-objective mode, holonomic information or 'omniscient wisdom', pushes even further beyond the boundaries of mainstream Western thought. Lacking the open-mindedness and the insightfulness to escape their indoctrinations, mainstream Western thinkers cannot transcend their cultural limitations and preconceived notions. Yet these are the same Westerners who boast that they alone possess the one true Universalist understanding of the universe as we saw with the likes of Stephen Hawking and Sheldon Glashow in Chapter 2.

American Cognitivist 'Consciousness theorist' Bernard Baars is first-named editor of MIT Press book *Essential Studies in the Scientific Study of Consciousness*. In this book, Baars makes the stupendously ignorant statement, "We cannot vary our own consciousness from the inside... decrease it, lose it"[116]. Physics graduate turned Buddhist scholar Alan Wallace says, at present there is no scientific evidence even for the existence of Consciousness. Modern science does not even have a theoretical framework for experimental research[117]. In the MIT Press book *Neural Correlates of Consciousness* published in 2000, academic philosopher Antii Revonsuo says that nothing remotely resembling a scientific research programme on Consciousness currently exists[118]. Physicist Nick Herbert says that Consciousness is science's biggest mystery[119].

Indeed, around the time I was identifying the physical correlate of the Light of Pure Consciousness, the 'New Age' Institute of Noetic Sciences sponsored the first of the *Towards a Science of Consciousness* conferences held at Tucson Arizona where a lot of Western "consciousness researchers" and "philosophers" expended a lot of hot air. However, in spite of all the huffing and puffing and the media brouhaha surrounding these events, the Westerners made little progress. Rajiv Malhotra, a US-based entrepreneur who founded the Infinity Foundation to promote wider appreciation of Indian contributions to global culture, raised an audience question of certain platform speakers using Westernised reformulations of Indian ideas at one of these Tucson conferences. He was largely met with a silence born out of embarrassment. As Malhotra pointed out, speakers who had first learnt about Mysticism from Indian Yoga and notions like Dependent Co-Origination and the Momentariness or throbbing pulses of experience from Buddhism and Kashmir Saivism, tended to 'legitimise' making references to such notions by referring to recent Western individuals such as Jung or to Whitehead rather than Indian traditions which actually pioneered such notions. This is what Malhotra refers to as the 'U-Turn'

We find at the back of the Tucson 3 Conference Proceedings, a final section on Phenomenology which was absent in the first two conferences. Note that Phenomenology was placed at the back supposedly because most Anglo-American scholars don't understand what it is and dislike its links with Non-European knowledge. The likes of B. Alan Wallace, a Physics graduate whose Buddhist studies were sponsored by Malhotra, were allowed to argue that a phenomenological approach like those already existing in the East were the way forward. Ironically, Charles Laughlin, in essays such as one in Willis Harman's *New Metaphysical Foundations of Modern Science* (NMFMS) and one given at the 3rd Tucson Consciousness conference, spoke approvingly of profound Eastern mystical knowledge, attacked the ethnocentric naivety of Western theories of Consciousness (no knowledge of altered states), Western phenomenological naivety (limited personal experience, often unaware of their conditioned attitudes towards their own states of consciousness), and discussed the phenomenology of Causation[120]. But Laughlin naively concurred with his 'Biogenetic Structuralist' colleague Eugene D'Aquili's reduction of our sense of Causality to the (vacuous) notion of a 'Causal Operator' along with his other equally vacuous and unspecified 'Operators' for basic cognitive modes (as is repeated by d'Aquili's colleague Andrew Newberg in recent books such as *Why God Won't Go Away*). Such unspecified so-called 'operators' are an example of what Whiteman refers to as the 'Fallacy of the Linguistic Blanket', the false belief that giving a name to a problem it immediately solves (or explains) the problem[121]. Another example is the vacuous Western notion of the *Emergence* of Consciousness out of insentient matter; it is no more than exclaiming *abracadabra* or producing a puff of smoke to mask a childish appeal to Magic.

In Tucson 3 Laughlin notes Husserl's great disappointment that students failed to develop the requisite skills[122]. In NMFMS, Laughlin stated[123]:

> *No matter how solipsistic, sceptical or realistic these and other more complex versions between mind and reality (including even the phenomenology of Husserl) are, they nonetheless tend to be conditioned by different transformations of the same mind-body dualism that also informs Euro-American theological and scientific views.*

Yet, having said all this, Laughin (in Tucson 3) immediately reverts to his own Eurocentric, ontological naivety, referring to *material reality* and an Emergent Materialist trivialisation of his previous talk about Eastern knowledge of Altered States, nonlocal causality etc. Amusingly Laughlin immediately follows this Emergent Materialist view with the heading "Reality is Transcendental"[124]

Ironically, such facile Emergent Materialism and notions of Causal Operators displays Laughlin's own Western naivety and complete misunderstanding of true Transcendentalism. In contrast, we have seen that Willis Harman understood the Primacy of Consciousness and also that the Western notion of Causality could be incorporated into the (transcendentalist) Indian metaphysics. Laughlin says[125].

> *How does biogenetic structural theory conceive of consciousness... Experience is the internally produced play by which the body enacts the world for its own consumption. The body is the producer, the projectionist, and the audience of this ongoing play, which unfolds within the functional space we call consciousness".*

Once again, Mind is conflated with Consciousness *per se* (sentience or awareness) in what is no more than crude, crass Behaviorist Functionalism. As if by reducing egoic or mental processes to bodily processes, *Abracadabra*, the ontological problem of Consciousness magically resolves itself!

This resembles the "Embodied Enactivism" of Buddophile Evan Thompson[126], the protégé of Francisco Varela who ignored his friend the Dalai Lama's views in his neurophenonenology[127, 128]. In fact, as I pointed out to Thompson, his mentor Varela was not the first to use the term "neurophenomenology". Laughlin and d'Aquili had already used the term in a similar misguided attempt to link Buddhist *Abhidhamma* to Cognitive Science in a book subtitled *Toward a Neurophenomenology of Human Consciousness*[129]. Laughlin's view also resembles somewhat Nobel laureate Roger Sperry's preposterous claims, also found in NMFMS, that Emergent Materialism lifts science beyond culture, tradition, metaphysics, etc., and grounds Science directly in the interactions of Reality itself – it constitutes a new cosmology that makes possible the derivation of transcendent moral guidelines[130] ! And pigs can fly! Split-brain researcher Sperry seemed to have a split personality with his Mr Hyde side being a Biblical lawgiver-prophet with a direct line to God who dictates supposedly moral laws for Humankind! Similarly we saw that neurologist James Austin (S&MN member) cannot see beyond his naive ethnocentric Emergent Materialism in his *Zen and the Brain* in spite of 25 years of Zen Buddhist practice and teachings[131].

In spite of the obvious failings of Western philosophy and science to "get a handle" on the seemingly intractable problem of Consciousness, few Western academics dare to contemplate that this failure might implicate the validity of Physicalist-Materialist metaphysics. Like Nationalist ideologies, fanatical support for a football club, fundamental frameworks of mind constituting metaphysical world-views, become deeply entrenched components of personal identity and ideas challenging these frameworks are subconsciously appraised as threats. Even the few who do question basics often remain steeped in the hubris of Western Eurocentrism and refuse to acknowledge that, Easterners, having studied Consciousness for thousands of years, may have something to teach them! As we have seen 'Postmodern' Western academics continue to conflate 'scientific' with 'European', a subtle form of White Supremacism.

The asymmetric treatment of Indian philosophy by the supposedly neutral, value-free scholars of Western "Euroversities" (the term "University" is rather misleading given the ethnocentrism) is seen most brazenly in the proceedings book from the, Honolulu-based, 6th East-West Philosophers' Conference entitled *Culture and Modernity: East-West Philosophic Perspectives*[132]. It was edited by the American scholar of *Advaita Vedanta*, Eliot Deutsch. However, as I have mentioned in Chapter 3, pride of first place in the book is given to the well-known US academic Richard Rorty. Rorty is most famous for having advocated the most extreme form of Materialism, 'Eliminative Materialism' which actually remains honest to monistic Materialist assumptions in that it denies the real existence of the most basic, seemingly indisputable, fact; that we possess conscious awareness. Fashionable Emergent Materialism is, in contrast, 'dishonest' tacit Dualism as philosopher of science Mario Bunge pointed out decades ago. Emergent Materialism sneaks in a new ontological 'substance', an imaginary Consciousness that, supposedly, only appears with the evolution of complex brain functioning, into the *insentient* Material universe.

Rorty supposedly 'eliminated' Consciousness from the cosmos by arguing that it is just an imaginary by-product of our "Folk Psychology", the common parlance we use to talk about our mental states. The convenient notions used in linguistic expression of thoughts and feelings supposedly mislead unsophisticated folk into thinking that our linguistic terms reflect the actual nature of the Mind. According to Rorty, clear-thinking philosophers like himself who 'understand Science' can see-through such "Folk Psychology" and understand that *only physical brain states actually exist*.

> *The problem is not to take account of the special difficulty raised by the 'inside-character' of consciousness, but to convince people that there is no reason to grant that persons have more of an inside than particles.*
>
> — Richard Rorty (1982) [133]

Neuroscientist Edoardo Bisiach, who used this quote from Rorty in a paper on Consciousness, remained unconvinced[134]. Rorty's references to 'brain states' and 'particles' are rather amusing given that his philosophical writing resembles Literary Criticism, like that of the Gallic Post-Structuralists, rather than serious metaphysical and scientific analysis. Rorty's Freudian dismissal of Transcendentalism was in an essay on novelists Charles Dickens and Milan Kundera. Not only did Rorty present absurd and pseudoscientific Freudian arguments against Transcendentalism, he also denigrated traditional philosophers in general as having been elitists and, supposedly, misogynists. Yet in his simultaneous glorification of Charles Dickens as a great Liberal social reformer, Rorty made no mention of Dickens' racism. Dickens had opposed the abolition of (African) slavery and wrote of exterminating Indians after the 1857 rebellion.[N13] Behaviorist Rorty also reduced humans to Skinner's laboratory pigeons, apparently incapable of feeling anything beyond mere pleasure and pain. Rorty's term "Folk Psychology" is much in vogue amongst arrogant and deluded Western academic philosophers who adhere to the Materialist dogma, tossing the label at non-Materialist views in order to tarnish their opponent as (supposedly) unsophisticated *without actually resorting to serious argument or facts*. This resembles the Christian misuse of the word 'Pagan' or the demonising of the victims of State Terrorism who fight back asymmetrically as violent, irrational 'terrorists'!

I recall that the when I purchased *Culture and Modernity* from a central London bookstore in 1991, the bookish sales assistant (obviously a status-conscious graduate) made a big fuss, saying "good choice", etc., seeming extremely keen to indicate that that he had read it himself and was into the fashionable Postmodern 'Cultural Criticism' indicated by the title! In the first conference paper presented in this book, Rorty argues along Freudian lines that mystics and semi-mystical philosophers like Heidegger (or Rorty's "ascetic priests") are fakes who sublimate the sex drive to make themselves appear "more manly than the warriors" by pretending to "penetrate the veil of appearances". Thus, as with the Kantian Constructivists in Comparative Religion, Rorty makes out that 'true philosophy', in the sense of transcending the sensory world of appearances to 'see' Reality is just a self-aggrandising lie! Why this lie should be repeated with such similar descriptions of the Inner Light and associated phenomena in all cultures by very different types of people, Near-Death Experience subjects and, wait for it, 'penis-envying women' such as Mechthilde of Magdeburg or Hildegard of Bingen, escapes 'clever dick' Rorty's limited attention. Only pseudo-intellectuals and the vulgar masses take Freudianism seriously so, as I wrote in O/OM, Rorty's views are, at best, entertaining Literary Criticism (not real 'Philosophy') based on "Joke Psychology".

The largely Anglo-American participants at the Tucson Consciousness conferences are like fish oblivious of the ocean, unable to grasp that they cannot grasp Consciousness because Consciousness *per se,* (i.e., Raw Awareness) is the unitary ground of our existence, containing within itself the entire phenomenal universe. Limiting themselves to scientific approaches will get them nowhere for as was known by some even in medieval England where the anonymous mystic who wrote *The Cloud of Unknowing* realised; What it is to be is to be conscious[135]. In 1994 the Royal Society meeting on Consciousness revealed the consensus that Science understands none of the central aspects of Consciousness; what it is, even what it is for[136]. Note that the emphasis on 'what it is for' over 'what it is' again reveals the tacit Materialist presupposition that Consciousness is merely egoic (conflating Consciousness with Mind) and that it must have evolved for a purpose. My RAS-brainwave correlate of Pure Consciousness demonstrates the distinction between Consciousness in itself and the mentally-conditioned (objective) consciousness that superimposes it constituting mental activity. Psychologist Harry Hunt recognises that the Western concept of Consciousness as subjective and interior emerged within a (Christian) social order that valued the autonomous individual as the ideal[137].

Modern Western scientific thought takes for granted Galileo's division of the properties of objects into so-called 'primary (measurable) qualities' (such as their weights and speeds) and his so-called 'secondary qualities', the sensory qualities such as colours and smells which we actually experience. Galileo's distinction was based Plato's notions of sensory knowledge being subjective whereas knowledge of Geometry was objective[138]. This

'Quantification of Nature' by Galileo also reflects the Pythagorean myth that Reality is Number. Of course, Bohr's Copenhagen interpretation of Quantum physics speaks only of Intersubjectivity (discarding Objectivity), but as d'Espagnat noted, most practising physicists are not so sophisticated philosophically and still adhere to the Galilean Ontology. Science treats only the 'primary', quantifiable properties as 'real', supposedly intrinsic to the object itself, and overlooks the subtle, but undeniable and inescapable, fact that Galileo's so-called 'primary qualities' all presuppose the existence of a conscious observer to make the measurements, etc., which abstract these quantities. That is, Galileo's "primary" qualities cannot actually exist without the pre-existence of observations involving the conscious "secondary" qualities.

Isaac Newton had recognised this contradiction[139]. Both Relativity and Quantum theories have shown that what we measure is not independent of the observer (and also the observer's relative motion) but such inconvenient facts are overlooked. Most scientists simply assume the correctness of Physicalism or Materialism on the basis of authority or faith just like true believers in Semitic religions. Christian mythology held Nature to be devoid of Spirit and Western science, rooted in this Christian mythology, produces a de-spiritualised conception of Nature by abstracting mathematical quantities describing stable and regular patterns of phenomena from the psychophysical reality of our experience. As Whiteman puts it, loosely put, the *physical universe* is what we can see, hear, smell, taste, touch, or sense in any other way in some spatiotemporal organisation whilst we are in our normal physical (i.e., Waking) state. But Science denudes existences of all knowable qualities, for all sensory observations are explained as effects of an unobservable causal structure. Measurability becomes a criterion of 'physicality' or 'Physical Reality'[140].

Beyond the Limits of Scientific Constructs: Looking Far out into our Minds

Returning to the metaphysical claims of the *Sanatana Dharma* such as that Nondual distinctionless, Pure Consciousness is the Ultimate Reality and the Ground of all Being, we can all easily appreciate the following simple fact. For the vast majority of humans who have not experienced Mystical Union or the less profound ego dissolution in Nature Mysticism, there is nothing we can know which exists outside our own individuated ego consciousness. Thus the primary epistemological fact is not that there is a 'Physical World' *out there* but that everything we experience, including the external world, is known to us only *in our own consciousness*. This is the basis of the epistemological Primacy of Consciousness. We saw above how Husserl's first phase of phenomenological 'reduction' resulted in dissociation from the 'Natural Attitude', our habitual delusion that we actually have an immediate acquaintance with the world outside of our individuated field of consciousness.

The well-known perceptual illusions involving Gestalt switches of perspective such as the Necker Cube show that what we perceive is a construction in our brains and not the external world as it really is. Recent Cognitive Science research into perceptual illusions is reinforcing this understanding amongst scientists who all too easily lapse into the myth of epistemological Realism. NeoDarwinism is relevant in regard to understanding that we have evolved sensory systems which seek out selectively and construct perceptual models of the information which has proven most useful for the survival of our ancestors. Discriminating food sources and potential dangers are vital needs; experiencing unmediated reality serves no purpose and leads to information overload. Hence habituation screens out persistent but harmless noise from our hearing. The likes of William James and Carl Jung stressed that Perception acts like a filter. Sensory input reduces our apprehension of the world to a manageable level. The use of Infra-Red night vision, etc., shows the limitations of our sense perceptions to certain aspects of the external world. Perceptual 'colour constancy' under varying light conditions debunks the commonly held Materialist belief that colours are simply correlated exactly with physical wave-lengths of visible light. Thus we can easily see that the so-called 'Physical World' we experience around us is not Reality in itself but in fact our interpretation of *phenomena* (appearances), the perceptual constructions in our own consciousness. Scientific theories, as is nowadays quite generally appreciated, are in fact models of the world and, in this sense, theories resemble the models of the world in the brain which we perceive.

We saw that d'Espagnat is prepared to go a little further than the supposedly 'sublime' Immanuel Kant and argues that the successes of Physics in predicting the behaviour of phenomena must reflect something of the actual Mind-independent, 'Veiled Reality'[141]. d'Espagnat is correct in arguing that Quantum Physics does reflect something of transcendental (his "Veiled") Reality. In response to Ken Wilber's facile conflation of the 'Material plane' of mystics with the 'Matter' of Physics (*see Ch. 6*), I stressed that we never actually perceive directly the entities of atomic and subatomic physics. Fritjof Capra pointed out correctly that the physicist, like the mystic, also has extraordinary perceptual capabilities by virtue of his instruments extending the range of his perceptions[142]. David Bohm also recognised the epistemological importance of Perception and scientific constructs as abstractions of invariant or regular aspects of the information available to us[143]. As d'Espagnat stressed, the so-called photo-images of individual 'atoms' are created in highly artificial situations of isolation in fields not normally found in Nature[144]. Gribbin points out that individual atoms still display wave-like interference fringe patterns in two-slit experiments[145]. This indicates their underlying nonlocal wave structure. Thus atoms are not the ultimate reality, nor are so-called 'fundamental particles' which can be 'annihilated' generating energy, (i.e., increasing the wave frequency in the underlying nonlocal field) and created out of energy.

Physicist Olivier Costa de Beauregard argued that the universe of Physics is not the whole Reality but indicates the existence of another 'psychic universe' of which the material one is only a passive and partial double[146]. In his *Nature of the Physical World*, Arthur Eddington pointed out that the symbolic (abstract) nature of the entities of Physics makes it almost self-evident that Physics is revealing but a partial aspect of something wider. He also stated that the physical significance no less than the mystical significance of a scene, such as sparkling waves as if moved with laughter, does not exist out there but here in the mind. The external phenomena simply satisfied certain differential equations for which mathematicians have a partiality[147]. Franklin Merrell-Wolff said that much in modern Physics sounds more like Transcendentalism than Naturalism[148]. We have also seen that Stanford Electrical Engineering professor turned philosopher, Willis Harman understood that Consciousness was ontologically prior to Matter and pointed out that the scientific picture of causality can be incorporated into the Indian cosmology as a limited case, the reverse is not true[149].

In *Science as Cognitive Process*, Rubinstein *et al.* show quite clearly that the so-called 'paradigms' (Thomas Kuhn's term for conceptual frameworks within which scientific research programmes operate) function in a manner remarkably similar to our understanding of how the cognitive frameworks of our perception function, selectively seeking out certain information which can be assimilated into existing knowledge[150]. The anthropological analysis of 'doing Science' (or 'Sciencing') shows that scientific activity is a class of normal cognition which is ritualised; that is it follows formal rules. As with Perception, scientific paradigms selectively discriminate the information they accept, picking out only that which fits harmoniously into the existing framework and rejects the anomalous information. The perceptual and behavioural constraints on the scientist, along with indoctrination, function to reinforce the reigning paradigm in a manner which *parallels the belief systems of primitive tribal cultures* {*e.m.*}[151].

Recently, the theoretical physicist Lee Smolin has published an excellent overview of the failings of Theoretical Physics over the previous 25-30 years entitled *The Trouble with Physics: The Rise of String Theory, the Fall of a Science, and What Comes Next*. Smolin shows that the once revolutionary paradigm of String Theory has become dominant in Theoretical Physics research even though it has severe limitations and has failed to provide any experimental predictions with which to test its validity. In fact, given its failure to make experimental predictions, it is more a String "conjecture" than a proper "theory". In spite of the failings of the String Theory paradigm, it has seized the lion's share of research funding and academic tenures at elite institutions. Smolin's explanation of this perverse situation involves analysis of the Sociology of Science showing how basic human *tribal behaviour patterns, power relations, etc., lead to "us and them" attitudes* within the String Theory community and the phenomenon of "groupthink" where *an orthodox dogmatic line is adhered to preserve the status of the group (like a priesthood)*. The dominance of String Theory has led to the lack of funding for alternative hypotheses based on other mathematical models which might have more bearing on the progress of Physics rather than the constant *ad hoc* modifications of countless String models in order to try to fit the experimental data {*e.m.*}[152]. I would add that the lack of experimental verification makes String models little more than a mathematical form of speculative metaphysics which Positivist science frowns upon. The idea of 'strings' seems to me no less an idealised human construct than point particles.

In Milo Wolff's holonomic wave model of the electron, the Light Horizon (the 13-14 billion light-year limit which orthodox Science says is the age of the universe since the Big Bang) is interpreted as the limit of the holonomic 'in-waves' coalescing at a particular point from the rest of the cosmos from which particle like phenomena manifest. Thus, if this view is correct, nonlocality would have a limit rather than extending infinitely and this limit would correspond to the knowable universe. Each 'particle' phenomenon that we call an electron would exist at the centre of its limited universe, its extended wave structure not reaching out to infinity but reaching out 13-14 billion light-years, corresponding to the Light Horizon, but the actual universe of galaxies would be infinite[153]. However, orthodox interpretation of the Hubble telescope's Deep Field image suggests that the most distant visible (hence, according to the orthodox view, the oldest) galaxies exhibit less evolved forms[154]. The authors (in Ref. 154) do not explain what 'less evolved' actually implies; presumably it means smaller galaxies (as larger galaxies form by absorbing smaller ones) that are deficient in the heavier elements which form in supernovae and hence the proportion of heavier elements in the universe increases with time. If correct, this would support the Big Bang scenario which Wolff rejects. The WMAP satellite purporting to show the Cosmic Background Radiation from the Big Bang seems to indicate an ancient 'Dark Shell' region where galaxies had not yet formed beyond the 'oldest' visible galaxies. Even beyond this, the WMAP image is said to indicate the first light emitted by the original formation of atoms from the cooling superheated plasma of the Big Bang[155]. None of these interpretations is 'fixed in stone'; given the way our cognitive structures make us see what we expect to see, it could be that orthodox science only seeks and thus finds that information which seems to corroborate its Big Bang model and fills the explanatory-gaps with suitably shaped jigsaw-piece' concepts such as the very problematic notion of 'Inflation' added on *ad hoc* to make the model fit the observed data.

Human beings have never travelled farther than the moon yet Science claims authoritative knowledge of the entire "known" or 'Hubble' universe, which is itself, to all human intents and purposes, of near-infinite proportions. Mathematician Charles Seife says that most cosmologists now believe in an infinite universe (or multiverse) although the 'known universe', within the light-speed determined horizon, is finite[156]. Scientists do not have direct experience of other galaxies or even of subatomic phenomena far removed from our everyday realm of experience. What physicists actually have is mathematical models utilising the limited information we can detect, especially from remote objects, with which they attempt to simulate limited aspects of the behaviour of the external world. Where these models make successful predictions they usually become mistaken as factual descriptions of reality, (i.e., the Fallacy of Misplaced Concreteness) until new evidence turns up which reveals the inadequacies of the reigning models. We saw above that three different versions of Quantum Mechanics, based on different models, give exactly the same predictions. There has been much debate in Physics and Cosmology following the recent discoveries of a seemingly accelerating expansion of Space between galactic clusters (usually interpreted as the Big Bang expansion) as to whether our theories of gravitation, which work so well in the solar system, can simply be extrapolated, both spatially and temporally, without modification onto the large-scale universe and onto all the eras of its existence.

Thus, although modern Materialist Science claims to be giving us an unquestionable framework for understanding everything about the universe, the deeper we examine it the more we can see that scientific models are, in fact, partly the by-product of the human brain and its intrinsic categories of organising information into models of the external world. As stated in the quote from Brian Josephson in Chapter 4, Physics is being reformulated utilising Information Theory, related to Communications Theory[157]. Seife tells us in *Decoding the Universe* that such research is revealing more insights about Physics and Astronomy as modes of gathering and manipulating information[158]. Such mathematical models are never free of metaphysical assumptions because they can only deal with limited abstractions from all the actual information. For those who still remain trapped within the Positivist frame of mind which rejects Metaphysics and believes that Science deals only with actual measurable phenomena, let me quote from physicist Wolfram Schommers' *The Visible and the Invisible*[159]:

> *Does there exist for each element of the theory an element-specific deflection at the measuring instrument? In other words, has each element of the theory a counterpart in actual reality? If not, then the theory contains metaphysical elements, i.e., elements which have no counterpart in reality? ...there are obviously no theoretical conceptions of the world which are free of metaphysical elements.*

Schommers holds a Kantian view that Mind-independent Reality is impossible to access directly. Letting it pass that he also assumes incorrectly that an event in a measuring instrument constitutes "actual reality", rather than a Bohrian 'instrumental' (or operational) phenomenon, his larger point still remains valid; there can never be a one-to-one correspondence between a theory and actual reality. A better argument for revealing a hidden metaphysics is the one I have used in Chapter 3 in regard to Kafatos and Nadeau's claim not to have indulged in Metaphysics. If a system of thought or conceptual-mathematical models is based on assumptions which are not based on direct experiential confirmation, then those assumptions constitute a tacit metaphysic. Science's assumptions that energy is insentient, that Consciousness is only present in ego-like minds and that Consciousness arose through evolution are metaphysical assertions. The variety of multidimensional models constituting so-called 'String Theory' is of course highly metaphysical as they introduce many new unproven assumptions.

Thus when looking outwards into the universe we are still, in a sense, looking inwards into the deeper nature of our own minds. Paradoxically, by looking inwards through yogic practises, not only can we uncover the phenomenological processes underlying this human world-construction, but, paradoxically, through such yogic insight or intuition it has been discovered that our limited individual consciousness (ego) can dissolve and our awareness can expand, transcending spatial limitation, to nondual awareness of Cosmic Consciousness. It can also shift to nondual awareness of the infinite supracosmic Plenum of Pure Distinctionless Consciousness (*nirguna Brahman*) transcending Time itself (i.e., Eternity). Although transcending normal Space and Time, Merrell-Wolff describes this Absolute Consciousness as having something of the character of an unlimited Absolute space which, unlike 'Einsteinian space', is unaffected by the presence or absence of Matter. He found this description preferable to the misleading Buddhist use of "Void" hence his first book was entitled *Pathways Through to Space*[160]. In fact, based on LSD experiments, Grof asserts that Consciousness can become one with any finite aspect of the universe (from atoms to galaxies)[161]. It is human conceptualisation, utilising dichotomous categorisation of phenomena that generates paradoxes for human minds when these conceptual systems conflict. *Paradoxes do not exist in Reality, only in human thought constructs*. In Transcendental states, such thought-paradoxes dissolve in the supra-rational harmony. It is such deeper, mystical connections that have led to many great scientific insights although the scientist may not have been aware of how the insight actually came to him except as a sudden flash of intuition.

Arthur Eddington, as we saw in Chapter 4, was philosophically sophisticated enough to see through the errors of the Materialist metaphysics of Science as he explained in his *The Nature of the Physical World*.

> *...those who in the search for truth start from consciousness as a seat of self-knowledge with interests and responsibilities not confined to the material plane, are just as much facing the hard facts of experience as those who start from consciousness as a device for reading the indications of spectroscopes and micrometers.*
>
> — Arthur Eddington[162]

As stated above, scientists studying the fundamental nature of Matter at the subatomic level are far removed from the Reality they investigate through the mediation of various sophisticated instruments which bring into their consciousness only limited information which they have to reconstruct imaginatively using their mathematical models. Hence we find that Einstein's General Theory of Relativity (GTR) which models Gravity and Quantum Theory which models atomic and subatomic matter have so far stubbornly resisted any unification into a common mathematical model which can describe both types of phenomena.

It is not only the (speculative-metaphysical) String "theory" models with their varying number of postulated extra hidden *dimensions* of space (or *degrees of freedom* for vibratory activity to occur)[N14] but numerous other approaches to unification which have failed here. However, Milo Wolff's holonomic wave model of the electron, although very inchoate, begins to indicate that Gravity can be understood as an epiphenomenon (a non-causal by-product) created by the actual, causal wave activity in the holonomic Quantum realm that manifests macroscopically as Electromagnetism[163]. The little-explored Aharanov-Bohm Effect (Bohm here is David Bohm) also suggests that the Electromagnetic and Gravitational forces are different manifestations of the same underlying 'Electro-gravitational' potentialities of the Quantum Vacuum (Zero Point Field)[164]. I mentioned in Chapter 1 that Anatoly Sakharov (father of the Russian 'layer-cake' Hydrogen bomb) suggested in the 1960s that Gravity may be but a collective phenomenon like 'pressure' which does not exist in individual entities such as atoms and molecules[165]. Recall that *phenomena* means appearances (i.e., not Reality). I also mentioned that Einstein's highly abstract GTR had already transformed (Newton's occult force) Gravity into a derivative phenomenon resulting from the underlying supposed curvature of the mathematical Space-Time Continuum due to the presence of mass.

Milo Wolff asks his readers, if energy is the wave activity in Space, **what then is Space itself** {*e.m.*}[166]. We saw that in his 1967 *Philosophy of Space and Time and the Inner Constitution of Nature*, Whiteman argued as follows. The metaphysical interpretation of QM gives us *indirect* knowledge of the transcendental substructure of Nature and that Matter (energy and momentum) in QM is derived from an underlying Wave Structure. However, this transcendental substructure can be known *directly* through meditation {*e.m.*}[167]. Eddington noted that, whereas Science deals only with measurements far removed from Reality, we do possess an insight which is not limited to such instrument readings; the experience of the thoughts in our own brain. *Our thoughts have a background of Consciousness*. If we assume the continuity of Nature, (i.e., metaphysical Monism) then we should expect that the *background Reality underlying Science's measurements to be of the same nature as the background to our thoughts*. Thus Eddington concluded that the only hint we have into background Reality is that it has a nature capable of manifesting as mental activity {*e.m.*}[168]. As we saw in Chapter 4, in *Science and the Unseen World*, Eddington revealed his view that Reality is Spiritual. The Material World is only the waves, not the ocean or substance of Reality[169].

Thus, unlike the scientist, the yogi can actually come 'face to face' with this background Reality which manifests as mental activity and finds that it is of the nature of Pure Consciousness which manifests mental activity through its energetic activity. But transcending normal Space-Time in the deep planes of subtle manifestation and becoming one with other aspects of Nature, the realisations come to the yogi that, not only our own minds, but all phenomena throughout Nature are manifestations of this underlying unitary Ground, this background existence of Pure Consciousness and its energetic activity. We have seen that nondual Pure Consciousness is established as the Ground by *sublation*. Therefore, in answer to Milo Wolff's question above, the answer is that Space is *akasa* (the first phase of Creation). Space is subtle matter characterised by (energetic) vibrations. Mind and Matter are found to manifest according to the same underlying principles and matter, which Science knows to be a manifestation of an underlying Energy, arises from this unitary ground of all energetic activity creating phenomenal manifestations, the background plenum/void of Pure Consciousness. It is not surprising then that what we perceive as Light is said by Science to be electromagnetic radiation, a form of energy. It also becomes clear as to why both the New Physics and highly developed forms of yogic philosophy, such as monistic Kashmiri Saivism, both describe the manifestation of Nature as a process arising through myriad energetic vibrations. We saw above that a theory can never have a one-to-one correspondence with Reality but our individuated consciousness can dissolve and become One with transcendental Reality and we can attain 'Knowledge by Identity'. Thus we can begin to see that the *Sanatana Dharma* is not merely a Perennial Psychology but has broader metaphysical and cosmological significance as yogis have repeatedly claimed throughout the millennia.

References

1. Grosso, Michael "The Archetype of Death and Enlightenment". In Lee W. Bailey and Jenny Yates (Editors) (1996) *The Near-Death Experience: A Reader*, Routledge.
2. Goldner, Diane (2003) *How People Heal: Exploring the Scientific Basis of Subtle Energy in Healing*, Hampton Roads. (Originally title: *Infinite Grace* (1999)).
3. White, John "Some Possibilities for Further Kundalini Research". In John White (Editor) (1979) *Kundalini: Evolution and Enlightenment*, Anchor Books.
4. Merrell-Wolff, Franklin (1994) *Franklin Merrell-Wolff's Experience and Philosophy: A Personal Record of Transformation and a Discussion of Transcendental Consciousness*: Containing his *Philosophy of Consciousness without an Object* and *His Pathways through to Space*, State University of New York Press.
5. Deikman, A.J. (1966) "Deautomatisation and the mystic experience". *Psychiatry*, Volume 29, excerpted in Ornstein, R. (1986) *The Psychology of Consciousness*, Penguin.
6. Schwab, Raymond (1950, French) English translation *The Oriental Renaissance: Europe's Rediscovery of India and the East 1680-1880* (1984) Columbia University Press.
7. Schwab, Raymond (1950) *ibid.*
8. Sorman, Guy (2001) *The Genius of India*, McMillan India.
9. Radhakrishnan, Sarvepalli (1940) *Eastern Religions and Western Thought (2nd Edn)*, Oxford University Press.
10. Bowes, Pratima "Mysticism in the *Upanisads* and in Œankara's *Vedânta*". In Karel Werner (Editor) (1989) *The Yogi and the Mystic: Studies in Indian and Comparative Mysticism*, Curzon Press.
11. Merrell-Wolff, Franklin (1995) *Transformations in Consciousness: The Metaphysics and Epistemology* (Containing His *Introceptualism*), State University of New York Press.
12. Werner, Karel "Mysticism and Indian Spirituality". In Karel Werner (Editor) (1989) *The Yogi and the Mystic: Studies in Indian and Comparative Mysticism*, Curzon Press.
13. Whiteman, J.H. Michael (1993) *Aphorisms on Spiritual Method: The "Yoga Sutras of Patanjali" in the Light of Mystical Experience*, Colin Smythe.
14. King, Richard (1999) *Orientalism and Religion: Postcolonial Theory, India and 'The Mystic East'*, Routledge.
15. Guenther, Herbert V. (1989) *From Reductionism to Creativity:rDzogs-chen and the New Science of Mind,* Shambhala Publications.
16. Varela, Francisco J. (Editor) (1997) *Sleeping, Dreaming, and Dying: An Exploration of Consciousness with the Dalai Lama*. Wisdom Publications.

17. Hunt, Harry T. (1995) *On the Nature of Consciousness: Cognitive, Phenomenological, and Transpersonal Perspectives*, Yale University Press.
18. Varela, Francisco J. (1999a) "Present-Time Consciousness". In Francisco J. Varela and Jonathan Shear (Editors) (1999) *The View from Within: First-person approaches to the study of consciousness*, Imprint Academic.
19. Varela, Francisco J. (1999b) "The Specious Present: A Neurophenomenology of Time Consciousness". In Jean Petitot, Francisco J. Varela, Bernard Pachoud and Jean-Michel Roy (Editors) (1999) *Naturalising Phenomenology: Issues in Contemporary Phenomenology and Cognitive Science*, Stanford University Press.
20. Thompson, Evan (2007) *Mind in Life: Biology, Phenomenology, and the Sciences of Mind*, Belknap Press (Harvard University Press).
21. Thompson, Evan (2007) *ibid.*
22. Lama, Dalai "Understanding and Transforming the Mind". In B. Alan Wallace (Editor) (2003) *Buddhism and Science: Breaking New Ground*, Columbia University Press.
23. Clarke, John J. (1997) *Oriental Enlightenment: The Encounter Between Asian and Western Thought,* Routledge.
24. Ramaswamy, Krishnan, de Nicolas, Antonio and Banerjee, Aditi (Editors) (2007) *Invading the Sacred: An Analysis of Hinduism Studies in America*, Rupa and Co.
25. Kapstein, Matthew T. "The Divine Presence of Light". In Matthew T. Kapstein (Editor) (2004) *The Presence of Light: Divine Radiance and Religious Experience*, University of Chicago Press.
26. Ramaswamy, Krishnan, de Nicolas, Antonio and Banerjee, Aditi (Editors) (2007) *ibid.*
27. *Ibid.*
28. *Ibid.*
29. Hixon, Lex (1992) *Great Swan: Meetings with Ramakrishna*, Shambhala Publications.
30. Ramaswamy, Krishnan, de Nicolas, Antonio and Banerjee, Aditi (Editors) (2007) *ibid.*
31. *Ibid.*
32. *Ibid.*
33. *Ibid.*
34. *Ibid.*
35. *Ibid.*
36. Indich, William, M. (1980) *Consciousness in Advaita Vedânta*, Motilal Banarsidass.
37. Clarke, John J. (1997) *ibid.*
38. Thompson, Richard F. and Madigan, Steven, A (2005) *Memory: The Key to Consciousness*, Joseph Henry Press. (Reprinted 2007, Princeton University Press).
39. Grof, Stanislaw (1985) *Beyond the Brain: Birth, Death and Transcendence in Psychotherapy*, State University of New York Press.

40. Bakan, David (1958) *Sigmund Freud and the Jewish Mystical Tradition*, D. Van Nostrand Company.
41. Joseph, Rhawn "Sex, Violence and Religious Experience". In Rhawn Joseph (Editor) (2002) *NeuroTheology: Brain, Science, Spirituality, Religious Experience*, University Press, California.
42. Persinger, Michael (1987) *Neuropsychological Bases of God Beliefs*, Praeger.
43. Stevens, Anthony (2002) *Archetype Revisited: An Updated Natural History of the Self* (2nd Edn), Brunner-Routledge (Taylor and Francis).
44. Ramaswamy, Krishnan, de Nicolas, Antonio and Banerjee, Aditi (Editors) (2007) *ibid.*
45. May, Robert, M. (1991) *Cosmic Consciousness Revisited: The Modern Origins ahd Development of a Western Spiritual Psychology,* Element.
46. Odajnyk, Volodymyr W. (1976) *Jung and Politics: The Political and Social Ideas of C.G. Jung*, New York University Press.
47. Stevens, Anthony (2002) *ibid.*
48. May, Robert, M. (1991) *ibid.*
49. Kirkpatrick, Robert and Williams, Forrest (1960) "Translators' Introduction" to Jean-Paul Sartre (1957) *The Transcendence of the Ego: An Existentialist Theory of Consciousness*, The Noonday Press.
50. Sartre, Jean-Paul (1960, English translation) *The Transcendence of the Ego: An Existentialist Theory of Consciousness*, The Noonday Press.
51. Merrell-Wolff, Franklin (1995) *ibid.*
52. Schwartz, Jeffrey M. and Begley, Sharon (2002) *The Mind and The Brain: Neuroplasticity and the Power of Mental Force*, Regan Books (Harper Collins).
53. Stevens, Anthony (2002) *ibid.*
54. Griffin, Joe and Tyrrell, Ivan (2004) *Human Givens: A New Approach to Emotional Health and Clear Thinking*, HG Publishing.
55. Griffin, Joe and Tyrrell, Ivan (2004) *ibid.*
56. Wulff, David M. "Mystical Experience". In Etzel Cardeña, Steven J. Lynn and Stanley Krippner (Editors) (2000) *Varieties of Anamalous Experience: Examining the Scientific Evidence*, American Psychological Association.
57. Jordens, J.F.T. "Prakriti and the Collective Unconscious, Purusha and Self". In Harold Coward (*with contributions by* J. Borelli, J.F.T. Jordens, and J. Henderson) (1985) *Jung and Eastern Thought*, State University of New York Press.
58. Sokal, Alan and Bricmont, Jean (1999) *Fashionable Nonsense: Postmodern intellectuals' abuse of science*, Picador.
59. Gross, Paul, R. and Levitt, Norman (1994) *Higher Superstitions: The Academic Left and its Quarrels with Science* , The Johns Hopkins University Press.
60. Ramaswamy, Krishnan, de Nicolas, Antonio and Banerjee, Aditi (Editors) (2007) *ibid.*
61. Hixon, Lex (1992) *ibid.*
62. Bridgeman, Jacqueline, H. (Editor) (1992) *Huxley and God: Essays*, Harper Collins.

63. King, Richard (1999) *ibid.*
64. Bauwens, Michel (No date) "The Cult of Ken Wilber" (Web article: www.kheper.net/topics/Cult_of_Ken_Wilber.html).
65. Whiteman, J.H. Michael (2006) *Universal Theology and Life in the Other Worlds*, Colin Smythe.
66. Newport, John P. (1998) *The New Age Movement and the Biblical Worldview: Conflict and Dialogue*, William B. Eerdmans Publishing Company.
67. Smith, Huston (2000) *Cleansing the Doors of Perception: The Religious Significance of Entheogenic Plants and Chemicals*, Tarcher Putnam.
68. Lott, Eric (1980) *Vedantic Approaches to God*, MacMillan/Harper and Row.
69. de Quincey, Christian "The Promise of Integralism: A Critical Appreciation of Ken Wilber's *Integral Psychology*". In Jensine Andresen and Robert K.C. Forman (Editors) (2000) *Cognitive Models and Spiritual Maps*, Imprint Academic.
70. Bowes, Pratima (1989) *ibid.*
71. Dyczkowski, Mark, S.G. (1987) *The Doctrine of Vibration: An Analysis of the Doctrines and Practises of Kashmir Saivism*, State University of New York Press.
72. Stroumsa, Gedaliahu G. "Titus of Bostra and Alexander of Lycopolis: A Christian and a Platonic Refutation Manichaean Dualism". In Richard T. Wallis (Editor) and Jay Bregman (Associate Editor) (1992) *Neoplatonism and Gnosticism*, State University of New York Press.
73. Evangeliou, Christos "Plotinus's Anti-Gnostic Polemic and Porphyry's *Against the Christians*". In Richard T. Wallis (Editor) and Jay Bregman (Associate Editor) (1992) *Neoplatonism and Gnosticism*, State University of New York Press.
74. McEvilley, Thomas (2002) *The Shape of Ancient Thought: Comparative Studies in Greek and Indian Philosophies*, Allworth Press.
75. Obeyesekere, Gananath (2002) *Imagining Karma: Ethical Transformation in Amerindian, Buddhist and Greek Rebirth*, University of California Press.
76. Fischer-Schreiber, I., Erhard, F-K., Friedrichs, K. and Diener, M.S. (1989, English translation) *The Encyclopedia of Eastern Philosophy and Religion*, Shambhala Publications.
77. *Ibid.*
78. *Ibid.*
79. Capra, Fritjof (1975) *The Tao of Physics: An exploration of the parallels between modern physics and Eastern mysticism*, Wildwood House.
80. Reported in *Daily Telegraph* (Newspaper) 26th November 2011.
81. Beckford, Robert (2008) *The Nativity Decoded*, Television documentary, Channel 4 UK.
82. Clarke, John J. (1997) *ibid.*
83. *Ibid.*
84. *Ibid.*
85. Stokes, Eric (1959) *The English Utilitarians and India*, Oxford University Press.

86. Clarke, John J. (1997) *ibid.*
87. *Ibid.*
88. *Ibid.*
89. King, Richard (1999) *ibid.*
90. Forman, Robert, K.C. (1999) *Mysticism, Mind, Consciousness*, State University of New York Press.
91. Clarke, John J. (1997) *ibid.*
92. Wallace, B. Alan (Editor) (2003) *Buddhism and Science: Breaking New Ground*, Columbia University Press.
93. Lama, Dalai (2003) *ibid.*
94. King, Richard (1999) *ibid.*
95. Dallmayr, Fred (1996) *Beyond Orientalism: Essays on Cross-Cultural Encounter*, State University of New York Press.
96. Guenther, Herbert V. (1989) *ibid.*
97. Guenther, Herbert V. (1989) *ibid.*
98. King, Richard (1999) *ibid.*
99. Kaw, Maharaj, K. (2000) *The Science of Spirituality*, Full Circle.
100. Esherick, Joseph, W. (1987) *The Origins of the Boxer Uprising*, University of California Press.
101. Malhotra, Rajiv and Neelakandan, Aravindan (2011) *Breaking India: Western Interventions in Dravidian and Dalit Faultlines*, Amaryllis.
102. Mangalwadi, Vishal (1997) *India: The Grand Experiment*, Pippa Rann Books.
103. Davis, Mike (2001) *Late Victorian Holocausts: El Niño Famines and the Making of the Third World,* Verso.
104. Dutt, Romesh Chunder (1908) *The Economic History of India in the Victorian Age; From the Accession of Queen Victoria in 1837 to the Commencement of the Twentieth Century*, Kegan Paul.
105. Davis, Mike (2001) *ibid.*
106. Heisenberg, Werner (1958) *Physics and Philosophy: The Revolution in Modern Science,* (US Edition 1962), Harper and Row.
107. Pribram, Karl, H. (1991) *Brain and Perception: Holonomy and Structure in Figural Processing*, Lawrence Erlbaum Associates.
108. Bruzina, Ronald (2004) *Edmund Husserl and Eugen Fink: Beginnings and Ends in Phenomenology 1928-1938*, Yale University Press.
109. Brown, Daniel P. "The Stages of Meditation in Cross-Cultural Perspective". In Ken Wilber, Jack Engler and Daniel P. Brown (Editors) (1986) *Transformations of Consciousness: Conventional and Contemplative Perspectives on Development*, Shambhala Publications.
110. Bruzina, Ronald (2004) *ibid.*
111. Bruzina, Ronald (2004) *ibid.*
112. Bhattacharya, Sutapas (1999) *The Oneness/Otherness Mystery: The Synthesis of Science and Mysticism,* Motilal Banarsidass.
113. Lancaster, Brian (1991) *Mind, Brain and Human Potential: The Quest for an Understanding of Self*, Element.

114. Grof, Stanislaw (1985) *ibid.*

115. Sutherland, N.S quoted in Wallace, B. Alan (2000) *The Taboo of Subjectivity: Toward a New Science of Consciousness*, Oxford University Press.

116. Baars, Bernard J, Banks, William P. and Newman, James B. (Editors) (2003) *Essential Sources in the Scientific Study of Consciousness*, Bradford Books, MIT Press.

117. Wallace, B. Alan (2000) *The Taboo of Subjectivity: Toward a New Science of Consciousness*, Oxford University Press.

118. Revonsuo, Antii "Prospects for a Scientific Research Program on Consciousness". In Thomas Metzinger (Editor) (2000) *Neural Correlates of Consciousness: Empirical and Conceptual Questions*, MIT Press.

119. Herbert, Nick (1993) *Elemental Mind: Human Consciousness and the New Physics*, Dutton.

120. Laughlin, Charles, D. "Biogenetic Structural Theory and the Neurophenomenology of Consciousness". In Stuart R. Hameroff, Alfred, W. Kaszniak, and David J. Chalmers (Editors) (1999) *Toward a Science of Consciousness: The Third Tucson Discussions and Debates*, MIT Press.

121. Whiteman, J.H. Michael (1967) *Philosophy of Space and Time and the Inner Constitution of Nature: A Phenomenological Study*, Muirhead Library of Philosophy, George Allen and Unwin and the Humanities Press.

122. Laughlin, Charles, D. (1999) *ibid.*

123. Laughlin, Charles, D. "On the Relationship Between Science and the Life-World: A Biogenetic Structural Theory of Meaning and Causation." In Willis Harman with Jane Clark (Editors) (1994) *New Metaphysical Foundations of Modern Science*, Institute of Noetic Sciences.

124. Laughlin, Charles, D. (1999) *ibid.*

125. Laughlin, Charles, D. (1999) *ibid.*

126. Thompson, Evan (2007) *ibid.*

127. Varela, Francisco J. (1999a) *ibid.*

128. Varela, Francisco J. (1999b) *ibid.*

129. Laughlin, Charles, D. Jr, McManus, Hohn and d'Aquili, Eugene, G. (1992) *Brain, Symbol and Experience: Toward a Neurophenomenology of Human Consciousness*, Columbia University Press.

130. Sperry, Roger "Holding Course Amid Shifting Paradigms". In Willis Harman with Jane Clark (Editors) (1994) *New Metaphysical Foundations of Modern Science*, Institute of Noetic Sciences.

131. Austin, James H. (1998) *Zen and the Brain: Toward an Understanding of Meditation and Consciousness*, MIT Press.

132. Deutsch, Elliot (Editor) (1991) *Culture and Modernity: East-West Philosophic Perspectives*, University of Hawaii Press.

133. Rorty, Richard quoted in Bisiach, Edoardo "Understanding Consciousness: Clues from Unilateral Neglect and Related Disorders". In A. D. Milner and M.D. Rugg (Editors) (1991) *The Neuropsychology of Consciousness*, Academic Press, Harcourt Brace Jovanovich.

134. Bisiach, Edoardo (1991) *ibid.*

135. Forman, Robert K.C. "Introduction: Mystical Consciousness, the Innate Capacity, and the Perennial Philosophy". In Robert K.C. Forman (Editor) (1998) *The Innate Capacity: Mysticism, Psychology, and Philosophy,* Oxford University Press.
136. Wallace, B. Alan (2000) *ibid.*
137. Hunt, Harry T. (1995) *ibid.*
138. Burtt, E.A. (1954) *The Metaphysical Foundations of Modern Physical Science, 2nd Revised Edn*, Doubleday.
139. Burtt, E.A. (1954) *ibid.*
140. Whiteman, J.H. Michael (1967) *ibid.*
141. d'Espagnat, Bernard (2006) *On Physics and Philosophy*, Princeton University Press.
142. Weber, Renée "*The Tao of Physics* Revisited: A Conversation with Fritjof Capra". In Ken Wilber (Editor) (1982) *The Holographic Paradigm and Other Paradoxes: Exploring the Leading Edge of Science*, Shambhala Publications.
143. Hiley, B.J. and Peat, F. David "General introduction: The development of David Bohm's ideas from the plasma to implicate order". In Basil J. Hiley and F. David Peat (1987) *Quantum Implications: Essays in Honour of David Bohm*, Routledge and Kegan Paul.
144. d'Espagnat, Bernard (2006) *ibid.*
145. Gribbin, John (1995) *Schrödinger's Kittens and the Search for Reality*, Weidenfield and Nicolson.
146. Von Franz, Marie-Louise (1966) "Time and Synchronicity in Analytic Psychology". Reprinted in Marie-Louise von Franz (1992) *Psyche and Matter*, Shambhala Publications.
147. Eddington, Arthur, S. (1928) *The Nature of the Physical World*, J.M. Dent and Sons.
148. Merrell-Wolff, Franklin (1995) *ibid.*
149. Harman, Willis "The New Science and Holonomy". In Ken Wilber (Editor) (1982) *The Holographic Paradigm and Other Paradoxes: Exploring the Leading Edge of Science*, Shambhala Publications.
150. Rubinstein, Robert, A., Laughlin, Charles, D. Jnr, and McManus, John (1984) *Science as Cognitive Process: Toward an Empirical Philosophy of Science*, University of Pennsylvania Press.
151. Rubinstein, Robert, A., Laughlin, Charles, D. Jnr, and McManus, John (1984) *ibid.*
152. Smolin, Lee (2006) *The Trouble with Physics: The Rise of String Theory, the Fall of a Science, and What Comes Next*, Houghton Mifflin.
153. Wolff, Milo (2008) *Schrödinger's Universe: Einstein, Waves and the Origin of the Natural Laws*, Technotran Press.
154. Steinhardt, Paul J. and Turok, Neil (2007) *Endless Universe: Beyond the Big Bang – Rewriting Cosmic History*, Broadway Books.
155. Steinhardt, Paul J. and Turok, Neil (2007) *ibid.*

156. Seife, Charles (2006) *Decoding the Universe: How the New Science of Information is Explaining Everything in the Cosmos, from Our Brains to Black Holes*, Viking Penguin.
157. Josephson, Brian, D. (2001) Quoted in Steven, H, Strogatz (2003) *Sync:The Emerging Science of Spontaneous Order*, Hyperion.
158. Seife, Charles (2006) *ibid.*
159. Schommers, Wolfram (1998) *The Visible and the Invisible: Matter and Mind in Physics*, World Scientific.
160. Merrell-Wolff, Franklin (1994) *ibid.*
161. Grof, Stanislaw (1985) *ibid.*
162. Eddington, Arthur, S. (1928) *ibid.*
163. Wolff, Milo (2008) *ibid.*
164. Woodhouse, Mark, B. (1996) *Paradigm Wars: Worldviews for a New Age*, Frog Ltd.
165. McTaggart, Lynne (2001) *The Field: The Quest for the Secret Force of the Universe*, HarperCollins.
166. Wolff, Milo (2008) *ibid.*
167. Whiteman, J.H. Michael (1967) *ibid.*
168. Eddington, Arthur, S. (1928) *ibid.*
169. Eddington, Arthur (1929) *Science and the Unseen World*, The MacMillan Company.

10

The New Transcendental Physics and the Scientific and Ontological Superiority of Indian Metaphysics over Greek and Western

> *Indeed, the mood there* [Harvard University, mid-20th Century] *was that ancient civilisations were fit only for the pages of history books. The death of Brahmanism and therefore of Hindu civilisation was being seen as inevitable despite the rescue operation led by stalwarts of 'modern' Hinduism like Vivekananda, Dayanand, Tagore and Gandhi.*
>
> — S.N. Chopra[1]

The Unacknowledged Role of India in the Rise of Modern Science

The 'Oriental' or 'Sanskritic Renaissance' in late 18th to early 19th Century Europe was associated primarily with Romanticism and transformed European culture just as thoroughly as the Italian Renaissance. It was not just Western poetry that was inspired by the translations of Sanskrit texts. Linguistics, Comparative Studies and Theatre were transformed also. The translation of Kalidasa's Sanskrit poem-play *Sakuntala* was one of the great literary events shaping 19th Century European literature[2]. William Jones considered Kalidasa an equal to Shakespeare[3]. The notion of Biological Evolution and the study of Palaeontology were inspired in part by Indological research (*see below*)[4]. Anderson reminds us that it was the vastly greater extension of historical time and that of Creation, along with cyclical time, in Hindu thought that impressed free thinkers. The first heretical and blasphemous saying attributed to Elizabethan playwright Christopher Marlowe by an informer was that the Indians had records going back (supposedly) 16,000 years. Kepler believed the universe began in 4004 *b.c.e.* Isaac Newton also stuck to a Biblical 6,000 year history of Creation, even suggesting that God made the Earth rotate much slower in the first six days in order to do so much[5]. Schwab recognised the influence of William Jones' 18th Century discovery of the common origins and evolutionary diversification of Indo-European languages on the famous

French Natural Historians who proposed evolutionary theories in Biology. Cuvier, Lamarcke and Delambre were linked with Indological researches. Cuvier, the founder of Palaeontology, started re-examining chronologies through his interest in India but the dogmatic pastor could not rid himself of faith in the authority of (the fictional) Moses and Biblical genealogies. Charles Bonnet coined the term 'evolution' in the late 18th Century. Thus the origin of evolutionary ideas was, in part, the result of the Indian-inspired 19th Century Sanskritic Renaissance[6].

Most recent British TV 'Natural History' and Biology documentaries continue to make it appear that the idea of evolution suddenly appeared out of thin air to Englishman Charles Darwin during his voyage on the *Beagle.* [N1] Although Darwin's theory of Natural Selection (independently formulated by Alfred Russell Wallace) did undoubtedly transform human understanding, British NeoDarwinist 'Darwin-worshipping' biologists fail to mention that Darwin's actual theory, as some scientists soon pointed out, did not actually work. It was only the rediscovery of Mendel's work on hereditary factors and the rise of Genetics around 1900 which resolved the paradox. Furthermore, whereas Darwin is presented usually as a daring radical, he actually held back from publishing his ideas for twenty years fearing the from the response Christian clergymen who dominated British universities in early Victorian times. The idea of 'Evolution' was not new but had become associated with French Revolutionary Republicanism and its revolutionary political ideas which rejected the supposedly 'God-given' hierarchical social order. It was only when Wallace came forward with essentially the same idea that Darwin was persuaded to publish his findings[7].

Sir Henry Rawlinson wrote that the study of Comparative Religion, which arose in response to the translation of Sanskrit texts from India, had an effect upon modern thought comparable only to Darwin's *Origin of Species*[8]. However, the most dramatic impact of the Sanskrit translations was on European philosophy. We have seen the influence of Indian philosophy on the likes of Schopenhauer, Carus and others whose Indian-influenced ideas then influenced the likes of Mach and Schrödinger. It was this philosophical revolution that would lead Heisenberg and Schrödinger to state that their co-invention of the revolutionary New Physics in the mid-1920s was inspired by Indian philosophy. As we have seen, both had recognised the parallels between the new Quantum Mechanics and Indian philosophical views long before *The Tao of Physics* brought such parallels to a wider audience. In fact 21st Century Mathematics, Physics and Cosmology actually reflect Indian metaphysics which is both scientifically and ontologically superior to Ancient Greek and Modern Western metaphysics. But you would never guess this fact given the tacit White Supremacist presuppositions lurking behind the purportedly impartial presentations of Western scholars!

James Mill was the racist British historian who demonised Hinduism whilst working for the piratical East India Company of which he became the Second-in-Command. Bernal tells us that James Mill and the German theologian Friedrich Schleiermacher both played key roles in 19th Century Classics' misrepresentation of Plato.[N2] Plato's writings were whitewashed of Oriental influences and their supposed meanings decontaminated of (supposedly primitive and false) Mysticism[9]. White Europeans were not supposed to learn from supposedly inferior Non-White Oriental races (even in the ancient world). Nor were the Ancient Greeks, whose heritage was misappropriated by Northern Europeans as part of their own 'Germanic' ancestry, supposed to be mystics. The Ancient Greeks, or the Hellenes, who settled the Eastern Mediterranean including Afro-Asian lands, were not even 'Europeans' in the modern sense, let alone Westerners[10]. Numerous communities descended directly from Hellenes live in the Arab world where Hellenes settled in ancient times. The 'Sea Peoples' who became the Philistines (giving the name Palestine to Canaan) around 1200 *b.c.e.* are now known to have been Greeks. Hellenes lived in Egypt from at least 750 *b.c.e.* Ancient Hellenes never lived in Northern Europe or in Britain, although Germanic writers made up historical fantasies linking Germany to Greece. The Hellenes did actually settle in lands like Afghanistan and Syria. Yet North-Western Europeans presenting themselves as their descendants.[N3] *Franks* and *Latins,* (i.e., real Westerners) remain dirty words in Greek to this day given the Greek memory the barbaric Western Crusaders' pillaging of Constantinople[11]. We have seen that, in reality, many Ancient Greek philosophers were in fact Shamanic healers but they have been presented by Classics and the History of Science as proto-modern 'scientists' and their philosophies as just rational speculations rather than based on mystical insights.

McEvilley notes that E.R. Dodds in his *The Greeks and the Irrational* (1951) made a stark distinction between **rational** Greeks and **irrational** Orientals. Irrational elements were relegated to Asia Minor. As McEvilley notes, the implication was that thought was even more irrational further to the East {*e.m.*}[12]. In his *History of Greek Philosophy* (1962-1981) published by Cambridge University Press, British W.K.C. Guthrie dismissed Indian Philosophy. He wrote that the motives and methods of Indian schools with their theological and mystical backgrounds were so *utterly different from those of the Greeks* that there was no point in comparisons {*e.m.*}[13]. The extremely Eurocentric Cambridge historian Hugh Trevor-Roper wrote in his 1965 *The Rise of Christian Europe* that European techniques, European examples and European ideas shook the non-European world out of Barbarism[14]. G.C. Nayak noted that some Western scholars such as P.R. Coleman-Norton (1980; *Encyclopaedia Americana*) dismissed Hellenistic Neoplatonism as 'Poetry' rather than Philosophy. As for Indian Philosophy, Nayak added, "*a band of self-appointed custodians of philosophy customarily dismiss the whole of Indian philosophy as mere mysticism, poetry, primitive thinking* and so on {*e.m.*}[15]. Cognitivist theorist Thomas Metzinger's dismissal of four-fifths of humanity as irrational (*See Ch. 5*) shows that such, tacitly racist, Colonial Era attitudes continue to permeate supposedly 'Postmodern' Western academia.

How Hindisat Laid the Foundations of the Scientific and Financial Revolutions in Europe

In his highly Eurocentric and misleading book *The Unnatural Nature of Science* Lewis Wolpert pondered, "one may speculate with concern how

Renaissance scientists would have fared without Euclid and Archimedes". Developmental Biologist Wolpert had been Scientific Advisor to Academic Press, for whom I worked in the 1990s. In 2008 I read this book and debunked numerous myths peddled by Wolpert in support of his rehashing of the 'Greek Miracle'.[N4] In this book Wolpert asked, how was Aristotle to know that the world is constituted in a way that bears no relation to common sense[16]. I noted in my debunking of Wolpert's claims that, had Aristotle not rejected the mystical nature of true philosophy as taught to him by Plato, he might have understood the Indian notion of *Maya* and related notions which distinguish sensory perception of (*common sense*) Space/Time/Causality (or the Empirical world) from the deeper transcendental reality (or the Noetic Realm) which Quantum Physics is revealing.[N5] Wolpert located the Greek origins of 'scientific thinking', most ironically, in Empedocles' famous theory of the Elements which utilised general concepts to categorise a wide variety of natural phenomena[17]. No mention was made of Empedocle's shamanic status or that his Elements were also considered to be deities[18]. I pointed out the Indian origins of the Theory of the Elements and that, whereas Empedocles' theory was now nothing more than a 'museum relic', the original Upanishadic version (the *Panch Bhuta*) with *Akasa* as the first element paralleled 21st Century Physics. Wolpert of course assumed that Materialism was correct, stating that we just had to take subatomic particles and the Laws of Physics for granted[19]. I had just read Milo Wolff's *Schrödinger's Universe*[20] which had just been published and so was able to undermine Wolpert on this point as well. I also pointed out the fact that my RAS brainwave correlate of Pure Consciousness and its elaboration confirmed the scientific validity of the phenomenological assertions of the Upanishads in regard to Consciousness.

At the UK Publishers' Association Centenary Conference (1996) Richard Dawkins quoted Wolpert's view of the 'unique invention of Science' by the Greeks with approval. Dawkins also spoke about the publishing of "mystical rubbish" and hoped that in the next millennium the publishing of mystical 'pseudoscience' (*inverted commas mine*) would wither away[21]. The notion that it was the ('White') Greeks alone who invented Science is a brazen falsehood rooted in the Scientific Racism of the 19th Century. In fact, the revolutionary ideas which overthrew the Aristotelian-Ptolemaic, (i.e., Greek) cosmology, first amongst the Arabs, then the Sephardic Jews, and finally amongst the Christians in the West, and also allowed the medieval Arabs and Europeans to consider Atomism as a possibility, originated in Indian mysticism. Forms of Atomism appeared in India before Leucippus and Democritus[22]. In fact the Ancient Indian views of atoms flashing in and out of existence resembles modern Physics view of subatomic particles more closely than Greek-style point particles. In *Science and the Modern World* (1925) A.N. Whitehead wrote that each primordial element is a vibratory ebb and flow of an underlying energy, an organised system of vibratory streaming energy. The electron is nothing at any instant of time. It requires its whole (cyclic) period in which to manifest itself[23]. Merrell-Wolff recognised that the general insight of the Greeks was not as profound as Westerners assume. We remember the great exceptions like Plato and Plotinus. The Greeks focused on bodies rather than on space. Our modern spatially-oriented mathematics is nearer to the typical feeling of the Indians than to the typical Greeks[24].

It was the impact of the new Hindu mathematics (especially the concepts of Zero and Infinity) on the medieval Mediterranean, which led to the overthrow of the Aristotelian rejection of the vacuum allowing Atomism to be reconsidered. Scholars have noted how the medieval Kabbala introduced new concepts of *ayin* (nothingness) and *ein sof* (infinity) inspired by the new maths from India with its concepts of Zero and Infinity. Both Zero and Infinity were derived from Indian mystical knowledge of the 'Void' transcending the manifest world[25]. Moorish Kabbala and Sufism from Spain influenced Renaissance Natural Philosophy[26]. Hindu concepts of Time, both historical and cosmological along with the Hindu notions of the incredible vastness of the universe also had profound effects on Western cosmology.[N6] Previously, the 'universe' was limited to just the Babylonian planetary spheres encircling the Earth up to Neptune and the fixed stars. Western scholars claim falsely that Nicholas de Cusa and Giordiano Bruno were the first to suggest an infinite universe with countless worlds[27]. The mystical Cardinal de Cusa received his doctorate from Padua which we have seen was a major port for entry of non-Western knowledge from Moorish Spain and he, like Bruno, was associated with the medieval Kabbala of Ramon Lull. Domenico Berti revived the legend of Bruno, the philosopher and 'mathematician', making him out falsely to be a martyr for Science. Bruno was an Occultist, Kabbalist, heretical theologian and his supposed 'mathematics' was in fact Numerology [N7] [28]. Bruno designed magical mandalas meant to make an impression on the memory and transform a person into a religious personality[29].

It was the new Indian system of numerals and much other mathematics new to the West, which the West calls "Arabic numerals", Arithmetic, Algebra, Trigonometry (including the Sine function), Negative and Imaginary numbers, and the solution to general equations (especially indeterminate ones), etc., along with the concepts of Zero and Infinity which actually played a revolutionary role in the Renaissance, transforming the cosmology, banking, art, etc., as well as laying down the mathematical basis without which the Scientific Revolution of Galileo, Descartes and Newton, etc., would have been impossible[30]. As long ago as 662 *c.e.*, the Syrian astronomer Severus Sebokht had written[31]:

> *I shall not now speak of the knowledge of the Hindus.... of their subtle discoveries in the science of astronomy – discoveries even more ingenious than those of the Greeks and Babylonians – of their rational system of mathematics, or of their method of calculation which no words can praise strongly enough – I mean the system of nine symbols. If these things were known by people who think that they alone have mastered the sciences because they speak Greek they would perhaps be convinced, though a little late in the day, that other folk, not only Greeks but also men of a different tongue, knew something as well as they.*

In fact Indian Brahmagupta (born 598 *c.e.*) arrived at solutions credited to Fibonacci (1202 *c.e.*) and Vieta (1580 *c.e.*)[32]. The so-called 'Fibonacci Series' was known in India by Pingala (200 *b.c.e*) and by Virahanka (*c.* 700 *c.e.*). Pingala even developed the Binomial Triangle 1800 years before Blaise Pascal[33]. In his 2008 British TV series *The Ascent of Money*, the Glaswegian Neocon Niall Ferguson[N8] wrongly presented the new methods of arithmetical calculation introduced by Fibonacci to Italy from Algeria as Arabic. So too did a British professor presenting the 2009 TV series *A History of Christianity* and the Professor Bartlett who presented the recent 2008 BBC TV series *Inside the Medieval Mind* which presented Hindu mathematics falsely as being Arabic. Nor is the term 'Hindu-Arabic' fair as all that the Arabs did was to change the shape of the numerals in translation. However, Ferguson recognised the importance of this number system to the rise of banking and finance in Europe, essential to economic development.[N9] In his highly influential book *The Clash of Civilisations*, Samuel Huntington claimed that "Arabic numbers are the world's way of counting"[34].

In a 1980 episode of the classic US children's TV series *Little House on the Prairie* (Series 7, Episode 6) Pa Ingalls complains of not being able to check his son's algebra homework as he can't understand it. Ma Ingalls replies that he shouldn't blame Laura (their daughter who is now the schoolteacher), "Blame the Greeks". Such Eurocentric falsehoods continue to be taught in many Western schools today. Milo Wolff in his 1990 book[35], rehashes Eurocentric myths indoctrinated in Western schools, claiming that the Ancient Greeks like Euclid, Archimedes and Pythagorus [*sic*] were immensely productive in the creation of *algebra* and geometry {*e.m.*}. Pythagorean triplets were known to Egyptians in 2,000*b.c.e.* and in the Indian *Sulva Sutras* which also predate Pythagoras. The earliest actual proof of the so-called Theorem of Pythagoras actually appears 500 years after Pythagoras in Euclid and it was first accredited to Pythagoras by Cicero in 50 *b.c.e.*[36]. Rawlinson wrote that it is likely that Pythagoras was influenced more by India than by Egypt as almost all the religious, philosophical and mathematical ideas taught by Pythagoras (which he famously learnt from Orientals) were known in 6th Century *b.c.e.* India[37, 38]. Even Sanskrit-literate mathematical physicist and mystic J.H.M. Whiteman wrote of the unbelievably primitive state of mathematics in pre-Renaissance Europe. However, whereas he mentioned the Indian roots of Greek Philosophy, he seemed unaware (in 1967) of the Indian origins of the new mathematics that revolutionised Europe in the Renaissance[39].[N10]

In fact, as A.L. Basham and Goonatilake note, the Arabs called mathematics ***Hindisat*** {*e.m.*}[40] or ***Hindsat*** {*e.m.*}[41], the **Hindu Art**. G.N. Banerjee mentions the Arabic term ***ilm hindi*** (Indian Science) for Arithmetic {*e.m.*}[42]. The Arabs called these numerals *Argam-I-hindi*[43] or *hinds*[44] and they were in definitely in use in India by the 3rd Century *b.c.e.* in the famous inscriptions of Emperor Asoka[45]. However, Conrad Rauhfuss (1769) tried to argue that these numerals were derived from the Greek alphabet even though the Byzantine Greeks attributed the invention of Arithmetic to the Indians[46]. The true Zero (as a number – not the Babylonian placeholder symbol) was invented in India around the 2nd Century *b.c.e.* The earliest Arab use of Zero was one thousand years later in 873 *c.e.*[47]. Mohammedans also translated the major Indian medical texts. The 11th Century Arab astronomer and historian of Science, al-Andalusi placed India as the leading scientific nation of the age[48]. The famous Persian polymath Al-Biruni went to India early in the 11th Century *c.e.* in search of India's legendary Philosophy, Mathematics (and Astronomy)[49]. Note that Muhammad ibn Musa al-Kwharizmi (the word *algorithm* arose as a corruption of his name), the main translator of Indian Arithmetic and Algebra was actually a Persian, (i.e., Aryan) and not an Arabian (Semite), as were most Mohammedan philosophers. Like the Jewish and Christian Gnostics before them, the Mohammedans tended to corrupt older Mediterranean (including Greek) philosophy by introducing anthropomorphic and historical religious elements. In fact, whereas Islamic scholars such as al-Khalili point to the rise of the House of Wisdom in Mohammedan Baghdad as the great centre of learning, a similar cultivation of learning had taken place three centuries earlier in pre-Mohammedan Persia. The Latin translation of Al-Khwarizmi's main text made in Cordoba in 1000 *c.e.* by al-Majriti is called *Algorithmi de numero* ***indorum*** {*e.m.*}[50]. The rules of arithmetic using the Indian numerals and zero, already commonplace in India, were clarified by Brahmagupta in 628 *c.e.*[51].

This is not a trivial point for as the Cambridge mathematical physicist John Barrow states, the **Indian number system** is probably the *most successful intellectual invention ever invented by humans*. It is the nearest thing we have to a universal (human) language {*e.m.*}[52]. I read a quote from a contemporary French Historian of Mathematics who compared the invention of this Indian number system to Mankind's first use of Fire. In 1814 the great French mathematician and astronomer Laplace wrote[53]:

> *The ingenious method of expressing every possible number using a set of ten symbols (each having a place value and an absolute value) emerged in India. The idea seems so simple nowadays that its significance and profound importance is no longer appreciated... The importance of this invention is more readily appreciated when one considers that it was beyond the two greatest men of antiquity, Archimedes and Apollonius.*

Laplace himself remains Eurocentric in considering only Greeks amongst the greatest men of Antiquity. In fact, Apollonius's ancient biographer wrote that he learnt Astronomy from India[54]. What Laplace also noted (in the ellipses) in regard to this greatest mathematical invention of all time was the just how remarkably simple and easy calculations became with this Indian system. It was the medieval equivalent of a powerful new tool, speeding up all calculations and allowing Science to expand its horizons, like the electronic computer is nowadays. In medieval Italy doing multiplication the Indian way was as amazing to the general public as magical tricks and they paid to watch such incredible feats as multiplying 27 by 14 (presumably done mentally without writing) performed by travelling mathematicians at town fairs[55].

Hindu origins of Infinitesimal Calculus, Trigonometry, Modern Algebra and Analysis

In 1941 the Cambridge mathematician E.H. Neville gave a BBC radio broadcast on the life of the, then recently deceased, great Indian mathematical genius Srinivas Ramanujan whom, as we have seen, got his insights through meditative imagery. But the BBC censored the section of his prepared speech in which Neville asserted that Ramanujan proved to the English that India could produce geniuses to match England's greatest men[56]. It is easy to forget that prior to 1945, the British were little different from the Nazi Germans in regard to White Supremacist colonial crimes and propaganda. German Alexander Tille had Germanised British imperial Social Darwinist ideology with Nietzsche's 'Superman' whilst at Glasgow in the 1890s leading to Ratzel's 1901 notion of *Lebensraum*[57]. Hitler declared the 1941 invasion of the USSR a 'War of Extermination'. His use of this phrase was based on precedents set by British and American colonial exterminations of natives (*see Note 1*)[58]. It is only the post-war revisionist history of the Anglo-American victors that makes it appear to their own people that only the Germans were capable of such racial genocide and other atrocities (as in the 1914-18 war). Even now in 2014, British comedians on TV shows continue demonising the Germans as if the British never committed similar crimes. In response to such jibes on a BBC TV show in January 2014, the British-based German comedian Henning Wehn commented that he calls Britain's "Remembrance Day" (*a.k.a.* 'Armistice Day'; November 11th) as "Selective Remembrance Day"!

On a recent episode of the BBC's supposedly very 'highbrow' quiz show *QI (Quite Interesting)*, the smug and supercilious 'know-all' presenter Stephen Fry, claimed absurdly that modern Physics, (i.e., that of Newton) would have been impossible without Euclid's Geometry. Anyone with an iota of real understanding would know that modern Physics was actually based on Infinitesimal (or Differential) Calculus. US mathematician Charles Seife notes that the mathematical inventions of both Descartes and Newton would have been impossible without the new Indian maths, especially the Zero[59]. Contrary to Western presentations, subsets of Infinitesimal Calculus had been invented by the Keralan mathematician Madhava over 200 years before Newton and Leibniz[60, 61]. In fact there is strong evidence that Bhaskara II pioneered Differential Calculus in the 12th Century, five hundred years before Newton[62].

Westerners have suppressed the fact that Copernicus copied Arab mathematics such as the Urdi lemma and the Tusi couple in his astronomy. The Arabs had solved mathematical problems that had plagued the Greeks. Copernicus' work contains identical notation and arbitrary details identical to al-Tusi[63]. Although Aristiarchus of Samos put forward a heliocentric model in the 3rd Century *b.c.e.*, the details remained unknown to Renaissance Europe although Copernicus mentions Aristiarchus[64]. Nor did Aristiarchus have knowledge of 'modern', (i.e., largely Classical Hindu) mathematics. However, the Indian astronomer and mathematician Aryabhatta put forward a heliocentric model, in which the Earth rotates around the stationary Sun, dating from around 499 *c.e.*; over a thousand years before Copernicus' supposed 'revolution' in 1542. In the 6th Century *c.e.*, Varahamihira wrote the *Brihatsamhita* in which he stated that the moon rotates around the Earth and the Earth around the Sun[65]. In *Sphutanirnaya* Acyuta Pisarati (1550-1621) enunciated the reduction to the ecliptic that would be presented by Tycho Brahe (1546-1601). Pisarati later produced a simplified formula. In his *Tantrasangraha* (1500) Nikilantha Somasutvan (1444-1545) had a heliocentric scheme with eccentric orbits. He also revised models for Mercury and Venus not bettered until Kepler 100 years later. Tycho Brahe, at the end of the 16th

Century, presented a similar model but Brahe formulated incorrectly the equations for the centres of Mercury and Venus[66].

Aryabhatta invented the basics of modern Trigonometry. Aryabhatta's work, the *Aryabhatiya* was translated into Latin in the 13th Century *c.e.* (long before Copernicus) allowing Europeans to learn Indian methods of calculating volumes of spheres, square and cube roots etc.[67]. The 5th Century Indian mathematics of *Aryabhatiya* only appeared as so-called 'modern' methods in Europe in 1546 and 1613 [68]. Aryabhatta put forward the notion of relative motion 900 years before Oresme in Europe[69]. Although Teresi claims that this *Aryabhatiya* translation did not influence the heliocentrism of Copernicus, Professor Martin Bernal suggested to me that the work of Swerdlow and Neugebauer on the mathematical astronomy in Copernicus[70] would indicate that Copernicus read a Greek translation of *Aryabhatiya*[71]. Teresi, himself of Sicilian origin, does however note that, for Galileo, 'Mathematics' meant 'Geometry' and, contrary to Western textbook presentations, he did not use Algebra. Galileo never actually wrote the equation $s=At^2$ but rather expressed his relation in ordinary written language[72]. Galileo had asserted famously that the 'Book of the Universe' was written in the language of Geometry. The West learnt 'Algebra' from the Arabs who learnt it from the Indian *bijaganita* not from Greek sources[73]. Al-Khwarizmi's *Hisab al-Jabr w'al-muqabala* (Calculation by Restoration and Reduction) was translated into Latin as *Liber algebrae et almucaola* in the 12th Century [74]. The Arabs called the rules of computation *hisab-al-Hind* [75].

In his famous 1817 paper on Hindu Algebra, H.T. Colebooke examined the question, as to whom the invention of algebraic analysis is due. He noted back then that it was highly unlikely that the same mathematician, (i.e., al-Khwarizmi) who studied Indian Arithmetic and taught it to his Arabian brethren could have 'hit upon' the methods of 'Algebra' unaided by the older Hindu Algebra. Colebrooke noted that al-Khwarizmi had also translated an Indian Astronomical work which must have utilised Hindu Algebra. He then framed astronomical tables based on those of the Hindus. *In the 5th Century, perhaps earlier, the Hindus had already developed algebraic methods extending to the general solution of both determinate and indeterminate problems of the 1st and 2nd degrees.* They subsequently advanced to the special solution of biquadratics wanting the second term and of some simple cubic equations {*e.m.*}[76]. In India and China mathematics was largely algebraic whilst in Greece, mathematics was typified by Geometry. Feminist Bethany Hughes' hyped up the female Greek Hypatia's contributions to algebra on her recent UK Channel 4 TV programme on Alexandria, whilst suppressing the fact that Hypatia was primarily a Neoplatonist mystic. In fact, the Greeks had inherited Babylonian algebra but did not make any significant improvements to it[77]. A method of resolving maths problems by reduction to equations was not to be found in any Greek until the work of Diophantus in about 360 *c.e.* Colebrooke notes that Diophantus's work is very far behind that of the Hindus. *The Hindu Algebra was far superior to that of Diophantus*, with a better and more comprehensive algorithm; management of equations with more than one unknown term; the resolution of equations of a higher order and anticipating the modern discovery of solutions for biquadratics; general methods for solution of indeterminate problems of 1st and 2nd degrees going far beyond Diophantus and anticipating discoveries by 'modern', (i.e., European) algebraists; and the application of Algebra to astronomical investigation and geometrical demonstration where again the medieval Hindus made mathematical discoveries and methods that were repeated centuries later in 'modern' Europe {*e.m.*}[78].

The Sanskrit-inspired European Renaissance Leading to the New Physics and the New Age

The Eurocentric presentation of the rise of Renaissance science as a uniquely Greek-inspired phenomenon, which continues to be peddled by Western Historians of Science, does not hold water. But this is still leaving aside the Eurocentric omission of the Second European Renaissance in 19th Century Germany inspired by the translation of Sanskrit texts. J.J. Clarke[79]:

> *The interest in Eastern ideas during the Romantic period was as pervasive as was the interest in China during the earlier epoch, and it was the extent of this interest that led the Orientalist Raymond Schwab to revive the idea of an 'Oriental Renaissance'. He believed that the introduction of Indian thought into Europe from the late eighteenth century onwards and its integration into the cultural and philosophical concerns of the period amounted to a cultural transformation of the same order of that of the Renaissance of fifteenth century Italy,...*

However, both Schwab and Clarke failed to appreciate that the Italian Renaissance was not due to a purely Greco-Roman inspiration as I have just demonstrated. Oriental influences on European thought and technology were not just limited to these two periods of course. German mathematician and philosopher Gottfried Leibniz (1646-1716) is most famous for his development of Infinitesimal Calculus into the method we now use today. Leibniz's Panpsychist metaphysics incorporating holonomy, known as the Monadology, may have been inspired by his familiarity with the Hua-yen school of Buddhism[80]. Citing various writings from the early 19th Century, Schwab demonstrated amply that nearly every major European intellect in that period knew that they were living through a new 'Renaissance' inspired primarily by the translations of Sanskrit texts by the Asiatic Society of Bengal in Calcutta. Schwab states that the profound Orient, *especially India*, was of greater concern to the French Romantics than it has been to their biographers {*e.m.*}[81]. This 'selective remembrance' resembles the attempts by Jung's biographer Jacobi to suppress the Indian influences on Jung, which Jung himself had openly admitted[82] and the suppression of Schrödinger's Vedantism by the likes of Bitbol and Malin today.

The reactionary Barbey d'Aurevilley, alarmed by ideas such as Unity of Religions expressed in Musset's French poetry, blamed all the evils of the 19th Century on Indian influence[83]. Wilhelm and Rawlinson state that Sanskrit philosophy profoundly affected German Transcendentalism. Kant's central doctrine, that things of experience are only phenomena of the thing-in-itself, is essentially that of the *Upanisads*[84]. Early in the 19th Century a British judge Sir James Mackintosh studied the Brahman doctrine with native Brahmans in

Bombay. He was surprised to find in the ancient Indian philosophy an 'Idealism' (*inverted commas mine*) similar to that recently developed in Germany by Fichte and Schelling[85]. Halbfass considered Schelling to be the German Idealist most heavily influenced by Indian thought, more so even than Schopenhauer[86]. Whiteman described Fichte's system as a remarkable Western reformulation of Eastern mystical teachings[87]. In fact Anquetil Duperron, in his notes to his *Oupnekhat* (Upanishads), had already established a clear relation between Brahmanism and post-Kantian metaphysics. Brahmanism-inspired Schopenhauer was later emphasising this same link and in 1841 Edgar Quinet wrote that this link had long been understood[88]. At the beginning of the 19th Century Madame de Staël wrote that the philosophy of the Indians can only be thoroughly understood through the German Idealists[89]. Although this claim is totally absurd it, nonetheless, reveals the fact that German Idealism was inspired by Brahmanism.

In 1833 in the *Revue Encyclopédique*, Jean Reynaud complained bitterly that it was "unbelievable" that German schoolchildren were all taught about Sanskrit whereas French children were stilled confined to the Greco-Roman. He found it equally shocking that not a single Paris library kept a complete set of the Calcutta publications[90]. The aforementioned influence of Indian mystical ideas on Heisenberg and Schrödinger, the two men who invented the radically new physics called Quantum Mechanics in the mid-1920s (Bohr's 1913 quantum model of the Hydrogen atom had not broken fully with Classical Mechanics) may be seen as the culmination of the Indian-inspired new Renaissance which Schopenhauer had predicted. It will come as no surprise that Christopher Isherwood, whose book *Goodbye to Berlin* about the decadent Weimar Republic was made into the musical *Cabaret*, was himself an advocate of Brahmanism co-editing *Vedanta and the West* with Aldous Huxley.

The Indian influence continued beyond the Weimar Republic of course in the Aryanism of the Third Reich.[N11] The young artist Adolf Hitler in Vienna had been an avid reader of the Ariosophists' journal *Ostara* which in 1908 had two special editions on the *Manusmriti* (Code of Manu) and supposed 'race cultivation' amongst the Indo-Aryans. The Ariosophists' founder G. Lanz-Liebenfels was one of the early propagators of the swastika, a symbol associated primarily with Hinduism[91]. Numerous other factors influenced Hitler's racial ideology such as the fashionable Eugenics movement also associated with the likes of Francis Galton and Henry Ford. But as Hitler himself stated in *Mein Kampf*, his inspiration behind the conquest of Eastern Europe and the enslavement of the 'subhuman' Slavs to the 'Master Race', was the White Supremacist British Empire with its enslavement and exploitation of Indians in order to enrich Britain (*see Note 6*).

Contra the naive Eurocentric claims of Philhellenic Madame de Staël, the speculative systems of the German Idealists with their abstruse, unverifiable metaphysics attracted much ridicule and, unlike Yoga-based Brahmanism, remain of interest only to historians. After Vivekananda's 1893 speech in Chicago, Americans began to ask, "Why send missionaries to a country which produces men like this?" Another Bengali Paramahansa Yogananda was invited to Boston by the American Unitarian association in 1920 where he spoke on 'The Science of Religion'. In 1924 a transcontinental lecture tour drew huge crowds across the USA. In January 1925 thousands were turned away from a sold-out talk at the Philharmonic Auditorium in Los Angeles. In 1927 record crowds attended his lectures in Washington D.C. and he was received by President Calvin Coolidge at the White House[92]. Based on his own experiences, Merrell-Wolff confirmed the Brahmanic doctrines, including the Primacy of Consciousness, for himself and called Sankara the greatest 'Idealist' philosopher[93]. However, in reformulating ancient Brahmanic doctrines, even he made self-aggrandising and Eurocentric claims of going beyond others and bringing about a 'Copernican Revolution' in philosophy. He also played down the influence of Sankara on him in his later writings[94].

We have seen that, between the two great wars of the 20th Century, French Nobel laureate poet Romain Rolland promoted 'India's Genius', primarily in the forms of Vedanta and cultural Pluralism, as the great hope for the salvation of Mankind in the face of tribal, European Nationalism and Totalitarianism. In the 1930s Englishman Paul Brunton, after travelling around India, presented the Wisdom of Ancient India as a message of hope to a Western world in the midst of the Great Depression and the rise of Fascism. His first book *A Search in Secret India* (1934) sold a quarter of a million copies in several languages. In later works reflecting upon the *spiritual failure of Western civilisation*, Brunton argued that the only hope for the future lay in a *harmonisation of Western science and Eastern mysticism* {*e.m.*}[95].

Winkelman says that Asian traditions were central influences in the development of 'Transpersonal Psychology'[96]. The massive but largely unacknowledged influence of Hindu 'Vedanta-Yoga' on the US culture over the last two centuries, beginning with President John Quincy Adams, has been publicised in Philip Goldberg's recent *American Veda: How Indian Spirituality Changed the West*[97]. The New Age movement has transformed religious worship in much of the USA. Harvard University Christian scholar John Newport points out that many liberal Christians make Monistic and other metaphysical pronouncements, derived from Vedanta, which contradict official Christian theological doctrines. Newport, who like the earlier Western Romantics conflates Pantheism and Transcendental Monism (or Panentheism), wrote in his *The New Age Movement and the Biblical Worldview* {*e.m.*}[98]:

> *The New Age bottom line can be stated in three words "All is One". The cosmos is seen as a pure undifferentiated, universal, energy-interconnected process...God is seen as an impersonal energy, force or consciousness. ...**In most respects New Age can rightly be classified as a Western expression of classic Hinduism.***

Rajiv Malhotra has drawn attention to Western Christians and New Agers misappropriating Hindu knowledge and reformulating it as Christian or Western. Malhotra calls this distancing of oneself from the Hindu sources, the 'U-Turn'. To some extent those undertaking the U-Turn have sought to aggrandise themselves as supposedly original thinkers by such distancing and relabeling rather than just pandering to xenophobia. Harmon Bro says that it is a conscious fraud to promote indiscriminately the widely studied *A Course in Miracles* as literally the words of Jesus. Helen Schuchman's bestseller claims to have come to her through her Inner Voice but the text implies that the source is the Biblical Jesus! This overlooks the *obviously Vedantic substance* of the teaching denying the crucifixion and ontologically existent Sin and Evil {*e.m.*}. 'Miracle' is taken to mean a new perception of ourselves as Sinless Sons of God, never actually separated from God. Along with Sin, the notion that the execution of Jesus serves as vicarious atonement for our sin is dismissed as false. Such, clearly non-Christian misappropriation of Brahmanism, robs students of a legitimate study of Hindu philosophy[99]. Newport comments that Evangelical Christianity can learn from Tantric Hinduism given the latter's balanced view of the human body and sexuality[100]. Malhotra has pointed out how Christian groups have sneaked in such Tantric Hinduism into their practices pretending that they are old Christian practises by labelling them with Christian terminology.

In her 2002 book *Original Sin: Origins, Developments, Contemporary Meanings*, Christian Feminist Tatha Wiley has a chapter on the work of Jesuit Bernard Lonergan (died 1984). According to Lonergan *Consciousness is the Empirical base from which concrete meanings of Theological terms may be derived*. The 'inner Word' of God is (esoteric) religious experience. The need is to ground Theology in the dynamics of Human Consciousness. He wanted Christianity to shift from medieval Speculative Metaphysics to a Methodological Theology based on concrete experience, moving from abstract medieval concepts to *empirical realities verifiable in inner human experience*. This approach would ask questions like to what psychological or existential experience does Infusion of Sanctifying Grace or Sanctifying Grace as supernatural habit refer. Sin is alienation from one's authentic being. Such a *contraction of Consciousness into Egoism is basic Sin* {*e.m.*}[101].

In the previous chapter Wiley told of how the 20th Century theologians, Jesuit Piet Schoonenberg and Protestant Reinhold Niehbuhr had reinterpreted the notion of 'Sin' as Egotism which is alienation from God[102]. In his his recent book *Being Different*, Malhotra stressed the Exclusivism of Christian belief based on adherence to the Nicene Creed which he spelled out in full. If Christians are to be true to their dogmatic faith then they cannot truly respect other religions as this would compromise the Nicene Creed. In Note 9 for Chapter 9 I mentioned that, in 2000, Cardinal Ratzinger and the late Pope John Paul opposed the changing of the wording *Toleration* (of) to *Mutual Respect* (for) other religions (originally proposed by Malhotra). Wiley says that creating Us/Them distinctions is sinful. Hence Christian exclusivism in regard the status of Christ and the Church, when allied to political power, is sinful in denigrating non-Christians and becomes religious imperialism[103]. Malhotra also stressed how Christianity has suppressed development of the notion of the indwelling Holy Spirit as this contradicts the Theist separation of God and Man[104]. Whilst stressing Hindu difference Malhotra championed the Doctrine of Non-egoic Action (or 'Action without desire/attachment'; *niskama karma*) from the *Bhagavad Gita*. I pointed out that a deeper mystical understanding of the Christian doctrine of Redemption as infusion of Holy Spirit reveals that it is in fact referring to largely the same Non-egoic Action.

Lonergan referred to St Paul: God's Love poured into our Hearts through the Holy Spirit that has been given to us. The Power of the Spirit offsets the power of Sin (Egotism). Live by the Spirit whose fruits are love, joy, peace, patience, kindness, generosity, gentleness and self-control. The Divine indwelling (of the Holy Spirit) effects a transformation of our values, opening the heart to seek the Good. Its authenticity counters the inauthenticity engendered by alienation (Egotism). Self-sacrificing love of others constitutes redemption. Lonergan wrote that the originating value is *Divine Light* and Love while the terminal value is the *whole universe*. By sustained authenticity, humans participate with God in the realisation of the universe {*e.m.*}[105].

What is striking but also typical in Wiley's presentation of Lonergan's ideas is her complete omission of the fact that Lonergan was 'Indianising' or 'Hinduising' Christianity. Consciously or not, Lonergan was reinterpreting Christianity in a manner resembling Yogic phenomenology which he must have been aware of. *The grounding of Theology in the dynamics of human Consciousness* is exactly what was achieved in the Upanishads a thousand years before the alleged birth of the Gospel character Jesus.[N12] Alienation from our 'authentic being' is another way of stating 'ignorance of our True Self' as in the Vedantic *avidya*. In referring to Divine Light (Inner Light) and the 'whole universe' Lonergan appears to be referring the experience of the *Atman* leading to Cosmic Consciousness (*Saguna Brahman*).

This attempt to re-derive Christian theology from the transformations of Consciousness is a tacit acknowledgement by such spiritually-literate Christians of the Universal status of the Vedantic methodology and metaphysics based on Yoga. The popularity of Yoga around the world has been based on the superficial preliminary *Hatha Yoga* processes rather than real *Yoga* as a method to attain mystical union. However, some British clergymen have banned the superficial exercise Yoga classes from their church halls as they recognise it is the preliminary stage of Hindu meditative practise leading to Hindu philosophy. We have seen that, in 2011, the Vatican's Chief Exorcist Gabriele Amorth asserted publicly that Yoga was 'Satanic' as it leads to Hinduism[106]. Cover-ups of the dirty deeds of paedophile Catholic priests by the ex-Hitler Youth member Pope Benedict (when still Cardinal Ratzinger) was however not the 'work of the devil'!

Christian true believers (e.g., Creationists) and defenders of the mafia-like papal imposters peddling superstitions to the gullible masses fear both Yogic phenomenology and Science. In contrast, non-dogmatic Hinduism has never feared Science but rather welcomed it. Hinduism was seen as being in tune with Science given its claim to be based on repeatable yogic disclosures (rather than unique revelation). Numerous Hindu Reformers in 19th Century India attempted to give 'scientific' interpretations of the *Atman*[107]. Of course, poorly educated Indian writers have continued to peddle pseudoscientific nonsense about the scientific basis of Hindu thought which is easily dismissed by critical minds. Nonetheless, the very search for a scientific interpretation shows that Hinduism, unlike the Semitic 'religions', does not simply accept dogmatically prescribed doctrines to be held unquestioningly on the basis of 'Faith'. Klaus Klostermaier wrote in his 1989 *A Survey of Hinduism* that what we see happening with Hinduism today may be the formation of a truly new world religion. Hinduism is articulating its essentials, it is modernising. It would not be surprising to find Hinduism the dominant religion of the 21st

Century. Hinduism is more open than any other religion to new ideas, to scientific thought and social experimentation[108]. He added[109]:

> *A fair number of leading physicists and biologists have found parallels between modern science and Hindu ideas. An increasing number of creative scientists will come from a Hindu background and will consciously and unconsciously blend their scientific and their religious ideas. All of us may be already much more Hindu than we think.*

When I read this in 1990 I did not consider myself a 'Hindu' in any real sense. But as I wrote in O/OM, the deeper I looked into my own thought, the more Hindu I began to appear, even creating a philosophical *sutra* which poured forth from my subconscious in 1991. This was over 15 years before I read about the Vedic true *brahmana* seeking Divine Inspiration to 'word the world' (*see Ch. 7*). Then whilst trying to elaborate on the meaning of my philosophical poetry in the early 1990s, experiencing numerous synchronicities, I identified the physical correlate of the *Atman*, based on evidence mainly from Hindu and Buddhist yogic knowledge. Jung wrote that the *unus mundus* (equivalent to Cosmic Consciousness) can intervene in (egoic) consciousness usually under conditions of stress related to the individual's search for deeper truth (or meaning in life). Through synchronicities the *unus mundus* level of Reality orchestrates events at the mundane level. Struck by such 'meaningful coincidences', the individual's life is transformed so that the individual moves towards realisation of the deeper truth[110]. From personal experience there seems to be much truth in Jung's view although synchronicities are not anthropocentric and do not play out some predetermined drama.

We see that the Neo-Brahmanic New Age metaphysics appeals primarily to the well-educated classes in the West along with those who have personal experiences of a psychical and/or spiritual nature. We have seen that Whiteman argued that creation of the new Quantum Mechanics (QM) of the 1920s actually resulted in a new science indicating an underlying Wave Structure that provided Universal Cohesion. The interpretation of QM leads to indirect knowledge of the Transcendental Substructure of Nature which can be known directly through mystical contemplation[111]. We also saw that Nobel laureate physicist Brian Josephson made similar assertions of experiencing Transcendental Quantum Reality through meditation at the 1986 Bombay conference on the Synthesis of Science and Religion[112]. The later books by David Bohm on the interpretation of QM, less scholarly than Whiteman's work and not based on personal experience, were influenced by Bohm's friendship with famous mystic guru Jiddu Krishnamurti and Rosen refers to Bohm's Vedantism[113]. We shall see that the new QM which indicated a deeper, Transcendental Quantum Reality, actually helps to confirm the ontological validity of the Hindu Brahmanic and Tantric metaphysics developed by the ancient Indians. This Indian inspiration leads back to Indian metaphysics and the one true Ontology.

Ontological Superiority of Indian Transcendental Process Metaphysics and Mathematics over Greek Geometric Idealism and Platonism

At the beginning of his TV Series *The Story of Maths*, Professor Marcus de Sautoy asserts that one discipline reveals the underlying reality beneath the physical universe; that discipline is Mathematics[114]. We saw above that Merrell-Wolff recognised that our modern spatially-oriented mathematics is nearer to the typical feeling of the Indians than to the typical Greeks oriented to static geometric objects[115]. Goonatilake states that, (dynamic) 'operations' were more basic in Indian maths than (static) 'being'. Indian maths emphasised Becoming rather than (formal) Being[116]. I have added the word *formal* in parentheses here to differentiate 'static' forms of objects from Being *per se*. Goonatilake refers to "Physical Reality" so, presumably, he is a Physicalist and does not appreciate the deeper transcendental formless, Nondual Consciousness (*cit*) as Being *per se* (*sat*). A.O. Lovejoy in his *The Great Chain of Being* stressed the contradiction inherent in the Platonic tradition of the static, immutable supposed perfection of the Platonic Absolute co-existing with its generative and diverse material Creation. For Plato 'Good' meant 'perfect' and excludes change, development, progress and novelty. Lovejoy saw 18th Century Romantic Evolutionism temporalising the Platonic Chain of Being[117]. This metaphor of a 'chain', as rehashed by Ken Wilber, is very misleading suggesting a linear atomistic system rather than the phase-transition-like process occurring throughout the whole universe implied by Plotinus in his Emanationism. What the Romantics temporalised was actually the 'Planes' or 'Levels' of Being corresponding to Plotinus 'hypostases' which emanate out of the One. Western Romantic evolutionary, temporal process ideas were primarily inspired by Indian Philosophy with its cyclic *kalpas* of creation and dissolution, vast time scales and also by notions of the phenomenal world as *samsara* ("ceaseless") or dynamic flux. Western Classics' view of Heraclitus, based on believing Plato's interpretations, as teaching that All is Flux has been challenged by modern research based on the few extant fragments of Heraclitus.[N13]

Greek-style formal geometrical structures are, as already indicated in regard to the underlying Wave Structure of Matter (WSM), idealised abstractions from (conscious) experience. In a section entitled 'The Mathematisation of Nature' in his *Crisis of the European Sciences and Transcendental Phenomenology*, Husserl discussed the origins of Geometry in the abstraction of idealised *limit-forms* from the actually amorphous, shifting forms of experience[118]. As Whiteman says, the Greeks abstracted ideal intuitive properties from the actual ones[119]. Ideal Geometry exists only in human imagination. Thus Western thinkers who imagine that Ultimate Reality is 'Geometry' or that 'Physics reduces to Geometry' are again guilty of the Fallacy of Misplaced Concreteness. Susantha Goonatilake states,"The Indian tradition considered Mathematics as a natural science, an area of empirical reality and not of absolute truths", and, as in natural sciences, observations and experiments were utilised. Results were generally given without the detailed reasoning. The Indian demonstration of proof, *upapatti*, was primarily found in commentaries[120]. Indians used the Principle of Mutual Exclusion without formulating a general law. Goonatilake adds that modern Intuitionists do not view the laws of logic as either eternal or *a priori*. Logic changes according to circumstances and so the logic that applies in the field of finite objects would be invalid if applied to the infinite realm[121]. Such understanding ties in with Indian Philosophy where mundane logic (*tarka* – atomising logic) and spatiotemporal categories of Language become inappropriate in the suprarational, nondual realisations of the Transcendental Realm. Similar notions have arisen recently in regard to the interpretation of Quantum Theory requiring a Quantum Logic in a nonlocal reality transcending mutually exclusive, extensive objects.

Due to the Indian stress on operations, the Rational/Irrational number dichotomy did not arise in India unlike 'Greece', (i.e., the Hellenistic world) where numbers were considered rational (perfect ratios)[122]. Indians thus utilised fractions and irrational numbers in the *Sulva Sutras* (dating between 800-500 *b.c.e*)[123]. The so-called 'Pythagorean theorem' plays a leading role in the older *Sulva Sutras*[124]. In fact von Schroeder argued that Indians should be ascribed a very considerable influence on Greek geometry. But Cantor and Weber tried to claim an Alexandrian Greek origin for the *Sulva Sutras* which was absurd as these *Sutras* were part of the rigidly preserved sacred ancient knowledge of the Brahmins, including the Vedas, which were not tampered with[125]. Bernal tells us that the Ancient Greeks themselves state that they learnt Geometry from the Egyptians[126].

We have seen that Barrow has called the Indian arithmetical number system the greatest intellectual invention of all time[127]. Indians invented what became 'modern' Algebra which is indispensible to the mathematical modelling undertaken by Science. Indians began the development of Infinitesimal Calculus which was the basis of modern Physics. Indians invented Negative numbers, Imaginary numbers and Zero without the metaphysical and theological concerns that plagued their introduction in the West[128]. The secrecy of the Pythagoreans in regard to the existence of Irrational numbers is well known. The Pythagorean myth of Ultimate Reality as Numbers finds echoes in Galileo's Quantification of Nature with his ontological myth of quantifiable so-called Primary Qualities. Even in 16th and 17th Century Europe, Indian Negative numbers were considered absurd (by the likes of Descartes). As late as the 19th Century influential European mathematicians such as Kronecker attempted to rid Mathematics of Irrational, Imaginary and Transfinite numbers[129]. I have mentioned above the rejection by the medieval Church of the Zero and Indian numerals (partly to prevent fraud) leading to their secretive use by bankers. The Indian number Zero as Seife describes it was a 'Dangerous Idea' challenging the Aristotelian rejection of Voids in Nature[130] and it took a long time for the Europeans to accept it [131].

Zeno's paradox was never considered seriously in India[132]. As stated above the use of dichotomous Greek logic culminated in such *reductio ad absurdam* arguments for which Catholic Scholasticism was famous whereas Science originated more from Magic (Occultism) and Empiricism. Henri Bergson argued correctly that such paradoxes as Zeno's arise from the myth of the infinite divisibility of Time whereas, in reality, Time is discontinuous with discrete durations[133], the 'specious present' of William James. I would add that Zeno's paradoxes of motion are based on a false ontology of autonomous entities moving in supposedly empty space whereas, in reality, the translocation of a phenomenal form involves holonomically interdependent manifestations in a dynamic flux which, in reality, cannot be broken up into discrete spatiotemporal steps of 'Cause and Effect' except in our imagination. Indian metaphysicians familiar with the Momentariness of the Temporal Stream of Consciousness and dynamic, holonomic process views of Nature would not fall for such Idealisations. *Paradoxes exist only in the human mind*, due to erroneous assumptions and conceptions, they do not pertain to Reality. Mystical Indian Philosophy knew that seeming conceptual contradictions are derived from the illusory world of sense perception, dissolving into supra-rational harmony (beyond the opposites) in the Transcendental Reality. We have seen that the Wave/Particle dichotomy only exists for those who cling to the Democritan/Geometric myth of point particles. Empty space is again a Greek idealisation that never actually exists. It was introduced by Democritus to allow his mythical 'atoms' to move about. Indian philosophy interpreted the Transcendental Reality more correctly, as contemporary mystics with scientific backgrounds appreciate, in terms of the dynamic, energetic vibrations of *Akasa*.

One such contemporary mathematician-mystic is Ralph Abraham whose own LSD and Yogic experiences under the guidance of gurus in India have led him toward the Indian Tantric *Trika* philosophy of Kashmir Saivism which emphasises the Doctrine of Vibration and the related Brahmanic-Yogic notion of the *Akasa*. Thus Abraham has researched the relations between vibrations and the manifestion of forms (Cymatics). In a 2008 paper entitled *Mathematics and the Psychedelic Revolution*, before moving on to the subject of 'Vibration and Forms', Abraham reveals how the 1960s psychedelic drug culture played a key role in Silicon Valley Computer Revolution, Computer Graphics innovation, and also the development of new Mathematics, especially the so-called 'Postmodern Maths' of Chaos Theory and Fractal Geometry[134]. He states {*e.m.*}[135]:

> *Another event in 1990, followed the publication of a paper in the International Journal of Bifurcations and Chaos when an interesting article appeared in the monthly notices of the American Mathematical Society, the largest union of research mathematicians in the world. The article totally redefined mathematics, dropping numbers and geometrical spaces as relics of history, and adopting* ***a new definition of mathematics as the study of space/time patterns.*** *Mathematics has been reborn, and this rebirth is an outcome of both the computer revolution and the psychedelic revolution...*

Remember that Galileo claimed that the 'Book of the Universe' was written in the language of Geometry and that Galileo did not use algebraic equations. Albert Einstein's General Theory of Relativity (GTR) is very much rooted in Geometry, albeit non-Euclidean. As stated above Arthur Eddington asserted that the Space-Time Frame of GTR was a fictitious and arbitrary human mental construct overlaid on Nature[136]. In his 1967 *Philosophy of Space and Time*, Whiteman discussed the Myth of 'Physical' Geometry and the Abacus Fallacy. Briefly, this involves the confusion of the 'order of approach' with the 'order of reality'. He concludes that it is far more true to say that we have applied a prescribed geometry (regardless of whether it is prescribed by us or by Nature) to Nature in order to measure it. It is clearly false to say, in the manner of Galileo with his 'Primary Qualities', that the measures we read off from nature are uniquely given. Measurement applies only to the 'Actual', (i.e., the 'actualised' phenomenal manifestation) not to the potentialities (represented in Physics by fields)[137]. In his January 2010 BBC TV *Horizon* documentary "How long is a piece of string", de Sautoy showed that, ultimately, measurements reflect human interests and impositions rather than being simply inherent in Nature[138]. However, he failed to recognise the more profound implications of this in regard to contradicting the ontological basis of Galilean Science.

Whiteman's distinction above between the 'actual' and the potential in regard to measurement parallels the Vedantic philosophy relating to the famous notion of *māyā* (the creative power of the Absolute which is often rendered as 'illusion'). The book *Māyā in Sankara* which I bought in 1994 and contained the Hindu myth of Sutapas (*see Ch. 12*) was subtitled "Measuring the Immeasurable"[139]. Kaplan tells us that *māyā* is the limitation of that which is without limitation. *Māyā* is related to *mātrā* (measure) and states[140]:

> *Māyā understood in terms of mātrā superimposes categories of quantification such as space and time on the amatro 'nantamātrśca. Māyā is the traversing of the non-objectifiable with structures and limits which appear to make it into objects.*

Kaplan's reference to the Sanskrit term *mātrā* ties us in with the so-called *tanmātrā* (that matrix) which is the Yogic technical term in the Yoga Sutra tradition for the flow of the Inner Light constituting the Time/Space Matrix of (empirical) Perception[141]. *Māyā* is also the cosmic generalisation of *avidya* (ignorance of Reality) which refers to our mistaking the perceptual world of spatiotemporal phenomena for Reality. As such, *Māyā* (the mysterious creative power of the Absolute) can be understood as the emergence of a spatiotemporal order in the cosmos at large, out of the Transcendental Realty, which is mirrored in our perceptual world.

Wolfram Schommer's reformulation of Quantum Mechanics (QM) so as to incorporate the ('Buddhistic' according to Einstein) Mach's Principle does away with an *a priori* Space-Time. Instead Space-Time arises from an underlying 'prespace' of fundamental energy/momentum processes[142]. We have seen that Schrödinger stressed that there are no trajectories in QM, only manifestations of 'particle-like' phenomena[143]. David Bohm had also argued that Space-Time should not be viewed as *a priori* but as an abstraction. Bohm saw QM as describing the 'enfolding' of a localised event from a deeper Nonlocal reality (his implicate order) involving the whole universe[144]. As we have seen, in QM relates energy to *wave* frequency and momentum to *wave*-length. Therefore, Schommers' work actually points towards the WSM view as indicated by Whiteman (1967)[145], Bohm (1992)[146] and developed by Wolff (1990, 2008)[147,148]. As with the Einstein- Podolsky-Rosen thought experiment, Einstein's challenges to the worldview of Quantum Theory have all met with failure. Indeed, Leonard Susskind has a chapter entitled "Einstein, Don't Tell God What to Do" in his 2008 book *The Black Hole War: My Battle with Stephen Hawking to Make the World Safe for Quantum Mechanics*[149]. Only the metaphysically naive such as Hawking and other hard-line Relativity theorists would consider Einstein's idealised, geometric GTR to be more fundamental than QM. The Quantum Revolution in Physics, inspired in part by Indian mystical philosophy, has led to modern Physics and Cosmology paralleling Indian Brahmanic metaphysics in key respects (rather than Greek Philosophy). Similarly this shift to a broader view of Maths is a move away from Grecian Static Idealism towards a dynamic process view that is more in tune with the traditional spirit of Indian Mathematics and Metaphysics.

Eurocentric writers such as Shimon Malin[150] hype up the metaphysics of Plotinus as the most sophisticated mystical philosophy. Ironically, Whitehead's Process Philosophy, which Malin also hypes up as '*rigorous*' and '*magnificent*' {*e.m.*} actually lacks any Space-Time transcending deeper reality, (i.e., the very Noetic Field of Potentialities beyond spatiotemporal phenomena that Malin attempted to elucidate). In regard to philosophical rigour, Whitehead's *Process and Reality* resembles the works of medieval Scholastics which often result in *reduction ad absurdam* arguments. A true ontology can only be established by super-Empirical (Willis Harman's 'Radical Empiricism') observation of the Transcendental not by rigorous logical reasoning! Malin even cites a J.M. Burgers who wrote in 1963 that Whitehead's philosophy accounts for the weird aspects of QM[151]. This is nonsense as one cannot interpret QM without Transcendence of Space-Time. Whiteman points out in his critique, Whitehead's Process Philosophy (of the late 1920s) amounts to a *one-level actuality* view of Space-Time which is asserted on *a priori* grounds to be 'flat'. There is no going beyond the actual entities to find anything more real. For Whitehead, even God is a 'primordial actual entity'[152].

Whitehead's obscurantist and inchoate, yet much hyped, Neo-Scholastic attempt at creating a system of speculative metaphysics in *Process and Reality* (P&R) is full of neologisms such as 'actual occasions', 'prehension' and 'concrescence' which make the book almost impenetrable to the uninitiated. Whitehead remained obsessed with Reason, basing his God concept on the Rationalist's need for a self-subsisting, unexplained, basis to the rational superstructure. This resembles the medieval Scholastic attempts to provide a rational proof for the existence of God. P&R was not based on mystical experience of the Divine and Whitehead remained ignorant of the Reality that transcends rational concepts. As Jack Goody points out, contrary to the naive presentations of Classicists and Historians of Science, Greek logic was not essential to the rise of Science during the Italian Renaissance. Aristotelian logic was adopted by the Catholic Church after Aquinas's synthesis of Aristotle with Christian mythology. Thus Greek logic actually culminated in medieval Christian Scholastic nitpicking which had little to do with the actual rise of Science. Formal logic and Euclidean presentation has little to do with real scientific research outside Pure Mathematics[153]. Early modern science was based on experimentation which Ancient Greeks like Plato had detested in contrast to Pure Thought. 'Magic' (Occultism) in the form of Alchemy was in fact more important than Logic and biographer J.M. Keynes described Isaac Newton as the last great magician. Aristotelianism was very explicitly rejected by Newton. E.A. Burtt stated that "It is obvious to the most cursory student of Newton that he was as thoroughgoing an Empiricist as he was a consummate mathematician". Mathematics was to be constantly modelled on *experience* and, if lengthy deductions were made from principles, Newton insisted zealously that such results were purely conditional until they could be *verified by experiment* {*e.m.*}[154]. In fact, in criticising the Greek myth of *Logos*, Whitehead himself wrote[155]:

> *Also it illustrates the anti-rationalism of the scientific public that, when Hume did appear, it was only the religious implications of his philosophy which attracted attention. This was because the clergy were in principle rationalists, whereas the men of science were content with a simple faith in the order of nature.*

In his "Philosophy of Organism", presented in P&R, Whitehead projects qualities of the human ego onto the electron. The supposed 'Panpsychism' of Whitehead and his so-called 'Process Philosophy' acolytes conflates the emergence of organised process (*organism*), starting with the electron, with Creation *ex nihilo* (actually implying the *magical appearance*) of Consciousness. This view is thus better labelled "Pan-Emergentism" as with other Western ontological fantasies of ('Non-Idealist') 'Pluralistic Panpsychism' that deny a monistic Universal Consciousness and so have to 'create' or 'sneak in' Conscious Awareness *de novo* into an insentient Material universe that supposedly possesses no trace or 'seed-potentiality' of Awareness in its ultimate constituents. Whitehead, as is typical of modern Westerners, thought that Consciousness appears with the individuated ego and extrapolates this notion down through the various levels (or scales) of spatiotemporal order onto electrons, his primary 'organisms'. Whitehead and other 'Pluralist Panpsychists' are therefore more consistent, logically, than the absurd Emergent Materialism which dominates today's Western 'Philosophy of Mind'. In order to avoid heretical 'Panpsychism' (tainted by Mysticism) Emergent Materialists limit their conflation of Consciousness with the appearance of the ego alone. This results in a brazen Dualism as we have discussed at length in Chapter 5. They conflate Consciousness *per se* (Awareness) with egoic mental processes which can, in principle, be reduced to supposedly insentient physical processes and gloss over their disguised use of ontological Dualism.

In Whitehead's case this disguised Dualism is spread out over the whole of Nature rather than limited to the brain. This is more logical than today's commonplace Emergent Materialism because, as we have seen, emergent phenomena are present throughout Nature as scientific theories usually cannot predict the appearance of higher-level, organised processes from their constituents. But this does not solve the Ontological Problem of Consciousness as it is no less a disguised form of Dualism than standard Emergent Materialism. Advocates of such 'Non-Idealist' views may call their views 'Panpsychism' as they imagine Awareness suddenly appearing in organised processes throughout Nature (though not permeating the whole universe) but this is only an 'Imaginary Panpsychism' that exists only in the minds of its advocates. As they do with Wittgenstein's pseudo-mystical utterances and Heidegger's etymological ramblings, many simple-minded Western 'intellectuals' conflate Whitehead's obfuscation for profundity. As we shall see, I managed to avoid such glaringly obvious metaphysical errors with my original Panpsychist theory of Consciousness at age eighteen.[N14]

Process Philosophy exponent N.P. Jacobson wrote that Buddhism anticipated by over 2,000 years some of the ideas which have been attributed to Westerners such as Bergson, Dewey, Darwin, Fechner, James, Hartshorne and Whitehead and Peirce[156]. Malin stresses that Whitehead's metaphysics holds 'throbs of experience', (i.e., his so-called 'actual occasions') as the building blocks of the universe[157]. Whitehead did in fact use the expression 'throbs of experience' but only on one occasion in P&R. Kashmir Saivism stressed a similar view based on mystical experiences of the pulsations (*spanda*) of the underlying Ground of Universal Consciousness. Malin, who I am told was deeply into Indian Yoga[158] probably knew this but makes no mention of Kashmir Saivite parallels. J.J. Clarke says that Whitehead eventually came to see the kinship between his own metaphysics and Eastern philosophy especially Buddhism[159]. Judith Cressy says that a Howard Storm told her that P&R was based on a Near-Death Experience[160] De Quincey says that, while it is true that Whitehead did not practise Yoga, he did report a lucid dream. De Quincey clearly does not really understand what Yoga entails. He conflates the Sanskrit *Jnana* (in *Jnana Yoga*) with 'Intellect' in order to claim that Whitehead did undertake some form of spiritual practice , saying that Whitehead exemplified as much as anyone the 'path of *jnana yoga*'[161]. But *Jnana* does not mean 'Intellect' in the modern sense in which de Quincey uses it (rather than the ancient mystical sense of 'Intellectual Vision' in Platonism or 'Pure Intellect' of Eckhart). *Jnana* means supra-rational mystical *Gnosis*. The English translation of the German *Encyclopedia of Eastern Philosophy and Religion* translates *Jnana* as 'spiritual wisdom and illumination; knowledge of ultimate reality'[162]. De Quincey stresses Whitehead's emphasis on temporal movement leading from Subject to Object preceding Spatiality[163]. This knowledge, as it is confirmed in mystical experience, might have actually been based on an NDE. We have seen that Perennial Mythology based on mystical experience asserts that the temporality of the Time Stream associated with the Godhead (or Highest Self) precedes Spatialisation[164]. The Pure Consciousness is Pure Subjectivity and its waves (experienced as our stream of 'Now' moments) become superimposed by object-laden consciousness. But this primacy of temporality also reflects Whitehead's understanding, stated above, of the electron as itself a temporal process of streaming vibratory energy which manifests cyclically as an object[165].

However, even if Whitehead had some experience of deeper states of Consciousness, he did not base his ideas on mystical disclosures but on rational speculation based on his false 'Pan-Emergentism'. Whitehead famously states in P&R that Western philosophy is but a series of footnotes to Plato (supposedly the father of 'Western philosophy') whilst simultaneously referring to Plato's atavistic (retention of primitive characteristics) mysticism[166]. He states[167]:

> *In other words, philosophy is abstraction, and not of concreteness. It is by reason of their instinctive grasp of this ultimate truth that, in spite of much association with arbitrary fancifulness and atavistic mysticism, types of Platonic philosophy retain their abiding appeal; they seek the forms in the facts.*

Whitehead failed to appreciate that mysticism, purification of the soul and escape from the Wheel of Transmigration was central to Plato's *philosophia*. So Whitehead did not actually understand the true esoteric Plato! Plato distrusted written philosophy and taught his real doctrines only orally in private[168]. Although it is true that Greek philosophy and Western philosophy became but abstraction, Plato's *Sofia* was meant as Divine Wisdom associated with Divine Illumination, not conceptual abstractions. When Plato refers to 'drinking' and 'singing' in his *Laws* he is not advising that all citizens get drunk but referring to Drinking-in the Spirit, as in the Gospel myth of turning 'Water' (normal consciousness) into 'Wine' (Spirit) or many Vedic references to drinking *Soma*[169]. Whitehead also failed to recognise the mystical basis and Oriental roots of Pythagorean thought which he praised[170].

Whitehead stated famously that the 'Fallacy of Misplaced Concreteness' (the mistaking of abstractions for concrete facts) derailed Western Philosophy. Rather ironically, Whitehead's admirer de Quincey reduces Ontology to human conceptual abstractions, (i.e., 'relations', 'processes') in his Tucson III paper on Intersubjectivity. De Quincey argues for a Buddhist and Whiteheadian ontology in which individuated loci of Consciousness arise from (intersubjective) 'relations' or 'processes' from a field of such relations/ processes linking together all conscious entities[171]. But unless they are grounded in *concrete facts* (e.g., energy waves) these relations remain just human abstractions. The same applies to those who mistake the abstract concept of 'Information' to be the Ultimate Reality. As mentioned previously, at one of the Tucson *Towards a Science of Consciousness* conferences, Rajiv Malhotra raised the question of Western New Agers, having learnt about Consciousness from Indian Philosophy, suppressing in public all reference to Indian Philosophy and referring to the likes of Whitehead and Jung. We have seen the deficiencies of Jung's understanding, reducing Gnostic metaphysical cosmology regarding Creation to his so-called 'Collective Unconscious' and the ego[172]. Jung claimed that Indian philosophy had over-reached itself in extrapolating grand cosmology from psychic processes. Indian Philosophy, he claimed, was 'pre-Kantian'[173]. Jungian psychology itself has degenerated into anthropocentric, dream interpretation mumbo jumbo. We have seen that Fritjof Capra reduced Eastern Mystical metaphysics to Emergent Materialist 'Systems' views and was overtly dualistic in misusing the term 'emergence' in the sense of being *irreducible*, in principle, to physic-chemical processes. I also showed that Ken Wilber misunderstands the basic mystical meaning of the Material Plane, conflating it with the 'Matter' (atoms, particles) of Physics. This resulted in his tacit Dualism and his false claim that Science and Mysticism could never be synthesised!

Yet such Western thinkers are presented as the intellectual 'Great White Hopes' to maintain the myth of White Supremacism in 'Science', again tacitly assuming that the White Man's thought is 'scientific' and acceptable whereas references to non-European thought is taboo. These Westerners learn from Indian thought but then, when writing or speaking for a Western audience, pander tacitly to mainstream Western preconceptions that Indian thought is religious superstition and that White Men are innately 'rational' and 'scientific'. This pandering to racial stereotypes is implicit in their suppression of references to Indian philosophy. Goldner tells us that Dolores Krieger dropped all references to *Prana* to make 'Therapeutic Touch' palatable to US medical staff[174]. Similarly we saw in Chapter 6 that the notion of Space-Time transcending 'Morphic Resonance' which Rupert Sheldrake publicised in his controversial *A New Science of Life: The Hypothesis of Morphic Resonance*[175] was in fact the *Akasa* notion as found in Patanjali's *Yoga Sutras*. Sheldrake mentioned in his preface that he had written the book in a Christian ashram in India, but the text tried to validate these ideas by appealing to Aristotle's unrelated notion of Formal Causation. Amongst fellow New Agers Sheldrake did state that it was his first trip to India in the late 1960s which led to him breaking free of his Materialist indoctrination[176]. In fact, Sheldrake's friend US mathematician Ralph Abraham admitted (in a Calcutta conference paper) that both he and Sheldrake were undoubtedly influenced by the Hindu notion of the *Akasa*, originally presented in the Upanishads[177].

J.H.M. Whiteman's friend and fellow South African, Professor John Poynton invited me to speak at the Society for Psychical Research in London in 2000. He pointed out that the members are in the main sceptics trying to debunk claims of paranormal phenomena. Furthermore, they are also hostile to people who cite Sanskrit or Pali terms as they don't understand what such terms can have to do with 'scientific' studies. Of course, these same Europeans remain in ignorant bliss in regard to the fact that the Zero and other key elements of modern Mathematics, Astronomy, Chemistry, Metallurgy; the discovery of isotopes, wireless communication, the EEG, numerous developments in computing, the Polymerase Chain Reaction; giants of Physics such as Newton, Schrödinger, Heisenberg, Pauli, Eddington, etc., were all linked in some way to Occultism or Mysticism. Whiteman himself tells us in his book on the *Yoga Sutras* and in his final book *Universal Theology* (2006), that in mentioning seemingly weird notions such as Fathers (*pitara*), Ancestors/Relatives (*bhratrivyah*) and Co-Minds (*nirmana-cittani*), the *Rg Veda*, *Upanisads* and *Yoga Sutras*, respectively refer to actual phenomenological experiences. The Indian texts contain yogic technical terms which non-mystics, including supposed academic authorities misunderstand. In default of such deep mystical knowledge, dismissive characterisations have been imputed to *Rig Vedic* hymns[178, 179].

To be fair to A.N. Whitehead, in his 1925 *Science and the Modern World* (SMW) he had written that Space-Time can't be considered as a self-subsistent entity; it is an abstraction and must it be explained with reference to that from which it is extracted. Space-Time is related to the mutual ordering of events[180]. Idealism explains Nature as Ideas in an Ultimate Mentality. Whitehead also saw Platonic Ideas as derived from Pythagorean Numbers as real ultimate entities. Whitehead claimed that the original error of Mechanistic Materialist philosophy was the error of simple location, i.e., that Matter has a definite spatial and a definite temporal location[181]. His Principle of Relativity in P&R is the same as what I have referred to as 'holonomy' related to traditional mystical doctrines of 'Internal Relations' as opposed to Mechanistic views of causality as external relations. Malin and de Quincey stress that Whitehead's 'actual occasions' are said to arise out of processes involving all the other 'actual occasions'[182, 183]. The latter notion is clearly the same as the Buddhist *pratitya samutpada* (Dependent Co-origination). Such notions are not actually part of mainstream Western philosophy (Pythagoras, Plato, etc., were 'Eastern Mediterranean' people not Westerners) but are central to Eastern Philosophy, especially Buddhism. We saw above that notions of atoms as flashing in and out of existence paralleling modern particles in QM existed in Ancient India. Whitehead did mention in the final chapter of P&R that the Indians posited God as the ultimate philosophic principle before the Greeks[184]. Huston Smith says that, later on in the USA, Whitehead reportedly asserted that Vedanta was the most profound metaphysics ever invented by Man[185].

Although Merrell-Wolff calls Sankara the greatest Idealist and refers to his *Advaita Vedanta* as Absolute Idealism, I disapprove of the term 'Idealism' based on Platonic abstractions. As Merrell-Wolff himself stressed, it is Pure Nondual Formless Consciousness which is Primary. He also stressed the Ultimate Formless Reality as Indifferent paralleling the Vedantic concept of *udasina* (Total Indifference). Good and Evil are human constructions. Whitehead-influenced Christian turned Taoist R.C. Neville says that Plato gave different accounts of the Form of the Good at different points in his career. In the *Republic* Plato describes the Form of the Good as the 'Creator of the World' and *condition of possibility of relating knowable entities to knowing faculties as Light relates visible objects to vision*. The Form of the Good is *not itself an object* that can be known but known only in its expressions {*e.m.*}[186]. Plato's description of the 'Form of the Good' here as *not* being *itself an object* and as the basis or background of Knowing is a circumlocution around a concept of **Consciousness**.

The Good, the True and the Beautiful is merely poetry beside the older Brahmanic triad of *sat* (Pure Being), *cit* (Pure Consciousness) and *ananda* (Divine Bliss). The Platonic view that an object is beautiful (or good etc.) if it participates in the Eternal Form of Beauty (or of Good etc.) is utter nonsense. As Merrell-Wolff says, there is no such thing as objective beauty. Beauty in perception is superimposed upon the object by the observer, (i.e., it is in the eye of the beholder)[187]. At the end of the 2005 version of the film *King Kong* we are told that it was "beauty which killed the beast". Letting it pass that such myths of 'gorillas' (which actually come from Africa) attracted to White women reflected subconscious fears of Afro-American males, a real male gorilla would have evolved to find female gorillas attractive; not a blonde human female! Pretentious Western historians of Art often present famous Western paintings as if they possess universally-acknowledged beauty and value when, in fact, I and others see little of beauty in many of these works. Nor does everyone find works by Beethoven, Mozart and other Western Classical composers 'pleasing to the ear'.

The Constructivist thesis is of relevance here as such claims are conflating what has been indoctrinated into the Western elite culture with supposedly 'universal' values. Similarly, Biblical images are meaningful only to those who have had these images drummed into them by organised religion. Superimposition of value judgements here ties in with the Vedantic notion of *adhyasa* (mutual superimposition). This unconsciously superimposed value judgment can be disentangled from its objective content and viewed apart from all objects in the introceptive function[188]. It is clear here that, as with the

Greek myth of *Logos*, Plato's Forms are generic concepts taken from the relative mind of humans and projected falsely onto the Absolute. The Platonic cosmos was static, without evolution, so that anything beyond mundane perception was mistaken to be Eternal! Meyer points out that traditional Platonism is not consistently Monistic given the duality between the (supposedly) unchanging, perfect realm of Forms and the chaotic, temporal domain[189]. As we have seen, Sankara's *mayavada* is also tacitly dualist with its denial of the transformation of Brahman.

McEvilley points out that the longstanding Western prejudice of treating Plato as a logician, rather than a mystic, colours the translations. He himself translates Plato's *phronesis*, not as 'reason', but as 'wisdom' as with the Sanskrit *prajna* (supra-rational wisdom)[190]. But this is confusing as McEvilley also claims that *phronesis* is the same as Buddhist Mindfulness. Mindfulness does not lead to *prajna*; the mind must be cleared or 'emptied' of superimposed objective content to attain the subtle holonomic information, (i.e., 'omniscient wisdom') inherent in the Light of Pure Consciousness. 'Stopping the Mind' is a prerequisite for Basis Enlightenment. McEvilley, though recognising that true Greek *Philosophia* (Love of Divine Wisdom) resembles Indian Yoga and that it goes beyond mere concepts derived by Thought, does not (at least publicly) seem to acknowledge enlightened Gnosis (knowledge of Divine Wisdom) as having a basis in facts of experience[191]. He points out that the *Brihadaranyaka Upanisad* says, "Whoever knows thus 'I am Brahman' becomes this All. Even the gods cannot prevent his becoming thus, for he becomes their self". Thus attainment of this 'knowledge' of oneself as Brahman is associated with claims to omniscience on the ground that, if one knows the substrate, one knows all manifestations before they are manifest. He also cites the *Prasna Upanisad* saying, "He who knows thus, become omniscient, becomes All"[192]. Many passages from the Upanishads clarify this (omniscient) knowledge as non-discursive, supersensible knowledge of underlying unity[193].

But, later on in his collection of 25 essays (published together as *The Shape of Ancient Thought*) which vary in original publication date from 1970 to 2000, McEvilley asserts that Mahavira was the first religious teacher in India to claim omniscience. I presume that McEvilley distinguished the philosophical claim to knowing the substrate of all things found in the Upanishads from *religious* teachings of the Jains and Buddhists with their mass followings. Subsequently, states McEvilley, such claims became common amongst the Jains. Even some of the Ajivikas (a now extinct sect) seem to have claimed omniscience which he says is strange for teachers of scepticism. The claim to omniscience first arises in the Buddhist tradition in the *Milindapanha* at the very end of the Pali Canon. McEvilley concludes, fairly, that the claims for the Buddha attaining omniscience may have been added retrospectively in order to compete with the Jains (for prestige). The only place in Greek philosophy where complete omniscience is taught is in Plato's doctrine of Recollection; knowledge of all things in the universe is innate in the human soul but obscured at birth by the soul's immersion in matter[194]. Plato's 'True Philosopher' will not rest until knowledge of the true nature of every essence is attained by *a sympathetic and kindred power* in the soul {*e.m.*}[195]. I have emphasised Plato's reference to 'a sympathetic and kindred power' as this resembles the Yogic notion of resonance through similarity ('kinship') of form. In Mediterranean Occultism such powers were known as 'Sympathies'. Through this power in the soul the True Philosopher becomes One with every being. Plato's Special Knowledge is not like Intellectual knowledge in that it requires a redirecting of one's entire being and opening an 'Eye' (of Wisdom). The mind is flooded with light and 'wisdom'[196].

We have seen Plato's passage about 'Destroying the Hypotheses' of Mathematics and Astronomy in Chapter 3. McEvilley says that it is no coincidence that we must reject *all* our hypotheses. This reflects Plato's Parmenidean inheritance of Absolute Reality as the One, more ultimate than Ideas[197]. Aristotle said that, in spite of the plurality of Forms/Ideas, Plato's attitude remained fundamentally Monistic. For Plato, as with Parmenides, the One alone was the Real[198]. We have seen that Parmenides was in fact the founder of an Order of Shamanic Healers near Naples. For Parmenides, as modern Westerners tells us, Being and Thinking/Intellect have always been and shall forever be the same indivisible Reality (the One). Francisco Garcia Bazàn argues that, following careful scrutiny of Parmenides, it is seen to be the *Consciousness* that asserts itself as a constant *Awareness* as does the Reality that is known. *Therefore* **Being** *and* **Conscious Awareness** *are really one and the same* {*e.m.*}[199]. McEvilley says Plotinus interpreted Plato's *Parmenides* as the demonstration of the ineffability that attends any attempt to express the Absolute[200].

Brian Hines tells us that an Indian friend introduced him to Plotinus. Hines adds that Plotinus's explication of the Perennial Philosophy is framed in a thoroughly "Western" fashion. He admits that (Western) scholars play down the fact that Plotinus believed in Reincarnation. It is easier for Westerners to be convinced by another Western mind although, to be fair, Hines says that one's mindset is the product of one's education not of race[201]. This is still misleading given that Plotinus was not a Westerner at all. He came from Alexandria in the Middle East, albeit Hellenic, before the 'West' had even come into being following the Germanic conquest of Rome and the Western Roman Empire! As in the cases of Hippocrates and Plato, the English have suppressed the texts or passages displaying the 'Otherness' of such Ancient Greek thinkers[202]. Now, if it is easier for Westerners to be convinced by another Western mind, it is strange that right from the start Hines clarifies Plotinus's teachings for the reader by referring to Indian-style teachings of Consciousness, Universal Consciousness and Innermost Consciousness. Right at the start he says that Plotinus's goal is to discard from Consciousness all that is not the One[203]. But Plotinus himself does not actually refer to Consciousness although he presupposes it. Christian apologist Philip Cary, a Westerner, find Plotinus's metaphor of Inner Vision worse than incoherent and ugly although he reads it literally as an eyeball somehow turning inward[204]. In regard to the Eurocentric Husserlian phenomenologists, John Pickering commented that Eastern techniques and their objectives can be described in beautifully simple language. In contrast (European) Husserlian Phenomenology, including the elucidations in this book (*The View from Within*), is difficult to follow[205].

Hines rehashes the well-worn cliché that the roots of 'Western thought' spring from the fertile ground of Ancient Greece. He quotes Richard Tarnas from the *The Passion of the Western Mind*, "For the deepest passion of the Western mind has been to reunite with the *ground of its own being*" {*e.m.*}[206]. What Hines does not tell us is that Tarnas, who was associated with the New Age Esalen Institute ends up reducing such mystical reunion with 'the Ground' to Freudian superstitions of a 'Return to the Womb' experience. Although Tarnas praises Stanislaw Grof whose LSD research focused on reliving womb and birth experiences, Grof himself also stressed transcendental experiences of Cosmic Consciousness and the Supracosmic Void as we saw in Chapter 2. Grof himself favours the Hindu Tantric Kashmir Saivism[207]. Eurocentric and Christocentric Tarnas seems to be implying, in the quote above, that the (unspecified) 'Western mind' has its own *separate Ground* in the womb; he says "ground of *its,* (i.e., the Western mind's) own being" {*e.m.*}. He does not say the Ground of All Being! Nor does he specify what qualifies a mind as 'Western'. I presume that this reflects a naive adherence to Constructivist dogma which views all Mysticism as rooted in culture! True Spirituality, as we have seen involves transcending cultural constructions to the Universal Humanity (symbolised by the *Anthropos*) or Common Core Mysticism of the Inner Light.

I began Chapter 7 by restating Sarah Iles Johnston's comment from *The Presence of Light* that notions that Divinity was Light and that mortals might interact with it or receive it were uncommon in the Ancient Mediterranean[208]. We have seen that the famous Christian theologian Hippolytus of Rome wrote in the early 3rd Century *c.e.* that the Indian Brahmins taught that God was Light and that the likes of Sylvain Levi, Ara Alexandru Sismanian and Thomas McEvilley have all stressed Indian influences upon Plotinus (*see Chapter 7*). We also have seen that, before the Council of Nicaea outlawed such mystical views, Augustine of Hippo was deeply immersed in the writings of Plotinus and had referred to Christ as the Inner Teacher. The pre-Nicene Augustine described the **Light** or **God** as the *potential for all knowing*. God is the Light, found by the inward turn, which makes intellectual vision possible. The inward turn ends with the insight that it is *Truth that makes all knowing possible* and this insight is a glimpse of the nature of God {*e.m.*}[209]. The Inner Light is the 'Truth' or 'God'. Again Augustine's phraseology (potential for all knowing) is a *circumlocution around the concept of* **Consciousness**.

Even Whiteman in his 1967 book, after referring to the *Rig Veda* and Upanishads and the Indian origins of the Ancient Greek Theory of the Elements, claims that Plotinus gives the most developed form of this mystical teaching[210]. The Tantric Kashmir Saivite Doctrine of Vibration (derived from the Upanishads) was little known in the English-speaking world until the 1980s. Specialist scholars of Plotinus point out that his metaphor of Emanation from the One is fraught with irresolvable problems. Steeped in his view of a static universe and immutable forms, Plotinus even attacked his Gnostic contemporaries who argued that noetic Forms were dynamic and Creation was temporal[211]. On this point the Gnostics were correct. Plotinus also projects the Planes of Emanation, (i.e., Planes of Consciousness) onto the Babylonian Astrology with the Celestial Spheres of the (known) planets and the 'fixed stars'. In stark contrast, Brahmanic philosophy is not just rehashing the view of one mystic but is derived from the testimony of countless mystics, a philosophy gradually refined over thousands of years and still being refined as in this work. As the likes of (ex-Biochemist) Ken Wilber have emphasised, it is the repeatable nature of Eastern yogic methods that allows Eastern Philosophy to be 'testable' in a manner resembling scientific experiments. If you follow the same procedure you get the same results[212].

We have seen that the speculative metaphysical systems of 19th Century German Idealists, inspired by Brahmanism, have been discarded as these unverifiable systems were but the fantasies of individuals. Aldous Huxley mocked the preposterous Western over-valuation and infatuation with words, notions and the niceties of Language. The Upanishads, said Huxley, like other great Eastern philosophies, were not systems of speculation; rather they taught a doctrine which could be *made to "work"* {*e.m.*}[213]. The Vedantic-Yogic doctrine of *Akasa* and its gradual vibratory densification into matter resolves the problem of the emergence of Planes. The Planes are understood as perceptual abstractions at different levels of dynamic, vibratory process-structures as subtle ethereal matter condenses into the gross forms of the Material Plane. J.J. Clarke tells us that the common core truth underlying the world's spiritual traditions was most closely identified with Indian *Vedanta* (*Advaita Vedanta*) by Aldous Huxley in his influential *The Perennial Philosophy* (1946)[214].

This Indian knowledge, though older than Greek philosophy in origins, also remains far more accurate scientifically as demonstrated in my identification of the direct physical correlate of the Inner Light derived from this knowledge. My correlate confirms the Upanishadic claims of the existence of *cit* (Pure Nondual Consciousness) during Deep Sleep and the *Prana/Atman* Identity. The famous 4-state model of the States of Consciousness found in the *Mandukya Upanisad*, represented by the Hindu AUM (or OM) symbol still remains valid scientifically. The AUM symbol also represents the concept of *Sabdabrahman* and the Vibratory Creation of the phenomenal universe which parallels QM and especially its deeper interpretation involving the nonlocal WSM. We have seen that physicist Nick Herbert author of *Quantum Reality* advocates what he calls Quantum Tantra. He is in fact associated with the likes of Ralph Abraham and Rupert Sheldrake. Based on personal experiences, Jamesian scholar G.W. Barnard also advocates a Hindu-style Tantric ontology in his *Exploring Unseen Worlds*[215]. Leading LSD researcher turned 'Transpersonal Psychologist' Stanislaw Grof also favours Hindu Tantric Kashmir Saivism[216]. Biophysicist Mae-Wan Ho tells us that vibrational resonances, related to Quantum Coherence, can theoretically extend to infinity[217]. The currently fashionable String Theories are based on QM and also represent matter and forces as modes of vibratory activity. Susskind refers to the extended structure of electrons spreading over the entire universe in String Theory[218]. Although he finds this amazing, we have seen already that this reflects the underlying holonomic interpenetration of all phenomenal 'objects' which is stressed by Eastern philosophies with notions such as All in One and One in All in Vedanta and, *dharmadhatu* (holonomy) and Dependent Co-Origination (*pratitya samutpada*) in Buddhism. In fact this holonomy was also present in Plotinus with his 'Integral Omnipresence'[219] of Forms in *Nous* which are described poetically as existing Everywhere and Nowhere. All things in *Nous* are transparent. Each (in *nous*) has everything in itself and sees all things in every other[220].

We also see such self-imposed paradoxes, for instance, in W.J. Edgar's 1976 paper *Continuity and the individuation of modes in Spinoza's physics* in which Edgar, like Spinoza himself, remains steeped in the Geometric and Mechanistic Western ontology. Edgar refers to spheres and dynamics (in the sense of Newtonian mechanics)[221]. From the standpoint of Indian transcendental process metaphysics, individuation of seemingly (phenomenal) distinct entities from the indivisible Oneness is far less problematic. Individuation may be described metaphorically as like a vortex in the energetic flux where no individual is actually separate from the Whole (from the point-of-view of Universal Consciousness but only appears to be so from both subjective and objective perspectives of individuals). In deeper Universal Consciousness opposites (the One and the Many) are transcended. We have already seen the false notion of a point particle reflecting the Euclidean notion of a dimensionless point, creating paradoxes in Physics. I noted above David Hume's dismissal of the Greek myth of *Logos* as a primitive superstition. J.H.M. Whiteman, remained largely a Platonist, and in his 1967 book he defended the notions of a Rational Order in Nature saying that it is the error of modern Phenomenalism to assert that all Logic/Order exists only in the subjective mind with Nature deluded of all Reason. There must be necessary connections in the Real if we are to be able to apply Logic or Mathematics to it at all[222].

Whiteman tended to conflate human Reason mirroring the regular behaviour, (i.e., repeated patterns of spatiotemporal activity) or the 'Order of Nature' (or *Logos*) with *Nous* or the realm of archetypal Forms. Recall Wolpert's comment regarding how Aristotle was to know that Nature does not operate through Common Sense. *Common Sense* is linked with what we refer to as *Reason* and the *Rational*. Malin goes so far as to claim that the Laws of Nature can be recognised as objectivised Platonic Forms[223]. But Platonic Forms are immutable so nothing would ever develop from the original conditions; there could be no evolution. Perfect Ideal Forms admit no variation essential to evolution. They are merely human Generic Ideas writ large! So-called Laws, (i.e., seemingly universal dynamic regularities of phenomena) and fundamental constants are nowadays understood more as emergent stabilities not fixed eternally as in the static universe of Plato and Plotinus! Chaos Theory helps elucidate how Nature self-organises into stable patterns or *attractors* as in traditional Indian and Chinese views. The human mind has evolved to mirror the superficial *phenomenal order of Nature* in what we nowadays call *world-modelling* or simulation of gross features of the environment. This leads to the superficial myth of *Logos*. Or as Pagels says[224]:

> *[T]he geometry of space and time became an empirical problem with the advent of general relativity. ...The lesson of quantum theory can be interpreted to imply that the logic of the physical world is non-Boolean. Logic, usually thought to be prior to any experience, becomes empirical—depending on our experience—just like geometry.*

To be fair to Whiteman, in 1967 he did not use the term *Logos* but referred to a developing (evolving) 'Eternal Design' resembling the 'Akashic Records' in Aurobindo or the 'Collective Unconscious' of Jung. But, nonetheless, his use of terms like 'Reason' and 'Design' smacked of Anthropomorphism. In his final book in 2006, he even refers to the Archetypal *Logos* and asserts that the word 'God' (*Theos*) must be taken to stand for the Archetypal Reason in all, including the 'I AM', (i.e., the ego) and consciousness, if the ancient testimonies are to be understood[225]. Whiteman (1967) also argued that the problem of Communal Objectivity, which modern Western philosophy fails to explain is due to each individual mind having access to a Universalised Consciousness (in the informative sense of *nous* or *akasa* rather than merely Awareness). This is related to the origin of Kantian *a priori* concepts and the notion of 'Karmic' inheritance psychical characteristics. My point here is that *Nous* or Akashic Information is *supra-rational*; it transcends the limitations of human logic with its subject/object duality, dichotomous polarities, temporality, and locality. We saw in Chapter 3 that Plotinus himself stressed that there is *no discursive thought in Nous* and that everything in *Nous* is also everything else. The philosophical meaning of 'discursive' is *proceeding by argument or Reason rather than by Intuition*. As mystics, psychics and NDE patients testify, transcendental knowledge does not proceed in rational steps but comes in intuitive bursts of all-inclusive, supra-rational insights or realisations. Such insights require 'disentanglement' after the experience to express them in rational form. Thus the real Order underlying the apparent Order of Nature transcends Reason or *Logos*.

I agree with Lakoff and Johnson's *Philosophy in the Flesh: the Embodied Mind and its Challenge to Western Thought* in regard to Western Logocentric myths of disembodied Mind (*Logos*)[226]. The Western tradition conflates the egoic 'Mind', which depends upon bodily structures for its Thinking, Intellection and simulation of phenomenal behaviour, with Consciousness *per se*, which is the Ground of Being. Reasoning is associated with the Jamesian fringe of the egoic centre of attention, the nexus of potential relations which become actualised as soon as attention turns to some aspect of them. *Reason* is dependent on innate and habituated patterns of organisation in the human brain; it *cannot exist in a disembodied state*. As I have stated previously, the Eastern *bija* (seed-potentialities), Hermetic *archetypes*, or the *dharman* of the *Rig Veda*[227] are better understood as resonant, vibratory 'Principles of Manifestation' of phenomena as contrasted to the *spatiotemporal regularities of phenomenal appearances* which tend to be what is referred to by 'Laws of Nature'. We saw that Petitot has argued that Physics describes only the (regular) dynamic activity not the substance of Nature. However, such mystically-experienced 'Principles of Manifestation' may be related to the establishment of certain fundamental constants determined by Physics.

William Blake was brought up in the tradition of Protestant Dissenters who sought the Divinity within. For him, all religions were One as all deities reside in the human breast[228]. He read the first English translation of the *Bhagavad Gita* published by Charles Williams in 1785. Given his family upbringing within the Swedenborgian New Jerusalem Church, he may be excused for his obsession with and conflation of Biblical fantasies with true

Spirituality although he distinguished the God of the Old Testament from his own. Blake quoted Bishop Berkeley in regard to Plato and Aristotle considering God as abstracted or distinct from the Natural World whereas the Aegyptians [*sic*] considered God and Nature as making one whole[229]. The reference to Aegyptians is actually to *Poimandres* (*Pimander*) from the 2nd Century *c.e.* Hellenistic *Corpus Hermeticum* which falsely claimed to be of Ancient Egyptian origin. Blake added that Plato and Aristotle also considered God as abstracted or distinct from the Imagination. Blake called Man's Divine core the 'Divine Imagination'. The Divine Image (*Imago Dei*) is eternal and infinite and gives God a human face. For Blake, the purpose of the Human Reason was to order and analyse the sense world through abstraction and reduction to general rules. In contrast it is the 'Human Imagination' which discerns the spiritual essence which is eternal and infinite in every living detail of the created world[230]. Thus Blake stated[231]:

> *He who sees the Infinite in all things sees God. He who sees the Ratio, sees himself only. Therefore God becomes as we are, that we may be as he is.*

Thus Blake also wrote in his poetry the famous line, "May God us keep from single vision and Newton's sleep"[232].

In regard to a true understanding of *Rig Veda* Antonio de Nicolas discusses the differences between Indian and Western philosophical traditions. He quotes from Nietzsche's *The Will to Power*[233]:

> *Philosophers are properly those who have the most difficulty in freeing themselves from the belief that the fundamental concepts and categories of reason belong by nature to the realm of metaphysical certainties. They always believe in reason as a fragment of the metaphysical world itself; this backward belief always reappears for them like an all-powerful regression.*

De Nicolas notes that the Vedic Rishis understood the intelligible *Vac* (Word) operating to transcend conceptual spaces. Thus Western frames of interpretation are not appropriate for understanding *Rig Veda*, not even the most general of the Western conceptual frameworks; the metaphysical frame of Being and its subservience to Thought as universal human ground[234]. In Western philosophy Thought is taken for granted, Thought itself was never questioned in this sense and was taken uncritically for what it was not. The Platonist/Aristotelian dichotomy led to the priority of Ideas on the one hand, (i.e., Rationalism) and the priority of sensation and material substance (Empiricism) on the other. The teleology of Thought is imposed on the World and on Man[235].

Whereas mainstream Western Philosophy continues the Scholastic tradition of logical argumentation leading to vacuous artificial paradoxes, the dominant Indian Brahmanic tradition, based on yogic access to metaphysical knowledge of Transcendental Reality beyond natural phenomena, successfully resisted the naive 'Atomising Logic' and Atomistic Materialism which, as we have seen, was mooted in India before the time of Leucippus and Democritus in Greece. Reality is One not Many; a mysterious unitary whole. As modern Quantum Physics is rediscovering, the seeming multiplicity of individually-existent phenomena is illusory. Thus modern Science, though unquestionably of enormous value in so many respects, arose in Renaissance Europe not due to the superior insight of Europeans as Eurocentric historians imply tacitly. Rather it arose because the Europeans were actually puerile in regard to Metaphysics and projected various myths onto phenomenal Nature; myths of Ultimate Reality as insentient Matter; of god-given Laws and mind-mirroring *Logos*; of Nature as mechanical and multitudinous rather than Nature as merely the phenomenal manifestations of the indivisible, transcendental One, *Brahman*. Thus 21st Century Western academics who continue to peddle the myths of the supposedly unique 'Greek Miracle' in Philosophy and Science and that scientific Reality is as Greek philosophers said it was are not stating facts; they are peddling White Supremacist, racial fantasies.

References

1. Chopra, S.N. (1997) *India and China: Perspective on the Culture of the Hans and the Hindus*, Vikas Publishing House.
2. Schwab, Raymond (1950, French) English translation *The Oriental Renaissance: Europe's Rediscovery of India and the East 1680-1880* (1984) Columbia University Press.
3. Kejariwal, O.P. (1988) *The Asiatic Society of Bengal and the Discovery of India's Past 1784-1838*, Oxford University Press India.
4. Schwab, Raymond (1950) *ibid.*
5. Anderson, William (1996) *The Face of Glory: Creativity, Consciousness and Civilisation*, Bloomsbury.
6. Schwab, Raymond (1950) *ibid.*
7. Desmond, A. and Moore, J. (1991) *Darwin*, Michael Joseph.
8. Schwab, Raymond (1950) *ibid.*
9. Moore, David C. (Editor) (2001) *Black Athena Writes Back: Martin Bernal Responds to his Critics*, Duke University Press.
10. Vlassopoulos, Kostas (2007) *Unthinking the Greek Polis:Ancient Greek History beyond Eurocentrism*, Cambridge University Press.
11. Browning, Robert "Greeks and Others: From Antiquity to the Renaissance". In Thomas Harrison (Editor) (2002) *Greeks and Barbarians*, Edinburgh University Press.
12. McEvilley, Thomas (2002) *The Shape of Ancient Thought: Comparative Studies in Greek and Indian Philosophies*, Allworth Press.
13. Ibid.
14. Ibid.
15. Nayak, G.C. "Plotinus and Sankara: Some Significant Affinities and Divergences". In Paulos Mar Gregorios (Editor) (2002) *Neoplatonism and Indian Philosophy*, State University of New York Press.
16. Wolpert, Lewis (1992) *The Unnatural Nature of Science*, Faber and Faber.
17. Wolpert, Lewis (1992) *ibid.*
18. Kingsley, Peter (1995) *Ancient Philosophy, Mystery, and Magic: Empedocles and Pythagorean Tradition,* Clarendon Press (Oxford University Press).

19. Wolpert, Lewis (1992) *ibid.*
20. Wolff, Milo (2008) *Schrödinger's Universe: Einstein, Waves and the Origin of the Natural Laws*, Technotran Press.
21. Dawkins, Richard (1996) In *Bookseller* (Magazine UK), 12th April.
22. Goonatilake, Susantha (1998) *Toward a Global Science: Mining Civilisational Knowledge*, Indiana University Press.
23. Whitehead, Alfred North (1925) *Science and the Modern World*, The McMillan Co.
24. Merrell-Wolff, Franklin (1995) *Transformations in Consciousness: The Metaphysics and Epistemology* (Containing His *Introceptualism*), State University of New York Press.
25. Seife, Charles (2000) *Zero: The Biography of a Dangerous Idea,* Souvenir Press.
26. Yates, Frances (1964) *Giordano Bruno and the Hermetic Tradition*, Routledge and Kegan Paul.
27. Seife, Charles (2000) *ibid.*
28. Yates, Frances (1964) *ibid.*
29. von Franz, Marie-Louise (Undated) "Some Historical Aspects of C.G. Jung's Synchronicity Hypothesis". English translation in Marie-Louise von Franz (1992) *Psyche and Matter*, Shambhala Publications.
30. Seife, Charles (2000) *ibid.*
31. Basham, Arthur L. (1954) *The Wonder that was India*, Sidgwick and Jackson.
32. Goonatilake, Susantha (1998) *ibid.*
33. Goonatilake, Susantha (1998) *ibid.*
34. Huntington, Samuel P. (1996) *The Clash of Civilisations and the Remaking of World Order*, Simon and Schuster.
35. Wolff, Milo (1990) *Exploring the Physics of the Unknown Universe: An Adventurer's Guide*, Technotran Press.
36. Goonatilake, Susantha (1998) *ibid.*
37. Radhakrishnan, Sarvepalli (1940) *Eastern Religions and Western Thought (2nd Edn),* Oxford University Press.
38. Goonatilake, Susantha (1998) *ibid.*
39. Whiteman, J.H. Michael (1967) *Philosophy of Space and Time and the Inner Constitution of Nature: A Phenomenological Study*, Muirhead Library of Philosophy, George Allen and Unwin and the Humanities Press.
40. Basham, Arthur L. (1954) *ibid.*
41. Goonatilake, Susantha (1998) *ibid.*
42. Banerjee, Gauranga N. (1920) *Hellenism in Ancient India*, Butterworth and Co.
43. Goonatilake, Susantha (1998) *ibid.*
44. Sharma, R.S. (2005) *India's Ancient Past*, Oxford University Press India.
45. Sharma, R.S. (2005) *ibid.*
46. Banerjee, Gauranga N. (1920) *ibid.*
47. Sharma, R.S. (2005) *ibid.*

48. Goonatilake, Susantha (1998) *ibid.*
49. Das, Gurcharan (2000) *India Unbound: the Social and Economic Revolution from Independence to the Global Information Age*, Alfred A. Knopf.
50. Goonatilake, Susantha (1998) *ibid.*
51. Barrow, John D. (2000) *The Book of Nothing*, Jonathan Cape.
52. *Ibid.*
53. *Ibid.*
54. Banerjee, Gauranga N. (1920) *ibid.*
55. Teresi, Dick (2002) *Lost Discoveries: The Ancient Roots of Modern Science – from the Babylonians to the Maya*, Simon and Schuster.
56. Kanigel, Robert (1991) *The Man Who Knew Infinity: A Life of the Genius Ramanujan*, Scribners.
57. Lvindqvist, Sven (1992) *Exterminate All the Brutes*. English translation (1996) The New Press.
58. Lvindqvist, Sven (1992) *ibid.*
59. Seife, Charles (2000) *ibid.*
60. Joseph, George, G. (1991) *The Crest of the Peacock: Non-European Roots of Mathematics*, I.B. Tauris.
61. Ramasubramanian, K. (Madhava scholar) quoted in "Not Newton, but Madhava" *Mumbai Mirror* (Newspaper) 29th July 2008.
62. Goonatilake, Susantha (1998) *ibid.*
63. Teresi, Dick (2002) *ibid.*
64. Yates, Frances (1964) *ibid.*
65. Sharma, R.S. (2005) *ibid.*
66. Goonatilake, Susantha (1998) *ibid.*
67. Teresi, Dick (2002) *ibid.*
68. Goonatilake, Susantha (1998) *ibid.*
69. Goonatilake, Susantha (1998) *ibid.*
70. Swerdlow, Noel, M. and Neugebauer, Otto (1984) *Mathematical Astronomy in Copernicus's De Revolutionibus, Volume 1*, Springer Verlag.
71. Bernal, Martin. Personal Communication July 2008.
72. Teresi, Dick (2002) *ibid.*
73. Sharma, R.S. (2005) *ibid.*
74. Joseph, George, G. (1991) *ibid.*
75. Goonatilake, Susantha (1998) *ibid.*
76. Colebrooke, H.T. (1817) "Hindu Algebra". Reprinted in Dharampal (1971) *Indian Science and Technology in the Eighteenth Century*, Impex India.
77. Goonatilake, Susantha (1998) *ibid.*
78. Colebrooke, H.T. (1817) *ibid.*
79. Clarke, J.J. (1994) *Jung and Eastern Thought: A Dialogue with the Orient*, Routledge.
80. Talbot, Michael (1992) *The Holographic Universe*, Harper Perennial.
81. Schwab, Raymond (1950) *ibid.*

82. Coward, Harold *with contributions by* J. Borelli, J.F. T Jordens and J. Henderson (1985) *Jung and Eastern Thought*, State University of New York Press.
83. Schwab, Raymond (1950) *ibid.*
84. Wilhelm, Friedrich and Rawlinson, H.G. "India and the Modern West." In *A Cultural History of India* (1975) edited by A.L. Basham, Clarendon Press (Oxford University Press).
85. Schwab, Raymond (1950) *ibid.*
86. Halbfass, Wilhelm (1988) *India and Europe: An Essay in Understanding*, State University of New York Press.
87. Whiteman, J.H. Michael (1967) *ibid.*
88. Schwab, Raymond (1950) *ibid.*
89. *Ibid.*
90. *Ibid.*
91. Halbfass, Wilhelm (1988) *ibid.*
92. Newport, John P. (1998) *The New Age Movement and the Biblical Worldview: Conflict and Dialogue*, William B. Eerdmans Publishing Company.
93. Merrell-Wolff, Franklin (1994) *Franklin Merrell-Wolff's Experience and Philosophy: A Personal Record of Transformation and a Discussion of Transcendental Consciousness*: Containing his *Philosophy of Consciousness without an Object* and *His Pathways through to Space*, State University of New York Press.
94. Leonard, Ron (1999) *The Transcendental Philosophy of Franklin Merrell-Wolff*, State University of New York Press.
95. Clarke, John J. (1997) *Oriental Enlightenment: The Encounter Between Asian and Western Thought,* Routledge.
96. Winkelman, Michael (2000) *Shamanism: The Neural Ecology of Consciousness and Healing*, Bergin and Garvey.
97. Goldberg, Philip (2010) *American Veda: From Emerson and the Beatles to Yoga and Meditation – How Indian Spirituality Changed the West*, Harmony Books, Random House.
98. Newport, John P. (1998) *ibid.*
99. *Ibid.*
100. *Ibid.*
101. Wiley, Tatha (2002) *Original Sin: Origins, Developments, Contemporary Meanings*, Paulist Press.
102. *Ibid.*
103. *Ibid.*
104. Malhotra, Rajiv (2011) *Being Different: An Indian Challenge to Western Universalism*, HarperCollins India.
105. Wiley, Tatha (2002) *ibid.*
106. Amorth, Gabriele. Reported in *Daily Telegraph* (Newspaper, UK) 26th November 2012.
107. Prakash, Gyan (1999) *Another Reason: Science and the Imagination of Modern India*, Princeton University Press.

108. Klostermaier, Klaus K. (1989) *A Survey of Hinduism*, State University of New York Press.
109. Klostermaier, Klaus K. (1989) *ibid.*
110. Dourley, John "The Innate Capacity: Jung and the Mystical Imperative". In Robert K. C. Forman (Editor) (1998) *The Innate Capacity: Mysticism, Psychology, and Philosophy*, State University of New York Press.
111. Whiteman, J.H. Michael (1967) *ibid.*
112. Josephson, Brian, D. (1982) "Science and Religion: Can the Two be Synthesised?" delivered as part of *1982-3 Isthmus Foundation Lectures on Science and Religion*, The Isthmus Institute. Revised as "Science and Religion: How to Make the Synthesis". In T.D. Singh (Editor) (1988) *Synthesis of Science and Religion: Critical Dialogues and Essays*, The Bhaktivedanta Institute.
113. Rosen, Steven M. "Time and Higher-Order Wholeness: A Response to David Bohm." In David R. Griffin (Editor) (1986) *Physics and the Ultimate Significance of Time*, State University of New York Press.
114. de Sautoy, Marcus (2008) *The Story of Maths* (Television Series) British Broadcasting Corporation.
115. Merrell-Wolff, Franklin (1995) *ibid.*
116. Goonatilake, Susantha (1998) *ibid.*
117. Hanegraaff, Wouter, J. "The New Age Movement and the Esoteric Tradition". In Roelof van den Broek and Wouter J. Hanegraaff (Editors) (1998) *Gnosis and Hermeticism from Antiquity to Modern Times*, State University of New York Press.
118. Husserl, Edmund (1936) "The Mathematisation of Nature" (from *Crisis of the European Sciences and Transcendental Phenomenology*). Reprinted in Donn Welton (Editor) (1999) *The Essential Husserl: Basic Writings in Transcendental Phenomenology*, Indiana University Press.
119. Whiteman, J.H. Michael (1967) *ibid.*
120. Goonatilake, Susantha (1998) *ibid.*
121. *Ibid.*
122. *Ibid.*
123. *Ibid.*
124. Banerjee, Gauranga N. (1920) *ibid.*
125. Banerjee, Gauranga N. (1920) *ibid.*
126. Moore, David C. (Editor) (2001) *Black Athena Writes Back: Martin Bernal Responds to his Critics*, Duke University Press.
127. Barrow, John D. (2000) *ibid.*
128. Goonatilake, Susantha (1998) *ibid.*
129. Goonatilake, Susantha (1998) *ibid.*
130. Seife, Charles (2000) *ibid.*
131. Goonatilake, Susantha (1998) *ibid.*
132. Goonatilake, Susantha (1998) *ibid.*
133. Bergson, Henri (1913) *Time and Free Will: An Essay on the Immediate Data of Consciousness*, George Allen and Co.

134. Abraham, Ralph (2008) *Mathematics and the Psychedelic Revolution*, (Internet paper on www.ralph-abraham.org ms#124).
135. Abraham, Ralph (2008) *ibid.*
136. Whiteman, J.H. Michael (1967) *ibid.*
137. Whiteman, J.H. Michael (1967) *ibid.*
138. de Sautoy, Marcus (2010) "How Long is a Piece of String". Episode on *Horizon* (Television Series), British Broadcasting Corporation.
139. O'Neill, L. Thomas (1980) *Mâyâ in Úankara: Measuring the immeasurable*, Motilal Banarsidass.
140. Kaplan, Stephen (1987) *Hermeneutics, Holography and Indian Idealism: A Study of Projection and Gaudapada's Mandukya Karika*, Motilal Banarsidass.
141. Brown, Daniel P. "The Stages of Meditation in Cross-Cultural Perspective". In Ken Wilber, Jack Engler and Daniel P. Brown (Editors) (1986) *Transformations of Consciousness: Conventional and Contemplative Perspectives on Development*, Shambhala Publications.
142. Schommers, Wolfram (1995) *Symbols, Pictures and Quantum Reality: On the Theoretical Foundations of the Physical Universe*, World Scientific.
143. Schrödinger, Erwin (1995) *The Interpretation of Quantum Mechanics: Dublin seminars (1949-55) and other unpublished essays*, Ox Bow Press.
144. Hiley, B.J. and Peat, F. David "General introduction: The development of David Bohm's ideas from the plasma to implicate order". In Basil J. Hiley and F. David Peat (1987) *Quantum Implications: Essays in Honour of David Bohm*, Routledge and Kegan Paul.
145. Whiteman, J.H. Michael (1967) *ibid.*
146. Bohm, David (1980) *Wholeness and the Implicate Order*, Routledge and Kegan Paul.
147. Wolff, Milo (1990) *Exploring the Physics of the Unknown Universe: An Adventurer's Guide*, Technotran Press.
148. Wolff, Milo (2008) *Schrödinger's Universe: Einstein, Waves and the Origin of the Natural Laws*, Technotran Press.
149. Susskind, Leonard (2008) *The Black Hole War: My battle with Stephen Hawking to Make the World a Safe Place for Quantum Mechanics*, Back Bay Books, Little Brown and Co.
150. Malin, Shimon (2001) *Nature Loves to Hide: Quantum Physics and Reality, a Western Perspective*, Oxford University Press.
151. Malin, Shimon (2001) *ibid.*
152. Whiteman, J.H. Michael (1967) *ibid.*
153. Goody, Jack (1996) *The East in the West*, Cambridge University Press.
154. Burtt, E.A. (1954) *The Metaphysical Foundations of Modern Physical Science, 2nd Revised Edn*, Doubleday.
155. Whitehead, Alfred North (1925) *ibid.*
156. Clarke, John J. (1997) *ibid.*
157. Malin, Shimon "What Does Quantum Mechanics Imply about the Nature of the Universe". In Stuart R. Hameroff, Alfred W. Kaszniak, and David J. Chalmers

(Editors) (1999) *Toward a Science of Consciousness III: The Third Tucson Discussions and Debates*, MIT Press.

158. Malhotra, Rajiv (Personal Communication).
159. Clarke, John J. (1997) *ibid.*
160. Cressy, Judith "Mysticism and the Near-Death Experienc" In Lee W. Bailey and Jenny Yates (Editors) (1996) *The Near-Death Experience: A Reader*, Routledge.
161. de Quincey, Christian "The Promise of Integralism: A Critical Appreciation of Ken Wilber's *Integral Psychology*". In Jensine Andresen and Robert K.C. Forman (Editors) (2000) *Cognitive Models and Spiritual Maps*, Imprint Academic.
162. Fischer-Schreiber, I., Erhard, F-K., Friedrichs, K. and Diener, M.S. (1989, English translation) *The Encyclopedia of Eastern Philosophy and Religion*, Shambhala Publications.
163. de Quincey, Christian (2000) *ibid.*
164. Von Franz, Marie-Louise (1981) "Meaning and Order", *see also* von Franz, Marie-Louise (1978) "The Psychological Experience of Time" both reprinted in von Franz, Marie-Louise (1992) *Psyche and Matter*, Shambhala Publications.
165. Whitehead, Alfred North (1925) *ibid.*
166. Whitehead, Alfred, N. (1929) *Process and Reality: An Essay in Cosmology* Corrected Edition (1978), Edited by David Ray Griffin and Donald W. Sherburne, The Free Press.
167. Whitehead, Alfred, N. (1929) *ibid.*
168. McEvilley, Thomas (2002) *ibid.*
169. Whiteman, J.H. Michael (2006) *Universal Theology and Life in the Other Worlds*, Colin Smythe.
170. Whitehead, Alfred North (1925) *ibid.*
171. de Quincey, Christian "Intersubjectivity: Exploring Consciousness from the Second-Person Perspective". In Stuart R. Hameroff, Alfred W. Kaszniak, and David J. Chalmers (Editors) (1999) *Toward a Science of Consciousness III: The Third Tucson Discussions and Debates*, MIT Press.
172. Segal, Robert A. (1992) *The Gnostic Jung*, Princeton University Press.
173. Coward, Harold *with contributions by* J. Borelli, J.F. T Jordens and J. Henderson (1985) *ibid.*
174. Goldner, Diane (2003) *How People Heal: Exploring the Scientific Basis of Subtle Energy in Healing*, Hampton Roads. (Originally title: *Infinite Grace* (1999)).
175. Sheldrake, Rupert (1981) *A New Science of Life: The Hypothesis of Morphic Resonance*, Blond and Briggs.
176. Sheldrake, Rupert (1994) *Noetic Sciences Review* (Summer, 1994), Institute of Noetic Sciences.
177. Abraham, Ralph (1996) "Vibrations: communication through a morphic field". Preprint for *Synthesis of Science and Religion, Calcutta, 1996* (Conference paper, MS#86 on www.ralphabraham.org).
178. Whiteman, J.H. Michael (2006) *ibid.*

179. Whiteman, J.H. Michael (1993) *Aphorisms on Spiritual Method: The "Yoga Sutras of Patanjali" in the Light of Mystical Experience*, Colin Smythe.
180. Whitehead, Alfred North (1925) *ibid.*
181. Whitehead, Alfred North (1925) *ibid.*
182. Malin, Shimon (1999) *ibid.*
183. de Quincey, Christian (1999) *ibid.*
184. Whitehead, Alfred, N. (1929) *ibid.*
185. Smith, Huston (2000) *Cleansing the Doors of Perception: The Religious Significance of Entheogenic Plants and Chemicals*, Tarcher Putnam.
186. Neville, Robert C. (1993) *Eternity and Time's Flow*, State University of New York Press.
187. Merrell, Wolff, Franklin (1995) *ibid.*
188. Merrell, Wolff, Franklin (1995) *ibid.*
189. Mayer, John R.A. "Plotinus's Neoplatonism and the Thought of Sri Aurobindo". In Paulos Mar Gregorios (Editor) (2002) *Neoplatonism and Indian Philosophy*, State University of New York Press.
190. McEvilley, Thomas (2002) *ibid.*
191. *Ibid.*
192. *Ibid.*
193. *Ibid.*
194. *Ibid.*
195. *Ibid.*
196. *Ibid.*
197. *Ibid.*
198. *Ibid.*
199. Bazàn, Francisco G. "The 'Second God' in Gnosticism and Plotinus's Anti-Gnostic Polemic". English translation in Richard T. Wallis (Editor) and Jay Bregman (Associate Editor) (1992) *Neoplatonism and Gnosticism*, State University of New York Press.
200. McEvilley, Thomas (2002) *ibid.*
201. Hines, Brian (2004) *Return to the One 6 ᒪ Plotinus's Guide to God-Realisation: A Modern Exposition of an Ancient Classic, the* Enneads, Adrasteia Publishing.
202. Moore, David C. (Editor) (2001) *ibid.*
203. Hines, Brian (2004) *ibid.*
204. Cary, Phillip (2000) *Augustine's Invention of the Inner Self: The Legacy of a Christian Platonist*, Oxford University Press.
205. Pickering, John "Words and Silence". In Peer Commentary and Responses section of Francisco Varela and Jonathan Shear (Editors) (1999) *The View from Within: First-person approaches to the study of consciousness*, Imprint Academic.
206. Tarnas, Richard. Quoted in Hines, Brian (2004) *ibid.*
207. Grof, Stanislaw (1998) *The Cosmic Game: Explorations of the Frontiers of Human Consciousness*, State University of New York Press.

208. Johnston, Sarah Iles "*Fiat Lux, Fiat Ritus*: Divine Light and the Late Antique Defense of Ritual". In Matthew T. Kapstein (Editor) (2004) *The Presence of Light: Divine Radiance and Religious Experience*, Chicago University Press.
209. Cary, Phillip (2000) *ibid.*
210. Whiteman, J.H. Michael (1967) *ibid.*
211. Evangeliou, Christos "Plotinus's Anti-Gnostic Polemic and Porphyry's *Against the Christians*". In Richard T. Wallis (Editor) and Jay Bregman (Associate Editor) *Neoplatonism and Gnosticism*, State University of New York Press.
212. Wilber, Ken "Physics, Mysticism and the New Holographic Paradigm: A Critical Appraisal". In Ken Wilber (Editor) (1982) *The Holographic Paradigm and Other Paradoxes: Exploring the Leading Edge of Science,* Shambhala Publications.
213. Huxley, Aldous (1956) "Knowledge and Understanding", *Vedanta and the West*. Reprinted in Bridgeman, Jacqueline, H. (Editor) (1992) *Huxley and God: Essays*, Harper Collins.
214. Clarke, John, J. (1997) *ibid.*
215. Barnard, G. William (1997) *Exploring Unseen Worlds: William James and the Philosophy of Mysticism*, State University of New York Press.
216. Grof, Stanislaw (1998) *ibid.*
217. Ho, Mae-Wan (1993) *The Rainbow and the Worm: The Physics of Organisms*, World Scientific.
218. Susskind, Leonard (2008) *The Black Hole War: My battle with Stephen Hawking to Make the World a Safe Place for Quantum Mechanics*, Back Bay Books, Little Brown and Co.
219. Cary, Phillip (2000) *ibid.*
220. Kealey, Daniel "The Theoria of Nature in Plotinus and the Yoga of the Earth Consciousness in Aurobindo". In Paulos Mar Gregorios (Editor) (2002) *Neoplatonism and Indian Philosophy*, State University of New York Press.
221. Edgar, W.J. "Continuity and the Individuation of Modes in Spinoza's Physics". In J.B. Wilbur (Editor) (1976) *Spinoza's Metaphysics: Essays in Critical Appreciation*, Van Gorcum.
222. Whiteman, J.H. Michael (1967) *ibid.*
223. Malin, Shimon (2001) *Nature Loves to Hide: Quantum Physics and Reality, a Western Perspective*, Oxford University Press.
224. Pagels, Heinz, R. (1982) *The Cosmic Code: Quantum Physics as the Language of Nature*, Simon and Schuster.
225. Whiteman, J.H. Michael (2006) *ibid.*
226. Lakoff, George and Johnson, Mark (1999) *Philosophy in the Flesh: The Embodied Mind and its Challenge to Western Thought*, Basic Books.
227. Whiteman, J.H. Michael (1967) *ibid.*
228. Van Meurs, Jos "William Blake and His Gnostic Myths". In Roelof van den Broek and Wouter J. Hanegraaff (Editors) (1998) *Gnosis and Hermeticism from Antiquity to Modern Times*, State University of New York Press.
229. *Ibid.*

230. *Ibid.*
231. *Ibid.*
231. *Ibid.*
232. *Ibid.*
233. De Nicolas, Antonio T. (1976) *Meditations through the Rig Veda: Four-Dimensional Man*, Nicolas-Hays Ltd.

Part Three

My Path to the Light

11

My 1980s Panpsychist Theory of Consciousness

The Background to My 1983 Paper on Consciousness

My Secular Western Upbringing and Indian Self-hatred

My journey towards my identification of the physical correlate of the Divine Light in 1994 probably began when I was twelve years old in 1977. I recall reading a translation of the *Bhagavad Gita* by Swami Prabhupada of the Krishna Consciousness Society which my late father, who died in January 1977, had acquired. My family had moved to London from Gauhati (now called Guwahati), the state capital of Assam, in 1967 when I was two and a half years old. My father had come to London in 1966. I think that the British Legion, of which he was a member following a spell in the Royal Indian Navy during the 1939-45 war, had suggested coming to Britain where there was a shortage of teachers. Although my father, who worked sporadically as a supply teacher teaching English, had also performed sacred rites as a Brahman *purohit* (priest)[N1] at a few *pujas* and funerals during the 1970s between periods of serious ill health with cirrhosis, we were not in any way a religious family. He had also read to us the Hindu epics, the *Mahabharata* and the *Ramayana* during the summer holidays when I was at primary school. These came across to me as Indian fairy tales little different from those of Greek mythology which I had read in library books. As a boy, the warrior heroes Achilles and Alexander appealed to my imagination. The Indian epics held little appeal to me, they seemed alien, backward and embarrassing like my temperamental and good-for-nothing, Sanskrit-literate father who made us to listen to them when we could have been watching television (TV).

When in 2006, to mark the 40th anniversary of *Star Trek's* first US screening (it started in the UK in 1969), the SciFi Channel started showing all the original series, I was filled with nostalgia. The mythological heroes who really captivated me in my pre-teenage years were James T. Kirk and Mr Spock of *Star Trek*. I not only saw *Star Trek* on TV but also read the stories in paperbacks borrowed from the local library from around age nine to twelve. In 2006, I noticed that a number of episodes of the original 1960s *Star Trek* referred to Mind or Consciousness transfer, Consciousness and Energy, intelligent computers, brainwave patterns decoded in universal translators etc. Back in my primary school days these philosophical issues had all gone over my head. Perhaps it was all those mini-skirted and bikini-clad women had attracted my pre-pubescent self to *Star Trek* but still it may well have helped engender in me an attraction to Science as I also read the stories in book form which lacked the titillating images of the TV series.

The summer of 1967[N2], when I arrived in London, was the much-hyped hippies' Summer of Love and, not far from where I lived, the Beatles were recording their psychedelic *Sargeant Pepper* album which included some Indian gurus on the cover image. Having experienced altered states of Consciousness using LSD, they would soon head off to Rishikesh to learn Yoga. The Beatles' 'seal of approval' soon made Indian spirituality hugely trendy amongst the young, educated classes in the West, especially the 'baby boomers' in the USA. I recently noticed in a 50th anniversary re-screening that the first episode of the BBC science-fantasy series Doctor Who starring Tom Baker in 1974 had the Doctor stating early on, "All energy is a form of Life". This clearly mystical statement reflected the hippy influence on popular culture in that era. But, as a youngster, I was oblivious of such cultural transformations. We did not face any serious racism in liberal, middle class Belsize Park in Hampstead, then full of Indian immigrants renting rooms in large, run-down Victorian houses. My father, who had come over in advance in 1966, had previously rented a room in a large house further up Haverstock Hill at the corner of Pond Street owned by an Indian known as 'Benarasi'.[N3]

Miss Kahn, the Jewish headmistress at our primary school was delighted to have little Indian boys and the elderly Jewish couple who ran a nearby delicatessen joked to my parents that they wanted to adopt one of the lovely little boys. During my first year at school (1969–70), following news of the death of my maternal grandfather, my brothers and I had to shave our heads according to Hindu custom. Arriving shaven-headed at school was extremely embarrassing given the teasing from other children. At age 6, as my reading and writing ability was way ahead of my own age group, I was given a double promotion and put in the class for seven year olds at my first primary school. During this year, 1970–71, I was best friend with an American boy, Peter Schlossman, from Boston who only stayed in London for one year. Perhaps we were both drawn to each other as we were both newcomers to the class. Peter would take me to his home in a luxury detached house in Keat's Grove opposite (the Romantic poet) Keat's House in Hampstead, one of the most exclusive streets in London. I recall that even at age six, I would feel deeply embarrassed and ashamed if his mother would escort us back to my home, one large room in the basement of a large decrepit house in Belsize Park, two doors from the Underground station. We lived there from mid1967–September 1972. At least Mrs Schlossman only went to the front door of the house.

While living in Belsize Park, I became friends at school with John Hughes, son of Scottish Member of Parliament Robert Hughes, Under-Secretary in the

Labour Government (who was Chairman of the Anti-Apartheid Movement in the 1980s). The Hughes' eldest son was a friend of my elder brother so our families became friends. They also lived in a large house near to our school and had a large Ford Zephyr car. As a Junior Minister, Hughes also had the use of a ministerial black limousine. I recall the embarrassment when they visited our home, the basement room, and John was repelled by the Indian-style boiled chicken my mother had cooked and she had to make fish fingers (fish sticks) for him. I recall my embarrassment also when a white woman social worker looked around snootily and rummaged through the oil-spattered drawers full of my mother's spices. Of course, nowadays, the much more aesthetically presented Indian curries made in so-called "Indian restaurants", mainly by cooks from the Sylhet province of Bangladesh, are a staple part of the British diet. Numerous other Indian immigrants lived in the same house and in other houses nearby which nowadays have become refurbished multi-million pound mansions often inhabited by the very wealthy and the famous. The same gentrification occurred in West London's original Afro-Caribbean ghetto of Notting Hill. Not all of my friends were so well off of course, although decades later I learnt that my friend Zad (this was his real name!) from my first year (1969–70), whc had invited me to a bonfire night party at their apartment, was the son of architect Richard Rogers.

In September 1972 we moved out of the single room in the basement into a 3 bedroom council apartment in a tower block near to Primrose Hill and Swiss Cottage a little to the North of Belsize Park. I think we moved on my 8th birthday. I recall pestering my parents relentlessly for an expensive present that they were reluctant to buy, £4.50 for an 'Adventure Kit'. The cost was largely due to the fact that it included a functional camera that I ended up never using as I could not afford the film. Although such pestering for toys is normal behaviour amongst children, I still feel embarrassed. The apartment in the tower block with three bedrooms, large sitting room, kitchen and storeroom was a huge improvement in our living standards and I remember the period with some fondness. Perhaps the fact that we also got a colour television makes this period in the council apartment seem so vivid in my memory. However, rather than wait for the delivery of a brand new TV from the factory, my useless father brought home the showroom display unit as he wanted to watch the 1972 Olympic Games in colour! But like many Indian immigrants from Camden, in May 1973 we moved to North-East London where my father had managed to buy a house.

Prices were cheaper in this largely working class area nearer to the outer suburbs of Greater London although, back then, the price of houses in the expensive parts of London had not become totally unaffordable for ordinary families due to millionaire financiers and foreigners buying up houses for millions of pounds as secure investments. At my new primary school one or two of my white friends had parents who voted for the racist National Front and some of my younger brothers' friends did not allow Non-Whites into their homes. Whilst walking home with me one day, one of my friends would even shouted out, with no sense of embarrassment that I was present, when he saw South Asians driving a car. He was obviously repeating what he heard his parents say; that they (Asians) come over here, take our jobs and they can even afford to buy cars. Another white working class friend told me how jealous he was when I brought to school a very expensive book on the history of aviation worldwide, full of colour pictures of the world's great aeroplanes. In fact, it had been given to me as a present by my old Camden school-friend's father, the MP Robert Hughes on my 9th or 10th birthday. My own parents would not have been able to afford it. At age eleven, I was able to show off with my father's sound cine camera on a school trip to Normandy (which my mother had paid for out of her savings). No one else had such a fancy camera. But I was too embarrassed to show the film footage at school as my father had started using the first reel at home. I pretended that the films had been lost in the post after processing at Kodak. Thus it was the stark contrast in living conditions compared to my middle class friends in Camden (which resumed when I returned to Camden for secondary school in 1976) coupled to the embarrassing rituals, food, etc., contributed to my childhood sense of self-hatred and embarrassment in regard to things Indian.

Thus when I looked through Swami Prabhupada's translation of the *Bhagavad Gita* in summer 1977, a year after I had started at secondary school, I was not a religious person nor did I think of myself as a Hindu. I did not study any books on Hinduism until the 1990s. In a footnote to the text, Prabhupada wrote that God was the underlying Ground of all things, or something similar to this. At age twelve, I only grasped this in a most vague Pantheistic sense that everything was God. The Christian hymns and fairy tales at school always referred to "God" as if "God" were a man, a father or a Lord or whatever, separate from us. Without any logical analysis, something deep inside me seemed to recognise the insight presented in Prabhupada's footnote; I intuited it to be profound and meaningful without knowing anything about Theism or Non-theism.[N4] I only recalled this incident in the mid-1990s when I was writing *The Oneness/Otherness Mystery* (O/OM) because I re-read an essay I had written in 1983 mentioning it (*see below*). In fact, in the years following 1977 this notion, which I had intuitively found so appealing had been largely forgotten as I began to acquire knowledge from Science and Western philosophy during my teenage years at secondary school. Although my family had moved to North-East London, I got a place in the 'Grammar' (selective intake) secondary school in middle class Hampstead/ Highgate in the borough of Camden where we had lived previously. My elder brother had got a place in 1973 just before we moved East and I did well in an entrance test for boys from outside the borough. My year was the last 'Grammar' year (selective intake for the brightest). As with most such schools, the Labour government's policies forced it to become a 'Comprehensive' school taking children of all abilities.

My Teenage Encounters with Metaphysics and Mysticism

I recall two incidents from my fifth year at secondary school (age 16) which indicate that such spiritual concerns were still in the background of my thoughts as I was deciding to specialise in Science. Both occurred just before I was about to take my first public examinations (Ordinary or 'O' Levels) in spring to summer 1981. During a French lesson, the teacher (a Mr Kaye from New Zealand), stopped the class and asked me what I wanted to do when I grew up. I think I was singled out as I was perceived by the teaching staff as having a particularly enquiring philosophical mind even though there were numerous academically bright pupils in my year which produced a high proportion of 'Oxbridge' entrants. I answered him with some vague talk about propounding the Vedanta. In fact, I had very little idea as to what the word 'Vedanta' actually meant; I had 'picked it up' from a tiny pocket-size book about Swami Vivekananda's speeches that my mother had brought back from India a few months earlier. That trip to India was her first visit after 13 years in Britain. Wealthier Indians living in Britain travel to India regularly but my poor widowed mother, with four schoolboy sons, could not afford to do so. Thus India was not at all familiar to me; it was a mysterious place. Although my mother, like most Hindu Bengalis, kept pictures of Ramakrishna, his wife and Vivekananda in our sitting room, I knew next to nothing about their lives. Yet, for reasons unknown to my 'normal mind' (my ego), the very word "Vedanta", especially with the nationalistic connotations given to it by Vivekananda, had captivated me. I felt a powerful resonance with it even though I had only the vaguest idea as to what it actually meant!

At around the same time, in summer 1981, due to the absence of a teacher, the headmaster Mr Russell Perry supervised my class. Mr Perry was a teacher of Religious Education (RE) and he had taught my class RE back in the second year (age 13) and had considered me to be the star pupil in RE Both Mr Perry and the other RE teacher Mr Brown, back in the second year (when we started RE lessons), had made pronouncements to my class basically saying that I was more "spiritually" advanced than my classmates, nearly all of whom were Europeans (including a high proportion of Jews). Whereas many people look back and criticise teachers for underestimating their potential, my secondary school teachers had seemed to sense something 'special' in me linked to my philosophically-inclined mind. Although not the best at Maths or Physics, I had a special 'insight' when it came to establishing the fundamental 'first principles', (i.e., the metaphysical assumptions). There had been another Indian in my class (an Agrawal) in the first year but he left the school after one year. The fact that I had the best exam results across all subjects in my year group in the first year exams obviously influenced opinions as well. Now three years after he had taught my class, Mr Perry wanted to see how our religious or philosophical thoughts had progressed in three years. I was the first person he asked. I responded with some vague notions I had picked up from Prabhupada and Vivekananda's speeches about God being "spiritual energy" which was somehow present in every man. Again, I simply uttered these words without any deep understanding of their meaning; as a teenager I probably thought that it sounded impressive. My word elicited a very favourable response from Mr. Perry who responded very positively about how he too was still learning about these matters and that we never stop learning.

However, my words provoked a sarcastic response from an English boy called Cabot who was possessed of a very stereotypical English middle class character (although the famous explorer John Cabot was of Italian origin). He was very friendly towards me so there was no malice in him when he expressed his opinion that such talk of 'spiritual energy' was just nonsense, a fanciful idea with no evidence to support it. This response is in fact typical of the shallow English common sense Empiricism, associated with Dr Johnson[N5], which frowns upon Metaphysics and deep intellectual pursuits as signs of psychopathology best cured with outdoor walks and sports. The British are probably the most ignorant of all the major cultures in the world when it comes to Metaphysics and Mysticism. Of course, nationalistic mythologies can affect one's perception of Metaphysics and Mysticism as in the response of a work colleague called Jim Denton-McClellan in 1994. This Physics graduate was something of a pariah amongst his colleagues who worked as copyeditors and proofreaders on scientific journals. This was due to his staunch support for the Conservative (Tory) Party and his British nationalist views amongst a youthful workforce who were largely left-leaning.[N6] I tried to explain my ideas on the physical correlate of the Divine Light to him by mentioning books like *The Tao of Physics*. The right wing Tory boy's response was simple: Physics was correct and Eastern mysticism was a load of rubbish.

I recall that at age fifteen to sixteen we were taught basic Newtonian physics. I could never come to terms with this system of thought. Notions of a world constituted of microscopic 'billiard balls' bouncing off each other simply did not make sense to my intuitions. This was part of the reason why I never managed to master Physics as it did not seem to make sense ontologically. However, with hindsight, it is clear that the quality of teaching in Mathematics and Physics was extremely poor even back then in the late 1970s and early 1980s. One Maths teacher, an Indian Muslim and one Chemistry teacher, who was Chinese struggled to speak clear English let alone explain anything clearly.[N7] Yet remarkably the latter had outstanding success at Ordinary Level exams as he got students to practice with past papers! Hence now, thirty years on, with an even greater shortage of properly qualified Maths and hard Science teachers, few British students take these subjects at Advanced level (age 17-18) even though the new style exams have become easier and easier since my time so that the new government targets for schools' performance are met.[N8] Recent news reports show how in South Korea (as was the case in Japan) most schoolchildren rise around 6 a.m. in the morning and then attend private tuition classes in the evening so as to become competent at Maths and Science. The state also invests heavily in ensuring that highly qualified graduates become Maths and Science teachers. Such a 'totalitarian' approach would never be tolerated in Britain.

Although I was in the top set in Maths, and considered good at it by fellow average-ability pupils, I was nowhere near as good at Maths some of the mathematically-gifted boys who went on to do Maths or Physics at Cambridge and I eventually stopped attending lessons in my final year. I was also too embarrassed to ask the teachers to try to explain things more clearly for fear of 'looking stupid'. The Indian Maths teacher who spoke 'broken English' would just work out the answers without really explaining the principles or steps but the native British teachers were little better at explaining. I noticed that outstanding achievement in Maths and Physics seemed to require too much "brain-space" for such abstract symbol manipulations which prevented development of other mental faculties. Such specialisation seemed to go with a lack of creativity and a broader knowledge of other fields. I saw myself as a "philosopher", interested in all knowledge but for a variety of reasons, including my aforementioned desire to understand Science, I chose to study Molecular Biology. The thought of studying "Philosophy" at university never crossed my mind as it was not a subject taught at school and nobody in my year seemed to have considered it.[N9] With hindsight, I was lucky to have avoided wasting my time as Anglo-American (Language Analysis) philosophy was definitely not what I thought of as either interesting or even worthwhile philosophy.

At my school, the brightest boys all tended to specialise in the sciences so peer pressure had a part to play. There was pressure from both my teachers and my mother to do Medicine but this was out of the question. Even the discussion of blood circulation in Biology lessons made me feel queasy and I was extremely squeamish. I recall watching a television programme involving human dissection and suffering a bout of rapid-breathing and almost fainting – having to go into the garden for fresh air. Quite obviously I am not descended from the 'Warrior Caste'! At that time, the new science of Recombinant DNA Technology had just been created and the media presentation of so-called "Genetic Engineering" made it appear glamorous and important. I did myself sit the Oxford entrance exams in 1982 before taking my Advanced Level exams in 1983. Oxford University, which had the most prestigious Biochemistry department in the UK awarded me an Exhibition award for good performance and an unconditional offer of entrance (not dependent on A'Level results). However, I only wanted to show that I could have gone to 'Oxbridge' had I wanted to. Boring Biochemistry did not appeal to me at all. I wanted to do Molecular Genetics and so chose a flexible degree course at London University that allowed me to study Molecular Biology, some Developmental Biology and Neurobiology as well. To be honest, we did not get any decent career advice and I knew nothing about real careers.[N10] Unfortunately, my specialisation at age 16 forced me into a science degree whereas, to be honest, I was totally unsuited to laboratory work and the hyper-specialisation required in post-graduate science. Also, in those teenage years, I was a naïve Reductionist thinking that, to understand Life we had to understand its smallest components.

When I spent the book tokens for the best student in Biology in 1982, I bought a history of Molecular Genetics but also spent my own money on a recently published book suggesting that Life on Earth may have begun in simpler, inorganic clay systems before becoming based on complex organic macromolecules[1]. The Molecular Genetics history book, by Stent and Calendar[2], later used as a standard text for my second year at university, mentioned in its introduction that Schrödinger had suggest in his 1944 book *What is Life* that new Laws of Physics might be required to understand Life. The main author Gunther Stent claimed that, on the contrary, Molecular Biology had found that Life simply involved the making and breaking of hydrogen bonds! Stent was reducing 'Life' absurdly to one small facet of the replication of DNA. In fact the 'making and breaking of hydrogen bonds' is something that occurs between molecules of water all the time but we do not say that water is alive! I obtained a copy of Schrödinger's *What is Life* from a local library and I recall feeling excited reading Schrödinger's view that understanding Life might require new principles. I also noticed his references to Vedanta in the appendix but did not pay much attention because, as stated above, I did not really know what Vedanta was.

I recall that I first heard about the famous paradoxes of Quantum Mechanics in 1982 when *New Scientist* magazine reported on the famous experiment by Aspect *et al.* in France, related to the Einstein, Podolsky, Rosen paradox, which confirmed Quantum Mechanics' prediction of nonlocal (instantaneous, action-at-a-distance) correlations which appeared to defy Einstein's limit on the speed-of-light. I recall that, when I first read of Quantum Indeterminism, I found it abhorrent as my scientific education had led me to believe that Reality must be deterministic. In the school library, I had read Nigel Calder's *The Key to the Universe* which told of Relativistic Quantum Electrodynamics and the recently formulated Quantum Chromodynamics of quarks in the atomic nucleus. The success of these Quantum Field theories, unifying electromagnetism and nuclear forces made it appear that a Unified Field Theory including Gravity was not far away. I also recall that sometime when I was in the school library, I saw in an issue of *Scientific American* an advert by the Transcendental Meditation movement which asserted something along the lines of the Grand Unified Field of Physics being equivalent to Hindu notions. Once again this made little impression on me. I was far more fascinated by the philosophical issues relating to Science, the "big questions" such as the origin of Life of Earth and the true nature of Life, than with the highly specialised studies undertaken by real scientists.

In 1983, whilst others were swotting up for their A' Level exams, I decided to broaden my mind learning about interesting philosophical topics as it was not going to be difficult to get the minimum Advanced Level grades offered to me to get into university. On my school-leaving form, I filled in the section asking what I hoped to be when I grew up with the words, "poet, priest, philosopher". I must have appeared a totally naive idiot to anyone with worldly knowledge about real scientific work and careers, etc., dreaming of being a "philosopher-poet" but if I had not messed up my career opportunities, I would never have eventually made the breakthrough in 1994. At this time, around April 1983, shortly before I took my final school examinations, I wrote an essay which won its section of a London Schools' literary competition. The essay was entitled "Something to Believe In" and I quoted the final lines from the hymn, "When a knight won his spurs" beneath the title:

And let me set free with the sword of my youth
From the Castle of Darkness, the power of the Truth

The opening paragraphs spoke of my "tempestuous marriage of instinctive passion and conditioned reason" sending me "careering through the worlds of subjective and objective knowledge, resulting in virtual schizophrenia". It went on to describe my eclectic approach drawn from "Newton's pebbles and the pearls of philosophical insight", never "wearing like Patroclus the seemingly impenetrable armour of any great hero" but, taking Alexander Pope's advice, making use of every friend or foe for, "A little learning is a dang'rous thing".

I wrote of my early childhood 'paganism' and contemplating as a child the worrying possibility of reincarnation as I was unhappy with my lot in life.

I wrote that, "I felt special, there was a Jungian synchronicity in my life" and that I came to see my suffering as a "preparation for the tough world which lay ahead of me". My discovery of the notion of synchronicity, which would play a major role in my path to the Light, came associated with an actual instance of synchronicity! I found a book in the school library by an Arthur Koestler entitled *The Act of Creation* about creativity. I first read about synchronicity in Koestler's *Act of Creation*. That same evening (3rd March 1983) I heard on the news that this same Arthur Koestler and his wife had committed suicide that day.[N11] My essay continued:

> *At the age of twelve, mainly because it seemed a trendy thing to do, I started to read the 'Bhagavad Gita'. All was one, all was God, it exclaimed; matter was just an illusory temporal manifestation of His energy. This unitary revelation struck a harmonious chord in my mind, its simple beauty still enchants the homunculi. Meanwhile, my ego had become suspicious and worried over my Lord's failure to deliver and matters related to free will. This eventually culminated in my metamorphosis; I dumped Him as a creation of my mind.*
>
> *Stepping out into the objective world of Science, I adopted biology after reading about how an inanimate virus comes to life. [In fact, I had read this at around age ten.] Here, I thought, was the key to a true understanding of life and, after initial hesitation, I deposed myself from my spiritual throne. I understood how I could be a product of blind cosmic evolution, my body a gene vehicle, my mind an abstract aspect of brain activity. However, I could not accept the blind faith of many a physicist in meaningless fundamental disorder. Surely there had to be a reason for the existence of the cosmos in the first place? On this issue my instinct and logic were accordant. And, if there was this ultimate reason, then it followed that everything in the cosmos had a meaning. I was aware that natural selection had designed my brain to distil order from apparent chaos in order to systematise the world but I found no conclusive evidence for a repudiation of my ultimate meaning in life.*
>
> *I had drifted into the ethereal world of metaphysics which convinced me that I was really a panentheist and not the pantheist I thought I was. I would meditate on the relationship between the conscious mind and the cosmos. The latter seemed to be an unconscious extension of the material human body; perhaps there was a sort of mind pervading the cosmos. Perhaps I was really a panpsychist. I found that most of my ideas had been entertained by the great metaphysicists [sic] of the past. My ego assumed that this was because great minds think alike but upon sober reflection realised that all human minds, fundamentally, think alike. The human brain fixed the parameters of human understanding. Metaphysics came to a full-stop in Spinoza's circular reasoning of the 'elementary substance' being a cause unto itself.*
>
> *'The point is to change the world', said Marx, words that sent an aura tingling to my scalp. I had little appetite left for the Buddhistic vegetation of philosophy...*

I was soon to 'eat my words' and become fully absorbed in philosophical questions. The son of the sociologist and Life Peer (non-hereditary parliamentary "Lord") Michael Young[N12], author of *The Rise of the Meritocracy*, co-author of the Labour Party's 1945 manifesto, etc., had joined my School in the sixth form (age 17-18) although he was a year older than us having apparently failed some of his O'Levels at age 16. Although he studied Politics and Economics, he had befriended me as the two of us were the most loud-mouthed and opinionated boys in the sixth form and he liked the fact that I had said no to Oxford. Unlike the rest of us who wore casual clothes, he wore a (non-uniform) blazer and owned a car. Ironically, although Michael Young coined the term "meritocracy" in regard to the comprehensive schooling debate of the late 1950s, his own son seems to benefitted from the fact that he was the son of a distinguished academic and Life Peer. Toby got into Oxford University even though he failed to attain the grades required to meet the terms of his conditional offer. I recall when we met again in 1986 Young was boasting about getting a First in PPE (Philosophy, Politics and Economics), that strange Oxford degree for posh political types, including an Alpha in the 'Philosophy of Mind'. At the time I was too ignorant to know that Oxford University has been a hotbed Anglo-American Analytical hot air and myth-making associated with names like Gilbert Ryle and J.L. Austin in Philosophy. Given its association with the British conservatism (in contrast to Leftist Cambridge) and the likes of Margaret Thatcher, Tony Blair and Neocon Niall Ferguson, I would consider Oxford to be the capital of Eurocentric academic White Mythology.[N13] The philosophically-sophisticated Germans refer to the English as 'Islander Monkeys'.

In May 1983 I decided to go along when he drove a few of his Economics friends down to the London School of Economics to hear a debate between the economists Wynne Godley and Alan Budd. The debate was of no interest to me but we happened to visit the LSE bookshop nearby. I recall that it was in the LSE bookshop that day that I first came across a copy of the English translation of Jean Piaget's 1968 book *Structuralism*[3]. The back cover blurb said that Structuralism was an increasingly important method of analysis in disciplines as diverse as Mathematics, Physics, Biology, Psychology, Linguistics, Sociology, Anthropology and Philosophy. I remember having a deep intuition there and then at the LSE bookshop that this book was going to be important for me, even though I did not have any money with me to buy it. This is the first time I can recall having such a sense of mental dissociation into my normal Self and a deeper Self where powerful non-articulated feelings arose deep within me manifesting as an urge or compulsion.

I think that the attraction to the book was not simply an intuitive feeling but also intellectual as it seemed to be offering an interdisciplinary approach to integrating knowledge from diverse fields. Although, my attraction to Molecular Biology was inspired in part by a Reductionist mind-set, I was also, simultaneously, attracted to the idea of a unitary understanding of everything, although back then my ideas were extremely immature. I recall scribbling stuff back the then about a "Quest for Enlightenment" although by "Enlightenment" I simply meant ultimate knowledge and understanding in a rational sense rather than any supra-rational, mystical notion. As if by synchronicity or meaningful coincidence, around this time I visited the library of one the two girls' schools adjacent to our own school where some of my friends used to hang out. At sixth form level some Arts and Humanities subjects had started to be taught jointly with these two adjacent schools and another school in Tufnell Park.[N14] There in the library I found another copy of Jean Piaget's *Structuralism* which I decided to take home with me. The library borrowing slip inside the front cover was blank, although the book was published in 1971 the female pupils and their teachers had never once borrowed the book themselves in 12 years. The book was far too advanced for teenagers. When I myself tried to read this English translation of Piaget's book, I found it incredibly heavy going and didn't really understand much of what Piaget was trying to say. However, it was in this book that I first came across notions from Gestalt Psychology about neurological Field theories etc.

The Events of July 1st to July 12th 1983

After finishing my Advanced Level examinations in June 1983, on July 1st 1983, when still technically a schoolboy (as the summer term finished in mid-July), I began to write entries in a hardbound notebook which I entitled *Certain Philosophical Questions*. I had just read Christian mystic Pierre Teilhard de Chardin's *The Phenomenon of Man*. I read this not out of any interest in Mysticism but rather because it was mentioned in the writings of the famous neurobiologist J.Z. Young whose *An Introduction to the Study of Man* I had read from the school library. I think I first read about Molecular Genetics in the form of Jacob and Monod's Operon hypothesis of bacterial gene function in this book so perhaps this subconsciously influenced my choice of degree. Such bio-molecular "cybernetics" of DNA and proteins conjured up in my mind Reductionist thoughts of explaining Life through such simplistic bio-molecular feedback loops.[N15]

I read another of J.Z. Young's popular paperback books on Biology and related philosophical matters co-written with his wife which I bought around 1982–83. We shall see later that another book by J.Z. Young would play a critical role in my identification of the physiological correlate of Divine Light. Thus my study of Biological Sciences proved to be critical in this regard. Young's fondness for Teilhard's mystical ideas was rather ironic given that the same J.Z. Young mocked the mystically-leaning philosophy of the German Idealists as great tuba blasts bellowing forth from the Rhine. It must have been because Teilhard's anthropocentric ramblings were supposedly inspired by Henri Bergson's Creative Evolution ideas which appealed to the biologist Young. In 2000 I learnt from the Infinity Foundation's Yogapsychology discussion forum (involving many of the USA's top scholars of Hinduism and Buddhism) that Christian missionary Teilhard (like the German Idealists) was much influenced by Eastern ideas including the famous Indian theistic Vedantin Ramanujan but Teilhard's Eurocentric followers ignore this fact to make Teilhard appear more original than he actually was.

Teilhard had written that he was fond of Spinoza's view in which Mind and Matter were, respectively, like the 'inner' and 'outer' attributes of reality[4]. In my very first entry in my new philosophical notebook, I jotted down that I thought that this view was "mystical nonsense". I presume that Teilhard's Christian anthropocentric focus on Man must have coloured my response to his views and thus tainted my view of Spinoza by association with Teilhard. I already knew Spinoza's ideas as I had some acquaintance with Western philosophy through reading entries in the *Encyclopaedia Britannica* which my late father had ordered in 1976 before he died in January 1977. My father wasted money on inessential luxury items like silent and sound cine cameras and projectors whilst neglecting essential household items.[N16] However, in purchasing the Britannica he probably realised that he was terminally ill from cirrhosis and was leaving something for his children. In the event of the death of the purchaser, the Britannica Company's policy was to let the family keep the expensive books even if the deceased, like my father, had only paid a few instalments.

I had also read Bertrand Russell's *A History of Western Philosophy* which I found in a bookcase in a school meeting room. In fact, in late 1982 I had bought a book reviewed in *New Scientist* entitled *The Mind's I* edited by Artificial Intelligence researcher Douglas Hofstadter and the academic philosopher Daniel C. Dennett[5]. The apologists for the Materialist, Behaviourist orthodoxy in so-called Cognitive Science studies including Francis Crick and the Marxian-leaning *The Guardian* newspaper hype up Dennett's Reductionist approach, reflecting contemporary research in Cognitive Science (*see Ch. 5*), and refer to Dennett as if he was a great philosopher. I would call such facile and blinkered Scientism, failing to transcend provincial, contemporary cultural mythologies (*see Ch. 5*), puerile 'Pop Philosophy'. *The Mind's I* contained a series of articles, mainly pop-culture style pieces by Science Fiction writers on issues related to the Mind with comments by the Materialist editors Hofstadter and Dennett. It included a reprint of Thomas Nagel's well-known paper "What is it like to be a bat" which argued that Materialist views of Mind as merely material processes fail to address what it is actually like (or 'how does it actually feel') to be something which is what *'being conscious'* really entails. However, in 1982, Nagel's view made little impression on me and I went along with the immature dismissal of his argument by the editors.

A few days later, a strange compulsion arose within me to go to one of the local libraries as if something deep inside me knew that there was something important awaiting me there. I found there a book called *The Self and its Brain* by British philosopher of science Karl Popper (born an Austrian Jew and famous for his argument that a scientific theory needed to be falsifiable) and the Australian-born Nobel laureate neurophysiologist, John Eccles (who did pioneering work on synaptic transmission between neurons)[6]. These seemingly illustrious authors turned out to be rather confused old men arguing for psycho-physical Dualism (historically associated in the modern West with Rene Descartes). In fact Popper called his view the 3-World hypothesis! If I recall correctly, the information physically stored in physical objects such as books constituted, according to Popper's absurd hypothesis, a separate ontological world from the physical (*see below for further discussion*). I noted that Popper ridiculed Spinoza's Panpsychism as a mystical notion with vacuous 'knee-jerk' response style arguments of his own that basically reflected orthodox scientific belief. I still considered myself a Materialist at this time.

But, suddenly, I found myself totally absorbed in the metaphysical problem of the Ontological Status of Consciousness.

Then on 9th July 1983, the realisation dawned upon me that it was impossible to construct a Physicalist (Materialist) model of Consciousness because Materialism was a fundamentally flawed metaphysical picture of Reality. I use "Physicalist" as I knew that the New Physics actually recognises that Matter is not the primary reality as it is created out of the rather undefined primary principle that physics labels as "energy". Matter was organised patterns of "frozen" energy which could be released from its material bondage in matter-antimatter annihilation. However, this deeper form of Materialism made no difference in regard to the question of conscious awareness. It also dawned upon me that the only viable approach to the ontological problem lay with the view I had, only a few days previously rubbished in my notebook; the Panpsychist approach associated with Spinoza.

This realisation dawned upon me by trying to pursue the ramifications of every type of Physicalist approach to the problem through in my mind, (i.e., 'thought experiments') and eventually I realised that all of them, due to the basic assumptions of this metaphysics, missed the point of what conscious awareness was. All that Physicalism actually does, in essence, is describe patterns of spatio-temporal activity or "*behaviour*" of insentient energy-matter with no reference whatsoever to any Awareness or even to any potentiality for Awareness. Physics cannot transcend its Classical roots in Dynamics and Kinematics (the study of moving objects). Even with the new Quantum Mechanics (QM) of the 1920s, the essential mode of description is dynamical even if so-called 'particles' have no individual trajectories, what is being described is the spatiotemporal behaviour of the underlying nonlocal wave dynamics manifesting particle-like events. The ontological shift here was from the old Materialism to a new 'Physicalism' (with a suppressed Transcendentalism). There was no shift to Panpsychism (meaning here the view that Awareness permeates the entire universe) thus, contrary to much 'Quantum Mind' pop philosophy and New Age nonsense QM says nothing directly about Consciousness. From the *Dynamics* of Galileo and Newton we now have today's relativistic Quantum Electro-*Dynamics* (QED) and Quantum Chromo-*Dynamics* as well as Thermo*dynamics*. In Engineering, structures have to be constructed that resist the natural tendencies for random motion and oscillations, etc., in atomic and molecular crystalline structures, so that they remain largely 'static' or stable at the macroscopic level at which they function for human convenience. Spatio-temporal patterns of (supposedly) insentient Matter are simply that, the motions of matter and no more. *The motions of atoms and molecules, however complex and organised, can no more give rise to Sentience (or Awareness) than the motion of marbles shaken in a jar*. The Physicalist picture precludes Awareness which simply cannot be reduced to such spatio-temporal patterns of activity or the *behaviour* of organised forms of insentient energy, which is what the mathematical formulae of Physics actually describe.

No amount of word-mongering to obfuscate the issue with talk about increasing *complexity* of such spatio-temporal patterns, (i.e., material processes) or talk of *self-referential loops*, or *emergent processes* could overcome this intrinsic flaw inherent in the basic assumptions of Physicalist and Materialist metaphysics. An obvious point which Materialists overlooked or deliberately suppressed was that their supposed explanations for the so-called 'emergence' of supposedly unique human consciousness could not be restricted to information processing activities in the human brain. If the oft-repeated claim that Consciousness is an emergent property were valid then why was it that Consciousness was not present in all emergent processes throughout Nature, the universe is full of emergent processes! The notion of *Emergence* technically refers to properties that appear in collective systems which *cannot be predicted from knowledge of the properties of the constituents*; the classic case being the inability to determine a collective (higher-level) property of a system from knowledge of individual molecules in gaseous or liquid states.[N17]

The fact is that Newtonian physics breaks down once more than two bodies (e.g. molecules) have to be described whereas macroscopic systems consist of countless trillions of molecules. Thus, in reality, Nature is replete with emergent systems because Particle Physics can only describe in detail the most simplified, unnaturally isolated, systems where particles are created in artificial experimental set-ups. Weather systems and Global Temperature are amongst countless emergent systems and the new Chaos Theory has shown that tiny changes in initial conditions can lead to vastly different outcomes making detailed forecasts unpredictable. Similarly, amplification of uncertainty and indeterminism at the quantum level can result in anomalous phenomena, such as freak giant waves on the ocean. The Physicalists or Materialists give no explanation nor even an indication as to what is so special about human brain processes that could account for this amazing new property of Awareness which was nowhere present, not even in some faint potential state, throughout the rest of the Physicalist conception of insentient Nature.

If one examined carefully what an emergent property is, it is found to be nothing more than a more complex level of spatio-temporal patterns of activity abstracted at a higher level of spatio-temporal or physical order. They are unpredictable or "incomputable" simply because of the complexity of all the interacting particle motions are way beyond the simple models of Physics not because any novel ontological property arises. Thus there is nothing special about them ontologically; in fact *emergent properties are the norm rather than the exception*! How could unpredictable collective motions possibly create Awareness, Awareness is not a complex motion or spatiotemporal pattern. Awareness is that mysterious qualitative background of our existence that experiences visual colours and forms, sounds, smells, tastes, feels and thoughts. The 'Laws of Physics' only describe dynamical attributes of supposedly insentient energy/matter not any sort of potentialities for sentience. *Emergence* refers to *incomputable dynamical complexity* (higher level spatiotemporal activity patterns not predictable from the dynamics of constituents due to sheer complexity) *not the magical appearance of entirely novel properties* with no links whatsoever to what is supposed to exist in the Physicalist ontology. Emergence is merely an epistemological concept referring to the limitations of scientific models to predict complex behaviour. A decisive argument against the Emergent Materialist position involving the difference between Life and Consciousness is given below in regard to my first Theory of Consciousness. In July 1983, I realised that the only logically consistent position for this line of reasoning was Panpsychism.

We can easily intuit that a higher level pattern of order does not imply a magical new appearance of Awareness. The numerical read-out on a liquid crystal display (LCD) calculator is a higher level collective property (abstracted by a mind) from the lower level pattern of dots or pixels. The dots themselves are also a collective property of a pattern of liquid crystal molecules. If the Emergent Materialists argued in a logically consistent manner, rather than obfuscating to hide their abject failure, then their argument would imply that a display on a calculator screen would be "conscious" and so too would each single dot etc. I could see where the Emergentists were 'coming from' as the notion of *emergence* does have relevance to Mind-related questions such as explaining how *meaningful information* arises at higher levels of order. But the appearance of 'meaningfulness' at higher levels, as in the LCD is obviously not the same thing as the appearance of conscious awareness. Those holding to the view that Consciousness was a property limited to human or higher animal brain processes only really had one ontological option, Dualism.

In fact, Emergent Materialism, the view most scientists seem to espouse is, for the reasons given above, a form of *disguised Psycho-Physical Dualism* although advocates purport to be Monistic Materialists. Completely unspecified and undefined "emergent brain processes" are tacitly afforded a separate ontological status from the rest of physical Nature as the simple property of emergence (unpredictable, complex higher-level behaviour) cannot actually distinguish them from the rest of Nature where such emergence occurs everywhere. Thus Popper and Eccles were correct in recognising the failure of Physicalist attempts to account for Consciousness. But their Dualist approach only creates countless new problems without really resolving anything. What is their separate "world" co-existing with the natural world and why does it only seem to be associated with certain unspecified brain processes. Popper said that the information in books constitutes another (ontological) world. But, of course, such *information* is actually part of the 'Physical World'. It only becomes '*meaningful* information' for humans when transmuted by human sensory and cognitive processes into another form of information in human brains. We do not experience strings of letters as printed in books, we actually experience Gestalt-quality (holistic) word-sounds and thoughts in our mind. Going through such lines of reasoning in my head, on 9th July 1983 it dawned upon me that the only viable approach was in fact Panpsychism.

However, although it became clear that Physicalism was simply incapable of accounting for conscious awareness and that Psycho-Physical Dualism was just too intrinsically flawed to be a viable alternative; beyond realising that Panpsychism was the only consistent Monistic approach it seemed impossible to make any more progress. Faced with questions such as why there was a plurality of conscious entities rather than just one all-pervading Universal Consciousness and why it appeared as if only certain brain processes (which we call our 'conscious mind') seemed to be conscious when all of Reality was in fact Psycho-Physical, I gave up trying to make progress. These questions appeared totally intractable and I thought that they were probably beyond the capacity of the human mind to comprehend. Then three days later, on July 12th 1983, as I sat and watched television I suddenly became aware that entering my mind was an image of what seemed to me intuitively to be a living neuron. I was somewhat sedated as I had suffered badly from hayfever since 1976 and, in those days, used old-fashioned long-action antihistamine tablets called Dimotapp LA which made me drowsy and caused serious problems for me at exam times (June-July). But such drowsiness had never resulted in such an image forcing its way into my consciousness before or since.[N18] On July 12th 1983, coupled to the vision of the 'living neuron' came a powerful intuition that this living cell was itself a *sentient entity* and that, if I followed this line of reasoning, I would arrive at the answer to the problems which had seemed so utterly intractable only three days earlier.

Following this brief vision experience, I was suddenly driven by a strong compulsion to look again at Jean Piaget's *Structuralism* book which a few weeks previously had made little sense to me although, when I first saw the book, my deeper Self had intuited strongly that it would be very important for me. Now on July 12th 1983 my deeper Self was insistent that the answer I was looking for was to be found in that book and the book just seemed to open exactly where the seeming answer was given. I later found that such "library angel" (Koestler's term) experiences of a book falling open at the right place for something very meaningful was common amongst mystical seekers. The book fell open near its beginning where Piaget discussed the concept of a 'structure' as an autonomous subunit; a concept derived from mathematical Group Theory. This autonomy of the structure was related to the concept of 'closure' and the fact that the 'structure' was, in the English translation, "self-regulating". I took "self-regulating" to mean the far more radical notion of "self-organising" (which is closer to Piaget's actual meaning as is clear from his book *Biology and Knowledge*, (*see below*)). A self-organising entity maintains its physical form whilst constantly transforming through dynamic processes. 'Self-regulation' implies simply that one parameter such as temperature of the system is controlled. The Western philosopher-of-mind David Chalmers has discussed thought experiments on 'What is it like to be a thermostat' without any adequate explanation as to why a thermostat (or a simple self-regulating network) should be considered an individuated sentient entity[7]. Somehow my subconscious intuition (perhaps my 'deeper Self') grasped the connections between these ideas such as individuation and the problem of Panpsychism and I just knew how to put these ideas together with my intuitive vision of the brain cell as a sentient individual entity in itself.

This resulted in my metaphysical picture of a nested hierarchy of topologically closed fields within fields wherein each closed field constituted an individuated sentient entity. Similar ideas had been put forward by others which I did not know of at that time. Piaget's book had also brought to my attention Gestalt Field theory which had arisen in Germany in the 1920s but had long gone out of fashion in mainstream psychology. I did not realise until a few years later that in our bookcase containing my father's old books there was a book printed in 1960 by Woodworth called *Contemporary Schools of*

Psychology. The original edition had been printed in 1931 and it contained a chapter on Gestalt Field Theory and its problems. But the fact is that it was Piaget's concepts of structures, closure and self-regulation that were important for me and not a detailed discussion of the old Gestalt Field Theory which was found in Woodworth[8].

There was another idea which I had that, with hindsight, I realise that I must have picked up from two sources. I recall reading a *Scientific American* article at school about how a chess-playing computer uses a simulation of the chess board and pieces etc. Furthermore Richard Dawkins in *The Selfish Gene* (which I read in 1982) had speculated that the conscious mind was a simulation of the environment in the brain and he speculated further, in his naïve Materialist way, that perhaps the evolution of such a simulation process in the human brain had (magically) given rise to Consciousness[9]. I think that the idea of the Mind as a model of the world had first been put forward by Kenneth Craik. I realised that, as with Emergent Materialism and Hofstadter's and others' self-referential loops of information processing, such a simulation process in itself completely failed to address the fundamental *ontological problem*. However, I realised also that these Materialist notions such as Emergence and World-Modelling had some partial truth in them relating to aspects of the nature of human mentation and were useful in understanding how 'meaningful experience' arose in a Panpsychist Reality. The Materialist Reductionists were like the blind men mistaking these partial aspects of the elephant for the whole picture.

My 1983 Paper on Consciousness: Structural Subjectivity

The 'Inherent Behaviorism' of Physicalism Precludes Awareness

I knew that this 'nested hierarchy' picture that came to me was just a model which seemed to resolve the problems with Panpsychism but I still felt very excited feeling that I had discovered a new metaphysical picture of the universe which could succeed in explaining Consciousness where Materialist Science was doomed to failure. I possessed a typewriter and amidst the heat, humidity and hayfever of summer 1983, I sat down to present my insights in an essay which I entitled *The Hypothesis of Structural Subjectivity*. The basic ideas presented in this paper were as follows although some points stated below were clarified in a later revised paper written in 1987 with the essentials unchanged. As stated above, I argued that Physicalism was "inherently Behaviorist" in that it was limited to describing phenomena in terms of spatio-temporal patterns of activity or in terms of the *behaviour* of the system under consideration. Put another way, Materialism cannot transcend its roots in the description of matter in motion; all it describes are complex patterns of the motion of matter. The more recent Physicalism, following Quantum Mechanics, simply views matter and forces as complex spatiotemporal forms of insentient energy but this remains inherently Behaviorist. Physicalist explanations generally involved showing how a complex phenomenon could be reduced to patterns of spatiotemporal activity occurring at a smaller scale of Space-Time which manifested the higher level activity as an emergent phenomenon.

Now this method of explanation was extremely successful in regard to the spatiotemporal phenomena such as the motion of cannonballs and planets, with which Classical Physics began its studies. Extension of this Materialist picture and explanatory method from Physics and Astronomy to Chemistry and even many aspects of Biology, overcoming the objections of Vitalists, had proven extremely successful. But in many respects this enormous success blinded most scientists to the intrinsic flaws in the basic picture. These flaws become apparent in regard to the problem of Consciousness but most scientists ignore them believing that the methods which succeeded previously will eventually overcome the objections of the "Mentalists". Most scientists believe that Life has been fully explained by Science as an emergent phenomenon arising out of the smaller scale chemical and physical phenomena which obey the so-called 'Laws of Physics'. Indeed, I agreed that 'Life', meaning here the maintenance of a stable macrocosmic organism, was described satisfactorily as such an emergent phenomenon; a complex pattern of spatiotemporal activity arising from the smaller scale patterns of activity corresponding to biochemical processes, which themselves arose from even smaller scale patterns of atomic activity and so on. But when scientists contend that this same Emergent Materialist approach will also eventually explain how Consciousness arose in the human or perhaps some other animal brain they are failing to grasp that this extrapolation is invalid. The crucial problem with *Consciousness* (meaning here *Awareness* in itself and not something like 'information processing' as many scientists misrepresent it) is that it cannot be reduced to such spatiotemporal patterns of activity or to the Physicalist metaphysical picture (ontology).

This is best shown by considering the *difference between Consciousness and Life* in regard to the concept of Emergent Phenomena. If we were to create a living organism *de novo* we would have little difficulty demonstrating this because all we needed to do was to show that it exhibited the same *behavioural patterns of activity* which we identify as the key features of living systems. Thus a living system is known to us as *living* because it *exhibits patterns of spatiotemporal activity* including some form of respiration, energy transduction, genetic information storage and replication etc. However, we cannot demonstrate empirically that another human being has conscious awareness using scientific methods, we only impute analogically that other humans have conscious awareness because they resemble us (the so-called 'Other Minds' problem). If we were able to look inside a subject's brain whilst the subject was awake, we would not expect to actually detect, let alone observe, the 'raw feels' (or so-called *qualia*) of our experiences. We may find physico-chemical processes *correlated* with experiences but Science can, *in principle,* never reveal anything resembling our experiences nor can Physicalist modes of explanation limited to 'Behaviorism' in the ontological sense, *in principle*, ever account for how such experience somehow co-exists with such physico-chemical processes.

If someone created an artificially intelligent computer that appeared to solve tasks intelligently, once again there is no scientific way to prove that it actually has any awareness. Some Artificial Intelligence workers and their supporters in academic philosophy hold to the ludicrous view associated with the so-called 'Turing Test' which holds that *behaviour* isomorphic to (or mimicking) that of a human in answering some questions is all that is required to prove the existence of Consciousness.[N19] But this is in fact just a vacuous tautology as we have seen above that the Physicalism is 'inherently Behaviorist' in that all it actually describes is behaviour or spatiotemporal patterns of activity. Physicalists tacitly assume that everything that really exists must be reducible to behaviour because that is all that the Physicalist ontology can actually describe. Thus the Turing Test actually proves nothing as a normal communicative human being, by default, passes this test but, as we have just seen, we cannot prove scientifically the existence of Consciousness in a living, awake human brain. Thus, for all intents and purposes, in the Physicalist ontological picture described consistently, a human being is necessarily reduced to the Behaviorists' *insentient automaton* as sentience simply cannot exist in any part of the Physicalist world-picture.

Indeed the extreme form of Materialism is Eliminative Materialism which tries to deny the existence of Consciousness as a real ontological fact claiming, for instance, that it is only a misconception we have associated with our everyday language based on naïve "Folk Psychology". This Eliminative position is associated the afore-mentioned Richard Rorty (*see Ch. 5*), who coined the term "Folk Psychology", and also with Paul and Patricia Churchland. Although this extreme position is ridiculed, even by other Materialists, the fact that it exists serves a useful purpose because it is in fact the only logically consistent form of Materialism. Thus Materialism, followed through in a consistent logical manner, ends up with the absurd denial of the reality of the most fundamental, indisputable fact of our existence, our conscious awareness! *Thus if Materialists followed their arguments through consistently, **all Materialists should all be Eliminative Materialists** as the existence of Consciousness is precluded by the ontology of Materialism (and Physicalism).*

Other supposedly 'non-eliminative' forms of Materialism such as Epiphenomenalism (Consciousness as a mysterious by-product which arises out of physical phenomena but plays no causal role) and Emergent Materialism, etc., can only 'include' Consciousness within the metaphysical world-picture using either 'Tacit Elimination' or 'Disguised Dualism'. Most attempts at Materialist Reductionism *eliminate Consciousness tacitly*, brushing it under the carpet, hoping that we will not see through the obfuscating cloak of the fancy words and metaphors of self-referential loops, complexity etc. These words (the 'Linguistic Blanket') just distract the layman from the fact that no explanation has actually been given; rather Consciousness has been *reduced falsely to some sort of behaviour*. We have also seen that Emergent Materialism, the most widely held view amongst scientists, is in fact tacit (or disguised) Dualism. The universe is full of emergent processes yet no explanation is offered as to why some, always unspecified, brain processes (constituting the 'conscious mind') should somehow, from out of nothing, possess this remarkable new property nowhere to be found or even hinted at in Material Nature. This is because the Physicalist metaphysical world-picture, originally developed to describe the motion or *dynamics* of planets and cannonballs and, even the New Physics (e.g. QED, QCD), is essentially limited to Dynamics.

All it can describe is spatiotemporal forms, patterns of activity, or the motions of Matter. The notion of imperceptible extra dimensions remains 'inherently Behaviorist' in that a *dimension* is a *degree of freedom* or spatial mode of energetic activity to occur.[N20] Because of the indisputable successes it has achieved, it has become a 'sacred cow' for Scientific Materialists and there is in fact only one way that Consciousness can be included in this picture, by an appeal to **magic** (i.e., creation *ex nihilo*).

My Panpsychist, Structuralist Solution to the 'Ontological Problem of Consciousness'

The solution to this failure of Physicalist metaphysics was, I argued, to shift to a view similar to that of Spinoza in which Reality is not just Physical but is Psycho-Physical and Panpsychist (consciousness permeates all of Reality). Recall that Teilhard de Chardin commented that he liked Spinoza's view that 'Mind' and 'Matter' were like the inner and outer attributes of Reality. In fact Spinoza's picture was that the Underlying Reality or Substance (identified with 'God') has an infinite number of attributes of which we can only know two, the Mental and the Material, which run in parallel. Thus what appears Material in one attribute is Mental in the other. I used such a Psycho-Physical Parallelist form of Panpsychism where the Mental and the Physical attributes of the underlying Reality were like two aspects of the same reality, viewed from within and from without (but with qualifications; *see below*). Later on in the 1980s, revising these ideas, I would stress that such Psycho-Physical Parallelism is actually only a construction of our minds, a metaphorical approximation to the Underlying Reality as such Parallelism if carefully analysed can be shown to be untenable. This has to do with notions of 'causal closure' of the Physical realm which such Parallelist views uphold with a form of tacit Dualism treating Consciousness like an epiphenomenon which runs in parallel with all Physical processes without affecting them in any way. The very fact that we talk about and write about our subjective experience shows that the subjective realm does in fact affect causally the so-called 'Physical world'.

Thus in later revisions I stressed that the Parallelist metaphor was only an approximation to a more subtle, intangible Underlying Reality which I called a Psycho-Physical Nonduality which our conceptual apparatus was incapable of grasping except through the tacit Dualism of 'Parallelism'. This view resembles the so-called 'Neutral Monism' postulated by William James[10] and, in one period, by Bertrand Russell; an atypical period when he was not too deluded by his infatuation with Logic and Atomistic Materialism. I was not aware of these views at the time. In fact 'Neutral Monism' resembles the ancient mystical philosophy of the 'ineffable' Ultimate Reality beyond the limitations of our concepts. This failure of our dichotomous concepts was also brought to light in the so-called Wave/Particle dichotomy and Bohr's Complementarity Principle in Quantum Theory but, as I have stated elsewhere, paradoxes such as this only exist because of false human assumptions and theoretical concepts. A fundamental particle is just a human concept abstracted from the underlying 'Quantum' (transcendental) realm of nonlocal, holonomic wave activity. This stems from the Western infatuation with Geometry leading to the ontologically absurd, idealised notion of 'point particles'.

The questions I still had to answer were, if Awareness or 'Subjectivity' must be a fundamental attribute of all Reality and thus permeated the whole universe, as it could not be created physically, then why did it appear to us that only certain unspecified brain processes in humans, and most probably other higher animals with brains, appear to be conscious. Why did the rest of the universe appear insentient? Related to this question was a more subtle one. If Awareness (or Consciousness) permeated the whole universe, then why was there a seeming plurality of conscious entities in the universe rather than just one all-pervading Universal Consciousness? In 1983, I did not know anything about Vedanta's Pure Consciousness or of the distinction between Nondual Universal and Transcendental Consciousness etc. However, I did put forward a notion of 'Raw Awareness' based on the Western philosophical use of 'raw feel' for the essential subjective experiences such as 'redness' or 'coldness' etc. 'Raw Awareness' was essential *awareness-in-itself*, not of anything in particular, the content of awareness was the spatiotemporal patterns of energetic processes (or information) which differentiated Raw Awareness. The point of this notion was that the physical processes may have something to do with the content of awareness but not with Awareness *per se*. Thus unwittingly, I had put forward an inchoate notion which resembled the Universal Pure Consciousness. However, it was not an important factor in my 1980s ideas as back then I was not concerned with altered states of Consciousness which I knew nothing about. I only had a basic acquaintance with Spinoza's philosophy and I did not even know his ideas relating to individuation before 1994 when I discovered that his view resembled my Structuralism-influenced ideas.

The answer to the first issue of why most of Nature seemed insentient was related to the issue of 'Other Minds'. As stated above in regard to creating Life *de novo*, we cannot demonstrate or prove the existence of conscious awareness in ourselves or anyone else by conventional scientific means. When neurosurgeon Wilder Penfield stimulated the brains of his still conscious patients there were no detectable physical indicators correlated with the experiences, including out-of-body experiences, he induced. In order to avoid Solipsism, we infer the presence of Consciousness in others *by analogy* with our own experiences, rather than consider other people to be insentient automata. Such reasoning seemed clearly related to the view that Consciousness was the 'inner aspect' of an entity whereas the Physical was the 'outer aspect'. This was also related to Thomas Nagel's question as to what it was like to actually be some entity as opposed to simply knowing about entities other than ourselves[11]. I realised that the only thing that we were ever aware of *directly,* (i.e., without mediation of the senses and concepts) was the contents of own personal 'conscious mind'. To be more precise this was actually, at any one moment a very limited 'Field of Attention' and the contents of this field usually changed from one moment to the next.

The fact was that *we never actually experienced the world outside our minds* save as representations within our mind of certain biologically relevant aspects of our environment in a sort of *model of the world or our local environment*. Thus all we actually experienced was our selves, the 'inner being' aspect of our conscious minds (or the changing 'Field of Attention').

Everything else in the universe was seen by us in its 'outer aspect'. Within a matter of days, this logical reasoning as to the nature of our 'self', Spinoza's Panpsychism, the notion of the Mind as a field process from Gestalt Field Theory and the notion Mind as world-modelling simulation was brought together with my intuitive insights relating to Piaget's autonomous, closed structures into my *Hypothesis of Structural Subjectivity* in July 1983.

The universe was Psycho-Physical, with both Physical and a Subjective (or Psychical) aspects, like the 'inner' and 'outer' aspects discussed above. The plurality of separate conscious entities arose because parts of the constant flux of phenomena (the spatiotemporal patterns of energetic activity described by Physics) 'closed themselves off' from the whole as self-organising processes. I knew that modern Quantum Field Theories described the universe not in terms of discrete particles but as spatiotemporal patterns of unimaginably intense activity (or localised dynamic processes) in the fields which permeated the entire universe. Even the proton, the most stable component of atoms would eventually decay. These 'subjectively closed' entities were like whirlpools in the ocean, not truly separate, only maintaining a temporary individuality through self-organising activity. From the Physical perspective, those '*closed*' entities which maintained a sense of *individuality* were probably subatomic particles, atoms, molecules, biological cells, multicellular organisms, perhaps planets, stars and galaxies. Though a non-gaseous planet like Earth appears to be a lump of rock held together by Gravity, it is in fact a fluid process of molten lava and what appears permanent to us is dynamic process on longer time-scales.

In the 1990s I learnt that Spinoza wrote that what there is (i.e., Ultimate Reality) is indivisible but there is individuation of 'modes'. These 'modes' are individuated by motion[12]. Spinoza's metaphysics was not based on actual experience but was a highly Rationalistic, speculative metaphysics which historians have noted must have been inspired by his knowledge of Kabbala mysticism hence Popper (himself of Jewish Ancestry) dismissed it as 'mystical nonsense' above. His Pantheistic views and his contempt for organised religion led to the young Spinoza's 'excommunication' from his Amsterdam Portuguese-Jewish community with the harshest writ they had ever issued. Spinoza went out of his way to distance himself from Judaism stating that "Love thy neighbour as you love yourself" is the only moral law. He dismissed the (tribal) Jewish self-image as "God's Chosen People" as childish; the Hebrews were neither intellectually nor morally superior to other peoples. Although Spinoza dismissed the need for priests or Rabbis, holding that the 'supreme authority' resides in each individual, he claimed that this 'authority' was the 'natural light' (of Reason)[13]. Given Spinoza's infatuation with Rationalism and Euclidean-style Geometry, it was difficult to picture his notion of individuation using notions of rotating spheres etc. Individuation is much easier to 'picture' in a Monistic Process metaphysics in which distinct entities that maintain an 'identity' appear as vortex-like processes which are not really separate from the rest of Nature's constant flux.

Returning to my own model; from the Subjective or Psychical perspective, these physically individuated processes became 'closed' or shut off both from the Universal Awareness of the whole universe. Thus a self-organising process individuates not only physically but concomitantly in its subjective aspect it becomes a Subjective Whole or a Unity of Experience. However, except for the most fundamental particles, all structures contain within themselves smaller-scale ('lower-level') structures which themselves are 'closed' from the subjective experience of the higher-level structures enclosing them. Such a picture of structures within structures within larger structures (reflecting different levels of Physical order) is known as a 'nested hierarchy' model.[N21] Thus an individuated sentient entity will contain within itself smaller substructures which are individuated sentient entities in their own right and this is repeated right through all levels of physical order until we reach the most fundamental 'particle' level.

Thus each structure only experiences the 'higher level' (larger-scale) patterns of activity, relations or information existing within it spatially as most of the 'lower level' information is 'closed' to its subjectivity within substructures. This arrangement has important consequences and is related to the reason why most contemporary Materialists favour the notion of Mind as an Emergent property. This is because the 'meaningful information' in our mind arises at a higher level of physical order from the smaller-scale, 'lower level' processes doing the underlying information processing. Recall the metaphor of the LCD calculator display. The *meaningful information*, the sequence of numbers, exists at a higher level of order from the lower level information which constitutes it, i.e., the individual dots on the LCD screen. These are in turn made from molecules and so on. Thus, in a superficial manner, my view resembles Emergent Materialism in restricting the content of our experience to higher level information which develops out of the activity of lower-level processes. Unlike Karl Popper's 3-World nonsense, I am not claiming that 'meaningful information' constitutes a separate ontological world! There is no ontological problem here as there is no need to explain how Awareness arises in my picture as Awareness is omnipresent throughout Nature.

Thus each individuated sentient entity (each 'closed autonomous process structure') experiences events correlated only with the higher level physical processes (or the higher level information) within itself as most of the lower level information is closed off in substructures. My metaphorical picture of individuated 'whirlpools' relates more concretely to the notion of a closed *field* used here in the sense of a self-organising process which has a sense of wholeness, interconnectedness and unity as well as a degree of ethereality. The individuated closed *field* notion helps convey the image of the individual as a dynamic spatiotemporal pattern of activity whose individuality is simply a temporary maintenance of an organised pattern of activity as the term 'field' may also be used to delimit such a spatial domain of activity. The lifetime of the individuated field can range from infinitesimally small periods of time for unstable particles to billions of years for galaxies. In contrast to such unitary *structures*, the Physical realm (but not the Psychic) also contains *aggregates*, systems which cohere in time through rigid interactions in a non-dynamic manner such as crystals, human artefacts such as tables and computers, rocks, and any other form which is not a dynamically maintained, self-organising process. The aggregate is not subjectively closed from the higher level 'structural subjectivity' in which it exists, although its component substructures (molecules, atoms etc.) are in themselves closed individuated sentient entities. The word *aggregate* indicates that such an entity is like a disorganised 'clumping together' of components rather than a self-organising whole.

Human 'Mindlike' Consciousness and 'Meaningful Experience'

All such self-organising, individuated entities are assumed to have an awareness that exists only on a moment-by-moment basis, changing in relation to the spatiotemporal, energetic flux with which their experience correlates. The Subjective or 'Awareness' aspect of the structure changes *in parallel* with the energetic flux, (i.e., Psycho-Physical Parallelism) thus at any moment, the Subjective aspect reflects the Physical state of the individuated system. Although such systems have an individuated Subjective aspect, essentially the same as our own conscious mind, they were '*Non-Mindlike*' structures as their awareness does not include a sense of Self nor a sense of Self-continuity through Time. In fact Non-Mindlike structures have no '*meaningful*' experiences whatsoever, only a moment-by-moment, 'vegetative' awareness of the changing state of their physical aspect. These physical states might be cyclical or random patterns of flux without any *meaningfulness* (we shall discuss below what constitutes 'meaningfulness'). In contrast to the general Non-Mindlike subjectivity that permeates most of Nature, I argued that our own subjectivity was '*Mindlike*' which meant possessing Self-apprehension, apprehension of Self-Continuity through Time (Personal Identity), and general 'meaningfulness'. I interpreted *meaningfulness* in an evolutionary sense in that the contents of our awareness have some sort of adaptive function serving the organism of which the conscious mind is a special substructure. We shall discuss the meaning of meaningfulness or '*meaningful organisation*' more fully below. However, the point I stressed was that there was *no essential or ontological difference between* our meaningful, *Mindlike awareness* (so-called 'Consciousness' in the everyday Wakefulness sense) *and* the meaningless, moment-by-moment *Non-Mindlike awareness* of most individuated sentient entities.

What my point above stresses is that there is **no Ontological duality** (i.e., of *Physical* phenomena and *Subjective* experience) involved in explaining our conscious mind as *our mind is, in essence, the same as the rest of Nature* where closed fields of self-organising activity become individuated sentient entities, with their own awareness shut off from the Universal Consciousness. Thus ,whereas most scientists, steeped in Materialism, resort to disguised Dualism to try to 'explain' how 'Consciousness' supposedly 'emerges' (*ex nihilo*) in Physical evolution from an *insentient* Physical Nature, the real question was not how 'conscious awareness' as such arose. Awareness cannot possibly be created *de novo* from *insentient* Physical Nature. The real issue of human consciousness was how a '*meaningfully organised*' or '*Mindlike*' sentience arose from the random and cyclical fluxes of phenomena in a *sentient Psycho-Physical Nature*. Once we have resolved this Ontological Problem, the remaining questions become much the same as the ones that Physicalist science can actually deal with. These include how mental phenomena as 'meaningful organisation' (unlike 'conscious awareness') can indeed be reduced to spatiotemporal patterns of activity (or physical 'behaviour') which is all that Physicalist science can actually describe. To account for this Non-Ontological, lesser 'Problem of Mind' (as distinct from the Ontological Problem of Awareness), I put forward an idea which drew upon Gestalt Field theory and the notion of the Mind as simulation of the environment, calling my idea the World-Model Field. This World-Model Field was the physical correlate of what we ourselves actually are, the closed structure corresponding to our conscious mind or the Field of Attention.

The Physical correlate of our awareness, our constantly changing 'Field of Attention' or conscious mind, I argued was a self-organising process in the electromagnetic field activity occurring in the cerebrum (the two cerebral hemispheres constituting the bulk of our brain). The psychical closure of the Field of Attention would presumably correlate with some sort of topological closure of this self-organising field activity in its physical aspect. This self-organising field process was associated with a World-Model or simulation process which had evolved in higher mammals culminating in the human form. Such a simulation of the key features of the animal's environment provided huge adaptive advantages to the animal in relation to reliance on primitive instinctual responses and the slightly more advanced conditioned learning exhibited by many animals. The human capacity for foresight, to visualise possible outcomes in one's head before undertaking an action would have provided a huge evolutionary advantage to those animals possessing this recently evolved capacity. Such a simulation process to foresee the consequences of one's actions would require some sort of self-representation of the organism within the simulation as well as well as a capacity for memory retrieval and basic spatiotemporal representations. Such foresight presupposes some capacity for imaginative reconstruction of perceptual images or, in other words, a capacity to simulate important features of the environment.

In 1983 we were well into the age of information processing and Artificial Intelligence (AI) research whereby humans were trying to recreate such simulation processes in computers. I recalled reading how a chess-playing computer had to make a model of its 'world', the chess board and pieces along with the transformation rules by which the chess game operated. Indeed, *The Mind's I* book was partly inspired by the over-confidence of such AI researchers as to the capabilities of their machines. I recall in the 1980s, AI zealot Marvin Minsky appearing on BBC's *Horizon* science documentary series boasting that, in the (not too distant) future, our computers would keep us as pets! In fact, other TV programmes showed how the real rationale behind AI research was not really to understand the nature of Mind but the Pentagon's desire to build computer guided cruise missiles which could correct their positions using Cybernetics to arrive at their specified targets. We saw the true fruits of such AI research in the 1990 Gulf War. The academic discipline of Cognitive Science had arisen in the USA in the 1950s through military funding following concerns about the Chinese practice of "brainwashing" American prisoners during the Korean War. Thus my use of terms such as spatial and temporal reference frames for a world-modelling process were a reflection of contemporary scientific advances with which we in the information processing age are very comfortable although philosophers in earlier centuries would not have had access to such notions. In 1983, I was not aware of Immanuel Kant's argument that Space and Time were *a priori* categories or forms built into our perception let alone Yogic and Husserlian phenomenological knowledge of the actual processes.

Unlike Non-Mindlike structures, the *World-Model Field is 'meaningfully organised'* because the events occurring within it are strictly controlled by evolved automatic brain functions to constitute a 'faithful' (in regard to *predictability* of events rather than reflecting Reality) simulation of the external world upon which the human organism bases life and death judgements. I stressed in O/OM that 'meaning' exists in relation to the 'whole', an entity only has meaning in terms of its relations to the other entities in the system under consideration. This is illustrated by the lock and key metaphor. A flat piece of metal with little ridges cut into it serves as a key if it opens a lock. If the key has been washed ashore on a remote island inhabited by a primitive society, the native islanders do not understand the piece of metal as a key. It has no meaning in their environment where there are no locks. *It does not fit in*. Something is *meaningful* if it fits harmoniously within the prevailing system of relations and concepts (such as a language) in a particular context. Of course, something that does not fit harmoniously is not absolutely devoid of 'meanings' within other contexts but it remains anomalous of relative meaning within the context where it does not fit. This is very relevant to the nature of Mind. In Chapter 9, I mentioned how a scientific paradigm (conceptual framework) operates very much like how we believe perceptual frameworks operate. Perception discriminates from the sensory input those patterns which fit in with inherited and learned cognitive patterns (called "neurognostic structures" by the so-called Biogenetic Structuralists[14] influenced by Piaget) relevant to the organism (such as predators and prey shapes) whilst tending to ignore patterns that do not fit. Our senses themselves have evolved primarily to select key features of the environment which are of importance to the organism's survival in a dangerous environment (information which is *meaningful* to the organism). I recall a famous scientific paper in *Scientific American* called "What the frog's eye tells the frog's brain", about the shapes resembling flies, etc., which elicit the instinctual projection of the frog's tongue to seize the prey.

Eddington pointed out in *Nature of the Physical World* that scientific concepts only have a meaning within a nexus of relations to other scientific concepts and are somewhat meaningless outside this nexus. If we ask what the property *x* means, we are told that *x* is related to properties *y* and z in such and such a manner. But then the meaning of *y* and *z* is defined by their relations to *x, a, b, c*..., etc., so we never escape this interconnectedness of meanings[15]. Thus our brains are to some extent 'pre-wired' to expect meaningful patterns of information and gradually we develop conceptual frameworks, etc., through reorganisation of neuronal connections etc. Thus the World Model Field is **meaningfully organised** *in relation to the organism's survival* in its environment and possesses self-reference frames, temporal frames and memory retrieval processes in order to maintain it simulations of relevant features of the organism's environment. Thus it constitutes a *Mindlike* structure. However, in essence (ontologically), it is no different from the *Non-Mindlike* structures in Nature as it too is only aware of its physical state (or informational pattern) in a moment-by-moment manner. However, due to the brain's capacity for meaningful organisation of information, including memory retrieval in a temporal frame plus self-representation within a world-model, our moment-by-moment awareness appears to us to have continuity (due to memory traces) and is meaningful (as discussed above).

It is worth noting that Anglo-American Analytical philosophy held to a dogma that Language is a prerequisite for Thought. Such naïve Rationalism ignores the facts of biological evolution, glorifying Language as with the Semitic religions. Evolutionary considerations would lead us to think that visual reasoning based on imaginative simulation was a precursor of abstract conceptualisation. In recent years the unscientific, mythological assumptions of Anglo-American and much of Western philosophy, undermined by knowledge from Cognitive Sciences, Phenomenology, Evolution etc., have been exposed by various authors [e.g.,[16, 17, 18]]. In stark contrast to the Logocentric, Anthropocentric myths of Anglo-American Philosophy, rooted in Christian superstitions holding Man to be alone amongst creatures in possession of a spiritual, 'Rational Soul', Ethological studies of animal intelligence have demonstrated in recent years the presence of foresight, self-awareness, problem-solving skills, etc., in animals such as chimpanzees, dolphins, elephants and even, to some extent, in Corvid birds (e.g. Crows, Ravens, Magpies).

As with Non-Mindlike sentient entities, the World Model Field is only aware of events *within itself* which are not closed off within sentient substructures (cells, molecules and atoms); this leaves 'open' to its awareness only the higher level patterns of meaningful electromagnetic field activity generated by neuronal information processing. The experience of *after-images* suggests that generation of a mental image involves sustained activation in certain neural representational patterns. The neural correlates of the image of a bright light-bulb may remain over-excited after attention has shifted from the light bulb. We seem to see an area of electrical excitation that dissipates gradually in the 'mind's-eye'. Furthermore, we only experience that which is spatially within the closed field structure of the Field-of-Attention and never anything spatially external to it (this was my view in the 1980s before I understood mystical ego dissolution and transpersonal experience). *Phenomena* (or percepts) of the outside world are events inside the World Model Field mostly generated by events outside the brain; information being transmitted into the field by the sensory transduction and nervous conduction and being organised into the field's internal information (spatiotemporal patterns of activity). Thus the so-called *Physical World* is actually our conceptual interpretation of such *phenomena* ('appearances' or percepts), which are actually part of the internal structure of our conscious mind, in terms of an 'outside world' of physical events. There is indeed an outside world of course in this metaphysical model but we cannot apprehend it as it is in itself (*noumenally*); we are restricted to phenomenal representations generated within ourselves (inside the World Model Field) through sensory transfer of information from external entities.

The problem of **Personal Identity** through Time or **Self-Continuity** poses no problem for the World Model Field notion even though our experience is only a moment-by-moment awareness due to memory storage and retrieval from the neuronal patterns in the brain combined with temporal and self-representational frames necessary for world-modelling. As stated above, memory traces from past states and the life history of the organism can be incorporated into the present moment so we have a meaningful experience of Self-Continuity even after Dreamless sleep when the World-Model Field is actually extinguished before being recreated with the return of Wakefulness. In 1983, I suggested that Dream states were the product of a 'Sister Model' activation occurring in the right hemisphere which, as it drew from the same life history memories maintained our sense of Personal Identity with the normal Wakeful World Model. No strict world-modelling staying faithful to the animal's environment is required during the sleeping state when the organism is not actively participating in the world and so the dreaming Sister Model can violate the strict laws by which the waking World Model operates in its simulations. During Wakeful states, the dreaming Sister Model would be inhibited by strict World Model generation for the purpose of survival. Research suggests that Rapid Eye Movement sleep is associated with learning critical behaviours, the animal acts out critical behaviours such as hunting prey or escaping predators in its dreams.

My Panpsychist hypothesis also gave an answer to the question posed in regard to AI research as to whether or not a future computer could attain Consciousness. As stated above, Materialist science confuses the emergence of meaningfully-organised Mindlike information processing systems with the 'emergence' of conscious awareness *per se*. Thus there is much nonsense spouted about self-referential loops of information feedback or higher level information processing supposedly creating Consciousness (*de novo*) out of (insentient) physical processes. But my hypothesis argued that such meaningful organisation of information does not constitute human-like 'consciousness' even though the entire universe is Psycho-Physical and permeated by Awareness. The reason being that such higher level meaningful information, along with its self-reference frame, temporal frame, memory traces, etc., must all be present as integral features of an individuated self-organising process, with the lower level substructures closed off. Even if such meaningful information existed in a computer it would only constitute a tiny part of the vast disorganised, meaningless information of the higher-level 'closed-structure' of which the computer circuitry was a tiny part, such as the planet Earth or, if the Earth is not a self-organising process, perhaps the galaxy! The current technology of 'silicon chip' microprocessors is not capable of facilitating the generation of self-organising fields of meaningful electrical information as the electrical activity was restricted to metallic circuitry. However, it was not inconceivable that, in the distant future, computers could be created out of biochemical, organic materials which would allow for self-organising activity of *delocalised electrical fields* which would integrate the meaningful information into a closed Mindlike system. Therefore, the possibility of (meaningfully-organised) Mindlike consciousness in human artefacts cannot be ruled out.

The Response to My 1983 Paper on Consciousness

The presentation of my 1983 *Hypothesis of Structural Subjectivity* above has been polished with three decades of further learning. With the benefit of hindsight, I also write now with the confidence that these lines of reasoning prepared me so that I was able to make the amazing breakthrough in 1994 when I identified the physical correlate of the Divine Light of Pure Consciousness and confirmed the basic validity of this approach. *In 1994 I became the first person in human history to identify the exact physical correlate of a state of consciousness*; indeed of what was historically the most exalted state of Consciousness identified with *Divinity* or the *Godhead.* Of course, the actual paper produced in July 1983 was the work of an eighteen year old schoolboy and immature in its presentation although the essential ideas were the same as presented above. I was very excited, thinking I had discovered something completely new. I now know that others who have realised the failings of Materialism have put forward Panpsychist ideas and they too also get very excited even though these ideas of academic philosophers do not come near to the consistency of argument that I managed to put forward as a teenager! Much so-called 'Panpsychism' such as the 'Process Philosophy' inspired by Whitehead's "Philosophy of Organism" involves denying a Universal Consciousness as this is associated with Mysticism. Such views are better labelled 'Pan-Emergentism' as they tacitly rely upon Dualism in positing a magical appearance of conscious awareness alongside certain types of material organisation. I also noticed that, in the proceedings of the Third Tucson Consciousness Conference, British academic Galen Strawson became very excited after realising things similar to some of my teenage insights prompting a conversion to 'Panpsychism'. But Strawson still referred naively to Physical reality etc.[19]

I sent out photocopies of my typed-up ideas to any Philosophy society or professor I could find addresses for including Peter Strawson at Oxford University, presumably the father of Galen Strawson, who noted a similarity to Neutral Monism.[N22] In August 1983, I received a letter from a J.J. Williamson DSc., President of *The Society of Metaphysicians* in Hastings. I found their address listed under philosophical societies in a reference book in a local library. Williamson wrote that "works of this sort are very important indeed if formal science is to extend its frontiers beyond limited frames of reference". He asked to publish it and I readily agreed. He did not seem to have realised that this was the work of an 18 year old schoolboy and he asked me in another letter as to how parapsychology fitted into the picture. At that time, I was still deeply entrenched in my scientific, rationalist indoctrination and, following the orthodox opinion, thought that Parapsychology must be irrational nonsense like Mysticism. Even though I knew nothing about Parapsychology, I replied that, given the problems of information transfer, etc., I could not see how Parapsychology could exist.

I recall now that in my early twenties, before I came to accept Mystical experience and Paranormal phenomena, 'life' (in the sense of my worldly existence) seemed meaningless and the universe '*disenchanted*'. A world-picture based on atoms, DNA and deterministic physical interactions remained devoid of any *cosmological relationship*, in the traditional sense, between the Individual and the Cosmos as a Whole. The original poetry part of my O/OM, written in 1991, was essentially about this 'cosmological relationship' and a sense of being connected to other 'wholes'. I recall as a youngster contemplating writing poetry based on questions such as; if each of us is an ever-changing collection of material particles, what then am I and what is the Love between two such collections of particles. One could raise similar questions in regard to Richard Dawkin's Reductionist 'Selfish Gene' ideas. Dawkins did stress early on in his book that the word 'Selfish' was just an Anthropomorphic metaphor connoting the *successful persistence* in the *random process* of cosmic evolution of stable, self-replicating structures. Genes were not really 'selfish'. However, as mentioned in the quote from my 1983 essay "Something to believe in" above, he also argued along the lines that our *bodies were merely vehicles for the perpetuation of our genes*. Alongside Dawkins' unwitting reformulation of the vulgar form of the Christian myth of 'Original Sin' (*see Chapter 1*) this '*body as gene vehicle*' view paralleled religious notions of biological bodies as vehicles for reincarnating immortal souls. His pop philosophy notion of a 'meme' or cultural unit of replication resembles notions of the Karmic persistence of memories in the *Akasa*. My own nested hierarchy of 'closed fields' hypothesis made me believe back then that, if the universe was considered as a 'God-like' Supreme Being, it would neither be omniscient nor aware of what the individual human experienced. As I believed that paranormal interventions in the law-like behaviour of Nature did not exist, then there could be no real 'Synchronicities' (only random coincidences) nor other sorts of special events which brought some sense of mystery, destiny or meaning into our lives.

In summer 1983 I also received a very positive response from Professor D.W. Hamlyn, who was the editor of *Mind*, the leading British academic journal of Philosophy. He wrote that he was "amazed" that an eighteen year old had written the paper commenting about some similarities to Leibniz's distinction between perception and "apperception" etc. He urged me to seek *scientific evidence* for my vision {*e.m.*}. Professor Thomas Nagel, based in the USA, also responded saying that he had passed on my paper to a friend of his at London University, Arnold Zuboff, who commented that, although the work was immature, the boy showed much promise and may go on to do things. The quite famous London-based Historian of Science Karl Popper, who peddled his naive "three-World hypothesis", also responded commenting that he thought that I had tried to tackle far too many things at once. I was then and still remain disdainful toward this 'specialist's attitude' as for *real understanding* you needed to comprehend *how all these different things fitted together*. Popper's co-author on *The Self and its Brain*, Australian-born Nobel laureate Sir John Eccles was also courteous enough to respond from his Swiss residence although only really acknowledging receipt. So too was the American Mathematical Physicist turned Computer Scientist, Douglas Hofstadter, the principal editor of *The Mind's I*, whose popular book *Godel, Escher Bach*, I had also read in 1982. He said that my ideas were interesting and sent me a little ring-bound booklet containing his own Emergent Materialist views. His co-editor Daniel Dennett, who was then less well-known than Hofstadter, did not respond. Dennett has since become very well known as an apologist for the Materialist orthodoxy, appearing on British television science documentaries about AI and the Turing Test and publishing books with misleading titles like *Consciousness Explained* (*see Chapter 5*).[N23]

Trying to publicise my ideas by attending the meetings of the Aristotelian Society in central London, I was befriended by an elderly English gentleman called M.F.H. Roe who said that he was associated Chinese Philosophy and was excited by my talk of fields as Gestalt Field Theory had been 'all the rage' when he was at Cambridge long ago. Roe invited me to come with the members to another building for the informal chats and wine after the presentation of a paper by the new president. The President, a Philosophy professor from Southampton University, called Manser if I recall correctly, gave a tedious talk involving the usual vacuous word-mongering that marked Anglo-American philosophy. Roe told me not to waste my time with these British academic 'philosophers' as they had no real interest in such traditional philosophical questions. I was wise to choose Science at university, he added. The academic philosophers simply attended these meetings to drink the free wine on offer rather than listen to the boring papers being read out by their boring colleagues.

After a few meetings in 1983, I saw Roe again in 2000 at my lecture to the Society for Psychical Research and discovered that he had been a diplomat in the Far East. In 1983, what excited me most was that Roe said he knew the American physicist David Bohm, whom Einstein had befriended at Princeton, before he had been driven out of the USA by McCarthy's witch hunt[N24] and who, in 1983, taught at Birkbeck College in central London. In 1982, I had bought and read Bohm's *Wholeness and the Implicate Order*[20] discussing the metaphysical problems associated with Quantum Mechanics after a science writer had discussed this book in *New Scientist* after the 1982 Aspect experiment. In fact, even before I typed up *A Hypothesis of Structural Subjectivity*, I had written a letter to Bohm trying to explain my views in a few paragraphs but I received no response. Roe, who considered Bohm's work to be "very important", said that Bohm was very ill at the time.

Roe invited me to come with him to listen to some seminars on AI, etc., at Chelsea College. I lent him some of the books I had recently purchased and he commented about the insightfulness of my pencilled notes in the margins. He was also excited by another book by Jean Piaget I had found called (in English translation) *Biology and Knowledge: An Essay on the Relations between Organic Regulations and Cognitive Processes* in which Piaget discussed the possible biological bases of learning using Structuralist and Gestaltist influenced ideas[21]. This was perhaps a sort of philosophical precursor to the new fields such as Synergetics associated with Hermann Haken and others dealing with self-organising cognitive processes. On visiting Foyles bookshop I had found an old book from 1974 called *Biogenetic Structuralism* by Charles Laughlin and Eugene D'Aquili which used Piagetian Structuralist-influenced ideas in regard to human neural and cognitive evolution[22].

I had also discovered in Foyle's bookshop's Philosophy and Psychology section an extremely interesting new book from the USA containing selected articles by various contributors to a journal called ReVision edited by an ex-biochemist called Ken Wilber called *The Holographic Paradigm and Other Paradoxes: Exploring the Leading Edge of Science*. The latter discussed new ideas associated with the radical ideas of neurologist Karl Pribram and physicist David Bohm[23]. In the 1990s I found that Pribram listed Piaget's *Structuralism* in the references to his 1991 book *Brain and Perception* indicating that he too had been influenced by Piaget's work. *The Holographic Paradigm* included an intriguing paper by physicist Fritjof Capra mentioning Heisenberg's discussions with Tagore which Heisenberg said helped him come to terms with the radical new Quantum world-picture. I either skipped this or, more likely, it meant little to me until I re-read this story in 1990 in Capra's book *Uncommon Wisdom*[24]. It also had a piece entitled "Field Consciousness and Field Ethics" by a Renée Weber and the aforementioned comments by Willis Harman playing down the Holography hype and stressing that the true 'New Paradigm' must be based on the **Primacy of Consciousness,** (i.e., Consciousness was prior to Matter ontologically). In fact, I recall that in my first week at university a fellow first year student, hearing about my ideas on Consciousness, asked me if I had read *The Holographic Paradigm*.

The Holographic Paradigm was a 'New Age' book discussing the parallels between new scientific understanding and Eastern mysticism. I had just turned 19 and knew nothing about Mysticism so this book, like Bohm's rather advanced *Wholeness* book, was intriguing but I couldn't really understand much of what was being discussed. In fact, it took me years to shift from my Psycho-Physical Nondualism to understand the Primacy of Consciousness; that Pure Universal Consciousness is ontologically prior to all that is Physical. Many people (including it seems Albert Einstein; *see Chapter 4*) who are not familiar with Mysticism misinterpret such 'Idealism' based on a Universal Formless Consciousness as implying that the human mind (or ego consciousness) is magically creating our perceptions independent of Physical laws etc. I picked up the term "Perennial Philosophy" from *The Holographic Paradigm* although I did not really understand what it meant either although I recall amending my paper to say that I liked the idea from the Perennial Philosophy that the universe created forms to look back through them upon its own creative evolution.

In spite of my inability to grasp all that was being discussed, this book left in my mind the reassurance that there were famous scientists out there who were prepared to challenge openly the basic assumptions of Science. I knew that my use of the term 'field' was vague and I was reassured to find Theoretical Physicist Bohm pointing out that nobody knew what a 'field' really was; scientists used the concept pragmatically to get mathematical results and they did not concern themselves with the deeper, (i.e., ontological) questions such as what the field concept actually represented. Of course, studying at university I was quickly disillusioned by the complete lack of interest in such philosophical issues by the academics who, learning more and more about less and less, managed to be engrossed by trivial questions about the narrowest fields of knowledge.[N25]

Facing up to Real life Problems and the Reality of India

After the initial burst of enthusiasm in autumn 1983 things quickly quietened down as life had other priorities as I started at university. I recall, in September (or October) 1983, that I felt very depressed when going by bus to the nearest bookshop from home to pick up some books I had ordered. In largely working class North-East London the small bookshop near our house in the 1970s disappeared and, by 1983, so had the next nearest one. I felt nauseated with myself as I had spent so much money, over £20, on a couple of philosophical books, unrelated to my degree course, when my self-sacrificing mother was in the midst of an employment crisis. Having commuted for miles to outer West London after the company where she worked as a lowly clerk had moved out of central London, she had in 1979 taken a job as an X-ray filing clerk at the London Hospital in Whitechapel, in London's historical 'East End'. It was a semi-manual job heaving around X-rays in dark basement store rooms and she complained of the physical strain it put upon her. In autumn 1983 she had been offered a job near to the hospital as a Bengali translator in this area full of Bangladeshi immigrants, the poorest borough in all of Britain placed right beside the exorbitant wealth of the City of London financial district. However, after resigning from the X-ray filing position, my mother panicked because the new job entailed a three month probationary period. Not having much of an education, she did not actually speak English very well and the Bangladeshis tended to be Sylhetis (as in Britain's so-called "Indian" restaurants) who spoke a provincial dialect of Bengali. She was in a state of panic because, if she lost the position after the probationary period, we could have lost the house. My good-for-nothing father had mistreated her and with, his death in January 1977, left her with 22 years of mortgage payments on the house and four sons, aged from eight to fifteen, to bring up.

Only around 2004 did I learn that in 1973 my father had possessed a Life Insurance Policy which would have paid out around £55,000 on his death; but he had cancelled it to get £2,000 towards the £3,000 deposit towards the £11,000 house. In 1977 £55,000 would have been enough to buy a nice house with plenty of money left over! I am still deeply saddened by my mother's reminiscence in 2005, a few months before she died, about how she had tried in the past to get a job as a Post Office clerk but had been told that if only her maths had been a little better she would have passed the tests. As the eldest of seven sisters and one brother, the cruel and outdated Indian dowry system had forced her father to marry her off as cheaply as possible. He did so to a man nineteen years older than her, my father, who had already been married with a son. My brothers and I only heard about this after my father's death. His first wife, the daughter of a wealthy Calcutta judge, had refused to put up with the violent tantrums any more and returned to her family with their child, a boy. My father's family had 'bad-mouthed' his first wife when courting my mother.

After her marriage my mother had kept quiet about his violent tantrums when questioned by her father, partly out of shame but also because she did not want to further burden her parents. Her own father, the only son of a reasonably well-off lawyer, had been a spoilt child and was hopeless with money. Thus her chances of getting a better education were thwarted partly by the fact that my temperamental, wife-beating father who never found himself a steady job and always blamed everyone other than himself. He would even sneak across the border into "East Pakistan" (now Bangladesh) to hide from the Indian legal system in regard to alimony etc. However, he had kept this quiet when, around 1972 in London, a Bengali woman friend of ours divorced from her husband. The wife was shunned from our family until my father's death; such was his hypocrisy! From at least 1961 to 1966 my parents lived in Guahati, the capital of the remote North Eastern province of Assam, populated largely by the Ahom, a branch of the Thais and numerous indigenous tribal peoples such as the Bodos.[N26] My elder brother, I and the third brother were born there.

My temperamental father always argued with other people and, in Britain, he never managed to secure a permanent teaching post. As stated above in 1972 he first went to hospital with cirrhosis and, unknown to us, had become terminally ill with frequent bouts of ill-health forcing him to stay off work for long periods. In spite of this, against my mother's wishes, he brought his elderly mother over to London in 1975 to burden my mother even more. Even as a young boy I recognised her plight at his hands and I had deliberately tried to disrupt his plans for bringing over his mother by pretending to post a letter to his relatives in India which I actually threw away in a bin. For some years before his death in 1977 my mother had become extremely gaunt and thin through the unbelievable stress. After his death she at last returned to normal weight and found a degree of freedom.

In September 1983, I had suggested that she tell her current employers about her predicament and see if she could withdraw her resignation. This in fact was what occurred, her employers being very sympathetic to her precarious situation as a widowed mother of four with a mortgage. However, this meant that my mother stayed on in that semi-manual post for another eleven and a half years until she got early retirement in February 1995. Even by 1990 when the Queen visited the hospital to rename it The Royal London Hospital, my mother was the longest serving member of her section and was thus chosen to have tea with the Queen. The point being that she was forced to stay on in a semi-manual, dust-filled, low status job for 16 years that most younger people left after a couple of years or. Our relative poverty had also influenced my decision to stay in London for university as I knew that my mother was not in a position to assist financially although two of my brothers went off to Scottish universities where the entrance criteria were easier to satisfy. This is why I was feeling so depressed on the bus to collect a couple of inessential books using up my student grant when our domestic situation was so insecure. My earlier book purchases had been financed by a very low-paid Saturday job my mother had got for me at a local chemist which I did from January 1979 to August 1983 although she had still paid my train fare to go to school.[N27] One of the two books that I picked up in September 1983 was called *The Self-Organising Universe* by an Erich Jantsch of the Management Research Centre at Berkeley California[25]. This book, first published in 1980, was dedicated to the Belgian physical Chemist of Russian descent, Ilya Prigogine, who had won the 1977 Nobel Prize for chemistry for his remarkable work on the thermodynamics of open systems. The old thermodynamics created largely in the late 19th Century had focused on closed systems such as reactions in sealed test tubes and beakers where no energy exchange occurred between the system and the environment. Such closed systems tended toward equilibrium. In Prigogine's open systems, dynamic, self-organising, non-equilibrium processes could occur in chemical reactions creating dynamically stable patterns or forms known as 'dissipative structures'. I learnt from Prigogine's popular book on his ideas *Order out of Chaos*, that Prigogine was also an admirer of Bengali poet Rabindranath Tagore[26]. In 1998 I discovered that Prigogine was a member of the Scientific and Medical Network, the international network interested in the relationship between Science and Mysticism. As living organisms were all open systems, Prigogine's new non-equilibrium thermodynamics of open systems had generated much philosophical speculation amongst open-minded scientists as to the relevance of such notions to the scientific understanding of Life. Jantsch extrapolated from such ideas about 'autopoietic' (self-organising) systems to argue that a new emerging paradigm of cosmic evolution was emerging, in which the universe was viewed as being full of self-organising processes at all levels of order from subatomic particles to galaxies and the universe itself[27]. This of course tied in beautifully with my own interpretation of Piaget's vague and rather abstract notion of "self-regulating structures" only two months earlier.

In fact in April 2004, I received a book from India called *The Chakras and Human Energy Fields*[28] which turned out to have nothing useful in it in terms of scientific study. But I did find in it a quote from Jantsch's *The Self-Organising Universe*:

> *If consciousness is defined as the degree of autonomy a system gains in the dynamic relations with its environment, even the simplest autopoietic systems such as chemical dissipative structures have a primitive form of consciousness.*

I wondered why I had not used this quote myself in my revised manuscript in 1987. Looking in Jantsch's book, I saw that back in 1983, I had written "CLOSURE" in the margin beside this text, but had obviously forgotten about it in 1987. Furthermore, the paragraph above this text began "An autopoietic regime includes the expression of a particular individuality, a particular autonomy from the environment"[29]. Of course, although Jantsch's view bore a striking resemblance to my "Structural Subjectivity", we cannot of course define *Consciousness* as simply the degree of autonomy of a system. Jantsch's view is merely another Emergent Physicalist Process view resembling Whitehead's 'Organism' view which is more accurately labelled 'Pan-Emergentism' rather than Skrbina's[30] label 'Pluralist Panpsychism', (i.e., Panpsychism without an all-pervading Universal Consciousness). Metaphorically, these speculative viewpoints grasp a small part of the 'elephant' (a partial truth) and take it to be the whole truth. In order to make sense, such self-organising, autonomous individualities had to be integrated into a truly Panpsychist metaphysics like my own in which Psyche or Awareness permeated all of space (I did not understand Transcendentalism at that time).

As indicated above, life's insecurities made me question my obsession with fanciful metaphysical notions in September 1983. In December 1983, as my mother was unable to take time off work, I was sent on her behalf to her one brother's wedding in Calcutta. I took my recently purchased copy of Fritjof Capra's bestselling paperback, *The Tao of Physics* to read on the plane but never read it. Instead, I gave it away to an unemployed physics graduate in Calcutta. When I did buy this book again in 1990 and read it, I found it more intriguing than truly informative as no clear indication was given as to what Eastern mysticism actually involved or entailed and I had no familiarity with Yoga myself. Thus it was totally unclear if there was anything of interest to be pursued in these parallels between the vague generalisations drawn from Physics and Mysticism. As discussed in Chapter 6, Capra reduced Mysticism to Emergent Physicalist, 'Systems Theory' pop philosophy and failed to appreciate the Primacy of Consciousness, the Transcendental etc. Capra stressed his Emergent Physicalist views in his later books such as the *The Turning Point* rather than in *The Tao of Physics*. I read a review of *The Turning Point*, by someone who wrote that they were sympathetic to Capra's aims. But, the reviewer wrote wryly, if this inchoate and wishful thinking about Eco-Feminism, etc., represents the "new paradigm" then the reviewer preferred the old Cartesian-Newtonian "paradigm" any day. I could easily appreciate the reviewer's distaste with the New Age fluff associated with the Californian counter-culture presented by Capra as the new holistic, eco-friendly world-view of Science.

Furthermore, in December 1983 it was my first encounter with the reality of my homeland, India, since I was two years old so I only possessed a few vague memories from my early life in India. The culture shock on arrival in Calcutta was overwhelming. All the more so as I was not a British tourist coming to see a very different country. I was the last member of my nuclear family to return to India. The other members of my family had gone there between 1979 and 1982 and I had seen the photographs. However I must have repressed in my mind the reality presented in those images and held on to an idealised vague image. These physically underdeveloped strangers surrounding me were my closest relatives outside my nuclear family and this chaotic, unplanned, underdeveloped, poverty stricken place was the India, my home country, of which my parents had spoken so fondly. In contrast, the relatively poor part of North-East London where we lived, increasingly becoming an 'alien' Pakistani and Afro-Caribbean ghetto with 'White flight', seemed like a land of milk and honey.

This encounter with India changed my priorities and I wanted to understand why there were these huge differences in living conditions between Britain and India and what could be done to raise India. Unwittingly these socio-political concerns about my roots and my true identity, which would later manifest in the 1990s as philosophical poetry and prose elaboration in *The Oneness/Otherness Mystery*, actually led me towards opening my mind to Indian mysticism and finding the missing pieces of the jigsaw puzzle in my quest to understand the true nature of Consciousness.

My Search for a Career and My 1987 Paper on Consciousness

I graduated in 1986 with outstanding distinction, not only getting a First Class honours in Molecular Biology but also having come top of the year in the School of Biological Sciences in both my second and final years. The professor who headed the School, himself a Geneticist, commented that I was the only student who really understood what was being taught. He even asked me in 1985 to meet with a wealthy businessman called Jacobsen who had indicated that he would provide London University with an endowment if it could undertake research which would promote his philosophical ideas.[N28] However, my degree in Molecular Biology was largely a complete and utter waste of time. Thankfully, the state paid the tuition fees and gave me the full maintenance grant, as my parent was so poor, so I did not end up in debt as well. As with the repression of the true nature of Indian living conditions as indicated from my relative's photos, I had also repressed the reality that I was useless at, and I hated, laboratory work. The final year research project gave students a feel for research and I found it unbearable standing around wearing lab-coats in hot, dark laboratories trying to culture microbes. It certainly was not glamorous. It was more like being a cook than a philosopher and I was hopeless at it. I must add that this was partly due to the fact that the experienced research assistants were not really available to show you how to do things properly and I detested it.

The more I tried to kid myself that I could perhaps change myself, the more an overpowering anxiety and dread arose from the depths of my being, a feeling that things were wrong and I could not possibly go on in scientific research. I know it sounds absurd but I knew nothing about careers in Science until well into my final year. I am not the only fool to have had the fantasy notion that simply going to university would mean that they would get a well-paid career as I this is what young British graduates now stuck in low paid, unskilled jobs were saying on a TV news report about the declining life prospects for Britain's younger generations in February 2014. In my defence I must point out that, due to my intellectual prowess, friends of the family, academics and fellow students all assumed that I would go on to become a professor. My mother thought naively that having the title Doctor would be of benefit to me. Whereas I was brilliant absorbing vast amounts of knowledge from books in diverse subjects and grasping its essence, I was just useless at practical classes which, partly due to lack of adequate funding, never seemed to work. Furthermore, I began to realise that continuing in Science meant ultra-specialisation and focusing on the most trivial of problems. I had deluded myself, having read James Watson's *The Double Helix*, about how he and Crick worked out the structure of DNA[31], that it was possible to get away with doing very little of the hated lab work and simply use one's creative mind and superior intellect to solve some really big problem which would make you famous.

In reality Science did not work that way and Watson was of course exaggerating. In any case, in my field of Molecular Genetics, the major creative breakthroughs establishing the paradigm of Recombinant DNA Technology had been made during the 1970s and all that most Molecular Biologists actually did was use the new technology in to sequence DNA from a new species. In fact such work was so uncreative and repetitive that a lot of it could be automated and even the experimental strategies reduced to computer programs. I recall the satisfaction I felt in the second year reading the aforementioned *Molecular Genetics* and following the logic of early pioneers who had to think up ingenious indirect methods to demonstrate facts about genes in past decades when direct DNA analysis was not available. There was a fair amount of ingenuity in devising decisive experiments to test hypotheses about a realm of bio-molecules which back then was far more inaccessible in regard to Electron Microsocopy and automated DNA sequencing from the tiniest sample. I suppose that this learning to see the heart of the matter in such scientific problems has helped in my work on Science and Mysticism, especially in regard to Consciousness where direct, invasive analysis of living brain processes is impossible. In 1992, I read an honest assessment of such issues in a *New Scientist* article entitled, "How to be a Ph.D. student"[32]:

> *You have to kid yourself. You have to hypnotise yourself into a state of religious fervour. You have to get yourself into that peculiar state of mind where you can go to an issue of Nature and read a paper entitle "Glucose is an essential cofactor for function of the glucose porter in vitro" from top to bottom and think "Wow" and then aim for similar lofty heights.*

I recall reading an article in *The Guardian* newspaper in the 1980s entitled "The three-year cycle that ends when your thirty", which described the short-term contracts of one-three years given to Research Biologists which offered no job security and meagre pay. Then at age thirty, you became too expensive and were replaced by cheaper younger people. No wonder countless disillusioned science postgraduates left university for secure, well-paid jobs outside Science especially in the financial sector where their numeracy was valued. In 2002 the British news had stories about a research scientist leaving to train as a gas boiler repair-man as this paid at least twice as much and gave security. The highest paid scientist at the Roslin Research Institute in Scotland where Dolly the sheep was cloned earned less than the man who came to re-stock the cold-drinks dispensing machine! A husband and wife couple of Molecular Genetics graduates who had worked at a Cambridge Genome Project, where the Nobel laureate in charge was paid only about the average London worker's wage, left to become window cleaners.

For many years after graduation I wished that I had not studied for a science degree but rather done something like History instead as then I could have continued into postgraduate studies. There was no career that appealed to me and, not being able to continue in Science, I just left university not really knowing what to do. I decided to try for the Civil Service elite "fast stream" exams in late 1986 but the old initial entrance tests were full of all sorts of grammatical gibberish suited for Classics scholars to concoct convoluted balderdash to befuddle the layman as ridiculed in the 1980s BBC TV comedy *Yes Minister.* Science graduates did not learn such outdated word-mongering and I did not pass the first test.[N29]

As I wrote in O/OM, although I might have appeared to be a "brown Englishman", my outlook on world affairs was distinctly Indian. From the 1970s through to the 1990s, London was subject to Irish Republican attacks.

In spite of the possible danger to myself, I wholly supported the IRA's cause of ridding Northern Ireland of English imperialist rule. When I started at university, I had also started subscribing to *New Internationalist* magazine, a popular Marxian-leaning magazine, covering international issues, which even had a column by the Finance Minister from Marxist run West Bengal. Left wing students were constantly rallying for the Coal Miners who had gone on strike around 1984 against the closure of most of Britain's coalmines by Thatcher. Thatcher's ally Reagan was involved with the murderous death squads in Central America slaughtering those challenging US imperialism. Thus a career in business did not appeal to me at all. I recall attending a 'jobs fair' at the Islington Business Design Centre in summer 1987 which seemed full of financial services jobs and countless would-be "yuppies" ahead of the 1987 "Big Bang" deregulation of the British financial sector. I couldn't bring myself to approach a single stall as I could not pretend to show any interest nor did I have anything of relevance to say. I read later that Accountancy firms like Bioscience graduates as they had the requisite numeracy to pass the Accountancy exams etc. However, after the 1987 Stock Market Crash and years of recession, I also read that the first to be made redundant by financial firms tended to be those who didn't really have their hearts in the job, having gone into Accountancy during the late 1980s boom.

Whereas passage through school and university was quite straightforward and based largely on merit, I suddenly found myself facing problems of racial and cultural discrimination in this 'foreign country'. I got a permanent job as an abstract writer, summarising scientific papers in Biotechnology, in August 1987 but the Biotechnology section were used as guinea pigs using computers rather than typewriters. Staring at a small screen (the old 6-7 inch type) of green text all day doing a formulaic, repetitive job gave me severe eyestrain and I felt extremely unwell after work due to eyestrain and depression. Thus I was forced to quit this job after 6 months without finding another one, even though they gave me an above average pay rise for good work, as I just could not bear the eyestrain. In fact even today typing this text on a 15 inch LCD screen with large black text gives me eyestrain and computers at work have continually been a problem for me. After my work was switched to near constant PC use in late 1997, I could no longer read anything after work due to eyestrain and I could hardly survive a full five-day week working on-screen. It took me almost three years to settle down into steady permanent employment after graduation in summer 1986. Given that my mother earned a pittance doing a semi-manual job, whilst paying off the mortgage, etc., life was even more depressing as I had dreamed of earning money to pay off our debts and improve our situation. The son of the afore-mentioned Bengali friend who divorced her husband for another man, after failing his Engineering degree was able to start again taking a degree in computing. His mother and stepfather had no children of their own so they could afford this. Another Bengali boy studying in the Biological Sciences department at my own college, the son of a doctor, had failed to pass the same exams where I had come top of the School of Biological Sciences. His parents paid for him to start another degree course!

Thus the years 1987 and 1988 were very bleak, nightmare years, for me and I was finding it hard to lift myself out of bed to face the world each morning to play the humiliating game of life. An invisible web of interconnected circumstances, partly psychological, seemed to tie me down in hopelessness in this alien society where I did not fit in. Yet during this time when I felt that I was being totally crushed by the world, from the depths of my being arose the urge to reinforce and preserve the greatest achievement of my brief existence. At this point of despair, when thoughts of doing away with myself sometimes crossed my mind, it was as if my deeper Self was surging forth and saying No. *My deeper Self was driving me on to create, to leave my message to the world and make my existence meaningful*. At that time it seemed as if my message would be like the plaque on the Voyager satellite, a message that would have to wait an 'eternity' to be discovered and deciphered, to be lifted from the vast cold indifferent void of the cosmos. Yet something inside me drove me on to keep working on the problem of Consciousness through the darkest days of that period even though it seemed like the most insane pursuit; when my priority should have been to find myself a job and start earning some money. With hindsight, I can look back on the purchase in 1987 of J.Z. Young's book *Philosophy and the Brain* as having been of crucial significance seven years later when the critical breakthrough came. The clarifications of Psychophysical Nonduality and the interpretation of the Physical and Subjective worlds in terms of *phenomenal* and *noumenal* realities in 1987 would also put me in good stead to start clarifying the relationships between Mysticism and Science in later years.

This effort during 1987 and 1988 resulted in a far more mature presentation of my Panpsychist model of Consciousness entitled *A Panpsychist Interpretation of Consciousness*. As stated above, rather than repeat myself, I included the clarifications I made to my 1983 ideas in the presentation above such as the realisation of a Psychophysical *Nonduality* rather than simple *Parallelism*. The understanding that the 'Physical World' was merely our interpretation of *phenomena* also came in 1987 after contemplating and clarifying the meaning of my earlier ideas. At a public library in middle class Swiss Cottage, I found a couple of academic philosophy journals which also included the addresses of some others and I approached them. But I found that there was no place for the outsider in the closed world of Anglo-American academic philosophy. One journal sent a brief set of comments from a reviewer who said that, although the work was well-written, it relied upon "Folk Psychology". I did not know at the time that "Folk Psychology" was the pejorative term introduced by Eliminative Materialist Richard Rorty, who also tried to reduce Mysticism to Freudian sex mythology, to dismiss any references to the validity of our own experiences as such. Anglo-American philosophy, based on false mythologies of the primacy of Language, etc., sees itself as 'scientific' or 'rational' and frowns sneeringly upon anyone referring to actual conscious experiences or to phenomenology (as is the case with those 'foreigners' in Continental Europe) as taking seriously the self-delusions of laypeople. One reviewer had commented that my use of Immanuel Kant's *noumenon/phenomenon* (things as they really are in themselves/things as they appear in our perceptions) terminology in regard to the Subjective/

Physical distinction was not what Kant meant by this! As if all that was important was to rehash 200 year old views without reinterpretation! Note also the 'prophet-like' authoritative status projected upon Kant by these Western academics as if he had some sort of irrefutable 'Divine Knowledge'. Contrary to what this reviewer said, I discovered in 2006 that Kant had in fact realised that the *noumenon/phenomenon* could be used to resolve the Mind/Body problem, in the way I had used it in the 1980s, although he had not emphasised this[33].

Although deeply frustrating at the time, with hindsight I can see that publication in such low circulation, Eurocentric clique-ridden circles would have been of no benefit to me as it would only have reached reactionary, muddle-headed, navel-gazing, academic philosophers rather than forward-looking scientists who might actually advance our knowledge and understanding. It was rather amusing reading newspaper articles in the early 1990s by British philosophy academics attempting to justify the worthiness of the Language Analysis that they taught as presumably it was under threat from government funding cuts. The general public, including cost-cutting Tory Party politicians, who supposedly deluded themselves with "Folk Psychology" when it came to understanding the 'Mind', could see that such Anglo-American 'Anal' academics were spewing out 'verbal diarrhoea'. Such linguistic and logical 'hair-splitting' was little better than sticking their heads up their own backsides (as one of my managers in the 1990s, a Chemistry graduate put it). In fact, looking up one's own backside was probably more worthwhile as it was of bio-medical interest!

I did in fact approach the *Journal of the Indian Council of Philosophical Research* whose address I found at Swiss Cottage library. The *JICPR* replied that I had given the Mind/Body dualism view a cursory dismissal, and were I to re-examine this point and resubmit the paper, they would reconsider it. In 1988, I knew nothing about the vast cultural differences between India and the West in regard to the understanding of Consciousness and that (mysticism-linked) Panpsychism did not conjure up such negative connotations amongst many Indians as it did in the Anglo-American West dominated by Behaviourist myths. Instead, after having spent a long time writing the paper, and feeling too proud to re-examine Dualism, which I considered to be totally untenable, I never took up the offer.

Such pride and arrogance also affected my career prospects as, with hindsight, I realised that I always tried to get in at the elite level as with the Civil Service exams rather than taking a job at a lower level in order to get into the system and then progress upwards. I was still trying to make use of my degree in Molecular Biology by trying to get into scientific publishing in some editorial capacity. In fact in late 1988 I came close to getting into scientific publishing at the commissioning editor level without any prior experience. In late spring, early summer 1988, I had been doing temporary clerical work on a week-by-week basis through a temping agency at the old Pearl Assurance building in central London which was gradually shutting down as Pearl had relocated to Peterborough. Although after a month or two, I was told I could stay on over the summer. However, I found the filing clerk work in the dark Victorian environment was again straining my eyes and as the football

European Championships was about to start I decided not to continue. In fact, I started drinking coffee at Pearl and suffered withdrawal affects at home falling asleep with no coffee to arouse me. When I left Pearl I not realise why I was feeling so unwell, thinking it must be depression putting me to sleep. Furthermore, as all the university students became available for summer temping, I remained unable to find any temporary work for about 4 months until in autumn the agency offered me some work. It turned out that the work was at Shell International at Waterloo in the Personnel department.

Now at this time, Shell, along with Barclays Bank, was a principal target of the Anti-Apartheid Movement (AAM) and I was a member of the AAM. Furthermore, TV documentaries had shown how the bosses of big British businesses including Shell were involved in a McCarthyite style organisation called the Economic League which secretly blacklisted left-wing activists and AAM members etc. I desperately needed work and, as I would technically be working for the Agency, I overcame my reservations and accepted the offer. I worked for a fortnight in the Personnel Records department under a woman who played cricket for the England Women's Team. She was also interested in my philosophical ideas and read my new manuscript. I was then offered a few more weeks work in the Graduate Selection section under the Head of Graduate Selection Procedures, psychologist Richard Scriven. In October 1988 Scriven was going off to a graduate recruitment fair called Enterprise '88 aimed at convincing top graduates that they should go into industry rather than service sector jobs. On the radio I heard a discussion of Enterprise '88 telling of how graduates wanted to get what they perceived to be glamorous jobs such as journalism or publishing rather than go into manufacturing industry which they perceived as manufacturing "nuts and bolts up North" in the cold, bleak, smokestack grey industrial North. Of course, during the 1980s the North had been economically devastated by Thatcherism and the closure of old manufacturing industries.[N30]

I pointed out to Scriven that I was just such a graduate and at that time I was applying for a job as a Biological Sciences Commissioning Editor with Chapman and Hall publishers in London. Scriven was very interested in my philosophical ideas as he said that he had taken a year off work as a sabbatical and studied under Sir John Eccles at Oxford. He read my paper *A Panpsychist Interpretation of Consciousness*. Although he recognised that my ontological and epistemological arguments were impressive and basically correct, what impressed him most was that my paper displayed the very quality which he was looking for in Britain's supposedly "brightest and best" graduates and couldn't find. Shell had the most elitist graduate recruitment programme in Britain taking mainly Oxbridge graduates and restricting themselves to graduates considered to be amongst the most intellectual in their years at the most prestigious universities with a minimum of an Upper Second Class Honours Degree. Although many graduates were being recruited each year, what Scriven found was missing was what Shell prized the most as an indicator of top management potential in one of the world's largest corporations. Indeed, they recognised that such ability was important for leadership and success in numerous fields, not just industrial management. Shell called this "helicopter ability", meaning an ability to view the situation, as if from above, *to see the whole picture* whilst being able to focus in and analyse the critical relevant points. My eclectic, interdisciplinary approach to the problem of Consciousness displayed exactly this holistic ability to see the whole picture whilst also showing analytical skills getting directly to the heart of the problems.

The irony was that Scriven was going out looking for such ability amongst Britain's supposedly "brightest and best" Oxbridge graduates whereas he found such rare ability right under his nose in a temporary filing clerk brought in to weed some files. Scriven thought that the few graduates who had such ability did not come onto the job market as they probably continued in academia but I thought that this is unlikely as academia forced one to narrow one's focus rather than take the interdisciplinary, holistic approach to understanding. It was rather that modern society required people to specialise into narrow fields of study to master the requisite technical skills. We have seen repeatedly in this book that scientists speculating about 'Consciousness' almost always tend to reduce its mystery to try to make it fit within their own limited field of knowledge as in naive Quantum Mind speculation. Thus 'Consciousness' no longer resembles what we understand as 'Consciousness' in such Reductionist speculation. They also display a staggering ignorance of factual knowledge outside the tramlines of their limited specialisations.

At the same time I had managed to impress the new head of Publishing at Chapman and Hall, an Anthony Watkinson, who told me that he was a Cambridge Theology graduate. My interest in philosophy went down well with him and he even suggested that I might later switch to their Arkana New Age list etc. this was extremely exciting as Chapman and Hall, a publisher of boring technical books, was then part of Routledge Chapman and Hall. Routledge, the Social Sciences and Psychology publisher was well known to me as the publisher of philosophical books by David Bohm etc. However, Watkinson pointed out that the role of a Commissioning Editor or "Publisher" was not at all as glamorous as people imagined. It mainly required listening to boring old science professors talking about their boring old subjects and pretending to be excited by it. The problem with me was that I did not come across as someone who would be happy to play "second fiddle" to others which is what the publisher's real role required. Also, it was not going to be his decision, but that of a woman who would be the new head of Life Sciences. In a precursor to a number of later experiences, whereas the male Editor-in-Chief empathised with my masculine self-confidence and self-promotion, the woman with the Ph.D. felt threatened by the brash young man and, although I got to the final two candidates, I v.as not chosen.[N31]

Richard Scriven had said that I should work for Shell but this was not something that could be undertaken easily or on his say so. Deep feelings of how could I live with myself if I did get a job with the company so despised for its Apartheid links; its full name was Royal Dutch Shell and was majority Dutch owned. Hence there was a closer affinity with the Dutch Boers who were at the forefront of the Apartheid regime supported by the Dutch Reformed Church. Then there was the question of the Economic League with its secret blacklisting. I later discovered from the left wing *Daily Mirror* newspaper's investigators that my name had not been on the list. But I was now so desperate that I succumbed for a while to 'temptation by the devil' and went for an interview. With hindsight, it was lucky that, as Scriven saw me as a "creative type", I was interviewed for a Marketing role by some dour man from the provinces (perhaps a Protestant Ulsterman from Northern Ireland). However, the actual jobs on offer would have been marketing chemicals for the Shell refinery at Stanlow[N32] in Cheshire in the far North of England which did not excite me at all. The images of dirty smokestacks, derelict coalmines and textile mills that a typical Londoner conjures up were all there as on the Enterprise '88 radio programme. I was more afraid of succeeding than failing the interview. I did not impress the humourless, nerdy provincial man who interviewed me and I did not progress. After a few more months temping, by losing my naïve pride and seeking a lower grade entry in scientific publishing as a Production Editor, I finally got another permanent job in April 1989 which did not give me severe eyestrain, etc., almost three years after I graduated.

References

1. Cairns-Smith, A.G. (1982) *Genetic Takeover and the Mineral Origins of Life*, Cambridge University Press.
2. Stent, Gunter, S. and Calendar, Richard (1978) *Molecular Genetics: An Introductory Narrative (2nd Revised Edition)*, W.H. Freeman.
3. Piaget, Jean (1968) *Structuralism* (English translation, 1971), Harper and Row.
4. Teilhard de Chardin, Pierre (1955) *The Phenomenon of Man* (English translation, 1961), Harper and Row.
5. Hofstadter, Douglas and Dennett, Daniel, C. (Editors) (1982) *The Mind's I: Fantasies and reflections on self and soul*, Bantam Books.
6. Popper, Karl and Eccles, John, C. (1977)*The Self and its Brain: An Argument for Interactionism*, Springer Verlag.
7. Chalmers, David, J. (No date) "What is it like to be a thermostat". On-line commentary article on: http://consc.net/notes/lloyd-comments.html
8. Woodworth, Robert, S. (1951) *Contemporary Schools of Psychology (Eighth Edition)*, Methuen and Co. Ltd.
9. Dawkins, Richard (1976) *The Selfish Gene*, Oxford University Press.
10. Cooper, Wesley (2002) *The Unity of Thought in William James*, Vanderbilt University Press.
11. Nagel, Thomas (1974) "What Is it Like to be a Bat?" Reprinted in Douglas, Hofstadter and Daniel C. Dennett (Editors) (1982) *The Mind's I: Fantasies and reflections on self and soul*, Bantam.
12. Edgar, William J. (1976) "Continuity and the Individuation of Modes in Spinoza's Physics". In James B. Wilbur (Editor) *Spinoza's Metaphysics: Essays in Critical Appreciation*, Van Gorcum.
13. Nadler, Steven "Baruch Spinoza and the Naturalisation of Judaism". In Michael L. Morgan and Peter Eli Gordon (Editors) (2007) *The Cambridge Companion to Modern Jewish Philosophy*, Cambridge University Press.
14. Lauglin, Charles, D. and d'Aquili, Eugene, G. (1974) *Biogenetic Structuralism*, Columbia University Press.
15. Eddington, Arthur, S. (1928) *The Nature of the Physical World*, J.M. Dent and Sons.

16. Lakoff, George and Johnson, Mark (1999) *Philosophy in the Flesh: The Embodied Mind and its Challenge to Western Thought*, Basic Books.
17. Margolis, Joseph (2003) *The Unravelling of Scientism: American Philosophy at the End of the Twentieth Century*, Cornell University Press.
18. Bailey, Andrew, R. "Beyond the Fringe: William James on the transitive parts of the stream of consciousness". In Francisco Varela and Jonathan Shear (Editors) (1999) *The View from Within: First-person approaches to the study of consciousness*, ImprintAcademic.
19. Strawson, Galen "Realistic Materialist Monism". In Stuart R. Hameroff, Alfred, W. Kaszniak, and David J. Chalmers (Editors) (1999) *Toward a Science of Consciousness III: The Third Tucson Discussions and Debates*, MIT Press.
20. Bohm, David (1980) *Wholeness and the Implicate Order*, Routledge and Kegan Paul.
21. Piaget, Jean (1971, English translation) *Biology and Knowledge: An essay on the relations between organic regulations and cognitive processes*, Edinburgh University Press.
22. Lauglin, Charles, D. and d'Aquili, Eugene, G. (1974) *ibid.*
23. Wilber, Ken (Editor) (1982) *The Holographic Paradigm and Other Paradoxes: Exploring the Leading Edge of Science*, Shambhala Publications.
24. Capra, Fritjof (1988) *Uncommon Wisdom: Conversations with remarkable people*, Century Hutchison.
25. Jantsch, Erich (1980) *The Self-Organising Universe: Scientific and Human Implications of the Emerging Paradigm of Evolution*, Pergamon Press.
26. Priogine, Ilya and Stengers, Isabelle (1984) *Order Out of Chaos: Man's New Dialogue with Nature*, Bantam Books.
27. Jantsch, Erich (1980) *ibid.*
28. Karagulla, Shafica and van Gelder Kunz, Dora (1989) *The Chakras and the Human Energy Fields*, Quest Books (Indian Edition, Motilal Banarsidass).
29. Jantsch, Erich (1980) *ibid.*
30. Skrbina, David (2005) *Panpsychism in the West*, MIT Press.
31. Watson, James D. (1968) *The Double Helix*, Athenaeum.
32. Wolff, Simon, P. (1992) "How to be a Ph.D. student" in *New Scientist* (magazine) 6th June.
33. Skrbina, David (2005) *ibid.*

12

Driven on by My Deeper Self: To Despair or to Destiny?

My Encounter with Indian Philosophy

My second permanent job beginning in April 1989 led ostensibly to my loss of interest in the seemingly futile study of metaphysical questions in a society that was almost totally unconcerned with such questions. However, with hindsight, even during my two years in this job with a scientific publisher, I had not completely given up. I saved, without actually reading, copies of books and journals containing information about electromagnetic fields and life, etc., which I felt that, one day, I would return to. The most famous man in scientific publishing was the late 'Robert Maxwell' (born Ludwig Hoch in Czechoslovakia) who owned Pergamon Press (which had published Jantsch's book; *see Ch.* 11) and Mirror Group Newspapers. He died in 1991 soon after it was revealed that he had stolen about £400 million from the Mirror Group's pension funds to cover the losses in the vast network of Maxwell front companies designed to hide his true finances from the taxman.[N1] In 1971 Maxwell had been declared "unfit to run a public company" after a Board of Trade investigation, but as always, he managed to avoid prosecution; he usually threatened potential whistleblowers with hugely expensive lawsuits. The threat of takeover by the notorious Robert Maxwell had led the US company Harcourt Brace Jovanovich (HBJ), the Scientific and Medical Publishing company I was to join in 1991, to take on a billion dollar 'poison pill' in the form of buying up debt-laden companies. HBJ's board knew that the crooked Maxwell could not actually service such a debt with real hard cash. His takeovers involved using shares in his own 'empire' grossly inflated by the false accounting by his front companies. Thus avoiding Maxwell's criminal clutches led HBJ to weaken its own financial wellbeing leading to it being taken over by General Cinema, a US company without any previous background in publishing, in 1992.

The second scientific publishing company I worked for, before I joined HBJ, was a rather mysterious business. Although founded in New York, its official HQ was in a small town in Switzerland and it also had offices in the British Virgin Islands and Lichtenstein. Once libraries subscribe to a scientific journal these journals tend to act as a guaranteed revenue stream regardless of the quality of the papers published in them. Their academic journals were the most expensive, least subscribed journals around and the papers published in them the least cited by other academics according to a study published in a prestigious science journal. The boss in New York was, like Maxwell, of Eastern European Jewish background. As with Maxwell, potential whistleblowers were kept quiet with the threat of expensive lawsuits if they ever dared to go public about the tax schemes etc. Rumour had it that a Finance Director who had allegedly spent £70,000 on his Company credit card for personal uses, including his daughter's wedding, was allowed to resign without prosecution as he "knew too much". As with Maxwell's Pergamon Press, it published lots of translated material from the Communist bloc countries which seemed to have been published due to grants from the Communist regimes. One Western reviewer of a translation of a Russian biology book wrote that the only use he could find for this book was as a doorstop but at $300 it would be a very expensive doorstop! However, the company had also published in the past some interesting academic material on Parapsychology and other unconventional scientific and humanities' fields which mainstream publishers avoided.

On 2nd December 1994, two and a half years after I had left, the *Bookseller* reported on a High Court case following the voluntary liquidation of the company in the UK. The London office landlord had not been paid the rent due for some time. But in court the publishing company's lawyers tried to dodge liabilities by claiming, at the last minute, that the company's main creditor was *not* the London landlord but some IT services supplier which was in fact *an affiliate of the publishing company*! The landlord pointed out that the company's cash position had fallen most suspiciously from £5.3 million stated in June 1991 to just £6,000 at the time of liquidation in September 1993. In spite of the liquidation, the UK part of the company actually continued operating as an academic publisher under a different name having completed its move out of London to the small town of Reading in Berkshire.

Furthermore, this unusual situation, publishing books which seemed to largely remain unsold meant that it was a very relaxed atmosphere with a lot of intellectual debate in the 'office' which often actually meant the pub.[N2] I started drinking alcohol with my colleagues (I disliked beer which I had tried on a school trip to Paris in 1979) and socialising with work colleagues and participating in Britain's main 'school of philosophy', the drunken gibberish of the pub.[N3] I stopped drinking alcohol around 1994 as alcohol and cigarette fumes inflamed my sinuses and I had better things to do than waste my life. However, such drunken "socialising" is an important component of climbing the career ladder in Britain with promotions usually going to those who "socialised" with you in the pub.[N4] There was little hope of promotion or of learning the proper publishing business methods in this little company. The editor-in-chief was largely interested in promoting pretty young women. Having some money for the first time in my life, and finding myself in this decadent environment, I wasted lots of money on restaurant meals and very expensive holidays to the USA and India (Delhi and Bombay) in 1989 and 1990 after having had no holidays abroad before 1989.

But amidst the fun and games of 1989-90, I also made some crucial steps which led to my breakthrough in 1994. While working there I worked on the production of a book by some Sankritist on Indian kingship and it became very clear to me that I knew nothing about my own Indian background. I also recall that the commissioning editor for this book, the son of an English Life Peer, telling me as we walked to the office from the underground that he was reading about mysticism. I recall that he challenged my view that Mysticism was "irrational". Thus around 1990 I still held a very negative view of Mysticism.[N5] An Indian called Deepak of about my age who worked in marketing left his job to join the Hare Krishna movement whose central London headquarters was nearby. I recall disputing his Literalist, mythological view of Hinduism. He claimed that Krishna really and truly was a spiritual being living in human form on Earth rather than a symbolic mythical character as I argued. (Deepak's view resembled that of Christian Docetists who argued that Jesus was not really a material human being). Visiting the Krishna centre with him, I was appalled by the 'end-of-world-is nigh' and "cannibals will roam the earth" type nonsense spouted by the Hare Krishnas' (American) priest and I sat upright whilst everyone else bowed before him. Although my colleague said that he believed this Hare Krishna stuff which I found absurd, he also mentioned his interest in a pretty English girl who was already a member. As we were located neaı to London's Charing Cross Road, famous for its bookshops, I would visit these shops at lunchtime and I recall that I bought a new copy of Fritjof Capra's *The Tao of Physics* (I had given away my first copy in Calcutta in 1983) and also his later book of interviews with progressive thinkers (including Heisenberg) entitled *Uncommon Wisdom* around this time. But more significant was a weekend trip to Dillons University Bookshop in central London in 1990 where I went to find out about Hinduism prompted by my need to challenge the Hare Krishna convert boy's superstitions.

On this trip to Dillons I found Penguin Classic paperbacks on the Rig Veda and the Upanishads, J.C. Chatterji's aforementioned *The Wisdom of the Vedas*, a book called *A Survey of Hinduism*[1] and a new Centenary Edition printing of Radhakrishnan's *The Principal Upanisads*. On the top shelf beyond my reach I noticed a purple dust jacket with the title *Vedantic Approaches to God*[2] and used a ladder to reach it. It was a volume in the MacMillan Library of Philosophy and Religion and clearly a lot more advanced than the introductory books that I had selected. However, the reason I hesitated before purchasing it at the time was its price, a hefty £38 which was about six times the price of some of the paperbacks. A few years later I would fork out £65 (reduced somewhat by Publisher's Discount) for a book entitled *Event Related Brain Potentials* (which turned out to be of no use to me) as I sensed my breakthrough in 1994. But back in 1990 I had no great sense of excitement and parted very reluctantly with £38 for an advanced level discussion of Vedanta.

Interestingly, near to the Hinduism section at Dillons, I perused a book by Jiddu Krishnamurti and the aforementioned physicist David Bohm entitled *The Ending of Time: Thirteen Dialogues*[3]. But in spite of the fact that it was a cheap paperback, I decided not to purchase it. Then, for a number of days after my visit to Dillons, I felt disturbed as my Deeper Self kept nagging me with the compulsion to go back to Dillons and acquire the Krishnamurti and Bohm book. I was receiving an intuition that this book contained something important. However, as with the intuitive recognition of Piaget's *Structuralism* by my Deeper Self at the LSE Bookshop back in 1983, when I did buy the book and read it, it seemed like gibberish or "psychobabble"; it meant nothing to me and I felt stupid having returned to Dillons another day to purchase it. However, after my breakthrough in September 1994, I re-read *The Ending of Time* and, this time around, I found it to be perfectly meaningful; Bohm was trying, rather unsuccessfully, to relate Krishnamurti's Yogic phenomenological knowledge to Philosophy and Science. As we saw in Chapter 6, in one dialogue Bohm asked if there was a function in the brain which is independent of the content, which is not conditioned by the content but that might still be a physical function. However, the rather simple-minded Krishnamurti thought that the "content" *is* the consciousness. Bohm responded that there could be another kind of consciousness, without content[4]. Back in 1990 I did not have a clear idea of the notion of Pure (contentless; actually without objective content) Consciousness (the *cit* of Vedanta) even though I may have encountered it briefly in *Vedantic Approaches to God* or *The Principal Upanisads* before I read *The Ending of Time*. However, Bohm made no further comments beyond raising this question with Krishnamurti about an *unconditioned brain function* so this book did not actually contain any useful information beyond raising this question *which I was to find the answer to in 1994*.

I did not return directly to the Ontological Problem of Consciousness until 1993 when I wrote the first versions of the essays elaborating on the aphoristic philosophical verses or *sutras* which poured out of my subconscious in summer 1991. This outpouring was partly the result of all the reading in Indian history and philosophy I had undertaken in the previous two years as part of a sort of search to discover my "roots". As discussed in the introduction to my *The Oneness/Otherness Mystery*, another major factor behind this sudden outpouring was the collapse of the Iron Curtain and the end of the Cold War which resulted in a concomitant dissolution of deeply rooted frameworks in my mind as I had grown up with the Cold War divisions as an unchanging background reality. The breaching of the Berlin Wall and similar incidents in November 1989 had been occurring whilst I was visiting Los Angeles and the Grand Canyon as part of my holiday to Las Vegas and, far from home, the news reports had seemed almost unreal. I had not written any poetry for ten years and had no plans to do so until the sudden impulse came to me in 1991. Indian philosophical knowledge was originally presented as aphoristic verses or *sutras* ("threads") summarising the key ideas for mnemonic purposes. Later various prose commentaries would be written upon the original *sutras* and commentaries responding to earlier commentaries and so on. I had produced about 500 quatrains divided into 16 separate but inter-related poems. Overall it constituted a *cosmology* in the traditional sense of exploring the individual's relationship to the whole universe, what I referred to in the verse as "my primal bondage", the essential mystery of our existence as individual selves faced with everything else as other to us. But I, who felt like an outsider in this world, recognised also that I was part of, or bonded to, numerous smaller-scale "greater beings" such as family, nation, race etc. The first poem was entitled "This Oneness/Otherness Mystery", a phrase drawn from this key quatrain around which the entire five hundred quatrain work revolved:

But can I truly claim myself
Free from nation, race and history
Clan, class, sex, species, cosmos, fate
This oneness/otherness mystery

The introductory poem came to the cosmological conclusion that, although I felt like an outsider, standing apart from and alienated from this meaningless world, in reality I was the product of the interplay of numerous "greater beings" of which I was a part such as nation, species, and cosmos:

No monad in itself has meaning
For meaning lives within the wholes
Its meaning is its greater beings
In which it plays so many roles

This work, based upon this rather mystical poetry of oneness and separation from my greater beings, eventually became my *The Oneness/Otherness Mystery* which eventually became two books rolled into one. It was the discussion of my earlier and more recent ideas on Consciousness in 1993 and 1994 whilst writing the original part of that book that led to my breakthrough in 1994. I then added a vast amount of new material unrelated to the original poetry relating to my ideas on how Science and Mysticism were to be synthesised, following my direct linkage of the two in September 1994, finally finishing the manuscript in October 1997 two years after having got the offer of publication from Motilal Banarsidass.

In summer 1993 I had suffered a nervous breakdown following the realisation of the totally unfair and discriminatory promotion processes at the London office of the larger and more respectable company Harcourt Brace Jovanovich (HBJ), which I had joined in May 1991. This unfairness seemed destined to keep me held down in the subservient Book Production Department. Some commented that I seemed more interested in my own writings than in wanting to become a publisher but in 1991 and 1992 I did really want to progress in terms of promotion and become a publisher. I had spent two relaxed years at the previous company where opportunities were limited and which was moving out of London to a small provincial town. However, with hindsight even the well-known Harcourt Brace, certainly in its London offices, was not a place of equal opportunities. When I joined the Managing Director was a woman who had risen from temporary secretary in the production department to Managing Director of the whole UK business. But this was also a woman whose very wealthy husband had purchased a significant stake in the company.[N6] Although jobs were advertised with Equal Opportunity statements, the reality was that most vacancies had already been earmarked for someone friendly with the selectors in advance of the 'charade' of advertising the job so as to make things appear as if there was real competition.

Furthermore, very soon after I started, I defied the norms of subservience expected of production staff after having chased up for an approval on a proof from a Life Sciences Commissioning Editor whom my colleagues seemed rather afraid of. She came to our office and answered one question on my memo and then referring to my chasing up on the proof, she said "as far as I'm concerned, you've got it you do it". I immediately retorted loudly, in front of my own manager[N7], "Oh no no no, it's your responsibility". I was praised by my male manager for standing up to this troublesome woman as, if any mistake went through to press, the editors always blamed production staff for missing the error when they too were responsible for checking and signing-off proofs. However, I was also warned by a senior colleague, training me, that such editors can make life difficult for you in future. She also told me that that this female editor had herself started in Journals Production herself and resigned after failing to get promotion to editorial. This may have been partly due to the Journals management not wanting to keep losing staff to the Editorial department but clearly her humourless and rather creepy personality had something to do with it. She later returned to the company as a Commissioning Editor. But, more interestingly, my trainer told me that this woman had been married to a brash young professor, who had published with Harcourt Brace, and was now separated with a child. Thus it seemed that this introverted, rather feminist Ph.D 'Doctor' woman, probably held bad feelings towards brash men like her ex-husband and I was most definitely a very brash young man.

Indeed in 1992 the same woman editor gave me much grief for a small error of omitting "Second Edition" from the title page of a book although it was present on the cover, etc., which she herself should have noticed on the proofs. Unfortunately, soon after I joined a new Editor-in-Chief (EiC) was appointed to the Academic Press (AP) division who promoted this woman to head of Life Sciences. But very shortly after his reorganisation of AP Editorial he himself was sacked. A male Commissioning Editor in Physics had been taken on in 1991 by this 'shortlived' AP EiC. He joined from Butterworths the same company that this EiC had also come from. This male Physics editor, a non-scientist, was a bit of an outsider in AP Editorial where women with Ph.Ds were in the majority and he seemed rather paranoid. He couldn't keep his mouth shut, constantly revealing the politicking that was going on in Editorial on his visits to other departments. He told me that the AP EiC's wife had left him for his old friend and colleague at Butterworths and thus he had been acting aberrantly during his brief spell at AP! The sacked EiC had been banned from re-entering the building but had tried to re-enter to say goodbye. He also told me that the sacked EiC had brought with him a personal letter for the woman whom I had got on the wrong side of. This male editor also told me that I had ruined my chances of getting promoted into AP Life Sciences by crossing the path of the woman now in charge. It also transpired that this chatterbox editor had worked at Butterworths with the woman with a Ph.D who had rejected me for the Commissioning Editor job at Chapman and Hall in late1988; he added that that woman had disliked having anyone with talent under her as she felt threatened by them. This also appeared to be the case with the women

'Doctors' in AP Editorial. This male Physics editor, an Economics graduate, admitted that he had been promoted to be a Commissioning Editor at Butterworths on the basis of longevity having served 18 years as a copyeditor.

In 1993 when I went for a job in the Medical division the newly appointed female Publishing Director told me things about how she would choose the successful applicant which events in the next few months proved to be untrue. In the informal pre-interview chat she said that she did not want anyone who wanted to be a Commissioning Editor (Publisher) to take the Development Editor role working under the Commissioning Editor even though everyone knew it was the understudy position whose occupants were best placed for promotion to Publisher. Of course, it was highly unlikely that anyone would apply for the Development Editor role who did not, like me, want to use it as a stepping stone towards becoming a Commissioning Editor. I was not even given an interview and then a young woman from my previous company phoned me to say that she had got one of the two jobs. This is what prompted the nervous breakdown following previous failed attempts. Although the Publishing Director had told me that she wanted people interested in doing the development role, both of the women who got these development jobs were promoted to the commissioning role with indecent haste.[N8]

The next development job in the Medical division went, unsurprisingly, to a young Anglo-Asian woman from our Journals department, whom my colleagues in Journals had forecast in advance would get the job as the new vacancy had been created for her by the Publishing Director. In fact, at this time there were no men serving under the Editor-in-Chief of the Medical division although this was not due to any lecherous behaviour but the fact that he only appointed people who responded "Yes" to him. Women, it seems, were more likely to be 'Yes-men'.[N9] Such brazen sexual discrimination in favour of women and jobs for the friends was it seems the norm in British publishing. Around this time the trade magazine *The Bookseller* carried a joke article about the creation of a new organisation called MENOPAUSE (Men Of Publishing Against Unfair Sexual Equality). There were a handful of decently paid Commissioning Editor (Publisher) jobs and most of these were re-circulated between the same old people who moved from one post to another before the chickens came to roost with the projects they had commissioned. When senior staff got senior posts in smaller companies, they tended to take their sidekicks with them as 'Yes-men'. The business was so small that everyone knew everyone else and there were only a handful of jobs to go around unlike normal businesses where people could easily find other companies to escape to.

In fact, with hindsight I realise that I would have had great difficulty fitting into the Stalinist "see no evil, hear no evil" hush, hush environment of the editorial departments as I felt the same sort of subconscious resistance as I had felt at Shell when I went for interviews for editorial posts. Had I been promoted I would have had to have kept my head down, my mouth shut and "play the game" as the aforementioned male manager in the Production Department used to call it. Although in the Life Sciences, the women with Ph.Ds tended to try to restrict entry to only women with Ph.Ds, alongside them we witnessed in the Physical Sciences men without any science backgrounds at all doing the equivalent jobs. As stated above, the paranoid male chatterbox Physics editor was an Economics graduate and other male editors in the Physical Sciences were also non-scientists. One young woman with no science background, only an English degree, joined the AP Physical Sciences Editorial as an Editorial Assistant around the same time as me. She was generally regarded by other members of staff as over-promoted, constantly making mistakes which others corrected for her, but somehow she kept getting promoted rapidly to senior level. She did not seem to actually commission new books just manage the backlist of conference proceeding put together as supposed new books by one professor. Thus it is not exaggerating to say that one of the most incompetent of my contemporaries really did have the most meteoric rise during my time at Harcourt Brace.

It was no wonder, given the totally Stalinistic approach which stifled real talent, that over the course of the 1990s, the smaller companies were all bought up and eventually in 2000 even the giant Harcourt Brace was sold off to the Anglo-Dutch journal publishing giant Reed-Elsevier and most of the old book publishing activity has largely disappeared. All that the reverse sex discrimination by both the 'sisterhood' and the lecherous old men had proven was that women were better at playing the hostess with professors churning out boring academic texts. Indeed, the aforementioned creepy woman whom I stood up to and thus angered used to say cynically that it was all about "massaging the egos" of these old professors to get them to produce manuscripts. Recall that Anthony Watkinson had said much the same in 1988 about having to play "second fiddle" to boring old specialists encouraging them to produce boring, technical texts in their boring old specialities. Although it was a nightmare continuing to work there in the immediate aftermath of my nervous breakdown, it was actually very light work for the most part and allowed me to continue with my writing as I did not have to worry about work at home.

My *sutra* or aphoristic verses of 1991 had included poetic summaries of my understanding of the famous, afore-mentioned, Rig Vedic creation hymn *Nasadiya Sukta* (The Hymn of Nonbeing) in which the universe is created out of a mysterious plenum/void as well as a summary of the key teachings of the Upanishads as I understood them. Furthermore, I had summarised my earlier Panpsychist theory of Consciousness, as presented in Chapter 11, into aphoristic quatrains with rhyme and meter! With hindsight, undertaking and completing such a task seems impossible. It is clear that the 1991 *sutra* was partly the product of inspiration (a modern-day real *Brahmana* 'wording his world through inspiration' as is his true vocation). The creation of *The Oneness/Otherness Mystery* book was also aided by inspiration surrounded in mystical synchronicities and compulsions, including compulsions from my Deeper Self which resulted in me sacrificing any hope of a career in Publishing. I tried to comment in the prose commentary upon my notion, developed in ignorance of Mysticism, of an underlying "Psycho-Physical Non-Duality" (which could only be grasped by our mind through our dichotomising Parallelist conceptual constructions of the "Physical" and the "Psychical"). I linked this notion ('Neutral Monism') with my vague notion of *Brahman* drawn from my rudimentary knowledge of Vedanta.

The Vedantic claims of a transcendental *nirguna brahman* (distinctionless Reality) caused me serious concern at the time as Sankara's dominant interpretation seemed to imply a Dualistic co-existence of this supposedly immutable, Non-Substantial realm alongside the Substantial existence of the Material World in a most problematic manner which Sankara's Illusionist arguments did not resolve. This was in spite of Sankara's authoritative standing amongst Neo-Hindus who were keen to stress the rational argument in his work. I knew from Lott's *Vedantic Approaches to God* [5] that other Vedantic schools disputed Sankara's Immutability Doctrine as the *Brahma Sutras* (summaries of the Upanishads upon which Sankara wrote a famous commentary) repeatedly asserted *Brahmaparinama* or the transformation of Brahman in the world-creation process. Sankara reinterpreted these assertions to suit his own tacitly Dualist Doctrine of Illusionism. The Sanskrit term *Maya* is usually translated as "illusion" following Sankara's usage but actually means the mysterious Power of Creation inherent in Brahman. We have discussed already the false status of Sankara's Illusionism as discussed by Pratima Bowes and Kashmir Saivism's assertion of the tacit Dualism of Sankara's supposedly absolutely Monistic *Advaita* (Nondualism)! In 1993, when attempting to elaborate upon the possible nature of my "Psycho-Physical Non-Duality", it came to me that what my notion of the mind as a self-organising electromagnetic field process actually implied was that the scientific principle of *energy* and my "Raw Awareness" (my vague notion of the essence of Consciousness which I came to equate increasingly with the Vedantic *cit*; "chit" or "Pure Consciousness") were two attributes of the same NonDual Underlying Reality which I now began to refer to as *Brahman*.

Moksa and Near-Death Experiences: An Intuitive Leap

Attempting to make some sort of comment about the Vedantic concept of *moksa* (moksha or "liberation" referring to union with *Brahman*) in relation to my own views on Consciousness, I found myself at a total loss. I could not imagine what a "Higher State" of Consciousness could be in terms of brain functions. The term "higher" seemed to imply a more ramified, complicated process involving new developments on top of existing processes. Whilst I was contemplating this problem, there appeared on television a preview for a religious programme about Near-Death Experiences (NDEs). A few years earlier I had seen a programme on NDEs in which patients talked about seeming to float above the body, etc., but had thought nothing more of them. Yet upon watching this preview in 1993 it suddenly came to me in a flash that this Light or "God" or whatever these patients claimed to have experienced had to be related to the *moksa* experience of unity with *Brahman*. In fact, although such connections were not indicated on the preview, the actual programme that evening discussed the same issue. It featured the anti-paranormal, sceptical psychologist Susan Blackmore saying that she believed that the NDE experience of the Light was related to Yogic enlightenment.

But this was not the only intuition that came to me upon watching the preview. The NDE linkage immediately provided me with another intuition. This was that the NDE must involve a retreat of the physical correlate of mental activity (which I viewed as a self-organising energy field) away from the outermost neocortical areas of the brain, which most scientists think are associated with Consciousness, towards the brainstem. The brainstem is the knob-like structure at the top of the spinal cord lying at the 'centre' or the 'core' of the brain and is the most primitive brain structure in terms of evolution. The brainstem is surrounded by subcortical structures (such as the bilateral amygdalae, the two bilateral egg-shaped thalami, the bilateral hippocampi etc.) which are, in evolutionary terms, primitive brain structures in relation to the outermost structures, the bilateral cerebral cortices). I knew from medical textbooks at work that that brain death was technically defined as the cessation of the activity of the Reticular Activating System (RAS) located in the brainstem. I also recalled reading about the RAS in J.Z. Young's *Philosophy and the Brain*[6] back in 1987. In a section entitled "Initiation of action by the brain", Young wrote:

> *Yet, so far as is known, there is no overriding central program that selects and supervises all the others. There is indeed down the centre of the brain a set of cells known as the reticular activating system that never come to rest. They rhythmically discharge nerve impulses that initiate the brain waves, which are essential for the action of all other parts. These impulses are fundamental for life, continually sending nerve signals that keep the other parts of the brain going. But the reticular system is not in any sense a supervisor.*

The Yogic path towards enlightenment, I reasoned, must resemble the dying process with deactivation of normal brain functioning. Enlightenment must involve a similar 'retreat of mental activity' *towards the brainstem*. I realised that so-called "Higher" States of Consciousness were not more ramified, more complex processes but that they must in fact be *less complex*, simpler underlying processes. Although I had read in Lott's book and elsewhere that the Vedantic *cit* (Pure Consciousness) was the Ground of Consciousness, (i.e., the basic type from which all others arose), this had not been absorbed into my understanding and the talk of Enlightenment involving "Higher" States of Conscious had left me confused. Most scientists would probably hold Consciousness to be a product of complex, specialised activity in the cerebral cortex and view the subcortical regions, and even more so the primitive brainstem (derived from our reptile-like ancestry), as devoid of any conscious activity. The misleading Freudian terminology of the 'Unconscious' for deeper processes only reinforces such mainstream Western views. Following these intuitions, it began to cross my mind that if one could somehow monitor the brain activity changes during NDEs one could show that Consciousness was not limited to the cerebral cortex as this would be deactivated near-to-death. My broader intention underlying such lines of thought was of course to argue that Consciousness, in the sense of some sort of generalised awareness rather than the meaningful world-modelling perceptions of our normal experience, was omnipresent. The NDE as a Retreat-to-the-Brainstem argument seemed to support my Panpsychist view of Reality. Although I had no evidence to back up my Brain-Deactivation and Retreat-to-the-Brainstem intuition, I had great confidence in the essential validity of my ideas. I believed that as Reality was ultimately One, the Scientific and Mystical perspectives had to be understood as different perspectives upon that One, the Underlying Psychophysical Reality.

In late 1993, having made these speculative assertions, I completed my first attempt at writing the prose commentary to the metaphysical poems in my *sutra*. I equivocated over my inchoate 'mystical' interpretations of my own existence in the verse, seemingly in the hands of fate. This sense was partly reinforced by my nervous breakdown in summer 1993 during which I had a feeling of realising a deeper interconnectedness of events somehow linked to my Deeper Self. I had felt that during job interviews, etc., my being had been torn in two directions with my Deeper Self resisting the worldly ambitions of my normal egoistic self and somehow seeming to subvert secretly my worldly plans through subliminal and synchronicitous influences. Indeed, it was during the years 1993-1994 that I was surrounded in synchronicities (meaningful 'coincidences') which seemed to be leading me toward some metaphysical breakthrough but at the cost of sacrificing my worldly ambitions. My late 1993 draft essay paralleled the equivocating attitude of the final poem in my *sutra* entitled *The Web Intricate*, blowing hot and cold over these mystical "coincidences", etc., and my essay ended upon a sceptical note born partly of my need to impress upon scientifically-minded people that I was not stupid. I stated that I was well aware of the fact that what I privately held to be "meaningful coincidences" might also be interpreted as just "accidental events" due to random chance.

A short while after I wrote this first draft, I began to experience a recurring rhyme rising up unintentionally into my mind, spinning in my head and refusing to go away. It was a verse I already knew from Ralph Waldo Emerson's poem *Brahma*:

They reckon ill who leave me out
When me they fly, I am the wings
I am the doubter and the doubt
And I the hymn the Brahmin sings

It gradually dawned upon me as to why I was experiencing this recurring rhyme in my head. I was repressing my true beliefs, not being "true to my Self", in writing equivocally about my synchronicity experiences and related experiences of being guided toward some as yet unknown destiny. People have often found my openness in discussing things which others keep quiet about, such as my father's violence and similar unpleasant facts or subconscious motivations, as unusual. This was especially the case in British culture where repression of one's true feelings is encouraged. This sense of being guided by some deeper wisdom was partly behind my feeling that had I been promoted at work, I would have fallen apart, as I could not have "played the game" or "lived the lie" that was required. Upon realising that this recurring rhyme was occurring because I could not live the lie of suppressing my true feelings on these matters related to synchronicity, I decided to change the ending of my essay and "come out" wholeheartedly in support of these "mystical" notions which seemed to be real for me. The recurring rhyme ceased. I rewrote the discussion of *The Web Intricate* poem stressing that the scientific concept of chance was, in fact, only the imposition of statistical, mathematical constructions based on Probability Theory upon the spontaneous "bubbling broth" of Reality. This imposition resulted in the artificial construction of "statistical normality" which most modern people confused for the real order of things.

This intuitive communication with my Deeper Self included another component which I, being the open person that I was, told other people about. Basically, the message coming to me from the depths of my being was that I had to come out with my true beliefs as the work I was writing would be of great significance. Although I would have liked to have thought this, even back then in 1993 I could tell, deep down, that the essay I had just written was not very good. I was not confident of my assertions and I had little background knowledge in regard to the questions that I was tackling and the issues that arose from them. At that time I was still thinking within the limited frames issuing from my Panpsychist notions from the 1980s and what little I knew of Indian philosophy was used as supporting evidence for such limited ideas relating to Metaphysics. In spite of my speculative linkage of *energy* and *Pure Consciousness*, I still had little time for the claims of yogis about their amazing experiences such as oneness with the cosmos. That my Deeper Self was telling me that the work I was writing would be of great significance seemed to me at the time to be typical of the exaggerated, bombastic nature of such encounters with the deeper realms of our being as Carl Jung had mentioned in his writings. At that time, knowledge I had acquired from very different realms remained compartmentalised in my brain. It had not clicked in my head that my interest in the problem of Consciousness which had arisen out of my interest in Science had led me straight to the 'heart of the matter' in regard to questions of Spirituality.

Learning the Meaning of Spirit

Early in 1994, after a TV dramatisation of the life of Ludwig Wittgenstein, Channel 4 Television advertised a so-called 'Talking Heads Club' debate to be held in central London which I attended. Before the hall had filled, an ignorant middle aged Englishman, assumed from my light-brown skin that I was a Mohammedan and so asked me what was meant by Khilafat. This was probably due to the appearance of small stickers or posters stuck on lamp-posts, etc., all over London with that word printed on them. I answered that these probably had something to do with the notion of re-establishing a Mohammedan Caliphate. It was most amusing to see, in the new post-Cold War era, Pakistanis in London holding up placards pronouncing "Communism is Dead, Capitalism is Dying; The Only Answer is Islam!" A few years after the Rushdie Affair, I found such reactionary delusions hilarious. As if the scientifically educated modern, secular people of the ex-USSR as well as those in the secular West were suddenly going to seek redemption in a 7th Century *c.e.* Bedouin mythology and medieval social mindset! It is not widely publicised that many Mohammedan Jihadis in Pakistan, claiming that they want to 'liberate' Kashmir (an Indian kingdom which their ancestors invaded and occupied) still fantasise about re-conquering supposedly 'idol-worshipping' and 'pagan' India to convert it to their 'One True Faith'. Yet as with the Taliban in Pakistan, we see the increasing influence of Saudi-funded Wahhabi brainwashing on the streets of London with most Mohammedan women nowadays covering their heads and some wearing burkas.[N10]

I recall that the elderly gentleman sitting to my left, during the Wittgenstein debate, told me that he had studied Philosophy at Cambridge whilst Bertrand Russell was still alive. At the end of the debate, he said to me that I had made by far the most valuable contributions to the debate; there were about two to three hundred people in the hall. An attractive English woman, about the same age as myself, who said that she was an unemployed journalist also sought me out after the close saying that I appeared to be on the verge of Enlightenment. As is usual, I presume that my rather 'dashing' features and my 'animal magnetism' (*see below*) got certain people rather carried away. I pointed out that I was just an intellectual investigating such questions through books; I had never practised meditation. I recall that my public comments included pointing out that Wittgenstein, in giving away his wealth and living as a hermit in Norway, was clearly a Western version of a 'Holy Man'. I had also pointed out that Wittgenstein's comments about "meeting God in the Face of Death", as on the TV drama, tied in with the notion that Enlightenment resembled Near-Death Experiences.

Later in about 1995, I would find in a newly published biography of Tagore the story about Wittgenstein told in full in Note 5 to Chapter 8; Whereas Bertrand Russell, supposedly under the spell of the young Logic-obsessed Wittgenstein, remained hostile to Mysticism throughout his life, Wittgenstein himself in the 1920s and 1930s became a devotee of the mystical poetry of Tagore. He even turned his back on meetings of the Vienna Circle to read out loud from Tagore[7]. In fact, around the year 2010 I read in Avrum Strolls' *Twentieth Century Analytic Philosophy* (2000), that the Logical Positivists of the Vienna Circle and the Anglo-American Analytic academics (obsessed with Scientism) ignored the overtly metaphysical and *mystical* last section of Wittgenstein's *Tractatus*. *Contra* Scientism, Wittgenstein even wrote that what is of *ultimate philosophical significance is something that transcends the possibility of Scientific study*. Some even assert that the **Mystica**l is the central theme of *Tractatus* {*e.m.*}[8]. So it is not only the Mysticism of the Ancient Greeks that Western academics have suppressed. Returning to 1994; When the 'Talking Heads Club' debate Chairman asked the audience if they believed that there was such a thing as "the Truth" which could be revealed, I did not put my hand up. When asked at the end by some young female Buddhophiles sitting in front of me what Enlightenment revealed, all that I could say was that it shows that Reality was Psycho-Physical rather than Physical.

In spring 1994, I had lunch with my best friend from my secondary school, Alexander Hudson-Crawford.[N11] The son of an Eton-educated curator at the British Museum, he had planned to study Classics, (i.e., Greek and Latin) at Oxford like his father but failing to get a place at his first attempt, influenced by my 1983 ideas on Consciousness, he had switched to Philosophy and Psychology, which he eventually studied at Edinburgh. As I tried to explain to him what I was writing about, he pointed out that what I was calling "psychophysical stuff" was what in the pre-modern West had been called *Spirit*. The word "spirit" had come to evoke negative connotations in my mind due to my scientific indoctrination. I had not thought of the Vedantic *Brahman* as *Spirit* prior to this, as I viewed the latter as an irrational conception associated with Semitic religious superstitions. In contrast, I had compartmentalised Vedanta as rational philosophy. My uncertainty and ignorance of such matters is reflected in the fact that in 1992 I had bought Swami Prabhavananda's (Aldous Huxley's Vedanta teacher) book *The Spiritual Heritage of India*[9], summarising the various systems of Indian philosophy but I had never paused to think as to why the Indian philosophical systems were called the "spiritual heritage".

Due to my preconceived notion that Yoga was some futile exercise best left to unthinking Buddhists and their like, I had skipped over the chapter on Yoga in that book just as I had skipped over the chapters on Christian thought when I read Bertrand Russell's *A History of Western Philosophy* at school. I had mentally distanced Vedantic philosophy from its Yogic sources due, partly, to my Western indoctrination resulting in my valuing words and writing over experience. It was also partly due to my lack of acquaintance with any practitioners of Yoga. One problem was that I could not understand how some sort of breath control could possibly give remarkable insights into the true nature of things. I had never paid any serious attention to Yoga so I did not understand what it was really about. I recall that on perusing Prabhavananda's book I was disdainful of an approach that considered dreams and their nebulous ilk to be of importance in understanding Reality. This seemed the opposite of my indoctrinated view of "objectivity" and "hard science", dreams were not only subjective but fluid, blending into one another, and impossible to capture and isolate for study. Dreams seemed to be exactly the opposite of hard scientific facts; indeed, they seemed to be the epitome of falsehood due to their linkage to fantasy and delusion! This was in spite of my having read some Jung who also studied dreams.

I also recall that when I read Prabhavananda's book around 1992, I found the *Sanhkya* concept of Nature as *Prakriti* rather alien and tantalising. The dualist *Sankhya* metaphysics, which we have seen was first written 600 years after the *Yoga Sutras* is usually superimposed onto the *Yoga Sutras* although the Monistic approach of *Advaita Vedanta* is prevalent in modern Hinduism. *Sankhya* involves an ontological Dualism of Pure Consciousness (*Purusa*) and Nature (*Prakriti*). As with dreams, I found the view of Nature as constant flux-like, dynamic *Prakriti*, a Process view, difficult to acknowledge even though in my own Panpsychist theories I had stressed that the Physicalists' universe was essentially but patterns of dynamic spatiotemporal activity. My mind was compartmentalised into different frames of thought and my scientific learning based on stable atoms and molecules (rather than dynamic flux) and my modern urban environment, far removed from the natural, organic growth and decay familiar to pre-modern society made such views of Nature as flux appear very alien.

A few months after my lunch meeting with Hudson, I saw a television programme about the famous Nobel laureate physical chemist Linus Pauling who had explained the chemical bonds between atoms in terms of the new Quantum Mechanics in his *The Nature of the Chemical Bond*. He had also worked out the structure of protein helices and had been 'pipped to the post' (overtaken at the very end of the race) in unravelling the molecular structure of DNA by Watson and Crick after he had made what he had referred to as a "schoolboy error". Watson and Crick had also benefitted from the use of the 'space-filling' molecular models displaying the outer electronic shells of atoms, which Pauling had first used successfully with proteins. However, Pauling, who won a second Nobel Prize for 'Peace' (the very controversial Western prize which has even been awarded to War Criminals but which was denied to Gandhi), had spent the latter part of his life promoting the benefits of taking Vitamin C as something of a cure-all. At work the next day I commented that Pauling's antics with Vitamin C reminded me of Isaac Newton's "spiritual bollocks" (the latter word being English slang for testicles) referring to Newton's profuse "mystical" writings which he held to be more important than his work in Natural Science. A colleague pointed out to me that I myself had been talking a lot about "spirituality" recently and wasn't this also "spiritual bollocks". Embarrassed, I retorted that Newton's mystical writings involved Biblical stories of the Israelites as the chosen people and searching for hidden prophetic codes in Biblical texts, (i.e., Kabbala) thus it was "a load of bollocks" whereas my writings on mysticism were based on the rational knowledge of the Vedanta. In fact, I still find it very irritating that the mass media includes all sorts of popular superstitions such as Astrology, Palmistry, Healing Crystals and Bible Code gibberish which are lumped together with serious spiritual philosophy under the label of "Mysticism" making it very easy for narrow-minded sceptics to 'lump together', ridicule and dismiss all aspects of Mysticism as if they were all nothing more than superstitious rubbish.

I knew that not all of Newton's mystical thought was Bible-based "bollocks". In a classic history of science book, which had been reprinted by the company I had worked for between 1989–91, I had discovered that, in a draft version of his *Opticks*, Newton had written[10]:

> *if there be an universal life and all space be the sensorium of a thinking being who by immediate presence perceives all things in it, as that which thinks in us, perceives their pictures in the brain.*

Thus even Isaac Newton, whose name is usually associated with crude Mechanistic Materialism, had in fact contemplated the possibility of an Universal "Mind" or Consciousness as well as the view that universe is in some sense alive (Hylozoism). We have seen in Chapter 1 that Newton actually looked down on the 'vulgar chemistry' of gross matter in comparison to the operations of subtle spirit[11]. As with my assertion in July 1983 that Spinoza's views were "mystical nonsense", very soon after this incident in which my normal self (ego) automatically rubbished spiritual views (albeit with some qualifications this time), I was to find myself engrossed in spiritual knowledge. It seemed to me that when my ego, indoctrinated into such as hostile stance towards Mysticism and Spirituality, made such strong assertions, it triggered some response from my Deeper Self, the depths of my being, teaching me what a fool I was in taking such a closed-minded attitude.

Spirit had seemed to imply something insubstantial, beyond all human enquiry, as with the Vedantic *nirguna Brahman*, with which I had so much difficulty due to Sankara's tacit Dualism. I had included in my *sutra* references to the Native American concept of the Great Spirit but this had not been included as a link to Vedantic concept of *Brahman* which was prominent later on in the *sutra*. I had only included this Native American material to show the hypocrisy of the West in demonising the recently collapsed Communist world as building its system upon the 'Red Terror' of Stalin and Mao when the Capitalist world market system was built, historically, on far greater terror in the extermination and enslavement of the peoples of the non-European world. As my *sutra* stated, *contra* the sanitised Western propaganda of Humanitarian progress, the true History of the rise of the West was "Writ large across the world in blood". I felt a deep intuitive resonance with the Great Spirit idea which I could not articulate, perhaps simply due to my feeling that this Naturalistic conception of a Supreme Being amongst this group of so-called "savages" was vastly superior, in my opinion, to the anthropomorphic concepts and the ridiculous personality cult of the man Jesus in the Christian beliefs held by the White settler-colonialists.

Once my old school-friend Hudson had put the word "spirit" into my mind, linking it to my own ideas, subconscious processes were brought into play as I toyed with the relationships between "Psycho-Physical NonDuality", *Brahman* and Spirit. With hindsight, it is clear that the notion of Underlying Unity or Oneness which had so appealed to my intuitions when I was twelve years old must have continued to operate subconsciously in my belief of there was but one Reality, one actual Ultimate Reality underlying diverse human perspectives rather than incommensurable dualities. At that time I did not understand the true, mystical nature of intuition and inspiration from which such Monism arises. Modern Western self-proclaimed 'sceptics' deride, in knee-jerk fashion, such talk as nonsense. We have seen that such people are pseudo-sceptic dogmatists as they fail to keep an open-mind toward what they are unfamiliar with as a true *sceptic* should. These same modern so-called 'sceptics' airbrush out of history facts such as how the belief in an Underlying Unity of all phenomena inspired the Evangelical Christian Michael Faraday who first put forward the notion of a Field-of-Force and demonstrated that Electricity and Magnetism were interrelated through his experiments on induction. This belief in Underlying Unity also inspired him to try to show the unity of Gravity and Electromagnetism back in the 19th Century.

The Deeper Self, Destiny, Animal Magnetism and My Changing Evaluation of Eastern Values

Whilst remaining ignorant of Mysticism, I recall that around this time I had another intuitive idea which my later discoveries would help to concretise. I kept referring to my Deeper Self in a vague manner in my writing and I tried to elaborate upon this in my prose commentary to my *sutra*. I recall that the idea came to me that there was some sort of presence deep in our mental being which, in some sense, could scan our brains and read the individual's "destiny". My intuition was that somehow this presence deep within ourselves could, in a flash, evaluate our potential for the future, perhaps even, in some sense, 'see' our future and subconsciously guide us towards our destinies. Such ideas were obviously based upon my own experiences of having a "Deeper Self" which seemed to lurk in the depths of my mental being and seemed to know things that I could not possibly have known. Although such ideas will sound very familiar to those well-versed in Mysticism and Spirituality[N12], to my scientifically indoctrinated mind at that time, these ideas were extremely speculative and far-fetched but seemed to make some sense based on my own subjective evaluation of how my life was proceeding.

In the spring of 1994, I found myself embroiled in a crisis situation and my sense of disillusionment with the ways of the world plumbed to even lower depths of disbelief combined with anger and frustration that fate seemed to have me trapped in such an intolerable situation from which there seemed to be no short-term way out. As stated above, due to the incestuous nature of scientific publishing in Britain, it was not easy for a person like me, marked as a loud-mouth dissenter, to escape as everyone knew everyone else in this stagnant little pond. After I had my breakdown in 1993, I had been very vociferous in castigating the Stalinistic system of promotions but the aforementioned appearance in *Harpers and Queen* magazine at that very time, alongside some journalists from my secondary school and also from Eton College, Britain's top so-called "public" (private) school, enhanced my status as someone who could hit back with public exposure of the system. The fact that my school colleagues regarded me as the cleverest boy in the school and I was from an ethnic minority would have made the company look even worse. In spring 1994, due to my ongoing negativity, the Personnel Director suddenly called me to her office and issued me with a final warning about my "behaviour" without going through the stipulated procedures of lesser warnings that should lead to a final warning. She had wanted to put the "fear of God" in me and assumed wrongly, that in order not to ruin my career prospects, I would finally succumb to their demands. However, as I was a member of the National Union of Journalists (NUJ) I decided to go to them and got the support from my colleagues who were members. In fact, the very threat of the NUJ intervening and exposing the hypocrisy of the actual practises employed by the Personnel Director who gave lectures on Personnel Management at the Publisher's Training Centre, etc., forced her to back down very quickly.

Although my self-confidence, articulate speech and my intellect led people to imagine that I was a public schoolboy from a well-to-do background, I was of course still trying to overcome the relative poverty of mother's impoverished situation and my own inability to get a good career. Thus when I was suddenly facing the Personnel Director snarling her warning at me, although I braced myself to go into aggressive mode to fight back against the unfair system, my first thought was that I must not do anything stupid so as to bring even more suffering and despair upon my poor mother who was hoping that she might be able to get early retirement in the near future. I had to stay in work and keep earning money. In fact I kept the whole warning and NUJ affair hidden from my mother so as not to upset her more. A crucial factor in such considerations was that I was approaching my thirtieth birthday and my mother, her friends and some of the more mature women at work were asking me if I had plans for marriage, etc., I must admit that, in spite of its Stalinist-like promotions system,

Scientific Publishing had some consolations such the light workload (most of the time) and being surrounded by numerous attractive young women.

Throughout my thirteen years in the business, from my mid-twenties to mid-thirties, I found that I had a presence which attracted countless attractive women of all types, of all races, all classes, levels of education, not just the well-educated middle class women drawn to genteel publishing. Of course, with well-educated women there is a tendency to seek males who are at least as well-educated as themselves and with middle class women a tendency to seek males whom their families would approve of as well as 'ticking the boxes' on their 'idealised partner checklists'. Soon after I joined Harcourt Brace in 1991 a very young, buxom and rather 'dizzy' blond working class secretary, resembling the young Diana Dors, was hugging me as we left the office to go home and wanting me to be her boyfriend. The fact that I had just written a five hundred verse 'poem', (i.e., my *sutra*) at that time played a role. Although flattered, I wisely and politely explained that we were too different from each other. I recall another young working class blond secretary with a strong Birmingham accent telling me rather uninhibitedly when I joined Harcourt Brace in 1991 how I was "superior" to the other men with my articulate speech, intellect and personality. She asked if she would be able to understand my poetry. The young women in the office teased me when a pretty young Celtic brunette Cambridge graduate, who had joined at the same time as me as a short-term temp before going off on some expedition in Namibia, enquired about me in a postcard.

One female Medical Publisher told me that I should be a Bollywood actor as I was so sexy. A Welshman colleague referred to my "animal magnetism", subconsciously women seemed to be drawn to me, both single women and women with partners. This *animal magnetism* tied in with the comments about Sutapas being on a 'higher plane' than others as it raised questions in my mind as to whether imperceptible transcendental connections operating at a subconscious level could influence or even override the normal egoic restraints upon our animal impulses. Perhaps there was some truth behind the 'folk psychological' talk of 'Female Intuition'. One middle class woman who joined us in 1995 admitted to me that she was a natural-born psychic who had experienced Past-Life Memories etc. The middle aged woman who also acted as the training supervisor asked me around this time me what I was going to become. She had later become a freelance after reorganisations to departments and I had sent her a copy of O/OM. When she visited us in the office in 1999, it appeared that I had begun to live up to my seemingly mad ambitions of a few years earlier. Thus my eclectic mind was developing an understanding of such *psychical influences* partly through the social interactions as well as the synchronicities affecting negatively my career ambitions.

I should add that I also had an influence on the humble, much put-upon mailroom staff in both HBJ and the previous company. I seemed to be the one they would always come to for help as I always treated them politely and as equals. In 1991, I helped the rather slow-witted young man, younger than myself, in the first company carry a very heavy printer between the two offices. He was from Romford in Essex and thus the butt of many jokes about stupid Essex people and I myself played many a joke on him. But he instinctively knew that I was not being nasty and befriended me and we sang karaoke together at his leaving party before he left to, follow in the footsteps of his brother, becoming a Purple Coat entertainer at Pontins' Holiday Camps. Similarly, the Mailroom men in HBJ were hard done by as they tended to be fired shortly before they managed to complete two years service and thus gained full employment rights under British Law. Again these working class men turned to me when they needed help knowing that I would always oblige without making a fuss and they befriended me. This says something about my State Grammar turned Comprehensive school where I mixed with boys from the full spectrum of British society from the poorest to sons of Life Peers and of CEOs. But I think there was also a subliminal recognition that I was not 'one of them', not one of the mainly middle class establishment but an Outsider like them and they could trust me.

A loudmouthed 'boy', the son of a plumber, who had joined HBJ in 1992 from my previous company's new provincial office in Reading, kept commenting that I was an Alpha Male. He would jokingly greet me with the phrase "well hellooooo" as I reminded him of the dashing, moustached cads of 1960s British cinema such as Leslie Phillips who used that phrase when they saw a pretty woman. He would comment, with a touch of envy, that I would be 'perfect', in the classical sense, if it were not for my largish nose. I recall one occasion in 1992 or 1993 when he expressed his amazement at my ability to draw to me, without saying or doing anything, an attractive, elfin young Irish secretary whom he thought was the most beautiful girl he had ever seen ('animal magnetism' or amazing 'pulling power' in working class vocabulary). I had actually spoken to her previously so my charm must have worked! Of course, a few people who are not really cut out for drudgery but are quick-witted and charismatic characters can make a living out of it as, radio presenters, TV chat-show hosts, etc., but I was it seems 'driven' or 'destined' to follow my 'true vocation' as a philosopher. It was thus that I commented in O/OM that I do not come across like the Western stereotype of a supposed 'philosopher' as a balding, bearded serious-minded figure but a man who loves to burst into song, brag, and brag about bragging etc.

Even in early 1996, when a young upper middle class woman in her mid-20s with Classical (film-star class) good looks joined our department, I drew envious glances from male colleagues. Although already engaged[N13], in her first week when we were filling up the seats in a meeting room, she immediately and quite obviously grabbed the seat beside me. On another occasion, when the senior woman was not around she feigned that she needed my help with some work and as I approached reached out and touched my hand sending tongues wagging amongst our colleagues. Being rather eccentric and uninhibited in expressing her feelings, she would later openly compliment me, out of the blue as I walked past her, that I looked extremely smart and elegant etc. However, during 1996 my mother was diagnosed with Parkinson's Disease and the great optimism of 1995 faded away rapidly. In 1995 my mother had taken early retirement from the semi-manual low-paid job at the Royal London Hospital she had started in 1979. I had also got the offer of publication from Motilal Banarsidass on my birthday in 1995. This posh young woman, in her uninhibited style, pointed out to me that my entire personality had changed dramatically since my mother was diagnosed with Parkinson's and I was no longer the fun person I had been before. I could not keep cracking jokes knowing that one would be burdened by this disease which would progressively get worse and destroy my mother's retirement.

In November 1997 when I was reassigned to Academic Press after the Book Production Dept was shut down, my old male manager from 1991 was deputy to the EiC of AP (*see Note 7*). I recall him commenting out loud about how little things had changed since 1991, as young women seeing that I gone into the tea-room followed me. I recall that on a couple of occasions between 1998-2000, one quite attractive upper middle class woman who made numerous advances tried to catch me in the tearoom or in the photocopier room only to find that another woman had already beaten her there! In 1999 a young woman from Newcastle, who was as attractive the now ubiquitous Cheryl (Tweedy) Cole, without all the fancy make-overs, became captivated. My reputation as a philosopher-poet, who had written a book, obviously helped in enhancing my mystique. However, as the same attraction was evident often with women who were complete strangers to me on buses and trains, it was clear that my looks alone were the prime factor. A rather posh upper middle class young woman in my department told me soon after I joined HBJ that all the women were talking about me; something that a rather effeminate young man had also said to me after I joined the previous company in 1989.

My rather classical cheek-boned features, wavy hair, moustache, self-confidence, intellect, poetry, smart dress, etc., obviously made me appear rather "dashing" as one upper middle class woman from another division of the company, who was obviously rather besotted with me though I didn't even know her name, put it in 2002. I recall that both at Shell Centre in 1988 and at Harcourt Brace in the late 1990s, groups of women from other departments entering a lift (elevator) in which I was alone joking that they were not going to let me go. This no doubt added to my sense of being someone 'special' but it also added to my frustration given my miserable economic situation of entrapment in a dead-end job in a dead-end business. In spite of persistent attention from attractive women, my personal circumstances were such that I had no security whatsoever in the low-paid production job which could end at any time thus I could not imagine settling down as I could never get a mortgage etc. Although relationships between work colleagues were common at Harcourt Brace, unlike more professional businesses, some of the women attracted to me also worked for some of the senior staff who had blocked my promotion chances so I could not imagine having to socialise with people I tended to snub. Furthermore, the fact that I managed to captivate the attention of numerous women meant that I could never focus on one as special who stood out above the others!

With hindsight of course, I know that being distracted by a woman would have destroyed my chances of 'fulfilling my destiny', completing my pursuit of the True Ontology explaining Consciousness, Spirituality and the Paranormal which I knew possessed world-changing implications and should of course make me very famous. Thus it seemed to me that my Deeper Self was somehow complicit in keeping me trapped and miserable in order to keep me on the path that it wanted me to follow. From my own perspective, during the early 1990s, I had also viewed turning thirty as a critical marker. I had hoped that I could put an end to the fooling around of my twenties that had got me nothing but failure and start taking work and training for work (such as learning about computers which did not appeal to me at all[N14]) seriously. One must note that as I had never had any ambitions to progress in book production work, I was never promoted in my 13 years in Scientific Publishing whereas colleagues who took the silly hierarchies in the Book Production Department seriously were constantly becoming "senior" or team leaders etc. After the showdown with the Final Warning, I decided to focus my energies on my writing which I hoped would lead to life changes.

In fact, although I do not normally take astrology seriously, on the day of my nervous breakdown in March 1993, I looked at the London *Evening Standard* horoscopes section and saw that my horoscope on that day read:

> *Provided you can accept that certain plans are no longer viable, what remains stands every chance of eventual success. So commit yourself only to what is essential and remind yourself constantly that limited expectations yield only limited results.*

I know that such horoscopes are deliberately very vague so as to be interpreted as one wishes but the meaningfulness of this statement seemed like a synchronicitous communication from my Deeper Self regarding my destiny, telling me not to waste my time with the vacuous delusions of a career in Scientific Publishing but to continue pursuing my own philosophical writing. Following the nervous breakdown of March 1993 I seemed to become aware of deeper connections between events, not normally perceived, which most people would immediately dismiss as the delusions of a madman. I seemed to be in a sort of mildly altered state of Consciousness. One aspect of this was the de-inhibition of normal socially encouraged repression of true feelings in public. I realised later that during such "breakdowns" or dissolutions of established cognitive frameworks, invoked by a reality that goes so contradictory to expectations, that one was perhaps more open to anomalous information in the environment that our normal habitual modes of perception would filter out. Thus in this slightly altered state, perhaps I was able to perceive subtle connections between events which social conditioning had filtered out of normal experience.

Following this crisis of early 1994, I concentrated with even more zeal upon rewriting the socio-historical essay elaborating upon the philosophical ideas contained within my *sutra*. It was whilst rewriting this essay that I began to realise that a positive transformation of human society required a shift away from Western-style Materialism towards a more Indian style introspective culture, which curbed egoistic excesses. In Indian history this approach had been taken by the likes of Emperor Asoka's conversion to Buddhism and Gandhi with his *satyagraha*. This was a point that many people had made, and increasingly so with the rising hysteria over manmade 'Global Warming', etc., but, for me, this constituted a major shift in direction as I had never taken such ideas seriously before. My examination of these social and historical questions led to a growing sympathy for the approach of the Indian tradition marking a complete turnaround from my youthful days. As a young man, steeped in Western Materialistic Individualism, I sneered at such a self-abnegating approach as primitive, superstitious delusions of pre-modern minds faced with the harsh realities of ancient life which for the vast majority was full of uncertainty, scarcity, suffering and the ever-present threats of disease, death or enslavement. The point to note is that, indirectly, a shift in my evaluation of Meditation had occurred. Yoga, which I had scoffed at back in 1992 when reading *The Spiritual Heritage of India*, began to acquire a positive value in my new frame of mind, my scheme of things. This arose, not because I believed in the metaphysical and cosmological claims of Yoga, but because I began to realise that Yoga might hold possibilities for transforming human behaviour through introspection and control of our rampant, instinctual drives which led to what society labelled as "immoral" actions.[N15] As stated previously, the deeper I pushed into the underlying structure of my metaphysical thought and now, partly as a result of seeking my roots combined with my general socio-political outlook, the more I kept discovering the resonances with the Indian tradition. I was uncovering my underlying 'Indianness' or 'Hindu' character which had been masked by my Western upbringing. Indeed, the poetry that had poured out of my subconscious in 1991 included the quatrain:

You live in me through archetypes
In me you resurrect your themes
Oh land surrounded in memory
Oh patchwork land made up of dreams

Learning from Jung and Synchronicities

I had picked up the notion of *archetypes* in the early-Jungian sense of a sort of ancestral or racial memory from a popular paperback book on Carl Jung by Anthony Storr[12] which I had read parts of back in late 1982 (hence the references to Jungian synchronicity in my 1983 essay quoted previously). Not only was I "Indian" but I was a Brahman, a scion of the Indo-Aryan priestly elite who had largely formulated most of Indian philosophy and, in recent times, largely formulated modern Indian Nationalism. Indeed, I had come to learn that my surname Bhattacharya (*bhatta* means a learned Brahman; *acharya* means "the master" in Sanskrit) was a title that, in the past, learned Brahman scholars acquired and was then used as a surname. I had found that India's most prestigious academic professor of (Indian) Philosophy of the 20th Century was a K.C. Bhattacharya (no relation of mine). I felt that the synchronicitous 'nudging' or "guidance" from my Deeper Self had something to do with these Jungian "archetypes", the frameworks and memories I had inherited from my ancestors. We saw in Chapter 7 that the *brahmana* of the *Rig Veda* 'worded the world' through Divine Inspiration and pursued the Divine Light. Thus it seemed to me, due to my heritage, I could intuit what Indian philosophy meant subconsciously, hence the strange intuitions etc.

In the summer of 1994, I pulled out Storr's book from my bookshelves to read again the section on Jung's concept of Synchronicity in order to reconsider what I had been writing about in my draft manuscript of *The Oneness/Otherness Mystery*. However, on perusing the book, I decided to read the whole book (which I did not do back in 1982) and I was struck by some of its contents. I came across the ancient Gnostics' concept of the *pleroma*, a sort of plenum/void from which the universe arises which I recognised as very similar to the plenum/void of the much older Rig Vedic hymn *Nasadiya Sukta*. In an extract from Jung's *On the Psychology of the Unconscious*, I read of how the idea of the Conservation of Energy came to the German physiologist Robert Mayer in a sort of mystical vision or realisation on his first visit to the tropics. Jung related Mayer's insight to the primitive 'dynamistic' religions with their universal magical power or energy called by various names such as the *mana* of the Melanesians. The historian of philosophy A.O. Lovejoy had called such primitive ideas of a primal power "primitive energetics". Jung argued that this same essential notion, this "archetype", of the conservation of the magical power manifests throughout history in metaphysical and theological notions. Thus the idea of the Conservation of Energy was essentially a modern reinterpretation of this perennial insight[13].

In the summer of 1994 a Bengali song that I had known since childhood kept spinning in my head. The words translate into something like, "Like a hibiscus at the feet of the Mother, Awake and flower my mind" where "the Mother" is the Great Mother goddess. A hibiscus flower that had stubbornly refused to flower in our kitchen in the summer of 1993 flowered in summer 1994. At work a female colleague called Sara, who had moved to our department earlier that year, would offer to make me a cup of tea asking me "Sutapas, is it your time?" She would burst out laughing as I would reply jokingly, slowly in deep voice, "My time has not yet come!"[N16] One day, at this time, I decided to take an alternative route to the station as I left work and came across a huge billboard poster announcing the visit of an American faith healer, Morris Cerullo, to London. The slogan slashed across the poster in huge letters said "YOUR TIME HAS COME". Deep down inside I felt that it was a message to me although, at that time, I was in dire straits not knowing what to do with my life, seeming to have no way to break free from the various interconnected traps of domestic and career insecurity which fate seemed to have set for me. Although I could see no way out, my Deeper Self seemed to acknowledge the message of the billboard poster linking it to my joking responses to my colleague's offer to make tea. Of course, these jokes arose from a belief deep down that one day people would start taking notice of my philosophical ideas. The day after seeing the Morris Cerullo poster, I caught the end of a television programme about the Shoemaker-Levy comet which was crashing into Jupiter at that time. At the very end of the programme, an astronomer was asked if he felt that the comet signified anything. The astronomer replied that it portended a "New Age of Enlightenment".

In July 1994, plagued by the feeling of being trapped by the invisible web of interconnected problems that framed my existence, I had a very strong impulse to learn more about the problematic relationship between the Transcendental and the Immanent, the *nirguna* and the *saguna* aspects of *Brahman*. This impulse arose partly due to my deep frustration with life, the failure of my worldly ambitions, making me inquisitive as to what this existence was all about, why did I exist? At the 'Books from India' shop in Museum Street (in front of the British Museum), I picked up a couple of books on

Sankara's thought as he was supposed to be the greatest of the ancient Vedantic philosophers. Back at home, I randomly opened one of the two books I had purchased, entitled *Maya in Sankara*[14] and there on the opened pages I noticed my name *Sutapas*. I had never before come across anyone, either real or fictional, called Sutapas so this was meaningful to me, another instance of the "library angel" as occurred in July 1983. As of December 2012, I have not come across another person named Sutapas (though many females have the name Sutapa). The Sutapas in the book was a sage in a Hindu myth who sought to learn from the god Vishnu the "Secret of Creation". Vishnu told Sutapas that even He could not tell him the answer to this but, if Sutapas really wanted to know the answer, he would have to "throw himself into the ocean". I intuitively interpreted the meaning of this myth, not explained in the book, as that the secret was ineffable; it could not be stated in words but it could be realised by attaining *moksa* ('Liberation' or mystical union with *Brahman*). The "ocean" of the myth was the ocean of Universal Consciousness into which individual identity was supposed to dissolve in mystical union. At the time, I could not understand how *moksa* could actually reveal secrets about Creation or the Meaning of Existence but this 'library angel' phenomenon with the mythical Sutapas who, like me, wanted to understand the Meaning of Existence or the Secret of Creation was extremely meaningful or synchronicitous.

I went around telling people that I was experiencing these synchronicities even though it seemed to raise questions about my sanity. This period in 1994 was replete with synchronicities, presumably due to my deep depression inducing connections with the depths of my being as I later discovered in the spiritual literature was often the case. However, the entire creation of *The Oneness/Otherness Mystery* was marked by synchronicities which cannot easily be dismissed. Moving ahead of the story of my path to the Light, on 11th November 1997, the Book Production department in which I worked was closed down by a new Managing Director at Harcourt Brace who had been getting rid of a lot of the old guard throughout 1997, whilst sitting in a temporary office in an old meeting room outside which my own production team sat as our main production area lacked space. I was reassigned to a new in-house production team for the Academic Press division and with, two old production functions combined into one, the workload increased dramatically and increased computer use gave me much more eyestrain. However, this dramatic change which prevented me from reading or writing at home occurred about two weeks after I finally finished the manuscript for *The Oneness/Otherness Mystery* and sent it off to the publishers who had offered to publish the finished work back in August 1995.

Indeed, even during 1993–1997, writing the book was not easy whilst in full time work; I had to use my weekends and all my holidays except in 1996 when my mother suddenly became ill and diagnosed with Parkinson's Disease, just one year after taking early retirement, and all my work holidays were used up with her emergencies. Furthermore, the manuscript was typed using a Canon bubblejet printer cum wordprocessor, holding only tiny text files and with a tiny viewing screen of two inches by about five inches with small blue text on a light blue background adding to my eyestrain. I had purchased it for £500 in December 2002 on credit after having spent most of my savings on a car, bought new, which was used only to transport my mother and then I gave my mother most of my remaining savings to help reduce interest on the loan for our new kitchen. Thus the four year preparation of the prose essays of *The Oneness/Otherness Mystery*, midway through which I identified the physical correlate of the Divine Light of Pure Consciousness, was completed just two weeks before my situation changed suddenly so as to stop me writing again until nearly ten years had passed (2007). With hindsight it seems remarkable that I managed to somehow seize the window of opportunity amidst such turmoil. It was my Deeper Self which kept driving me on and guiding me with synchronicities and insights as I stated in my Acknowledgements where I acknowledged no debt to any human teacher but only to my Deeper Self, the "impersonal spirit within" which guided me.[N17]

A far more remarkable synchronicity event, well beyond the realms of mere coincidence, occurred in March 1998 as I was checking the first proofs for *The Oneness/Otherness Mystery*. My home state of West Bengal in India had been run by the Communist Party of India (Marxist; CPI (M)) since the late 1970s.[N18] The Chief Minister Jyoti Bose was a close friend of the only relative of ours who lived in London and would stay with our relative on trips to London.[N19] In fact Bose's successor Buddhadev Bhattacharya is a very distant relative of mine. I thus know something about the history of Communism in India. It was introduced to India by the Bengali revolutionary Narendranath Bhattacharya (better known by his alias M.N. Roy) who went to the German Kaiser in 1915 to procure arms for India's freedom fighters. He had befriended Lenin after the Bolshevik Revolution, became a Communist and had adventures in China and Mexico as well as founding the Communist Party of India (CPI) which later split into various factions. However, he abandoned Communism after independence. I also knew that the first democratically elected Communist government in the world was the CPI government in Kerala led by a man called E.M.S. Namboodiripad. That was all I knew about the Keralan leader; even a book I had purchased in 1990 entitled *Marxist State Governments in India*[15] referred to him only by his initials as E.M.S. Namboodiripad.

In March 1998, I was enthused by seeing the proofs of *The Oneness/ Otherness Mystery* realising that my identification of the physical correlate of the Divine Light of Pure Consciousness, based on scientific evidence, overruled all the speculative interpretations of the Vedantic philosophers resolving debates that had raged for three thousand years. In my mind I kept thinking that the dominance of the false, tacitly Dualist, Illusionism of Sankara (known as Sankaracharya; Sankara the Master) would eventually be replaced by my new Science-Mysticism integration grounded on converging lines of empirical evidence, which I was seeing in print for the first time. Bhattacharya would replace Sankaracharya. Furthermore, whilst checking the proofs at this time, I had received an insight regarding Jung's vague concept of Synchronicity or "meaningful coincidence" which Jung had discussed for years with the great physicist Wolfgang Pauli in regard to so-called "acausal orderedness" or "acausal connecting principles". I realised that Jung's vague "synchronicity" which had played such an important role in my creation of *The Oneness/*

Otherness Mystery was in fact a limited case of the generic transcendental principle I had discerned as underlying paranormal psychic phenomena and Past-Life-Memory or Karmic phenomena.

This led to perhaps the greatest of my synchronicitous experiences. On, I think, 20th March 1998 I went home and due to eyestrain from work, just perused the headlines in the copy of *The Guardian* newspaper which my brother had purchased. Near the end of the paper was a photograph of an Indian face in the Obituaries section. I looked at caption and saw that the face was that of E.M. Sankara Namboodiripad, the famous Keralan Communist leader. Reading the text I discovered that he was named Sankara (or Sankaran[N20]) as he was a Brahman from the famous Namboodi Brahman clan of Kerala of which the great eighth Century philosopher of *Advaita Vedanta* Sankara or Sankaracharya had also been a scion. Thus as I saw my *The Oneness/Otherness Mystery* in print for the first time there was tremendous symbolic meaning in the fact that a famous Keralan "Sankara" of the Namboodis had just died!

References

1. Klostermaier, Klaus K. (1989) *A Survey of Hinduism*, State University of New York Press.
2. Lott, Eric (1980) *Vedantic Approaches to God*, MacMillan/Harper and Row.
3. Krishnamurti, J. and Bohm, David (1985) *The Ending of Time: Thirteen Dialogues*, Harper and Row.
4. Krishnamurti, J. and Bohm, David (1985) *ibid.*
5. Lott, Eric (1980) *ibid.*
6. Young, J.Z. (1987) *Philosophy and the Brain*, Oxford University Press.
7. Dutta, K. and Robinson, A. (1995) *abindranath Tagore: The Myriad-Minded Man*, Bloomsbury.
8. Stroll, Avrum (2000) *Twentieth-Century Analytic Philosophy*, Columbia University Press.
9. Prabhavananda, Swami (1979) *The Spiritual Heritage of India: A Clear Summary of Indian Philosophy and Religion*, Vedanta Press.
10. Jacob, Margaret, C. (1976) *The Newtonians and the English Revolution 1689-1720*, Cornell University Press.
11. Dobbs, Betty J.T. (1991) *The Janus Faces of Genius: The role of Alchemy in Newton's thought*, Cambridge University Press.
12. Storr, Anthony (Editor) (1983) *Jung: Selected Writings*, Fontana.
13. Storr, Anthony (Editor) (1983) *ibid.*
14. O'Neill, L. Thomas (1980) *Mâyâ in Úankara: Measuring the immeasurable*, Motilal Banarsidass.
15. Nossiter, Thomas (1988) *Marxist State Governments in India*, Pinter.

13

The Breakthrough to the Light

Learning the Significance of the Light

In summer 1994 I saw a television programme about Oxford English don turned Aurobindo Ashram disciple Andrew Harvey entitled *The Making of a Modern Mystic*. W.H. Auden had told Harvey that Auden envied T.S. Eliot (who had studied Sanskrit and Indian Philosophy at Harvard) as Eliot "had Spirituality". Harvey said that it was very difficult for a young *arrogant fellow at Oxford to learn that everything he had ever learnt was wrong* (*emphasis mine* {*e.m.*})[1]. Thus when I noticed a book by Harvey entitled *Hidden Journey* on display at Books from India (although it was not published in India) I bought a copy. This book was just a mass market paperback story about Harvey's search for spiritual awakening leading him to the Aurobindo Ashram in Pondicherry and an Indian girl called Mother Meera who possessed psychic powers. She held *darsanas* (sittings in her presence) for spiritual seekers. However, this lowbrow storybook was significant for me as Harvey kept referring to the "Light". Until then I had not actually equated *enlightenment* with actual *light* as popular expositions of Vedanta stressed *Saccidananda* (Pure Being (*sat*), Pure Consciousness (*cit*) and Bliss (*ananda*)) and the Buddhists spoke vaguely using negative terms such as the "void" and "nothingness" as far as I knew at that time. Even though I had made the link between *moksa* ("Liberation" or Mystical Union) and NDEs where a patient saw a Light, I hadn't really thought much about it beyond the fact that both *moksa* and NDEs must involve some sort of retreat of the 'mind' towards the brainstem. Reading Harvey's book, I was reminded of the fact that Halbfass had mentioned in his *India and Europe* that the early Jesuits in India had lauded the "natural light" of Brahmanism. I had taken this to be just a metaphor.

Intrigued by Harvey's mystical experiences and his references to the great Western mystics such as Meister Eckhart, I ordered a book entitled *Mysticism and the Religious Traditions* edited by the afore-mentioned Stephen Katz[2] which I saw listed on the back of another book in the same series in the Oxford University Press bookshop in London's Charing Cross Road. After picking up this book a couple of weeks later, I crossed Charing Cross Road on my way to Oxford Street when a book gleaming in a window display of another bookshop a little way back from the direction I was heading caught my eye. A powerful urge within me drew me back down the road a little to take a closer look at the window display. Emblazoned on the front of the white dust jacket in huge gold letters was the title *Embraced by the Light* [3]. It was a popular account of an American woman Betty Eadie's Near-Death Experience (NDE) although she claimed that she had actually died. In 2003 I learned that *Embraced by the Light*, which had originally been self-published by the author, had become a huge bestseller in the USA at the height of the 1990s explosion of interest in NDEs, hence the prestigious window display in a mainstream bookshop. Although it was obviously an unscholarly text hyped up for the non-discerning mass market, I decided to purchase the book simply in order to find out what these NDE subjects claimed to have experienced.

The next day, Sunday September 4th 1994 was my thirtieth birthday. In 2011 I discovered that US Evangelical Christian Harold Camping (famous globally for his 'End of the World' prediction in 2011) had previously calculated from the Bible that the Second Coming and End of the World would begin on 4th September 1994! The age of 30 is of course somewhat significant in that the Biblical Gospel character called Jesus starts his proselytising at around age 30. If one reinterprets the 'End Time' for Christians in a symbolic sense, Camping was closer to the truth with with his first guess of 4th September 1994. For on that day a sequence of events began leading ten days later to identification of the physical correlate of the True Light, the Spirit within us or the 'True Christ' and this will eventually lead to the end of Christianity and other Theistic superstitions, consigning them to the 'Dustbin of History'.

In 2009 I read in John Newport's *The New Age Movement and the Biblical World View* that US 'New Ager' Benjamin Creme had taken out adverts in major newspapers in 1982 claiming that the new *Maitreya*, new Christ or World Teacher was alive and living amongst the *Bengali community of East London* {*e.m.*}. My literary agent John White points out that Creme publicly identified someone whom he claimed to be his supposed *Maitreya*. Psychical mediumship is an inexact practice, routinely distorted by the human intermediary's own personal knowledge and memories such that the essential truth received is intermingled with and cloaked in imaginary, erroneous garb. I still find it a 'meaningful coincidence' that in the year when I first read about the mystery of Consciousness (in *The Mind's I)* and encountered the mysteries of the Transcendental (in regard to Aspect's Experiment and Bohm's *Wholeness and the Implicate Order*) some modern-day 'prophet' was proclaiming that the new World Teacher was living amongst the *Bengali community of East London*. I am a Hindu *Bengali* and *I was living in East London*. I do not claim to be some enlightened mystic or a spiritual exemplar; I am an intellectual 'philosopher'. But given my elucidation of the universal basis of human Spirituality in the brain, based on overwhelming evidence from authoritative Hindu-Buddhist yogic phenomenology, I do believe that the global Non-theistic Spirituality of the future, superseding religious superstitions, will be grounded upon my identification of the scientific correlate of the Spirit within us all. In the future no educated person will be able to discuss Spirituality seriously without reference to my work.

On the evening of 4th September 1994, I interrupted my reading of *Mysticism and the Religious Traditions* to have a quick look at *Embraced by the Light*. I began reading the foreword by a Melvin Morse, M.D. who was presented as an expert on NDEs. Morse pointed out that the author was actually talking about NDEs and not about what happens to you after Death as she claimed. Morse, to my great surprise, also claimed that a specific brain area had been identified which "allows us to have the experience"[4]. However, Morse was not at all clear on this point, neither stating *which brain area* nor *which experience(s)* he was referring to. Furthermore, Morse did not cite any sources for this claim (after all this was just a mass market paperback). Having put forward confidently my Retreat-to-the-Brainstem hypothesis, I was bewildered by Morse's statement. Could my intuition have been completely wrong! I was shaken but took hope in the fact that Morse was so vague. Perhaps he was only talking about part of the NDE experiences. I only had a vague idea of what happened in NDEs at that time, knowing only of an Out-of-Body Experience (OBE) and some sort of tumbling towards a light. Thus my Retreat-to-the-Brainstem hypothesis would still hold good if what Morse claimed was in fact true but applied to only part of the NDE. I had to find out more.

It was late evening on my thirtieth birthday. Following the Final Warning crisis a few months earlier which left me feeling very depressed about reaching this age with nothing concrete to show for all my efforts, all of my sacrifices over the years. My work situation, domestic situation and psychological make-up with the compulsions of my Deeper Self had seemed to conspire to trap me in a most miserable state of affairs from which there seemed to be no escape except possibly through my writing. Back in 1988 when I had been unemployed and doing temporary clerical work I had responded to the advertisement frequently placed on the front page of *The Guardian* newspaper from a so-called Writing School correspondence course which would guide you in developing writing skills wanted by publishers giving you your money back if you did not earn back the fee from published freelance article commissions. Stupidly I had paid the entire fee of over £200 up front and then got angry when the expert advisor responded to my initial material that I was too "highfalutin", meaning pompous or pretentious, and that I had to learn to write simple formulaic pieces which would appeal to magazine publishers etc. The advisor was presumably a writer on women's magazines which are notorious for being full of moronic drivel about celebrities, soap operas or the royal family. I had no intention of following the herd and churning out moronic cattle fodder in 'Journalese' and demanded my money back but they refused saying that I could continue again with the course at any time in future if I changed my mind! I was furious with myself for having paid up front rather than in instalments and losing £200.

Looking back with hindsight in 2007, churning out such formulaic junk may be acceptable for the New Age writers, portrayed as "philosophers" who somehow manage to produce a 'new' book each year; each one as superficial as the last. Obviously these books satisfy a demand from an uncritical readership who buy New Age junk splattered with hyperbolic quotes from the 'usual suspects', drawn from their fellow New Age writer friends. Even where a New Age writer presents some good ideas, they are juxtaposed usually with uncritical, unsubstantiated claims and naïve distortions of facts. But I took my writing seriously as true philosophical inquiry and I felt that I could only write something if I truly had something worthwhile to say rather than just churn out superficial drivel tailored to the lowbrow New Age market. Therefore I tried to check my facts as best as I could although I was not an academic with access to academic libraries. All of my research was paid for by myself. I wanted to be taken seriously by the best-educated minds, convincing even 'sceptical' establishment scholars, not just preaching to the 'converted' New Agers.

During the Final Warning crisis earlier in the year I had been supported by my Book Production colleague David who was the NUJ representative at Harcourt Brace. This was partly due to the fact that his female partner, a long serving member of our Journals department, had supported me strongly. I recall telling him that I wanted to be remembered as the first man in history to have truly solved the Problem of Consciousness. I had the feeling that I was really on to something. Thus Melvin Morse's statement about NDEs distressed me so much as it seemed like it might possibly undermine what, at that time, was my key idea, the Retreat-to-the-Brainstem hypothesis. Thus it seemed as if 'fate' was again playing a cruel trick upon me, as with my 1988 financial loss, rubbing salt into my wounds. Although the overall Panpsychist ontology I was presenting was not threatened by Morse's view, the loss of my Retreat-to-the-Brainstem hypothesis would have weakened the overall coherence of the ideas I was presenting.

I needed to get rid of this new cloud which had suddenly darkened my outlook. As I had already taken Monday September 5th as a holiday, I decided to go down to Foyles, the huge bookshop in Charing Cross Road to see if I could find out anything more about Morse's NDE-related brain area. As stated above, I did not have access to good libraries and there were not any readily available internet search engines then. Foyles, claiming to be the world's largest bookshop, did not return unsold books and thus one could find many older books, not available in most shops, along with the latest publications. In fact it did not take me long to locate a book by Melvin Morse. It was a small mass market paperback, entitled *Closer to the Light* [5], full of stories told by various NDE patients along with some discussion. I took the opportunity to look around Foyle's Philosophy and Psychology department and picked up a number of other titles. One was entitled *Gathering the Light: A Psychology of Meditation*[6]. Before returning to these two books, I will discuss what I learned from *Mysticism and Religious Traditions* which I had picked up two days earlier and I finished reading before reading Morse's book. This was because a quick perusal of Morse's *Closer to the Light* allowed me to find the information I had gone to seek at Foyles; it allayed my fears about my Retreat-to-the-Brainstem hypothesis being contradicted by Morse's exaggerated claim that there was a brain area known to be "responsible for NDEs".

Divine Light, Nothingness and *Saccidananda*

Most of the authors in *Mysticism and Religious Traditions* (edited by Stephen Katz)[7] were hostile to Perennial Philosophy type views, focusing instead on the diversity of mystical experiences. They stressed the supposed impossibility of separating out a 'Pure' or 'Common Core' Universal Mysticism from cultural tradition, the conservative affirmation of traditional orthodoxies by most mystics (reiterating the dogmas indoctrinated into them) and the social meanings of Yoga. The subtext of the book seemed to be, don't get carried away by the Perennialist 'hype', we are the scholarly experts and we know best. Katz himself wrote[8]:

> *Therefore, Christian mystics do not, in fact, experience nirvâna but rather encounter Jesus–'beloved bridegroom'. Make no mistake, even Eckhart's putatively attributeless 'Godhead' is not the Christian equivalent of nirvāna or sūnyāta, the metaphysical nature of the two being altogether different.*

The sort of argument presented as purportedly 'sufficient' to 'prove' their point by these religious scholars was simplistic to say the least and most unconvincing to someone like myself educated in Natural Sciences. As is usual in such 'Comparative Religion' studies, no scientific approaches of attempting to be impartial through controls and other self-critical procedures were applied to account for the contradictory evidence. In 1995 I was to read another OUP book entitled *The Problem of Pure Consciousness: Mysticism and Philosophy*[9] in which a group of pro-Perennialist academics provided a set of rejoinders to an earlier anti-Perennialist book on Mysticism also edited by Stephen Katz. These Perennialist scholars, led by Robert Forman, exposed the lack of any solid, coherent argument in Katz's assertions that there were no Universal Core mystical experiences such as the Pure Consciousness experience. Forman exposes the vacuity of Katz's anti-Perennialist arguments better in his monograph entitled *Mysticism, Mind, Consciousness* [10]. Katz appears to me as more of a zealot defending an unsubstantiated belief than as an impartial scholar examining the facts.[N1]

We have already discussed the vacuity of the Constructivist standpoint in academic Comparative Religion and seen that its central argument is simply to restate Immanuel Kant's personal beliefs is to deny any possibility of any unmediated, unconditioned perceptions! I say personal beliefs of Kant as nearly all Western scholars remain silent on Kant's secretive method used to reach his conclusions. We have seen that this was based on Thought Experiments and which Westphal claims actually support Realism[11]. *Thus Katz's central argument is nothing more than an appeal to the supposed 'authority' of a White Man, Kant, again conflating 'European' for 'scientific'.* Alan Wallace states that such Postmodern Relativism provides modern intellectuals with the easiest possible way out of coping with diverse world-views, avoiding precise analysis or experiential investigation. The *Constructivists interpret differences between traditions as real and commonalities as imagined* {*e.m.*}[12]. This denial of commonalities overlooks deliberately the glaring, inescapable commonalities between traditions in regard to the deepest experiences of the Divine Light as highlighted by myself in Chapter 7. Back in September 1994, before I knew all these counterarguments, I intuited that the hostility to Perennialism exhibited by Katz *et al.* was little more than crudely disguised prejudices provoked by the perceived threat from an underlying

Universal Spirituality (implied by Perennialism) to the mythologies of their cherished faiths, Judaism and Christianity. This point has also been raised by Perennialists such as Forman[13] and even by the Gadamerian, Postmodern Relativist Richard King[14]. Whilst Christian mystics mention mystical union which is at odds with theist Christian dogma, Judaism is strictly theistic with a strict separation of its so-called 'God' (actually the deity Yahweh) and Man. Given that Yahweh is not a personification of Divine Light, it is not surprising that union with Yahweh is not possible!

In one of the essays in Katz's book, the author Gimello set out ostensibly to challenge the assumption that Mysticism can be treated separately from the contexts of culture, history and tradition. Within Gimello's chapter I found quoted the views of Tsung-mi, a Ninth Century Chinese patriarch of two different schools of Buddhism. Tsung-mi distinguished the Buddhist *via negativa*, traced back to the great Indian Buddhist philosopher Nagarjuna, which emphasised the Doctrine of Emptiness from the Buddhist *via positiva* which stressed the omnipresence of the Buddha Nature:

> *Now if there were no such substantial realities as insight what could be revealed as the Buddha-nature, what could be said 'neither to be born nor to perish' and so forth? One must recognise that understanding in the very perception of what is presently at hand is precisely the Buddha-nature of the mind...*
>
> *Men of these days all regard negative discourse as profound and expressive discourse as shallow... This is all due to their mistaking purely negative discourse for profundity and to their failure to aspire after an intimate personal realisation of the substance of the truth.*
>
> — Tsung-mi (780-841c.e.) [15]

This authoritative statement by a Buddhist master intimate with Nagarjuna's *via negativa* helped clear up the confusion in my mind between the negative Buddhist terms "void" or "nothingness" and the Vedantic *saccidananda*. Those who followed Nagarjuna's "emptiness lineage" either failed to actually attain a personal realisation of the Buddha Nature (that which is neither born nor perishes; i.e., is *uncreated* and *eternal*) which is a substantial or essential reality. If followers of Nagarjuna's *via negativa* did actually manage to attain realisation of the substantial reality, they described it in seemingly profound negative terms such as "Emptiness" and "Void". As Tsung-mi pointed out, it is the **empty Awareness in itself** which **is** the **Buddha-Nature** {*e.m.*}[16]. As is also the case in modern Scientific Materialism with its Galilean Primary Qualities or with self-evident axioms, etc., Buddhist Negativists tacitly assume a Background Awareness which is taken for granted and not acknowledged. You cannot experience (or be aware of) a Void, an 'Emptiness' or whatever you call it without the presence of Awareness! We saw in Chapter 9 that Buddhist practitioner Herbert Guenther described *Sunyata* as the **background field behind Perception** {*e.m.*}[17].

Modern Western Neo-Buddhists such as some of the contributors to *Buddhism and Science*[18] including Michel Bitbol still find Nagarjuna's negative word-mongering as profound! We have also seen that Richard King's key argument against Neo-Vedantic claims to universal spirituality subsuming

Buddhism and other traditions was that Nagarjuna's Madhyamaka totally rejects a universal ground or essence[19]. However, we saw in Chapter 9 that Guenther tells us that Nagarjuna was a Logical Reductionist who thought in static terms and failed to gain a holistic understanding of lived reality. The dominant Tibetan schools consider Madhyamaka as Reductionistic and dogmatic in its intolerance. Thus Madhyamaka appeals to Logocentric Westerners who find in it elements reaffirming their own prejudices[20]. Wallace says that the followers of Tibetan *Dzogschen,* (seen as the final 'complete' interpretation[21]) do not see Nagarjuna's view as incompatible with their view of a Universal Ground Consciousness[22]. Dallmayr even states that Nagarjuna never really denied the Supreme Reality or *Brahman* of the older Brahmanic tradition[23].

In the final chapter of *Mysticism and Religious Traditions*, J.E. Smith[24] stated the following:

> *The Buddhists tell us that 'emptiness' is not to be understood on a relative plane as absence or extinction, but only on the basis of pure experience which is the mind reflecting itself and no other content. This is what is called* ***sunyata***...

Smith went on to briefly discuss the great Franciscan mystic St Bonaventure's thoroughly rational treatise *The Mind's Road to God* which speaks of the *uncreated light*, the significance of numbers and the Universe and of the Mind as both being mirrors of the divine {*e.m.*}[25].

> *Being as the condition for all beings, and light as the condition for all that is seen, become the final objects of contemplation, at the end of the process the mind passes beyond itself.*
>
> — St Bonaventure [26]

I realised that the Light, the "uncreated light" or the "eternal light" of Bonaventure was the *cit* or Pure Consciousness of the Vedanta. Bonaventure's Being and Light were equivalent to the Vedantic *sat* (Pure Being) and *cit*. Note also that Bonaventure's adjectives for the Light are *uncreated* and *eternal* which correspond to the Buddha's *That which is neither born nor perishes* as in the quote from Tsung-mi. I was soon to find confirmations of this Divine Light equals Pure Consciousness equation in both Vedanta and Nondual Kashmir Shaivism.

Scientific Hostility to Mysticism and Perplexity over the Light

I read Morse's book[27] in which I had already checked and found that the brain area that Morse associated with NDEs was the Sylvian fissure of the right cerebral hemisphere. However, contrary to Morse's exaggerated claims, this area was only associated with out-of-body experiences (OBEs) where it appears as if one is hovering above one's own body.[N2] The famous Canadian neurosurgeon Wilder Penfield had found that electrical stimulation of this area (in awake patients) induced OBEs and this same association with OBEs had been rediscovered more recently by some Chilean neurosurgeons. Morse touched upon various scientific attempts to explain NDEs, most of which were just crude attempts to debunk anything that went beyond the limits of the modern scientific world-picture using Reductionist myths about chemicals, oxygen depletion, etc., presented as if they were 'explanations'. These factors do *not* actually account for the actual experiences although some of these physiological factors might show some sort of *correlation* with the experiences.

Any factor whose presence or absence is associated with, or whose quantity varies in a repeatable manner, with a conscious phenomenon is a 'correlate'. Correlates which are just *associated factors* such as the amount of oxygen in the brain is not the same as what I have called the **Direct Physical Correlate** which is the physical process *corresponding directly or exactly with the conscious phenomenon* as in my RAS brainwave correlate of the phenomenon of the Divine Light. Of course oxygen depletion would be expected to be associated with NDEs but surely oxygen depletion also occurs in numerous critically ill patients who do not have NDEs. Oxygen depletion (anoxia) in itself is nothing more than one component of the complex physiological processes correlated with the experiences and it hardly comes near to a sufficient explanation (ignoring here, for simplicity, the more general fact that *Science cannot actually explain any sort of conscious experience whatsoever* let alone NDEs, as we have seen). Nonetheless, the Reductionist notion of oxygen depletion was touted like some magical formula supposedly 'explaining' NDEs by a number of scientists. Would anyone try to explain our normal Wakeful experiences by saying that they are just the result of sufficient oxygen supply to the brain! In fact, I discovered in 2003 that the only published study in which blood oxygen and carbon dioxide was measured during NDEs found no effects of either anoxia or hypercapnia on the experience[28].

The sort of argument put forward by orthodox scientists to explain away NDEs or mystical experiences was exemplified by some comments addressed to the Dalai Lama by a Harvard professor of Neurobiology which I read in another one of the books I had picked up at Foyles.

> *I am a cellular scientist and a notorious radical materialist. I have a question that may be shared by other scientists or neuroscientists, as to whether one should invoke a non-material mind in order to understand brain science, or increase our understanding of human behavior... the particular nerve cells upon which cocaine is known to act are neither clear nor formless; they are amazingly intricate in their shape and they occur in collections of nerve cells whose form is wonderfully intricate. They are not clear, they contain a pigment... though no one knows whether it is related in any way to these phenomena [referring to euphoria].*
>
> —David D. Potter [29]

Self-proclaimed "Radical Materialist" Potter may be a professor at Harvard but his arguments are so puerile a bright schoolchild can see through them. He asks how can you experience a "clear light" when *nerve cells are not clear* and have intricate dendritic forms (in response to the Buddhists' claims of formless awareness). If our experience was limited by the structure of nerve cells and their pigmentation we would certainly not be experiencing the everyday world of forms and colours we nonetheless do experience! However, in spite of Potter's staggering epistemological naivety, this question as to why the structures of the brain, known to Science, do not appear in our conscious experience does raise a valid question. The reader will recall that I used a notion of "subjective closure" in my Panpsychist model in order to exclude nerve cells and lower level structures from our experience. The nature of after-images indicates that excitation of vast networks of cellular patterns appears in our visual experience and that this excitation pattern can persist above some sort of 'energetic threshold' level required for egoic presence (or presence in the Field of Attention) although attention has moved to other things.

By chance, the very day I first typed this, the newspapers were reporting the Archbishop of Canterbury Rowan Williams' response to the simplistic, Atheistic fundamentalism of biologist Richard Dawkin's book *The God Delusion*. The Archbishop notes correctly that although our society holds Science in high esteem, this does not mean that a good scientist is necessarily a good philosopher. His own "inner jury" remained out in the case of Dawkins[30, 31]. Although, like Dawkins, I have no time for the mythologies and dogmatism of Religions, I would not be so reserved in my estimation of Dawkin's philosophical maturity.[N3] A myopic approach resembling Dawkins' is displayed by the British comedy actor turned 'know-all' guru Stephen Fry[N4] who is presented on BBC television as extraordinarily erudite. I watched Fry appear as a guest on the BBC's *Room 101* TV series presenting his pet hates. One of his 'hates' was 'New Age' stuff. Fry dismissed New Age thinking using the facile 'straw man' examples such as New Age healing crystals and other cranky popular nonsense, sneering in his snooty upper-middle class accent at New Age talk of subtle energies and vibrations etc. This simplistic rejection of alien ideas is the intellectual equivalent of the Englishman abroad who, ignorant of foreign languages, simply talks loudly and slowly in English assuming that everyone should be able to understand English. Ironically, both Lewis Wolpert and Fry, who take this simplistic 'God is an Englishman' approach to what they don't understand, typical of Anglo-Saxon culture, are both, at least partly, of Jewish background. I was amused to read in 2010 that the well-known UK female newspaper columnist Julie Burchill had retorted to some misogynous remarks by Fry by describing him rather aptly as "a stupid person's idea of someone clever".

Returning to my reading of Morse's book in September 1994; it was not surprising that the NDE Associations formed by people across the USA who have had NDEs resent such crude attempts by Materialists to try to 'wish away' their spiritual experiences with such crude, Reductionist pseudo-explanations. A surprisingly high percentage of the US population seem to have had such experiences according to one oft-cited survey. Morse decided to focus on the NDE reports of children as they were less likely to be indoctrinated into religious beliefs[32]. A Scottish woman called Christine whom I worked with in the mid 1990s told me that her heart had stopped when she was seven years old and she had seen the Light but the doctors just ignored her claim. Morse had found that the scientific establishment discouraged anyone from investigating NDEs. To his credit, Morse himself remained open-minded, accepting the testimony of his of his young patients even in regard to their claims of experiencing paranormal psychic phenomena. He noted that such Death-related experiences have been known since time immemorial all over the world. The Egyptian Pharaohs had to undergo an initiation ceremony involving suffocation for a period of time in a sarcophagus which would have induced such experiences. Morse referred to Jung, the *Tibetan Book of the Dead* and related texts from around the world. He also suggested studying brainwave patterns in NDE patients and comparing them to those found in meditation[33].

Of the Light itself, Morse stated[34]:

The Light is the one element of the near-death experience that brain researchers can't even come close to explaining. The testimony of children is clear on this point. The Light is the key element of the NDE.
How can we scientifically explain this light after death? I do not know of any biochemical or psychological explanation for why we would experience a bright light as the final stage of bodily death.

He continued:

And then – there's light? Where does this light come from? The brain has nearly stopped functioning … Then why the Light?

Faced with this mystery, Morse mentions beliefs that this Light represents some sort of rebirth. This view seems to be encouraged by the experience of 'tunnelling' that is experienced by some NDE patients prior to encountering the Light which leads one to imagine some sort of journey across some boundary between this world and the next[35]. In fact, it is Western NDE patients who tend to experience passing through a tunnel whereas NDE patients from other cultures tend to have other equivalent experiences such as of walking down a road or passing over a body of water[36]. Morse attempted to eliminate cultural bias by concentrating on the testimony of very young children, who spoke in simplistic language about Jesus[37].

But Morse also cited the testimony of a fourteen year old boy who stated[38]:

As I reached the source of the Light, I could see in. I cannot begin to describe in human terms the feelings I had over what I saw. It was a giant infinite world of calm, and love, and energy, and beauty. It was as though human life was unimportant compared to this. And yet it urged the importance of life at the same time it solicited death as a means to a different and better life. It was all being, all beauty, all meaning for all existence. It was the energy of the universe forever in one place.

Here, in this rather sophisticated testimony from a fourteen year old (probably given years after the actual NDE at age fourteen), the parallel with Vedanta and other mystical traditions was glaring with the Light experienced as all Being and all the Energy of the universe. The reference to "all meaning for all existence", etc., also ties in with the notion of the Light as the Ground of all Being containing the *bija* (seed-potentialities) or *archetypes* for all possible forms of existence. I was satisfied from these remarkable parallels between the more sophisticated NDE testimonies and the Vedanta that my association of *moksha* with NDEs was totally justified, at least in regard to the final stages of the NDEs when the Light made its appearance. The limitation of Morse's "brain area", the right Sylvian fissure, to OBEs and his bafflement over the Light restored my own confidence in my Retreat-to-the-Brainstem hypothesis.

The Puzzle of Coherent Alpha Rhythm

Perusing a book on Synchronicity[39] which I had purchased along with Morse's book, I discovered that the brainwave patterns of yogis, supposedly in a state of Enlightenment, had been measured. The pattern was a unique one, so-called 'coherent alpha rhythm' all over the scalp. The source for this information was an article by Orme-Johnson published in a journal entitled *Electroencephalography and Clinical Neurophysiology*[40]. The book on Synchronicity was merely a mass market New Age paperback by non-scientists and did not elaborate upon this information. Some months after reading this, I rediscovered an article I had cut out of a 1991 issue of *New Scientist* magazine and kept for possible future reference. It was by the afore-mentioned sceptical psychologist Susan Blackmore and entitled *Is Meditation Good for You*[41]. I had seen Blackmore on numerous television programmes attempting to debunk the claims of paranormal activity. In fact, another of my September 5th 1994 purchases from Foyles, a popular book on the paranormal contained background information about her. In the past Dr Blackmore had been actively involved in Psychical Research but had later become an arch-sceptic[42]. Her zealous anti-paranormal stance seemed to me to indicate a subconscious desire to regain respectability with the academic establishment after her earlier flirtation with the Paranormal.

In the 1991 *New Scientist* article Blackmore discussed the history of EEG measurements of meditators. She went on to discuss Orme-Johnson's work, especially a study claiming to show paranormal influences by groups of meditators, pointing out that much of the research into EEG patterns during meditation was carried out by members of the Transcendental Meditation (or TM) organisation and published in their own publications where it is not subject to peer review. However, the aforementioned journal *Electroencephalography and Clinical Neurophysiology* is not a TM publication; rather it is published by the world's leading scientific journal publisher Elsevier. Blackmore continued with the statement, "A strong motivation to 'prove' the efficacy of TM could bias the findings"[43]. This is a valid concern and I later found that the TM organisation has misinterpreted the simple meaning of EEG coherence data to make false claims that such EEG coherence and, hence enlightenment, involves some sort of global integration of all brain functions into a coherent whole[44]. But arch-sceptic Blackmore fails to register *her own interests and biases* or even contemplate the possibility that her own presuppositions may be wrong. As with Eurocentric historians and sociologists who mock aspects of non-European cultures whilst overlooking the same faults in their own culture, Scientific Materialism projects all ignorance and irrationality, etc., onto the 'Other', those who challenge their orthodoxy. I would take issue with the claims of many Psychologists, suffering inferiority complexes in relation to the 'Hard Sciences', that they are "Scientists" and, as with Dawkins, psychological or scientific training does not make you a competent philosopher.

For instance, Blackmore appeals dogmatically to the 'Laws of Physics' as an argument against the existence of paranormal psychic phenomena as if such so-called 'laws', based on Christian myths, are immutable, sacrosanct and indisputable! We have seen, as Immanuel Kant also recognised, that simple epistemology shows that we never experience directly the so-called "Physical World" of Materialism which Blackmore also assumes is a self-evident, primary and indisputable fact! Furthermore Michael West, the editor of a scholarly volume entitled *The Psychology of Meditation*, points out the deficiencies in all the scientific studies of Meditation which due to ignorance, misconceptions, lack of suitable subjects and time, etc., simply cannot do justice to Meditation[45]. Taylor notes that when the US Army commissioned a study of Meditation, they completely misunderstood and distorted the issues. The US Army study made vague generalisations, relying upon just one outdated review of Meditation Studies, one non-representative practitioner and the study concluded along the lines that *mantrayana* (chanting) was equivalent to the counting sheep cure for insomnia[46].

Nonetheless, reading Blackmore's sarcastic comment that increased EEG coherence is also associated with epileptic seizure, coma and death was 'music to my ears' as this again helped to confirm my linkage between Yogic enlightenment and the process of dying or NDEs. The *pranayama* or breath control of the yogi is known to result in minimal oxygen consumption, yet another parallel with NDEs and their anoxia. The comatose state of yogis deep in *samadhi* (meditative 'absorption') appeared a number of times in my readings of 1994 and I was to read soon afterwards that it was not possible to detect a heartbeat in Ramakrishna when he was deep in *samadhi*. Returning to the actual development of my thought in September 1994, I had discovered the information that EEG studies on enlightened yogis revealed a rare state of coherent alpha rhythm all over the scalp in the Synchronicity book[47] and had not yet seen Blackmore's 1991 article. I recall telling a friend at work, who herself claimed to be psychic, a day or two after reading it that this coherent alpha rhythm data meant nothing to me. However, unlike Blackmore, I registered this information in an open-mind minded manner, as I had no ulterior motive to rubbish such studies and it just lay at the back of my mind. I had around this time purchased the afore-mentioned book on Event-Related Brain Potentials which discussed EEG studies but had not got around to reading it. With hindsight this expensive book was of no use to me and would not have helped understand Orme-Johnson's coherence data[48].

The Ego Complex in Zen Meditation: Phenomenological Evidence Supporting My Theory

V.W. Odajnyk's book, *Gathering the Light* [49], which I purchased along with Morse's book, began its back cover promotional text with the sentence: What exactly happens in meditation?" It went on to claim that it was the first book to apply the insights of Jungian psychology to the process of meditation. It claimed that it would give a ground-breaking explanation of Zen meditation based on the notion of a "meditation complex", a psychological explanation of the "mystical union of opposites" and a "psychological definition of self-realisation". Unlike Englishman Anthony Storr's book on Jung, Odajnyk provided a number of insights which to me, at that time, were most revealing. He pointed out, for instance, that the Chinese text *The Secret of the Golden Flower* (translated by Richard Wilhelm) for which Jung had written a famous foreword was in fact a Meditation manual. Storr had referred to this Chinese text but had made *no mention of Meditation*! Storr's book, with hindsight, was typical of English Eurocentrism. He was either ignorant of or suppressing the Eastern influences on Jung as Jung's disciples had done. Odajnyk referred to Jung's visits to India and focused on Jung's study of Alchemy.

Alchemy, a most mysterious term for the Modern Mind, was really supposed to be a form of Meditation resulting in the *mysterium coniunctionis* or the Mystical Union. Western alchemists had projected the final stages of the alchemical/meditative process onto the external world resulting in the ideas of transmutation of metals to gold associated with mysterious terms such as the 'chymical wedding'. In contrast, the Chinese alchemical text, *The Secret of the Golden Flower*, immediately identified the alchemical 'gold' as a simile for the (Divine) Light. Thus the *philosopher's stone* and its transmutation into the *philosopher's gold* actually represented the mind/soul ('stone') and its union with the Light ('gold') {*e.m.*}[50]. In Storr's book, I had read that Jung had spent about a decade discovering that the seemingly nonsensical medieval Alchemical texts, full of what appeared to be medieval rubbish relating various groups which had no obvious logical basis, began to make sense when these relations were understood as symbolic representations of psychological processes[51]. Odajnyk stated that later post-medieval Western alchemists such as Gerhard Dorn and the famous Paracelsus (whose life inspired Goethe's *Faust*) had begun to realise the psychical nature of the entire Alchemical process[52].

Jung sought to find Western parallels to Eastern spiritual practises and parallel Western terminology. Jungian literature is thus full of references to the *unus mundus* representing the Unitary Ground of the Universe with which the 'soul' unites in Alchemy/Meditation. He claimed that the West had never developed anything comparable to Yoga because of Western fear of the contents of the personal unconscious, the inner fantasies that surge to the surface as soon as one begins to 'let go' of normal egoistic control[53]. Buddhophile Odajnyk praised the "remarkable accomplishment of Buddha" in that, although enlightenment was nothing new nor unique, he was "the first person known to history to describe Self-realisation in primarily psychological and non-religious terms. And he did this *two and a half thousand years ago* when most of humanity was still very deeply involved with primitive deities and supernatural forces".

> *There is no eternal soul or God to speak of: at the core of everything is only eternal Consciousness, the Enlightened Mind.*
>
> — V.W. Odajnyk[54]

Odajnyk also quoted the first lines of the Tibetan Book of the Dead:

> *O nobly born... listen. Now thou art experiencing the Radiance of the Clear Light of Pure reality... is the very consciousness, the All-good Buddha.*

The **moment of death**, Odajnyk noted, is supposed to provide a supreme opportunity for realising one's true nature {*e.m.*}[55], again reaffirming the link between Enlightenment and Death.

Buddha's teachings were remarkable in their lack of primitive deities and supernatural forces, two thousand years before the Renaissance in Europe, especially in the Buddha's denial of an immortal soul and positing that the Mind or Personality was constituted of *skandhas* (aggregrates). The Buddhist view of the Mind, (i.e., ego) as a bundle of dynamically constituted aggregates parallels my own view from 1983 that the Mind (ego) is a self-organising process. However, we have also seen that many Westerners, such as Michael Wood, have glorified egalitarian Buddhism whilst ignoring elitist Brahmanism, written in the restricted language of Sanskrit, which was reserved for the Aryan 'priestly' caste. We have seen that Buddha's teachings do not in fact constitute a systematic philosophy as he refused to answer important philosophical questions and thus leaving his followers in great confusion over key concepts such as *anatta* and *sunyata*.

The Tibetan Book of the Dead's emphasis on the Clear Light Consciousness as the primordial Reality is, as we have seen a very Vedanticised (Brahmanised) version of Buddhism which, even in its original version, had strong roots in the older Brahmanism of the Upanishads which remained largely secret doctrines. Odajnyk's glorification of Buddha is thus grossly exaggerated as Buddha's teachings hardly arose in a vacuum but in a melting pot of numerous competing philosophies including Brahmanism, Yoga, Materialistic philosophies and especially Jainism, which influenced Buddhism heavily with its notions of *ahimsa* and transmigration. The dismissal of supernatural forces may seem to be way ahead of its time, but Buddha's contemporaries included Materialist thinkers. Furthermore, the attainment of Enlightenment is accompanied by supernatural psychic abilities (*siddhis*), the demonstration of which by yogis claiming enlightenment would have been expected. Buddha did not deny supernatural psychic powers as Odajnyk claimed but forbade his followers from displaying them as such public display strengthened the ego. Thus, as A.K. Coomaraswamy stated decades ago, *Westerners tend to admire Buddhism largely for what it is not* {*e.m.*}[56]. We have seen this with the Logocentric Western Buddhophiles hyping up the Logical Reductionism of Nagarjuna. Similarly, I have pointed out how Naturalistic Westerners delude themselves that 'psychological' Buddhism is more 'scientific' than Brahmanism as the latter indulges in grand Cosmology and emphasises the Primacy of Consciousness.

Having read the beginning of Odajnyk's book, I was awoken from my slumber on the morning of Saturday 10th September 1994 by the doorbell ringing. It was about 8 am and I heard my mother downstairs paying the milkman. This was most unusual as the milkman normally delivered the milk early in the morning and then came back at about 11a.m. or later to collect the money. I was thus unexpectedly awoken and, not fully awake, I looked up above me to see four beams of light on the white ceiling of my room. The beams, a purely natural phenomenon, entered my room through a small gap at the top of the region of overlap of the two curtains. The window was at the end of the room nearest my feet so the beams entered and spread about above my head. The light beams kept shifting across my ceiling and diffracting into various colours of the rainbow. In the 18 months or so that I had had those curtains, I had never noticed these beams on my ceiling. In early 1993, the room had been refurbished following the knocking down of the old chimney breast in 1992, with new plug points added when previously there was only one. I recall that, upon refurbishment, I had a strong unusual feeling as if my Deeper Self was "looking through me" in anticipation of the work it wanted me to do in this room which should be continued regardless of what happened to me on the career front.

On the morning of Saturday 10th September I was mesmerised by these, seemingly animate, shimmering beams of light silently swaying and diffracting above my head. I felt a numinous presence in their ectoplasmic transformations and later, looking back upon the experience, the thought that arose from my Deeper Self was, "howsoever you shall conceive me, in that form shall I appear". I knew that the Brahmanic teaching was that the Truth is One but people imagine it in many ways. Half asleep and mesmerised by the light beams, I began to contemplate all the knowledge that I had been acquiring over the previous two weeks including Bonaventure's final meditative state of Being and Light paralleling the Vedantic *saccidananda*, the mystery of the NDEs and the insightful ideas I was beginning to acquire from Odajnyk. In that state, it was crystallising in my mind that the central element of Mysticism was Divine, *Uncreated* or *Eternal* Light; That which is *neither born nor perishes*. Pure Consciousness was this Divine Light. I kept recalling Bonaventure's statement that the universe and the mind, the external and the internal worlds, were both mirrors[N5] of the Divine, (i.e., the Uncreated or Unborn). It was dawning upon me, gazing at the diffracting colours in the light beams, that if Pure Consciousness was Divine Light, then *colours* were not just part of the human or animal visual experience but Universal experiences of Consciousness with nothing essentially to do with vision.

It seemed to me at that moment that I was beginning to understand intuitively why the visual mode of perception was so different from other sensory modes. The answer seemed to be related to the fact that vision involved higher energy processes dominating our perceptual modelling of the world and thus visual consciousness was differentiated into colours as colours seemed to be primary gradations of the Light of Pure Consciousness. It seemed to me as if the other sensory modes were operating 'below' the energetic threshold level of the visual mode and cast ghostly shadows of touch, smell, taste and sounds into the Field of Attention dominated by visual patterning. Nonetheless, these other senses and all the other forms of awareness such as thoughts and feelings were still differentiations of Pure Consciousness. Unusual experiences such as Synaesthesia indicated the underlying inter-relatedness of all the sensory modes as Synaesthetics experienced non-visual sensations (often sounds) or even thoughts as colours etc. Thus, whilst mesmerised by the diffracting light beams, it was dawning upon me how this one unitary Light of Consciousness, the Ground of Consciousness, could 'diffract' itself into becoming the multitudinous forms of experience.

Thoughts also crossed my mind about how I had, up till then, completely failed to consider the possibility of ever knowing what sort of experience individuated entities far-removed from human minds might be having in this

Panpsychic cosmos. My interpretation of *phenomena* had been that they were events (experiences) within our 'selves' (the world-model fields) generated by external events transmitted by information flow via the senses. In essence, I now understood that my position (developed in the 1980s) was a modern restatement of the Indian view that *knowing* is *being* and thus everything we ever experience (know) is a part of our self (our 'being'). It followed from this line of reasoning that we could not know directly things in themselves, except for that which was the physical correlate of our 'self;' i.e., we could not know what it is like to be something other than my postulated 'World-Model Field' (or the 'Field of Attention'), our conscious mind. My earlier draft essay of 1993 had tried to discuss the broader implications issuing from my inchoate Panpsychist ideas developed with only the most rudimentary acquaintance with knowledge from yogic mysticism. My Panpsychism had been based largely on abstract reasoning superimposed upon insights based upon the primary insight that nothing existed without Awareness; i.e., I intuitively understood that all existence had to be sentient existence. I had realised that the so-called 'Physical World' was but the descriptions of energetic patterns of behaviour exhibited by phenomena and not a description of Reality as it actually is.

Thus, having held that we could never know what the subjectivities of other entities were like in themselves and not having imagined that there were other states of Consciousness (apart from Dreams) it was coming as a shock to me to discover that mystics experienced altered states of Consciousness and claimed (transpersonal) experiences of oneness with other things. My own *Sutra* had repeatedly referred to "becoming one with" other beings but this referred to my own momentary, perhaps imaginative, flashes of identification with something else rather than some volitionally sustained altered state of Consciousness. I had of course heard of 'Higher Planes' of Consciousness but had not encountered, prior to reading Odajnyk's book, any serious attempt to describe such a 'Higher Plane' which tried to relate such experiences to knowledge I could begin to come to terms with. Thus I had never been able to develop in my mind even an inkling of what was being referred to in such talk of 'Higher Planes', if indeed such states existed at all. From my modern, evolutionary perspective, a 'Higher Plane' implied some more highly developed form of world-modelling, i.e., some process more complex than the processes correlated with our normal Waking consciousness. If such processes existed, what possible evolutionary function could they serve to maintain, whatever the brain structures underlying them, and why could we not easily attain these states. The reader will note that, back in 1993, I had already realised that Enlightenment must resemble NDEs and thus should involve a 'Retreat-to-the-Brainstem' of the ego. Thus *moksa* would not involve a more complex state but in fact a less complex one. In spite of this intuitive leap, I hadn't really clarified my thought as I had some idea that the Path to Enlightenment (*Raja Yoga*) was not the only yogic path and I did not know how these 'higher planes' fitted in relation to the Basis Enlightenment (mystical union) experience. I recall reading in one book around this time that the Hindu mystics explored all aspects of "psychic space". This indicated to me that there were different yogic paths with altered states of Consciousness which were not simply directed at attaining Enlightenment.

I also contemplated on that Saturday morning something that had given me an even greater shock to my own framework of understanding than the mystical claim to experiences of *becoming one with non-human entities*. This was the mystical claim that it was possible to transcend what I had called in my Pansychist model, '*subjective closure*' (individuation) and become one with an all-pervading, 'Universal Consciousness'. In fact, with hindsight, my Panpsychist model had had been largely consistent with such mystical notions but I had never before pressed deeper to contemplate the full ramifications of such lines of reasoning; never having experienced such states of ego dissolution myself. Such mystical views had seemed totally preposterous to my scientifically indoctrinated mind. Having had such thoughts cross my mind whilst half-asleep in the presence of the beams of light on my ceiling which seemed to be, mysteriously, illuminating my mind through their sheer presence, I fell asleep again before waking up fully some time later.

Later that Saturday, I continued reading Odajnyk's book and discovered that the Zen meditation he practised involved dissolution of the so-called "ego complex" and formation of a so-called "meditation complex" into which the ego must first merge before further progress occurs. The ego attempts to monitor and unify all psychic contents that enter its field of awareness. More interestingly for my purposes, the ego was described as a "***closed energy field*** *that strives to maintain its integrity and resists penetration*". Odajnyk defined the term *complex*, following Jung, as a "feeling toned cluster of psychic energy". The Jungian "complex" has its own ***personality*** and ***volition*** {*e.m.*}[57]. Odajnyk did not bother to explain what he actually meant by the term "closed" but it was clear from his usage that, as in my Panpsychist hypothesis, by "closed" Odajnyk meant *discrete* or *autonomous* in the sense of closing itself off from its surroundings by some means in order to maintain a sense of individuality or separation from the surroundings. It struck me upon reading this discussion of this Zen meditation process that these *closed energy fields* described as "complexes", each with its own personality, was much the same as I had pictured my self-organising field processes which constituted individuated sentient entities or 'closed structures'. These complexes or closed energy fields striving to maintain their integrity also resembled *dissipative structures*, self-organising processes generated by flows of energy under certain conditions, in the new far-from-equilibrium thermodynamics of open systems developed by Nobel laureate Ilya Prigogine. The reader will recall from Chapter 11 that, back in 1983, I had linked my self-organising, individuated or closed structures with the new notion of dissipative structures applied generally to all manner of systems throughout the universe as popularised by Jantsch in his book *The Self-Organising Universe*.

The Light as Experienced in the Slow, Mainstream Yogic Paths

The word *Zen*, glorified in Western bohemian pop culture due to bestselling pop philosophy books such as Robert Pirsig's *Zen and the Art of Motor Cycle Mechanics*, is a Japanese term derived from the Sanskrit *dhyana* via the Chinese *ch'an* (a Buddhist school founded by an Indian named Bodhidharma).

In Patanjali's *Yoga Sutras*, the term *dhyana* refers to stilling the mind. A new form of Zen Buddhism developed during the Meiji restoration and a decontextualised, Vedanticised form of Rinzai Zen, a minor sect in Japan, was publicised in the West by D.T. Suzuki[58]. Suzuki's 'Zen' captivated certain 'bohemians' (beatniks) partly due to the anti-intellectualism associated with it. This popular 'Zen' encourages nihilistic views including the mistaken view that nothing rational can be said about the highest states of Consciousness. Such Paths to Enlightenment are quick, unstable paths not involving the step-by-step progress of more conventional yogic paths. Similarly Swami Prabhavananda threw Aldous Huxley out of the Ramakrishna Mission for expediting Enlightenment through the use of drugs which prevent development of volitional control over the transformations of Consciousness[59].

Along with the unorthodox Zen methodology which bypasses the step-by-step progress which can help us understand the process of attaining Enlightenment, Odajnyk's use of Jung's obfuscating terminology, based on Jung's misunderstandings of Yoga and lack of acquaintance and acceptance of the deepest spiritual realms, made his presentation most confusing. There were sequences of Chinese or Japanese pictograms describing changing states which lead more to confusion than clarity. Contrary to the hype on his back cover, Odajnyk actually gave no clear psychological explanation as to what Mystical Union actually entailed. Nonetheless, assimilating the insights he did provide into my background knowledge, I was getting very excited. Odajnyk had described the Mind, on the basis of introspective knowledge of altered states of Consciousness, as a "closed energy field constituted of the Clear Light of Consciousness". I could sense that things were stirring in my subconscious; I had to find out more about what actually happened in Yoga; where should I look? I had the idea in my head that the sort of information I was looking for could probably be found only in American journals or studies published in America which may not be available in the UK. At that time I did not know about the almost complete avoidance of such topics in Western academia. I wondered how I, with no qualifications or academic position would get access to such knowledge which might require access to academic libraries.

In spite of such pessimism in regard to finding the information I required, during my lunch break on Monday 12th September I decided to go and look near my place of work near Camden Lock, North London, to see what I could find. I went to the local Waterstones bookstore, as it was the largest bookshop nearby in this rather bohemian area. I did not realise at the time that a smaller bookshop called Compendium, the nearest bookshop to my workplace was a far better place to look. I knew Compendium only as a stockist of Marxist and radical tracts in its dingy basement supplying the middle class, left-wing 'trendies' of Camden, the London borough in which my secondary school had been located. I did not know then that at the back of the ground floor, behind the mainstream mass-market books, Compendium was also one of London's largest New Age stockists containing both popular and also, difficult to find, scholarly university press texts on all mystical matters which would prove to be a 'goldmine' for my research. On September 12th I looked around the small Psychology section in the local Waterstones and found nothing of relevance as it stocked mainly mainstream books.

After about half an hour I gave up and turned to go when my peripheral vision was somehow guided to a green book spine bearing the Shambhala logo (Shambhala had published Odajnyk's *Gathering the Light*) and entitled *Transformations of Consciousness*. It was edited by Wilber, Engler and Brown[60] and I recognised it as one of the books I had marked in the bibliography given in the afore-mentioned Harvard MindScience Symposium book[61] (containing David Potter's views) as a book that I would like to get hold of if possible. I had not noticed it, partly because it had been misplaced out of its correct alphabetical order of authors presumably because, unlike most of the stock, it had remained unsold for eight years since its publication in 1986. I had looked for Wilber, who was also the editor of the afore-mentioned Shambhala book *The Holographic Paradigm*[62] which I had bought in 1983, but found nothing. Quickly perusing the contents and back cover promotional material, I realised that this attempt to synthesise Psychology/Psychiatry with spiritual knowledge of deeper states of Consciousness was just the sort of thing I had been looking for. With hindsight, I later realised that Compendium bookshop kept around three copies of this book in stock in its New Age section. However, as with my purchase of *Embraced by the Light* nine days earlier, I had followed my intuition to investigate a book glimpsed in my peripheral vision. It felt as if I was meant to find the single copy at Waterstones. Had I known that Compendium was a veritable treasure trove of New Age information and gone there first, I would probably have been distracted by dozens of other books of interest to my investigations and missed this book. Instead, in the mainstream bookshop, I had found nothing of use to me until I finally chanced upon this book, misplaced and having remained there unsold for eight years.

The key chapter in this book turned out to be Harvard psychologist Daniel Brown's detailed study of the "Stages of Meditation" compared across three authoritative Yogic traditions. These were the Tibetan (Mahayana Buddhist) *Mahamudra*, the 'Hindu' *Yoga Sutras* and the Theravada Buddhist *Vipassana*, describing the similarities and differences across the traditions[63]. Within a day or two of seeking more information on what actually happens in Yoga, which I realised might not be easy to obtain, *I had been guided, or so it seemed*, to the best available published description of what happens in the mainstream, slow Yogic paths leading to Enlightenment. Brown described Meditation as the "Deconstruction of the Perceptual Process", "Stopping the Mind" as one Buddhist tradition called the earlier steps, and uncovering the "subtle flow of the Light" hidden beneath our gross perceptual constructs. Amidst the wealth of amazing information I found in Brown's study, most of which I could not assimilate in one reading, one key piece of phenomenological information stuck in my mind.

The flow of the Light underlying our gross mental content was described by the Hindu *Yoga Sutra* tradition as *tanmatra* (literally "that matrix" translated as "coordinates of that previous gross content") or "*a continuously vibrating **energy field** in a state of **continuous wave propagation***". The Buddhists, focusing on the discontinuities, described the Light as coming in pulses or movements {*e.m.*}[64]. I realised that these were just differences in perspective, the Hindu focusing on the underlying continuity, the Buddhist indoctrinated into focusing on the wave peaks and thus experiencing the Light as pulses. I realised that such fundamental differences in the focusing of the yogi's attention led to differences in metaphysics; the Hindu *ekatattva* (the one, continuous, principle) as against the Buddhist *ksanika* (moments or "pulses") devoid of an underlying Ground or Essence. Clearly, the Hindu focus, not limiting itself to merely the (energetic) wave peaks of the Light, was inclusive of more of Reality. I also guessed that the very origins of the Buddhist focus on discontinuous aspects could have been a result of the Buddhist socio-political motivation to challenge the Vedic ('Hindu') *dharma* (social order) by challenging its metaphysical underpinnings of the one continuous Ground of all Being or *Brahman*.

In fact, as stated previously, I later discovered that both William James (in his description of the underlying "Stream of Consciousness") and Husserlian Phenomenology (in its description of the underlying flow of the Temporal (or Time-constituting) Absolute Consciousness which also constitutes the spatial matrix of perception[65]) discuss this paradox of discontinuous moments of Consciousness actually constituting a continuum at a deeper level. The moments are our perceptual abstractions from the underlying continuity. Franklin Merrell-Wolff's thought also parallels my view of attaining a more inclusive view of Reality through deeper Insight. He argues that a deeper insight would harmonise the apparent differences between Buddha and Sankara. We have seen that he argued that the supposedly discontinuous moments of Buddhism were just abstractions from the Underlying Oneness, the Transcendental Absolute Consciousness which he called the true *Nirvana*[66].

All of this fascinating knowledge presented by Brown could not be digested easily by my mind. I had vague mental pictures of the subtle pulses of the Light flowing through the Field of Attention, free of gross cognitions. I imagined the gross cognitions 'bouncing back' into attention if the yogi failed to maintain concentration. Brown had mentioned how the ordinary self-reference frame drops away as the Flow of the Light becomes clearer with practice. What remains is a sense of self-agency, awareness of directing attention, exerting oneself and rejecting or developing the subtle flow into gross cognitions. Eventually, as the yogi lets go of all activities that interfere with the Flow of the Light, even the sense of self-agency drops away. There follows exploration of fascinating subtle realms, beyond the Time and Space constructions of Perception, where reality operates through 'acausal' interactions in an undivided wholeness and the subtle karmic activity underlying the gross activity of the ordinary phenomenal world. Finally, awareness turns in on itself as the last remaining artificial activity, (i.e., that which is not the spontaneous activity of the primordial state) is brought to cessation. The yogi realises that Pure Awareness exists as a continuous backdrop to all activities and, if lucky, attains "Basis Enlightenment" in which all events, content and activity drop away leaving a "Vast Awareness" in which the observer becomes one with the observed (i.e., Nonduality)[67].

This Basis Enlightenment is the one step in the process for which all three authoritative yogic traditions in Brown's study gave identical descriptions. Brown went on to discuss further developments which the yogi could undertake where, again, the traditions differed. Brown claimed that his study showed, contrary to the Perennialist view of various paths leading to the same goal, that the various paths were essentially the same and the goals were different[68]. I disagreed with this perverse Relativist interpretation given by Brown. As Brown himself had argued, *the paths to Basis Enlightenment* undertaken in the different traditions were *essentially the same*. The dissolution of a sense of separate identity in *Basis Enlightenment was clearly the key stage*. The description of Basis Enlightenment was the *near-to-identical across the three traditions*. This **'Basis Enlightenment'** was the **Mystical Union** in which the sense of a separate self dissolves and the observer and observed become one. The later differences between traditions were Post-Enlightenment practises, bringing awareness of the underlying Light flow into normal states of mind ("Fruition Enlightenment", Insight Meditation etc.), which depended upon first realising the crucial stage of Basis Enlightenment as the ultimate ground state and then reversing the perceptual deconstruction process. In 1995 I found that the pro-Perennialist contributors to Forman's *The Problem of Pure Consciousness*[69] also challenged Brown's naïve interpretation as the Perennialist argument is that the experience of Nondual Pure Consciousness (Brown's 'Basis Enlightenment') or Mystical Union is the Underlying, Universal Core experience of Mysticism.

Eureka

All of this information had been pouring into my head over a period of eight or nine days since my thirtieth birthday on September 4th. I could sense that things were crystallising in the subconscious depths of my being. The answer, I felt, was coming to me. Speaking to a colleague at work, the female science graduate who had psychical experiences, I began to realise slowly that such phenomena could not be explained by simple information transmission models. Rather one had to realise that there was a distinction between our normal Space-Time realm and Transcendent realms where such limitations of Space and Time were not relevant as indicated in Daniel Brown's study with its reference to 'acausal' interactions after perceptually-constructed Space and Time were transcended. On Wednesday September 14th 1994, as I went out of my workplace to buy my lunch, the basic answer suddenly came to me as I walked down Jamestown Road towards Camden High Street. The pulsing waves of the Light were the pulses of activating energy from the brainstem Reticular Formation known as the Reticular Activating System (RAS), flowing through all of the component structures of the brain. The coherent alpha rhythm measured all over the scalp of an enlightened yogi reflected the fact that, as the self-organising process (or dissipative structure) that was the Field of Attention finally dissipated, the only major activity that remained in the brain, devoid of mental activity, was the flow of these activating waves from the brainstem RAS passing through to the scalp without interference. In fact, even if Basis Enlightenment or Mystical Union were simply a momentary experience, the yogic attainment of states verging on union where the mind had been stopped, with only a naked sense of self-agency remaining, would result in such EEG coherence as the residual mental activity would be minimal and the RAS activating waves would be passing through to the scalp largely undisturbed.

Here at last was the direct linkage of Science and Mysticism, the Physical and the Psychical/Spiritual! Energy and the Divine Light of Pure Consciousness, the 'Stuff of the Universe' in Science and the 'Essence of Reality' in Yogic Mysticism were two fundamental attributes of the One Reality. Although this answer came to me on 14th September 1994, I later noticed something that I had written in late 1993 at the time when I prepared the first draft of my prose commentary to the metaphysical sections of my *Sutra*. After re-reading parts of the book *The Holographic Paradigm* (which I first read in 1983), I had written the following in pencil on the final page of the text:

> *Although my attitude towards the mystical has transformed dramatically in the last 10 years, I am now of the inclination that moksa (or nirvana) far from being a higher state of consciousness, let alone mystical union, is in fact a rudimentary state of awareness, the primary brainwaves from which the conscious mind takes form — akin to near-death experience. What conclusions to draw from this I have yet to decide.*

Back in late 1993, I did not know that the adepts of authoritative yogic traditions could discriminate that the Light came in *waves* or *pulses*, and that *the Light constituted the background matrix for all cognition* that the *Yoga Sutra* tradition described as a *continuously vibrating energy field*. But my *moksa*/ NDE linkage to the brainstem and my electromagnetic field notions of the physical correlate of the Mind had led me towards the answer, (i.e., the "primary brainwaves") without having pressed further to clarify what was actually implied by this, (i.e., the RAS). Indeed, I had forgotten that I had even scribbled this down until about a year later.

This marginal note reiterates that, before September 1994, I was highly sceptical of Yogic claims that Enlightenment constituted some sort of 'Mystical Union' with the Cosmos. In September 1994, even after the breakthrough on the 14th, I remained largely sceptical at first in regard to the awesome metaphysical and cosmological claims made by many mystics in regard to the experience of Enlightenment. How could the dissolution of the mind processes into the activating flow of psycho-physical energy amount to an understanding of the 'Secret of Creation'. My primary interest was in confirming the Panpsychist insights that had come to me in 1983, which I viewed as a revolutionary achievement undermining the greatest intellectual construction of the West, its Materialist Metaphysics. As with the young women who were interested in Buddhism at the Channel 4 Talking Heads Club debate, I recall that a young, lanky, neo-beatnik type Englishman in our Journals department, whom I knew had an interest in Buddhism commented negatively that my 'identification' of the (physical correlate of) Divine Light with some brainwaves was very Reductionist. Obviously he felt that such an interpretation robbed Buddhism of its seeming cosmological profundity.

A young woman Physics graduate in my own department, with similar interests in Buddhism, seemed at first rather averse to my Perennialist, universal interpretation of the Light as something not unique to Buddhism. I sensed that, although having studied Physics which seeks universal underlying commonalities transcending superficial differences, she seemed to have thought that in Buddhism she had found a unique spiritual system with

Exclusivist claims to Truth. Although this Exclusivist claim is the orthodox dogma for Christians, who claim childishly that Jesus is the only Way the only Truth and the "Light", and for other Semitic religions, I suspect that a lot of Western neo-beatniks project such immature beliefs in exclusive revelation onto Buddhism. To be fair to the young woman, she quickly came to accept my view that we all have the same essential brains structures, etc., so why should Buddhist yoga, following near-identical methods to Hindu yoga, magically reveal something radically different and new. I suspect that the peer pressure from my other colleagues, most of whom had science degrees and who readily accepted my Universalist and seemingly "Reductionist" view obviously helped overcome her doubts.

Many people lack the confidence to accept new ideas however strong the evidence and the reasoning behind them. They rely upon peer pressure or guidance by some authority figure. The aforementioned middle class Cambridge graduate in Journals, who had tried to put me down erroneously thinking that I was a highly privileged public 'school-boy' commented that lots of people have suggested that Consciousness is associated with brainwaves. Again I had to correct him, pointing out that I was not making such a vague speculation. In fact Science does not even acknowledge the fact that Pure (objectless) Consciousness actually exists and I had linked this highly specific state of Consciousness with a very special and distinct set of brainwaves, the brainwaves of the activating system known to all Medical doctors. To his credit, he later gave me a copy of the 1994 special issue of *Journal of Theoretical Biology* on Mind and Matter, which he was the copyeditor and proofreader (Lewis Wolpert was one of the two main editors of this journal).

In fact one of the first people I told about my breakthrough was a Dutch female psychiatrist in Amsterdam, named Beulah McNab, who had written a book for Academic Press in 1992 which I had worked on. As she had mentioned writers such as neurologist Karl Pribram (as in *The Holographic Paradigm*) in her book, I had told her of my Panpsychist 'theory of Consciousness'. Indeed, on reading a copy of my late 1980s paper, *A Panpsychist Interpretation of Consciousness*, Beulah had tried to see if she could get it published in Holland. Holland after all was not only the home of numerous publishers but Amsterdam had been the city where Spinoza had lived. However she had not been able to help me although she had urged me not to be "lazy" and keep pressing forward. I was somewhat irked by her use of "lazy"; I was hardly lazy trying to do this philosophical work whilst in full time work and funding my own research, etc., as I have explained above.

In September 1994, I phoned Beulah and told her that I had identified the physical correlate of Pure Consciousness. Before coming to my conclusion I mentioned that I had now learnt from Mysticism and that Science was not the only means of acquiring true knowledge. Beulah agreed wholeheartedly. I then mentioned Odajnyk's *Gathering the Light* and his description of the meditation complex as a closed energy field; Beaulah had read it already. She mentioned that I ought to read Pribram's new book, which she had cited in her own book, as he also viewed the mind as being like a self-organising process in the brain's electric fields. I went on to mention Daniel Brown's study in *Transformations of Consciousness*; Beulah had also read this! She asked impatiently, "Well what is it then"? "It's the Reticular Activating System", I replied. She then replied, "Of course! You are a genius". Then, after I told her that I was writing a book, she said she would love to see a copy. [N6] She added, "Millions of people will think you are mad but *I know that you are right*!"

My 'ReAwakening' or 'Conversion' Transformation

In the days following 14th September, I experienced something akin to a mild nervous breakdown. I told people that my cognitive structures were reorganising, interfering with normal mental processes. I had already experienced a nervous breakdown in March 1993, a negative experience during which I had felt a sort of unstoppable spinning of thoughts in my head. That 1993 experience, due to the cynical promotions system at work, resembled this pleasant experience as both were induced by my facing up to a reality which so contradicted my largely innocent view of worldly affairs. The 1993 breakdown led to a drastic reappraisal of my worldly situation and my approach to the problems I faced had been permanently transformed as I focused single-mindedly upon my writing. The September 1994 experience was far more pleasant, slowing my memory recall and other functions a little. As in 1993, I was again 'waking up' to a new understanding, this time of the metaphysical problems I had been grappling with which had perplexed me for years.

It was dawning upon me that the so-called 'Perennial Philosophy', towards which I had remained largely sceptical was not as preposterous as it first appeared even though it made seemingly incredible, metaphysical and cosmological claims on the basis of phenomenological knowledge. I was intuiting that there was far more to it than met the eye. Indeed, I sensed that it was, in its various forms, stating fundamental truths which were only now beginning to make sense to me; now that I had begun to realise what Yoga really was. How ignorant and arrogant I had been to dismiss many of the claims of mystics in the past, confident that my scientific knowledge was vastly superior to this 'primitive nonsense' which I had perceived falsely to be irrational. How foolish I felt I had been not to have seen these things before, how totally and utterly naïve and stupid I had been in the past. I had been transfigured. In 2006 I read about William James' psychological description of the religious "conversion":

> *Conversion for James then is the psychological reorganisation of a person's personality structure, in which the "hot place in man's consciousness, the group of ideas to which he devotes himself, and from which he works... [i.e.,] the habitual centre of his personal energy" becomes religious in nature;*
>
> — G. William Barnard [70]

Merrell-Wolff referred to "unconscious frameworks" within which our consciousness operates. If a framework is challenged powerful emotions are aroused. Frameworks possess people with the nature of *conviction*. Transcending these frameworks is as difficult as or analogous to a 'Dying process' that precedes a 'new Birth'[71].

In one of his books which J.H.M. Whiteman had sent to me in 1999, Whiteman stated that, in the Yoga Sutras, the Sanskrit term *jati* (literally 'birth') is a Yogic technical term referring not to a new parturition (birth of a physical body from the womb) but a new personality phase in the mind. This notion of 'rebirth' had created much confusion in regard to notions of *karma*[72]. In 2006, I found this view confirmed by Peter Harvey in regard to early Buddhist concepts of personality and Self. *Jati* occurs not only at start of life but also at the start of each perceptual cycle. The Buddhist texts refer to the repeated 'birth' of the personality-factors as part of the ongoing process of Perception[73]. This Buddhist view ties in with my 1980s arguments about Self-Continuity or Personal Identity through Time; during Dreamless sleep, the Mind or World-Model Field is annihilated but is recreated upon awakening and has access to the same life history memory and so retains identity with previous manifestations. The point here however is that my September 1994 'breakdown' and cognitive transformation (or 'reawakening' experience) resembled somewhat the traditional 'conversion' experience as described by James. Furthermore, although Buddhist texts refer to each new perceptual cycle as a 'birth', the religious 'born again' experience should involve such a transformation of the personal 'centre'. However, the eradication of habitual patterns of personality structure in Yoga or in Evangelical practise can also induce so-called 'deautomatisation' of perception leading to each percept feeling as if novel, experienced for the first time, as if one is 'born again'. My 'reawakening' was not such a drastic eradication of habituated perceptual filters leading to such a –'Morning has broken, like the first morning'– deautomatisation, rather it was a re-patterning of my once separate compartmentalised conceptual frameworks, removing the boundaries between them so to allow me to begin to comprehend the world as a unitary whole.

Along with this cognitive restructuring, the breakthrough of September 14th 1994 brought me a sense of fulfilment. All my life, it had seemed as if things were terribly wrong in some deep sense. Everything seemed like a waste of time and of my potential. Whatever little things I was trying to do to try to pull me out of the mess life had created for me was just tinkering with the complex problems, failing to address the underlying sense of dissatisfaction with my lot. Life, and my sense of alienation from this society captivated by celebrities, consumerism, etc., seemed to keep forcing me into a rather hermit-like isolation which I had not wanted but was unable to do anything about. It seemed to me that only something drastically life-changing such as winning a lottery jackpot could rescue me from this nightmare. Something deep within me was driving me to pursue this seemingly forlorn ambition of tackling deep metaphysical questions which did not bring me any material benefit although I was still suffering from the legacy of relative poverty of my upbringing. In spite of outstanding qualifications and natural ability that had impressed my school-friends from upper middle class backgrounds, teachers, philosophers, university professors, editors-in-chief, etc., I had been unable to make any progress in my formal career, remaining but a lowly clerk.

I recall the comments in 1993, from the Managing Director of a scientific illustration company called Oxford Illustrators which redrew all the artwork for our Journal department. He was a tall, jovial ruddy-faced Englishman in his fifties with a gruff voice who used to visit our Journals department each week and I would open a security door for him. I would tease him that he only bought cakes for the Journals department as his (rather expensive) company monopolised artwork for the money-making journals. Although this man hardly knew me except for short witty conversations as he passed me by, he asked me one day, within earshot of my colleagues, "Sutapas what are you doing here? You're much too good for this". I showed him a copy of the 1993 *Harpers and Queen* magazine in which I was presented as the cleverest boy in a good school, my turning down an Oxford scholarship, etc., and referred to my 500 verse *Sutra* etc. The MD patted me on the back and replied along the lines; I knew you were much better than this.

The long-serving woman who helped train new staff in our department once asked me what I was going to become in the sense that you are obviously going to become something out of the ordinary. Over the years she had witnessed the intellect, creativity, insight, charisma, the effect on women, the irrepressible personality which took the blows and bounced back etc. Obviously, although I had not made it career-wise, she could sense that I was destined for things much greater than this little office. At home my mother never saw this extraverted side of my personality, my public persona. My failure to get a good career after such promising academic achievement obviously hurt my mother who must have had high hopes and who later went to her death, after quite terrible suffering in 2004-2005 never really appreciating the significance of my philosophical writing. A quatrain in my *Sutra* written in 1991, summed up my feeling of alienation (*varnadharma* is the Sanskrit for the 'caste order' but *varna* literally meant "colour" as the high caste Aryans were lighter-skinned hence the parallel with British society).

Cast out by modern varnadharma
Cast out as too true to his caste
This brahman true born of pariahs
Misfit, misplaced and so miscast

Following the breakthrough in 1994 it seemed as if these ordeals which I had had to face up to all of my life were meant to be, for they were leading me away from wasting my life pursuing normal ambitions and leading me towards my true vocation. All the status symbols of normal worldly achievement which I thought that I would have been happy with when, in my darkest hours, they seemed impossible to attain, given the hidden forces conspiring against me, now seemed trivial and ordinary, devoid of any deep satisfaction, of any real sense of fulfilment. In 2012 I read in Joseph Campbell's *Transformations of Myth through Time* that in the medieval European Grail myths, the 'Wasteland' (as also used by T.S. Eliot as the title for his famous poem) was the preliminary theme to which the 'Holy Grail' is the answer. The Holy Grail is that Fountain in the Centre of the Universe, and also in each of our hearts, from which the energies of Eternity pour into the world of Time. The Grail is a symbol of the highest spiritual fulfilment, of realising the Divinity within us. The Wasteland represents people who live the life society pressurises them to follow, an inauthentic life[74].

Early in 1994 I had again been in deep crisis seeing no way out of my entrapment. The deep depression that ensued seemed to have triggered something in the deeper realms of my being because now, in September 1994, only a few months later I had made a breakthrough which, although attained at remarkable speed with lots of intuitive leaps and very little background knowledge, had opened up the way for me to start finding my real role in the world. I realised the significance of what I had done even if those around me didn't fully comprehend it. For thousands of years the supposedly greatest minds in human history had largely speculated about the central questions of Philosophy, the nature and significance of the Mystical Union and, in more recently in the modern West, the question of the relationship between Consciousness and the Physical World (misleadingly called the 'Mind/Body Problem'). Whilst everyone before had just speculated upon such matters I had actually identified the 'direct' physical correlate, (i.e., the actual process directly correlated with the phenomenon, not just an associated factor) of the central element of all Mysticism and Spirituality, the Divine Light of Pure Consciousness, with a physical process which was well-established; the Reticular Activating System was known to all Medics due to its role in Brain Death!

Thus with this one simple stroke, I could cast aside all the speculations of three thousand years of Indo-European philosophy and begin to resolve clearly both the question of the Mystical Union (which lies at the centre of all Indian philosophy) and also the problem of the Ontological Status of Consciousness which is the central and most controversial problem in modern Western philosophy. Although numerous issues still arose following my linkage, the fact was that I had provided an indisputable solid footing from which such issues could now be tackled whereas previously there had been just a quagmire of seemingly contradictory paradoxes and confusion. Furthermore, the Divine Light was the central element of all Spirituality, Eastern Philosophy and of the great world religions; it was the 'Godhead' itself (the wellspring or fountainhead of Divinity). Thus my identification of its 'direct' physical correlate provides the basis of the future Universal Spirituality for the globe, which shall in due course, undermine and make redundant all the false Materialistic and Anthropomorphic mythologies associated with the world's organised religions which have played such a major role in the last 1700 years of history since Constantine. Of lesser temporal significance, the modern Western metaphysics of Scientific Materialism has become the globally dominant metaphysical world-view in the last two to three centuries with the rise of Science and European global hegemony. By showing that Pure Consciousness was correlated directly with the primary energy flow through the brain, a flow of energy fundamentally the same as that underlying everything else in the universe, I had undermined the Scientific Materialist metaphysics.

I remember telling a middle aged Jewish colleague, who worked in Journals and took an interest in my work due to his own interests in Mysticism[N7], that I had to pinch myself to believe this was really happening given all the mystical synchronicities that had surrounded me and the implications of my uncovering of the first clear link between the Psychical or Spiritual and the Physical realms. As stated above, with the transformation of my cognitive structures, it was dawning upon me that the Perennial Philosophy, with its assertions that the physical universe arose from a transcendental realm grounded in the Ultimate Being of Pure Consciousness was in fact correct. The snippets of knowledge drawn from Daniel Brown's study regarding the Time/Space Matrix of Perception and underlying holistic causal connections, etc., were making me realise that my dismissal of paranormal psychic phenomena had been based upon my false Scientific Materialist indoctrination.

I wondered out loud why others had not seen this before, especially someone like the New Age guru Ken Wilber who had access to the same information. I was to discover that, given his fundamental misunderstandings and confusion, such as his mistaken claim that the "Higher Planes" are emergent rather than being the more fundamental levels of being, he had claimed naively that it was impossible to integrate Science and Mysticism. He had even asserted that we would never find a "missing link" between these two realms although I had done just that! Wilber's ever-changing "models" of spiritual development as in the first chapter of *Transformations of Consciousness* were like modern Ptolemaic epicycles (*see Ch. 6*). Yet Wilber's works had been hyped up as the authoritative view by Western New Agers including the Institute of Noetic Sciences which claimed to investigate the scientific basis of Mysticism and Spirituality and the UK-based Scientific and Medical Network. In a sense I was grateful that, in worshipping Wilber as if he was some incredible genius, these New Age organisations had led others astray! As I wrote in O/OM, I was grateful that I had remained largely ignorant of such misleading New Age myths.

As Daniel Brown had stated, Yoga led to the 'Deconstruction of Perception' and it was dawning upon me that in "Higher Planes", the yogi perceived the deeper, fine (smaller scale) structure of Reality which paralleled modern Physics' understanding of deeper, fine structural levels of the 'Physical Universe'. Thus I began to see how it was possible to integrate Science and Mysticism through the understanding that Yoga allowed one to access and "perceive" deeper, fine-structural levels of the external world. I was determined to find out as much as I could about these bigger, deeper issues flowing from my identification of the Divine Light. Thus the book I had been writing, which was supposed to have been simply a discussion of the philosophical issues concentrated into my aphoristic quatrains or *Sutra*, was to grow into what was in effect two books, which I entitled *The Oneness/Otherness Mystery: Beginning the Synthesis of Science and Mysticism* (the publisher dropped the words "Beginning the") including much new material researched and written between 1994 tc 1997 concerning the integration of Science and Mysticism. It was during these days immediately following my breakthrough that, one day during my lunch hour, I was accosted by the Personnel Director as we returned to the company building. She enquired if I had finished my writing yet, seeming to imply, perhaps to her credit, that had I given up such unrealistic ambitions, she could start considering how to get me promoted into Editorial, after all nearly every supposedly open vacancy was fixed in advance. However, I responded by asking her if she knew what the Divine

Light was. She responded that she did, especially when I pointed out that it was the central element of all Mysticism, Eastern philosophy and all true Spirituality, also known as the *Atman*, Buddha Nature, Godhead etc. Well I have identified what it is in the brain, I responded, thus I am going to become historically famous.

References

1. Cvitanovich, Frank (Director) (1993) *The Making of a Modern Mystic* (Documentary Film), First Run Features.
2. Katz, Stephen, T. (Editor) (1983) *Mysticism and Religious Traditions*, Oxford University Press.
3. Eadie, Betty J. (1994) *Embraced by the Light*, BCA with Harper Collins.
4. Morse, Melvin "Foreword" to Betty J. Eadie (1994) *Embraced by the Light*, BCA with Harper Collins.
5. Morse, Melvyn with Perry, Paul (1991) *Closer to the Light: Learning from the Near-Death Experiences of Children*, Souvenir Press.
6. Odajnyk, V. Walter (1993) *Gathering the Light: A Psychology of Meditation*, Shambhala Publications.
7. Katz, Stephen, T. (Editor) (1983) *ibid.*
8. Katz, Stephen, T. "The 'Conservative' Character of Mystical Experience." In Stephen T. Katz (Editor) (1983) *Mysticism and Religious Traditions*, Oxford University Press.
9. Forman, K.C. (Editor) (1990) *The Problem of Pure Consciousness: Mysticism and Philosophy*, Oxford University Press.
10. Forman, Robert, K.C. (1999) *Mysticism, Mind, Consciousness*, State University of New York Press.
11. Westphal, Kenneth R. (2004) *Kant's Transcendental Proof of Realism*, Cambridge University Press.
12. Wallace, B. Alan "Introduction: Buddhism and Science Breaking Down the Barriers". In B. Alan Wallace (Editor) (2003) *Buddhism and Science: Breaking New Ground,* Columbia University Press.
13. Forman, Robert, K.C. (1999) *ibid.*
14. King, Richard (1999) *Orientalism and Religion: Postcolonial Theory, India and 'The Mystic East'*, Routledge.
15. Gimello, Robert, M. "Mysticism in Its Contexts". In Stephen T. Katz, (Editor) (1983) *Mysticism and Religious Traditions*, Oxford University Press.
16. Gimello, Robert, M. (1983) *ibid.*
17. Hunt, Harry T. (1995) *On the Nature of Consciousness: Cognitive, Phenomenological, and Transpersonal Perspectives*, Yale University Press.
18. Wallace, B. Alan (Editor) (2003) *Buddhism and Science: Breaking New Ground,* Columbia University Press.
19. King, Richard (1999) *ibid.*
20. Guenther, Herbert V. (1989) *From Reductionism to Creativity:rDzogs-chen and the New Science of Mind,* Shambhala Publications.
21. Guenther, Herbert V. (1989) *ibid.*

22. Wallace, B. Alan (Editor) (2003) *ibid.*
23. Dallmayr, Fred (1996) *Beyond Orientalism: Essays on Cross-Cultural Encounter*, State University of New York Press.
24. Smith, John, E. "William James's Account of Mysticism: A Critical Appraisal". In Stephen T. Katz (Editor) (1983) *Mysticism and Religious Traditions*, Oxford University Press.
25. Ibid.
26. Ibid.
27. Morse, Melvyn with Perry, Paul (1991) *ibid.*
28. Greyson, Bruce "Near-Death Experiences". In Etzel Cardeña, Steven jay Lynn, and Stanley Krippner (Editors) (2000) *Varieties of Anamalous Experience: Examining the Scientific Evidence*, American Psychological Association.
29. Potter David, Dalai Lama *et al.* "Dialogue". In Daniel Goleman and Robert A.F. Thurman (Editors) (1991) *MindScience:An East-West Dialogue (The Harvard Mind Science Symposium)*, Wisdom Books.
30. Williams, Rowan (Archbishop of Canterbury) *The Guardian* (Newspaper, London) 14th October 2007.
31. Williams, Rowan (Archbishop of Canterbury) *Observer* (Newspaper, London) 15th October 2007.
32. Morse, Melvyn with Perry, Paul (1991) *ibid.*
33. Ibid.
34. Ibid.
35. Ibid.
36. Talbot, Michael (1991) *The Holographic Universe*, Harper Collins.
37. Morse, Melvyn with Perry, Paul (1991) *ibid.*
38. Morse, Melvyn with Perry, Paul (1991) *ibid.*
39. Combs, Allan and Holland, Mark (1990) *Synchronicity: Science, Myth and the Trickster*, Paragon House.
40. Orme-Johnson, D.W. (1977) Higher states of consciousness: EEG coherence, creativity and experience of the siddhis. *Electroencephalography and Clinical Neurophysiology* (Journal), Vol. 4, p. 581.
41. Blackmore, Susan (1991) "Is meditation good for you". *New Scientist* (Magazine) 6th July.
42. Ritchie, Jean (1992) *Inside the Supernatural: An Investigation into the Paranormal*, Fontana.
43. Blackmore, Susan (1991) *ibid.*
44. Fenwick, Peter "Meditation and the EEG". In Michael A. West (Editor) (1987) *The Psychology of Meditation*, Oxford University Press.
45. West, Michael, A. "Traditional and psychological perspectives on meditation". In Michael A. West (Editor) (1987) *The Psychology of Meditation*, Oxford University Press.
46. Taylor, Eugene "Radical Empiricism and the Conduct of Research". In Willis Harman with Jane Clark (Editors) (1994) *New Metaphysical Foundations of Modern Science*, Institute of Noetic Sciences.

47. Combs, Allan and Holland, Mark (1990) *ibid.*
48. Rohrbaugh, John, W, Parasuraman, Raja and Johnson, Ray (Editors) (1990) *Event-Related Brain Potentials: Basic Issues and Applications*, Oxford University Press.
49. Odajnyk, V. Walter (1993) *ibid.*
50. Odajnyk, V. Walter (1993) *ibid.*
51. Storr, Anthony (Editor) (1983) *Jung: Selected Writings*, Fontana.
52. Odajnyk, V. Walter (1993) *ibid.*
53. Ibid.
54. Ibid.
55. Ibid.
56. Coomaraswamy, Ananda K. (1943) *Hinduism and Buddhism* (New Revised Edition, 1999), Indira Gandhi National Centre for Arts and Manohar.
57. Odajnyk, V. Walter (1993) *ibid.*
58. King, Richard (1999) *ibid.*
59. Bridgeman, Jacqueline H. "Preface". To Jacqueline H. Bridgeman (Editor) (1992) *Huxley and God: Essays*, Harper Collins.
60. Wilber, Ken, Engler, Jack and Brown, Daniel P. (Editors) (1986) *Transformations of Consciousness: Conventional and Contemplative Perspectives on Development*, Shambhala Publications.
61. Goleman, Daniel and Thurman, Robert A.F. (Editors) (1991) *MindScience: An East-West Dialogue (The Harvard Mind Science Symposium)*, Wisdom Books.
62. Wilber, Ken (Editor) (1982) *The Holographic Paradigm and Other Paradoxes: Exploring the Leading Edge of Science*, Shambhala Publications.
63. Brown, Daniel P. "The Stages of Meditation in Cross-Cultural Perspective". In Ken Wilber, Jack Engler and Daniel P. Brown (Editors) (1986) *Transformations of Consciousness: Conventional and Contemplative Perspectives on Development*, Shambhala Publications.
64. Brown, Daniel P. (1986) *ibid.*
65. Bruzina, Ronald (2004) *Edmund Husserl and Eugen Fink: Beginnings and Ends in Phenomenology 1928-1938*, Yale University Press.
66. Merrell-Wolff, Franklin (1995) *Transformations in Consciousness: The Metaphysics and Epistemology* (Containing His *Introceptualism*), State University of New York Press.
67. Brown, Daniel P. (1986) *ibid.*
68. Brown, Daniel P. (1986) *ibid.*
69. Forman, K.C. (Editor) (1990) *ibid.*
70. Barnard, G. William (1997) *Exploring Unseen Worlds: William James and the Philosophy of Mysticism*, State University of New York Press.
71. Merrell-Wolff, Franklin (1995) *ibid.*
72. Whiteman, J.H. Michael (1993) *Aphorisms on Spiritual Method: the "Yoga Sutras of Patanjali" in the light of mystical experience*, Colin Smythe.
73. Harvey, Peter (1995) *The Selfless Mind: Personality, Consciousness and Nirvana in Early Buddhism*, Curzon Press.
74. Campbell, Joseph (1990) *Transformations of Myth through Time*, Harper and Row.

Notes to Chapters

Notes to Chapter 1

Note 1

This reminded me of the concern voiced by the famous physicist Enrico Fermi in 1945 that testing of the world's first atom bomb might ignite the atmosphere, leading to a chain reaction that would kill all life on Earth.

Note 2

Indian ideas of the vastness of Time (historical and cosmological) played key roles in Renaissance challenges to Biblical mythology regarding the age of the Earth and Biblical and Greek myths of a universe extending only as far as Neptune (*see* W. Anderson, *The Face of Glory*, Bloomsbury, 1996). During the Age of Reason, Indian notions of progressive reincarnation through ever more complex forms played a key role in the origin of the notion of Biological Evolution in France (*see* R. Schwab, *The Oriental Renaissance*, Columbia U.P., 1984). Hindu tolerance of other religions with its lack of religious persecution and violence amazed Europeans and deeply influenced the new Religious Tolerance in early modern Europe (*see* G. Sorman, *The Genius of India*, MacMillan India, 2001).

Note 3

Joseph Campbell wrote in his *Transformations of Myth through Time* (Harper and Row, 1990) that in Ficino's translation of *Corpus Hermeticum* the symbols of the Christian cult which went back to the pre-Christian Classical period were re-interpreted in terms of Hermetic rather than Mosaic mythology. Whereas the Mosaic interpretation is Literal, the Hermetic interpretation is Symbolic.

Note 4

The 18th Century Bengali *sakta* poet Ramprasad Sen, following earlier precedents in the Indian tradition, wrote of the difference between learning of the sweetness of sugar and actually tasting it as a metaphor for spiritual experience (*see* A.P. Sen, *Swami Vivekananda*, Oxford U.P. India, 2000).This was obviously long before the Sallie King to whom Richard King attributes the same distinction, between indirect knowledge and actual experience, in regard to the taste of coffee (*see* R. King, *Orientalism and Religion*, Routledge, 1999).

Note 5

I do not accept the Eurocentric label of 'First World War' for the 1914 –18 European conflict which was restricted primarily to Europe with some minor secondary theatres such as Arabia.

Note 6

In 2012 the *Sunday Telegraph* revealed that Dawkins is descended from a slave-owner Henry Dawkins who owned over 1,000 slaves on his Jamaican sugar plantation. The Dawkins' family estate was bought with the proceeds of such forced labour. In 2013 research by historians at University College London showed that Britain's slave-owners received the equivalent of £16.5 billion (in today's money) compensation from the taxpayer after the British abolished slavery in the Caribbean, Mauritius and the Cape (but not in East India Company territories). Among these slave-owner families were the ancestors of British PM David Cameron. The ex-slaves of course got no compensation and were little better off. The British also developed new forms of indentured servitude. Many victims of the 1877 Madras famine were forced by British-inflicted starvation to become indentured labourers (*see* Mike Davis, *Late Victorian Holocausts*, 2001). Other poor and illiterate Indians were often tricked into indentured servitude on the brutal Tea plantations in Assam where the notorious 'Slave Laws' allowing brutal plantation owners to arrest 'coolies' trying to escape or trying to reach a police station persisted into the 20th Century (*see* E. Kolsky, *Colonial Justice in British India*, Cambridge U.P., 2010). In the 1860s, efforts to import Indian indentured labourers to Queensland, Australia were blocked by the Colonial and India Offices. This led to incidents such as the deliberate kidnapping and cold-blooded murder of natives of New Guineau by the British merchant ship *Hopeful* in 1884 seeking 'labourers' for Queensland sugar plantations (*see* M.J Wiener, *An Empire on Trial,* Cambridge U.P., 2009). The 1833 'Abolition' was of course largely due to the efforts of Christian Evangelist William Wilberforce.

Note 7

The brainstem Reticular Formation was widely known as the only brain centre whose loss of function eliminates all forms of Consciousness. More recently the thalamic intralaminar nucleus (ILN) closely associated with the brainstem Reticular Formation has also been discovered to be essential. This does not affect my Reticular Activating System brainwave correlation of Pure Consciousness. Input to the two (bilateral thalamic) IL-nuclei include a large fraction of the ascending brainstem Reticular Formation so the ILN appears to be part of the same basic brainstem-thalamic system (*see* Joseph E. Bogen, "Locating the Subjectivity Pump: The Thalamic Intralaminar Nuclei". In Hameroff *et al.* (Editors), *Toward a Science of Consciousness II*, MIT Press, 1998).

Notes to Chapter 2

Note 1

These Christian Vikings from Kiev clashed with the Central Asian Hunnic-Turkic Khazars who had previously settled in the Caucasus and had converted to Judaism in the 9th Century *c.e.* These (non-Semitic) Jewish Khazars were forced Westward by the 13th Century Mongol invasion and later would become the Yiddish-speaking Ashkenazi Jews including the early Zionists who refused to assimilate into modern secular European culture. This led to the second religiously-motivated European occupation of Palestine by these Ashkenazi Zionists who are not the real descendants of Biblical Judaeans and Israelites (*see* Shlomo Sand *The Invention of the Jewish People*, Verso, 2009 *and* Note 5 to Chapter 3 *below*). The Arabs view the Zionist occupation of Palestine as a new Western 'Crusader state'. I would add that the imperialist West (and the European Stalin) forced non-European Palestinians to pay the price for Europe's collective 'guilt complex' relating to historic European Christian persecution of Jews. Prior to the Nazi genocide of Jews, Gypsies, etc., the Zionist project was backed by British imperialists who had plans for a European Jewish colony in Palestine serving the imperialist cause by protecting the Suez Canal. After the collapse of British power, the Zionists have presented themselves as supposedly serving US imperialist interests although many would argue that they have damaged the USA's real long-term interests through their racist policies toward Palestinian natives and repeated aggression against neighbouring states.

Note 2

That Winston Churchill (WC) was a White Supremacist and Anglo-Saxon Supremacist is clear from Richard Toye's *Churchill's Empire* (MacMillan 2010). British scholar Toye still skips over Churchill's criminal responsibility for the Bengal Holocaust (*see Note 3*) with only a passing reference thus not giving a true indication of the consequences of Churchill's racism. Toye says that Churchill's biographers have tended to present his racism as typical of a Victorian British mindset. But not all Victorians where White Supremacists and Churchill's racism toward Indians and other Non-Europeans persisted into the mid-20th Century when he was out-of-step even with the Tory Party on eventual Indian Independence. In his prologue, Toye refers to Churchill's "unashamed belief in **white superiority**" (*emphasis mine*). As Madhushrie Mukerjee stresses in her *Churchill's Secret War: The British Empire and the Ravaging of India during World War II* (Basic Books, 2010) WC was obsessed with India as Britain's great power status was dependent on exploiting India and, according to WC, the livelihoods and Food Security of Britain's Working Classes depended on British control of India (this shows that WC understood that India's political and economic captivity enriched Britain at India's expense). Mukerjee points out that during the war, as PM, WC wanted to renege on Britain's $2bn war debt to India (the 2nd largest after that to the USA) spouting his usual hypocritical rhetoric of how India was doing nothing whilst benevolent Britain was sacrificing so much to 'protect' India. Wavell retorted that it was Indian troops that had actually saved the British Empire in the Middle East. Furthermore, India had been dragged into Britain's conflict by the Viceroy without consulting any Indian leader! *Contra* historical myths, WC devoted the 1930s primarily to campaigning as an Independent against Indian Independence, to keep India enslaved and not campaigning against Fascism. Indeed, he was enthusiastic toward Fascism until he realised that it threatened British imperial interests. Mukerjee's index has 14 entries for WC's "**white superiority**" views (*emphasis mine*) During the 1939-45 war, any mention of India by more Liberal Brits, Americans or by Stalin would trigger frenzied fits of rage in WC verging on insanity. His vicious racism towards Indians, especially Hindus included his stating in 1942, "I hate Indians, a beastly people with a beastly religion". Both Toye and Mukerjee mention that Tory India Secretary Leopold Amery *compared WC to Hitler in regard to his racial hatred towards India and his callous lack of concern for the death of millions of Indians* (*emphasis mine*). He was also reported to have stated that, if Bomber Harris could spare the planes, he (WC) would bomb all the Hindus to death. Toye quotes WC saying "I hate people with slitty eyes and pig-tails" and mentions the brutal British reaction to Gandhi's Quit India movement in which thousands of Indians were killed by British warplanes strafing them with machine-guns. Contrast this to the post-war Anglo-American propaganda which makes out that only the Nazis strafed unarmed civilians with gunfire from the air. Mukerjee mentions how this strafing of Indians from the air also occurred after two white airmen were killed. Both Toye and Mukerjee mention how in 1943 US Vice-President Wallace revealed WC's notions of White Superiority in WC's opposition to including Latin Americans in a passport-free zone. WC was opposed to racial mixing. Why apologise for Anglo-Saxon superiority, WC responded, after Wallace told him that his plans for post-war Anglo-Saxon world domination were offensive to many Americans as well as to other nations. In his *An Empire on Trial* (Cambridge U.P., 2009) M.J. Wiener cites Ranajit Guha in regard to the "self-satisfied English attitude" of the supposed 'radical' (Marxist) historian E.P. Thompson who wrote of the English notion of the 'Rule of Law' as of universal significance. Thompson came from a Colonial background; his father was a Liberal Christian Missionary in India. As I have noted elsewhere, Christian Missionaries were often the champions of Colonialism and, even today, peddle British myths demonising native Indian traditions and the supposed 'Eternal Poverty of India' which the British supposedly tried to alleviate. *Contra* British boasts of bringing the Rule of Law (Equality under the Law was supposedly the 'Gospel of the English'), Apartheid-like privileges for Europeans in criminal cases allowing Whites to get away with beating, raping, torturing and murdering Indians existed in British India right up until Independence. As Elizabeth Kolsky stresses in her *Colonial Justice in British India: White Violence and the Rule of Law* (Cambridge U.P. , 2010), *contra* the myths of Britain holding India peacefully with just a handful of White officials, it was the everyday brutality of 'White Violence' towards Indians in the knowledge that there would be no punishment along with a huge White army of occupation of around 70,000 after 1857 that really maintained British Rule! Richard Gott tells us in *Britain's Empire* (Verso, 2011) how British officers kept the Indian *sepoys* (mercenaries) on-side with terror including the infamous 'cannonading' which was practised on Indians long before 1857. In 1857 it was the news of the Brits disarming and slaughtering 'non-mutineer' Indian troops in some garrisons which inevitably encouraged *sepoys* elsewhere to join the revolt against the discriminatory Brits.

Note 3

Recent research by Dr. Sanjoy Bhattacharya of University College London at the Wellcome Foundation, London suggests that the actual death toll of the British-inflicted artificial famine of 1942-3 known as the 'Bengal Holocaust' (it was labelled such in an Indian book in 1944) was 6-7 million. Although there was a cyclone in late 1942, as ever, the cause of the famine was political. The British inflicted the Nazi-like War Crime of Collective Punishment on Bengal given its radical support for Independence (Indian National Army leader Subhas Bose was from Bengal). The British hoarded ('stockpiled') rice for their own purposes and did not allow foodgrains from the rest of India, where there was a surplus, to enter Bengal. The Brits censored news of the famine for a year presenting actual mortality rates of 40,000 a week as just 1,000 a week. They also destroyed the entire print run of a Bengali pamphlet on the famine called *Hungry Bengal*. When censorship was finally broken in 1943 and the US, Canada, Australia and even Japan offered food aid to Bengal, Indian-hating racist Winston Churchill got his cronies to lie that there was no shipping available to take the Food Aid when in fact there was a glut of spare merchant shipping at the time (this is also a War Crime). Churchill wanted to punish Bengal as the homeland of Subhas Bose and punish India for daring to seek Independence. White Supremacist Churchill diverted food shipments which could have gone to Bengal to Britain to stockpile food so that Britain could manipulate world food prices after the war. He also wanted to stockpile food for a planned invasion of Greece to feed White Greeks and even for White Italians (who had been enemies). In 1941 the Nazis had allowed the Red Cross to give aid to famine victims in occupied Greece. Churchill and his cronies even lied to potential donor countries that Bengalis could not digest wheat and that Bengalis would rather starve than eat wheat (when wheat bread was a staple part of the Bengali diet). In contrast the diet of Working Class Brits actually improved during wartime due to rationing which included jam and sweets. Other luxury foods were placed under price-controls to prevent speculation. Price control and rationing was not practised in Bengal so that, combined with British exporting and hoarding grain, a certain amount of hoarding by Bengali merchants exacerbated the famine (*See* Mukerjee's *Churchill's Secret War*). This was the last of around 37 such famines inflicted on India by the British. In 1877 Cornelius Walford published a paper in the *Journal of Statistics* showing that there had been around 30 famines in 120 years in British-occupied Indian territories. In stark contrast there had only about 17 serious famines in India in the previous two thousand years of recorded history. The reason for India becoming a land of famines under the Brits was because Indian rulers had acted to prevent and alleviate suffering whereas the Brits pursued Social Darwinist, 'Let Them Starve policy' (*see*

Mike Davis *Late Victorian Holocausts*, Verso, 2001 and Nick Robins *The Corporation that Changed the World,* Pluto Press, 2006). These facts are little known in Britain where Winston Churchill was voted the 'Greatest Ever Briton' by BBC TV viewers. As far as I am aware BBC TV has not once mentioned the Bengal (Famine) Holocaust.

Note 4

Hence Cyrus is hailed as the Messiah Koresh. Contrary to popular myths of Judaean Exile, only the Judaean ruling elite (aristocracy and priesthood) were exiled to Babylon by Nebuchadnazzer. When Cyrus allowed the Judaean elite to return, the vast majority chose to stay in wealthy Babylon. These non-Zionist Iraqi Jews only returned to Palestine in the 1950s after the USA and the Zionists put pressure on the Iraqi government to deport them against their will in order to try to justify the Zionist colonisation of Palestine by the non-Semitic Eastern European Ashkenazi Jews, descended from the medieval Hunnic Khazar converts to Judaism. In fact, the oft-repeated story of the forced exile of the entire Judaean population in 70 *c.e.* is quite clearly a myth given the Judaean Revolts against Rome in the 2nd Century. It is true that Rome took some Judaeans as slaves and they helped build the Coliseum. The myth of mass exile was invented by Medieval Christians to explain the presence of Jews in Europe after it had long been forgotten that Judaism had been a proselytising religion before Constantine forbade it. Most Jews always lived outside of tiny Judaea (*see* J. Rose *The Myths of Zionism*, Pluto Press, 2004 and S. Sand *The Invention of the Jewish People*, Verso, 2009).

Note 5

Einstein's famous mass/energy equivalence is not, in itself, as revolutionary as the mainstream historians of Science present it. The Brahmanic metaphysics had understood matter to be the product of the densification of the energetic vibrations of the *Akasa* for millennia. Vivekananda had apparently suggested to Nikola Tesla that the latter try to prove the energetic basis of matter before 1905 (*see* J. Dobson *Cosmic Beginnings and Human Ends*, Open Court, 1995). Einstein's $e=mc^2$ equation is in fact isomorphic to Newton's $f=ma$ as a velocity squared is an acceleration (i.e., $f=ma$ can be written as $f=mv^2$ which has the same form as $e=mc^2$). Forces are now treated as less dense forms of energy than matter although hypothetical subatomic nuclear particles such as gluons are hardly distinguishable from the associated forces. However, Einstein's exact quantification of the relationship and his linkage to the speed of light did of course have previously unimagined implications in regard to the development of nuclear energy and nuclear weapons technology.

Note 6

Many ideas were attributed to Pythagoras by the later Pythagoreans including the so-called Pythagoras's Theorem the formal presentation which first appeared in Euclid, 500 years after Pythagoras, and was first attributed to Pythagoras by Cicero in 50*b.c.e.* The so-called Pythagorean triplets associated with this theorem about right-angled triangles (e.g. 3, 4 and 5) were known to Ancient Egyptians in 2,000 *b.c.e.* or about one and one half millennia before Pythagoras (*see* S. Goonatilake *Toward a Global Science*, Indiana U.P., 1998).

Note 7

We shall see later more evidence that Yahweh is merely a tribal war-god associated with mystical arousal of the Amygdala and not a personification of Divine Light.

Note 8

Another famous French Orientalist Sylvain Levi also asserted that Christianity and NeoPlatonism must have arisen in the Middle East out of Indian influence (R. Schwab, *The Oriental Renaissance*, Columbia U.P., 1984). Scholars have also suggested that the Theraputae, associated with the Essenes, was a name derived from *Theravada* (*see* S. Radhakrishnan *Eastern Religions and Western Thought*, Oxford U.P., 1940; G. Sorman *The Genius of India*, MacMillan India, 2001).

Notes to Chapter 3

Note 1

Jesus obviously encouraged his followers to live in 'socialistic' communities based on egalitarianism, sharing one's resources, charity, caring for the poor, the needy and loving thy neighbour. Many of the Socialist organisations in the West arose out of earlier Christian Socialist movements. Thus it is amusing to hear right-wing US Republicans, claiming to be 'Christians' whilst demonising Socialism and any policies aimed at helping the poor and needy and demonising Socialist countries as 'evil'. What would Jesus have done?

Note 2

Alongside the male deity Mithra, worshipped by males, the Romans also worshipped the Phrygian deity Cybele known also as *Magna Mater* or Great Mother. Emperor Augustus made Cybele the chief deity of Rome and her temple stood at the site upon which now stands the medieval Basilica of St Peter in the Vatican.

Note 3

Sorman says in his *Genius of India* that Alexander's Greeks in Taxila depicted Buddha as emaciated and near-to-death. These images travelled toward the West where they prefigured the depictions of the Martyrdom of Christ. (Taxila was the great ancient centre of learning or 'university' in NW India. *Contra* Western myths, Taxila already possessed a library far larger than the library later built at Alexandria-on-the-Nile and far more subjects were taught at Taxila than at Plato's Academy.)

Note 4

In January 2009, the 1956 film *Alexander the Great* was shown on the BBC. A synopsis of the film rehashed the absurd myth about him conquering the entire "known world" (at least on the Sky satellite TV Guide), rather than actually conquering only the effete Persian Empire. Westerners continue to peddle myths about him supposedly conquering and supposedly bringing civilisation to India when in fact his army turned and fled rather than face the far more powerful Indian forces waiting for him and Indian civilisation had arisen nearly three millennia before him. The Indus region which his army held for a short period had already been conquered by the Persian Empire two centuries earlier (*see* Note 14 to Chapter 7 for full details).

Note 5

In fact, as Shlomo Sand tells us in *The Invention of the Jewish People* (Verso, 2009), contrary to the myth that the Romans exiled the entire Judaean population in 70 *c.e.*, the Palestinian *fellahin* (farmers) are the true descendants of the Biblical Judaeans and Israelites. This fact was acknowledged by early Eastern European Zionists (descended from the Central Asian Khazars) including Israel Belkind, Ber Borochev and even David Ben-Gurion had recognised (in a 1918 book Ben-Gurion co-authored with Yitzhak Ben-Zvi). The Jews of Palestine had welcomed and even aided the Arab conquerors of Jerusalem ridding them of the Byzantine Christian rulers who had oppressed Jews as 'Christ-killers'. The new Arab rulers were kind to the Jews (Mohammed's new 'Abrahamic religion' was heavily influenced by his association with the Jews of Medina whom he had even tried to convert before he converted his fellow Arabs after he was expelled from Mecca). However, Mohammedan subjects did not have to pay taxes whereas non-believers did, so the majority of Jews in Palestine converted *en masse* to the Mohammedan faith. This led to the medieval Islamic-Jewish cultural symbiosis in the Middle East.

Notes to Chapter 4

Note 1

Recently I discovered that Max Planck stated that all matter consists of a force and that we must assume a conscious spirit behind this force. He even added, "I regard matter as derivative from consciousness. We cannot get behind consciousness". (*from* Susan Martinez, "The Elusive Quantum of Consciousness" in *The Journal for Spiritual and Consciousness Studies,* Vol. 36, Number 3, pp. 159-168).

Note 2

Neutral Monism is the term for speculative ontological systems which hold that the Ultimate Reality is singular (Monism) but unknowable or Ineffable. The human mind can only grasp contradictory conceptual abstractions or aspects of the enigmatic underlying Reality. Hence Bohr's double-aspect view of Waves and Particles as with double-aspect views of Mind (Consciousness) and Matter such as Jung's underlying psychophysical 'Psychoid Realm' are forms of Neutral Monism.

Note 3

Tesla could easily have beaten Marconi in being the first to send a Trans-Atlantic signal but, rather than bother with sending wireless information across the Atlantic as he had promised his sponsor (J.P. Morgan), Tesla spent the funds on trying to transmit wirelessly quantities of energy sufficient for industrial power (*Tesla: Master of Lightning*, PBS Television, 2000).

Note 4

In the 1920s Romain Rolland wrote biographies of Ramakrishna, Vivekananda and M.K. Gandhi which greatly increased awareness of these Indians in Europe. Rolland saw the marriage of Indian (spiritual) genius with Europe's genius as the great hope for the future of Humanity (*see* Sorman's *Genius of India*).

Note 5

Given mainstream Science's antipathy, it is interesting to note that the 1993 Bohm and Hiley book *The Undivided Universe* presenting the highly mathematical 'Ontological Interpretation' was published by the Humanities publisher Routledge rather than a Science publisher!

Note 6

The Hermetically-influenced Cardinal Nicolas de Cusa wrote in his *Vision of God* (1458) that Eternity enfoldeth and unfoldeth succession, since the Clock which is Eternity doth alike enfold and unfold all things. Von Franz uses this to stress that, before Descartes depicted 'Nature' as a soulless automaton in the 17th Century, the image of Nature as Clockwork was closely tied to Christian theology (*see* M-L. Von Franz, *Psyche and Matter*, Shambhala, 1992).

Note 7

Weizsäcker, who befriended Indian yogi Gopi Krishna, became the head of an organisation in Starnberg called 'Eastern Wisdom and Western Science'.

Note 8

I mentioned this suppression of Schrödinger's Indian Brahmanic influence in a critique I wrote undermining Bitbol's late friend Francisco Varela's 'neurophenomenology' which I forwarded to Bitbol. Bitbol largely agreed with my critique as the physical correlate of the Inner Light which I identified is also the physical correlate of Husserl's flow of Absolute Consciousness which Varela misrepresented. Indeed the Dalai Lama in his book written with Varela entitled *Sleeping, Dreaming and Dying* (Wisdom Publications, 1997) and in his chapter in *Buddhism and Science* edited by B. Alan Wallace, Columbia U.P., 2003) in which Bitbol also has a chapter, gives authoritative Buddhist knowledge of the Light which provide two striking pieces of evidence in support for my brainstem brainwave correlation. Bitbol, however, denied my claims of ethnocentrism stating that he had mentioned Eastern influences in French publications although admittedly not in the Oxbow Press publication (Personal Communication). However, he never did forward these other papers to me as he said he would. Bitbol also denied my claims of subtle Eurocentrism in Varela's ignoring his friend the Dalai Lama's views, saying that they had been too shy in challenging Western views in the past and pointed out his own interest in Indian Nagarjuna's Madhyamaka philosophy (Personal Communication). I have quoted Guenther on Nagarjuna's sterile logic appealing to Westerners (like Bitbol) for all the wrong reasons in Chapter 1. Physicist Shimon Malin also suppresses references to Schrödinger's interest in Vedanta in his *Nature Likes to Hide* (Oxford U.P., 2001). Malin claims misleadingly that Schrödinger was so immersed in Greek Philosophy that he wrote a book about it making no mention that Schrödinger openly advocated *Advaita Vedanta*. Rajiv Malhotra tells me that his old friend Malin became interested in such mystical philosophies through his involvement in Indian Yoga (Personal Communication).

Note 9

I had planned to provide a detailed *argument by elimination* of the entire spectrum of alternative ontological speculations as to the nature of Consciousness but this time-consuming task would have been too repetitive as well as lengthy. This is of course possible, in principle, but I will give general arguments instead to show the One True Ontology so as not to bore the reader too much.

Note 10

I empathise very strongly with this sense of enslavement to the drive of the Inner Voice which acted against my own personal ambitions as I wrote in O/OM (without knowing all these parallel experiences of others that I know now). My Deeper Self or Inner Voice was clearly related to my experience of numerous synchronicities especially in the mid-1990s as I was led by this sense of Destiny toward completion of O/OM. It is not pleasant to be 'possessed' by a mysterious presence which dashed my career ambitions and dragged me through immense suffering to complete these works.

Note 11

In fact, as Schwab showed in his *The Oriental Renaissance*, the French Natural Historians who first advanced the notion of Evolution in the late 18th Century were influenced by translations of Sanskritic knowledge coming out of Calcutta through the British Asiatic Society of Bengal. Indian notions of the vastness of time and of Vishnu's Reincarnation into progressively more complex animals ending with Man along with William Jones' notion of a 'Common Ancestor' of Sanskrit, Greek and other Indo-European languages helped inspire the notion of Biological Evolution.

Note 12

I saw this story on the *Daily Mail* Website in March 2010, just an hour after watching an old episode of *Ironside* from 1968 called 'Trip to Hashbury' (i.e., Haight Ashbury) where hippies were tripping on LSD; Synchronicity!

Note 13

The Old Testament is not strictly Monotheistic. Yahweh, the deity of the hilltop of Mount Zion, was in fact a member of the Canaanite pantheon in which the supreme deity was El. Yahweh had a female consort Asherah who has been airbrushed out of patriarchal Judaeo-Christianity. (*see* Franceska Stavrakopoulou, *The Bible's Buried Secrets*, BBC Television, 2011 and John Rose *The Myths of Zionism*, Pluto Press, 2004).

Note 14

In fact the notion of 'Laws of Nature', which originated as orders from a Christian man-god, presupposes a Universal Coherence. Such Coherence or harmonious co-ordination of all parts of the universe requires some subtle intercommunication which is explained by such holonomic, Dependent Co-origination type models as everything is interconnected with everything else.

Note 15

On the night of December 25th 2004 I went to bed and could not get out of my minds unusual thought about a natural disaster. This was not at all usual. I was having thoughts like what would happen if the supervolcano under Yosemite National Park erupted. The next morning came news of the Indian Ocean earthquake and tsunami hitting Aceh.

Note 16

At around 10.40 pm on December 26th 2005, the clock in our kitchen stopped for good (rather than requiring a new battery). It transpired that my mother had passed away at about this very time in a hospital one mile away from our house.

Note 17

The Mossad motto is 'By Way of Deception Shall Ye Wage War'.

Note 18

Zwicky had suggested the 'Tired Light' hypothesis to account for the Galactic Redshift soon after Hubble discovered it. Mechanisms for redshifting (energy loss decreasing wavelength) of light travelling through intergalactic dust clouds have been proposed (*see* L. Ashmore *Big Bang Blasted*, BookSurge, 2004).

Note 19

Milo Wolff argues in his *Schrödinger's Universe* (Technotran Press, 2008) that the Light Horizon limit to observation misleads us into thinking that the material universe of galaxies has a specific age and is finite whereas it is infinite. I think that his holonomic model of particle creation can be compatible with a finite cyclic universe (within a larger multiverse including finite universes) and then Nonlocality would indeed interconnect everything within each finite 'Creation' or universe.

Note 20

Still unproven Dark Matter was introduced *ad hoc* to fill the huge discrepancy between observable galactic matter and the actual galactic masses indicated by rotational velocities. But the notion of the matter existing predominantly in the form of invisible Dark Matter has proven successful in relation to other astrophysical problems allowing the theoretical models to produce predictions matching the observed facts. Nonetheless the false hubris of those who boast of creating 'Theories of Everything' based on Standard Model of particles has been exposed by the fact that the forms of matter and energy known to Physics constitutes only a small percentage of the known Universe and the rest remains unexplained 'Dark Matter' and 'Dark Energy'.

Notes to Chapter 5

Note 1

This was my 'Creating Life *de novo*' argument against Emergent Materialism whose supporters often asserted that Consciousness was an Emergent phenomenon just like a Living System. If we created a new Life Form *de novo*, the **presence of Life**, could be determined by the behaviour of the system. *Contra* naive arguments like the Turing Test, the mimicking of human behaviour by an artefact does not prove the existence of Sentience in the artefact.

Note 2

Physics depicts various forms of matter and force as vibrating fields of energy described by mathematics, with all properties of matter described as vibratory waveforms of energy. A particle is a localised constellation of activity in the various types of energy fields constituting, electromagnetic charge, spin, etc. These potential-fields and waves are supposed to exist without any underlying substance in contrast to the 19th Century idea of the Luminiferous Aether that was vibrating. Even the Quantum Vacuum is replete with vast amounts of Vacuum Energy associated supposedly with ephemeral 'virtual particles'.

Note 3

Acknowledgements go to Rajiv Malhotra for coining the pejorative label 'intellectual *sepoy*'. A *sepoy* was an Indian mercenary soldier who served the interests of the European colonial powers in India (originally from the Portuguese *cipao*). These Indian writers often denigrate their own native cultures so as to pander to the racial preconceptions and Eurocentric myths of Westerners. As Richard Crasta writes in his satirical *Impressing the Whites* (Invisible Man Books, 2000) the more a Non-European writer challenges Western stereotypes, the less likely he is to get published in the West.

Note 4

The general sense of 'Behaviorism' to which the editors of *Naturalising Phenomenology* assert that Cognitive Science conforms is in accord with but not nearly as general as my 'Inherent Behaviorism' extrapolation of Behavorism in Psychology. My phrase applies to the whole of Physicalist Science and not just studies of the Mind! I have used the US spelling of Behaviorism to indicate the links to the Behaviorism of J.B. Watson and B.F. Skinner.

Note 5

Ponce is used here in the American sense of one who pretends to have intelligence and sophistication rather than the UK sense of being effeminate or like a pimp. In the spring of 2010 Michel Onfray's book *Twilight of an Idol: The Freudian Fabrication* (Grasset Publications) finally brought the French the facts on Freud. Freudianism was exposed as the last untouchable religion revered by (showbiz) "stars and footballers". Onfray revealed that Freud was a fraud, a charlatan, homophobe and a perverted misogynist obsessed with sexual abuse.

Note 6

The 'hard' in 'Hard Problem' means *difficult*. It is merely a fashionable new label for the centuries' old Problem of the Ontological Status of Consciousness, misleadingly labelled the 'Mind/Body problem'. Use of the 'Hard Problem' is pertinent in this chapter given that Cognitive Scientists often present superficial work on neural processes associated with mentation (the Soft Mind/Body question) as (supposedly) solving the Ontological problem of Consciousness. Even the use of 'Neural Correlates of Consciousness' is misleading as Cognitive Science does not actually know what the Consciousness or the Mind is, assuming non-egoic processes to be devoid of 'Consciousness' (the supposed 'Unconscious'), and focusing on neuronal impulses and neurotransmitters rather than higher-level field dynamics.

Note 7

The term *Mind* is in itself misleading in that it evokes the existence of a regular, uniform persisting entity in the same way Physicists talk misleadingly about subatomic 'particles' as individual 'building blocks' when no individual particle trajectories exist. Siddharta the Buddha recognised over two and a half millennia ago that there is no persistent individual or personal 'soul' (*jiva*). Thus **Mentation** (the *process* or result of *mental activity*) is a better term than Mind in reflecting the constantly shifting, effervescent and periodic appearance of the activity of the Field of Attention from which we abstract the concept of an ego along with the non-egoic processes which remain subconscious until they seize the energy of attention for themselves.

Note 8

The Gestalt Field Theory of Wolfgang Kohler and others was itself inspired by the new Quantum Mechanics invented in the 1920s and by the Phenomenological studies of Husserl. The Holism was probably influenced by the rather simplistic Organism-based holism of Kurt Goldstein.

Note 9

We have seen that recent neuroscience regarding perception of colour, earlier work on Colour Constancy, etc., demonstrate that we do not perceive the outside world as it really is. Bohr's 'Copenhagen Interpretation' also rejects Realism in favour of Intersubjective Consensus.

Note 10

We have seen that, late in his life, one Nobel laureate neuroscientist, George Wald received an insight into the fundamental nature of Consciousness which had eluded him through scientific knowledge and enquiry. This insight, which drew him towards Eastern philosophy, was that Consciousness ('Mind') was a principle pervading the universe, perhaps primary to Matter (*see* G. Wald "The Cosmology of Life and Mind". In T.D. Singh (Editor) (1988) *Synthesis of Science and Religion: Critical Dialogues and Essays*, The Bhaktivedanta Institute).

Note 11

We saw in Chapter 1 that research by Jay Neitz published in *Nature* in 2012 suggested that it is possible that different individuals perceive the same (inter-subjectively stated) colour (e.g. blue as in a normal blue sky) differently in their subjective experience.

Note 12

It is highly doubtful that all the reported 'spiritual experiences' of Western students in these magnetic field stimulation studies in both Persinger's and Granqvist's studies, especially those indoctrinated by Atheist, Materialist Persinger, were actually deep mystical experiences. The reader will appreciate that Persinger has little idea of what actual Enlightenment or Gnosis entails and any vaguely described, unusual experience seems to have been labelled 'the God Experience'. Actual spiritual experience of Divinity or Divine Light is the result of years of difficult practice not just some vague numinous feeling reported as reported by Persinger's students after magnetic stimulation. Pseudo-mystical experiences given false spiritual significance by novices on the Path to Enlightenment are well-known to masters in yogic traditions.

Note 13

The likes of Alain Daniélou (in his *India –A Civilisation of Differences*, Inner Traditions, 2003) and Guy Sorman (in his *The Empire of Lies*, 2008. Encounter Books) have argued that Totalitarianism has its roots in Exclusivist Semitic Monotheism and viewed Maoism as a pseudo-Monotheistic Cult.

Notes to Chapter 6

Note 1

In his incoherent rambling writings, Nietzsche thought that the 'Light of Truth' was just a metaphor for an ancient philosopher's own knowledge and that Consciousness existed only in egos and evolved alongside Language. He asserted that philosophers' pretension to *wisdom* has been the maddest and most immodest of all pretensions. In India as in Greece, Wisdom has been a hiding place of the philosopher. He derided Kant for reducing Philosophy to just Epistemology. He also wrote that none of our religious people questions the veracity of his own experiences of 'miracles', 'rebirths' and 'voices of angels'. Furthermore, *contra* ancient anthropocentrism, he recognised the evolutionary survival value of human logic and that Man mistakes words and names as eternal verities. He noted that it was dawning on a few that Physics is only an interpretation of the world and *not* an explanation. The duality of Cause and Effect probably never occurs in reality, rather humans isolate two parts of a single continuum (*see* R.J. Hollingdale (Translator) *A Nietzsche Reader*, Penguin, 1977).

Note 2

Sorman (*Genius of India*) says that the early Western Jesuits in China recognised, unlike Indian Philosophy which was a highly developed 'real' system of philosophy, the Chinese 'philosophical' tradition consisted of little more than precepts and aphorisms (the pithy old Chinese proverbs). We shall see in a later Chapter that the introduction of Sanskritic words, Indian Buddhist logic and Indian Mathematics helped the Chinese and Japanese to develop logical thought (*see* J.Goody, *The East in the West*, Cambridge U.P., 1996). The *Tao* may represent Psycho-Physical Energy but it is usually expressed as being just Energy with no mention of Consciousness.

Note 3

I was pleased to see on the Internet that Berkeley library announced my 1999 book as amongst its recent additions in 1999 or 2000.

Note 4

When I visited the Princeton Engineering Anomalies Research (PEAR) Laboratory in 2000, I was surprised to find their PR man denying that any of their experiments had been publicised on UK celebrity hypnotist Paul McKenna's TV show in the 1990s. Yet I am certain that PEAR researchers demonstrated the same psychokinetic influence between the selection of two computer-screen images experiments with the studio audience that I tried for myself at the PEAR lab. I even recall that the UK professor Arthur Ellison appeared on the show. Later that year I learnt that there was a controversy at Princeton over the tenure of a Physics professor who had publicly expressed interest in Eastern Philosophy and Consciousness, etc., arousing indignation from orthodox colleagues. I suspect that, given this ongoing controversy, PEAR were trying to keep a low profile as they too encroached upon topics which are taboo in Western academia!

Note 5

This is just one of many such examples, where contrary to Eurocentric historical myths, some elements of Ancient Indian knowledge were more advanced than anything in the West until relatively recent times. Most of the modern mathematics underlying the Scientific Revolution including the decimal place value number system including Zero (modern Arithmetic), Trigonometry and the Sine function, Algebra, negative and imaginary numbers and even the basis of Infinitesimal Calculus, etc., were invented in India (*see* C. Seife *Zero*, Souvenir Press, 2000 and S. Goonatilake *Toward a Global Science*, Indiana U.P., 1998).The West did not surpass Indian *nyaya* Formal Logic until the development of Boolean logic in the 19th Century. European Linguistic analysis was inspired by the work of the ancient Indian grammarian Panini on Sanskrit.

Guy Beck tells us that many of the insights found in the work of Ferdinand de Saussure, the French founder of modern Structuralism and Linguistics very likely emerged from his tenure as Professor of Sanskrit in Geneva in the 1880s. Ancient India, says Beck, speaks more to 20th Century Europeans than to medieval or even mid-19th Century Europeans (*see* G. Beck, *Sonic Theology*, University of South Carolina Press, 1993). Many Indian philosophical and cosmological ideas dismissed as nonsense by Colonial European scholars are only now beginning to be taken seriously by Western scholars in the 21st Century.

Note 6

In 2006 an ordinary member of Institute of Noetic Sciences (IONS) Alan Rhodes, who had been impressed by my O/OM in 1999, forwarded to de Quincey (then President of IONS), one of my emails showing the growing list of evidence confirming my RAS correlate of the Inner Light of Pure Consciousness. In its quarterly review magazines IONS had presented Wilber as the leading light in the scientific study of Consciousness. De Quincey responded to Alan, not knowing that Alan would forward the response to me. De Quincey tried to dismiss my work by claiming that this Sutapas Bhattacharya did not seem to understand what a physical correlate was! In a brief off-the-cuff email to my friend Alan, I may have referred at first to my "identification of the Divine Light" without using 'physical correlate of' before 'Divine Light but I did use 'physical correlate' later in my email and in my O/OM etc. De Quincey also picked up on my use of 'Panpsychism' for the restricted Non-Idealist form of Panpsychism and claimed (on the basis of one email to friends) that Sutapas Bhattacharya did not seem to realise that there were Western Idealist Panpsychists. In fact I had been referring to Skrbina's book *Panpsychism in the West* which I had just read and which restricted the term 'Panpsychism' to non-Idealist forms. I note that de Quincey himself uses Panpsychism in this restricted sense in his discussion of Wilber's criticism of Panpsychism. Back in 1999 Alan had emailed Marilyn Schlitz at IONS about IONS reviewing my O/OM. But Schlitz responded claiming that she had never heard of it. This was in spite of the fact that she had written to me asking for a copy in 1998 and had recently met me at the August 1999 'Beyond the Brain' conference where she also saw me steal the show from herself and fellow speakers at the end when I mentioned my work from the audience. The fact that I exposed Ken Wilber's false claims on Science-Mysticism synthesis in my O/OM at the time Wilber had received large funds from the so-called 'UFO-CEO' Joe Firmage obviously did not go down well with Wilber's associates in the USA who were keen to benefit from his good fortune. I suspect that my rubbishing Wilber led to IONS staying silent about my book although IONS claims to help disseminate knowledge about the scientific understanding of mysticism and spirituality.

Note 7

Yet a few years later, after Wilber received the large donation from Joe Firmage, Goswami was 'singing the praises' of Wilber in the IONS magazine. Goswami's own view (*see* Goswami, A. with Reed, R.E. and Goswami, M., *The*

Self-Aware Universe: How Consciousness Creates the Material World (Simon and Schuster, 1993) itself remains a form of uncritical mass market 'pop philosophy' making exaggerated statements and claims such as this book providing a paradox-free, coherent and satisfying interpretation of Quantum Physics. Goswami asserts that Monistic Idealism has been the basis of all religions worldwide. This assertion is not backed up and is of course clearly false as most religions are not Monistic but Dualistic Theisms! Basing his ideas on the so-called 'Schrödinger's Cat' paradox (or the 'Collapse of the Wave Function') in QM, Goswami defines Consciousness as "the agency that affects quantum objects to make their behaviour sensible". This seems to be a conflation of 'Perception' with 'Consciousness'. We have seen that Gabor and Pribram recognised that the QM formalism reflects the processes of Perception! Even if the von Neumann interpretation of the so-called 'Collapse' by a so-called 'Consciousness' is not a completely out-dated approach to an epistemological (not ontological) problem, replaced by modern understanding of Decoherence, how Goswami's vague definition of Consciousness based on this tenuous paradox from QM (far removed from Psychology and Phenomenology) obviously does not help in clarifying things.

Notes to Chapter 7

Note 1

Indich tells us in his *Consciousness in Advaita Vedanta* (Motilal Banarsidass, 1980) that *Advaita Vedanta* recognised Wish-Fulfilment as one of the many causes of dreams over a thousand years before Freud.

Note 2

Bruno championed heliocentrism for mystical reasons (*see* F.Yates *Giordano Bruno and the Hermetic Tradition*, Routledge and Kegan Paul, 1964). In fact the great Ancient Indian mathematician Aryabhatta had presented a heliocentric model in his *Aryabhatiya* which was translated into Latin two centuries before Copernicus (*see* D. Teresi, *Lost Discoveries*, Simon and Schuster, 2003). Bruno is also presented falsely by Eurocentric historians as having, with Nicolas de Cusa, as being the first to put forward the notion of an infinite universe with countless worlds. Charles Seife (in his book *Zero*) notes that these ideas first appeared in medieval Arabia and Renaissance Europe alongside the revolutionary new Mathematics from India with its concepts of Zero and Infinity. William Anderson tells us that Indians had long postulated not only countless worlds in an unimaginably vast universe but countless universes (*see* W. Anderson *Face of Glory,* Bloomsbury, 1996). Neville tells us that Hindu cosmology suggested both cyclic, oscillating universes and a multiverse including many such cyclic universes co-existing together in a greater timeless reality (R.C. Neville *Eternity and Time's Flow*, SUNY Press, 1993). Teresi tells us in *Lost Discoveries* that the Indian counting system appeared like magic to medieval Italians. They paid to see mathematicians, who knew the Indian system, perform calculations such as 7x14 rapidly in their heads at fairs. Cambridge mathematical physicist John Barrow has described the Indian number system as the greatest intellectual invention of all time; it is the nearest thing humans have to a universal language (J. D. Barrow *The Book of Nothing*, Jonathan Cape, 2000).

Note 3

James Mill also played a prominent role in 'decontaminating' Plato both of Oriental influences and of the true mystical character of his philosophy as part of the 19th Century White Supremacist, Eurocentric rewriting of Graeco-Roman Civilisation known as 'Classics' (*see* D.C. Moore (Editor) *Black Athena Writes Back*, Duke U.P. ,2001).

Note 4

The 'Dravidian' race was invented by missionary bishop Robert Caldwell who again conflated Language and Race (*see* R. Malhotra and A. Neelakandan, *Breaking India*, Amaryllis, 2011).

Note 5

Most Western and Leftist Indian academics assume that everything in the Vedas is myth and smear Indian opponents who may actually be presenting good scientific evidence and rational arguments as 'Hindu fundamentalists'. But as Guy Sorman points out in *The Genius of India*, the call for *Hindutva* (Hindu culture) in India is actually a desire for (Indian) cultural authenticity not, as outsiders and Leftists present it, for fundamentalism or Fascism. Sorman says that *Hindutva* does not represent a return to the past but seeking an indigenous Indian way of combining the Eternal Dharma with Modernity. India always favoured syncretisation. Leftists hate to admit the fact that BJP supporters are not illiterate peasants but educated middle classes. Sorman even quotes M.K. Gandhi who stated that independence was worthless if all it meant was aping blindly the coloniser (as is commonplace amongst Westernised Indians, especially Leftists). 'Indophile' Michael Wood sides with the white nomads from Southern Russia myth in his 2007 BBC TV series. Even Edwin Bryant in his 2001 book (which makes no mention of Bailly and Playfair's astronomical argument or of the potential of DNA studies to resolve this question) *The Quest for the Origins of Vedic Culture: The Indo-Aryan Migration Debate* (Oxford U.P., 2001) chose to 'sit on the fence' in regard to the competing arguments. I noted that the arguments Bryant presents against the AIT had far more scientific *gravitas* than the pro-AIT arguments of Europeans based on the 19th Century pseudo-sciences of Philology and Scientific Racism but he seems to give both sides equal weight. Another factor behind European distortions of Ancient Indian history was the hidden Western root assumption that human civilisation began with the myths of Abraham, the Tower of Babel, etc., as stated in the Bible, hence the Christocentric focus on Mesopotamia. Quite clearly, the *Rig Veda Samhita* is a collection of spiritual hymns by various sages not historical stories (*see* Sri Aurobindo's *The Secret of the Veda*, 1956). The hymns were put together and the format standardised much later than some of the original compositions (*see* T.R. Trautmann (Editor) *The Aryan Debate*, Oxford U.P. India, 2005). We also saw in Chapter 2 the presence of Indo-Aryan language speaking Mittani and Kassites in the Middle East in the mid 2nd M *b.c.e.* again contradicting the AIT and the myth of mainstream British historiography that Indians were just a submissive, always conquered 'race' lacking 'historical agency'.

Note 6

The composition of the fictional so-called 'Deuteronomist History' dates from the reign of King Josiah in the late 7th Century *b.c.e.* It is a self-aggrandising national mythology created by the Judaeans who were actually the backward hill-people of Canaan (i.e., they already lived in the so-called 'Promised Land') in contrast to the great civilisation of the Phoenicians of the coastal cities. The Ur of the Chaldees said to be the home of mythical Abraham did not exist before the 9th Century *b.c.e.* The Exodus, conquest of Canaan and the vast empire of Solomon, etc., are fictional creations. In contrast to the poor Judaeans, the Biblical kingdom of Israel was a polytheistic society which prospered by trade and cultural syncretism with the great civilisations of the Phoenicians, Egyptians, Assyrians and Babylonians (*see* I. Finkelstein and N.A. Silberman *The Bible Unearthed*, Simon and Schuster, 2001).The Old Testament however is itself a 1st M *b.c.e.* compilation including much older myths and fables which the Judaean latecomers picked up from older civilisations such as the Babylonians, Assyrians, Phoenicians, Egyptians and Persians.

Note 7

Note that Max Muller described the *Rig Veda* as crude and childish whilst simultaneously believing in the utterly infantile, anthropomorphic, tribal, miracle-filled fairy tales of the Bible as the factual History of the Earth!

Note 8

In truth, much of what is called *Hindutva* (Hindu culture) by the BJP is a mish-mash of Western and Semitic religion-influenced reinterpretations of tradition along, championing of unscientific mythologies along with some actual traditional elements. But then no major country in the world can boast a pure tradition not influenced by other cultures, ridden with myths and modern reinterpretations.

Note 9

The prohibition of Birth Control is an example of anti-National policies. So too the Christian missionary false historical propaganda demonising Brahmans as another set of foreign invaders and the peddling of British Indological myths that India had been poverty-stricken and unchanging for 3,000 years due to Hinduism until the coming of the altruistic Western Christians!

Note 10

Sorman (*Genius of India*) writes of the Indian yuppies in Bangalore aping the worst aspects of Western Consumerism and ostentatious display.

Note 11

I recall reading a newspaper article by Indo-British Sikh journalist Nirpal Dhaliwal who pointed out how Western publishers have published novels by

Anglo-Indian or Anglo-African 'halfcastes' such as Hanif Kureishi, Monica Ali, Zadie Smith and Hari Kunzru. These (much-hyped and supposedly 'ethnic') writers tend to look down on their darker relations through White eyes thus perpetuating Western racial stereotypes. Indian-born Richard Crasta points out in his *Impressing the Whites* (Invisible Man Books, 2000) how Western publishers refuse to publish stories by Indians who fail to follow the Western stereotypical characterisations of Indians. As Alain Daniélou has stressed in his *India–A Civilisation of Difference* (Inner Traditions, 2003) modern Western 'Egalitarianism' has led to either elimination of (by genocide) or theoretical assimilation of non-European ethnic groups. There is a subtle racism in the Western Liberal attitude that only accepts non-Europeans once they have been forced to abandon their native traditions and ape the colonisers as second-class citizens in the White Man's world. The Hindu Caste system allowed India's indigenous tribes and various Non-Hindu religious communities to continue living according to their own way-of-life.

Note 12

Sorman says that Western politicians and the media were so fond of Nehru because he was so thoroughly Westernised (*Genius of India*). However Nehru was not a compliant puppet given his refusal to bring India into the Western camp during the Cold War.

Note 13

Joseph Campbell points out that a 'Holy Land' or 'Promised Land' as also with myths of sacred Central Mountains are actually metaphors for spiritual goals to be reached and not geographical entities. The whole idea of Pilgrimage is based on this false layman's misconception (*Transformations of Myth Through Time* Harper and Row, 1990). *The Bible Unearthed* (*see Note 6*) shows that the Exodus from Egypt and conquest of Canaan were self-aggrandising myths created for the backward highland Canaanites who became the Judaeans. The Judaeans were themselves Canaanites and never lived apart from other Canaanites. The historical fact is that Egypt ruled over Canaan at the time of the Bible's supposed Israelite conquest of Canaan. The coastal cities of Canaan were destroyed around 1200 *b.c.e.* not by Joshua's Israelites from the Sinai but by the Sea Peoples who became the Philistines. The once-mysterious 'Sea Peoples', who destroyed Mycenaean and Hittite cities but whom the Egyptians defeated, are now known to have been Greek-speaking people from the Eastern Mediterranean.

Note 14

The West continues to peddle the hyped-up racist fantasies of Alexander's military and cultural achievements in India. We have seen that the British used to claim that Alexander brought civilisation to India! In his BBC TV series *In the Footsteps of Alexander*, Michael Wood presented Alexander's retreat from India as due to the homesickness of his war-weary troops. Perhaps, Wood told us, had they gone forward Al might have conquered China! In reality, as Hellenes and Roman historians told it, Alexander's army mutinied because they knew that they would be slaughtered if they dared to cross the river Beas and face the enormous Indian forces waiting for them led by Chandragupta Maurya's battle-hardened army of Maghada. Graeber tells us that the strength of the Army of Maghada was based on the vast mineral wealth of the kingdom. This abundance of gold and silver allowed Maghada to maintain a vast standing army of professionally trained mercenaries. Greek sources reported that Maghada could field an army of 200,000 infantry, 20,000 cavalry and 4,000 war elephants and this is why Alexander's men mutinied rather than have to face them (D. Graeber *Debt–The First 5,000 Years*, Melville House, 2011). Alexander had defeated only the declining Persian Empire which Greek writers had long considered decadent and ripe for conquest since the Greeks drove back Xerxes. Where once Persian nobles were trained in martial techniques, they were now raised in the harem. But the Greeks themselves were too divided to seize Persia's empire. Only when the Macedonians conquered Greece were the Greeks forcibly united against their will (*see* B. Isaac *The Invention of Racism in Classical Antiquity*, Princeton U.P.). Michael Wood claimed that Chandragupta got the idea of Empire from (White Man) Al, when Indians were familiar with the Persian Empire which held the Indus for nearly 200 years and the Mauryan Empire copied Persian rock edicts and pillars. After Alexander's retreat from the Indus territory, the great bulk of his empire (from the Bosphorus to the Indus) was seized by his general Seleucus Nikator. But Chandragupta Maurya defeated Alexander's satraps in the Indus and later defeated Seleucus's forces and forced him to concede both the Indus (originally conquered by Persian Darius) and Bactria (Afghanistan) to the Indo-Aryan Mauryan Empire. Seleucus's daughter married Chandragupta and Megasthenes was posted to Pataliputra (modern Patna), then the richest and largest city in the entire world. These facts deflating the overblown myth of Alexander were not mentioned by Wood!

Note 15

Some have suggested that the rather mysterious Ammonias Saccas got his name from a Latinisation of Shakyamuni (Sage of the Shakyas), a name for Siddharta Guatama who was a member of the Shakya tribe. Asoka's Buddhist missionaries had founded missions in the capitals of the Hellenistic kingdoms created by Seleucus, Ptolemy and the other Macedonians who carved-up Alexander's conquests. These included Alexandria-on-the-Nile and Antioch.

Note 16

The seminal 'Voyages of Discovery' of both Vasco de Gama and Christopher Columbus were in fact Crusades. Columbus sailed West wanting to find gold to finance the re-conquest of the 'Holy Land' (J.M. Hobson, *The Eastern Origins of Western Civilisation*, Cambridge U.P., 2004). The Christian Crusaders in Palestine had been notorious for their barbaric atrocities, with their massacres of non-believers and Anglo-French Jew-hater Richard the First's chronicler boasting of roasting heathen babies on spits. Earlier Western Crusaders had practised cannibalism. Columbus told his sponsors that he was seeking a route to India as India was famous for its wealth. Before each military campaign in the New World the Conquistador captain was required to read to the native 'Indians', without an interpreter, a long and rhetorical *Requirimiento* exhorting them to adopt the 'one true faith' (Catholicism) (E. Galeano, *The Open Veins of Latin America*, 2009, Serpents Tail):

> *If you do not, or maliciously delay in so doing, I certify that with God's help I will advance powerfully against you and make war on you wherever and however I am able, and will subject you to the yoke and obedience of the Church and of their majesties and take your women and children to be slaves, and as such I will sell and dispose of them as their majesties may order, and I will take your possessions and do you all the harm and damage that I can.*

Columbus's brother Bartholome burnt alive (in true Christian style) Caribbean natives who desecrated Christian images after they had been forcibly converted by the Spaniards (F. Dallmayr, *Beyond Orientalism,* SUNY Press, 1996). In the next 100 years, about 70 million natives died through killing by the Europeans, starvation, disease, enslavement and forced labour in toxic silver mines etc. This reduced the native population of Latin America from over 70 million in 1492 to 3.5 million in 150 years (*from* Galeano).

Note 17

The Indian Ocean had been the peaceful epicentre of world trade for a thousand years until the arrival of the Portuguese. On his second voyage to India in 1502 Vasco de Gama captured a merchant ship bringing back 700 pilgrims from Mecca, loaded it with gunpowder and sunk it along with the pilgrims. At Calicut he seized 20 trading vessels and butchered their crews. The hands, ears and noses of more than 800 Indian prisoners were hacked off, piled into a boat and sent to the Zamorin with a note telling him to make a 'curry' with what he found. The Vatican-sanctioned Portuguese pirates imposed a protection racket allowing only merchants who brought a Portuguese permit to do business on pain of confiscation and death, claiming that Free Trade was reserved for Christians (*see* N. Robins, *The Corporation that Changed the World*, Pluto Press, 2006). As with mass murderer Winston Churchill, Columbus and de Gama are great heroes celebrated in the West!

Notes to Chapter 8

Note 1

We have seen that the Ashkenazi Jews of Eastern Europe were descended from the Central Asian Hunnic Khazars. In his *Jewish History, Jewish Religion* (1994, Pluto Press) Israel Shahak reveals the true character of early modern German Jewish society which famous Jewish writers such as Hannah Arendt have suppressed. In the 18th Century burning of books, persecution of writers, disputes about the magic power of amulets, bans on the most elementary 'non-Jewish' education such as the teaching of correct German was commonplace. Under the Rabbinical totalitarianism of Orthodox Judaism, that persisted until modern European secularism liberated Jews from such superstitions, the ordinary Jew did not even have the freedom to think. Before about 1780, the Jews of Europe were marked by a supreme contempt and hate for all learning except for the Talmud (filled with hatred toward Gentiles) and Jewish mysticism. Indeed, it was this reactionary hostility to modern secular knowledge that led to the rise of Zionism amongst Eastern European Jews who feared assimilation into the German nation.

Note 2

Western Phenomenological investigation actually began with William James in the 19th Century. James was familiar with Indian Philosophy and famously met with Vivekananda who had a profound influence on him.

Note 3

This is not to be confused with the normal English meaning of "intentional" as deliberate, implying 'freely willed' or volitional.

Note 4

Philip Goldberg tells us in his *American Veda* (Harmony Books, 2010) that Mind Cure was also known as New Thought and began in New England around 1860 influenced by the Emerson (himself inspired by Vedanta), the (Sanskrit Literature-inspired) German Romantics, British Idealism, metaphysical interpretations of the Gospels, Swedenborg, Spiritualism and Mesmerism. It had one million followers in 1902.

Note 5

Bertrand Russell had been shaken by Ludwig Wittgenstein's critique of Russell's 1912 article *The Essence of Religion*. Wittgenstein accused Russell of being a traitor to the Gospel of Exactness, indulging in vague terminology. In contrast Rabindranath Tagore sent Russell a letter congratulating him quoting the Upanishads on the ineffability of *Brahman*. Russell published Tagore's letter in his 1967 autobiography but stated that Tagore's talk of the Infinite was "vague nonsense". Russell continued, "The sort of language that is admired by many Indians unfortunately does not mean anything at all". In contrast Wittgenstein himself, in the 1920s and 1930s became a devotee of Tagore. At meetings of the Vienna Circle, Wittgenstein would turn his back on the Logical Positivists (who suffering Physics Envy tried to ape Physics' Reductionism) and read out loud from the poetry of Tagore (*See* K. Dutta and A. Robinson *Rabindranath Tagore*, Bloomsbury, 1995). As stated in Chapter 12, Avrum Stroll tells us in his *Twentieth Century Analytical Philosophy* (Columbia U.P., 2000) that the Logical Positivists and Anglo-American Analytical academics (steeped in Scientism) have ignored the overtly metaphysical and mystical last section of Wittgenstein's *Tractatus logico-philosophicus*. In this section, Wittgenstein stressed that *what was of the highest philosophical significance was beyond the scope of scientific study* (*emphasis mine*).

Note 6

We are told by Ronald Bruzina in his *Edmund Husserl and Eugen Fink* (Yale U.P., 2004) that Fink's insights into deeper levels of phenomenological constitution beyond the egoic procresses were inspired by his knowledge of Neo-Platonism. I suspect that Fink must have known of Indian Philosophical notions as well as NeoPlatonic ones just as Husserl was well aware of Buddhist philosophy (*see Ch. 8*). But, as we have seen repeatedly, references to Non-European knowledge are deemed 'unscientific' by Western academia and so omitted by authors censoring themselves due to peer pressure and Orthodox dogma. Fink's 'Transcendental Witness' (which is not separate from but right in the midst of cognitive processes) parallels the Yogic *saksin* (Witness Consciousness) found in Hindu and Buddhist schools.

Note 7

I do not agree with Paracelsus's identification of the Inner Man ((Innermost being) with the Subtle Body. There is no consensus as to what represents the Subtle Body but we have seen that the Hindu temple represents the Subtle Body that surrounds the Innermost being or Light and most mystics refer to the subtle body as an intermediary stage associated with Dream-like states.

Note 8

We have seen that Pythagoreans often attributed newer ideas to their founder. The authority of a legendary great sage was of greater prestige than originality in the ancient world.

Note 9

As Gross and Levitt told us in *Higher Superstitions* (Johns Hopkins, U.P., 1994) such assertions that Natural Sciences are not universally valid (in the common to all humans sense) stems from so-called 'Physics Envy' that is found in the Humanities as well as in the soft-sciences such as Biology and Psychology.

Notes to Chapter 9

Note 1

Grosso's terminology is misleading in that he uses the word 'Christ' in the vulgar sense as a culturally conditioned image of the man Jesus from the Gospels. Europeans depict this legendary Afro-Asian Semite as a White European, often as a blonde! Similarly, Afro-American separatists in the USA have claimed that ancient Northern Indian Siddharta Gautama (the Buddha) was black whereas East Asians depict Buddha as a Mongoloid.

Note 2

In late 2008, I came across on the internet a very similar quote from the Hindu text *Tripura Rahasya*, stressing that how one portrays the 'goddess' was up to the imagination of individual.

Note 3

Although *Brahman* is impersonal Consciousness, if we are to have an anthropomorphic Chosen Deity then a bisexual figure is appropriate as Reality transcends the opposites. Otherwise, a Female is preferable to a Male as the

Mother is more symbolic of the Unborn that 'gives birth to' the Creation and the Feminine is more appropriate in representing Divine 'Love' meaning a transpersonal empathy or Oneness.

Note 4

Jungian V.W. Odajnyk noted the fascinating instances of the imagery associated with Norse war-god Wotan (Odin; a tribal war-god equivalent to the tribal Yahweh) surfacing sporadically in German psychiatric patients and some aspects of German culture, after the 1919 Treaty of Versailles, bearing ominous portents of the momentous cataclysms that were soon to come with the rise of the Messianic figure of Adolf Hitler. Such images, repeatedly imagined by millions may persist (in subtle, vibratory form) in the collective human psyche and these psychic 'forces' may even occasionally play a role in unusually turbulent periods of history such as the Crusades or Millenarian movements. The mass 'hysteria' or collective delusions often associated with such periods may involve large numbers of people becoming 'possessed' by such collective-psychic forces associated with the *Zeitgeist* or the 'Spirit of the Time' (*see* V.W. Odajnyk, *Jung and Politics*,1976, New York U.P.)

Note 5

Thompson himself did not respond when I pointed these things out in an email undermining his views although the afore-mentioned French Philosopher of Science and old friend of the late Varela, Michel Bitbol did respond. He acknowledged that they had perhaps been too shy in the past in regard to going against the grain of mainstream Western thought (Personal Communication). Interestingly, an American Brain Dynamics researcher Professor Scott Kelso, whom I copied in on the email, appreciating the strength of my argument did email me asking for more information about my brainwave-linked views on Consciousness (Personal Communication).

Note 6

We have seen that Nikola Tesla, the genius inventor of the alternating current (AC), was an admirer of Vivekananda and there are suggestions that Tesla looked for a scientific proof of the Brahmanic/Tantric knowledge of the energetic basis of matter (J. Dobson *Cosmic Beginnings and Human Ends*, Open Court, 1995). It was the new Westinghouse-built AC electric generators, designed by Tesla, that famously lit up the 1893 World Fair in Chicago and they would also be installed at Niagra Falls to help power the growth of New York City (*Tesla: Master of Lightning*, PBS TV, 2000). Thomas Edison, whose DC systems lost out to Tesla's AC, was himself a follower of another Brahmanism-Buddhism inspired Western movement which also had strong links to Indian Nationalism, Theosophy.

Note 7

The Post-1945 presentation of Woodrow Wilson as a great Liberal who helped establish the League of Nations is grossly misleading. As James Loewen reveals in his *Lies My Teacher Told Me* (Touchstone, 1995), Wilson was a

White Supremacist who expelled Afro-Americans from Federal Government jobs and cracked down violently on organised labour. The Ku Klux Clan was reborn and spread all over the USA thanks to the racist policies of Wilson's government along with Hollywood's release of *Birth of a Nation* (*The Clansman*) based on a book by an old classmate of Wilson. As a historian Wilson had helped fabricate the myth, peddled in the film, that post-Civil War Reconstruction had been corrupt domination of White Southerners by Blacks and Northern carpetbaggers. Racial violence escalated and lynching occurred as far North as Duluth under Wilson.

Note 8

I found that these doctrines were all present in the teachings of (non-Semitic) Zoroaster looking through McEvilley's *The Shape of Ancient Thought* (Allworth Press, 2002). Later I found that Joseph Campbell wrote in *Transformation of Myth through Time* (Harper and Row, 1990) that our whole Western tradition comes out of the Zoroastrian message. The Saviour and the Second Coming of the Saviour are found in Zoroaster. Jonathan Kirsch in *A History of the End of World* (Harper Collins, 2006) tells us that Angels, the Son of Man and the Apocalyptic tradition were all copied by the Jews from the Persians. Thus, I would conclude, given that Zoroastrianism is much older that Judaism (which only arose in the 1st M *b.c.e.*) and, given that Persian Emperor Cyrus (*a.k.a.* Jewish Messiah Koresh) was behind the rebuilding of the Yahweh Temple by Babylon-born Judaean 'Agents of Persia' such as Ezra and Nehemiah, the Zoroastrian basis of the crass, core myths shared by the Semitic religions seems valid.

Note 9

In his recent book *Being Different* (Harper Collins India and India Today, 2011) Rajiv Malhotra tells of how he challenged the use of the word 'tolerate' in Inter-Faith dialogue as 'tolerate' implied a putting-up with something one disapproves of. Rather than 'tolerate' each other religions should have 'mutual respect' for each other. This change was urged by Hindu Swamis in the declaration of the UN Millennium Inter-Faith Conference in 2000 but resisted vigorously by Cardinal Ratzinger (Pope Benedict) who was the previous pope's 'enforcer'. Although the Vatican accepted the change in wording at the last minute, it quickly issued a press release reasserting the Pope's unique and exclusive status as God's representative on Earth. Thus, as Malhotra states, Christians (not just Catholics) pay lip-service to tolerating other beliefs but they know deep down that such tolerance contradicts the fundamental Exclusivist position of the Nicene Creed which Malhotra reprints in full. I would agree as I have found that practising Christians who claim to agree with the Perennial Philosophy still tend to cling to exoteric Christianity even though such 'Churchianity' (as Vivekananda called it) is at odds with the Perennial Philosophy. I suspect that this reflects a subliminal racism in that Jesus is seen, falsely, as a White Man and Europe is conflated, falsely, with 'Christendom'.

Note 10

Mike Davis tells us in his award-winning *Late Victorian Holocausts* (Verso, 2001) how journalist Edwin Arnold peddled the official propaganda that the British ruled India for the sake of Indians first and that revenue, reputation and power came afterwards. This was in response to criticism by American Missionaries that the British lied to deceive the world about their real purposes. This involved killing tens of millions of Indians through starvation and in Buchenwald-like camps for famine victims where 94 per cent died on dirt-mixed flour rations (less food than Nazi's gave in Death Camps) for hard labour. Simultaneously record amounts of India's food-grains were exported lowering world market prices for Westerners and providing Food Security for Britain. The British even introduced an Anti-Charitable Donations Act in 1877 to prevent private aid to Indians forced to starve by the Brits. Thus Christian Missionaries have done some good for India!

Note 11

The famous Florentine House of the Medici sponsored and protected many artists and philosophers including Galileo Galilei. Revisionist Historians of Science have pointed out that, *contra* the modern historiography of Galileo which makes the Church look totally stupid, things were not so one-sided. The Vatican employed many of the best-educated minds of the time and the Church put forward rational arguments against Galileo and other Natural Philosophers who challenged Catholic Aristotelianism. It was the hard power accruing from the New Science (and its technological offshoots) to its sponsors (especially at the time of the Protestant Reformation) that allowed the New Science to overcome resistance from the Catholic Church.

Note 12

As I edited this text (28th July 2012) physicist US Max Tegmark appeared on *Russia Today* TV discussing the recent news about CERN's claim to have verified the existences of the Higg's Boson. Tegmark asserted that we will never be able to answer certain 'Why' questions and deeper problems such as how the 'Laws of Physics' themselves arose. This contradicted in part his earlier claims that physicists were not dogmatic and that they were open to accepting past views as erroneous. We have seen the idea of 'Laws of Physics' is rooted in the Christian myth of Creation *ex-nihilo* and that a deeper understanding of the Transcendental and the holonomic Wave Structure of Matter can begin to start explaining how such so-called Laws arose.

Note 13

As stated previously Rorty's work, as with Postmodern followers of Derrida, Gadamer, etc., reads more like Literary Criticism than serious metaphysics. In his essay dismissing mystical claims to perceive the Transcendental, Rorty characterised traditional philosophers such as Brahmins and Nietzsche as 'ascetic priests' who were elitists, etc., unconcerned with the suffering of the masses. In fact, as we have seen, Nietzsche dismissed the Transcendental as a worthless self-deception and mocked traditional philosophers' claims to attain Wisdom. In contrast to such elitist philosophers, Rorty glorified novelist Charles Dickens as a great Liberal and Social Reformer. Here again Rorty misled the reader. Like many Western 'Liberals', Dickens was only a Liberal at home in regard to his own people. After the 1857 revolt in India, Dickens wrote that he wished that he were commander-in-chief in India so that he would be able to do "my utmost to exterminate the [Indian] race..." (*see* N. Robins' *The Corporation that Changed the World*, Pluto Press, 2006). Dickens also applauded the barbaric execution of Hindu (meaning Indian) prisoners-of-war by so-called cannonading (placing them directly in front of the cannon muzzle before firing). Dickens own writings reveal him to be a racist who denigrated various races and who opposed the Abolition of Slavery campaign of Wilberforce and criticised Harriet Beecher Stowe for her stirring up conflict aimed at overthrowing the White Race (*see* Esther M. Zimmer Lederberg's web article "Dickens and Racism" on www.estherledergberg.com).

Note 14

A number of writers have speculated that Consciousness may be like a 5th Dimension or another dimension. Such writers do not understand that a dimension is merely a *Degree of Freedom* for vibratory, energetic activity to occur. A dimension is thus a purely 'Behaviorist' spatiotemporal concept, describing patterns of energetic activity. New dimensions cannot broaden the Physicalist ontology to encompass the ontologically distinct property of Awareness.

Notes to Chapter 10

Note 1

It is true that "Nature is red in tooth and claw". But certain contemporary historical influences upon Charles Darwin's formulation of his hypothesis of Natural Selection are suppressed by Darwin's British hagiographers. In his *Exterminate All the Brutes* (US Edition, The New Press, 2007) Sven Lindqvist tells of the hypocritical Anglo-Saxon demonisation of the Spaniards for their cruelty and bloodthirstiness whilst blaming Divine Intervention for the extermination of natives in North America. Later, the wiping out of darker-skinned peoples by European 'Whites' was rationalised as a Natural Law of Race. The famous Anthropologist J.C. Prichard in his "On the Extinction of Human Races" (1838) had concocted the alibi that extermination of "the savage races" was inevitable. That same year Herman Merivale in a series of lectures at Oxford dismissed such myths, pointing out that it was the uncontrolled violence of the European settlers who can murder natives at will without any punishment that was to blame. In 1832, when Darwin arrived there, the Argentine government decided to exterminate the native 'Indians' of the Pampas. This genocide was still going on, financed by a bond loan, when Darwin wrote *The Descent of Man* in 1871. In 1836 Darwin visited Tasmania just after the British had exterminated the native population during the previous few years. Darwin had read Georg Gerland's 1868 book *On the Extinction of Primitive Peoples* in which Gerland, like Prichard, exposed the real cause as the bloodthirsty European settlers. But in his 1871 *Descent of Man* Darwin sided with the British Scientific Racists who saw such extermination of 'inferior races' by the White Race as a 'Darwinian' process.

Note 2

We have seen that Isaac Newton's Cambridge Platonist friends including Ralph Cudworth accepted the traditional view that Plato's doctrine of Ideas originated in Egypt and the numerous Oriental influences on Greek philosophy which the Ancient Greeks themselves had acknowledged.

Note 3

The 19th Century German scholar Jacob Fallmerayer had pointed out that the modern Greeks were not the real descendants of the ancient Hellenes as they imagined themselves to be but actually a hotchpotch of Slavs, Bulgars, Albanian Turks and others who had mixed over two millennia with the Hellenic population (*see* S. Sand, *The Invention of the Jewish People*, Verso, 2009). David Lowenthal has shown that the Greek state is itself a recent creation of Romantic Western Philhellenism. European support for the Greek War of Liberation from the Ottomans was predicated on the idea of resuscitating Ancient Greece. This Romantic vision of Classical Greece was not familiar to the natives who were made to embrace this romanticised version of their supposed Classical identity by the Western Philhellenes. The inhabitants of Greece were not Classical 'pagans' worshipping Olympian gods but Christian who called called themselves 'Romii' and spoke a language called Romaika. Most actual Greeks lived outside the Greek state and many centres of Greek culture lay beyond its borders. Philhellenes lumbered Greek nationalist protocols with archaic Classical Hellenic language that was unintelligible to most Greeks. Nationalists purged villages of their Turkish and Balkan folklore so as to construct a sense of continuity with the Classical Hellenes and refute the taunt that *the modern Greeks were actually Slavs* (*emphasis mine*) (*see* D. K. Chakrabarti, *Colonial Indology*, Munshiram Manoharlal, 1997). I have stressed that the actual Hellenes were not 'Europeans' but a people of the Eastern Mediterranean including North Africa and Western Asia. Note also that the Northern Germanic Lombards invaded Byzantine Italy in the 6th Century and see themselves as distinct from the darker-skinned Southern Italians, the true descendants of the Eleatic Greeks and the Romans. The Roman's mythological ancestry from the 'Trojans' of Asia Minor is supported by Latin's close kinship with Hittite and Indo-Iranian languages.

Note 4

I copied Wolpert in on my email which I also sent to Martin Bernal and J.M. Hobson; two scholars who have challenged the Eurocentric myth of the Greek Miracle. Wolpert's responded that no Ancient Indian had put forward a mathematical model but my friend Air Vice-Marshall V.M. Tiwari, an expert on Vedic Maths, pointed out Aryabhatta's work. Wolpert also asked me to name any Ancient Indian who had put forward the view that organisms were made of cells. But Cell Theory was not Ancient Greek. It was Robert Hooke who first observed cells.

Note 5

This is assuming the standard Empiricist view of Aristotle (derived from Aquinas) as opposed to transcendental Platonic Forms; a view which Phillip Cary challenges. Aquinas's exaggeratedly Empiricistic interpretation ignored a great deal of ancient commentary on Aristotle's Platonist epistemology. Aristotle's most important ancient commentator, a member of Aristotle's own School, was the Peripatetic philosopher Alexander of Aphrodisias. Aristotle's early Empiricism influenced Stoicism but his more mature Platonist writings were of great value to the Neoplatonists (*see* P. Cary *Augustine's Invention of the Inner Self*, Oxford U.P., 2000).

Note 6

At the end of the PBS TV's Science show *Nova* entitled *Just Where Are all the Aliens* (shown 30/7/2012 in UK) Neil de Grasse Tyson made the highly Eurocentric assertion that only a few centuries ago we thought that we were the centre of the universe. William Anderson says that Western science is rooted in the Christian linear time rooted in the Judaic obsession with tribal history supposedly ending in a New Jerusalem under a Jewish tribal redeemer. Anderson contrasts this conception with the Hindu view of the immensity and countless numbers of the universes each with its Brahma, Vishnu and Shiva (representing Creation, maintenance and dissolution). The universes float on the fathomless pure waters that form the body of Vishnu. Out of every pore a universe bubbles and breaks. A *mahayuga* or one Day of Brahma lasts 4,320,000 years. Against such immensities what is the worth of the individual human soul. The uniqueness of humanity is redeemed by the concept of the *atman* or Supreme Self, which subsumes all gods, all possible universes and all periods and cycles of time, and this *atman* is present in every human being (W.Anderson *The Face of Glory*, Bloomsbury, 1996).

Note 7

Ten years after Yates' *Giordano Bruno and the Hermetic Tradition* exploded these myths, the 1974 *Encyclopaedia Britannica* still presented Bruno as an astronomer and mathematician. In the 21st Century, both physicist Shimon Malin in his *Nature Loves to Hide* (Oxford, U.P., 2001) and also Oxford Neurobiologist Professor Colin Blakemore, in his Eurocentric UK TV programme *God and the Scientists* (Channel 4, 2009), repeat the Bruno as martyr for Science myth. The Church actually burnt him for his theological doctrines not for any scientific ideas.

Note 8

Glaswegian Neocon Niall Ferguson (NF) peddles Rudyard Kipling's fictional propaganda myths about British imperialism as if they were facts. D'Amato points out that, in his 2003 book *Empire,* NF contradicts himself. NF quotes positively Kipling bemoaning the supposed 'fact' that British officials in India "die, or kill themselves by overwork, or are worried to death...in order that the land may be protected from death and sickness, famine and war and may eventually become capable of standing alone". This totally absurd claim is contradicted later by another quote from a district tax collector who worked from 11am to 5 pm collecting taxes from Indians and finding time for hunting wild animals during work hours (P. d'Amato "When Britannia waived the rules". *International Socialist Review*, Issue 32, Nov-Dec 2003). H.M. Hyndman wrote that, on average, Britons in the ICS were paid more than five times the salary paid to the native for doing the same job. Of 960 civil offices which really control the civil administration of India, 900 are occupied by Britons and only 60 by natives. India is administered by a successive relay of English carpet-baggers, with no real interest in the wellbeing of the people they govern, who return to England at age 45 or 55 with large pensions (H.M. Hyndman, *Ruin of India by British Rule*, 1907). R.N. Cust, who himself drew a pension from Indian revenues equal to about 1700 times the annual income of the average Indian, wrote:

> *There is a constant drawing away of the wealth of India to England, as Englishmen grow fat on accumulation made in India, while the Indian remains as lean as ever... Every post of dignity and high emolument, civil and military is held by a stranger and a foreigner... it is the jealousy of the middle-class Briton, the hungry Scot, that wants his salary, that shuts out all Native aspirations... The consequences will be terrible.*

(Cited in W. Digby (1901) *'Prosperous' British India: A Revelation from Official Records*). In October 2001 in the right-wing *Daily Mail* NF had a two-page essay entitled (if I recall correctly) *The White Man's Burden* in which he presented Kipling's fictional claims (in his story *William the Conqueror*) about British officials heroically saving starving Indians in the 1896 famine as if they were historical facts. The *Daily Mail* (19/10/01) did publish my letter responding to these falsehoods. It was the British who actually created these 'Late Victorian Holocausts' as in the title of Mike Davis's award-winning book about the manmade famines in British-ruled India. Davis had debunked Kipling's propaganda citing an actual British official associated with the 1896 famine. Official British policy was to let the poorest Indians starve (as this was supposedly the Natural Law of Free Trade). In 1877 they even passed an Anti-Charitable Donations Act preventing private individuals aiding starving Indians and, as seen in Note 10 to Chapter 9, created Buchenwald-like Death Camps for starving Indians. Things were no different in 1895. By 1900 one quarter of Britain's wheat was imported from India. In 1901, *The Lancet* estimated conservatively from the Census that 19 million Indians died from starvation in Western India during the 1890s as a result of British 'Let-them-starve' policies (M. Davis *Late Victorian Holocausts,* Verso, 2001). In his letter to *The Guardian* (12th June 2010) responding furiously to journalist Seumas Milne's attack on the Tory Party's plans to get Ferguson to help rewrite the English schools' History curriculum, Ferguson ranted:

> *Those like Milne, who equate British imperialism with Nazi imperialism – who describe natural disasters [sic] like famines as "Victorian Holocausts"... are guilty of the worst kind of relativism.*

Once again Ferguson was being deceptive. Davis had told us in *Late Victorian Holocausts* Alfred Russell Wallace (who put forward the Theory of

Evolution by Natural Selection with Darwin) wrote that mass starvation in India was not due to 'natural disasters' but avoidable political tragedies. H.M. Hyndman noted caustically the hypocrisy of the British rulers: "We attribute all suffering under native governments to native misrule, our own errors we father on Nature".

Note 9

This new Arithmetic that revolutionised banking and commerce, science and philosophy was invented in India and translated into Arabic. Even in late January 2010, on BBC London News, the Muslim news presenter Riz Latif and a Muslim scholar at an Islamic Science exhibition at the Science Museum in London, both stated that the numerals, now in everyday use across the world, have their *roots* in Arabic culture! In a recent BBC TV programme on Science and Islam, hosted by Anglo-Iraqi Jim Al-Khalili, the achievement presented first as the most significant was in fact the counting system which Hindus invented! It can hardly be called 'Islamic' (*see below*). Playing fast and loose with historical facts by Mohammedans is common. Iranian Reza Aslan has appeared on Jon Stewart's *The Daily Show*. In a January 2010 History Channel TV programme called *Secrets of the Koran* in the series *Decoding the Past*, Aslan asserted that within 50 years of Mohammed's death the Muslims had conquered vast territories including most of the Indian Subcontinent! In fact the Muslims first conquered part of Northern India 600 years after Mohammed. In fact it was only about 1,000 years after Mohammed that Mughal Aurangzeb invaded central India provoking a Hindu backlash by the Marathas who eventually defeated the Mughals. On December 27th 2008 former Indian government minister Arif Mohammed Khan revealed in the *Times of India* the ridiculous fabrications of Indian history and anti-Hindu hatred inculcated in Pakistani state schools. Note that this was state-funded Pakistani schools not the misogynous Taliban-creating Madrassahs, funded by the feudal House of Saud, which indoctrinate poor children with Wahhabi fundamentalism.

Note 10

This was probably because he was born in 1906 and his upbringing in colonial Britain with its twisted historical propaganda inculcated in schools such as the myths of the (largely fabricated) horrors of the 'Black Hole of Calcutta' (*see* J. Dalley *The Black Hole*, Penguin, 2006) and the (largely fabricated) Cult of Thuggee (*see* N. Dirks *The Scandal of Empire*, Harvard U.P., 2006). These myths were concocted by the Brits to supposedly prove the barbaric savagery of Indians. As Dalley tells us, in 1915 distinguished historian J.H. Little reassessed the records and concluded that only nine prisoners-of-war had been locked up overnight in the 'Black Hole' (a British-built prison cell) and only three of them had died from the previous day's battle wounds. Contrast these facts with Thomas Macaulay's hyperbolic presentation of the Black Hole incident as the most horrific atrocity in history! Indeed, one survivor of the 'Black Hole' was Mariah Carey, the Anglo-Indian wife of a British sailor who had been refused permission to board a ship evacuating Brits from Calcutta as she was not White! The same British discrimination preventing Non-Whites evacuating besieged cities continued into the 1940s with the Japanese invasion of British-occupied Malaya and Singapore.

Note 11

Recently Sheldon Pollock, Professor of Sanskrit at Columbia University, has put the blame for European Racism and Nazism falsely upon Indian Civilisation. He claims 'high Brahmanism' ultimately led to the legitimisation of Nazi genocide. Wilhelm Halbfass built on Pollock's false thesis to equate the Hindu philosophical school of *Mimamsa* with Nazism, calling Kumarila and William Jones 'deep Nazis' and Adolf Hitler a 'deep Mimamsaka' (*See* Malhotra and Neelakandan, *Breaking India*, Amaryllis, 2011). This resembles the Russian attempts to deflect blame for the 1945 mass rape of German women by Russian troops from 'Europeans' onto the Soviet Central Asian descendants of Genghis Kahn or the claim by Stalin's father-in-law to blame Stalin's despotism on the 'fact' that he was an 'Asiatic' when in fact Georgians are Europeans often of Hellenic-Greek descent. I noticed that Halbfass's German-born friend Fred Dallmayr, in his tacitly Eurocentric 'postmodern' *Beyond Orientalism* (SUNY Press, 1996), referred to Halbfass's seeking of Caste ideology in Sankara whilst hiding the fact that Dallmayr's own hero Heidegger was an open Nazi. Such asymmetric treatment is also seen in regard to the European romanticisation of medieval Chivalry as if knights supposedly cared for the welfare of the poor. In fact the Chivalric Code was a barbaric system relying on terrorising the serfs so that they remained too frightened to challenge the warrior elite who kept them in servitude. Westerners peddle myths about how 'Liberty' and 'Individual Freedom' were supposedly incipient in Western society from Ancient Athens to the present day! In 2010 Pollock was honoured by the Government of India with a *Padma Shri* award (from *Breaking India*). Indian billionaires are now donating funds to the likes of Pollock and Harvard University without bothering to check what sort of demonisation of Indian tradition such Western scholars are actually perpetrating (Rajiv Malhotra, Personal Communication). The fawning Indian businessmen of course seek prestige by having their names associated with top Western (i.e., White Men's) academic institutions. Pollock's claims are absurd, projecting the blame for European crimes against Jews onto Hinduism, just as Zionist fabricators of history have done in blaming Arabs for expulsions and persecutions of the Jews which were actually perpetrated by Christian Europeans (*see* S. Sand *The Invention of the Jewish People*, Verso, and J. Rose *The Myths of Zionism*, Pluto Press, 2004). The medieval Jews and Arabs actually lived in a peaceful cultural symbiosis; Moses Maimonides was physician to Saladin. Jews in Muslim countries had no Zionist tendencies. The anti-Black racism of Maimonides and the anti-Gentile hate ideology of Orthodox Judaism have been hidden from Gentiles by Jewish scholars like Martin Buber who eulogised the whole Hassidic movement including the virulent Habbad (*see* I. Shahak, *Jewish History, Jewish Religion*, Pluto Press 1994). Such religious sanctions to cheat and harm non-Jews in the Talmud, Jewish genocide against non-Jews in Yemen, and the fact that the Jews aligned themselves with oppressive imperial aristocracies like the Normans and Czars, leading to anti-Jewish sentiments amongst European peasantry are brushed under the carpet. So too is the fact that genocide was not uniquely inflicted upon the Jews. The fact that the first 1939–45 war atrocity labelled a 'holocaust' was the British-inflicted Bengal Holocaust killing up to 7 million Indians has also been swept under the carpet (*see* Gideon Polya, *The Forgotten Holocaust*, 2005 web article and his related web articles). Norman Finkelstein, whose own mother (like Israel Shahak) was a survivor of Nazi genocide, has written about the US-based 'Holocaust Industry' which arose after the 1967 Zionist invasion of Egypt, Gaza and the West Bank (which as Rose shows in *The Myths of Zionism* was a war of expansion planned by the Zionists in the 1950s). The 'Holocaust Industry' misappropriates the legacy of the Jewish victims of the Nazi genocide to distract attention from the criminal activities of the Zionist regime (*see* N. Finkelstein *The Holocaust Industry*, Verso, 2000). Zionists actually supported Hitler's anti-Jewish policies as it furthered their anti-assimilation, Separatist ideology and Zionists even acted to prevent Jews escaping from Nazi Germany to the UK or USA as it compromised their settler-colonial ambitions to dispossess the Palestinians (*see* Lenni Brenner *51 Documents: Zionist Collaboration with the Nazis*, Barricade Books, 2002). Sven Lvindqvist in his *Exterminate all the Brutes* (US Edition, New Press, 2007) and Madhushrie Mukerjee in her *Churchill's Secret War* (Basic books, 2010) tell us of the real influences behind Nazi ideology. Hitler stated in *Mein Kampf*, the Nazi conquest of Eastern Europe with its War of Extermination was actually an attempt to emulate the British Empire. Lindqvist notes that the concepts of *lebensraum* and extermination of inferior races were derived from 'Germanisation' of White Supremacist British imperial ideology by a German academic Tille who taught in Glasgow in the 1890s. Brenner tells us in *51 Documents* that Churchill's official biographer Martin Gilbert was one of the leading Zionists who in 1987 tried to block the staging of the play Perdition, directed by Ken Loach, based on Brenner's book on Zionist-Nazi collaboration entitled *Zionism in the Age of the Dictators*.

Note 12

Halbfass wrote in *India and Europe* (SUNY Press, 1990) that early Christian visitors to India had lauded Vedanta as the 'natural light' or a natural conception of God devoid of ritual trappings and superstitious distortions. The Jesuits hoped to apply such ideas to Christianity.

Note 13

Western scholars hype up the minor figure of Heraclitus who is said to have put forward a Process Ontology. Heraclitus's links to the much older and much more developed Indian Process ontologies are ignored (*see Chapter 7*).

Note 14

I see that leading Whiteheadian 'Process Philosopher' David Ray Griffin became a September 11th conspiracy theorist!

Notes to Chapter 11:

Note 1

The Sanskrit surname *Bhattacharya* derived from *bhatta* (learned Brahmin) and *acharya* ('master', 'preceptor') is itself an elite title amongst the elite Brahman caste although the surname is quite common in West Bengal. In North-East India, local rulers imported Brahmans with grants of land to bring Indo-Aryan Sanskritic civilisation to these lands. I recently read a book on Bankim Chandra Chattopadhyay's writings in which he lauded the Bhattacharyas of the *tols* (native Sanskrit schools) in Bengal.

Note 2

In fact my good-for-nothing father had stayed in London and forced my mother to travel across India by train to Bombay, then by ship to Marseilles, then across France and the English Channel with three young children. Our ship the French *S.S. Vietnam* was in fact the last ship to go through the Suez Canal before the Zionist regime launched its premeditated invasion of Egypt annexing the Sinai, and simultaneous annexation of the West Bank, Gaza strip and the Golan Heights in the so-called '6-Day War'. The Western media portrays these wars of aggression as little 'Israel' defending itself when in fact it was planned long in advance and seen by the Zionist leaders as part of the Greater Israel fantasy; they claimed on the basis of absurd historical myths that all the land between the Nile and the Euphrates should belong to the Jews (*see* Rose's *The Myths of Zionism* and Shahak's *Jewish History, Jewish Religion*). In his *Zionism, Militarism and the Decline of US Power* (Clarity Press, 2008) James Petras tells of how the Congressional Hearings into the 1967 war Zionist attack on the American spyship *USS Liberty,* killing and maiming over 100 US service personnel was delayed by 40 years by the Israel Lobby. The explosive findings that Israel was guilty of deliberately killing and maiming over one hundred US servicemen in this attack were published in the Congressional Record but never appeared in the US print or broadcast media. Both Petras and Stephen Sniegoski in his *The Transparent Cabal: The NeoConservative Agenda, War in the Middle East, and the National Interest of Israel* (Enigma Editions, 2008) highlight George Washington's 1796 Farewell Address in which he warned of American citizens who betray the USA by devoting themselves to their favourite (foreign) nation. Billions of dollars of so-called 'aid' (Petras labels it more accurately as 'tribute'), including massive amounts of military hardware, keep being paid by the US to Israel! Imagine the huge and disproportionate US retaliation had an Arab warplane attacked the US spyship!

Note 3

In 2003 I read an article in the right-wing *Daily Mail* by the Indian born Sociologist Bikhu Parekh (made a Labour Life Peer). Parekh said that he had started life in England in Benarasi's house when he first arrived in the mid-1960s and that Benarasi made his money selling incense sticks at some major railway station in swinging London! The *Daily Mail* is often lampooned by comedians given its notoriety for sensationalist headlines about immigrants cheating the welfare system or committing crimes. During the 1930s, the paper supported Hitler, Mussolini and Oswald Moseley. Thus it seemed to me that Parekh was pandering to the English about how supposedly anyone could make it in England just because he and his sons had had some success. Two of his sons had become Oxford dons. His third son a banker is a close friend and associate of my elder brother. But I am certain that he also wrote that the two Oxford don sons had gone to private schools, called 'Public Schools' in the UK. Only 7 per cent attend private schools yet the privately-educated dominate all the top professions. Furthermore, Parekh denigrated Indian society for its lack of social mobility claiming that he was from some lower stratum, some fishermen's community or something. But I recall him writing rather oddly that his father was actually a village *moneylender* and that he himself got a place at Bombay University which seemed to contradict his overall argument of pleading poverty and lack of social mobility. Parekh also ignored the fact that Britain's prosperity and social reforms were built partly on the wealth gained by looting India for 200 years (after profiting hugely from the Atlantic Slave Trade) . Furthermore, under the Mughals, Hindus had attained high office whereas the British did their utmost to prevent Indians, regardless of merit, from rising to senior positions within the Raj. Solemn pledges made by the British Government and by Queen Victoria of Equal Opportunity for Indians were never redeemed. The Brits used all manner of dirty tricks, such as moving Indian Civil Service exams to Britain to deny Indians a fair chance. Of course there were numerous Indian collaborators who prospered by serving British interests as middlemen or subordinate bureaucrats, etc., serving the wishes of the Brits with no concern for the plight of their fellow countrymen.

Note 4

In his *The Oriental Renaissance* (English translation: 1984, Columbia U.P.), Raymond Schwab told an interesting story vouched for by Mr E.W. Emerson, a relative of Ralph Waldo Emerson. A teacher told a little American schoolgirl to learn some verses of Emerson. The next day she recited to him Emerson's poem *Brahma*. The astonished teacher asked why she chose *Brahma*. She replied that she had tried several poems but couldn't understand them at all. But this poem was so easy to understand, it just means, "God everywhere".

Note 5

Dictionary compiler Dr Samuel Johnson claimed to have 'disproved' Bishop Berkeley's Idealism (external objects exist in the 'Mind of God') by simply kicking a stone.

Note 6

I was told by those who worked with him that he collected militaria and supposedly sang along to "Land of Hope and Glory" at the end of the Tory Party conferences on television.

Note 7

In our Third Year we had a diminutive female Maths teacher from New Zealand who could not maintain authority faced with 30 or so mainly rowdy 14 year old boys most of whom just ignored her. I was not one of the few 'swots' who sat in the front row and tried to learn. I was friends with the less-academic 'bad boys' like Billy (*see Note 9*) so I learnt no maths that year. With hindsight, of course, I feel terrible about the way we behaved and the negative effect it might have had on her career through no fault of her own.

Note 8

I noticed that the sons of Bengali friends who went to private schools also often got private tuition at home. Having been asked whilst I was an undergraduate to give some tuition to the privately educated sons of two of my mother's friends who had helped her a lot, I got the clear impression that the British private schools had decent Maths and Science teachers or at least much better ones than in the State schools like my own. Given that my own school had been in a wealthy middle class area where most of the parents were themselves well-educated, I dread to think how bad the teaching is in most State schools in poor areas.

Note 9

Alexander Hudson from Islington, who was my best friend at school, had tried to get into Oxford to study Classics have studied Greek and Latin. His father was an eccentric Old Etonian, Oxford Classics-educated curator at the British Museum. But having waited to take the Oxford entrance exams after taking his Advanced Level exams, he was inspired by my summer 1983 work on Consciousness to study Philosophy and Psychology which he did at Edinburgh. In contrast to his background, my best friend in the early years at Secondary School was a blonde cockney boy from the rough part of Islington, Billy Harp. Billy's father, divorced from his mother, owned a pub in Clapton and Billy's half-brother (not in our school) was a member of the Neo-Nazi British Movement who would apparently have assaulted me, due to my ethnicity, outside our school had I not been his half-brother's friend. I never spoke to Billy's half-brother but I did befriend a muscular skinhead thug, a West Ham football hooligan with 'battle-scars', who had initially threatened to beat me up when the two of us were alone in an empty train carriage at Kentish Town over-ground rail-station. My talkative charm won him over and it transpired that he worked at the Royal Mint Chocolate Liqueur factory in Kentish Town owned by the Halgarten family whose son had been a friend of my older brother's at primary school. Thus I also had some leverage over him if he did misbehave. Such hooligans tend to behave badly when egged-on by friends in groups. Billy left school without any qualifications at age 16 to become an apprentice printer on the newspaper presses where his relatives already worked. In the past these unionised manual labourers earned very high wages. But Billy entered the trade not long before Rupert Murdoch's Wapping dispute (involving an Eddie Shah) and the electronic printing revolution led to the loss of thousands of such antiquated printing jobs.

Note 10

In fact, a search on the internet reveals that two boys in my class at secondary school became professional Molecular Biologists. Both were North Americans living in London and at least one was the son of a Biochemist. This was Canadian born Jordan Raff who had in fact been my friend in my first year at my first primary school (1969–70). But, as I was so far ahead of my age-group, I was given a double promotion to the year above where I befriended aforementioned American Jew Peter Schlossman and Scot John Hughes amongst others. I think that the first birthday party I attended was at Raff's house although I think his mother was divorced from his Biochemist father. We met again at age 12 (1976) when we were both assigned to the same class in our secondary school after I had returned to my own age-group at my second primary school. Raff did not make the top sets in Maths and Science in later years when we streamed on ability. I did not know the other boy Sean Colloms that well, who was in the top sets and went to Cambridge, but I think at least one of his American parents may have been a scientist. An academically very mediocre boy from my class Joe Swift is now a presenter on the BBC's *Gardeners' World*. I heard after I left school that his father was a fairly well-known actor and his mother a well-known novelist Margaret Drabble. This just seems to corroborate the fact that family connections are still very important in terms of career opportunities in the UK. In 2000, Joe Swift recognised me as I walked to work up Jamestown Road in Camden and he expected that I should recognise him (presumably because he was on TV). But I had not watched *Gardeners' World* since the 1970s and Joe had lost all of his bright ginger hair at a young age.

Note 11

It was Koestler's endowment which funded the new Parapsychology department at Edinburgh University. I later read that Koestler used to mistreat women and had raped Jill Craigie, wife of the famous Labour Party politician Michael Foot.

Note 12

He also seems to have been associated with the trendy, arts-based Dartington Hall school in Devon which was inspired by Rabindranath Tagore's Santiniketan in Bengal. His *Rise of the Meritocracy* was influential in inspiring the Labour Party to eliminate Grammar and Secondary Modern schools in favour of Comprehensive schools. This has actually resulted in a widening of inequality as poor children can no longer rise up the social ladder through free selective intake Grammar schools. On 8th July 2011 it was reported in the press that 4 elite private schools (Eton, Westminster, St Paul's Boys, St Paul's Girls) charging over £30,000 p.a. fees (more than the average worker's yearly salary), and the State run school in Cambridge teaching the children of Cambridge dons, together send more pupils to Oxford and Cambridge Universities than all Britain's two thousand plus Comprehensive schools put together! There is no Meritocracy in 21st Century Britain!

Note 13

In my *The Oneness/Otherness Mystery* I had a section entitled 'The Philistinism of the English Establishment' referring to their Materialist-Empiricist and tacitly White Supremacist disdain for Non-European knowledge. I quoted Andrew Harvey who had been the youngest fellow at All Souls College, Oxford in 1973. But Harvey discovered Indian Spirituality and went off to India. In the TV documentary *The Making of a Modern Mystic*, Harvey told of how difficult it had been for an arrogant young fellow at Oxford to learn that everything he had ever been taught was wrong.

Note 14

The other school was Acland Burleigh School in Tufnell Park. The aforementioned Labour MP Robert Hughes had sent his sons to this State Comprehensive as it was Labour Party policy to turn all the selective intake Grammar Schools into Comprehensives. This was in spite of the fact that, back then in the mid-1970s Acland Burleigh had a notorious reputation as a bad school where teenagers would come back to class drunk after lunch etc. Most Labour politicians do not seem to practice what they preach and seek privileged selective education for their own children whilst pushing Comprehensive education on the masses. Note the case of PM Tony Blair sending his son to a prestigious State School outside the London borough where they had lived and left-wing Afro-Caribbean firebrand MP Diane Abbott sending her own son to a very expensive private school. In 2014 I read in a newspaper that Labour Shadow Chancellor Ed Balls' father had been an anti-Grammar School zealot who sent his own sons to a private school. During the 5th Form, my best friend was Nigel Meacher, son of left-wing Labour M.P. and later Environment Minister Michael Meacher. In 1988 Meacher Snr would lose a famous libel case against journalist Alan Watkins of *The Observer* who accused him of claiming to be of Working Class background to get on in the Labour Party.

In fact Michael Meacher's father had been an accountant who later retired to his family's farm and MM had been sent to elite private school Haileybury (the East India Company School) before going on to Oxford University. Michael Meacher had also condemned second-home owners (I think he had once written that property should not be for social need and not for profit). But as Environment Minister promoting Green measures urging people not to be wasteful, etc., the Press revealed that Meacher had a built up personal portfolio of nine properties.

Note 15

I also recall that in 1981 or 1982 I read in my Advanced-Level Biology textbook about summation in synaptic connections in the brain and this conjured up Reductionist fantasies about how Mind could be explained by such simplistic cybernetic activations and inhibitions of synapses by dendrites from other neurons. Note especially in Chapter 5 how most scientists do not mature but seem to remain stuck in simplistic, adolescent Reductionist mindsets envisaging Mind and Consciousness simply in terms of Information Processing analogies and other such Reductionist ideas.

Note 16

Decades later my mother told me that he had said that he spent money on unnecessary luxuries like the cameras and projectors deliberately and selfishly, given that he was going to die from his cirrhosis, whereas we were going to live.

Note 17

We saw in Chapter 5 that D.S. Clarke has pointed out that Popper's example of solidity as an Emergent property is false. For most molecules, solidity is a 'Resultant property' (meaning that we can predict the formation of a solid structure at an appropriate temperature from molecular structure).

Note 18

The nearest parallel came in 1994-5 after reading a book on hypnagogia I tried to relax with my eyes shut and stop all thinking. On a couple of occasions, a cartoon-like image manifested spontaneously.

Note 19

We have seen that Alan Turing himself argued that the strongest argument against a computer passing the test was that, unlike a human being, it would not have **paranormal psychic experiences** such as ESP and Telepathy (*see* N. Herbert, *Elemental Mind*, Dutton, 1993).

Note 20

Einstein's presentation of Time as supposedly a 4th Dimension in GTR is essentially a mathematical trick. As the likes of Whitehead, Bergson and Whiteman have noted such a 'Block Universe' is extremely misleading in regard to the true nature of Time. Lee Smolin sees Descartes' use of a space-like axis for Time in his Analytical Geometry (Cartesian Co-ordinates) as a fundamental error underlying standard Physics (L. Smolin, *The Trouble with Physics*, Houghton Mifflin, 2006). Physics may present the Time axis as reversible but in reality Time is not such a reversible degree of freedom.

Note 21

I do not agree with those pop philosophers who call themselves fancy names like 'Systems Theorists' that loosely inter-related systems such as social insect colonies, human societies, cities, ecosystems, the biosphere, etc., can be considered unitary entities in the same way as an atom, molecule, cell or an organism constitutes a unitary self-organising entity (*see discussion in Ch. 6*).

Note 22

In my rush of excitement, I even sent a copy to the Queen at Buckingham Palace! I actually received a polite response from a Palace equerry saying that Her Majesty had instructed him to write thanking me for sending her my ideas which she found interesting. Assuming that she did indeed read it, I like to joke that as she is a German (Saxe-Coburg) she should be more open to notions associated with Mysticism such as Panpsychism. Her response also demonstrates the general politeness of distinguished British and American people in contrast to Indians who have 'made it' in the West. One prominent Bengali-American New Age figure claiming to doing something similar to my work, never responded to my synopsis of my book, even though two of his White American acquaintances assumed, in communications to me after hearing of my work, that this fellow Bengali would be excited by my book. One of these White Americans even forwarded my synopsis to him not knowing that I had already sent a copy to him myself a year before. As Richard Crasta tells us in *Impressing the Whites*, prominent Indians in the West seem unwilling to associate with or even respond to their fellow Indians. This may be due to them thinking that they have now risen above the lowly Indian to become 'honorary' Whites or they may want to deny any competitors to their cherished positions as 'native interpreters' for the White masters in regard to Indian culture. This is not to say that all Indians are like this. Furthermore, most White academics whose views are criticised, exposed as Eurocentric myths, undermined, etc., by my work tend to keep silent even when they boast publicly that they welcome new ideas and debate. They only really welcome that which reaffirms their own prestige; faced with threatening challenges to their authority, they keep silent and pretend such things will go away. In 2013 when I sent the British PM, Deputy PM, Leader of the Opposition and the Queen letters complaining about the plan to put White Supremacist War Criminal Winston Churchill on the new British Five Pound Note, only the Office of the Deputy PM, the Liberal leader Nick Clegg, responded, but only to pass the buck to the Treasury.

Note 23

At that time, my local Member of Parliament was a man called Bryan Magee, a historian of philosophy who appeared on British television hosting a programme called *Men of Ideas* and who appeared to be an acolyte of Karl Popper. I did try phoning him but he did not want to talk.

Note 24

For the truth about the consummate liar and homosexual molestor of underage boys Senator Joe McCarthy see the recent book about the racist, transvestite homosexual, blackmailer of politicians and Godfather of the FBI and his lover and deputy *J.Edgar Hoover and Clyde Tolson* by Darwin Porter (Blood Moon Productions, 2012).

Note 25

Recently I have come across a number of physicists, writing in popular books, expressing similar disappointment with academic Physics, where philosophical questioning means career suicide. Lee Smolin in his *The Trouble with Physics* wrote of the disillusionment of many young physicists who had been attracted to the subject by the philosophical paradoxes of Quantum Mechanics were faced with the "shut up and calculate" approach advocated by Feynmann and others.

Note 26

Assam was in the news in 2012 given the attacks by the Bodo tribals on the illegal Mohammedan settlers flooding in from the overpopulated Mohammedan state of Bangladesh (the old East Pakistan).

Note 27

Ironically, in 1995 at the time I got the publisher for my earlier book, etc., a young middle class Cambridge graduate, who worked as a journal copyeditor/proofreader at my workplace, assumed that I was a privileged public schoolboy due to my manner of speech and lofty interests in Philosophy. Due to my secondary schooling in an upper middle class area, and the self-promoting activities of Michael Young's son Toby, which resulted in my appearance in an article about my old school in the posh *Harpers and Queen* magazine in 1995 and a pilot TV programme in 1995 that never got aired, certain work colleagues assumed naively that I was more privileged than them. I pointed out to the Cambridge graduate that, on the contrary, I was brought up by a widowed mother and went to a state school, etc., and that he, in fact, was obviously from a far more privileged background than me. With hindsight, it is possible that my surname Bhattacharya (a hereditary title meaning *learned Brahman master* which is supposedly acquired by a distinguished Brahman ancestor) influenced my publishers Motilal Banarsidass. I later noticed in their catalogues that the most common surname for their authors is Bhattacharya. This is not surprising given the focus on Indian philosophy and tradition. In the 1995 *Harpers and Queen* article by Daisy Waugh (granddaughter of Evelyn and daughter of Auberon), Young and another journalist Sean Langan (who at school was something of a Fashion Victim and Party Animal; I noticed in the late 1980s that he did nightclub reports for the London *Evening Standard*) claimed that I was the cleverest boy in our year at school. It was pleasing to see that the non-scientist types were more impressed by my broad and enquiring mind rather than the swotty academic success of the Maths geeks. Freelance journalist Langan was recently the subject of a BBC4 'docu-drama' based on his capture and imprisonment by the Taliban in Afghanistan.

Note 28

In November 2009, I met my former Course Supervisor Professor Casselton at the Royal Society in London. She had become the Vice-President and Foreign Secretary of the Royal Society. She told me that Jacobsen did in fact give London University an endowment in the end although they would perhaps not be fulfilling his original unrealistic aims.

Note 29

At the same meet in Nov. 2009, Professor Casselton was interested to hear that such an outstanding science graduate was excluded from the Civil Service Fast Stream by these notorious language-based tests. In 1987 a "fly on the wall" TV documentary about the elite Civil Service entrance system showed how an intelligent lower middle class Oxford graduate, who questioned holding Olympics in authoritarian, human rights violating, South Korea was rejected by the final selection procedure as a civil servant does not question politics. An upper-middle class female with a posh accent who had attended the expensive Charterhouse School and Cambridge, who thought that the blacks in South Africa were all "tribals", etc., was selected for the Foreign

Service as the Selection Panel thought she would "fit in". Although, she came across as less intelligent than the aforementioned male, members of the Selection Panel thought that her poor performance in regard to intellectual ability was not really important as the backroom jobs were mainly just "paper-pushing". Such insights made me start to think about my identity in Britain as, my left-wing outlook on world affairs, active membership of the Anti-Apartheid Movement, etc., did not go down well with the British establishment. This was during the time of Margaret Thatcher's premiership. Thatcher's husband, like much of British industry and commerce, had financial stakes in the Apartheid economy and Thatcher denounced Nelson Mandela as a terrorist. She later helped her friend the US-installed Chilean dictator Pinochet escape on false 'ill-health' grounds after he was arrested in London for his Crimes against Humanity.

Note 30

I recall a number of Northerners who had found work in London bemoaning the fact that as soon as Southerners heard their Northern accents, they thought they must be unintelligent. But the same assumption applied to those with Working Class Cockney London accents and those from Essex, neighbouring NE London.

Note 31

My intuition about her was later confirmed by a male Commissioning Editor at my main employer Harcourt Brace, who had known her in her previous company and he thought that she felt threatened by confident people beneath her. In fact, Life Sciences and Medical commissioning became virtually monopolised by such women, usually with Ph.Ds, who would only promote fellow females to junior positions until not a single male was left in the Biological Sciences and Medical editorial departments. This "reverse" sexual discrimination was a more important factor than the institutional racism inherent in British companies, even in such businesses full of left-leaning graduates such as publishing. All this only showed that Watkinson was correct in that the role was really that of the "hostess" listening to boring professors talking about their boring technical books.

Note 32

Early in 2011 I read in the news that Stanlow Oil Refinery had been bought by the giant Indian business conglomerate, the Tatas who already owned Corus (British Steel) and Jaguar/Land Rover.

Notes to Chapter 12

Note 1

The criminal Maxwell was buried on the Mount of Olives in Jerusalem lending credence to the claim that he was a Mossad agent or at least closely associated with Mossad, using the businessman role as a front, especially behind the Iron Curtain.

Note 2

In 1997 when I worked for Harcourt Brace, an Irishman who had been a publisher in this company's Tokyo office, whilst I was working in one of the two London offices, joined Harcourt Brace. He told me that he remembered my name from seven years back as I was the only one in the London office who seemed to do any work, actually responding to his faxes.

Note 3

In fact my friends at secondary school had started the British national pastime whilst still underage. They spent most of the time on a school trip to Paris in 1979 (age 14-15) and a day trip to Brussels in 1980 drinking alcohol and playing Space Invaders in a cafe rather than sight-seeing. On the Brussels trip, Nigel Meacher (son of Labour M.P. Michael Meacher) and I went off alone after the formal visit to the EU HQ. He bought some beer and some bottles of wine, the latter supposedly as a gift for his parents. But he drank all the alcohol himself and then, as we rested our weary legs in a cinema hall vomited and fell asleep snoring loudly just before the film started. Luckily I had decided to sit in a side row by the wall so he vomited into the aisle rather than onto adjacent seats or people. I had to slap him awake as the film ended to get us out of there as Belgians, who had given us a wide berth, enquired as to whether he was ill.

Note 4

This point is also stressed by Mohammedans who are supposed to be teetotal. In July 2011 the media had been reporting on British employers denouncing British workers as lazy and workshy, hence they preferred immigrants from Eastern Europe etc. One employer was saying on BBC Radio 5 that British staff went to the pub every Friday evening (and presumably other weekdays) and then called in sick on Mondays. Their frequenting the pub also led to them filling their heads with false rumours about the employers leading to friction with management and high turnover of staff. On a BBC 2 *Newsnight* programme in 2012 a female Polish entrepreneur in the UK stated that the British seemed to think that they were above menial labour jobs as they once ruled 'half the world'.

Note 5

Incidentally, in mid-1989 this same editor went to Berlin where, at an institute for the study of East-West German relations, he was offered a manuscript on possible reunification of Germany. Our editor replied that nobody was interested German reunification!

Note 6

In fact, as HBJ had recently taken on a billion dollar 'poison pill' of debt to avoid takeover by Robert Maxwell, this debt resulted in a takeover of HBJ by General Cinema in 1992 and the installation of an American as the new boss in London.

Note 7

Indeed, I recall telling my friend David, the NUJ representative in 1994 when I had to take on the Personnel Director that I would beat everyone else to solving the Problem of Consciousness. Later that year I would say, I told you I would! This male manager and the 'paranoid chatterbox' Commissioning Editor mentioned below both expressed some amusement at my claims to be a 'Philosopher'. I recall the former showing signs of embarrassment when I claimed to be a Philosopher soon after I joined. This was on a North London Line train which we both used to come to work and I was saying this in earshot of the other passengers. The chatterbox joked to others that he (Sutapas) thinks he is a Philosopher-King etc. The man who had been my manager in 1991 had become 2nd in command at AP London after the new AP EiC had taken a liking to him and taken him to AP Editorial much to the bickering of the female editors who moaned that this managerial type man, an outsider had not been part of their set-up in the past and quickly became senior to them. I had given a copy of O/OM to a Marketing friend of his, an Irishman whom I also knew as he had previously worked at the company where I worked from 1989-91 and he was a Philosophy graduate. This Irishman had gone off to another company where another friend of his had been made a Director and had asked him to join him (such recruitment of one's friends was the norm in Publishing). Obviously the Irish Philosophy graduate, who was extremely impressed by my work, had told my old 1991 manager, who in 1999 was No. 2 in a reorganised AP where I had been reassigned in 1997 after the old Book Production Dept had been shut in November 1997. This was because the same man who had been embarrassed in 1991 on the train, was talking to his friend the Dutch AP EiC within my earshot (he sat right near me in the cramped offices) and referred to me as the 'Great Man'.

Note 8

This Publishing Director repeatedly stressed in the informal chat that what she was looking for was 'enthusiasm'. This vague word was used by many such senior women as a means of justifying their rejection of people with better qualifications and ability for less-able but 'enthusiastic' young women. Enthusiasm does not give you competence. Of course, the real meaning of *enthusiasm* is to be filled with Divinity! Following my nervous breakdown, which led to me ranting and raving out loud in the office about the cheating in regard to equal opportunities and promotions, the next day was a Saturday so I did not need to go to work. My mind seemed to be spinning uncontrollably and I could not get myself out of bed. Realising that I was unwell my mother asked what was wrong. I told her that I was very depressed by how unfair and corrupt the promotions system was at work. I recall her response as it typified the Macaulayite (i.e., the class of English-educated Indians that Thomas Macaulay and the British created to act as intermediaries and junior bureaucrats for the British occupation of India) mind-set of Westernised Indians. My mother responded that I should not get myself unduly upset by such things. After all the English only wanted us to serve as their juniors, especially so in their own country. Although not stated explicitly, I suspect that the majority of Indians in the West take this attitude that they should not 'rock the boat' and create a fuss. The English-educated Indian after all was created by the British to be a subaltern class serving the White Man and he can only expect, in reality, Second-Class Citizenship in the White Man's world, taking the professional jobs that most of the White 'masters' do not want such as doctors in the Inner City ghettoes, tax accountants, divorce lawyers or backroom IT staff. The English-educated Indians have largely internalised British Colonial White Supremacy and often play along with White prejudices as pandering to the White racial preconceptions leads to approval, praise, profit and promotion. Bankim Chandra Chattopadhyay wrote of how the British in India promoted those Indians who deliberately misspelled English words and grovelled to their British superiors as Indians were not supposed to be viewed as equals to the British. The self-respecting, well-educated Indians were not promoted by the British as they threatened to expose the myths of White superiority and prestige.

Note 9

One of my first book project meetings with the Medical Editors involved this Medical Editor-in-Chief (EiC) and a young male medical graduate he had hired recently as an understudy Associate Editor whom I also used to talk to on the North London Line. I noticed in this meeting that the young doctor had a penchant for saying "Yes" followed by the EiC's forename in a rather obsequious manner; although he soon quit the job leaving no males working under the EiC for a number of years. In this meeting for a 2nd Edn of a Neuroanatomy book the EiC discussed the features of the Medical Division's (W.B. Saunders's) bestselling Medical Textbook. The EiC listed a number of features which enhanced its sales potential. Looking at the voluminous tome being displayed, I, the 'new boy' who had just joined the Company joked that I thought that Medical students simply looked at the size of the book and thought, "Never mind the quality, feel the width". In fact, the day he quit HBJ the young medic (a tall handsome man) plucked up the nerve to ask out a beautiful young Irish girl who started off as the paranoid chatterbox's editor's secretary and they stayed together, getting married. After O/OM was published this woman, who was also best friend of the woman who used to ask me 'Is it your time' said that her partner said that you had said years ago (back on the North London line trains) that you were going to solve these problems.

Note 10

The British-Pakistani terrorist Omar Sheikh involved in the hijacking of an Indian airliner to Afghanistan and the later murder of US journalist Daniel Pearl had gone to the same private school in Snaresbrook as the sons of one of our closest family friends. Before being brainwashed into religious hatred by Mohammedan radicals, he had been quite normal and visited our (Hindu) friend's house.

Note 11

The double barrelled surname had only been acquired after he left school. His maternal (Crawford) grandmother fell out with her own son but wanted her surname to be continued by her grandson.

Note 12

In Chapter 4 we saw that Pauli suffered neuroses if he ever tried to disobey the will of his Inner Voice.

Note 13

The fact that a woman was already engaged did not seem to make much difference. I recall in 1993 that a girl who only worked with us for about six months before she went off to get married was equally captivated.

Note 14

I also detested work using computers as viewing things on-screen gives me severe eyestrain. I was unable to even read a book after work following the November 1997 transfer to Academic Press.

Note 15

We saw in Chapter 10 that both the Hindu doctrine of *Niskama karma* (Non-attached action) Christian Redemption involve a spiritual transfiguration of the individual so as to replace self-centred Egotism with actions, sanctioned by the *Atman* or Holy Spirit, conducive to the collective good involving empathy for others, compassion, kindness and charity.

Note 16

Her laughter was not mockery. She was rather captivated with me leading to snide remarks from my male friend who was her immediate supervisor whom she used to mock ruthlessly as did other women. I presume the fact that in 1995, I took part in the filming of a pilot TV programme for Channel four with Toby Young and some other boys from my old school added to my mystique. She was however also fascinated by my book and mentioned that her father was of Russian origin which may have indicated a more open attitude to spirituality. I even bought her a copy of Michael Talbot's *The Holographic Universe* for her birthday in 1995 to provide her with a more accessible introduction to ideas related to my own work which she went round telling people about.

Note 17

In the Acknowledgements to O/OM I referred to the Inner Voice of the Deeper Self based on personal experience and interpretation without knowing that the Inner Voice was linked in the Perennial Philosophy to the Inner Light of Conscience which is also the Witness Consciousness or Innermost Self.

Note 18

In fact the 34 year rule of the CPI(M) in West Bengal was finally ended in 2011 by the Trinamool Congress Party led by populist firebrand female leader Mamata Banerjee.

Note 19

In 2010, an old Bengali friend of the family told me that Jyoti Bose had rented a room at the house of an old German woman when he lived in London (presumably as a student) decades ago. Bose, whom I belief built upon an image of honesty, had deliberately cheated her out of her final instalment of rent by giving her a dud cheque just before he returned to India. The CPI(M) government in West Bengal won plaudits for non-nepotistic politics contra the appalling nepotism of the ruling Congress (I) Party with its Nehruvian 'Gandhi' dynasty. It has also won plaudits from the Westernised Indian media for its commitment to 'Secularism' but as critics point out, the so-called 'Secularism' is based on Leftist pseudo-religious Marxist mythology which demonises the native Hindu tradition. The CPI(M) has pandered to the countless illegal Bangladeshi Mohammedans in West Bengal, even forcing Bangladeshi Feminist writer Taslima Nasreen out of her sanctuary in Kolkata at their reactionary behest. One presumes that these CPI(M) supporting illegal immigrants managed to procure votes in the rigged-elections until the strictly supervised elections of 2011. The British Left has also pandered to reactionary Mohammedan Vote Banks which preaches misogynous, homophobic doctrines running totally contrary to their supposedly Progressive values.

Note 20

EMS's initial S may have been for Sankaran but I seem to recall *The Guardian* referring to him Sankara. Even if it did say Sankaran the Synchronicity was amazing given the Namboodi Brahman clan name; this is hardly a common name that appears frequently in the UK Obituaries sections (*contra* the closed-minded, pseudo-sceptics who dismiss Synchronicity as merely Coincidence).

Notes to Chapter 13

Note 1

In Norman Finkelstein's *The Holocaust Industry*, Stephen Katz is listed as prominent participant in this post-1967 'born-again' Zionist clique who hijacked the legacy of the Nazi genocide of Jews to distract public attention from the crimes of the Zionist regime against Palestinians and neighbouring states. In the preface to his *Exterminate all the Brutes*, Sven Lvindqvist refers to Stephen Katz's disdainful dismissal of those who point out parallels between the Nazi genocide of Jews and other genocides. As Finkelstein says, the Holocaust Industry perpetuates the myth that the Jews are a unique 'People' supposedly chosen by God as well as misrepresenting the Nazi genocide of Jews as an unprecedented unique event in world history. This reflects the Zionist 'Eternal Victimhood' myth that Jews in the diaspora were always persecuted by non-Jews covering up the pre-Zionist Jewish-Islamic cultural symbiosis and the complete lack of persecution of Jews in India.

Note 2

I do not think that the Out-of-Body Experience (OBE) poses a great mystery although Extrasensory Perception (ESP) is needed. Given that our normal embodied experience requires a World Model of the body in the brain, we believe the illusion that our ego is coextensive with the physical body rather than with brain representations. The OBE appears to be some form of alternative world-modelling using ESP which switches on in emergencies such as in a car crash giving a perspective from above the physical body. Note that Perception filters out most of the infinite information from the universe impinging upon us. ESP would involve using some of this untapped information that we usually ignore in normal sensory world-modelling.

Note 3

I once knew someone who attended Richard Dawkins' public lectures. She was the posh, eccentric upper middle class girl I worked with in 1996-97. Although extremely good-looking with classic features, she was something of a loopy dimwit. In spite of a degree in Chemistry, she had difficulty with basic grammar and seemed to have been raised simply with one aim in life; the traditional one for such upper middle class females of marrying a rich man. When our supervisor was not at her desk, this girl spent all her time phoning friends and chatting inane drivel. She thought that Dawkins was a genius but, given that her intellect did not extend much beyond the reading of the regular television soap opera updates sent by another young woman in our department, her judgement of lofty philosophical issues left much to be desired.

Note 4

Amusingly in November 2008, the BBC presented Fry as the quintessential Englishman in his series *Stephen Fry in America*. Fry is openly homosexual, spouting *double entendres* about sodomy on episodes of *QI* in late 2008. This resembles the James Bond films with Scottish and Irish actors playing the supposedly upper class English spy bedding all the women when in fact the most famous English Cold War spies were posh private school and Cambridge-educated homosexuals like Fry. Also unlike fictional Bond, these actual upper class Brit spooks served Communist Russia. On his TV tour of all 50 states of the USA, the sceptical Fry visited the TM headquarters in Fairfield, Iowa and listened to Fred Travis (whose EEG study-based Junction Point model of the Pure Consciousness as the background state of the cortex supports my brainstem brainwave correlation) talk about EEG slow wave coherence etc. Fry focused on the silly 'yogic flying' mattress hopping 'levitation' of the TM people which of course is ludicrous (the 'bathwater'). Soon afterwards at the Los Alamos National Labs in New Mexico, Fry drooled with delight as the Director spoke ludicrous 'Physics-babble" about creating '*self-aware materials*'. Ironically the 'smart arse' and 'clever dick' Fry was condescending toward some Western desert state cowboy types for never having heard of Phenomenology. Fry remained oblivious of the irony in that, if one had real understanding of Husserlian Phenomenology's central notion of Intentionality– with its unities of *noesis* and *noema* (related to Subject/Object duality), one would laugh at preposterous claims of creating 'self-aware materials'. Solid materials cannot mutually superimpose in the manner of the brainwaves constituting Pure Consciousness (as subjective moments) with brainwaves incorporating objective content or self-representational information allowing for reflective, self-awareness.

In 2011 I watched a repeat episode of the BBC 'highbrow' quiz-show *QI* (*Quite Interesting*) Fry. Fry asked a question about which man (singular) had prevented the death of about 1 billion people. The 'correct answer' was the astonishingly naive and tacitly racist assertion that American Norman Borlaug's introduction of 'Green Revolution' agricultural techniques into India in the 1960s had prevented the death of about one billion people. Fry was presumably reading an autocue based on behind-the-scenes research. But this demonstrates that, still today, the British are peddling the myth of 'Timeless Hunger' from which the British claimed cynically that they had rescued India. We have seen above that famine and starvation in India was largely the consequence of British bloodsucking colonialism not due to shortage of food. Native Indian rulers, both Hindu and Muslim, acted to prevent famines from developing. Rather the British stole the food right out of the mouths of the poorest Indians. Thus there were over 30 famines in British-occupied India in the first 120 years of British Rule up to 1877 compared to just 17 in the whole of India in the previous 2,000 years. Even without the Green Revolution, independent India would have imported food if there were serious shortages rather than follow the racist and genocidal 'Let them Starve' and Buchenwald-like Death Camp policies of the British Raj and the denial of food aid Crimes against Humanity of Churchill. *The QI thesis that a billion Indians would have died without Borlaug shows the tacit racism of assuming that hundreds of millions of Indians were merely passive and helpless spectators totally dependent upon the White hero figure coming to save them.* In fact, it was Food and Agriculture Minister C. Subramanian, appointed by PM Lal Bahadur Shastri, who sought out Borlaug and his high-yield Mexican dwarf wheat varieties (*see* Gurcharan Das, *India Unbound*, Anchor Books, 2000). This follows the archetypal pattern of British historiography! The BBC did not respond to my complaint about this racist nonsense even though I quoted well-sourced facts.

Note 5

Years later I read, probably in von Franz's *Psyche and Matter* that by 'mirrors' or 'reflections' of the Divine medieval writers such as Bonaventure meant 'manifestions' of the Divine.

Note 6

Unfortunately, in January 1999 when O/OM was published, I could not find Beulah's address in Amsterdam having lost a letter she had sent to me. So I never did send her a copy.

Note 7

This was the same person who gave me the review copy of *Archetype and Atom* as mentioned in Chapter 4.

Appendix

Evidence confirming RAS-Brainwaves as the Direct Physical Correlate of the Divine Light

What is the Reticular Activating System (RAS)?

The brainstem Reticular Formation (bRF) nucleus projects axons into all brain centres and fires rhythmically and continuously, activating the brain. The technical definition of brain-death is cessation of the RAS. The brainwaves generated by the RAS underlie all other gross brainwave activity continuing even during dreamless sleep and only ceasing at death. Modern medicine distinguishes the *Arousal* component of Consciousness due to the RAS activity and the *Contents* which medicine presumes to arise in the cerebral cortex.

Evidence for Divine Light/RAS correlation

1. All three major Hindu traditions, Vedanta, Kashmir Saivism and Sankhya (Yoga Sutras) describe the Pure Consciousness as shining like a Light in split second temporal gaps in the flow of experiences. There exist Buddhist parallels to this Hindu knowledge.

2. The Dalai Lama says that the highest Tibetan Buddhist Vajrayana knowledge asserts that the Clear Light is constituted by a continuous series of (mind) Moments whereas states such as Waking and Dreaming start and stop.

3. The Dalai Lama asserts that he likes Travis's Junction Point model (Based on EEG studies) of the Pure Consciousness as being a background state of the Cerebral Cortex as this ties in with Buddhist knowledge of the nature of the Clear Light. Travis vague "background state" is undefined but the brainwaves of the RAS constitute the background state of the entire brain including the Cortex. Expert on Buddhism Herbert Guenther says that *Sunyata* is the Background Field of Perception.

4. Daniel Brown showed that 3 major yogic traditions, Mahamudra, Vipassana and the Yoga Sutras, all describe the Underlying Flow of the Light, revealed after yogic "stopping the mind". The Yoga Sutra tradition asserts that this *Light flow* is the *background matrix* of gross cognitions/perception (*tanmatra*) and that it is a vibrating energy field in a state of continuous wave propagation.

5. In "The Innate Capacity" edited by Robert Forman, the authors show that nearly all the great philosophical mystics from all cultures [e.g. Plato in *Republic*] assert that Enlightenment involves uncovering something that is always present in everyone; i.e., there is no Evolution of Consciousness. The Light is always present but clouded over by mentation and needs uncovering.

6. Patanjali's Yoga Sutras begin: *Yogas Cittavritti Nirodhah* meaning Yoga is the cessation of the *waves* (Sanskrit *vritti*) of the mindstuff.

7. The Vedantic *Prana/Atman identity,* first clearly stated in the Kausitaki Upanishad, asserts that in death and in dreamless sleep, the normal consciousness dissolves into the so-called *Prana*. This so-called Life Energy is in fact the *Atman*. It is called Life Energy as if it stops you die (note RAS cessation = brain-death). Edmund Husserl also refers to the underlying, ultimately constituting flow of the Absolute Consciousness (*a.k.a* Time Consciousness) as the Life Stream as the Ego Life is maintained by this flow. There are Buddhist parallels regarding the Life Principle and the Brightly Shining Citta (Bhavanga) and in the work of 20th Century US mathematician and enlightened mystic Franklin Merrell-Wolff. There are also parallels with the *Zoe* (Life) and *Phos* (Light) of Hermetica and the Christian Holy Spirit as the Life-Giver.

8. In Husserl's phenomenology the mysterious underlying and ultimate level of cognitive constitution is the flow of the Absolute (Temporal) Consciousness; its moments constituting the Now moments. Husserl's collaborator Eugen Fink challenged Husserl's ego-centred focus and argued for nonegoic consciousness at the deeper levels like the Vedantic Pure Consciousness. This flow of the Temporal Consciousness is the same as William James' Stream of 'Thought' [or Consciousness] in which the mind moments flow into one another. Both James and Husserl discuss the paradoxical continuity/discontinuity of the Moments as in Hindu/Buddhist disputes. [Husserl's colleague Eugen Fink also began to realise that this flow also constitutes the Space horizon (or 'world concept') of perception – Yogis have long known that the flow of the Inner Light constitutes the Time/Space Matrix of Perception]. In her book *Psyche and Matter* von Franz states that, throughout world mythology, the Time Stream has always been linked to a culture's highest God Image or the Image of the Self. She adds that Spatialisation seems to be a concept derived from the experience of Time and not *vice versa*.

9. The Vedantic concept of *Adhyasa* (mutual superimposition) asserts that the Pure Consciousness becomes superimposed by sensory percepts in the constitution of normal (modified) consciousness.

10. Indian Buddhism says Nirvana is only slightly different from Death – this fact fits my RAS interpretation perfectly as the RAS is the last remaining gross brain activity before death.

11. The Light Near Death as in NDEs also fits as in 10. Enlightenment has been associated with Dying since time immemorial. As Rumi stated, Mysticism is practice in the Art of Dying.

12. The Light at the Centre descriptions or the Innermost Sanctum, the 'Sun' at the centre or Meditation as a Return to the Centre – the brainstem is at the "centre" of the brain and the energy waves flow outwards in the Stream of Consciousness.

13. The Light as the Ever-present Ground; the RAS is the ever-present background to all mental phenomena. (This ties in with point 3 above and the comments from the likes of Buddha and Edmund Husserl that the underlying River or Stream of Consciousness never ceases flowing). The RAS is active even during Dreamless Sleep confirming the claim that the Pure Consciousness is present in Deep Sleep made in the Upanishads.

14. The fact that the RAS brainwaves are a universal human process common to all humans undermines the Comparative Religion dogma of Constructivism which claims there can be no Common Core Universal Mysticism of the Light as there is no unconditioned mental process. The RAS arousal activity is not tainted by memory or cultural conditioning (Medicine distinguishes Arousal due to RAS from the Content of Consciousness) and so it is a common underlying, universal process!

15. Orme-Johnstone and others, using EEG, claimed to find a unique state of Coherent Alpha Rhythm all over the scalp of allegedly Enlightened yogis. Indeed, the TM movement made grossly unscientific claims about such EEG coherence, falsely interpreting EEG Coherence as global integration of brain activities.

However, as the likes of Susan Blackmore and others pointed out, Coherent alpha rhythm is also found in coma and near-to-death. This is not surprising for as I stated, Indian Buddhism considers *Nirvana* to be only slightly different from *Death* and *Enlightenment* has long been associated with Death although many New Agers want to believe the *myths of the Evolution of Consciousness* associated with the likes of Bucke, Gopi Krishna, Aurobindo, Wilber and Laszlo, etc., which assert that Enlightenment involves some sort of brain evolution (*see* Point 5– nearly all philosophical mystics say the Light is present in everyone at all times). Gopi Krishna even put forward ridiculous notions of sperm rising up the spine to nourish the brain cells, yet his ideas have been taken seriously by many New Agers.

In fact the Coherent Alpha Rhythm all over the scalp data fits perfectly my RAS interpretation of Enlightenment as Near-to-Death and in enlightened states near Mystical Union, the entire brain will be deactivated leaving only the underlying activity of the RAS. Thus as the scalp electrodes will measure brainwaves coming from this sole underlying source, the readings will be *coherent* (meaning only that they are at the same Frequency; not TM myths of global brain integration!).

16. My 'Retreat to the brainstem' interpretation of Enlightenment ties in with Eugen Fink's concept of deeper phenomenological 'reduction' (than Husserl's limitation to Wakeful object perception) as a process of "*Unhumanisation*" as the individuated consciousness of the yogi leaves behind the uniquely human structures of the neocortex in the Path to Enlightenment. In conjunction with knowledge of the Time/Space Matrix of Perception created by the underlying flow of the Light, this also allows us to understand yogic realisation of Transcendental Realms, beyond the limitations of Wakeful Space-Time-Causality, which tie in with the Nonlocality and Nonseparability of Quantum Mechanics. Such experiences of underlying *holonomy* whereby everything is dependent on everything else and of the *Akasa* (Space as subtle matter characterised by Vibration) tie in with the true

mystical meaning of *philosophia* as Gnostic "Love of Divine Wisdom" or 'omniscient' realisations. Such ideas undermine the dogmatic views of Immanuel Kant, Existentialists (based on Heidegger's views), Constructivists in Comparative Religion and Mysticism as well as most of Western Philosophy which imagines that it is impossible to transcend sensory phenomena. In fact, I also show how it is possible to understand scientifically the claim to apprehend Ultimate (unmediated) Reality as it actually is.

Index

D

I

J

K

L

M

N

O

P

Q

S

T

U

Y

□□□

Some Comments about *The Oneness/ Otherness Mystery*

Your outline seems to show that you have found the solutions to many of humanity's deepest philosophical problems and I shall look forward eagerly to reading your book.

Professor Arthur Ellison DSc(Eng)
Ex-Head of Electrical Engineering, City University, London
Vice-President, Scientific and Medical Network, Ex-President, Society for Psychical Research

I was pleasingly struck first by the way you "saw through" the muddled or otherwise seriously inadequate thinking of various much-publicised writings – for instance, those by Hawking, Wilber, Capra, Jung, and even Einstein.

Professor J.H.M. Whiteman
Taught Relativity and Quantum theories; had contacts with Heisenberg and Dirac;
author of books on scientific study of mysticism who has attained mystical union; also literate in Sanskrit/Pali

...delighted by its breadth and its understanding. It is a most wonderful reference book, and I am very pleased to have it on my shelf.

Professor Peter Fenwick
Maudsley Hospital and Institute of Psychiatry
Chairman of Scientific and Medical Network for 16 years
Expert on EEG studies of meditation and Near-Death Experiences

This is a remarkable book by an unusual young man...a polymath of very considerable ability...

Oliver Knowles OBE
From review in *De Numine*, newsletter of Alister Hardy Centre for the Study of Religious Experience, Oxford, UK

outlining his epoch-making synthesis of Indian spirituality and European science...

Karel Werner

Leading scholar of Eastern Philosophy and of Mysticism from review in *Journal of the Royal Asiatic Society*

I haven't been able to put it down. It is quite a tour de force. You cover so many things, so many ideas and it is full of the most interesting bits of information. Congratulations! I'm sure this book will make you famous.

Professor Subhash Kak

Computer and Electrical Engineering, Louisiana State University
Co-author with neurologist Karl Pribram and expert on ancient Indian knowledge systems.

It is noteworthy that the book is a definite pointer to a synthesis of science and mysticism, with strong evidence to support the activity in the brain region (RAS) during meditation.

Professor Uma Erry

From 8 pp review in *Bhavan's Journal* one of India's most famous and widely circulated serious magazines.

essential reading...this remarkable book presenting some ideas that will need serious consideration in any attempt to integrate contemporary science with Hindu philosophy and the phenomena of mystical experience.

Dr. Alan Mayne

Mathematician (University College London) from review entitled 'East-West Synthesis' in *Scientific and Medical Network Review*

...much of the scientific research on mysticism has had either of two purposes: either to support and confirm a particular group's claims for the superiority of their method (witness the work on TM in the seventies, and the revival of such scientific investigations in the recent investigation of Buddhist meditation; or alternatively to be used as a tool for reductive explanations that explain away mystical experience and meditative practice as reducible merely, to brain chemistry, brain electricity and so on. I am pleased to see that your work appears to take neither of these tacks and seeks rather an intelligent adjustment between these two modalities of knowledge...

Professor Paul Muller-Ortega

Professor of Religion, University of Rochester N.Y
Expert on Tantric Kashmir Saivism and has himself 'Seen the Light'

THE BRAINSTEM BRAINWAVES OF *ATMAN-BRAHMAN*

THE BRAINSTEM BRAINWAVES OF *ATMAN-BRAHMAN*

The Synthesis of Science and Spirituality

(In Two Volumes)

(Volume 1)

Sutapas Bhattacharya

GYAN

ISBN : 978-81-212-1221-2 (Set)

ISBN : 978-81-212-1282-3 (Vol. 1)
Price : Set (₹ 1850) Price : Volume 1 (₹ 925)

First Published, 2015

Published by

Gyan Publishing House
23, Main Ansari Road, Darya Ganj
New Delhi-110002
Ph. : 23242060, 23261060
Fax : 011-23285914
E-mail: books@gyanbooks.com
Website : www.gyanbooks.com

Laser Typesetting : Gyan Prints (AB-II), Delhi
Printed at : G. Print Process, Delhi

Cataloging in Publication Data—DK
Courtesy: D.K. Agencies (P) Ltd. <docinfo@dkagencies.com>

Bhattacharya, Sutapas, 1964-
The brainstem brainwaves of Atman-Brahman : the synthesis of science and spirituality / Sutapas Bhattacharya.
2 v. cm.
Includes bibliographical references and index.
ISBN 9788121212212

1. Âtman. 2. Brahman. 3. Science and spiritualism. I. Title.

DDC 201.65 23

Contents

VOLUME 1

VOLUME 2

Part Two

THE ONE TRUE ONTOLOGY

Part Three

MY PATH TO THE LIGHT

Preface

Ekam sat vipra bahudha vadanti
(That which exists is One, sages call it by various names)

[*Rig Veda* 1.164.46]

Indian air surrounds us, and original thoughts of kindred spirits. And oh, how thoroughly is the mind here washed clean of all early engrafted Jewish superstitions!

[Arthur Schopenhauer]

...Schrödinger and Heisenberg and their followers created a universe based on superimposed inseparable waves...This new view [for Schrödinger] *would be entirely consistent with the Vedantic concept of the All in One.*

[The doctrine of the *Atman-Brahman*] *the essence of Vedanta, is to him* [Schrödinger] *the grandest of all thoughts.*

[Walter Moore, *A Life of Erwin Schrödinger*]

What a yogic feat, what a giant leap for one of the world's oldest, greatest, and philosophically exalted cultures: from becoming one with Brahman... ...to impressing the whites... we have surrendered our souls to white worship... *and self-hatred... Inside our heads, Indian civilisation has been defeated by Western values and materialism.*

[Richard Crasta, *Impressing the Whites: The New International Slavery*]

I have used the terms *Atman* and *Brahman* in my title in order to stress the Indian origins of the philosophical knowledge of the Divine Light. The doctrine of the *Atman-Brahman* is the central element of Vedanta (Brahmanism) as first presented in the *Upanisads* (also known as the Vedanta or the 'end of the Vedas') dating from around 3,000 years ago. The *Atman* is the impersonal 'Self' (meaning Consciousness or Spirit) within us that is one with the Universal 'Self' or Universal Consciousness known as *Brahman*. The *Upanisads* stressed that the *Atman* is the Inner Light or the Pure Consciousness (*cit*), the (background) Ground-Consciousness underlying all other forms of Consciousness. This Pure (objectless or non-dual) Subjectivity becomes mutually superimposed with perceptual and conceptual consciousness which provide the objects of our dualistic experiences of Self and Other. The Sanskrit term *Prajna* (Luminous Wisdom Consciousness) was formulated to describe another aspect of the Divine Light, its subtle, non-dual content (i.e. it is part of one's Self), realised only in deep altered states of enlightened *jnana* or gnosis. This follows cessation of all mental activity clouding the Pure Light with percepts and conceptual 'objects'. This *Atman* was also found to be identical with the *Prana* or the Life Energy, so called because cessation of this energy entailed death. This fact correlates perfectly with the primary brainwaves generated by the brainstem nucleus known as the Reticular Formation which I identified as the physical correlate of the Divine Light (*see* Appendix for the full evidence confirming this correlation). The rhythmic impulse-firing activity of the Reticular Formation reaches out to all other centres of the brain and is known as the Reticular Activating System (RAS). These RAS 'brainwaves' underlie all other so-called brainwave activity in the human brain as detected by the Electro-encephalograph (EEG). They constitute the background field underlying all other brainwave activity. Cessation of the RAS activity constitutes so-called 'Brain-death'.

But as the Divine Light is the central element of all true Spirituality and of true Philosophy in its original sense of *Philosophia* (Love of [the Light of] Divine Wisdom), the knowledge presented in this book transcends cultural limitations and is of universal significance. This Divine Light (in its Inner Light, Background-Consciousness, Life Energy or Luminous Wisdom Consciousness aspects) has been known by many mystique-laden names throughout History including the following: *Agni* ('the divine 'Fire' within our hearts' found in the *Rig Veda*), *Atman*, *Cit* (Pure [objectless] Consciousness), *Prana*, *Saksin* (Witness Consciousness), *Bhavanga* (Brightly Shining Mindstuff of early Buddhism), *Sunyata* (Emptiness), the Buddha Nature or Buddha Mind, The Clear Light of Death, *Sophia* (the Cosmic Light of Wisdom), the Light of Truth, the Godhead, the Archetypal Light, *Nous poietikos,* the [Inner Light of] Christ, the Holy Spirit, the Inner Light of Conscience, the Light of Life, The Living God, the Fountain of the Water of Life, *al haqq* (The Reality in Sufism), The Fount of All Wisdom, The Philosopher's Gold, The Fountain of Youth, The Elixir of Life, The Divine Spark, the Eternal Flame, the Uncreated Light, the *Imago Dei*, the Inner Man, the Innermost Self (or 'Heart'), the Twin of Mani, the Stream of Consciousness, the Absolute Consciousness, the Time Consciousness, The Holy Grail, The Subliminal Self, The Hidden Observer, the 'Christ Consciousness' and the Near-Death Experience Light.

I identified the RAS brainwaves as the physical correlate of the Divine Light back in 1994 whilst I was writing my first book *The Oneness/Otherness Mystery: The Synthesis of Science and Mysticism* (O/OM) published in 1999. O/OM constituted a 'cosmology' in the traditional sense of the word. It was an attempt to elaborate fully on my own existence as an individual being in relation to all other aspects of my world (the 'greater beings' of which I am a part) up to the Cosmos itself. O/OM grew out a set of philosophical poems (*sutras*) covering all aspects of philosophical discourse, including socio-political and historical questions, which I began to expand upon in prose essays. My interest in the metaphysical problem of the ontological status of Consciousness had begun even earlier in 1983 when, as an 18 year old, I first tried to explain Consciousness using a Panpsychist metaphysics. I had realised that the Physicalist-Materialist ontology underlying Science could only describe the spatiotemporal behaviour of patterns of energetic activity which we describe as physical phenomena. It had precluded Subjectivity from the start and could never account for Consciousness (as Awareness in itself). The standard notion peddled by Western Physicalists/Materialists that Consciousness somehow 'emerges' out of insentient energy and matter is in fact a tacit appeal to Magic and a disguised form of ontological Dualism. As we shall see, simple epistemological analysis reveals that the so-called 'Physical Universe' of modern Science exists only in the imagination of believers!

Soon after I identified the physical correlate of the Divine Light (Pure Consciousness or Godhead), I began to realise that the so-called 'Perennial Philosophy' (*see below*) was actually hinting at the true nature of Reality, the True Ontology. Given the remarkable, world-changing importance of my discovery of the RAS-brainwave correlate of the Light, I spent another three years expanding the metaphysical essay in O/OM well-beyond the limits of the ideas discussed in my poetry. Although I was in full time work and suffered severe eyestrain from the increasing reliance on computers, I tried to find out all that I could about the interrelationship between Science and Mysticism from the books available in London's bookshops; I was not an academic with access to good libraries. Typing my manuscript on a word-processor with a tiny two-inch by five-inch screen display, causing further eyestrain, I prepared my 'Science-Mysticism Synthesis' essay which almost doubled the length of the manuscript and made O/OM rather like two books in one.

The importance of my RAS-brainwave correlate of the Light and my 'Science-Mysticism Synthesis' far outweighed the socio-political and historical discussions of the first half of the book. With one simple stroke my RAS-brainwave correlation undermined both the Physicalist ontology underlying Science and the Theistic mythology of most religions which imagine that 'God' or the Divine Spirit is totally distinct from material Nature. Theism asserts that Mystical Union with the Divine is impossible even though mystics in Theistic Christianity and Islam have testified to attaining such union. My correlation also resolved clearly and definitively the central problem of Hindu-Buddhist Philosophy, the nature and significance of the Mystical Union of the core individual consciousness (or subtilised ego) with the Divine Light. Furthermore my work began to resolve clearly and definitively the dominant paradox of modern Western Philosophy, the problem of the Ontological Status of Consciousness (often referred to misleadingly as the 'Mind/Body Problem').

As I indicated in the Preface to O/OM, such paradoxes actually arise as artificial products of human reasoning creating false conceptual dichotomies based on false assumptions. Reality is really much simpler than the conceptual confusions of most scientists and philosophers. Faced with such central questions of Philosophy, some philosophers and scientists find themselves so befuddled and entangled by their own conceptual errors that they conclude that clear and definitive resolution is impossible or beyond human understanding. They tend to obfuscate the reader with technical jargon and present the naive products of their own confusion, usually some fancy words which sound good but reveal nothing, as supposed insights into such intractable mysteries. Others, usually Materialists, simply resort to the common practice of philosophical sophistry, using verbal 'sleights of hand' to mislead the inattentive reader and claim that their reduction of such paradoxical issues to their dogmatically-held Materialist frame of reference has actually resolved the paradox in a satisfactory manner. In *explaining away Consciousness*, Materialists appeal tacitly to Magic, tacitly assume Panpsychism, suppress the logical implication of Panpsychism in their own arguments, and twist the real meanings of terms in order to disguise their own failings. I shall expose numerous such Reductionist deceptions in this book, including those by Nobel laureate scientists and other supposedly 'great minds' of the West.

I also expose those Westerners, including Taoism-influenced Fritjof Capra, Buddhophiles Francisco Varela, Charles Laughlin and James L. Austin, and 'neurotheologist' Andrew Newberg who pay positive lip service to the mystical philosophies of the East which they have themselves practised. However, regardless of how long they have practised and studied these Eastern techniques, these same Westerners cannot bring themselves to accept that non-European philosophers may have actually interpreted the facts correctly and rationally in regard to positing the Ontological Primacy of Consciousness (i.e. that Energy and Matter are created out of Universal Consciousness), distinguishing Pure Consciousness from the ego, and other such claims. These authors proceed to ignore the Eastern interpretations and, like their anti-mystical Western counterparts, reduce such Eastern mystical knowledge to tacitly magical explanations based on the Physicalist-Materialist myth of the 'Emergence of Consciousness'.

This reflects a major subsidiary theme of this book, the 'Institutional Racism' of Western Academia. We shall see that mainstream Western academia conflates 'European' with 'scientific'; credence is given to the speculative ideas of 'White' European thinkers regardless of how false or absurd their ideas may actually be. In stark contrast, non-European notions are dismissed as unacceptable regardless of the fact that some of these ideas are actually veridical. This is manifest in the ongoing perpetuation of the colonial era White Supremacist myth of the 'Greek Miracle' and supposedly unique invention of Philosophy and Science by the Ancient Greeks. The Ancient Greeks are also presented falsely as anti-mystical, proto-modern Western scientists when in fact they were not even 'Europeans' in the modern sense, let alone 'Westerners'. Furthermore, mainstream Western History and Philosophy of Science suppresses the fact that many such supposedly miraculous Greek 'proto-scientists' were actually shamanic healers and mystics and many of their most famous ideas were copied from supposedly irrational Orientals!

This tacit racism of the West is found even in the Western 'New Age' movement which hypes up as original geniuses contemporary Westerners who have repackaged Ancient Indian ideas in modern Western and Christian terms. Often these New Agers will have learnt about Consciousness and the Transcendental from Easterners but when it comes to writing books or speaking at Western conferences they will refer only to Ancient Greeks such as Plotinus and modern Europeans such as Jung, James or Whitehead. This book demonstrates the Indian origin of true conceptual *Philosophy* and numerous suppressed Indian influences upon modern Science such as the invention of modern Arithmetic, Algebra, Analysis and Infinitesimal Calculus, the Sanskritic Renaissance in Europe in the 19th Century (including Indian influences behind the idea of biological Evolution) and the later Indian inspiration behind the invention of Quantum Mechanics in the 1920s. I even have a chapter demonstrating the ontological and scientific superiority of the Vedantic-Tantric metaphysics over Ancient Greek and modern Western metaphysics. In fact, contrary to Western academia's White Supremacist propaganda, contemporary 21st Century scientific Cosmology, Physics, Phenomenology and Cognitive Science are far more in tune with Ancient Indian ideas than they are with those of the Ancient Greeks.

My 1999 book O/OM received remarkable plaudits from the likes of Professor Arthur Ellison and Professor J.H. Michael Whiteman (*see* Comments about *The Oneness/Otherness Mystery* page following Index) and some other academics who already knew something about Science-Mysticism interrelationships. However, to attain wider recognition beyond the limited circle of such cognoscenti, I required publicity in the USA and hopefully a Western publisher to reprint the book. In spite of the remarkable letters of praise from professors, I found that the main US New Age organisation claiming to promote the scientific study of Mysticism suppressed my book, not reviewing it in their magazine. In late 1999, when an American supporter of mine named Alan Rhodes who was an ordinary member, emailed the Director of Research asking when they would review it, she responded that she did not know of the book. Yet, as Alan knew, this same woman had in 1998 written to me asking for a copy of O/OM after I put up a post about my book on their website discussion forum. Furthermore, just a month or so before her denial of knowledge, she had witnessed me 'steal the show' from the invited 'big name' New Age speakers at a conference in Cambridge, UK sponsored by this US organisation and a UK counterpart called the Scientific and Medical Network (SMN). The final question from the audience to the speakers during the final discussion session was from a British woman who stated something along the lines of: There is a man in the audience called Sutapas Bhattacharya who knows a lot more than any of you speakers and we should all hear what he has to say. In fact, the Conference (and SMN) Chairman Professor Peter Fenwick tried to stop me from speaking about my own work. Fenwick had just read my O/OM and, throughout the conference had pressed the newly appointed Templeton Prize[1] judge Professor Ravi Ravindra to speak to me. Thus he was obviously aware that I could upstage the invited speakers and thus he tried to stop me but I went ahead anyway creating a sensation amongst the audience.

It later transpired that the American Director of Research had most probably denied knowledge of my book to Alan Rhodes because this US organisation had long presented the US New Age guru Ken Wilber as being the foremost original thinker on Consciousness and the Science-Mysticism interrelationship. In O/OM I had pointed out Wilber's glaring errors regarding the Planes of Consciousness amounting to tacit ontological Dualism along with his naive claims that we would never find a 'missing link' between Science and Mysticism, let alone attain a synthesis of the two. Around the time my O/OM was published Wilber had received considerable donations from a US Internet millionaire who had been pushed out from his CEO position from the company he had helped create due to his public pronouncements about UFOs (including extraterrestrials performing Biblical miracles). As Wilber's old friend Michel Bauwens states in his Web essay "The Cult of Ken Wilber", Wilber's associates in the US New Age movement were keen to share in this financial windfall. Bauwens pointed out that that even some of Wilber's erstwhile critics made U-turns and began singing his praises. As discussed in this book, Wilber's early books stuck closely to traditional Indian Vedantic notions, especially the famous 4-state AUM model of the States of Consciousness. These books made his name. Later on Wilber, churning out a new book every year or so, attempted to be original. But in putting forward his fallacious 'Pre/Trans Fallacy', 'Height Psychology', Quadrant (actually a mandala) and ever changing 'models' with over 2,100 'consciousness-variables' (!) he got everything absurdly wrong. Thus the glorification of Wilber by sections of the Western New Age movement reflects the tacit racism of Western society in which a White Man or 'Elvis' figure restating Non-European ideas is presented as a 'revolutionary genius' rather than give credit to the genuine pioneers of the philosophical study of Consciousness in Ancient India.

In regard to finding a Western publisher for O/OM, it became apparent that no Western publisher would reprint a 700 pp book with such a unique and diverse structure. My supporters suggested as I myself had already thought, that I rewrite the Science-Mysticism Synthesis half of O/OM as a short book in order to facilitate publication in the West. After being made redundant from my dead-end job in scientific publishing in August 2002 with a large pay-off, I started preparing a publishing proposal for just such a book (entitled *The Godhead in the Brain*) which in January 2003 I posted to the US publisher Paragon House. In October 2003 I received an offer of publication sent via Literary Agent John White (who had previously been the Editor at Paragon House). John White had also been Ken Wilber's original Literary Agent back in the 1970s and he had been a Director of Education at the main US organisation investigating the Science-Mysticism interrelationship (as mentioned above). However, in November 2002 I had become my mother's full-time carer as her Parkinson's Disease got worse and she lost her independence due to bouts of dystonia (causing her body to 'freeze') as the l-dopa levels reduced. Furthermore she suffered a number of other health crises, sometimes requiring hospital attention, etc.,which totally prevented me from pursuing the new book project at that time. Thus I decided to reject the Paragon House offer which I had not been totally happy with given their 200 page limit on the length and their tight schedule.

However, after my mother's death on Boxing Day 2005, I was finally freed from the nightmare that had cast such a shadow over my life for ten years since her diagnosis in 1996. I was also left with considerable savings meaning that I need not seek work immediately so I could once again resume my postponed project to prepare a new book presenting my Science-Mysticism synthesis. I decided that I would finish the manuscript at my own pace before seeking a publisher rather than be rushed to keep a tight schedule hence compromising quality and content. Rather than just rewrite the second half of O/OM, I decided to write a completely new work after seeking out all the new evidence and relevant information supporting my ideas that I could find. Back in the 1990s I did not have access to the internet to search for books. The eyestrain from office work had increased dramatically after I was reposted to a new more demanding job in late 1997. Thus for five years from November 1997 (just after I had finished the O/OM manuscript) to my redundancy in August 2002, I had hardly been unable to read a single book as my eyes were so tired. The revolutionary implications of my RAS-brainwave correlate of the Light and my interpretation of enlightenment etc. could not be demonstrated comprehensively and authoritatively within a mere 200 pages. My aim was not to preach to the converted (i.e. Indian Hindus and Western New Agers) but to convince the most sceptical, scientifically-literate Western Materialists. The vast majority of well-educated people, especially scientifically trained specialists, simply do not possess the broad scholarly knowledge of Mysticism, Comparative Religion, Western Esoteric traditions, Eastern Philosophies, Ancient Mediterranean Philosophies and Mystery Traditions, Western Philosophies, Western Phenomenology, Cognitive Science and the metaphysical interpretation of Quantum Mechanics required for an adequate background understanding to my own ideas on Science-Mysticism integration. Indeed, I only gained this knowledge for myself in the period 2006-2012 as I prepared this new book.

Small-minded people, especially those whose vested interests are threatened by my ideas, will highlight the fact that I am not an academic. Neither Charles Darwin nor the young Albert Einstein in 1905 was an academic. An academic simply could not have produced a multidisciplinary work of synthetic philosophy within the compartmentalised confines of a university, nor confronted publicly the institutional racism and related Eurocentric myths peddled by mainstream Western academia. Spokespeople for vested interests will no doubt pick up on the most tangential issues such as my historical and socio-political contextualisation of Western scholarship in order divert attention from the metaphysical substance of my work which they will not be able to challenge seriously as my work is not one of mere speculation; this two volume book is so long as it presents a barrage of evidence to back-up my highly rational, evidence-based arguments. I mention in this book the 'demonisation' by Freudian US 'scholars of Hinduism' of Hindu critics led by Indian-American philanthropist Rajiv Malhotra who exposed their misrepresentations and defamation of Hinduism. In fact, in 2000 Rajiv Malhotra offered to sponsor me through his Princeton-based Infinity Foundation to study for a Ph.D at a top US university saying that this would make it easier for me to get my ideas heard. My mother's deteriorating condition and my expectation of a large redundancy pay-off after the takeover of the company I worked for prevented me from considering the offer seriously. However, even if I had not been so constrained, I knew that no doctoral student or academic specialist could possibly undertake the truly interdisciplinary work that I had in mind for this book project.

Progress in academic careers usually depends upon churning out little papers on the most specialised subject matters and the academic learns 'more and more about less and less'. Such narrow specialisation contributes to the Reductionist mindset that is rife in Western academic studies of Consciousness and Spirituality. Scholars in the Humanities and the soft sciences have been accused of 'Physics Envy' and the abstract, predictive models of Physics provided the tacit exemplars for Western academic methodology in other fields of study however inappropriate this might actually be. The scientific attitude of Objectivity [with its denial of Subjectivity] is also copied by scholars in other disciplines even though Science's claim to Objectivity is clearly false epistemologically, as was recognised by Niels Bohr in his Copenhagen Interpretation of Quantum Mechanics. I expose in this book the 'Physics Appeasement' displayed by Western Philosophers including Thomas Nagel, John Searle and Evan Thomson who refuse, at least publicly, to challenge the basic Physicalist-Materialist ontology of modern Science when faced with the ontological problem posed by Consciousness. Actual scientists who try to tackle such philosophical problems tend to reduce the unknown (e.g. Consciousness) to the limited theoretical frameworks within which their own minds have become indoctrinated. This Reductionism is also apparent in the profusion of speculative so-called 'Quantum Mind' 'physico-babble' peddled by certain physicists who possess little, if any, knowledge of the Philosophy of Mind and no understanding of how to present a consistent philosophical argument. They do not bother to learn facts about Consciousness from the obvious fields such as Neurobiology, Psychology, Phenomenology and Eastern Philosophy or even define clearly what they mean by "Consciousness". Some try to 'blind' the reader with obfuscating, arcane Quantum Theoretical jargon about the supposed role of a vaguely defined "Consciousness" in the supposed 'Collapse of the Wave Function' as was postulated by John von Neumann. Others link 'Consciousness' to their own arcane studies in Quantum Gravity models or Quantum Thermofields and invoke bizarre notions such as 'inverse tilde universes' and Nambu-Goldstone bosons as supposedly relevant for our understanding of 'Consciousness'.[2] This is almost as ludicrous as the use of the term 'God Particle' for the so-called Higgs Boson by pseudo-intellectual journalists. The Bengali-American 'New Age' physicist Amit Goswami claimed in his 1993 book *The Self-Aware Universe: How Consciousness Creates the Material World* that we could define *Consciousness* as "the agency that affects quantum objects to make their behaviour sensible". Though Goswami is not a Reductionist in the sense of being a Physicalist or Materialist, this is still a form of '*Reduction to the limited knowledge of the Physicist*'! No serious philosophical work on the nature of Consciousness would start off by considering the misleading and probably outdated controversies associated with the interpretation of Quantum Mechanics such as the so-called Schrödinger's Cat paradox. I say 'outdated' as new notions of Decoherence involving interaction with virtual particles of the Quantum Vacuum have been introduced in regard to the so-called 'Collapse of the Wave Function'.

Obviously, a philosophical analysis of the nature of Consciousness (if limited to Western knowledge) should focus on knowledge from Philosophy of Mind, Phenomenology, Neurobiology, Psychology and perhaps Cognitive Science. Even the writings of the theoretical physicist David Bohm on the metaphysical interpretation of Quantum Theory were marked by Bohm's failure to learn in depth knowledge from outside his own speciality. Although much-hyped by acolytes, Bohm's ideas were, in the main, neologisms for traditional philosophical terms relating to the Transcendental Realm and he never got to grips with Consciousness. Where Goswami ventures outside his speciality he usually makes bland assertions including the false generalisation that all religions are based on Monistic Idealism! Although this statement may appeal to the popular interpretations of the 'Perennial Philosophy' view held by uncritical New Agers, no serious scholar of Religion would accept this. All the Semitic religions, Sikhism and most popular forms of Hinduism are Dualistic Theisms. Huxley's 'Perennial Philosophy' referred to esoteric mystical experiences not to exoteric religions and, even then, many esoteric traditions, including Theistic Vedanta, do not adhere to Monism even though this is the logical implication of Mystical Union. In stark contrast to the wild speculations made by 'Quantum

Mind' physicists, modern Bio-Medicine has established that the brainstem Reticular Formation (which generates the RAS brainwaves which I have correlated with Pure Consciousness) is the only brain structure[3] whose proper functioning is essential for the presence of any form of Consciousness in humans.

As we shall see in this book, the reason why the unusual aspects of Quantum Mechanics are so often conflated haphazardly with the Mystery of Consciousness is because the metaphysical interpretation of Quantum Mechanics indicates the same Transcendental Substructure of Nature (that some call 'Quantum Reality') which can be realised directly in deeper states of Consciousness attained through meditation. This is not mere speculation. This was the main conclusion, based on personal experience of mystical states, made by mathematical physicist and mystic Professor J.H. Michael Whiteman in his scholarly 1967 book *The Philosophy of Space and Time and the Inner Constitution of Nature*. He also wrote that there exists a Universalised Consciousness transcending appearances in Space and Time which is also the innermost core of our own consciousness. This is a modern restatement of the Vedantic knowledge of the *Atman-Brahman*. Anti-mystical self-proclaimed 'sceptics' in the West assert that they are more rational and understand science better than those who support such mystical claims. Anyone supporting mystical and paranormal claims is demonised by these blinkered, pseudo-sceptic[4] dogmatists as mistaking hallucinations for Reality. Note that Werner Heisenberg himself checked the chapter on Quantum Mechanics in Whiteman's 1967 book and that Paul Dirac (the man who invented the notion of antimatter) invited Whiteman to Cambridge to discuss the book with him. We shall see that many of the truly great and creative fathers of the New Physics were deeply interested in or even advocates of Mysticism (as Isaac Newton himself had been) whereas it is the little-minded scientists and philosophers who dismiss all Mysticism as deluded nonsense. These little minds, incapable of transcending the mythologies instilled in them by modern Western cultural indoctrination, are often hyped-up as 'great thinkers' or 'geniuses' by the celebrity-obsessed mass media. Due to constraints on space and time, this book focuses primarily on Spirituality, leaving aside the analysis of other aspects of Mysticism (primarily Occultism associated with paranormal psychic phenomena).

Many people are afraid of accepting radically new ideas, however strong the evidence and logic supporting them, due to lack of conviction in their own ability and lack of courage in regard to facing up to critics. Such people will only 'come on board' with new ways of thinking if such ideas are supported by established 'authority figures'. As we shall see, the basic metaphysical picture presented in this book has also been espoused by such scientific greats as Schrödinger, Eddington and, to some extent, the self-proclaimed mystic Wolfgang Pauli. The likes of Isaac Newton, Ernst Mach, Albert Einstein, Werner Heisenberg and David Bohm have written positively about such mystical notions. *This book may not be the work of a professor but it carries far greater authority than any academic qualifications or scientific reputation could possibly convey. It possesses the Authority of Evidence.* This is not a work of speculation, but presents an overwhelming barrage of converging lines of evidence. I challenge anyone to look at all the evidence confirming my

RAS-brainwave correlate of the Divine Light (*see* Appendix) and then try to dismiss it. As in legal assessments of the evidence in a court of law, it is 'beyond reasonable doubt'. Once in possession of all the facts presented in this book, the impartial, open-minded, rational reader will see that I have interpreted these facts in the most parsimonious and rational manner. Indeed, given that I simultaneously deconstruct in great detail alternative metaphysical interpretations, debunking their false claims, the impartial reader should also appreciate that what I claim to be the One True Ontology thrusts itself upon us as almost obvious given the overwhelming evidence and arguments supporting my conclusion.

The Science-Mysticism part of O/OM focused on Hindu and Buddhist yogic knowledge and demonstrated that this ancient phenomenological knowledge conformed to scientific knowledge of the RAS and the Transcendentalist metaphysical interpretation of Quantum Theory. As indicated above, this book was written primarily for a Western audience. Thus it focuses more on Western spiritual, esoteric and phenomenological traditions. I will demonstrate that Platonism, Gnosticism, Hermeticism, Neoplatonism, Esoteric Christianity and modern Western Phenomenology can all be explained in terms of the RAS-brainwaves as the physical correlate of the perennial spiritual Light, 'Fountain', 'Godhead' or the phenomenological 'Stream' or 'Flow' of Consciousness sustaining the ego. My 'Brain-deactivation and Retreat-to-the-Brainstem' interpretation of Enlightenment, based on Hindu and Buddhist knowledge, presented in O/OM works just as well in understanding these Western esoteric and phenomenological traditions including the seemingly unrelated Christian myths such as those of the Virgin Birth, the Son of God and of needing to be 'Born Again' so as to see the 'Kingdom of Heaven'.

As stated above, my RAS-brainwave correlate undermines both Physicalism and Theism. It also resolves definitively the central problem of Indian Philosophy (the nature and significance of Mystical Union) and the modern Western philosophical problem of the Ontological Status of Consciousness. But, as we shall see, combined with my neurobiological interpretation of Enlightenment, it also provides us with clear, scientifically-grounded answers which brush aside as unscientific, dogmatic myths the dominant Western philosophical arguments that are used repeatedly to dismiss the reality of unmediated mystical apprehension of (metaphysical) Reality, the reality of a 'Common Core' Universal Mysticism based on the deepest mystical experiences of the Divine Light (i.e. the 'Perennial Philosophy'), and the reality of the existence of Pure (objectless) Consciousness.

Given such profound implications, it is perhaps not surprising that my work has largely been denied any significant publicity. It is 'dangerous knowledge' that threatens the authority and the prestige of too many persons and groups whose vested-interests involve preserving the myths undermined by my work. This is taboo knowledge which debunks numerous myths peddled by Western academia, the scientific establishment and of course by organised religions. Even Hindu organisations claiming to advance the Vedantic world-view through scientific corroboration feel threatened by my work as it demonstrates that notions of a soul (*jiva*) and its supposed transmigration are untenable myths which must be discarded. Academics in Indian Philosophy feel threatened as my work is grounded scientifically, resolving clearly in physical terms the central questions, and makes their speculative efforts at interpreting yogic knowledge largely irrelevant and redundant. Western New Agers feel threatened by my work as it undermines their myths such as the 'Evolution of Consciousness' as well as exposing their false claims to originality and Einstein-like genius status.

It should already be obvious that this is not just another work of uncritical 'New Age' pop philosophy which preaches only to the converted. Although I am not an academic, this work is written at a scholarly level using knowledge drawn largely from books published by University Press publishers. Unlike New Age pop philosophy, which rehashes incestuously the same old ideas from the fashionable names of fringe scientists linked to the New Age networks, this book incorporates mainstream scientific, philosophical and spiritual knowledge referring to ideas of the greatest philosophers from the East and the West as well as to the greatest scientists. Far from being rooted in the rather crazy, psychedelic, guru-worshipping hippy counter-culture of the 1960s USA, this book is rooted in the dominant Indian spiritual tradition based on the Vedas and Vedanta (*see below*) which has survived critical scrutiny for millennia. It is also rooted in the Neo-Hinduism linked to the likes of Ramakrishna and Vivekananda which became associated closely with early elite Indian Nationalism.

Many a Westerner will recoil from my mentioning the word 'Nationalism' given that I am claiming simultaneously to present the One True Ontology, the truly *universal* picture of what really exists that underlies a truly Universal Science of the future. This science would accommodate Consciousness, Creativity, Spirituality and anomalous psychic phenomena precluded by the pseudo-universalism of Western Physicalist science. How can a nationalist viewpoint also be universal? This appears self-contradictory. But, as I discussed in O/OM, unlike the 'tribal nationalisms' of modern Europe which were based on supposed racial and linguistic exclusivity, *the 'Idea of India' was based on inclusivity*, itself rooted in the pluralism of Hindu tradition associated famously with the phrase '*Unity in Diversity*'. The countless diverse cults and sects of the Indian Subcontinent constituted the 'Little Traditions' brought together and integrated under the unifying umbrella of Brahmanism, the 'Great Tradition'. Even before the rise of Brahmanical Hinduism the Vedas had recognised that That which exists is One [commonly stated as 'Truth is One'], though sages call it by various names. The Brahmanic philosophy (Vedanta) of the elite Brahmans, especially in its Nondualist (*Advaita)* form – in which there is no dualistic separation of the Divine Spirit and Nature as is the case in Theistic religions – represented the underlying true philosophy (the *Sanatana Dharma* or 'Eternal Truth') which the diverse religious cults and sects attempted to describe in symbolic myths. As elaborated in this book, it was this notion of the underlying *Sanatana Dharma* that was expanded by Ramakrishna to include the great World Religions in his notion of the 'Unity of Faiths' or the common mystical truth underlying the diverse symbolic mythology of different religious traditions.

Later in the 1940s, whilst a member of the Ramakrishna Mission in California, the British writer Aldous Huxley would restate this same essential truth in his influential book *The Perennial Philosophy*. Huxley and his colleagues

Christopher Isherwood and Gerald Heard viewed *Advaita Vedanta* as the nearest example of the underlying Universal Spirituality which Huxley had realised for himself in attaining Enlightenment with the aid of drugs as well as meditation. He and his colleagues recognised, as Erwin Schrödinger himself had already recognised, that such Nondualist Brahmanic metaphysics was compatible with the New Physics of the 20th Century. In fact both Werner Heisenberg and Erwin Schrödinger have testified to the influence of this Indian Vedantic metaphysics on their invention of the revolutionary New Physics called Quantum Mechanics in the mid-1920s. However, as stated above, such Indian influences are usually suppressed by Western historians of Philosophy and of Science given the institutional racism of Western academia.

Tagore and Gandhi did not view India as a 'nation' like European nation-states but as a 'civilisation'. Early Indian Nationalists even aspired to leading the whole world toward an Universal Civilisation inspired by the Brahmanic Nondualist metaphysics which reveals that, when one transcends the Self/Other viewpoint of the personalised Ego, in Universal Consciousness (*Brahman*) – what St Paul refers to metaphorically in Galatians as "In Christ Jesus' or as "In the Sight of God" – there are no dualities of Self and Other; everything in the universe is realised as part of the Oneness of this Universal Self. Paul Deussen wrote that the Gospels call upon to 'Love thy neighbour as thyself' but do not explain *what it actually means to see others as part of your own Self.* Deussen added that the true philosophical basis of this injunction had been explained about a thousand years earlier in the Upanishads [i.e. in the central doctrine of the *Atman-Brahman* – that the True Self within us (*Atman*) is 'one with' or inseparable from the Universal Self (*Brahman*)]. Indeed, as Sarvepalli Radhakrishnan stated, this doctrine is the central teaching of all Hinduism.

The likes of Bankim Chandra Chattopadhyay (the 'Father of Indian Nationalism') and Jawarharlal Nehru wrote of the need to counter the one-sided, imbalanced Materialistic development of the modern West with a new Indian Modernity integrating, as Nehru put it, "Flesh and Spirit". Such ideas had inspired early Neo-Hindu Indian Nationalists who argued that Hinduism, especially in its supreme Nondualist expression, was a 'naturalistic', 'scientific' philosophy based on experiential evidence. This was in stark contrast to the superstitious myths of Christianity which many prominent British colonialists and their scholarly propagandists in so-called 'Indology' had dreamt of foisting upon Indians. Most of the British of course took it for granted that Christianity, the 'White Man's religion', was superior in terms of theological and world-historical truth to the supposedly primitive indigenous tradition. This Neo-Hindu ideology countered the self-serving denigration of Hinduism by the colonial British parasites. The British bloodsuckers depicted India as a land of 'Eternal Poverty and Famine' and blamed all its woes on Hinduism when in fact, prior to British occupation, India had been known throughout history as a land famous for its great wealth. In truth, not only did the British loot[5] India's wealth in the form of jewels, silver, captive markets and financial tribute, they also stole India's food-grains, to export for British profit and to provide Food Security to Britain forcing millions of the poorest Indians to starve. British occupation and plunder of India resulted in some three dozen of these man-made famine holocausts in 190 years killing tens of millions of Indians.[6] Mainstream British historians continue to cover up the horrendous truth and epic scale of the British Crimes Against Humanity in India which played a major role in making Britain the richest country in the world under Victoria. Having brutally and systematically destroyed India's world-leading textile industry which had created a 'silver drain' on Britain's economy, they also stifled any prospects of industrial development in India such as shipbuilding so that India was reduced to a giant plantation economy serving Britain's needs at India's expense. The Brits forced about ninety percent of Indians to live constantly on the edge of starvation through the brutal extortion of the imperial tribute of agricultural produce. American Buckminster-Fuller described the British Empire as the most successful pirates in History.

At the start of the 20th Century, some of the first generation of India's modern scientists led by J.C. Bose, dreamt of challenging the Mechanistic, Materialist science of the modern West with a new, holistic Indian science inspired by Vedantic metaphysics. In the mid-20th Century British historian Arnold Toynbee prophesied that, during the 21st Century, India would conquer her conquerors with her (philosophical) ideas. Many Indian gurus and writers of pop philosophy make similar claims. The late Professor Willis Harman (Electrical Engineer and ex-Head of Stanford Research Institute) stated the following at a 1986 Bombay conference on synthesising Science and 'Religion'. Harman predicted that the New Science that will supersede the inadequate Materialist Science that dominates today will be based on Indian metaphysics with its Transcendentalism and the Ontological Primacy of Consciousness. After receiving a copy of my O/OM in 1999, Japanese physicist Shiuji Inomata wrote to me. He mentioned that he had quoted Harman's prediction in his own inaugural address to a 1998 Tokyo Conference on 'Science and Eastern Philosophy'. Ten million Japanese television viewers had watched the TV programme about the conference.

In spite of grandiose claims made by Indian gurus and by uncritical Indian and Western New Age pop philosophers, this triumph of Indian metaphysics over Materialist Science (as well as over Western philosophies and Theistic religions) is not going come about using the existing resources of Indian Philosophy. Nearly all Indian books and Western New Age books purporting to reveal the scientific truth contained in Hinduism/Buddhism, or claiming to integrate Science and Mysticism, are uncritical, and usually pseudoscientific works which will never be taken seriously by 'sceptical' Western, scientifically-literate thinkers. This includes Aurobindo Ghose's voluminous *Life Divine* which squanders its entire second half on baseless, pseudo-scientific speculation, inspired by Nietzsche and Western Romanticism, fantasising about enlightened mystics constituting the progenitors of a new breed of 'Gnostic Supermen'. Indians who, out of nationalistic fervour, hype up such inadequate works as India's own indigenous 'science' tend to lack any notion of what constitutes rigorous philosophical argument and, even if scientists themselves, usually display a lackadaisical understanding of what constitutes convincing, coherent and consensual scientific evidence.[7] As indicated above, I am well aware that the dominant Western scientific approach based on the Galilean preclusion of Subjectivity and the myth of 'Objectivity' is inappropriate for the study of Consciousness-related phenomena. Nonetheless, Indian philosophical schools have failed to come to any general consensus on key critical questions relating to yogic phenomenology and continue to intertwine totally unsubstantiated speculation about souls, karma and transmigration, and superstitious nonsense about astrology, etc., alongside repeatedly-verified, intersubjective phenomenological knowledge of altered states of Consciousness. Given this mixture of facts with fiction, they do not constitute scientific systems of knowledge in a modern sense. It requires far more critical and insightful examination in order to overcome the deep-rooted objections of the Western orthodoxies underlying mainstream academic thought.

In India, the colonial legacy has left a tendency to ape Western fashions in a fawning manner and play 'follow the leader', waiting for the White Man to give the nod before Western-educated Indian academics will accept original ideas from, or discoveries made by, fellow Indians. Both colonial Macaulayite and Marxian influences have led to naive and self-hatred filled Leftists demonising anything related to the native 'Hindu' tradition. This was evident in regard to the controversies surround Indian challenges to the colonial concoction of the historical fantasy of the Aryan Invasion of India which has finally been debunked recently by DNA evidence. Indians presenting logical and empirically-substantiated arguments were often misrepresented as 'Hindu Fundamentalist Revisionists' and many Leftists still refuse to accept the countless lines of scientific evidence debunking this myth. To overcome such resistance based on mainstream Western preconceptions (and of course subtle racism) it is necessary to demonstrate the falsehood of famous philosophical objections to the possibility of unmediated mystical apprehension of Reality (or of 'penetrating the veil of appearances'). Such Western preconceptions have led to Mysticism becoming a taboo topic in Western scientific thought even though modern Science is rooted in Renaissance Nature Philosophy which pursued the *mystical* enterprise of seeking 'God's hidden order in Nature' and Isaac Newton was himself a mystic.

These preconceptions and objections include:

1. The Kantian denial of the possibility of a mystical Third Mode of Knowledge (beyond the senses and concepts) allowing Unmediated Direct Apprehension of Metaphysical (noumenal) Reality as it is in itself.

2. The mainstream Western philosophical dogma, derived misleadingly from Catholic ex-theologian Brentano's Scholastic notions[8], that conscious experiences are always 'Intentional' (i.e. always has some sort of object within them). This dogmatic assumption that all experience is intentional leads to the denial of the existence of the Vedantic *cit* (Pure Consciousness) which is empty of all objects.[9]

3. Jung's claim that Indian Philosophy had over-reached itself in basing its grand metaphysical and cosmological claims on the 'introspective' [more accurately 'phenomenological'] investigation of our inner psychic constitution.

4. The Constructivist dogma dominating mainstream Western academic Comparative Religion in recent decades which denies the possibility of a 'Common Core' Universal Mysticism (or 'Perennial Philosophy') based on the deepest experiences of Divine Light which are described in near-identical terms across traditions. Constructivists appeal to the authority of Kant (*see point 1*), Brentano (*see point 2*) and to the Social-or Cultural- Construction argument which asserts that there are no Unmediated, Universal mental processes in humans as all mental processes are socially- or culturally-conditioned or 'constructed'.

5. The Existentialists' claim that the human ego can never escape the sensory-conceptual 'lifeworld' of our everyday human experience. This implies that we can enter altered states of Consciousness and experience non-mundane, 'other-worlds' or 'planes of Consciousness' as claimed by mystics.

6. Arguments such as those put forward by Richard King in his *Orientalism and Religion* that the Neo-Hindu assertion that *Advaita Vedanta* (Nondualist Brahmanic) philosophy represents the true Universal Spirituality underlying the diverse mythologies of spiritual traditions from around the world [as was also argued by Huxley, Isherwood and Heard] is just self-aggrandising propaganda peddled by Neo-Hindus.

Academic scholars in Indian Philosophy rarely, if ever, attempt to counter even one of these Western arguments against the reality of Mystical Realisations and the Universal 'Common Core' Mysticism (or 'Perennial Philosophy). In fact no academic scholar of Indian Philosophy could overcome these Western objections as such scholars usually come from a linguistic rather than a scientific background. They have buried their heads in the barren sands of the worship of the Sanskrit language, churning out speculative etymological renderings of Sanskrit terms and yet more new translations of the same old ancient texts. Indian academics also copied outdated Western academic fashions and models already dismissed as Charlatanism or as 'failed projects' in the West just as Hindustan Motors churns out new variants of a1950s Morris Oxford motorcar decades after it was abandoned in the West.[10] Thus Indian Philosophy remains an irrelevant, reactionary relic, a realm of outdated exotica or curiosities left for Humanities students and far-removed from the dynamic, forward-looking world of Science and Technology that dominates the modern world.

Even if one were able to overcome these Western objections, a more daunting hurdle remains. This would be to demonstrate decisively the false status of the Physicalist ontology underlying modern Science. Physicalist Natural Science purports to constitute a universal system capable of accounting for all the phenomena that can possibly occur in this universe. It can only maintain this pretence by hoping that believers maintain their faith in the magical 'emergence' of an imaginary 'Consciousness' out of supposedly *insentient* energy and by denying the existence of mystical and paranormal psychic phenomena which do not fit into its conceptions limited to the 'Physical World' of Wakeful Spatiality, Temporality and Causality. In spite of these glaring failures, the undoubted successes in explaining predictable natural phenomena and the incredible technological successes of Physics-based Natural Science has blinded most scientifically-educated secular rationalists to the shortcomings of this approach. These shortcomings were more apparent in earlier centuries when the fundamental preconceptions of Natural Science, often founded in anthropomorphic Christian and Greek myths, were still being formulated. Most Materialists presume incorrectly that such debates were resolved clearly and decisively due to superior rationality on the part of the pioneers of Natural Science. In truth, some highly pertinent and rational criticisms were brushed aside given the tangible material benefits, including military and economic hard power, accruing from technological applications of the new scientific methods. Given that Natural Science has overcome some false counter-arguments of the past, most famously those put forward by superstitious Christian fundamentalists, naive Physicalist and Materialist believers tend to assume that *all* anti-Reductionist arguments about Spirituality, Consciousness, Paranormal Psychic Phenomena, etc., must also be the delusions of those believing in primitive superstitions. Such 'heretics' refusing to accept Physicalism are often also accused of being both *irrational* and not understanding Science when in fact, as we shall see, these critics may be more rational and actually possess a better understanding of what Science really is than the Reductionist scientists and their cheerleaders in mainstream academic Philosophy. The scientific establishment has, in the main, airbrushed out of scientific history the fact that the likes of Newton, Mach, Einstein, Eddington, Heisenberg, Schrödinger and Pauli wrote positively about Mysticism or, in some cases, were mystics themselves.

The good news is that the relegation of Indian Philosophy to inferior, third-rate status (fit for a 'Third World' society in the Western Mind) need not continue to be the case. My RAS-brainwave correlate of the Pure Consciousness combined with my Brain-deactivation/Retreat-to-the-Brainstem interpretation of Enlightenment and Mystical Union undermines Western objections 1, 2, 4, 5 and 6 above. Having overcome these objections, my RAS-brainwave correlate of the Pure Consciousness immediately undermines Physicalism by showing that Pure Consciousness is not some rare product of complex material evolution in animal brains but correlated simply with the primary or underlying flow of (electrical) energy through the brain that is *essentially no different* (nor more complex) from the energetic activity that underlies all physical phenomena. Therefore, such Pure Consciousness must be assumed to be present throughout the entire universe constituted by such Psycho-Physical energetic activity. My broader analysis demonstrates clearly the false status of Physicalism by exposing the fundamental epistemological errors of Galileo and other pioneers of Natural Science and also by debunking in great detail Physicalist/Materialist attempts to 'explain away' the anomalies of Consciousness (and spiritual phenomena) by reducing them falsely to the Behaviourist notions to which the Physics-model limits all Natural Science explanations. It goes on to demonstrate the epistemological and the ontological Primacy of Consciousness as the Ground of all Being, of which *Energy* (the vibratory activity of this Ground) and *Matter* (complex localizsed constellations of energetic wave processes) are derivatives, as has long been realised phenomenologically by Indian yogis through sublation and transcendence of the Material and the deeper subtle energetic planes of Perception. In his *Synthesis of Yoga*, Aurobindo Ghose famously quoted the *Mundaka Upanisad* which stated that "By energism of Consciousness (*tapas*) Brahman is massed; from that matter is born".

Few philosophers, if any at all, have actually attempted to answer the Jungian objection which is shared by many thinkers, even those who accept the validity of yogic methodology as a means of disclosing the deeper mental processes underlying Perception. It is after all an extremely challenging task to demonstrate how Phenomenology can disclose not only ontological truths but also grand cosmological ones. I believe that in Part II ('The One True Ontology') I have given as good a response as can be given as of today. My task is facilitated by the fact that both Yoga and Continental European Phenomenology have discovered the fact that it is the underlying flow of the Light of Pure Consciousness (or Husserl's 'Absolute Consciousness') constitutes the Time/Space Matrix of Perception. Thus my RAS-brainwave correlate of this Light-flow and my explanations of Enlightenment and enlightened Gnosis allow us to begin to understand how mystical realisations in deeper states of Consciousness can indeed transcend the Space-Time limitations of mundane perception and gain access to information linking us to all other phenomena in the universe. The answer to this Jungian objection also relies heavily on the metaphysical interpretation of Quantum Mechanics including the now well-established facts of Nonlocality and Entanglement in terms of a Space-Time transcending Wave Structure underlying Matter. This underlying Wave Structure was understood by the likes of Schrödinger (whose Wave Mechanical Equation lies at the heart of Quantum Mechanics) and Michael Whiteman (who experienced this Transcendental Substructure for himself). It was also implied in the work of theoretical physicists David Bohm and Wolfram Schommers, both of whom reformulated Quantum Mechanics to disclose the deeper Nonlocal realm. A model of this deeper Nonlocal Wave Structure has been developed for the electron by my acquaintance the US physicist Milo Wolff. Indeed this deeper understanding of what underlies Physics even begins to allow us some insight into how paranormal psychic phenomena such as Precognition may actually operate as well as accounting for the universal coherence or cohesion that is presupposed, though not explained, in Physics' assumption of universal so-called 'Laws' and Constants.

In the long run, my work should help define India's national identity. It marks the transition of Vedantic-Tantric metaphysics from being merely one school of Philosophy among many to becoming the basis of the new truly Universal Sciences based on the Ontological Primacy of Consciousness and Transcendental Causation. This is a transition as great as that of the earliest Upanishads which marked the world's first shift from mythological theology (as found in the earlier Vedas) to conceptual 'Philosophy' some three thousand years ago. This was centuries before the advent of such Philosophy in the Hellenic Mediterranean. The first Mediterranean philosophers, the Miletians, were almost certainly influenced by the older Indian Philosophy given the intermingling of Indo-Aryans and Ionians (*Yavana*) in the Persian Empire. Remarkably, the world's first Philosophy, the Vedanta remains the closest approximation to ontological Truth! The Tantric knowledge of the energetic manifestation of Matter was already present in the Upanishadic notion of Space (*Akasa*) as subtle matter characterised by vibration. This book's continuity with Indian tradition goes back even further. Western Indologists have distorted completely both the historical background and the meaning of the *Rig Veda*. J.L. Mehta wrote that the [true] central theme of the *Rig Veda* is [Divine] Light. This Light [of Truth (*Rita*)] is the concept which holds all the *suktas* ('hymns') and *padas* ('books') together in a coherent whole. The *brahmana* pursues The Light unceasingly. Aurobindo Ghose stressed that the key themes of the Vedas were Light (Consciousness) and Energy and that the *Arya* (noble) is one who pursues The Light. Though vastly different in content from the ancient Vedas which were originally composed perhaps some 4-5 millennia ago in the Saraswati-Sindhu civilisation, *this book represents the supreme fruition of this five millennium long Indian quest to understand the Divine Light of Truth within us.*

The earliest myths were refined into abstract, conceptual philosophies although still grounded on the same phenomenological facts of Consciousness.

Such phenomenological facts were embroidered with vague philosophical speculations to fill in the gaps in knowledge. This led to diverse interpretations with no means of resolving disputes between divergent Schools beyond reasonable doubt. Even the great Sankara whose name has become rather synonymous with the pre-eminence of *Advaita* (Nondual) or Absolute Monist interpretation of Vedanta in post-Buddhist India was in fact, as his Nondual Tantric Kashmir Saivite critics pointed out, actually a tacit Dualist! NeoHindus countering Western demonisation of Hinduism have stressed Sankara's logical (actually rather Scholastic) arguments but his *mayavada* remains Dualist and self-contradictory! Now such unsatisfactory philosophical speculations are rendered redundant as I have established the actual scientific basis of this supreme knowledge resolving long-standing controversies. This work also marks a significant breakthrough in modern India's maturation as a free-thinking independent civilisation no longer enslaved mentally to subservience and submission to Western hegemony and Western agendas in regard to the rational advancement of knowledge.

The new understanding of Spirituality presented in this book obviously has profound implications for the future of all religions. It will no doubt go on to influence society globally as the dominant metaphysical picture of Reality influences subtly both individual human behaviour and collective modes of social organisation. The reversal of the 'de-spiritualisation' and 'dis-enchantment' of Nature in the Modern Age brought about by the Galilean 'quantitative' mythology underlying Natural Science (along with the eradication of the Renaissance Occultists' *anima mundi* or World Soul notion by Descartes' tutor Mersenne) will no doubt be marked by future historians as the true beginning of a 'New Age'. The undermining of the Western Physicalist picture of the universe and debunking of numerous Western myths will no doubt help chasten the Westerners in regard to their arrogant and tacitly racist preconceptions in regard to innate European superiority in Rationality, Metaphysics, Universalism and Historical Agency. How these new historical developments will actually manifest is not for me to say but for my readers to start bringing about themselves.

Notes

1. In regard to the Templeton Prize, which was supposed to be for progress in our scientific understanding of Religion, it transpired that this primarily Christian organisation's actual mission appears be to defend Monotheism. Ravindra himself was a Theistic Hindu rather than a Nondualist. My work of course undermined Theism!

2. Roger Penrose's 1994 book *Shadows of the Mind: A Search for the Missing Science of* Consciousness, if it were a normal consumer item, would be guilty of violating the UK Trades Description Act. This book actually says nothing whatsoever about the search for a scientific understanding of Mind, let alone of Consciousness, except for one or two brief and extremely unconvincing speculations about Quantum Coherence in microtubules in the brain in the concluding chapter. The rest of the chapters simply summarise Penrose's actual research on mathematical models trying to harmonise Quantum Theory with General Relativity or 'Quantum Gravity'. The publisher presumably wanted a book about Consciousness but Penrose obviously did not produce such a book but simply wrote about his own speciality! Nambu-Goldstone bosons and the bizarre speculative notion of inverse tilde universes are conjured up in the 1995

book *Quantum Brain Dynamics and Consciousness: An Introduction* edited by physicists M. Jibu and K. Yasue.

3. The brainstem Reticular Formation was widely known as the only brain centre whose loss of function eliminates all forms of Consciousness. More recently the thalamic intralaminar nucleus (ILN) closely associated with the brainstem Reticular Formation has also been discovered to be essential. This does not affect my Reticular Activating System brainwave correlation of Pure Consciousness. Input to the two (bilateral thalamic) IL-nuclei includes a large fraction of the ascending brainstem Reticular Formation so the ILN appears to be part of the same basic brainstem-thalamic system.

4. As scientist and paranormal researcher Dean Radin has pointed out, a true sceptic is supposed to retain an open mind. The Western 'sceptics' who pounce on any claims of paranormal and mystical phenomena and deny that they can possibly exist are dogmatists living in denial of facts that don't fit their preconceptions, not true *sceptics*.

5. The English word *loot* comes from the Hindi word to rob and plunder. The Mafiosi-like British state corporation known as the East India Company looted Bengal after their conquest in 1757 resulting in the Great Bengal Famine of 1770 which killed up to ten million (or one third of the population) in Bengal, Bihar and Orissa. Whilst Indians starved to death in their tens of millions in countless British-inflicted famine holocausts, many East India Company men came back to Britain as super-rich 'nobs' (from *nawabs*) having extorted vast sums from rich and poor alike in India.

6. In 1877 Disraeli's regime set-up Death Camps for Indian famine victims killing 94 per cent of the inmates given less food rations for hard labour (dirt-mixed flour) than Nazis gave to inmates in Buchenwald Death Camp (not all Death Camps had Gas Chambers). Simultaneously record amounts of India's food-grains were exported providing Food Security for Britain and lowering market prices for Westerners. In 1942-3 the Hindu-hating, White Supremacist War Criminal Winston Churchill was responsible for creating the 'Bengal Holocaust' as a form of Nazi-like Collective Punishment for Bengal. It was the last of about three dozen such manmade famine holocausts and this holocaust killed 6-7 million Indians according to recent research. After British censorship was broken a year into the disaster, Churchill also prevented the USA, Canada, Australia and Japan from sending food aid to the victims, diverting the food instead for White Europeans and to stockpile in Britain so as to manipulate world food prices after the war.

7. This may be partly due to the unquestioning rote-learning still common in Indian education geared solely to passing exams without real developing real understanding or appreciation of alternative viewpoints. Many Indian educators, doctors and other figures of authority are notorious for their pomposity and rigidity especially in dealings with uneducated and illiterate Indian masses and this may be reflected in the didactic and unsophisticated 'theorising' of certain Indians who, having obtained some official qualification, imagine themselves to be all-knowing having never faced serious critical questioning.

8. Brentano's confusing notion of *Intentionality* is derived from Medieval Scholasticism involving extremely confusing phrases such as the intentional inexistence of an object! It is not the same as 'intentionality' derived from the common use of 'intentional' as volitional (or resulting from Free Will). In fact, as Robert Forman points out in his *Mysticism, Mind and Consciousness*, Brentano never claimed that all mental phenomena or experiences are intentional but was referring to a class of mental

phenomena. Similarly, Husserl's use of 'Intentionality' referred to that class of experiences related to objects which Husserl called Acts.

9. The Vedantic Pure Consciousness is empty of all 'objects' or 'dualistic content' in the sense that perceptual and conceptual content is superimposed upon Pure Consciousness forming the normal modified consciousness (*citta*) possessing subject/object (self/other) duality. In fact, although the Pure Consciousness appears at first devoid of all content, the enlightened yogi can proceed discriminate its subtle seemingly 'omniscient' content (the Infinite Divine Wisdom or *Prajna* aspect of the Light). This subtle Wisdom content is nondual; it is not experienced as non-Self like objective contents but as inseparable from the Self in Universal Consciousness.

10. Humanities scholars, as with scholars in 'soft sciences' such as Psychology, have been accused of 'Physics Envy' given the supreme prestige of Physics in Western academia. Such envy was surely a reason behind the false philosophising by the scientifically-illiterate, 'Postmodern' English Faculty professors who, inspired by Jacques Derrida and others, claimed to 'deconstruct' Natural Science and supposedly show it to be just culturally-constructed relative knowledge. Such deconstructive doggerel (which included passing off Literary Criticism and Freudian superstitions as metaphysical analysis) was exposed as Charlatanism by real scientists in books such as *Higher Superstitions* by Gross and Levitt and *Fashionable Nonsense* by Sokal and Bricmont. Even after such disclosures, Indian academics continued to ape this already-outdated and ridiculed Western academic fashion. Western-educated Indians seem to know only how to produce poor imitations of the West, following obsequiously the lead of their White mentors and the White heroes whom they idolise. They could not dream of doing some original, disapproved of by Western academia (which holds the lucrative jobs and 'First World' lifestyles they lust after) let alone challenge the foundations of Western knowledge. As late as the early 1990s, some Indian academics were writing that the 'way forward' for Indian Philosophy was to follow the Language Analysis of Anglo-American Analytic Philosophy. Once again the subaltern mindset of such Indian academics could only envision copying an out-dated Western model which level-headed Westerners had already dismissed as a failed project which is taken seriously only by the most blinkered Logical Reductionists whose heads appear to be stuck up their own backsides leading to tunnel-vision!

Acknowledgements

In my first book *The Oneness/Otherness Mystery* (O/OM) I acknowledged only one teacher, the 'inner tuition' or guidance that I had received from my deeper Self, the impersonal Spirit within or *Atman*. O/OM was the product of much inspiration in the form of poetic outpourings in 1991 and various compulsions and synchronicities, linked to my deeper Self, seeming to force me out of the 'Wasteland' of pursuing what society expects us to desire and leading me toward my destiny. Since childhood I had intuited that I was destined to be a philosopher and that my destiny was associated with Indian Nationalist aspirations even though I had been raised in England since I was just two years old. When I left school at age 18, before going on to study Molecular Biology at University, on my school-leaving form I wrote (only half in jest) that what I wanted to be when I grew up was a poet, priest and philosopher! This work lacks the creative inspiration of O/OM being written in a far more 'mechanical' manner with little, if any, inner guidance. But, as it is the product of seven years of full-time 'research' and repeated revision, it is a far more mature and refined work than O/OM. The Science-Mysticism part of O/OM was written over nearly five years between 1993-1997 when I was just beginning to understand the true relationship between Science and Mysticism following my 1994 identification of the physical correlate of the Divine Light. Back then I was constrained by having only a few hours of free time each week during the weekend. The increasing use of computers at work gave me severe eyestrain stopping me reading any books from just after I had finished writing O/OM. Furthermore, in 1996 my mother was diagnosed with Parkinson's Disease causing huge disruption to my writing plans as I lost all my holidays dealing with her medical crises. In the1990s my research was limited to the books I could find in London bookshops. The preparation of this book was not disrupted by having to fit it into holidays and weekends. I also had access to a far wider range of books thanks to the internet. Still, given limitations of time and space, this book focuses only on the deeper 'Spiritual' levels of mystical experience and phenomena or else it would have required numerous extra chapters.

But, as with O/OM, I have had to produce this work in isolation, with no material support from anyone else. As stated in the Preface, Western academic 'Philosophy' and Science is hostile to Mysticism and Metaphysics. Western academic specialisation does not permit any academic the freedom to pursue such truly 'integral' studies. Thus there were no formal avenues providing grants, income, security and officially-sanctioned prestige which I could have followed to produce this work. Furthermore, I ignored the advice to omit from my work contextual information about the numerous British Crimes Against Humanity in India and the tacit racism of Western academia which does not go down well with Anglo-American publishers. As stated in my Preface, knowing the truth about British colonial crimes in India helps contextualise the British establishment's demonisation of Hinduism and Indian Philosophy. Thus it was not too surprising that I could not find a publisher in the UK or USA. As Richard Crasta wrote in *Impressing the Whites*, the more an Indian writer challenges Western stereotypes the less likely he is to get published in the West. I have been forced to risk my own life-savings and future security in order to live frugally off my own savings since 2006 in order to be able to prepare this book unhindered by the need to work. Given that using computers gives me bad eyestrain and having envisaged this book as providing a comprehensive and authoritative presentation capable of convincing even 'sceptical' Western readers, it was seven years before I felt a sense of completeness. This 'completeness' involved checking that I had not made any unsubstantiated statements which critics could seize upon and a feeling that there was nothing more of significance that I could find.

I knew from my experience with O/OM that some reviewers would focus on any weakness in my text, magnify it and distort it out of all proportion so as to try to distract from or to diminish my achievements. This is especially the case with those whose own metaphysical beliefs, political views or vested interests are challenged by my work. This was the case with the late Oliver Knowles OBE who had been sitting next to me when I 'stole the show' from the speakers at the end of the August 1999 'Beyond the Brain' Conference in Cambridge. He promised me a review in *De Numine*, the newsletter of the Alister Hardy Centre for the Study of Religious Experience at Oxford, if I sent him a copy of O/OM. Knowles was in fact very impressed by my Science-Mysticism Synthesis writing to tell me that he had recommended my book to a doctoral student at the Alister Hardy Centre and he also attended my lecture to the UK Society for Psychical Research. However, having been a veteran of the war in Burma during the 1937-45 conflict[1], Knowles was infuriated by my praise for Subhas Chandra Bose and my sympathetic attitude toward the professed war aims of the Japanese. He pointed to the Japanese treatment of Western captives as being far worse than the misdeeds of Western colonialists in Asia. A year later I learnt from Mike Davis's award-winning *Late Victorian Holocausts* that Prime Minister Disraeli's henchmen in India had created Buchenwald-like Death Camps for victims of the 1877 British-created famine holocaust in South India killing 94 per cent of the inmates. More recently in 2010 Madhushrie Mukerjee revealed in her *Churchill's Secret War*, how Indian-hating White Supremacist Churchill prevented the USA, Canada, Australia and Japan sending food aid to the victims of the British-created 1942-3 Bengal Holocaust which killed up to seven million Indians. This constitutes a 'War Crime' as does the Collective Punishment of Bengal (for Subhas Bose's leadership of the INA by Churchill's regime) which created this Bengal Holocaust in the first place. The Anglo-American West, ever eager to demonise other societies, doesn't want the world to know that they themselves perpetrated such racist Crimes against Humanity killing millions!

Though left to my own resources, I have received moral support and praise from a number of people which has helped me to keep going in spite of the numerous hurdles and the setbacks I faced over the last two decades. This encouragement has helped reaffirm my own unceasing conviction in the world-changing importance of this work and the need to make it known to the wider public even though I may not benefit materially from this seemingly endless and materially-fruitless endeavour. First of all I must thank Rajiv Malhotra whose Princeton-based Infinity Foundation (IF) was created from the proceeds of the sale of his software company in order to increase global awareness of the many, usually unacknowledged, Indian contributions to global culture. As already discussed in the Preface, in 2000 Rajiv offered to sponsor me to undertake a Ph.D. at a top US university so as to facilitate getting my ideas heard by a wider audience. In fact in 2007, after he discovered that I had resumed my writing he again asked if I needed sponsorship. However, at the time I was quite well-off financially, before the 2008 Credit Crunch created by the 'Banksters' and ensuing Great Recession and near-zero interest rates robbed prudent savers like myself of interest. Thus, in 2007, I decided that I would wait until I had finished the manuscript and then ask for financial help with book promotion. However, when in 2012 I did enquire about some sponsorship to help promote the book I discovered that, soon after he made the offer in 2007, Rajiv's IF had stopped handing out such grants.

I must also thank US Literary Agent John White[2], even though he was not involved in my finding this Indian publisher (Gyan Publishing House). As stated in the Preface, John reviewed the original proposal for this book for Paragon House in 2003 resulting in an offer for publication of a 200 pp. book which I was unable to accept. Nonetheless John has stuck patiently with the project following my progress through email communication. He tried to help me find a Western publisher in 2012 even though I have savaged the ideas presented by some of his old friends such as Ken Wilber and Gopi Krishna and the fact that my views contradict some of his own views. However, in spite of his backing, and in spite of the remarkable letters praising my O/OM from professors such as Arthur Ellison and Michael Whiteman, I was unable to find a US 'New Age' publisher willing to take on this long and scholarly work by an unknown, non-academic. We could not approach Western academic publishers as they do not publish works including personal narratives and political opinions. However, John's experience was useful in making me cut out the excessive historical and political material as publishers would be put off by this. His encouragement also led to my preparation of a short paper about my work which is to be published in April 2014 issue of the American *Journal for the Scientific Study of Spirituality and Consciousness* published by a US organisation[3] with which he is associated.

I am also grateful to the late Professor Arthur Ellison DSc (ex-Head of Electrical Engineering at City University, London; VP of the Scientific and Medical Network (SMN) and a President of the UK Society for Psychical Research (SPR)). On contacting the SMN via Chairman Peter Fenwick in 1998, I asked for Ellison's contact details as I recalled reading his paper from the 1986

Bombay "Synthesis of Science and Religion" conference book. Fenwick sent me Ellison's phone number but Ellison was, at first, not keen on receiving my synopsis material for O/OM. I did not know that he was terminally ill with throat cancer. He insisted that I prove the scientific credentials of my work to him before he accepted. However he quickly agreed to give me his address when he heard that his friend Professor Robert Jahn (the ex-Head of Aeronautical Engineering at Princeton who set up the famous 'PEAR' Psychokinesis study lab at Princeton) had already asked for a copy of the book after receiving the same synopsis. Jahn wrote that he would try to get reviewed in the *Journal for Scientific Exploration* (another US fringe science publication[4]). Thus I must thank Professor Jahn on three counts as, his name also persuaded Ellison to read my synopsis and, thirdly, Rajiv Malhotra also learned of my book after Jahn showed it to him when Rajiv visited Jahn's PEAR lab.

After reading my synopsis Ellison wrote to me stating that it seemed like I had "found the solution to many of humanity's deepest philosophical problems" and that he looked forward to reading my book. He mentioned the 1986 Bombay conference where he had received a standing ovation from the audience (of mainly Indian scientists and public officials) after he stated that, in their haste to learn Western knowledge, Indians should not forget their own systems of knowledge based on the Vedas and Upanishads. He also asked me if I would send a copy of my O/OM, when published, to his friend Professor J.H. Michael Whiteman in Cape Town. Whiteman was a Mathematical Physicist who taught Relativity and Quantum Theory. Whiteman was also a mystic who had experienced every sort of psychical and mystical experience including mystical union. He had also learned Sanskrit and Pali so as to read the Indian texts in their original forms rather than the misinterpretations of academic scholars who did not really understand the true mystical meanings of these texts. Thus Whiteman was probably the best-qualified person in the world to assess my work.

I am also thus very grateful to Professor Whiteman who wrote to me after reading O/OM stating that he was pleasingly struck first by the way you "saw through the muddled, half-baked or otherwise seriously inadequate thinking of various much-publicised writings – for instance, those by Hawking, Wilber, Capra, Jung, and even Einstein". Whiteman noted the fact that I was only 34 years old although he added that I still had much to learn. As Ellison himself had recognised when I met him at SMN and SPR meetings before his death in 2000, Whiteman (then in his mid-90s) seemed to realise that I was the young man who could probably get this proper understanding of the Science-Mysticism relationship across to a much wider audience. He suggested that I read his 1967 book *The Philosophy of Space and Time and the Inner Constitution of Nature* and he had asked his publisher to send me copies of his two most recent books. I only got around to finding a copy of his 1967 book in 2006. This book directed me towards investigating Continental European Phenomenology which Whiteman had recognised reformulates knowledge long known to Indian Philosophy. Whiteman's final book *Universal Theology* (2006), which I read in 2010, was also most useful in regard to understanding the true mystical meaning of Christian myths (copied from the older Mediterranean

Mystery Religions) such as Virgin Birth, Son of God, Turning Water into Wine etc. I later found that this interpretation, which fitted in exactly with my neurobiological interpretation of Hindu-Buddhist enlightenment in O/OM, had earlier been hinted at by the great scholar of World Mythology Joseph Campbell.

Thanks to Professor Peter Fenwick (Neuropsychiatrist, Maudsley Hospital and the Institute of Psychiatry, London) who had been the Chairman of the SMN when O/OM was published. He read the synopsis which I posted to him in 1998, asking me for a copy of the published book as well as supplying me with Arthur Ellison's phone number. In August 1999 at the SMN's 'Beyond the Brain' Conference at Cambridge, he brought the newly-appointed Templeton Prize judge ex-physicist Professor Ravi Ravindra to sit at my table at the first breakfast and throughout the conference kept pressing Ravindra to speak with me.

Thanks to Air Vice Marshall (Retired) Vishwa Mohan Tiwari who is also a scholar of Vedic Mathematics amongst other things. After meeting me at a conference in Hoboken in 2000, he became a supporter of my work and has remained so to this day. In 2000 he tried to get *The Hindu* and *India Today* to publish his own review of O/OM. *The Hindu* responded that they had already done a review although this was a short piece of waffle by someone who seemed not to have read the book and who never mentioned my key achievement, the identification of the physical correlate of the Divine Light. *India Today* had promised me a review in 1999 but only printed a thumbnail of the cover with the words 'Marriage of Science and Mysticism' along with the title and placed this under a review of a mass market book. As in 1999, they refused Tiwari's review saying that the book was much too 'metaphysical' and 'highfalutin' for their readers.

Thanks are due to Alan Rhodes of Kansas who was probably the first American to purchase my book in 1999 after he had read my 1998 posting about the book on the Institute of Noetic Sciences (IONS) web discussion forum and asked me to send him more information. In both 1999 Alan chased up the Director of Research at IONS about when they would do a review of my book; after all, their primary purpose was supposed to be the scientific study of Noetic ('spiritual') phenomena.[5] She replied telling Alan that she had not heard of the book even though, on seeing the 1998 web forum posting, she had written to me asking for a copy and she had met me at the August 1999 'Beyond the Brain' conference a week or so earlier where she, as one of the speakers, witnessed me 'steal the show' right at the very end. In 2006, after I had emailed Alan with the new pieces of evidence confirming my correlation of the Divine Light with the RAS-brainwaves, Alan forwarded the emails to the new IONS President the 'New Age' academic philosopher Christian de Quincey. De Quincey, an admirer of Whitehead and Ken Wilber, dismissed the information responding to Alan with an absurd comment about this Sutapas Bhattacharya not understanding what a 'physical correlate' was. This was probably based on my informal email to Alan not using the phrase 'physical correlate' when I referred to my 'identification of the Light' although I always used 'physical correlate' in formal presentations and had indeed done so later in the email! De Quincey also stated that Sutapas Bhattacharya did not seem to know that there were Western Panpsychists who agreed with the mystical notion of Universal Consciousness. I knew this full well of course. In my 2006 emails I was using 'Panpsychism' in the restricted sense that David Skrbina had used in his 2006 book *Panpsychism in the West* which limited its use to 'Pluralist Panpsychism' such as Whitehead's Philosophy of Organism rather than Universal Consciousness views which Skrbina referred to as 'Idealism'.

Thanks to Maharaj Kishen Kaw who was Union Minister of Education in Delhi in 2000 when I sent him information about O/OM after I heard about his little book *The Science of Spirituality* in which he called for a scientific understanding of Spirituality. Kaw was impressed by O/OM and said that I should visit him if I was in Delhi. Thanks also to psychiatrist Dr Beulah McNab (associated with the University of Amsterdam) who, in September 1994, was the first scholar to agree with my RAS-brainwave correlate of the Light. In 1992 as an author with Academic Brace London, she had tried to help me find a publisher for my unpublished 1988 paper 'A Panpsychist Interpretation of Consciousness'. In 1994 when I phoned her to tell her of my discovery she told me that she had already read *Transformations of Consciousness*, the key book which had supplied me with the critical information about the yogic experience of the Light. Once I told her what the Light was in terms of its physical correlate she said 'Of course' and that I was a genius. She added that millions of people will think that I am mad but I know that you are right! She also mentioned to me Karl Pribram's new book *Brain and Perception* which included his new 'Holographic Quantum Field Neurodynamics' model of the mind which lent support to my own views of the mind (i.e. ego) as a dissipative structure in the brains electromagnetic energy fields. She was keen to see my book when it was published. However, when O/OM was published in 1999, I found that I had lost her 1992 letter and never found her contact details using the Internet.

Others I must thank include Dr Wolfgang Fischer of Munich who was excited by my work after I made contact in 2007 and has hosted draft versions of Chapter 1 of this book on his website since. Thanks to Professor Subhash Kak who was excited by my O/OM back in 1999 and expected that it would make me famous [which of course it should have, at least in India.[6] Thanks to the late Professor Karel Werner for his lengthy review of O/OM in *Journal of the Royal Asiatic Society*. Thanks to Professor Uma Erry who published a very positive 8pp review in *Bhavan's Journal*. Thanks to Dr Michele Caponigro, physicist and epistemologist at the University of Bergamo, for her praise for my work and pointing out to me the papers on Ralph Abraham's website. Thanks to the late Professor Willis Harman (Electrical Engineering, Stanford and ex-Head of Stanford Research Institute) who responded positively to my letter in 1995. As President of IONS until his death in 1996 he had urged Western 'Consciousness Researchers' to learn from India and predicted that the Science of the Future would be based on Indian metaphysics. He sent me one of his own monographs containing useful bibliographical references.

Thanks also to the following people who have either supported me or shown interest in my work on Consciousness: Professor Peter Stewart DSc (physicist and engineer; ex-Head of Rolls Royce Aero-Engines and psychic); Professor Michael Paidoussis, Dr Peter Hardwick, Professor J.M. Hobson, Professor David Yount, Professor Paul Muller-Ortega, Professor Harry Hunt,

Dr Richard Tieszen, Dr Nick Herbert, Dr David Peat, Professor Scott Kelso, Professor D.W Hamlyn, J.J. Williamson DSc, Professor Thomas Nagel, Dr Arnold Zuboff, and Dr J.J. Clarke. Finally a special thanks to Paul Nash, chemistry graduate and scientific indexer who had indexed books for Professor Roger Penrose and Professor D.W. Atkin before helping me index O/OM in 1998. He wrote to me thanking me for letting him help me with the index saying that O/OM had taught him what Quantum Theory was really pointing towards and what Spirituality was actually all about. He had been delayed on the indexing because my book was 'too interesting' and he kept reading it. He even paid for an extra copy of O/OM to give to his son who was then in postgraduate study. He stated on the phone that, if just one major newspaper published a proper review of the book (highlighting its central idea – the physical correlate of the Divine Light – which is of course world-changing importance) then this would create a 'snowball effect' or a 'chain reaction' as others would pick-up on it and repeat it.

Notes

1. Eurocentric historians date this global conflict as starting from 1939 even though the Japanese invasion of China began in 1937. They also refer to it as the Second World War as they label the 1914-18 'Great War' in Europe, with minor secondary theatres in Arabia etc. was a 'World War'.

2. John White had also been a Director of Education at the Institute of Noetic Sciences founded by Apollo 14 astronaut and physicist Dr. Edgar Mitchell during the period when Willis Harman had been President. John was also the Literary Agent for Ken Wilber when Wilber published his first book back in 1977 and also for Professor Amit Goswami (*see* Note 5).

3. Mainstream Western science is totally hostile to knowledge derived from Mysticism and Indian Philosophy; this is a 'fringe science' journal rather than a mainstream scientific journal.

4. Although Professor Jahn submitted it for review to this fringe science journal, I later received a letter from some Humanities professor from a (Catholic Jesuit) Marquette University in Milwaukee, saying that this book (which included poetry, historical and political material) was unsuitable for review.

5. In fact between 1998-2001 Rajiv Malhotra had sponsored Bengali-US physicist Professor Amit Goswami to spend 3 years as Scholar in Residence at IONS. Goswami stated that his project was to investigate the possibility of integrating Hindu-Buddhist Nondualism with Western Physics, Psychology and Philosophy. I sent him a synopsis of my O/OM in 1997 after reading his 'Quantum Mind' book *The Self-Aware Universe*. In 1998 the new President of IONS (after Harman's death) Winston Franklin had written to me saying that he had taken the liberty of forwarding my synopsis to Goswami stating that Goswami will be excited by this [as indeed he should have been]. Later in 1998 when I put up my posting on the IONS web forum, an American woman who knew him said that I should contact him as he would be excited by my work. I replied that I had already had done so in 1997 and that Franklin had forwarded my material to him a few months earlier. Goswami never replied to me. Indian Philosophy Professor Arvind Sharma of McGill Universitydid not respond either after Michael

Paidoussis (a Mechanical Engineering Professor at McGill who became a supporter of my work) told me that he had spoken to Sharma and urged me to email Sharma.

6. The fact that my O/OM did not get more publicity in India, even though it should have been a matter of national pride, reflects in part the obsequious attitude of most Western-educated Indian intellectuals toward Western opinion. They remain stuck in the subaltern mindset in which, in order to advance up the career ladder, one must follow the lead of the White Man and not question his superior knowledge! The Ramakrishna Mission got an Indian physicist to review O/OM. O/OM was actually confirming the Vedantic-Tantric metaphysical world-view that Ramakrishna himself had espoused. Even though the reviewer was sympathetic, he concluded with an absurd comment about how he doubted that Einstein would have agreed with me. It is of no consequence whether or not the late Albert Einstein, whose philosophical insight has been greatly exaggerated by the Anglo-American West [as I show in this book], might agree with my view. In regard to Panpsychism and the Indeterminist and Transcendentalist implications of Quantum Theory (which so disturbed Einstein), it is not important what one man thought when the overwhelming evidence and logical argument indicates that he was wrong on such questions!

Part One

The Light of Truth

1

The Mysteries of Existence and Creation

Hubris, Hyperbole and Humbug in Ontological Phantasies of Physics

It is wrong to think that the task of physics is to find out how Nature is. Physics concerns what we can say about Nature.

Niels Bohr[1]

In discovering that everything is made of atoms, modern Physics has solved the "Mystery of Existence". Thus spoke Professor Jim Al-Khalili, an Anglo-Iraqi physicist, at the start of his 2007 BBC television (TV) series *Atom*. He also proclaimed that, in discovering how heavier atoms are made in stars and supernovae and that much helium was created along with hydrogen in the Big Bang, Physics has also solved the "Mystery of Creation". Furthermore, in discovering the radioactive transmutation of elements, Al-Khalili added, physicists were the first "true alchemists". He admitted that Consciousness still remained a mystery but assumed that Consciousness posed no problem for the Atomic metaphysics; it was, he asserted confidently, a mystery related to amazingly complex arrangements of atoms[2]. To be fair to Professor Al-Kalili, he was only voicing publicly a view held widely amongst scientists and such hyperbolic claims are made regularly for pet theories by scientists presenting television (TV) documentaries.

In 2008 the world's media reported the start-up of the Large Hadron Collider (LHC) at CERN (the European particle physics research centre) with apocalyptic headlines about the possibility of planet-destroying black holes appearing in recreating conditions similar to the (hypothetical) Big Bang.[N1] The pseudo-intellectual journalists displayed their staggering ignorance by regurgitating the sensationalist claptrap of semi-educated scientists that the so-called Higgs Boson (posited to account for *Mass*), which they hoped to prove the existence of using the LHC, being the **"God Particle"**. Again in 2012, the media has been spouting this specious "God Particle" gobbledegook given the claim by CERN to have detected this boson (a term derived from the name of the Bengali physicist S.N. Bose). In this age of secular, Materialist myth-making this is the nearest that Science has come to 'gazing upon the face of the

Creator'. The British media fails to point out the fact, noted by Lee Smolin, that Briton Peter Higgs put forward his hypothesis independently, a few months after Francois Englert and Robert Brout in Brussels put forward essentially the same idea. Smolin says it should be called the EBH phenomenon[3].

We are told repeatedly by the Materialists that these fundamental particles are like the *building blocks* of the universe. We shall see that, in reality, the supposed individual fundamental particles (the modern equivalent of Democritus's *atoms*), are actually superficial phenomena (appearances), abstractions or mental constructs. Fundamental particles are neither ultimately real, nor distinct 'atomistic' entities as presented by al-Khalili and mainstream Physics. Referring to the Higgs Boson the 'God Particle' is worse than just putting an eye-catching, hyperbolic spin on media presentations of science which the general public would otherwise find boring. It is a shameless display of ignorance by pseudo-intellectuals in regard to the true source of the notion of a Creator God related to the notion of Divinity. This true source is the **Divine** (or *Uncreated*) **Light** (*a.k.a.* the Godhead, *cit* or Pure Consciousness, *Atman*, Buddha Nature, *al haqq* or The Reality, *Sofia* or the Cosmic Light of Wisdom, the Inner Light of Conscience, the Christ, the Holy Spirit, the Philosopher's Gold, the Holy Grail, the Fount of all Wisdom, the Fountain of the Water of Life etc.).

In the first episode of his 2004 BBC TV Series *Light Fantastic*, Cambridge Historian of Science Simon Schaffer claimed that the Divine Light was an ancient myth which had been discredited by Newton's work on Optics. When I saw this programme (repeated in 2010), I emailed the BBC to complain, both about Schaffer presenting Eurocentric myths about Greek culture supposedly dominating India but also about his myth that Divine Light was a myth (I could not find Schaffer's email as he was on a Sabbatical). After all I had identified its 'direct' physical correlate with a well-established brain process known to all medical doctors and this correlation was supported by overwhelming evidence based on authoritative Hindu and Buddhist yogic knowledge as well as the limited scientific studies of Enlightenment (*see Appendix 1*). I have used *direct* physical correlate here to indicate that it is the physical process that actually corresponds with the experiential phenomenon of the Divine Light. It is not just some minor associated factor such as a chemical whose presence or quantity may be correlated with the phenomenon such as blood-oxygen in Near-Death Experiences (NDEs). Schaffer's Producer at the BBC, one Anne Laking, read my long list of evidence supporting my correlation and then read the draft versions of the early chapters of this book which I had posted on-line in 2009. Obviously impressed by this, she emailed me back to say that she had even ordered my 1999 book, *The Oneness/Otherness Mystery: The Synthesis of Science and Mysticism* (O/OM), in which I first presented this knowledge and that she would show the book to her colleagues in the BBC Science department.

But as with my old university course supervisor Professor Lorna Casselton, who was the Vice-President of the Royal Society (when I visited her at the Royal Society to tell her about my work in 2009), I will get no publicity through such contacts. This is because to acknowledge publicly the validity of my physical correlate of the Divine Light or Pure Consciousness (which is beyond all reasonable doubt given the overwhelming evidence supporting it – *see Appendix*) would be to acknowledge the fact that the Physicalist ontology of modern Science is false. Furthermore, my identification of the physical correlate of the so-called Godhead, *al haqq* or Holy Spirit also undermines the Dualist mythology of Theistic religions which peddle superstitions about the complete Otherness of God from Man! It also undermines the false mythology believed by most New Agers that enlightened mystics are some sort of 'leading shoot' of a new, more highly-evolved form of human being.

We shall see that, regardless of the confident assertion of orthodox scientists that their theories describe actual reality, extremely simple epistemological analysis reveals that the so-called 'physical universe' of modern Science is a false ontological picture. The *physical universe* of modern Science can only exist in the imagination of self-deluding Materialist and Physicalist believers. The 20th Century shift from matter to energy as the fundamental stuff of the universe in Physics has led to the new 'Physicalist' ontology in which *energy* is held as the 'primary substance'. The atoms, particles and forces of the old Materialism are derivative forms of energy. We are told that the LHC is recreating conditions that supposedly pertained very shortly after the Big Bang. In fact the so-called 'Big Bang' hypothesis is not as certain a fact as the scientific establishment PR (Public Relations) presentations would have us believe, given the evidence which seems to contradict it, threatening to burst the "Hubble bubble" dogma. Such evidence is suppressed by orthodox science and its proponents usually dismissed as misguided 'heretics'. This includes extensive X-ray telescopic evidence gathered over decades showing that highly red-shifted quasars are clearly associated with (or linked to) nearby Seyfert galaxies that are low red-shifted and known to be relatively 'close' to the Milky Way. This contradicts the orthodox view that increased red-shifting is correlated necessarily with increasing distance from the Earth upon which the notion of the expanding universe originating in a 'Big Bang' is based[4].

Contrary to the popular misconception rehashed by Al-Khalili, true Alchemy did not aim at transmuting metals like Lead into Gold but transforming the base, mundane mind of the Alchemist into the "philosopher's gold", developing the True Self, to lead out the 'gold' within[5]. These were symbolic terms referring to transformation of the mundane mind of the alchemist into the Divine Light, a spiritual transmutation. The first known Alchemical text was by the 4th Century *c.e.* (Common Era) Graeco-Egyptian Zosimus of Panopolis who was a mystic associated with the Empedoclean-Pythagorean tradition[6]. Alchemy was also known as Islamic Hermetica in medieval Europe. The Greek deity *Hermes* (the Roman *Mercury*) was a symbolic reference to the mercurial, 'quicksilver-like' flowing quality of the Spirit (Divine Light) and its role as the Messenger between Heaven and Earth. Zosimus wrote:

> *For those who wish to save and purify the divine soul which is bound in with the four elements, or who seek to rescue the divine Pneuma from out of the body, a symbol of chemistry may be deduced from the Cosmogony,...*[7].

Alchemy came to Europe via Moorish Spain as Islamic 'Hermetica'. Some spiritually ignorant medieval Western alchemists took the texts literally, projecting such mystical transformation onto the natural world. Eventually Western alchemists such as Paracelsus realised the error[8]. True alchemists looked down disdainfully upon the deluded trying to produce metallic gold with their bellows etc. calling them 'puffers'[9]. We shall see that, contrary to orthodox histories of Science, the rise of modern Natural Philosophy (today's Natural Sciences) owed more to Magic (Occultism) than to Logic. Isaac Newton, himself deeply involved in Alchemy, distinguished the "vulgar chemistry" of the common chemists relating to 'grosser' particles of matter bringing about sensible changes and the more subtle, secret and noble, vital subtle matter diffused through the mass, the 'tender spirit'[10]. Medical psychiatrist Anthony Stevens[11] tells us:

> *The post-Renaissance view of alchemical purpose is a travesty, a base projection of our own barren spirit; what he wanted was not so much to enrich his coffers as to transform his soul. In order to acquire the 'golden understanding one must..., observing and contemplating by means of that inner light which God has lit in nature and in our hearts...*

Nobody who is familiar with the dynamics of Consciousness and mental states revealed in advanced forms of Mindfulness Meditation (which, following Edmund Husserl, modern Westerners call Phenomenology – *see Chapter 8*), with their characteristic wholeness or Gestalt quality and intensive (rather than extensive or spatially exclusive) mutual interpenetration, would think that mental phenomena are made of discrete impenetrable atoms. Distinguished French physicist Bernard d'Espagnat argues correctly in his recent book *On Physics and Philosophy* that Democritus's notion of ultimate particles or 'Multitudinism' (the view that Reality consists of many discrete elements) is no longer a tenable ontological perspective even though most physicists still cling to the old 'Galilean ontology'[12]. Contrary to the popular image of tiny particles whizzing around particle accelerators, there are in fact no moving elementary particles which can be followed as individual entities from one location to another.

In the plaza outside the CERN building in Geneva, stands a human-size statue of the Hindu deity Shiva in the famous *Siva Nataraj* posture, dancing within a fiery ring. On the plinth below are inscribed two quotations from famous Anglo-Sri Lankan scholar Ananda Coomaraswamy and from Fritjof Capra[13], the physicist whose 1975 pop philosophy book *The Tao of Physics: An exploration of the parallels between modern physics and Eastern mysticism* became a bestseller:

> *It is the clearest image of the activity of God which any religion can boast of.*
>
> Ananda Coomaraswamy[14]

> *In our time, physicists have used the most advanced technology to portray the patterns of the cosmic dance. The metaphor of the cosmic dance thus unifies ancient mythology, religious art and modern physics.*
>
> Fritjof Capra[15]

In her 1981 essay *Meaning and Order*[16] Marie-Louise von Franz, a close friend of the great physicist Wolfgang Pauli, wrote:

The God of modern physicists resembles more the God-image of Hinduism, or generally of the Far East, and has been, as Ruyer points out, actually influenced by it.

We shall see later that even Fritjof Capra, like many others, has reduced Eastern mysticism erroneously to Materialism (Emergent Materialist 'Systems' mumbo jumbo). We shall see below that the ancient Indian texts known as the *Upanisads* constituted the world's first conceptual philosophy. Indeed, the Greek Theory of the Elements was a corrupted form of the Indian *panch bhuta* (five spirits or five elements) found in the *Upanisads.* In one famous cosmology from the *Upanisads*, which developed into the Tantric Philosophy of Hinduism and Buddhism, the first created element was ***Akasa*** (Space as subtle matter characterised by *vibration* – or 'Ether')[17]. It was through the progressive vibratory densification of *Akasa* that the elements which we perceive as types of matter were created. This parallels the deeper metaphysical understanding of modern Physics as we shall see. In fact the famous AUM symbol of the *Mandukya Upanisad* represents both the Four States of Consciousness (a model which still retains scientific validity) as well as the Vibratory Creation of the Universe. We shall see that 21st Century Physics, Mathematics, Cosmology and Cognitive Science/Psychology are more in tune with ancient Indian Brahmanic-Buddhist philosophy than with the myths of the Ancient Greeks hyped up by Eurocentric Westerners in their racist 'Classics' as if they had created all Philosophy and sciences.

In the preface to his *Toward a Global Science*, Susantha Goonatilake says that a pervasive Eurocentric bias guides today's dominant perspective on Science. He notes that atomic ideas appeared in India before they appeared in Greece and were associated with Pakudha Katyayana, an older contemporary of Buddha[18]. I would add that some Ancient Indian atomic theories involved 'atoms' flashing in and out of existence; in fact such views accord better with modern Quantum Theory than with Democritus's indestructible atoms moving in an imaginary vacuum-like space. Note that the concept of space as empty of all substance was created by Democritus in order to allow the supposed atoms to move. This pervasive Eurocentrism is seen in the Western academic fabrications regarding Ancient Greek philosophers being proto-modern 'scientists' when in fact most of them were actually shamanic healers, occultists and mystics concerned with escaping the Wheel of Transmigration etc. Cicero wrote of Democritus, who believed in Dream Telepathy, that he never knew of anyone who talked nonsense with greater authority[19].

As with Kepler, Newton and many other fathers of modern Science and of 20th Century Quantum Physics, the occultist and mystical interests linked to their scientific work have been airbrushed out of History. Francis Bacon studied paranormal psychic phenomena and their study was one of the first uses he proposed for the new Natural Philosophy[20]. Similarly Giordano Bruno was actually obsessed with Hermetic Occultism (Alchemy, Cabbala etc.), Numerology and Astrology. He has been misrepresented as a mathematician (rather than a numerologist) and a martyr for modern science as he championed Heliocentrism, a notion that long preceded Copernicus. Bruno was burnt at the stake, not for scientific views but for his occult practices! Bruno, like

Copernicus himself, actually adhered to Heliocentrism on mystical grounds and Copernicus quoted the mythical Hermes Trismegistus in regard to the Sun as the visible god, reflecting the mystical sun (Inner Light)[21]. We shall see later that Europe's Financial and Scientific Revolutions were preceded by medieval Europeans translating Hindu mathematics and astronomy, which included Heliocentric models, centuries before Copernicus's supposed 'Revolution'. One thousand years ago, prior to the Mohammedan conquest of Northern India, Hindu India was acknowledged by the Arabs as leading the world in Science. Indeed, contrary to Western racial fantasies presented as 'History', the Scientific Revolution was largely based on Hindu not Greek mathematics and it was such Hindu influences that actually led to Atomism becoming acceptable again in medieval Arabia and Renaissance Europe.

The great physicist Erwin Schrödinger, whose wave-mechanical Schrödinger Equation lies at the heart of modern Physics, was himself an advocate of the *Advaita Vedanta* (Nondual Brahmanism) metaphysics derived from the *Upanisads*. He never accepted the notion of actual particles. In his *The Interpretation of Quantum Mechanics* he stressed that there are no individual particle trajectories in Quantum Mechanics (QM), i.e., particles do not exist except in relation to our measurements (or interactions with Nature)[22] implying a collective (delocalised) wave existence underlying the appearance of 'particle' phenomena[23]. He considered quantum waves to be as real as water waves, they were **matter waves** propagating continuously in space[24]. In his *The Nature of the Physical World*, the great astrophysicist Arthur Eddington depicted Schrödinger's Wave Mechanics as a sub-aether oscillating with ripples a million times faster than those of visible light, too fast to come within the scope of our gross experience. What we humans can appreciate (or abstract) is a disturbed area created by the convergence and coalescence of waves which we think of (or conceptualise) as a material particle such as an electron[25]. The earlier Matrix Mechanics invented by Werner Heisenberg was merely a calculating tool with no conceptual model behind it[26]. Heisenberg himself wrote in 1955 that that it is not possible for us to return to the ontology of Materialism (meaning the old Classical notion of particles whose trajectories we can follow through space)[27].

Furthermore, *contra* al-Khallili, it is rather obvious that the Big Bang hypothesis doesn't actually solve the Mystery of Creation as it offers no explanation as to the source of all this energy, along with rapidly expanding space which supposedly just burst into existence out of nothing (i.e., magically) some 13-14 billion years ago. In fact, as we shall see, modern Materialist Science is the disaffected child of Christian and Greek mythology with roots in the Christian anthropomorphic myth of *Creatio ex nihilo*. This involves the Christian God, resembling a male human personality, creating the Earth, Sun, Moon and six planets up to Neptune (the entire Christian universe) out of absolutely nothing (not some pre-existing substance). Something out of nothing implies Magic; usually framed as the miraculous power of the omnipotent Creator for whom nothing supposedly is impossible. In putting forward notions such as there being supposed 'Laws of Nature', existing independently of material Nature, the founding fathers of modern Science (in particular Isaac Newton) were assuming explicitly that this myth was true and that a man-like Creator God, resembling a human "sovereign" or a Roman emperor, laid down the rules specifying the mechanical (like clockwork) operations for the inert, inanimate and insentient material Nature that He had created miraculously out of nothing. Due to such tacit Christian roots, modern Physics comes full circle and presents us with an unsatisfactory, magical *Creatio ex nihilo*, which furthermore, completely ignores the fact that our existence is sentient possessing primarily a conscious or spiritual aspect.

Professor Al-Khalili assumed that the mystery of Consciousness posed no problem for Atomic metaphysics (i.e., Materialism), it was simply a problem due to the immense complexity associated with atoms organised into brains. If we examine such questions impartially, we will see quite clearly that Physics, including QM, actually has no explanation whatsoever for the existence of the most basic fact of our existence, the fact that we are conscious of existing. This Spirit/Nature (Consciousness/Matter) dichotomy stems from the Christian concept of insentient, inanimate Nature resulting from *Creatio ex nihilo*, a doctrine also held by Jews and Mohammedans (actually originating with the Persian mythmaker Zoroaster). Even Isaac Newton, who stressed the inanimate picture of matter to retain his theistic God as the Prime Mover and Upholder of the Laws[28], noted the glaring logical error in Galileo's metaphysical doctrine of Primary Qualities which removed subjective qualities from supposed Reality leaving behind just quantities[29]; a view that was challenged famously by Alchemists such as Robert Fludd[30]. Simple epistemological analysis reveals that Consciousness, as conscious intuition, is presupposed in the supposedly self-evident primary definitions of Physics just as it was presupposed in the axioms of Frege and Russell in their failed attempts to reduce Mathematics to Logic.

All Materialist or Physicalist approaches to the problem (except the ludicrous Eliminative Materialism of Richard Rorty and Patricia Churchland which denies its existence) tacitly presuppose the existence of Consciousness even though it has been precluded right at the very start of Natural Science. Thus Materialist or Physicalist speculations about it, including the countless papers churned out by most modern Western 'Philosophers-of-Mind' on Consciousness (as Awareness), are no more than vacuous sophistry, presupposing surreptitiously the very Consciousness they seek to explain. Such sneaking-in of Consciousness into the insentient 'physical universe' of Natural Science, using verbal 'sleights-of-hand' to disguise the desperate recourse to a magical creation of Consciousness *ex nihilo* (usually labelled **Emergence**), is the dominant approach amongst most contemporary Western 'Philosophers of Mind'. Blinkered by Scientism, they peddle this tacitly Dualist, magical Emergent Materialist mumbo jumbo. The use of 'emergence' resembles the use of 'Abracadabra' by conjurors. It is an example of the 'Fallacy of the Linguistic Blanket' where a fancy word is concocted to disguise vacuity of explanation. Simultaneously Emergent Materialists parade their supposedly scientific credentials by regurgitating the latest fashionable jargon from 'Cognitive Science' whilst demonising opponents of Physicalism as believers in mysticism who don't understand Science!

The orthodox scientific reviewers then heap praise on these supposed 'philosophers' for having reaffirmed their faith in the official dogma of Scientism.

Given this tacit Physicalist recourse to 'magic', it was amusing to hear that 'High Priest' of Scientism, Daniel C. Dennett, describing himself at one of the Toward a Science of Consciousness conferences held at Tucson in the 1990s as feeling like a 'cop' (policeman) amongst the New Age aging-hippy types[31]. If by this he meant that he felt like an establishment figure or a 'square', then fair enough. If, on the other hand, Dennett was implying that he was 'policing' the drug-induced fantasies regarding consciousness held by the hippy-types, then Dennett himself was the dope. The New Age, hippy-types probably possessed a better understanding of what Consciousness really is than Dennett with his Reductionist and vacuous 'cop-out' appeals to the (supposedly) unquestionable authority of Physics.

Furthermore, the Physicalist ontology presents us with the (originally) God-given Laws of Nature, nowadays treated as 'transcendental' (i.e., extraneous to the intrinsic nature of matter) and hence supposedly inexplicable. Some do try to account for them using pseudo-ontological modern myths like the brazenly tautological Anthropic Principle; the Laws and Fundamental Constants of Physics have the forms and often extremely precise values that we find as, if they didn't, there could be no evolution of Life and Mind in this universe to look back and discover them. We even find well-known scientists, usually apologists for Christian and Jewish Monotheism associated with the Templeton Foundation, using the supposed paradox of the unexplained and remarkably precise values of the supposedly universal physical constants to reintroduce their Neo-Christian 'God-of-the gaps' (i.e. an anthropomorphic God concept filling in the lacunae in understanding resulting from the failings of Physicalist ontology). I say "supposedly" universal as it has not been proven that the so-called 'Laws' and Fundamental Constants discerned in the proximity of the Earth actually apply throughout the known universe. The aforementioned paradox of highly red-shifted quasars connected by gas jets to low Redshift Seyfert galaxies has led to theories, by the likes of Jayant Narlikar (conforming to Mach's Principle) wherein the mass of newly created material particles may not be constant but starts off at zero and increases as the extent of interaction with the rest of the universe increases[32]. Mach's Principle, which Einstein tried to incorporate into his General Theory of Relativity (GTR), was that *inertia* (i.e., the resistance to acceleration due to *mass*) arises as a relativistic consequence of interaction with the rest of the entire universe. There are also alternatives to the Big Bang hypothesis which treat the speed of light as variable at different epochs of cosmic creation.

Indeed, building on the aforementioned ideas of Schrödinger, Mach's Principle, as well as the views of Einstein, Mach, Clifford and others, my acquaintance the US physicist Milo Wolff[33] has put forward a remarkable new holonomic (each seemingly discrete 'thing' exists by virtue of relativity to everything else) Wave Structure model of the electron, resembling Indian Tantric (phenomenal universe as energetic manifestations) metaphysics. Though still in its infancy, this approach begins to show how it is possible to account for both the emergence of particle-like material phenomena from the underlying wave dynamics and also for the self-organising appearance of fundamental constants and so-called 'laws'. It also casts some light on the intriguing relationships between microcosmic and macrocosmic physical constants pointed out by Paul Dirac (the great physicist who put forward the notion of Antimatter). In fact, the physicist David Bohm, famous for his metaphysical notion of the 'implicate order' (a neologism for the 'transcendental' realm underlying Nature) had suggested a model similar to Wolff's in the last chapter of his last book[34].

In 1967, over a decade before Bohm put forward his 'implicate order' ideas, mathematical physicist and mystic J.H.M. Whiteman had argued that the Universal Cohesion, (i.e., coherence) of the universal laws applying to physical phenomena and the true underlying Causality, connecting the discontinuous events registered by our instruments, indicated the presence of such a mutually interrelated, (i.e., holonomic) transcendental substructure to the discontinuous events or spatiotemporal phenomena described by Physics, (i.e., an order of reality prior to physical phenomena). The 'discontinuous events' referred to here are the particle-like phenomena which we detect with our instruments given that QM does not describe 'particle trajectories' linking together such phenomena. The reader will probably be familiar with the supposed paradoxes involving supposed 'particles' passing through two slits simultaneously (actually based on the false assumptions regarding the existence of individual particles moving around on their own like objects in the macroscopic world).

Whiteman also argued that the great success of QM in predicting physical phenomena implied that this transcendental substructure was a Wave Structure. In QM, *energy* (and hence *mass* due to mass/energy equivalence) are associated with ***wave-frequency*** and *momentum* with ***wave-length***[35]. I had argued in *The Oneness/Otherness Mystery*[36] that the so-called Laws were such self-organisational properties emerging from the resonant interactions of the energetic waves and vibrations underlying material phenomena. This deeper, transcendental reality was what Carl Jung was hinting at in regard to his vague and seemingly anthropocentric notion of Synchronicity (meaningful coincidences) which represented a special case of the more general 'Acausal Orderedness' underlying the predictable regularities of Space-Time-limited 'Causality'[37].

In *On Physics and Philosophy*, d'Espagnat mentions the arguments of Jean Petitot on Science and Ontology (the study of Being or of what actually exists). Petitot has put forward the valid argument that Physics gave up seeking to discern the true substantial nature of Being long before Niels Bohr. Bohr's orthodox Copenhagen Interpretation of QM interpreted QM and Science in general as being descriptions, not of anything like a given external reality, but merely of intersubjective (interpersonal consensus), communicable human experience. Thus for Bohr, scientific "Reality" is actively constructed not only by human thought but also by our operational (experimental set-up) decisions[38]. The latter point of our operational (or instrumental) decisions is most apparent in regard to the wave/particle paradox for, as indicated above, 'particles' are really constructs abstracted from our interaction with Nature associated with energy transfers which occur in discrete, quantised packets. Mathematical physicist Richard Thompson states that scientific statements refer only to patterns of correlation in (human) sense data[39]. D'Espagnat himself notes the highly artificial nature of isolating individual atoms in recent so-called 'photo' images and, given that 'particles' do not have trajectories, the particle aspect should strictly be considered as merely aspects for human observers with no implicit assumptions about actual properties[40]. In fact, single atoms still display interference patterns in a two-slit experiment[41], i.e., pass through both slits simultaneously so they cannot be discrete entities. Petitot argued that, in seeking law-like ordering of Nature rather than its intrinsic (substantial) features, the Galilean-Cartesian revolution in Physics (i.e. Classical Physics) had already discarded Ontology (questions about the true intrinsic nature of Being) before Bohr's interpretation of the New Physics which remains the orthodox view[42]. We shall see that this ontological vacuity of modern Science, describing only the regular patterns of phenomena whilst ignoring substantial questions about the nature of Being is related to the famous Brahmanic notion of *Maya*.

There are wackier speculations regarding our Existence and Creation put forward by some distinguished scientists faced with such grand metaphysical questions. The British Astronomer Royal and President of the Royal Society, Martin Rees, was recently promoting in the popular media the contemporary, Computer Age myth that our existence may be only a Virtual Reality type simulation in some 'cosmic computer'. Rees, following his friend Nick Bostrom, makes a facile literal extrapolation from the simple computer simulation known as the 'Game of Life' in which the following of a few simple rules for motion and interaction results in the generation of somewhat complex and unpredictable two-dimensional forms from an initial set of 2-D forms. Rees and Bostrom assume without question notions such as Laws and atoms and they conclude that our universe was created by more intelligent beings in a multiverse (a larger reality containing many universes). In this puerile fantasy, it is claimed that the "God of our ancestors" (suggesting all humans were monotheists worshipping the same 'God') is this greater intelligent being creating our simulated universe.

This myth assumes that we can never uncover the Secret of Creation, never look beyond the spatiotemporal order of phenomena and discover how it is actually being generated, so, for all we know, our very existence might just be a giant computer simulation! This modern Computer Age myth is little different from the Christians' projection of a Cosmic Lawgiver or Sovereign, or the ancient view that the Earth rides upon an elephant, which rests upon turtles. These are fantasies created by those who are ignorant of the fact that we can transcend the realm of spatiotemporal phenomena to realise within ourselves the source of the universe, or of Creation. In 2011, the Templeton Foundation, a Christian organisation which promotes Monotheism and Creationism, awarded their £1 million prize to Rees. This was presumably related to some comments made by Rees including that he still attended Church and some mild comments criticising the radical Atheistic proselytising of some well-known British scientists. Harry Kroto, a Nobel laureate in Chemistry commented[43], "There's a distinct feeling in the research community that Templeton just gives the award to the most senior scientists they can find who's willing to say something nice about religion." The prize is supposed to be for Progress in Religion (especially scientific understanding of it). I doubt that many people would be able to list the actual 'achievements' which have 'advanced scientific understanding of Religion' for which any Templeton Prize has been awarded.

The Brahmanic concept of *Maya* (the mysterious creative power of the Absolute which is usually mistranslated as 'Illusion') may at first appear somewhat similar to Rees' Virtual Reality computer simulation notion. But *maya* does not really mean that the physical universe is all an illusion or dream, rather that the spatiotemporal phenomena perceived through our senses do not constitute Ultimate Reality. In October 2010 the BBC TV's science flagship series *Horizon* showed how the study of illusions in Cognitive Science is revealing, *contra* naive Realism, just how subjective and constructed our perceptions are. Perceived colours need not be correlated with wavelengths of visible light as has long been known in regard to Colour-Constancy under changing light conditions. Perceptual tricks to fill in missing sensory information evolved to enhance our survival chances. On 30th June 2012 the *Daily Mail* reported on a research paper published in *Nature* by a Jay Neitz of the University of Washington which suggested that neurons controlling colour perception are not predetermined and that it was possible that one person's experience of the colour red may be what another person experienced as blue. Such studies show just how wrong is the naive epistemological Realism held by many Physicalists which holds that colours are nothing more than the wave-lengths of visible electromagnetic radiation. There is no objective Empirical Reality witnessed through our senses, there is only intersubjective (interpersonal) consensus.

Bernard d'Espagnat stresses that Physics is limited to direct knowledge of 'Empirical Reality' (actually meaning the world of sensory perception and its supra-biological extension via our scientific instruments) and, following Kant he imagines that the (human) mind-independent 'veiled reality' (the realm of Kant's *noumena*) is impossible for humans to apprehend[44]. Wilhelm and Rawlinson are not alone in arguing that Kant's *noumena/phenomena* distinction was inspired by the Brahmanic *Maya* as it is essentially the same[45]. We shall see later the overwhelming evidence, commonly known at the time, proving that post-Kantian German so-called Transcendental Idealism was derived from the European translations of the Hindu *Upanisads*. These translations excited numerous famous European philosophers and poets who hailed this, deeply profound and rational, spiritual philosophy in contrast to the myths and superstitions of the Bible (the mythical chapters of the Old Testament were actually composed after the oldest *Upanisads*). This so-called 'Brahmanic Revelation' posed the first major challenge in the West to the supposedly unique status of the Christian (spiritual) Revelation[N2 46]. Westphal says that Kant did not reveal much about his method of so-called Transcendental Reflection. Kant indicated that he used a speculative method involving Thought Experiments designed to try to determine the prerequisites of sensory perception. In fact Materialist Westphal claims that Kant's arguments actually point to Realism, (i.e., that our senses perceive the true Reality) rather than the 'Transcendental Idealism' Kant claimed to prove[47]. I have just shown above that recent Cognitive Science research has exploded the naive myth of Realism.

Brahmanism knows that, *contra* Kant's beliefs (Kant was extremely hostile to mystical claims[48]), it is in fact possible to transcend spatiotemporal perceptions and 'see' (with the 'Inner Eye') or 'realise' mystically how the phenomenal universe is generated. The 20th Century US mathematician, mystic and philosopher Merrell-Wolff admitted that he had failed to disprove convincingly the Kantian dogma that there is no **Third Mode of Knowledge** (beyond Sense Perception and Reason) which reveals Metaphysical Knowledge[49]. At the end of the following section, I shall briefly show how my identification of the physical correlate of the Inner Light of Pure Consciousness allows us to begin to understand in scientific terms, both how it is possible for the individuated consciousness of the human being to transcend the spatio-temporal limitations of the Empirical world and experience transcendental realms. But also I will also undermine Kantians, Existentialists, Constructivists and more or less the whole of Western philosophy by revealing how it is possible for the individuated human consciousness to go completely beyond the structural limitations of human embodied being and experience the (metaphysical or 'noumenal') Reality-in-itself, attaining *unmediated knowledge* independent of human mental constructions, in this mortal life.

The True Temple of the Spirit and Human Access to Metaphysical Reality beyond Sensory Appearances

The secrecy of ancient Mystery Traditions and the problematic notion of ineffability

You might have heard it said that the human body is the Temple of the Spirit. Indeed, a Hindu temple is said to symbolise, in its architecture, the so-called subtle body (*a.k.a.* etheric body or energy body)[50], well-known to Western psychics and healers, with its so-called *chakras* or vortex-like energy centres along the spine which, according to some, are opened in Yoga. Whereas the Christians build their churches to look upwards to the sky above as a representation of an imaginary heaven, the most sacred part of the Hindu temple is the innermost sanctum, hidden deep within the structure. As William James asserted famously in his *Varieties of Religious Experience*, beneath the surface of what seems to us most familiar and unassuming, our own consciousness, there lie hidden wonders, exotic planes of Consciousness very different to our everyday existence. *No account of Reality, no account of the universe in its totality can be complete*, noted James, *which ignores these other forms of Consciousness.*

But James appreciated that most of us may well go through life without even suspecting the existence of these altered states of Consciousness[51]. Thus Materialist scientists and writers who insist stubbornly on the non-existence of mystical experience of non-material realms and of paranormal psychic phenomena are like Edwin Abbot's inhabitants of *Flatland* who deny the existence of a Third Dimension because they have never experienced it. Contrary to naive secular misrepresentations of Flatland's intended meaning, ordained theologian Abbott was quite clearly using higher dimensions in *Flatland* as a metaphor for transcendental religious experience (which in fact can involve experiences non-Euclidean ordering of space and time). William James' own experiences were based on experimentation with nitrous oxide[52] and largely restricted to more superficial Nature Mysticism (*see below*) as expressed in his inchoate Panpsychist metaphysics of Pure Experience.

However, many a person may become aware of the greatest secret of human existence, of which James remained largely ignorant, only in the final moments of life. This revelation at the Moment of Death is not one that can usually be transmitted to others. A Cambridge taxi-driver who had been a soldier told me that many a dying soldier, who had been lifelong Atheists or Agnostics, uttered the word 'God!' with their last breath. Intimation (proclamation) of such intimate (Latin: *innermost*) secrets has long been suppressed by Jews, Christians and Mohammedans as it undermines their religious beliefs, exposing them as superstitions susceptible to disproof in spiritual experience. Such spiritual experiences are repeatable and verifiable by interpersonal consensus analogous to the intersubjective consensus which actually underlies the, epistemologically false, claims to 'objectivity' made by Physical Science. Modern (Materialist) Science, rooted in Judaeo-Christian and Greek anthropomorphic mythology, also tries to suppress discussion of this Great Secret (in the form of modern-day Near-Death Experiences) as its own dogmatically held beliefs are also undermined by such inconvenient facts.

Tacit intimations of this Great Secret are to be found all around us even in such well known cultural artefacts as the Mughal mausoleum in India, the Taj Mahal, the anthem of the European Union and the Great Seal of the United States of America as depicted on the Dollar bill. Each of these artefacts used to symbolise these great supranational unions also hints at this Great Secret (*see Chapter 2*). This secret has been wrapped up in arcane symbolism and often deliberate secrecy. Indeed, the word *mystic* originally referred to someone initiated into secret and sacred rites. Throughout around five millennia of civilised history this secrecy has helped contribute to the jungle of confusion and misunderstanding of such rare and exalted experiences. The exclusive association of the *mystical* with Religion (and Spirituality) is a product of modern secularisation dating from around the late 17th Century in Europe (the Age of Reason). Prior to this, the 'Natural Philosophy' or 'Science' of the Renaissance was viewed as one way of uncovering the hidden meaning of God's Universe. Thus Natural Science was itself originally a mystical pursuit[53]. This is clear in Kepler's references to Hermetic 'archetypes' and the highly mystical Isaac Newton's writing about seeking out God's laws by experimentation rather than through Divine communion[54].

We shall see that European scholarship has misunderstood and misinterpreted the esoteric mystical symbolism of the ancient Indian hymns known as the *Rig Veda* leading to absurd racialist fabrications of Ancient Indian history which remain the orthodox dogma of mainstream Western historians. There is remarkable astronomical and archaeological evidence (as well as more recent DNA studies) supporting the traditional Brahmanic view of the Indian setting and the true antiquity of the *Rig Veda*, the oldest parts of which probably date from the 3rd Millennium (M) *b.c.e.* This is about two millennia before Siddharta Gautama, the so-called Buddha (or 'Awakened One'), whom some ignorant Western Buddhophiles seem to think was the first to attain so-called Enlightenment.

Numerous uncritical writers regurgitate the myth, believed by Renaissance Occultists including Bruno, that the esoteric Greek texts known as the *Corpus Hermeticum* associated with so-called 'Alchemy' was written around 3,000 *b.c.e.* in Egypt and constituted the *prisca theologia* or original pristine wisdom which had become increasingly corrupted through the ages. The mythical author Hermes Trismegistus was seen by Latin translator Ficino[N3] as the first *priscus theologus*. But as long ago as 1614, using critical textual analysis, Isaac Casaubon had exposed the true age of the *Hermetica* as dating from the early Christian era around the 2nd Century. Casaubon noted that there was not a word about Hermes Trismegistus in any major pagan writer and he believed that the *Hermetica* were forged to make the new Christian doctrine more palatable to non-Christians. The *Hermetica* even pretends to prophesise that the old religion of Egypt will be superseded by Christianity[55]. A related falsehood peddled by some Afrocentric myth peddlers and some others, (e.g., Yoshihuko Kimura) is that Yoga originated in Egypt and was transmitted to India. As we shall see, archaeological artefacts clearly indicate that Yoga was first practised in the oldest Indian civilisation, the Saraswati-Sindhu in the 3rd M *b.c.e.*

The ancient Vedic wisdom of India, eventually developed into the world's first conceptual 'Philosophy' in the poetic texts known as the *Upanisads* (Upanishads; starting *c.*1000 *b.c.e.*), which were guarded jealously by the Brahman caste. Contrary to racialist Western academic presentations, we shall see that this Brahmanic philosophy, older than the earliest Greek Philosophy (which copied many ideas from Oriental philosophies and science), is actually more veridical both ontologically and scientifically than that of Ancient Greeks. As indicated above, 21st Century Physics, Cosmology, 'Postmodern' Mathematics and Cognitive Science/Psychology are more in tune with ancient Indian rather than Greek philosophy. The Ancient Hindus actually outclassed the Greeks in Mathematics, Astronomy and Logic and modern Science was based largely on Hindu, not Greek, maths. I identified the direct physical correlate of the Divine Light with a well-established brain process known to all medical doctors largely using the factual phenomenological descriptions of the Light found in Hindu and Buddhist philosophy (*see Appendix*). Given my correlations between Upanisadic knowledge of Consciousness and modern scientific and phenomenological knowledge, the *Mandukya Upanisad's* famous 4-State Model of the States of Consciousness (represented by the AUM symbol) remains a scientifically valid categorisation!

In India, the seeker of salvation went to a guru and learnt the "secret" knowledge or *rahasyam*. This was also true of the non-Brahmanic wanderer schools which co-existed with the orthodox Brahmanic tradition. This resembled the Greek *paradosis* or transmission of esoteric knowledge, often on a one-to-one basis[56]. Initiates in the Greek Mystery Religions were famously sworn to secrecy (*see Chapter 3*). The post-Christian *Corpus Hermeticum* claims that the ancient Egyptian priesthood also kept their esoteric, occult knowledge secret from the vulgar masses. This is a reasonable assertion given that Greeks had lived in Egypt from at least 750 *b.c.e.* (at Heliopolis, now part of Cairo) and probably much earlier, thus Hellenistic writers would have some knowledge of the Ancient Egyptian traditions. Rather like today's vulgar pop writers who are captivated with the pyramids, the Classical Greeks, awestruck by the ancient stone monuments, believed mistakenly that all Civilisation and Culture originated in Egypt'; the so-called *Greek Mirage of Egypt*. Herodotus claimed that the Egyptians are quite certain of dates going back 15,000 years before Amasis[57]. We now know that Sumerian civilisation in Mesopotamia was older than that of Egypt and the Babylonians were more advanced in intellectual activities like maths than the Egyptians. Now, about twenty six centuries after Siddharta Gautama (*a.k.a.* the Buddha) tried to learn for himself this secret mystical wisdom, and to reveal it (or at least methods to attain it) to the masses, we have reached a stage of collective human knowledge where we can now largely reject with some confidence an ancient argument, habitually rehashed by most writers on Mysticism, which has introduced tremendous confusion into all discussions of Mysticism.

William James reinforced this argument in *Varieties of Religious Experience* in which he listed the first characteristic of mystical experiences as their *ineffability*. Most Western scholars of, and popular writers on, Mysticism have simply taken it for granted that mystical experiences are ineffable. This implies that mystical experiences are completely beyond the limited capacity of our languages and our abstractive and dichotomising thought processes to convey their true character, hence the use of often self-contradictory attributes and of negative terminology (the *via negativa* – asserting what they are not to dispel the error of exact description) to describe them and insisting that they can only be understood properly through experiencing them. Mystical realisations may be extremely numinous or 'meaningful' (in a supra-rational sense) whilst in such states, sometimes involving identity of subject and object (or "becoming one with" aspects of Reality). Once one returns to normal modes of cognition, locked into subject/object dualities, and mundane spatiotemporal causality which are intrinsic to all languages, the mystic struggles to capture the experience of an alternate 'world' in words framed in the context of our everyday world of experience.

But if we are truthful, our words and concepts are insufficient to convey fully even simple experiences such as the taste of avocados to someone who has never tasted this exotic fruit[N4]. However, with sensory experiences, it is usually quite easy for the uninitiated to attain the sensation themselves. On the other hand, deep mystical realisations are notoriously difficult to attain, with the traditional prerequisite of world-renunciation and Asceticism. Decades of effort may result in failure, false pseudo-realisations or incomplete and partial insights. Over-exaggeration of ineffability and overuse of negative terminology associated with it has created endless confusion and controversy especially amongst various sects purporting to be the followers of the Siddharta Gautama, the so-called 'Buddha'.

In fact, ancient literature such as the *Iliad* used only about three or four colour concepts. In the antiquated Sanskrit language many words are polyvalent, having different meanings in different contexts, indicating a lack of conceptual differentiation. Studies have shown that primitive tribes-people can discriminate various distinct colours but lack the concepts to differentiate them. This is related to the Sapir-Whorf hypothesis stressing the importance of linguistic concepts in our 'dissecting' and categorising the phenomena of

Nature. Both Brahmanic and Greek philosophy developed abstract philosophical concepts from phenomena previously symbolised by anthropomorphic deities as we shall see. Contemporary science and technology provide us with numerous new concepts allowing us to describe and discriminate subtle, nebulous, and highly abstract phenomena such as those associated with Information Technology (IT), Electricity, QM or Relativity which would have appeared more or less ineffable to the Premodern Mind. We shall also see that numerous Ancient Indian mathematical, logical, grammatical, cosmological and metaphysical concepts were too sophisticated for the supposedly 'modern' mainstream European Mind of the Renaissance, Enlightenment, 19th and even 20th Century academics to grasp.

Although grounded on Christian superstitions and Greek myths (*as we shall see*), modern Western Science has nonetheless advanced remarkably our understanding of natural phenomena such that, with the advent of the new QM of the 1920s, Science has actually trespassed into the domains of the Supernatural and Transcendental which Descartes' compromise with the Catholic Church had left outside the realm of Science. Nature alone was to be the domain of the new Natural Philosophy which we now call Science so as not to create conflict with the Church. Concepts now exist within our language, drawn from the New Physics and its interpretation, (e.g., holonomic inter-relatedness of all phenomena, nonlocality, coherence, entanglement, nonseparability) and elsewhere, (e.g., Virtual Reality, non-Euclidean geometries, Cymatics – the creation of dynamic forms through wave phenomena associated with Sound) which, as we shall see, allow us to say much more in positive terms about the deepest mystical experiences which in the past could only be expressed in symbolic metaphors, myths or inadequate ancient philosophical concepts. Furthermore, the invention of psychedelic drugs, such as Albert Hoffmann's LSD (Lysergic Acid Diethylamide), has allowed numerous Western psychiatrists, scientists and technologists to experience altered states of Consciousness without the hassle of Asceticism leading them to seek out Indian philosophical knowledge.

Franklin Merrell-Wolff lamented the fact that many enlightened men throughout history lacked well-developed intellects and thus failed to explicate the path clearly for others to follow. He acknowledged that a powerful intellect can, though need not, be a barrier to enlightenment[58]. The famous *Brihadaranyaka Upanisad* states that it is harder for the learned to know Brahman than the unlearned. Radhakrishnan comments that spiritual attainment is not perfection of the Intellect but an energy pouring into it from beyond, vivifying it[59]. The source of this Life Energy (*prana*) which is also the Light of Pure Consciousness (*atman*) which gives access to metaphysical omniscience and Cosmic Consciousness etc. has perplexed philosophers throughout history leading to dualistic separation of the Spiritual (or of the Transcendental) and Nature. American New Age guru and prolific writer Ken Wilber, having peddled naive errors regarding the Planes of Consciousness (*see Chapter 6*), claimed that even a linkage, let alone a synthesis of Science and Mysticism (including Spirituality) was impossible[60]. But as one of the hymns from the ancient *Rig Veda* asserted famously, To what is One, Seers/Sages (*vipra*) give various names. Willis Harman (who had been a Stanford professor of Electrical

Engineering and Director of Stanford Research Institute) argued that Reality is One, so if Science and Spirituality could not be harmonised, either one or both of them had to be wrong[61].

Contemporary mystic and Religious Studies professor, Christopher Bache, who has realised mystical union etc., thinks that ineffability is overrated as a sign of genuine mystical experience. If you can't represent even to yourself where you have been, he says, you probably just got lost[62]. Ironically, whilst highlighting the ineffability of mystical experience, William James (in *Varieties*) also mentioned that the expression 'field of consciousness' had come into vogue (in the early 20th Century). He added that psychologists (referring primarily to German Gestaltists) tend to view the actual unit as more probably the total mental state (Gestalt), the entire **wave** (*emphasis mine*) of consciousness or field of objects present to the thought at any time (note that James used 'Stream of Thought' for Stream of Consciousness).

In fact, about two millennia before James, the great Indian philosopher Patanjali, began his famous *Yoga Sutras*:

Atha Yoganusanam/Yogas citta-vritti-nirodhah

Meaning, "Now an exposition of Yoga/Yoga is the cessation of the **waves** of the mindstuff" (*emphasis mine*). Note that, although supposedly authoritative scholars have translated the Sanskrit term *vritti* in many English renderings, it literally means *waves* reflecting the actual phenomenological facts rather than the various alternative etymological ramblings of word-monger academics. Merrell-Wolff attained enlightenment and mystical union in the mid-1930s, after 24 years of effort, attaining the deepest mystical Realisations after studying the writing of the great Brahmanic philosopher Sankara. Merrell-Wolff stated that Consciousness (or 'Life') is in some sense like electrical energy fields[63]. We shall see that this equivalence of 'Life' with Consciousness is a rediscovery of the *Prana/Atman* (Life Energy/Impersonal Spirit within) identity of the aforementioned ancient Hindu texts known as the *Upanisads* (Upanishads). Electrical engineer and psychical researcher Dean Radin states in his *The Conscious Universe* that the idea that Consciousness may be field-like can also be traced back to the Upanishads, with their concept of *Brahman*[64] (pronounced "Brummon"), the Absolute Transcendental Consciousness from which the phenomenal universe (empirical world of spatiotemporal forms) manifests. However, discussion of such philosophical issues within the Western academic Physics establishment has largely been rendered taboo as many open-minded physicists, interested in going beyond mere technical problems, have testified[65]. A similar dogmatic attitude resembling Medieval Scholasticism with the brazen suppression of heretical voices by the established orthodoxy appears to permeate Western academic (primarily Anglo-American) Astronomy/Cosmology[66].

In fact the rise of the new QM in the mid-1920s actually involved two European physicists, German Werner Heisenberg and the Austrian advocate of *Advaita Vedanta* (Nondual Brahmanism), the aforementioned Erwin Schrödinger, who have both put on record the influence of Indian philosophy upon their revolutionary ideas in physics (*see Chapter 4*). However, Western academia clings to its, subliminally racist, Eurocentrism and largely suppresses mention of such non-European influences on important Western ideas.

Heisenberg, the prime inventor of QM, himself checked the manuscript of the chapter on QM in *The Philosophy of Space and Time and the Inner Constitution of Nature: A phenomenological study*[67] written in 1967 by mathematical physicist and Sanskrit/Pali-literate mystic, Professor J.H.M. Whiteman. In this book, based on his actual experiences, Whiteman argued in favour of a Universalised Pure Consciousness, transcending appearances in space and time, which is the real core of our Consciousness (equivalent to the *Atman-Brahman* of the *Upanisads*), and other notions resembling Indian philosophical ideas although Whiteman remained primarily a Platonist. Chapter 21 was entitled "The Direct Knowability of Transcendental Constitution", and headed with mystical quotations from Plato's *Republic* and Patanjali's *Yoga Sutras*. In Chapter 20, entitled "Indirect Knowability of Inner Constitution: The Interpretation of Quantum Theory", Whiteman wrote that the change from the old Quantum Theory, (i.e., Bohr's model of the Hydrogen atom) to the new QM about 1925 created virtually a new science.

The concepts of *energy* (and hence *mass*) and *momentum* in QM are associated with Wave Frequency and Wavelength, respectively. 'Particle-like effects' or scintillations, says Whiteman, are more accurately characterised as localised quantum absorption effects[68], a view pre-empting Milo Wolff's elucidation of 'elementary particle-like phenomena' as resonant energy transfer processes arising from interactions in the underlying Wave Structure. Whiteman[69] even states:

> *The closeness of agreement [between QM and measured phenomena] indicates, perhaps, that the originating causal laws of movement and forces in nature are to be found in an ultimate wave-structure in fields and concentrations. The outward manifestations that we call momentum, energy and force are end-results in which the unobserved causal world, [i.e., the transcendental substratum to the phenomena of the physical world] has taken on, in our imagination, a sensory character in accordance with its effect on our sense of touch and bodily resistance.*

The aforementioned inventor of the notion of antimatter, Paul A.M. Dirac, the second greatest English physicist after Isaac Newton (although Dirac's father was French), invited Whiteman to Cambridge to discuss the book with him personally. Whiteman's emphasis is on the Transcendental Substructure as a realm of infinite *potentialities* which actualise upon occasion and tie in with Heisenberg's notions of *energy* and the Quantum Wave Function representing *potentia*. As Germany's senior most physicist, Heisenberg was chief of Hitler's atomic bomb project during the 1939-45 war and thus the Anglo-American West has largely ignored his ideas although both Heisenberg's and especially Schrödinger's philosophical ideas (along with those of Eddington and Pauli) and, in general, the metaphysical implications of QM are far more profound and ontologically more fundamental than those of the relatively superficial and abstract GTR. Yet Einstein has attained the status in Western popular culture as the celebrity "icon" (a pseudo-intellectual media buzz word) even though he tried to refute the implications of the new QM that has proven itself amazingly accurate in all tests of its validity. In fact, we shall find that many of the hyped-up intellectual 'icons' lionised by the

Western media such as Einstein, Bertrand Russell, Sigmund Freud, Stephen Hawking, Francis Crick, Richard Dawkins, Richard Feynman, Immanuel Kant and countless other Western 'intellectual giants' were or are, in some respects, 'little minds' incapable of transcending the false mythologies culturally indoctrinated into modern Western societies.

We shall see that the previous lack of adequate concepts concerning the ego or individuated consciousness, in spite of Siddharta Gautama's teachings that it is a self-organising process (complex of aggregates), has led to much confusion and controversy. Much of the confusion stems from Gautama's own rather vague and misleading concepts and terminology, especially the so-called Doctrine of *Anatman*. The confusion over this manifests not only in regard to the great questions of What am I, and What is our relation with Divinity where major philosophical schools collide but also leads to great confusion over issues such as the yogic state of Deep Sleep Consciousness (*susupti*) which, supposedly authoritative, Indian commentators misunderstand. The oft-repeated arguments that a 'feeling of refreshment' upon waking or the lack of memory during deep sleep argument used to defend the existence of Pure Consciousness in Deep Sleep in scholarly books on Indian Philosophy appear totally unconvincing when compared to my activating brainwave correlate of Pure Consciousness which Science knows remains active during Deep Sleep. It is not surprising that the scientifically-illiterate scholars in the academic study of Indian Philosophy have largely kept quiet about my work as it threatens to make redundant their endless, etymological speculations and self-aggrandising pretensions based on their ability to read Sanskrit.

Once we have a much clearer picture, based on converging lines of empirical evidence, as to what the physical correlate of ego consciousness is, it becomes much easier to clarify these great questions which, even those who have experienced enlightenment can easily misinterpret. Experience in itself is not sufficient as, unless one has advanced intellectual training along with adequate conceptual constructs to label the subtle processes of yogic transformation, one is likely to sow only confusion amongst those who rely upon the written word. Thus we find that there is no consistent description of a supposed 'subtle body' that has been claimed to exist by many mystics. The doctrine of Ineffability is a product of the historic inadequacy of human concepts to capture the essential features of transcendental realisations. Merrell-Wolff states correctly that clinging to traditional methods and interpretations is a subtle form of attachment and hence a barrier to enlightenment[70]. However, by identifying the direct physical correlate of the central element of all true Spirituality with a well-established physiological process, related issues such as the nature of the ego consciousness and Deep Sleep consciousness, begin to fall into place. Countless false interpretive speculations can be dismissed with confidence now we have a solid 'handle' to grasp the deepest, most central and ubiquitous component of mystical transformation, the Inner Light. The likes of Aurobindo Ghose and Merrell-Wolff have described the ego as being like a **vortex** in the underlying flow of the Stream or Current of (Pure) 'Bliss' Consciousness. Anthony Damiani, a famous advocate of Eastern spirituality in the USA, wrote that the Real Self is the Nothingness, the empty centre of the **vortex** of thoughts[71].

Reductionist science, EM fields, Consciousness and transcending Material Nature through 'Unhumanisation'

As with Physics, Life Sciences also made remarkable progress in the 20th Century *c.e.* This was in part due to the influx of physicists into Biology just after the 1939-45 war[N5], partly shocked by Hiroshima and Nagasaki, and partly inspired by a little book by Erwin Schrödinger called *What is Life*[72] in which Schrödinger again propounded his monistic Vedantic (Brahmanic) philosophy in the appendix. This book helped stimulate the revolution in Molecular Biology which was my own field of study at university. This revolution, combined with the fact that most biologists (as indeed most scientists) do not yet understand the deeper implications of the new QM, has led to a naïve, reductionist conception of Life as being merely the result of the replication and transmission to offspring of DNA macromolecules which encode for other macromolecules called proteins.

Archbishop of Canterbury Rowan Williams wrote rather aptly in regard to the views of biologist (and proselytising pop philosopher) Richard Dawkins, just because you are a scientist doesn't make you a good philosopher[73]. I have thought that Professor Dawkins should have used the more pithy 'Dick Dawkins' for his mass market Atheist proselytising; his literalist interpretations reveal him to be the alter-ego of the religious fundamentalists he lambasts. As a non-religious, Non-Theist, I share Dawkins' disapproval of the dogmatic superstitions of the Semitic religions, especially the unsavoury tribal war-god Yahweh, and the fundamentalists' rejection of Evolution. But Materialist-Reductionist Dawkins completely fails to recognise his own dogmatically-held beliefs and the fact that Spirituality *per se*, stripped of Semitic religious codswallop, is much more than just outdated, manmade Bronze Age mythology. Goodwin points out that Dawkins' 'Selfish Gene' views are an (unconscious) reformulation of the vulgar form of the Christian myth of Original Sin in which humans are born into Sin but through Faith and moral effort, Humanity can be saved.[N6] In Dawkins' secularisation, we are (supposedly) born innately selfish but can become altruistic[74].

The real meaning of Augustine's myth of Original Sin is related to the human development of ego consciousness and volition from the earlier unreflective, Nature Mystical consciousness of primitive hunter-gatherers which Australian Aborigines refer to as the Dreamtime. Indeed, both Christian notions of Sin and Eastern notions of karmic attachment are centred on voluntary action undertaken by the (self-centred) ego. Human beings are not simply vehicles created by (metaphorically) 'selfish' DNA for the perpetuation and increase in frequency (within gene pools) of certain combinations of DNA sequences. I am not denying that there is much truth in such arguments in regard to biological evolution and animal behaviour. Human selfishness and altruism are closely associated with the distinction between Egotism and spiritual states of reduced Egotism which involve experiences of transpersonal empathy or Oneness with other creatures associated with terms like Compassion and (metaphorically) God's Love or the Sight of God.

Not surprisingly some have referred to Dawkins as the Mad Mullah of Neo-Darwinism. The Reductionist, Neo-Darwinist view of Life as the transmission of self-replicating hereditary factors between generations of organisms is certainly not what most people throughout history have thought of as *Life* or the sense of being *alive*. Pseudo-intellectual biologists and journalists even refer in reverential terms to the Human Genome Project as the supposed "Book of Life"! Viruses (which may have evolved from rogue cellular genes) replicate their RNA or DNA molecules but, in itself (outside of a living cell), a virus is not a living system. We will see, in regard to the myths of the Elixir of Life, Water of Life, etc., that the true understanding of Life requires a much broader understanding which accounts for why ancient philosophers in both East and West, and the likes of Husserl and Merrell-Wolff, have associated Life with Consciousness and Energy. The Christian Baptism as with Hindus washing away sins in the river Ganges are practises that arose from mental projection of the flow of Spirit or Pure Consciousness onto physical water and rivers. The real Spiritual Baptism, Rebirth or Resurrection is a transformation of the Egoic-Consciousness ('mind') in the Flowing Spirit or Inner Light.

Similarly, in regard to the mind and brain, it is commonplace for Reductionist scientists and philosophers to propound the Behaviourist myth of *Neuronal Man*. "Neuronal Man" first appeared as the eponymous title of a pop science book by French Nobel laureate J-P. Changeaux. There is no mind, nothing psychic, only neurones. Consciousness is but the functioning of the regulatory system and it 'emerges' **literally** as an iceberg emerges from water (*emphasis mine*)[75]. This is an absurd simile glossing over a complete vacuity of explanation; we do not posit a (magically appearing) sentience to parts of floating objects protruding above the water! Nor do we lose consciousness by swimming underwater! Of course, Even if we take the iceberg metaphorically as referring to our self-conscious ego sitting atop much vaster psychical processes of which we are normally unconscious, this does not, in any way, even begin to explain what Consciousness is!

The Neuronal Man myth is perhaps best expressed by the better known English Nobel laureate famous for discovering the double helix structure of DNA, Francis Crick. In his 1994 book *The Astonishing Hypothesis: The Scientific Search for the Soul*[76], Crick states.

> *The Astonishing Hypothesis is that "You", your joys and your sorrows, your memories and your ambitions, your sense of personal identity and free will, are in fact no more than the behavior of a vast assembly of nerve cells and the associated molecules. As Lewis Carroll's Alice might have phrased it: "You're nothing but a pack of neurons."*

Neurons are important in understanding the nature of the mind or 'mentation' but, as we shall see, cannot account for Consciousness *per se* (primarily in the sense of Awareness). The truly astonishing, unashamed puerility of Crick's 'Neuronal Man' view resembles more the over-hasty jumping to immature conclusions of a teenage 'Hormonal Boy' than the reflections of a mature thinker.

Crick makes another revealing statement in this book. He says that for Western religions, the vast scale of the universe known to Science was almost inconceivable. But he adds "certain Eastern religions, such as Hinduism, took pleasure in inflating times and distances for the sheer joy of it"[77]. Once again we find a distinguished scientist exhibiting unashamedly his astonishing ignorance along with his Eurocentric arrogance. Most scientists (indeed most academics) reveal the limited breadth and depth of their knowledge, often quite embarrassingly, the moment they venture outside their ultra-specialised technical domains, revealing themselves to be "glorified technicians" rather than the "philosopher-scientists" they imagine themselves to be. Crick's second chapter is entitled "The General Nature of Consciousness" yet Crick says nothing (and probably knew nothing) of altered states of Consciousness. It was Crick who had a grossly inflated view of the scope of his own understanding and whose ego is, metaphorically, over-inflated like a balloon full of hot air that needed to be pricked!

The underlying nature of Consciousness has long been of central concern to Hinduism and, by exploring this, Hindu mystics gleaned insights into the vastness in Space and Time of the universe as deeper states of Consciousness transcended the perceptual limitations of normal Space/Time/Causality and the ego dissolved into an unlimited or infinite expanse of Cosmic Consciousness. Such insights have been confirmed by scientifically-educated modern Western mystics and LSD researchers. We saw above how the notion of *Akasa* parallels the New Physics in describing Space as subtle matter characterised by vibration which 'densifies' into gross matter. Modern scientific cosmology is only recently beginning to appreciate the seemingly startling prescience of ancient Indian concepts of the distinctionless "plenum/void" transcending space and time (*nirguna Brahman*) from which the material universe (or Creation) manifests and of notions such as the holonomic (or relativistic) interpenetration of all phenomena in the transcendental. Recent notions that three quarters of the Universe is 'Vacuum Energy' or 'Dark Energy' parallel the claim in the *Chandogya Upanisad* that three fourths of Supreme (*nirguna*) Brahman remains unmanifest in the heavens. The Hindu *kalpas* (cosmic cycles of Creation and dissolution) could be successive (cyclic) or co-existent (multiverses) with Time existing only in relation to the dynamic evolution of each individual universe[78]. We shall see later how Hindu notions revolutionised Western cosmology and scientific thought in the late medieval Renaissance and again during the 18th Century 'Enlightenment'. Only now in the late 20th and early 21st Century are Cosmologists beginning to produce models of multiverses bubbling forth universes and cyclic universes manifesting and dissolving back into Dark Energy, etc., paralleling ancient Hindu insights. To dismiss such insights as mere fantasies made up for the joy of exaggeration, because they are so remarkably different to the Judaeo-Christian-Greek geocentric cosmos (with the Sun, Moon and six planets), reveals more about how small-minded, arrogant and culturally-blinkered are the supposedly "visionary" thinkers of mainstream Science.

Zoological neurologist J.Z. Young pointed out in his 1987 book *Philosophy and the Brain*[79] that the convenience of probing live monkey brains with micro-electrodes has led to the fixation of contemporary neurologists with the activity of individual neurons whilst failing to see the "forest for the trees". In this case the forest being the electrical field dynamics of the brain which seem intuitively to be far more likely candidates for the direct physical correlates of what we call mental activity as we saw above in regard to William James and

Gestaltism etc. The Field Theory of the Gestalt psychologist Wolfgang Köhler, was itself inspired by the new QM and also by Husserl's Phenomenology with its notion of the Field of Pure Consciousness. Hans Berger invented the electroencephalogram (EEG) in 1925 after a telepathic incident with his sister and he hoped to use the EEG to study telepathy[80], another fact which the Western scientific orthodoxy would like to brush under the carpet. In spite of new brain-imaging techniques, the EEG remains the most useful monitor of real-time gross brain activity correlated with behaviour. Yet even today, according to the recent *Electric Fields of the Brain*, very little is known about the so-called brainwaves and field activity believed to underlie the electrical potentials detected by the scalp electrodes of the EEG[81]. Nonetheless enough is known for me to show, beyond reasonable doubt, that the deepest and most profound mystical phenomenon, the Inner Light of Pure Consciousness, is correlated directly with a very special set of brainwaves, whose source structure has been known since 1949[82]. In fact, I first learnt of the brainstem Reticular Formation which generates these brainwaves underlying all other brainwave activity in J.Z. Young's book in 1987, seven years before I made the correlation with the Inner Light. Modern Medicine has long recognised the central and essential role of the brainstem Reticular Formation activity as the key prerequisite for any form of Consciousness.[N7]

This correlation should not be interpreted in a reductionist way as that the Inner Light (Divine Light) is nothing more than the "activating brainwaves". To understand how this brainwave correlation leads to the Great Secret of Existence we need a much broader and deeper understanding of Reality than the technically-limited concepts of Science. We can then appreciate that "brainwaves" and other scientific concepts are, in part, the product of the limitations of technology which can only abstract certain discrete patterns of information at certain levels of spatiotemporal order from all the information available in an unimaginably complex, multilevel psychophysical reality. Thus the idealised abstractions or concepts of science, pick out intellectually-manageable, discrete, "skeletal" forms omitting the "flesh", and should not be confused with actual, substantial, (i.e., ontological) Reality.

This bigger, deeper Reality transcends the Empirical realm of natural phenomena limited by the mundane order of spatiotemporal events, and involves supernatural, holistic modes of connectedness involving participation of the whole universe including the 'incoming' wave-potentialities of future events which actually constitute the deeper nonlocal 'true causality' underlying the discontinuous sequence of events monitored by our physical instruments. I used the Buddhist term **Dependent Co-origination** (*pratitya samutpada*) for this deeper, holistic, true causation as it evokes the holonomic interdependence of all phenomena[83]. Thomas McEvilley states that the Buddhist term for such 'holonomy' is *dharmadhatu*[84]. Although orthodox science continues dogmatically to deny all the evidence, paranormal psychic phenomena really do exist which do not conform to the law-like behaviour patterns abstracted and modelled by Physics. Most scientists are in what psychologists call 'denial' about the existence of phenomena which would undermine their 'world' or lead to dissolution of their habituated and comfort-giving frameworks of mind. As with the constructed illusory nature of

Perception, Cognitive Science is also revealing just how much we perceive what our brains *expect* to 'see' depending on contextual cues and anticipation of commonplace scenarios. Anomalous information, not matching expectations of habituated cognitive frameworks may be filtered out. We shall see that the invention of numerous invaluable scientific ideas and techniques, ancient, medieval and contemporary involved mystical insights or occult inspiration. J.H.M. Whiteman, who has experienced such psychic phenomena, quotes from *The Personality of Man* (1947) by a G.N.M. Tyrrell[85]:

The major part of the scientific world...is not animated by a scientific desire to know the truth but is in the grip of a psychological urge to disallow what is distressingly unfamiliar...

The Great Secret of Existence is hidden in a 'temple'and, although the Hindu temple architects were on the right track when they viewed the human body as the Temple of the Spirit, they were not quite correct. The 'opening' of so-called *chakras* along the spine is, largely, imaginative symbolism for use by yogic neophytes to represent the stages of yogic progress. As with the common metaphor that God dwells in the human heart, representing the centre of our being, these are projections onto the human body of mystical transformations although there might indeed be some secondary activity associated with the *chakra* regions, where the experience appears to be occurring, that can even be detected with instruments[86]. Yet the spine does play a key role in the Great Secret as the true Temple of the Spirit is in fact the human brain and the secret is linked to its innermost sanctuary where the primitive, in evolutionary terms, chordate spine enters the human brain as the brainstem.

Contrary to Kantian, Existentialist and Constructivist naivety and dogma permeating Western thought, the human being-in-the-world (or *Dasein* as the Existentialists, following Heidegger refer to the normal sensory or empirical world) can be transcended. As Husserl's colleague Eugen Fink began to realise in the 1930s, it should be possible to go deeper into the constitutive processes of mind than the superficial (Continental European) phenomenology of Husserl, limited largely to object perception in the mundane waking state. Fink realised that such a deepening would amount to an "**Unhumanisation**" (*emphasis mine*). He also realised that the underlying flow of Husserl's so-called Absolute (or Temporal) Consciousness established the spatiotemporal field horizons or 'world-concepts' for perception[87]. In fact Fink was merely beginning to rediscover ancient Indian yogic knowledge that the underlying flow of the Inner Light of Pure Consciousness constitutes the Time/Space Matrix of normal perception. The yogi can transcend this normal field to attain transcendental realisations not limited by the mundane perceptual ordering into strict spatiotemporal relations. Von Franz states that, throughout world mythology, the Time Stream has always been linked to a culture's highest God Image or the Image of the Self. She adds that Spatialisation seems to be a concept derived from the experience of Time and not *vice versa*[88].

We shall see that my **brain-deactivation** and **Retreat-to-the-Brainstem** interpretation of *Raja Yoga* (the path to Enlightenment) begins to account for how such Unhumanisation and Time/Space Transcendence occurs as the yogic 'vehicles' of consciousness (transformed foci of attention or subtilised or purified forms of individuated consciousness) leave behind the uniquely human structures of the neocortex as they retreat toward the primitive brainstem. Such **subtilisation** of the ego is equivalent to stripping the 'soul' (*jiva*) of its 'worldly attachments' which accrete around the basic individuated nucleus. These correspond to the Vedantic *kosa* or sheaths which have to be removed step by step. By retreating from the cerebral cortex, the yogic vehicle escapes the spatial and temporal-causal limitations imposed on wakeful perception by the flow of the Inner Light through the cerebral cortex allowing experience of underlying transcendental realm where all phenomena interpenetrate unlimited by normal (extensive; mutually exclusive) spatiality and true causation is holonomic (operating through internal-relations or interconnectedness to everything else that exists). Eventually in mystical union the naked, translucent, most subtilised form of individuated consciousness (*anandamayakosa;* 'Bliss sheath' or Bliss vehicle') dissolves into the Inner Light, the underlying, background flow of electrical energy from the brainstem.

As solid-state physicist and IT pioneer, C.A. Mead (a colleague of the late Richard Feynman) states, with the phenomena of superconductivity etc., experimental physicists are beginning to realise that Electromagnetism (EM) is the macroscopic manifestation of the deeper Quantum Reality[89]. It is well-known that the nuclear forces and EM are all manifestations of the same underlying energetic activity. However QM and GTR, (i.e., 'Gravity') continue to resist unification long after Michael Faraday first tried to show the unity of EM and Gravity based on his spiritual belief in the Unity of Nature. Einstein had already reduced Newton's imaginary force of Gravity (with its paranormal action-at-a-distance) to a mere phenomenon in his GTR. Eddington stated correctly, in his *The Mathematical Theory of Relativity*, that GTR overlays a fictitious and arbitrary human mental construct, the Space-Time Frame, onto Nature[90]. Leonard Susskind points out that the rubber-sheet and ball model use to give a mental picture of Space-Time curvature is "all wrong" as it uses the Earth's gravity to model Gravity (tautologically) and it has no Time curvature[91]. In recent years, assuming that the 'standard-candle' Supernovae data indicating an accelerating expansion of the universe is not flawed, Astrophysics has had to introduce a new Lambda anti-gravitational 'force' which most theoreticians seem to associate with the Zero-Point energy of the Quantum Vacuum. GTR is a highly abstract (idealised), geometric model which overlooks all the small-scale processes occurring in Nature (described by QM).

Gravity is not a force or a form of energy that can be detected directly. No one has detected hypothetically-postulated Gravity waves. We impute its presence indirectly from the behaviour of objects possessing mass. The great Russian physicist, and father of the Soviet ('Layer Cake') Hydrogen Bomb, Anatoly Sakharov had suggested in the 1960s that Gravity was not a fundamental reality but rather a gross, collective phenomenon rather like a pressure[92]. In Milo Wolff's holonomic wave model of the electron, gravity appears as a secondary phenomenon to the primary electromagnetic activity in a manner resembling Einstein's space-time curvature model of the Gravity phenomenon. Thus if in mystical union, the individuated consciousness dissolves into the underlying flow of electric energy waves, it is dissolving into the singular, directly detectable, primary principle of modern Physics, electromagnetic energy. In fact we are told in *Electric Fields of the Brain* that the magnetic component is not of much significance in brainwave activity[93]. We have seen that Physics is not Ontology. Physics models spatiotemporal patterns of energetic activity (the regular behaviour of phenomena) rather than describing Reality-in-itself. This is not the place to discuss the relationship between *energy* (the dynamic activity of the underlying Reality which QM relates to wave-frequency) and its substantial basis in the vibration of the underlying Pure Consciousness which is in itself undivided and One. This distinction underlies the paradox of the dual aspect of the Divine Ground as Unmoved Stillness and Creative Temporal Flux. This brief overview should allow the reader to begin to appreciate that, unlike Science and Western philosophy, Indian yoga-derived metaphysics is not limited to human mental constructions or phenomena but is actually based on direct apprehension of Reality as it is independent of human mentation!

References

1. Bohr, Niels. Quoted in "The philosophy of Niels Bohr" by Aage Petersen, *Bulletin of the Atomic Scientists* (September 1963).
2. Al-Khalili, Jim (2007) from Episode One of *Atom*, British Broadcasting Corporation (BBC) Television.
3. Smolin, Lee (2006) *The Trouble with Physics: The Rise of String Theory, the Fall of a Science, and What Comes Next*, Houghton Mifflin.
4. Arp, Halton (1998) *Seeing Red: Redshifts, Cosmology and Academic Science*, Apeiron.
5. Voss, Karen-Claire, *Spiritual Alchemy: Interpreting Representative Texts and Images*. In *Gnosis and Hermeticism: From Antiquity to Modern Times* (1998) Edited by Roelof van den Broek and Wouter J. Hanegraaff, State University of New York Press.
6. Kingsley, Peter (1995) *Ancient Philosophy, Mystery, and Magic: Empedocles and Pythagorean Tradition,* Clarendon Press (Oxford University Press).
7. Von Franz, Marie-Louise (1960) *The Idea of the Macro-and Microcosmos.* Reprinted in Von Franz, M-L. (1992) *Psyche and Matter*, Shambhala Publications.
8. Odajnyk, V. Walter (1993) *Gathering the Light: A Psychology of Meditation*, Shambhala Publications.
9. Yates, Frances (1964) *Giordano Bruno and the Hermetic Tradition*, Routledge and Kegan Paul.
10. Dobbs, Betty J.T. (1991) *The Janus Faces of Genius: The role of Alchemy in Newton's thought*, Cambridge University Press.
11. Stevens, Anthony (2002) *Archetype Revisited: An Updated Natural History of the Self* (2nd Edn), Brunner-Routledge (Taylor and Francis).
12. d'Espagnat, Bernard (2006) *On Physics and Philosophy*, Princeton University Press.

13. Goldberg, Philip (2010) *American Veda: From Emerson and the Beatles to Yoga and Meditation – How Indian Spirituality Changed the West*, Harmony Books, Random House.
14. Goldberg, Philip *ibid.*
15. Goldberg, Philip *ibid.*
16. Von Franz, Marie-Louise (1981) *Meaning and Order.* Reprinted in von Franz, M-L. (1992) *Psyche and Matter*, Shambhala Publications.
17. Radhakrishnan, Sarvepalli (1953) *The Principal Upanisads*, (Centenary Edition 1989), Unwin Hyman.
18. Goonatilake, Susantha (1998) *Toward a Global Science: Mining Civilisational Knowledge*, Indiana University Press.
19. Radin, Dean (2006) *Entangled Minds: Extrasensory Experiences in a Quantum Reality*, Paraview and Pocket Books (Simon & Schuster).
20. Radin, Dean (2006) *ibid.*
21. Yates, Frances (1964) *ibid.*
22. Schrödinger, Erwin (1995) *The Interpretation of Quantum Mechanics: Dublin seminars (1949-55) and other unpublished essays*, Ox Bow Press.
23. Mead, Carver (2000) *Collective Electrodynamics: Quantum Foundations of Electromagnetism*, MIT Press.
24. Malin, Shimon (2001) *Nature Loves to Hide: Quantum Physics and Reality, a Western Perspective*, Oxford University Press.
25. Eddington, Arthur, S. (1928) *The Nature of the Physical World*, J.M. Dent & Sons.
26. Malin, Shimon (2001) *ibid.*
27. Whiteman, J.H. Michael (1967) *Philosophy of Space and Time and the Inner Constitution of Nature: A Phenomenological Study*, Muirhead Library of Philosophy, George Allen and Unwin and the Humanities Press.
28. Jacob, Margaret, C. (1976) *The Newtonians and the English Revolution 1689-1720*, Cornell University Press.
29. Burtt, E.A. (1954) *The Metaphysical Foundations of Modern Physical Science, 2nd Revised Edn*, Doubleday.
30. Yates, Frances (1964) *ibid.*
31. Dennett, Daniel C. quoted in "Zombies, dolphins and blindsight. Is Consciousness the hardest of problems?", *New Scientist* 4th May 1996.
32. Arp, Halton (1998) *ibid.*
33. Wolff, Milo (2008) *Schrödinger's Universe: Einstein, Waves & the Origin of the Natural Laws*, Technotran Press.
34. Bohm, David and Hiley, Basil J. (1993) *The Undivided Universe: An Ontological Interpretation of Quantum Theory,* Routledge.
35. Whiteman, J.H. Michael (1967) *ibid.*
36. Bhattacharya, Sutapas (1999) *The Oneness/Otherness Mystery: The Synthesis of Science and Mysticism,* Motilal Banarsidass.
37. Von Franz, Marie-Louise (1992), *Psyche and Matter*, Shambhala Publications.
38. d'Espagnat, Bernard (2006) *ibid.*

39. Thompson, Richard, L. (1981) *Mechanistic and Nonmechanistic Science: An Investigation into the Nature of Consciousness and Form,* The Bhaktivedanta Book Trust.
40. d'Espagnat, Bernard (2006) *ibid.*
41. Gribbin, John (1995) *Schrödinger's Kittens and the Search for Reality*, Weidenfield and Nicolson.
42. d'Espagnat, Bernard (2006) *ibid.*
43. Kroto, Harry quoted in *The Independent* (Newspaper, London) 7th April 2011.
44. d'Espagnat, Bernard (2006) *ibid.*
45. Wilhelm, Friedrich and Rawlinson, H. G. "India and the Modern West." In *A Cultural History of India* (1975) edited by A. L. Basham, Clarendon Press (Oxford University Press).
46. Schwab, Raymond (1950, French) English translation *The Oriental Renaissance: Europe's Rediscovery of India and the East 1680-1880* (1984) Columbia University Press.
47. Westphal, Kenneth R. (2004) *Kant's Transcendental Proof of Realism*, Cambridge University Press.
48. Perovich Jr, Anthony, N. "Does the Philosophy of Mysticism Rest on a Mistake?". In *The Problem of Pure Consciousness: Mysticism and Philosophy* (1990) edited by Robert K.C. Forman, Oxford University Press.
49. Leonard, Ron (1999) *The Transcendental Philosophy of Franklin Merrell-Wolff*, State University of New York Press.
50. Green, Elmer, E. "Science and Psychophysiology, Psychophysics and Mythology" in *Ancient Wisdom and Modern Science* (1984) edited by Stanislaw Grof, State University of New York Press.
51. James, William (1902) *The Varieties of Religious Experience*, Longmans, Green, and Co.
52. Barnard, G. William (1997) *Exploring Unseen Worlds: William James and the Philosophy of Mysticism*, State University of New York Press.
53. King, Richard (1999) *Orientalism and Religion: Postcolonial Theory, India and 'The Mystic East'*, Routledge.
54. Hesse, Mary "Hermeticism and History: An apology for the internal history of science" in *Historical and Philosophical Perspectives of Science* (1970) edited by R.H. Steuer, University of Minnesota Press.
55. Yates, Frances (1964) *ibid.*
56. Obeyesekere, Gananath (2002) *Imagining Karma: Ethical Transformation in Amerindian, Buddhist and Greek Rebirth*, University of California Press.
57. Naddaf, Gerard (2005) *The Greek Concept of Nature*, State University of New York Press.
58. Merrell-Wolff, Franklin (1994) *Franklin Merrell-Wolff's Experience and Philosophy: A Personal Record of Transformation and a Discussion of Transcendental Consciousness*: Containing his *Philosophy of Consciousness without an Object* and *His Pathways through to Space*, State University of New York Press.

59. Radhakrishnan, Sarvepalli (1940) *Eastern Religions and Western Thought (2nd Edn,* Oxford University Press.
60. Wilber, Ken (Editor) (1984) *Quantum Questions: Mystical Writings of the World's Great Physicists*, Shambhala Publications.
61. Harman, Willis quoted on back cover of White, John Warren (1990) *The Meeting of Science and Spirit: Guidelines for a New Age*, Paragon House.
62. Bache, Christopher (2000) *Dark Night, Early Dawn: Steps to a Deep Ecology of Mind*, State University of New York Press.
63. Merrell-Wolff, Franklin (1994) *ibid.*
64. Radin, Dean (1997) *The Conscious Universe: The Scientific Truth of Psychic Phenomena*, Harper Edge (Harper San Francisco).
65. Smolin, Lee (2006) *ibid.*
66. Arp, Halton (1998) *ibid.*
67. Whiteman, J.H. Michael (1967) *ibid.*
68. Whiteman, J.H. Michael (1967) *ibid.*
69. Whiteman, J.H. Michael (1967) *ibid.*
70. Merrell-Wolff, Franklin (1995) *Transformations in Consciousness: The Metaphysics and Epistemology* (Containing His *Introceptualism*), State University of New York Press.
71. Malin, Shimon (2001) *ibid.*
72. Schrödinger, Erwin (1944) *What is Life,* Cambridge University Press.
73. Williams, Rowan (Archbishop of Canterbury) *The Guardian* (Newspaper, London) 14th October 2007.
74. Goodwin, Brian C. (1994) *How the Leopard Changed its Spots: The Evolution of Complexity*, Charles Scribner.
75. Changeaux, Jean-Pierre (1986) *Neuronal Man*, English Translation, Oxford University Press.
76. Crick, Francis (1994) *The Astonishing Hypothesis: The Scientific Search for the Soul*, Simon and Schuster.
77. Crick, Francis (1994) *ibid.*
78. Neville, Robert C. (1993) *Eternity and Time's Flow*, State University of New York Press.
79. Young, John Z. (1987) *Philosophy and the Brain*, Oxford University Press.
80. Radin, Dean (1997) *ibid.* Also mentioned in Pockett, Susan (2000) *The Nature of Consciousness: A Hypothesis*, iUniverse.
81. Nunez, Paul, L. and Srinivasan, Ramesh (2006) *Electric Fields of the Brain: The Neurophysics of EEG, 2nd Edn*, Oxford University Press.
82. Baars, Bernard J, Banks, William P. and Newman, James B. (Editors) (2003) *Essential Sources in the Scientific Study of Consciousness*, Bradford Books, MIT Press.
83. Bhattacharya, Sutapas (1999) *ibid.*
84. McEvilley, Thomas (2002) *The Shape of Ancient Thought: Comparative Studies in Greek and Indian Philosophies*, Allworth Press.
85. Whiteman, J.H. Michael (1967) *ibid.*

86. *See* Bhattacharya, Sutapas (1999) for original sources.
87. Bruzina, Ronald (2004) *Edmund Husserl and Eugen Fink: Beginnings and Ends in Phenomenology 1928-1938*, Yale University Press.
88. Von Franz, Marie-Louise (1981) "Meaning and Order", *see also* von Franz, Marie-Louise (1978) "The Psychological Experience of Time" both reprinted in von Franz, Marie-Louise (1992) *Psyche and Matter*, Shambhala Publications.
89. Mead, Carver (2000) *ibid.*
90. Whiteman, J.H. Michael (1967) *ibid.*
91. Susskind, Leonard (2008) *The Black Hole War: My battle with Stephen Hawking to Make the World a Safe Place for Quantum Mechanics*, Back Bay Books, Little Brown and Co.
92. McTaggart, Lynne (2001) *The Field: The Quest for the Secret Force of the Universe*, Harper Collins.
93. Nunez, Paul and Srinivasan, Ramesh (Editors) (2006) *ibid.*

2

The Great Secret of Existence

The Taj Mahal's Marble, the EU Anthem and the Great Seal of the USA

The Vedic culture of India's first civilisation and the mystical commonality beneath the clash of Mohammedan and Hindu traditions in India

I have one piece of artwork in my bedroom. It is a large plate made of white marble inlaid with roses created out of semi-precious stones of deep blue lapis and pearl in the famous *pietra dura* style of the Taj Mahal. Indeed, I bought it at the Red Fort in Agra in 1990 as the striking blue and silvery pearl roses immediately stood out from the other plates and items that had the more typical red and green stone set in the white marble. We encounter here a fundamental issue of perception in the fact that I focused on the figures inlaid in the white background. Our visual system has evolved to distinguish the *figure* from the (back-) *ground*. Such perceptual abstraction of the obvious forms, resembling the conceptual abstraction of particle-like phenomena, is one of the many subtle reasons for the failure of Western Philosophy and Science to account for Consciousness. The intrinsic properties of the largely blue and white plate, apart from its relative difference from the other plates, may also have attracted my attention as I have supported Chelsea Football Club (the "Blues") since I was five. Thus blue would be engrained deeply in my subconscious frameworks as something of value to me.

The tourist guides at the Taj Mahal also focus on the intricate artwork inlaid in the white marble and none mentioned the reason why the white marble itself was chosen for the Taj. Indeed, as the Taj Mahal is not only a mausoleum but has mosques on either side of the mausoleum along with minarets, it is obviously a Mohammedan shrine. The Taj Mahal is often used to represent India in films such as *Independence Day*. As if alien invaders of Earth would identify Agra as a strategic, military target! It is a Muslim shrine built by barbaric, Turko-Mongol (*Mughal* or *Mogul* comes from Mongol) alien invaders of India who claimed ancestry from both the bloodthirsty, mass-raping, man of the millennium, Gengis Khan (who had wanted to exterminate the entire Chinese peasantry) and the even more bloodthirsty barbarian Turk Timur Lenk (Tamerlane), who left gruesome towers of skulls of his victims from Persia through Delhi to Russia.

Gengis Khan's notion of the 'Greatest Happiness for a Man' was to exterminate others, destroy them to their roots, loot their wealth, cause misery and rape their women. Having just defeated the Western European Crusaders occupying parts of Syria-Palestine, the Muslim Arab civilisation was devastated by the Mongol conquest of Persia and Mesopotamia. The Arabs remember it as the 'Mongol Catastrophe' although the Mongol rulers later converted to Islam as had the Ottoman Turko-Mongols who captured the remnants of the Byzantine Empire (the last bastion of Hellenistic-Roman Classical civilisation). It is perhaps significant that these descendants of Gengis and Timur converted to warlike Mohammedanism rather than the pacific Buddhism from India adopted by most Mongols in the Far East. Scandinavian Vikings also had a bad reputation as rapacious barbarians. In medieval Ukraine the Viking founders of Kiev had chosen to convert to Orthodox Christianity in order to become more civilised after having heard from representatives of Catholicism, Mohammedanism and Judaism.[N1] Unlike the Anglo-Saxons, who converted voluntarily to Catholicism, many Europeans had been forced to convert to Roman Christianity first by the Roman Empire, then later by the Frankish Charlemagne, the so-called 'Holy Roman Emperor'. The Mohammedans were more tolerant toward their fellow Semitic religions but pressurised non-Muslims to convert by subjecting them to a selective poll tax.

Babur, the first of the Moghul invaders of India actually came from Persia where the descendants of Genghis and Timur had settled, hence the Persian style of the Taj Mahal. Thus many Hindus feel that this Persian-style Mohammedan mausoleum is not a suitable symbol of India, home of the great, continuous civilisation of at least five thousand years age, which foreigners call "Hindu". The famous Hindu temple complex at Madurai in South India represents the true dominant Indian tradition which originated in the Vedic culture of ancient Saraswati-Sindhu Civilisation (*a.k.a.* 'Harappan' or 'Indus') that arose in the North-West of the Indian Subcontinent around 5,000 years ago. Various invaders of India, such as Macedonians, Scythians and Huns had converted to native spiritual traditions and had become 'Indianised'. The early Mohammedan invaders of India from Afghanistan (who formed the Delhi Sultanate) as well Mohammedan raiders like Timur and, later on, the Mughals destroyed countless Hindu, Buddhist and Jain temples. They massacred monks and built mosques on the ruins of their monasteries and temples (hence the famous Ayodhya dispute where Babur built a mosque on a holy Hindu site).

Today's Mohammedan *jihadis* in Pakistan still harbour ludicrous fantasies of religious conquest, not only of Kashmir, but the conquest and conversion to the 'One True Faith' of all of 'pagan', idol-worshipping India! The simplistic tenets of Mohammedan monotheism leads to rabid hostility toward what Mohammedans perceive as 'idolatry' in Hinduism and the 'Atheism' of Buddhists. The medieval Mohammedan barbarism led to the lack of major ancient Hindu structures in Northern India. Even the city by the confluence of the Ganges and the Jamuna known as Prayaga, the most sacred site of the Hindu *Kumbh Mela* ("spiritual fair"), officially retains the distinctly non-Hindu name *Allahabad* although Calcutta, Bombay, and Madras (cities built by the

British) have been given native-sounding names (Kolkata, Mumbai and Chennai). In fact, Prayaga is supposed to be the site of the confluence of *three* rivers, not two, as the legendary Saraswati river is also said to join the Ganges and Jamuna here.

The most ancient Indo-European texts, the *Rig Veda Samhita* is a compilation of about one thousand largely sacred poems. This is the oldest of the Hindu scriptures known as the Vedas which eventually culminate in the Upanishads or Vedanta (end of the Vedas). The *Rig Veda* refers to this river Saraswati as the main river of the Land of Seven Rivers (*sapat sindhu*; i.e., the 'Punjab' – which is a much later Persianised Mughal term referring to five rivers). The Veda even names the six extant rivers of the Punjab and placed the Saraswati between the Sutlej and Jamuna. Satellite imagery and archaeology shows that this huge river actually flowed North-South, between the Sutlej and Jamuna, through Rajastan to the East of the present course of the Indus. Earthquakes in the Himalayas around 1900 *b.c.e.* diverted tributaries of the Saraswati into the Indus[1]. The Indus (*Indu*) is the second most frequently mentioned river in *Rig Veda*. Indeed the geography actually presented in the *Rig Veda* coincides more or less exactly with that of the Saraswati-Sindhu civilisation.

However, the 'Aryan Invasion' fantasies concocted by colonial European Indologists and philologists continue to be peddled by Western academia although totally discredited both by archaeology and more recent DNA studies. Given the common ancestry of North Indian (Sanskritic) and European languages, White European colonial conquest was projected into India's ancient history by the self-proclaimed 'scientific' scholars from Europe. The Vedic Aryans who wrote *Rig Veda* were portrayed ludicrously as blue-eyed blonde Nordic nomads invading India in mid-2nd M *b.c.e.* This 'Aryan Invasion Theory' added to the self-justifying mythology created by the colonial British historians beginning with James Mill who presented Indian civilisation as totally debased and never capable of creating anything good. All positive elements and rational developments in India had to have come from outside India[2], brought in by White-skinned invaders. Brits like Mill demonised India's native 'Hindu' tradition to justify the savagery of British plunder, deindustrialisation and economic exploitation which turned the subcontinent, once-famed for its wealth, into a land of hunger, poverty and famine. Captain William Sleeman fabricated the so-called Thuggee cult to cover up the true causes of such Highway Robbery. Sleeman wrote sensational accounts of his campaign against this imagined religious cult which helped reinforce in the minds of the Brits that Hinduism was supposedly the source of India's social evils[3]. The diversionary myth of Thuggee allowed Sleeman to cover up his detention without trial and execution of hundreds of Indians. The primary cause of such Highway Robbery in British-occupied India was in fact the economic devastation and pauperisation of people in conquered territories by British plunder, destruction of native industries and their creation of countless famines.

Many Westerners continue to regurgitate the false myths they have heard about 'Hinduism' yet know nothing of the Buchenwald-like Death Camps set up by Benjamin Disraeli's henchmen in India[4]. Nor does the Anglo-American dominated West publicise the fact that Winston Churchill was a White Supremacist[N2] who committed racist Crimes against Humanity. He was responsible for the genocide of up 7 million Indians in the 1942-3 'Bengal Holocaust', the first racist genocide atrocity of the 1939-45 war labelled a 'Holocaust' [N3 5,6]. This was in fact the last of some 37 or so artificial famine holocausts inflicted on India by the British in 190 years killing tens of millions of Indians. At the same time vast amounts of India's foodgrains were looted by the Brits in order to subsidise and provide Food Security for White Britons and other Europeans. In 1900 one quarter of Britain's wheat was brought in from India. In 1901, *The Lancet* estimated conservatively from the Census that 19 million Indians died from starvation in Western India during the 1890s as a result of British 'Let-them-starve' policies[7,8].

Many British still believe the Malthusian myth that famines in India were due to over-population. The Reverend Thomas Malthus, as with historian James Mill, worked for the state-owned corporation the (mafia-like) East India Company (EIC) which was responsible for many Crimes-against-Humanity in India. Two hundred years ago nearly all the wealthiest families in Britain had stakes in the EIC through shareholdings and lucrative jobs for their sons. In truth, 19th Century India had a much lower population density than Britain and India as whole always grew enough food to feed all Indians. It was the British Social Darwinist policies which led to India's food-grains being exported for Britain's benefit whilst millions of the poorest Indians died of starvation. Many Westerners continue to buy into the British-created myth that India was a land of Eternal Poverty and Famine. This is the height of ignorance given that, throughout most of civilised history in Eurasia, India was famed and envied for its vast riches. The British made themselves the richest country in the world in Victorian times by their parasitical colonial looting, deindustrialisation, 'plantationisation' and captive market exploitation of India. It was the British Rule that left the land once-famed for its vast wealth as a land known for poverty and hunger. But you would never guess this from the false propaganda peddled by the mainstream British historians and media.

Even though in the early 1920s the Indus Valley cities of Mahenjo-Daro and Harappa were rediscovered by Indian archaeologists, proving that Indian civilisation long preceded the supposed Aryan Invasion, the vast majority of Western scholars refused to acknowledge their mistakes and concocted ever more elaborate *ad hoc* fantasies about ancient Indian history. The darker-skinned South Indian 'Dravidian'-language speakers, having been portrayed as ugly 'Black' tribal savages conquered by the 'White' Aryans were now re-imagined to have been the builders of the Indus Valley Civilisation (now known to be the much larger and older Saraswati-Sindhu Civilisation) who were driven to the South by the invading Aryans. It was not explained how these people somehow forgot how to build such cities as they were (supposedly) driven South.

In recent years two Saraswati-Sindhu type cities have been detected under the Gulf of Cambay, invoking Hindu myths of Krishna's submerged city of Dwarka. If Cambay was submerged when geologists say it was then questions must be asked about Western archaeology's subliminal Christocentric focus on Mesopotamia as the 'Cradle of Civilisation'. The Western archaeological focus on Mesopotamia is rooted in the fictional Biblical fantasies of Abraham, the Tower of Babel, etc., discredited by archaeology, and the myth that Mankind originated there. The Sumerians themselves said that their ancestors came to Sumer (near modern Basra) from the East in ships from a place called Dilmun (perhaps Bahrain)[9]. Around 1600 *b.c.e* the Indo-Aryan speaking Mitanni, worshipping Vedic gods and expert horsemen, ruled over what is now Kurdistan in Turkey and Iraq and over principalities in Syria and Palestine. Soon afterwards Indo-Aryan speaking Kassites conquered and ruled over Babylon[10]. Note that these people spoke Indo-Aryan, (i.e., North Indian) not Iranian languages. Yet Western historians persist with the racist myth that India was just the passive receptacle for vigorous and creative light-skinned invaders from the North-West as if native Indians lacked historical agency. This vigorous invaders creating Indian history narrative was clearly discernible in Michael Wood's 2007 BBC TV series *The Story of India*. Furthermore, Wood skipped over the British plunder of India's wealth and made no mention of the three dozen or more British-inflicted famines that killed tens of millions of Indians. The British media never hesitates to mention the famines created by Mao Zedong and by Stalin or the crimes perpetrated by Nazi Germany.

In fact recent DNA analysis suggests that the first wave of modern humans leaving Africa went around the coast of Arabia and India to Indonesia and Australia. Their descendants include communities possessing the Ancestral South Indian (ASI) genetic markers who are generally more dark-skinned than North Indians. A second wave left Africa perhaps as late as 50,000 years ago travelling around the coast of Arabia to the North-West of the Indian Subcontinent (largely modern Pakistan). It seems as if it was from NW India that all the modern humans who later created the first civilisations spread out to cover Eurasia (including Mesopotamia), North Africa and the Americas. This second wave included people with Ancestral North Indian (ANI) genetic markers who are genetically quite close to the modern Europeans (hence the Indo-European linguistic linkages). But *contra* Western Indological myths about 'Aryan' and 'Dravidian' racial apartheid, there are neither pure ANI nor pure ASI communities in India. All Indian genotypes are mixed, with varying proportions of ANI and ASI DNA. The only populations harbouring pure ASI DNA are the isolated, primitive negroid tribes on the Andaman and Nicobar Islands which are located closer to Malaysia than to India[11].

Thus contrary to colonial European racial myths projecting European colonialism onto antiquity, the Vedic Aryans (the people who wrote the *Rig Veda*) were not white-skinned nomads who invaded India in the 2nd M *b.c.e.* from some unspecified location between India and Europe. Indeed suggestions for this mythical Aryan *Urheimat* (original homeland) put forward by the 'scientific' minds of Europe reached from the North Pole to the South Pole[12]! Rather, as their Brahman descendants claimed, the Vedic Aryans lived in an Ancient Indian civilisation. They were almost certainly the builders and residents of the vast and ancient civilisation, contemporaneous with the much smaller Sumeria, along the Indus (Sindhu) and the nearby now dried-up course of the earlier main river, the Saraswati.

Such facts undermine the false propaganda peddled by certain Marxists, tribals, Dalits (Untouchables) and South Indian separatists that the Aryan Brahmans are just another lot of foreign invaders of India, like the Mohammedans or the British, who supposedly destroyed 'Dravidian' civilisation in the Indus and drove the dark-skinned natives to the South. Not only were the Aryan Brahmans descendants of the original North Indians, the Indo-Aryans were the first civilised Indians who brought the benefits of civilisation to the rest of the Subcontinent and also to South-East Asia (as we shall see). Furthermore, in stark contrast to the genocide, ethnic cleansing and forced assimilation of uncivilised primitive, tribal indigenous people and of religious minorities by the Europeans all over the world, the Indo-Aryans allowed the countless primitive tribes present in India to continue to live in their traditional homes in their traditional ways. India was a sanctuary for persecuted religious communities including Jews, Christians and Zoroastrians thousands of years before the English colonies in North America. Alain Daniélou challenged many of the, often hypocritical, Western myths about the so-called 'Caste System' showing that there were positive reasons behind it. In *The Caste Institution* he wrote[13]:

> *Traditional India...has always recognised the primitive tribes' right to survive with their own way of life....Recognition and respect for the various communities and varieties of the human species...has made India a refuge for all persecuted peoples, elsewhere threatened with extinction or assimilation. ...The caste institution...is certainly not without its faults, but is still a model showing how the most different human groups can co-exist. We have much to learn from [this] institution...*

Whilst ancient Egypt was building pyramids, resembling somewhat the grandiose monuments of the centralised Soviet state, contemporaneous India covered a vastly larger area with numerous grid-pattern cities built of fired-brick. Covering nearly one million square miles the Saraswati-Sindhu civilisation spread out over a territory four times larger than any contemporary civilisation[14]. Western archaeology tends to exaggerate the importance of monumental architecture. The ancient Indian pattern of civilised development indicates a less centralised civilisation building smaller structures over a much wider area. With the odd exceptions such decentralisation has remained a feature of Indian history and is of course a key characteristic of Hinduism. In the 19th Century, the newly translated ancient Hindu literature was described by the likes of German Wilhelm Schlegel and Frenchmen Victor Cousin and Francois Lenormant as poetic and philosophical monuments comparable to the (physical) monuments of Egypt[15].

This lack of centralised authority also distinguishes Hinduism from Middle Eastern spiritual traditions. The famous *pasupati* (Lord of the beasts) seal from the Harappan excavations was over-confidently identified by the English archaeologist Sir John Marshall in 1931 as a prototype of the Hindu god Siva[16]. The actual identity of the figure is not known but what is clear is that this and other figures are shown in yoga postures. These figures once again hint at the Great Secret. The Sanskrit word *Yoga* has common Indo-European roots to the English word Yoke. Yoga thus refers to a yoking together, in fact the yoking together of the individual consciousness with the Absolute Consciousness in the *mystical union*. Yoga lies at the heart of the mystical spiritual traditions of India that permeate every aspect of Indian culture. The word 'Hindu' is the Persian form of the river name Sindhu and originally meant the people of the Indus region. This decentralised so-called 'Hindu' tradition is very different from the closely related, dogmatic Middle Eastern 'Semitic religions', Judaism, Christianity, and Mohammedanism with whom authority lies in sacred texts. In fact, the Persian Zoroaster seems to have introduced such dogmatism and absurdly materialistic religious doctrines which the Judaeans later adopted and passed on to the Christians and Muslims. The Persian Emperor Cyrus became the Messiah 'Koresh' for Judaism (*see below*). Thus a figure of a yogi in one of the classic yogic postures is far more representative of India than the Persian-style Mohammedan mausoleum built by a descendant of Turko-Mongol invaders.

Although the Taj Mahal is alien to India's indigenous culture, beneath its overtly Mohammedan symbolism hides a deeper, esoteric symbolism reflecting our common humanity. The official name of the Taj Mahal is 'The Illumined Tomb'. The white marble was chosen to represent Divine Light as scholars at the Mughal court were intimate with the philosophy of Divine Illumination propounded by the medieval Persian mystic Suhrawardi[17]. Shah Jahan's grandfather, Akbar the Great, was mystically-inclined, engaged in debates with Hindu, Parsi, Jain and Christian scholars and even mooted a syncretic religion drawing on numerous traditions. Akbar was keen to translate major Sanskrit texts into Persian so that Hindu knowledge once confined to the Brahmans could diffuse widely[18]. Jahangir, Akbar's son and successor as Emperor, was deeply interested in Vedanta and Sufism (the mystical tradition within Islam). He even called Vedanta the 'Science of Sufism'[19].

In fact, Islam in India, cut off from its Arabian desert roots and heavily influenced by Sufi mysticism (itself heavily influenced by Hinduism), has generally been less rigid than in the Middle East. This fact is stressed by French scholar Guy Sorman in his *The Genius of India*, in which he also points out that the early French Indologists named the Indian spiritual tradition (which the British later labelled 'Hinduism') as *Tolerationism*. The Europeans were amazed at the lack of religious persecution, sectarianism and violence in the Indian tradition and this deeply influenced the newly arising religious toleration in Europe's Age of Reason[20]. Sorman notes that liberal Indian and Javanese Muslims outnumber Arabs. Arabic Islam is largely recitation of the Koran whereas traditional Indian Islam has songs and music, saints and worship at their mausoleums. Shah Jahan's son and heir, the liberal mystically-inclined Prince Dara Shukhoh commissioned a Brahman pundit to translate the great Brahmanic texts, the Upanishads, into Persian. Dara Shukhoh was killed by his Mohammedan fundamentalist zealot brother Aurangzeb who seized the Peacock Throne. But the Persian translation of the Upanishads commissioned by Dara would later be translated into French by Anquetil Duperron helping to bring about the Sanskritic Renaissance of the 19th Century, transforming European culture and philosophy. This Renaissance in turn inspired the rise of the New Physics known as Quantum Mechanics (*see Chapter 4*).

Aurangzeb resumed the destruction of Hindu, Jain and Buddhist temples and the murder of monks. But his incursions into Maharashtra in Central India provoked the rise of the Hindu Marathas, originally led by the legendary Marathi warrior-king Shivaji after whom Mumbai's old 'Victoria Terminus' railway station, a target of the November 2008 Pakistani Mohammedan fundamentalist terrorism, has been renamed. Contrary, to most British historical presentations, the newly created Maratha Confederacy was the dominant military power in India in the mid 18th Century. Having defeated the Mughal army the Marathas retained a Mughal figurehead 'emperor' in Delhi. The piratical British invaders led by Robert Clive exploited this power vacuum. The original Mohammedan Arab imperialists who conquered the Southern Roman world had occupied the province of Sindh (from "Sindhu" or Indus) now in Southern Pakistan, in the 8th Century *c.e.* but were driven out after about 60 years by the Hindus.

Contrast this fact with the ludicrous assertion of the Pakistani leader Zulfikar Ali Bhutto that 'Pakistan' was always a part of the Middle East. This was the same Bhutto who declared that Pakistanis would eat grass if that was what was needed to get them a nuclear weapon! In fact it was the savage, murderous Chinese Communist dictatorship, ever keen to do down rival India, that gave a nuclear bomb blueprint to the failing, fractious and feudal Mohammedan entity. Though not grazing on grass, the 'flocks' of the Semitic religions are expected to obey their clergy like sheep fed on pseudo-spiritual fable fodder. As Sorman tells us in *The Empire of Lies: The Truth about China in the 21st Century*, the Communist Party of China stole nuclear secrets from the USSR and Western powers to build their own nuclear weapons. Mao Zedong exported China's food-grains to pay for the nuclear weapons programme and held lavish, expensive banquets for foreign dignitaries in Beijing, whilst tens of millions of Chinese died from the manmade famines[21]. However, whilst Sorman castigates such manmade famines in Communist countries, he overlooks the fact that the British in India created far more artificial famines and killed more people due to their worship of the false idol of the 'Free Market' (which was in fact not free but a Captive Market) and their White Supremacist racism. In 1877 Disraeli organised the biggest feast in human history, the Delhi Durbar to celebrate Victoria being crowned Empress of India, whilst 100,000 Indians a week were dying of starvation in Madras Province. Record amounts of India's food-grains were exported, making up for Britain's shortfalls in food production and lowering prices in Western markets, whilst Indian famine victims were murdered by the British regime in Buchenwald-like Death Camps[22].

The Turko-Mongol Mughals were largely liberal Muslims and this Hinduism and Sufism influenced anti-clerical strain of Islam persists in India. William James, in his *Varieties*, says that Sufism has existed in Persia since earliest times and that it has been suggested that Sufism must have been inoculated into Islam by Hindu influences[23]. In recent decades, the influence of Saudi Arabian funded Madrassahs teaching the fundamentalist Wahhabi form of Arabian Islam has led to the rise of reactionary fundamentalism, especially in Pakistan where the Taliban originated. Ibn Saud's takeover of Saudi Arabia involved killing 400,000 with 1,000,000 fleeing into exile. In the numerous rebellions that followed Ibn Saud executed 40,000 in public executions and amputated the limbs of 350,000. The Wahhabi sect believes in killing all dissenters and enslaving their wives and children. Women were killed just for appearing outdoors and men killed for smoking cigarettes. Colonial Secretary Winston Churchill admired this 'friend of Britain' and increased his funding facilitating further barbarism. The British Army in Iraq also intervened to help Saud crush a rebellion[24]. As with the corrupt Nawabs serving the British in India by looting their own treasuries, the barbaric House of Saud, far more reactionary than Shia Iran, remains an agent of Anglo-American imperialist interests and hence avoids Western demonisation. The Pakistani state schools themselves teach absurd fabrications of Indian history instigating anti-Hindu hatred in their official textbooks as revealed by Indian Muslim parliamentarian Arif Mohammed Khan in the *Times of India* in December 2008. For most of its history India has maintained the religious pluralism and tolerance that was common in the ancient Mediterranean world prior to the rise of Constantine.

The mystical inspiration and message of the EU anthem

Roman Emperor Constantine's politically convenient adoption of monotheistic Christianity, to symbolise a unified empire with one emperor, after it had been divided under three regional emperors. This led to the creation of a totalitarian theocracy under the Nicene Creed. Constantine himself only converted to Christianity on his deathbed[25]. It was the later emperor Theodosius I who enforced the exclusive adherence to the Nicene Creed in 380 *c.e.* throughout the empire, suppressing unorthodox Christian sects such as the Arians. The First Council of Nicaea in 325 *c.e.* fixed the Biblical canon and the official Church dogma, denying that Divinity was to be found within us, denying religious freedom, outlawing unofficial mystical exploration and imposing an absurd dogma that only one human being, in all history, was of Divine nature! French scholars such as Daniélou have linked the development of Totalitarian political systems to Semitic Monotheisms with their exclusivist pretensions to being the 'One True Faith'. Under Stalin, Hitler and Mao the people were forced into a sort of monotheistic Cult of the Great Leader[26].

In fact, in the late 2nd and early 1st Century *b.c.e.* Judaea, the Hasmonean Dynasty (the 'Maccabees') had modelled their new Rabbinical Judaism on Plato's description of the brutal Spartan regime. The Rabbis were to be a sort of 'Thought Police' stifling independent thinking amongst the Judaeans[27]. This was the first truly Monotheistic period in Judaean history, in which the Judaeans were forced into the exclusive worship of Yahweh (god of Mount Zion; one of the many deities in the Canaanite pantheon) reinforced by the destruction of temples dedicated to rival Canaanite gods such as that of the neighbouring Israelite Samaritans on Mount Gezirim[28, 29]. King Josiah had attempted to impose this exclusive worship of Yahweh along with the 'Deuteronomic ideology' during his short-lived reign before the Babylonian conquest in 597 *b.c.e.* So too had the very few members of the Babylonian-exiled Jerusalem elite (aristocracy and priesthood) such as Nehemiah and Ezra who chose to return to backward Judaea as agents of Persian emperor Cyrus[N4] (who conquered Babylon in 539 *b.c.e.*) and rebuilt the Temple of Yahweh in spite of great opposition from the polytheistic Judaean masses[30, 31]. The Samaritans claim that theirs is the true religion of the Israelites in contrast to the 'Judaism' (based on Josiah's Deuteronomist revisionism) enforced by these agents of Persia which also introduced numerous new Babylonian and Persian elements.

The well-educated liberal, mystically-inclined Roman emperor Julian succeeded Constantine. He is demonised by the intolerant Christians as he tried unsuccessfully to reverse Constantine's Christian totalitarianism. The Christian demonisation stems from the fact that Julian got Christians to compensate non-Christians for the temples that Christians destroyed and the property that Christians stole from non-Christians' houses[32, 33]. Julian had studied at the Platonic Academy in Athens which survived in a Neoplatonic form until Christian Byzantine emperor Justinian forced it to close in 529 *c.e.* (a date some consider the end of Classical Antiquity). Lactantius tells us in his *Divine Institutes* that Julian attempted to return to the philosophical "Religion of the World" and to the Mystery Cults. Along with the supreme God represented by the Sun, Julian wrote of 36 lesser deities associated with equal divisions of Babylonian Zodiac[34]. Neoplatonism was feared as a dangerous adversary by the Christians. After a decree of the Council of Ephesus (431 *c.e.*) and a Law of Theodosius II in 448 *c.e.* the books of Plotinus's great student Porphyry (who had rubbished the Christian superstitions) were burnt. The female Alexandrian Neoplatonist teacher Hypatia was publicly stripped and dismembered by Christians who also burnt down the famous Library[35]. In his BBC TV series *The Story of Maths*, Marcus de Sautoy presents Hypatia solely as a mathematics teacher, suppressing the fact that she was primarily a Neoplatonic mystic (as also does Classicist Bethany Hughes) and de Sautoy claimed falsely that the Arabs had destroyed the Library!

Most people around the world will not know what the European Union's anthem is although, if they heard it, they would recognise the tune. It is in fact Friedrich von Schiller's *Ode to Joy* which Schiller's friend Beethoven set to music as part of his famous Ninth Symphony. Schiller's poem expresses his vision of the human race becoming brothers. The *joy* to which Schiller refers is not simple pleasure but Divine Joy (*ecstasy* – nearer to the *ananda* or 'Bliss' attribute of *Brahman* which is more a blissful freedom from material-worldly bondage), the "spark of Gods" or the "spark of Heaven", the Divine Spark which is within each of us so that, according to Schiller, beggars become princes' brothers[36]. This Divine Spark within each of us is better known as the Divine Light and in the 19th Century *c.e.*, the great Indian Neo-Hindu reformer Vivekananda would argue similarly for a common Humanity along similar lines. William Anderson, in his book on the role of Divine Inspiration in truly great artistic genius entitled *The Face of Glory: Creativity, Consciousness and Civilisation*[37], tells us that both Schiller and Beethoven believed in the existence of a Universal Consciousness (equivalent to the *Brahman* of Hinduism) and that their artistic lives were heavily influenced by this belief.

As Anderson highlights in his book and we shall also see, true creative genius would not exist if the Great Secret were not true. Nowadays the shock displays of unmade beds and pickled sheep carcasses of British so-called Conceptual Artists are awarded the infamous Turner Prize. Giving a seemingly-profound label to a pile of dung does not make the dung something truly worthy of acclaim. Both artists and the Turner judges have either had mental development arrested at pubescent levels or are colluding an elaborate charade to make money selling worthless chaff. Anderson has a revealing quotation from Pablo Picasso (*emphasis mine*)[38]:

> *I am not bold enough to think of myself as an artist in the great and ancient sense of the word. ...I am merely an **amuseur public**, an entertainer who has understood his time and milked as best he could the imbecility, the vanity, and the greed of his contemporaries. It is a bitter confession..., but it has the merit of being sincere.*

It is worth noting that, not only great artistic geniuses, but also many of the greatest creative geniuses of the New Physics have understood something of the Great Secret of Existence (*see Chapter 4*). However, as we saw above, most scientists nowadays are little more than 'glorified technicians', learning more and more about less and less, yet quick to dismiss such mystical knowledge as primitive superstition or nonsense without understanding what they are talking about. This may be because they are mere journeymen technicians operating unquestioningly within the established frameworks set by the mystically-inspired true geniuses of science. Otherwise, if they themselves have been truly inspired, they have repressed the true sources of their creativity. As discussed in Chapter 4, Christianity literally 'demonised' such mystical potentialities within us. Westerners have been indoctrinated culturally not to recognise mystical influence or to accept it as such, if indeed they are aware of them at all. As William James stated about other forms of Consciousness lying hidden, we may go through life never suspecting their existence.

This cultural ignorance of the true nature of Divine Inspiration is seen in the story of the remarkable, mathematical genius Srinivas Ramanujan Aiyar (known as Ramanujan)[39]. Kanigel notes that many mathematicians do not consider Ramanujan to be a mere genius, but a magician. With a normal genius, given hindsight, you can see where he was coming from. For instance, a physicist will recognise the origins of Einstein's theory of Special Relativity in the Lorentz Transformations.[N5] Whiteman, like others, has noted that the clear point of origin of Special Relativity was in an insight of the French mathematician Henri Poincaré that, if the failure to measure an ether-drift was absolute, then the postulation of an absolute Space-Time frame would be unjustified. Poincaré had the further insight in 1904 that, if this was so, the Lorentz Transformations must then be interpreted as new kinematics of Space and Time. This is exactly what Einstein achieved in his 1905 Special Theory of Relativity[40]. Ramanujan often put together mathematical functions from such disparate fields that it appears as if he plucked them out of thin air. People are still working out proofs of his theorems almost a century after he died[41].

The India/West dichotomy is seen in the scepticism of his atheistic patron G.H. Hardy, then Britain's leading mathematician, towards Ramanujan's explanation as to the true source of his inspiration. Hardy considered his association with Ramanujan as the greatest thing that ever happened to him. Furthermore, in terms of natural creative ability, if Ramanujan were to score one hundred then Hardy rated himself as scoring only four. However, Hardy could not accept that Ramanujan was telling the truth when he claimed that his insights came to him in visions when he meditated upon his village deity, Namagiri (Ramanujan was a Brahman but Brahmans still participate in the countless polytheistic cults of popular Hinduism). So in Britain, Ramanujan kept quiet about this whilst speaking openly about the source of his inspiration in India[42]. In the ancient world Mathematics was closely associated with Mysticism but this link continues to be suppressed by Western historians (as in the case of Hypatia). Mathematician turned mystic, Merrell-Wolff realised the mystical origins of esoteric mathematics, impossible to visualise in the normal framework of human mentation, and thought that such mathematical training might provide a path for Westerners seeking enlightenment[43]. In fact mathematician Ralph Abraham reveals that the new so-called 'Postmodern' mathematics of Chaos Theory and Fractal Geometry was to a large extent inspired by psychedelic drug-induced experiences of altered states of Consciousness[44].

Modern Western Philosophy of Mathematics[45], Philosophy of Physics[46] and Epistemology cannot really account for the invention of non-Euclidean geometries, not limited by normal perceptual Space and Time. Such non-Euclidean orderings of Space and Time are actually experienced in deep mystical realisations, attained either through yoga or through the use of LSD[47]. Existentialist Maurice Merleau-Ponty tried to dismiss the supposed 'transcendental illusion' of past philosophies, including those of Kant and Husserl, with their 'supernaturalism' (trans-empirical realms). Merleau-Ponty's superficial phenomenology reduced human creativity to merely the expressive play of indeterminate potentialities in the (Jamesian) 'fringe' or (Gestalt) background field of our experience[48]. Merleau-Ponty rejected the (seemingly) Platonic and Kantian *a priori* approach of Husserl's phenomenology in regard to Mathematics with its 'Free Variation' of the experienced 'object' (which could be a non-physical idea) in the imagination, exploring its possible transformations. Husserl viewed mathematical insight as the discovery (uncovering) of *a priori* invariants in our cognitive processes through such imaginative Free Variation[49].

Merleau-Ponty's emphasis on many possible creative pathways unique to individuals fails to account for why, in Maths, there is usually only one actual true solution which a mathematician may re-**discover** rather than create *de novo*. We shall see that Infinitesimal Calculus originated with Bhaskara II and Madhava in India centuries before Newton's presumably independent work. Merrell-Wolff states that, since non-Euclidean geometry it has been evident that Mathematics is not an independent existence beyond thought but rather the 'necessitarian' aspect of thought[50]. This is in agreement with Husserl's view as 'necessitarian' here implies the basic constraints or limitations on possibilities of experience. This understanding contradicts the anthropomorphic Greek myth of *Logos* that permeates Western scientific thought. This is the notion that human Reason merely reflects an eternal, immutable order intrinsic to Nature; i.e., that Nature is an analogue of the human mind. We shall see that although Kant and Husserl were essentially correct on the notion of *a priori* conditions of human experience, they both remained ignorant of true 'transcendence' in the traditional sense of going beyond the Space/Time/Causality limitations of sense perception. Kanigel notes that in the Ancient 'West', the Greeks and Romans knew of the link between the "Unconscious" and the transcendental realm[51]. This again points to the outlawing of mystical exploration (e.g., Gnosticism, Hermeticism and Neo-Platonism) by the totalitarian Nicene Church as the period when the Western world started to become so ignorant of the Great Secret of Existence.

The true Holy Grail, the All-Seeing Eye and the mythological objectification of mystical glory

At the end of his 2006 TV programme on the Holy Grail[52], presenter Richard Hammond concluded by saying that such grail myths persist because people want to believe in an *object that is secret* and which *holds the key to great mysteries*. However, he seemed unable to grasp what he had been told at a New Age gathering in Glastonbury that perhaps the 'Holy Grail' represented the goal of inward spiritual progress. Joseph Campbell wrote that The Inquisition stopped the Grail romance for the Grail romance is of 'God in your own heart'. The Christ becomes a metaphor for that transcendent power which is the support and being for your own life[53].

The recent popular interest with the Holy Grail followed the enormous success of Dan Brown's fictitious novel *The Da Vinci Code* which highlighted the fact that the Catholic Church has suppressed various inconvenient truths about the origins of Christianity and the life of Jesus. Such rehashing of conspiracy myths about a supposed bloodline of Jesus detracts from the related, yet far more profound and historically sound so-called "heresy" which the Christian Church suppressed brutally and wrote out of official Christian teachings and history, Gnosticism. The Gnostics' teachings that true spirituality involved looking within oneself to find the Divinity within each one of us was anathema to the Church as it undermined the role of the Christian priest as the mediator between God and the laypeople and hence the authority of the Church.

Following the success of *The Da Vinci Code*, TV has also jumped on the bandwagon of another book by Brown, *Angels and Demons*, which revives the conspiracy theory of the Illuminati. This need not concern us save for the fact that it involves the so-called All-Seeing Eye on the Great Seal of the USA as depicted on the back of the US Dollar bill. This All-Seeing Eye (or Eye of Providence), an eye within the apex of a pyramid, is linked by Brown with the so-called Illuminati and the Freemasons. The actual Illuminati secret society was a short-lived group of late 18th Century Enlightenment freethinkers in Bavaria who wanted society to be rid of organised religion. At the time the Church played a key role in justifying the existence of absolute monarchies in Europe. The Illuminati conspiracy theory was propounded by 18th Century European reactionaries who felt threatened by the liberal ideas of the European 'Enlightenment' such as Liberty, Equality, Republicanism and, of course, the Brotherhood of Man as expressed in Schillers' *Ode to Joy* written a few years before the French Revolution. The paranoid reactionaries saw in the New Order sweeping Europe, the hidden hand of a secret anti-establishment, anti-Christian movement in which they placed all the liberal philosophers of the

'Enlightenment'. The All-Seeing Eye on the Great Seal is surrounded by rays of light known as a *glory*. Freemasons claim that they use a triangle linking the All-Seeing Eye of Deity supposedly with the Christian Trinity rather than a pyramid (which indicates Hermetic influence).

The surrounding Light-Glory points to the subtle esoteric links to true spiritual (rather than socio-political) *Enlightenment*. This is seen in Alexander Korda's famous 1940 film version of the Arabic One Thousand and One Nights' tale *The Thief of Baghdad* , in which the boy thief Abu has to steal a magical jewel from the forehead of a Hindu-Buddhist style statue of the Goddess of Light on the highest peak of the highest mountain range on Earth, (i.e., the Himalayas). Note the Mohammedan conflation here of the omniscience of the All-Seeing (Inner) Eye with the height of the mountain indicative of the Semitic Heaven in the Sky myth. Thus the All-Seeing Eye is a symbol of the 'Third Eye' or 'Eye of Wisdom' which is opened when one attains spiritual enlightenment. For as Anderson states in *The Face of Glory*[54]:

> *Glory in Judaeo-Christian terms is first the splendour of the godhead and, second, the experience of the transformation in which we, temporarily on Earth and for eternity in Heaven, are taken up into the sharing of that splendour. ...In Indian terms it is the participation in the rasa, the taste of the glory of atman mediated through the bliss of contemplation... Glory is another aspect of the imagery of light associated with the nature of consciousness: it is another name for the halo...*

Thus when Richard Hammond speaks of people wanting to believe in an object which is secret and which holds the key to great mysteries, he is misunderstanding the fact that such myths project properties of rarefied spiritual experiences of the universal Self (**subject** or consciousness) onto imagined physical **objects** such as a mythical Holy Grail, a Fount of All Wisdom, an Elixir of Life (or Fountain of the Water of Life) or an All-Seeing Eye. The eye at the apex of the pyramid symbolises that only a tiny few possess this Divine Illumination or Gnosis, whilst the vulgar masses remained trapped in the Ignorance of the sensual world (mistaking sensory phenomena for Reality). The New Testament myths of 'Virgin Birth', of the 'Son of God' as the Unique Earthly Incarnation of the Divinity, actually refer, not to some historical Hebraic healer Jesus (who is only mentioned outside the Gospels in a fleeting remark in Josephus), but to mystical experiences well-known to the older Mystery Religions of the Mediterranean[55, 56]. *Dionysos* meant Son of God in Phrygian[57]. The Virgin Birth referred to the rebirth of the soul in the spiritual realm (in the Pure or 'Virgin' Spirit). Campbell tells us that Christian missionaries thought that the devil was tricking them when they found versions of the Virgin Birth myth all over the world amongst people who had never before encountered Christianity[58]. We shall see that all these mythical metaphors refer to what Vedanta calls the *anandamayakosa* (Bliss Sheath) or the Causal Body.

The hymns of the *Rig Veda* linked true nobility (the *Arya*) to those who seek and find the Light within by 'sacrificing himself' (the Inner 'Sacrifice' of the egoic self). Campbell famously linked the archetypal *Hero* of world mythology to the person who seeks and encounters the Divinity within in order to find a solution to some personal or collective crisis and brings back to the mundane realm some new insight or course of action[59]. The All-Seeing

Eye, the Fount of all Wisdom and the Elixir of Life myths are all based upon the mystical experience of merger and union with the Divine Light (the Divine Spark of the Gnostics, the *Atman* or the *Cit* (Pure Consciousness) of Brahmanic Hinduism (*Vedanta*), Mahayana Buddhism's Buddha Mind or Clear Light of Death, Islamic Sufism's *Al haqq* (the Reality), the Eternal Light or Uncreated Light of Christian mystics etc.) into which the ego (the individuated consciousness) of an enlightened yogi or mystic dissolves after the ego has been stripped of worldly attachments or subtilised into the 'naked', translucent individuality of the *anandamayakosa*. This dissolution results in an experience of impersonal (without a sense of "I" or of being a separate being) Universal Consciousness, an experience of Oneness, devoid of subject/object distinctions, (i.e., "nondual"), with the entire Cosmos. It is this experience of a Universal or "Cosmic Consciousness" (known in Brahmanism as the *saguna Brahman*; Reality with distinctions) in which our individual boundaries dissolve into a limitless, impersonal Oneness, an all-pervading Light of Awareness permeating the entire Creation, that has led to the popular myth of the All-Seeing Eye which now graces the Great Seal of the United States.

In Tudor England Thomas More started adopting Neoplatonism to Catholicism and his *Utopia* published in 1516 showed Hermetic influences in its appeals for religious tolerance. The Protestant Reformation in England under Elizabeth Tudor replaced the tolerance of Erasmean education with scriptural Puritan thought, following narrowly theological and anti-Catholic historical propaganda. But in private circles Hermetic influence remained. Intellectual courtiers led by Philip Sidney chose her astrologer-in-chief John Dee as their teacher[60]. According to tradition, the Stewart king Charles I, on the scaffold before his execution, quoted a passage from Philip Sydney's *Arcadia* beginning: "O all-seeing light and eternal life of all things…"[61].

Nature Mysticism, Transcendental Cosmic Consciousness, the Plenum/ Void and Creative Manifestation

Merrell-Wolff called the power of the Light of Consciousness to turn upon itself, (i.e., rather than flowing outwards towards sensory perception of the external world) "introception" (which he noted is the same as the Indian *nirbija* ('seedless') meditation without a subtle object that leads to enlightenment[62]. In contrast, *introspection* involves objective content. Successful introception means that Consciousness loses all content other than itself[63]. This is what is usually called 'Purification of Consciousness' to attain Pure Consciousness as implied in Patanjali's definition of Yoga as cessation of the waves of mindstuff (which cloud over the inner Light). Merrell-Wolff says that introceptive consciousness is realised in a way independent of both Time and Space, at least as these notions are predicated of the external world[64].

Whiteman says in his *Philosophy of Space and Time*, there is no need to regard the term 'transcendental' as unscientific. He uses it to refer to features of contemplation which come to light when one passes beyond 'simple location' in Space and Time[65]. This is most evident in QM (and also in String Theory derived from QM) in which so-called 'elementary particles' such as the electron exist nonlocally, and only manifest locally, (i.e., like a localised particle) when an interaction (or energy transfer process) occurs as in an electron detecting instrument. In my introductory overview to my Science-Mysticism synthesis in O/OM entitled "The Bigger, Deeper Picture", I wrote[66]:

Similarly, the term transcendental is widely misunderstood. I use it to mean beyond the realms of our ordinary perceptions involving normal spatiotemporal categories of organisation... Even simple contemplation of the modern scientific understanding of sensory reception of information from the environment can reveal to us the seemingly paradoxical issue as to why we perceive the world as moving smoothly through normal space and time when, clearly, the information from past states of entities must still be present in some form in the environment...

A.N. Whitehead asserts in his *The Concept of Nature* that "the meaning of **nature** reduces itself principally to the discussion of the character of **time** and the character of **space**" (*emphasis mine*)[67]. In his 1925 *Science and the Modern World* Whitehead claimed that the original error of Mechanistic Materialist philosophy was that of **Simple Location**; holding matter to have a definite spatial and a definite temporal location[68]. Whitehead is correct in regard to Mechanistic causality with its External Relations as opposed to the traditional mystically-inspired Doctrine of Internal Relations related to holistic causation. But the original error of Materialism is clearly the myth of the Ontological Primacy of Matter; Whitehead never truly understood Consciousness, conflating it with the appearance of organised process ('organism') in the speculative metaphysics of his much-hyped *Process and Reality*.

Arthur Eddington's description of the quantum 'particle' as the coalescence of more fundamental, imperceptibly fast-vibrating waves of a deeper 'sub-aether' (*see Chapter 1*) neatly explains what we actually mean by **Matter**. 'Matter' refers to the gross forms abstracted by our sense perceptions (the material world or 'material plane'). It also refers to the microscopic, seemingly distinct forms such as molecules, atoms and even subatomic particles abstracted by our physical instruments (which greatly extend the range of our information discrimination beyond the limitations of our senses). *Matter is derivative*, not primary. Matter is not Ultimate Reality. The true Ontology, as we shall see in Chapter 9, is one that must be based on the **Primacy of Consciousness**, meant here in the sense of nondual, formless Pure Consciousness (*cit*) beyond the vibratory-energetic manifestation of spatiotemporal forms (*nirguna Brahman*).

I would add that the use of "space" here for a characteristic of Nature really means Wakeful, sensory perception of **spatiality** and **causality** as *Space* as such is not absent in transcendental realms as we shall see below. Normal spatiality is related to perception of generally discrete forms of surfaces or impenetrable, extensive objects distinct from one another (mutually exclusive) along with normal causality with temporal succession of events in the familiar manner of cause always preceding effect in a linear manner. Time is generated by dynamic activity, i.e., it is an abstraction from process, and the **temporality** of events may change in transcendental realms unlimited by normal spatiality and causality. The term **eternity,** implying total transcendence of Time (*atemporality* rather than 'endless time'), applies to the *nirguna Brahman*. This is Ultimate Reality without distinctions or forms, devoid of all activity or change. I do not accept the Platonic and Neoplatonic views, repeated by the likes of Shimon Malin[69], that the Neoplatonic transcendental realm of supposedly immutable Ideas/Forms (*Nous*) is an 'eternal' realm. Plotinus asserted that *Nous* is eternal but makes various contradictory statements which he claims are justified as being necessarily paradoxical[70]. Carl Jung's mature conception, based on actual experience, of 'archetypes' in the *unus mundus*[71] (equivalent to Platonic Ideas in *Nous*) parallels the Indian dynamic view of such *bija* ('seeds'; potentialities of forms of experience) in the *akasa*. Jung even stated that his mature understanding of 'archetypes' was that they were the same as the yogic *samskara* (reverberating memory impressions)[72].

The usage of the term 'transcendental' by the likes of Immanuel Kant and Edmund Husserl was not the same as this traditional meaning referring to extrasensory experiences of supernatural realms beyond mundane spatio-temporality. Husserl referred to the actual (non-phenomenal) object in the external world (Kant's 'thing-in-itself') transcending the limited perspectives of perceptual adumbrations, etc., and both Kant and Husserl used 'transcendental' to refer to the non-experienced, and supposedly inapprehensible, processes of Consciousness underlying the constitution of our 'empirical' perceptual consciousness. Although both Kant and Husserl remained ignorant of the reality of mystical realisation of transcendental realms of existence, in a sense, their usage conforms to the traditional usage as such 'transcendental experience' is usually contrasted to the normal sensory ('empirical') experience which is limited by our Wakeful apprehension of Space, Time and Causality (where effect follows cause in distinct succession). Thus the traditional distinction is also making a distinction between Empirical consciousness with its Wakeful apprehension of Space, Time and Causality and Transcendental consciousness although this involves mystical realisations of realities beyond our normal experiences. In the speculative thought of Kant and Husserl, the transcendental was inapprehensible things-in-themselves (Kant's *noumena*) and deeper constitutive processes generating the *a priori* categories of thought such as Kant's 'Transcendental Unity of Apperception' (or 'Transcendental Ego') which, according to Kant, is always present as a prerequisite of experience but cannot be perceived or discerned by introspection.

Thus we are in a position to distinguish what I will call **Nature Mysticism** from what I have already referred to here as 'Cosmic Consciousness' or the *Saguna Brahman* (Reality with distinctions). The famous physicist Ernst Mach had a deep influence on both Einstein and Heisenberg (*see Chapter 4*). He was also the godfather of Wolfgang Pauli[73] and a close friend of the Buddhist scholar Paul Carus[74]. Mach's so-called Pan-Sensist ontology and the very similar Pan-Experientialism of William James are based on such superficial Nature Mysticism experiences. Such experiences have also been described by Jean-Jacques Rousseau[75], the poet Alfred Tennyson and neurologist James Austin (his *kensho* experience) in his Emergent Materialism and 'Neuronal Man' reductionist myth-ridden *Zen and the Brain*[76]. This involves attaining momentary ego dissolution in the normal waking state of Consciousness and an experience of impersonal, nondual consciousness where one loses the sense of separation from the surrounding sensory world. Mach had such a Nature Mysticism experience (or 'panpsychist epiphany' as the anti-mystical Skrbina refers to it) and abandoned his Kantian view that the noumenal Reality underlying perceptual phenomena can never be apprehended[77]. In fact this led Mach to dismiss Kant's notions of *noumena* and an unchanging ego as nonsense[78]. Mach described the experience as "the world with my ego suddenly appeared to me as one coherent mass of sensations". This led Mach to believe that noumenal Reality consisted of sensations, (e.g., colours, tones, pressures, spaces, times) but with no observing mind[79]. The latter point is a description of Nondual Consciousness where there is no objectification of these senses by an observing mind creating subject/object duality. William James' Pluralist Pan-Experientialism is essentially the same Nature Mystical view as is clear from the 'plurality' of experiences. Skrbina says that James, after the manner of Mach, asserts that 'pure experience' is the ultimate reality[80].

Mach's vague use of 'spaces' and 'times' is interesting as, if senses are active and functioning normally, then one should be limited to normal Space, Time and Causality. It seems that Mach had some experience of altered states beyond merely the Material plane of Nature and such 'Buddhistic' experience, as he and Einstein referred to them[81], must have influenced his relativistic, nonlocal "Mach's Principle'. The key point to note here is that such Panpsychist (Consciousness or Awareness pervades the entire material world) views limit Ultimate Reality to the **Space-Time world** or '**Nature**' but have no conception of a greater transcendental 'Reality' from which Nature emerges. Whitehead's *Process and Reality* falls into this category. Such views parallel Spinoza's limited Pantheism in which his impersonal 'God' was simply the totality of Nature rather than a deeper 'Panentheism' which understands that the impersonal Spirit, although pervading and being the substance of Nature, is not limited to simply the realm of Nature but transcends Nature. On a recent British TV new report about contemporary British 'pagans' being allowed religious holidays, we were told that such pagan's worship what they can see around them like trees and rivers. Thus there is an element of truth in Christian criticisms of some pre-Christian traditions in Europe as not being truly spiritual, being ignorant of the Unseen Reality.

The translations of the Upanishads dramatically impacted Europe at the end of the 18th and beginning of the 19th Century, influencing profoundly the Enlightenment critics of Christianity and especially the Romantic Movement. But these Europeans conflated the 'Brahmanic Revelation' with Pantheism. The yogic Path to Enlightenment and true Mystical Union (*Raja Yoga*) involves "stopping the mind"[82]. Stopping the mind means cessation of mental activity; this primarily means withdrawing attention from the senses leading to their deactivation. Recall that Patanjali began his *Yoga Sutras* with the assertion that Yoga is the cessation of the waves of the mindstuff. Cessation of mental activity (equivalent to Merrell-Wolff's introceptive turning away of the Light of Consciousness from the objective world towards Consciousness itself) uncovers the underlying flow of the Inner Light of Pure Consciousness which, as I have already stated, creates through its pulsating flow the Time/Space Matrix in which gross perceptions manifest[83]. As indicated previously, new modes of attention or lucidity (the so-called 'vehicles of consciousness' – of which the normal waking ego is but one case) are stabilised in deeper processes of consciousness.

Unlike Mach's overhasty conclusion that Ultimate Reality is a coherent mass of senses, the Vedantic tradition utilises the process of **Sublation** to Ultimate Reality. Sublation (cancellation) is the criterion of Truth in *Advaita Vedanta* (Nondual Brahmanism). The less capable some content or object of Consciousness is of being sublated, the *more real it is*[84]. Briefly speaking, the introceptive retreat into Consciousness leads to the normal perceptual world being sublated, it is revealed to be generated by deeper planes of manifestation within Consciousness. Through such processes, passing through a number of planes of manifestation, it eventually becomes clear that the only non-sublatable realm is that of Pure self-luminous Consciousness which reveals itself as the **Ground of all Being**. Through yogic sublation Ultimate Reality is revealed as the Pure Being (*sat*) and Pure Consciousness (*cit*) of the Inner Light or *Atman*, which, when the subtilised, translucent 'naked ego' (*anandamayakosa*) dissolves into this transcendental Light into an unlimited or infinite Awareness. (Note that this is not the Waking ego dissolving into the field of sense-perception as occurs in Nature Mysticism). This is the true **Mystical Union** or 'becoming one with' the Universal Light of Nondual Consciousness or *Brahman*. However, as indicated previously Brahman is realised in two different modes of being which can transform between one another like a Gestalt switch between two alternative perceptual constructs in apprehending an ambiguous figure.

Merrell-Wolff uses the term Cosmic Consciousness for any mystical (transcendental) plane of Consciousness which has content or any kind of multiplicity[85]. This distinguishes a variety of levels of subtle manifestation of forms from the pure formless (nondual) consciousness, the plenum/void (the *nirguna Brahman*; Reality without distinctions) which, Merrell-Wolff calls the High Indifference and says has something of the character of an infinite space[86]. Stanislaw Grof, referring to both LSD subjects and others experiencing mystical states through his own variations on Yoga, Dervish practises, etc., which he calls "holotropic breathwork", says that such individuals claim to witness the emergence of creative Cosmic Consciousness from the Void or, conversely, its return and disappearance into the Void[87]. Artist Mellen-Thomas Benedict claims his Near-Death Experience (NDE) took him beyond the Big Bang into the energetic Void of Nothingness[88]. Merrell-Wolff[89] states:

> *The immediate effect of a state of consciousness having...no object is that of a vast void. It is an I suspended in an utter voidness. At once a process of 'enantiodromia' transforms the voidness into the value of substantial fullness. ...this quality of fullness, which is the actual palpable presence of Divinity itself. It is nothing so crude as a vast person in space, but a Presence that permeates all space, interwoven throughout the objects of ordinary consciousness, yet more completely present where those objects are not. The effect is a radical reversal of all former values...*

This description from a 20th Century mathematician and mystic is reminiscent of the famous statement attributed to Pythagoras[N6], itself reminiscent of earlier Vedic cosmology; 'the One breathed in the Void to fill up the space between things'. It should be added that the normal experience of objects as mere surfaces disappears as nondual Consciousness penetrates the depths of entities with which it is one[90]. As Aurobindo Ghose says, in supramentalised seeing the material world and space and material objects cease to appear material as in our sense perceptions but are seen as Spirit itself in a form of itself[91]. Aurobindo stressed the vibrant energetic activity of Consciousness which underlies and manifests the perceived gross forms, quoting the Upanishads, "By energism *(tapas)* of Consciousness, Brahman is massed and matter is born"[92, 93]. Plotinus tells us that *Nous* is not another place; it is this very world of appearances seen with complete penetration, to see all things as the living substance of God. Distinctions remain on the surface of each being but in common depth all is seen as Oneness[94].

Thus we begin to see that sense-perception is not so much a transparent 'window' on the world but more a screen or filter allowing in only selective information, the gross forms of the 'Material World/Plane' or Nature. Aurobindo tells us, "the last knot of our bondage is at that point where the external draws into oneness with the internal, the machinery of the ego itself becomes subtilised to the vanishing point... [95]. Merrell-Wolff [96] also gives a very clear description of **mystical union** or dissolution of the most basic individuated vehicle of consciousness into the Light:

> *The self stripped of all extraneous elements, of everything that can possibly be an object for consciousness, is very small indeed. It is a bare point of Light... If, at this point, the introceptive process continues..., then there follows a tremendous enantiodromedal transformation. The self as a bare point becomes an unlimited Space whose nature is Light or Consciousness. Divinity fuses with the self, thereby becoming the Self which is at once both God and I. Again, this is not speculation –it actually happens. This changes the whole view of the nature of being and supplies... the true basis of absolute idealism.*

Note the striking resemblance here to the famous testimony of 13th century theologian and mystic Meister Eckhart, denounced as heresy by the Christian (Catholic) Church which fears such revelations of Truth, given below.

In regard to the Brahmanic understanding based on such realisations (constituting in a sense a sort of 'experimental' evidence) along with logical argument that the Light of Pure Nondual Consciousness in its formless mode as the plenum/void is the Ground of all Being, it is worth briefly considering the following. The Galilean ontology, which most physicists still adhere to[97], surreptitiously presupposes Consciousness which is logically prior to Galileo's imagined 'primary qualities' (measured quantities). You cannot make measurements without observations based on subjective experiences (so-called 'secondary qualities') and all measurements (attaching numbers to phenomena) presuppose a manmade convention or standard superimposed on Nature regardless as to whether or not these standards are based on naturally occurring phenomena[98]. As Professor Marcus de Sautoy showed on a recent BBC documentary entitled 'How Long is a Piece of String', 'objective' quantitative measurements are not pre-existent values simply read-off from Nature but, as we saw with so-called 'elementary particles', products of human interaction with Nature[99]. The Galilean ontology leads also to Positivistic myths which deny reality-status to anything which cannot be measured or measured in a repeatable supposedly 'objective' manner.

Indeed all Physicalist ontologies of an insentient Ultimate Reality are merely the **'phantasies' of physicists** as they actually exist only in the imagination of humans and cannot actually be realised; nor can Consciousness be somehow made to 'appear' in these speculative ontological systems by 'emergence' or otherwise as metaphysically-naive Physicalists imagine. As in the case of the Big Bang with its Creation *ex nihilo*, notions of *Emergence* are verbally-disguised appeals to *magic*, the magical appearance *ex nihilo* of an imaginary 'Consciousness' which supposedly exists only in the 'minds' (again an unspecified notion) of humans (and perhaps other higher animals) in an otherwise insentient universe. Far from being monistic Emergent Materialism is a tacit form of ontological Dualism; the unspecified 'conscious minds' cannot be of the same intrinsic nature as the rest of the insentient material universe. Furthermore, as Thomas Nagel has stressed, the concept of Emergence is epistemological not ontological, it actually refers to *human ignorance* (or lack of information) making it impossible to predict a higher-level 'emergent' phenomenon from *scientific models* describing smaller-scale processes. Emergence refers to human theories or mental constructions, not to Reality[100]. *Emergence* does not explain anything; it covers up the explanatory failure of scientific models. Merrell-Wolff says that Consciousness is essentially indefinable; it is presupposed even in the possibility of definition, but is never itself the object defined[101]. This point is related to the famous Godel's Theorem which undermined the Formalist program in the Foundations of Mathematics associated with Gottlob Frege and Bertrand Russell. Kurt Godel and Herman Weyl, both admirers of Husserl, realised that the fundamental, unproven 'self-evident' axiomatic definitions in any formal system are themselves established by conscious intuition[102]. Thus neither Physics nor Mathematics, under careful epistemological scrutiny, can escape the fact of the **Primacy of Consciousness.**

The realisation of Cosmic Oneness or the Universal Self is not the ultimate realisation. The deepest realisation is that of the formless plenum/void (the *nirguna Brahman* or the Clear Light of the Void), transcending all dualities or polarisations including the limitations of normal Space, Time and Causality. The Sanskrit *nirguna* means "without *distinctions* (qualities or forms)" which relates to the use of the term "void" (*Sunyata*) by some branches of Mahayana Buddhism or Nothingness by those fond of negative terminology. The famous negative predications of this Ultimate Reality in the Upanishads which assert that *Brahman* is 'neither this nor that' highlight the inadequacy of concepts (which are of necessity relative and abstractive) to grasp the ineffable Absolute which transcends all relative predications, all dualities. Our concepts can only indicate in a limited and inadequate manner something of the *nirguna Brahman*. Our minds can only grasp things if distinctions are present to distinguish things.

Thus in Neoplatonism *Nous*, the first emanation (plane of being) from Plotinus's 'ineffable One' is referred to as the *Intelligible* World paralleling the Brahmanic concept of *Saguna*. We saw above Plotinus's description of *Nous* (*a.k.a.* the 'One-Many' or 'All-in-One') as Oneness in which distinctions still remain. In claiming knowledge (or nondual realisation) of the One (beyond Creation) Plotinus actually presupposes the presence of Consciousness as *to Know* or *to Realise* presupposes Awareness. Rather paradoxically, the seeming nothingness (better "no-thing-ness") is the formless Plenum or Fullness of Pure Absolute Consciousness which is the substantial, Ultimate Reality or Ground of All Being which contains the possibility or potential for all forms of existence. Merrell-Wolff says that Voidness is only *Sunyata* from the relative perspective; when realised in its inherent nature it is absolutely substantial and is the one and only self-existent Substance. He notes that (the original) Buddhism abandoned the notion of Substance entirely leading to a nihilistic view that there is nothing but movements inhering in nothing else[103]. In fact, modern Physics' conception of electromagnetic energy is of waves in Space without any underlying substance which is 'waving' or vibrating.

Although mystical union, or loss of individuality in the uncovered Light of Pure Consciousness, appears to be the ultimate goal in some yogic texts, it is the end of the deconstruction-of-perception process of Raja Yoga leading the yogi to the Ultimate Reality. The yogi needs to realise this Ground of all Being from which all the planes of manifestation are found to arise before he or she can begin to explore the manifestations. It is also necessary to attain mystical union to demonstrate that our individuated selves (or egos) are themselves manifestations and not absolute (or permanent) entities as claimed by Theists ('immortal souls') and by the likes of Kant and Husserl. But in order to retain some clear memory of nondual realisations, the yogi in reaching the depths of being will have reduced the ego to a 'naked', translucent individuality, a subtilised individuated-consciousness stripped of personal attachments (the *anandamayakosa* or bliss sheath/bliss vehicle) which floats almost transparently in the Light of Godhead without clouding over the Light. It is by developing the capacity to generate such subtilised 'vehicles of Consciousness', stripping the ego of habitual, worldly attachments, that the yogi can remain lucid in deeper planes which appear 'unconscious' to ordinary people and form memories in such deeper states. So-called *Yoganidra* (Yogic Sleep) is like Lucid Dreaming but lucidity can also be developed in deeper states equivalent to Deep Sleep. We normally forget dreams unless we attain a degree of lucidity just before we awake.

It is such capacities for stabilising lucidity that is beyond the, presumably sincere, Dualist Vedantin Theists, who may 'black out' (lose personal consciousness) attempting to stabilise the 'naked ego' on the verge of mystical union. Thus such Dualists may deny oneness with the impersonal Godhead due to their own lack of yogic skill rather than on dogmatic grounds as is the case with Semitic religious orthodoxy. It may be that, like Semitic religions, some Theist Hindus project anthropomorphic emotions onto the impersonal Light. I recall in 1999 at the UK/US New Age sponsored *Beyond the Brain* conference at Kings College, Cambridge, the Chairman, Professor Peter Fenwick, who had just read my O/OM kept pushing an Indian-born Canadian professor of Physics and Religion , Ravi Ravindra in my direction even sitting him opposite me at the first breakfast. Ravindra had just been made a judge by the Templeton Foundation. However, Ravindra showed little interest. He, like the Monotheists from Semitic religions, peddled a Theistic theology based on the *Bhagavad Gita* which was an attempt to harmonise the Vedanta of the Brahmanic elite with the Theistic devotionalism or *Bhakti* tradition that developed in popular Hinduism. Aurobindo tells us that the Supreme *Purusa* (Self) is **not the personal God** of popular, (i.e., Theistic) religions, a being separate from all others[104]. Of course, my physical correlate for the Divine Light or Godhead shows that the Theistic myths of the complete separation of God and Man and of an immortal soul are untenable! The ability to reduce the ego to subtle vehicles of Consciousness to access deeper planes is presumably important, along with the highly developed discriminative skills, to the post-mystical union practises in which the yogi can remain aware of the Light-flow in the midst of normal Waking consciousness.

It becomes clear to the yogi that the Absolute Distinctionless Plenum is both the source and substance of the phenomenal universe (the objective world of appearances in dualistic, relative consciousness) or 'the Creation' which is a manifestion arising within the Plenum. Manifestation does not imply a one-off event occurring in time, but rather that the entire universe of matter and space is a process continuously arising out of the infinite Absolute Plenum, a continuous creation. The underlying vibratory process that continually manifests material forms or 'Becoming' creates Time. The naive *mayavada* (Doctrine of Maya) ontology of the so-called *Advaitin* or Nondualist Sankara has been exalted by many Neo-Hindus. Merrell-Wolff called Sankara the greatest 'Idealist' philosopher. But, ironically, Sankara's Illusionism which denied that the *nirguna Brahman* transforms itself into the manifest Creation (*saguna Brahman*) is in fact tacit Dualism as the truly Nondualist Kashmir Saivites such as Abhinavagupta recognised[105]. The original Vedantic summary the *Brahmasutras* repeatedly asserts *Brahmaparinama* or transformation of Brahman[106]. Sankara's tacit Dualism was later criticised by the likes of Ramakrishna and Aurobindo Ghose who, as with Abhinavagupta, stressed Tantric views of Creation through energetic vibrations emanating within the distinctionless Ground of *nirguna Brahman*.

As Pratima Bowes states, the Upanishads taught of two levels of reality, the Sensory (or Empirical) Reality and the Suprasensory Reality that could only be realised by extrasensory means. Contrary to the usual reading of Sankara, the Empirical level is still real and not merely illusory[107]. In fact the standard *Advaita Vedanta* doctrine is that of *anirvacaniya* (indefinable), that the *Maya* world is neither identical with Ultimate Reality (*sat*) nor different (*asat*). Merrell-Wolff elucidates this point saying that the empirical world is a mirage, insubstantial and ghostlike. The concept of *Maya* (actually meaning 'the mysterious creative power of the Absolute') when taken as 'illusion' refers to mistaking this illusory phenomenal appearance for the Ultimate Reality[108]. The Upanishadic doctrine of *Panch Bhuta* (Five 'Elements') asserted that the first created element is *Akasa* (Space as subtle matter or 'Ether') whose characteristic is *vibration*. Material phenomena manifest by the progressive vibratory densification or grossification of *Akasa*[109]. The Tantric

Doctrine of Vibration in Nondual Kashmir Saivism began to elucidate the actual process of creative manifestation of the phenomenal universe. From our contemporary perspective, we can appreciate the insubstantiality of the phenomenal manifestations of the physical world in terms of the Wave Structure of Matter indicated by QM.

The mystical realisation of the *nirguna Brahman* (plenum/void) parallels the QM notion of the Quantum vacuum ('Zero Point Field') actually being full of unimaginably vast amounts of energy. The *saguna Brahman* or manifest Creation is like an overspill or rippling over of the infinite formless plenum of Transcendental Consciousness. The Creation, at both the tiniest microcosmic level and at the cosmic cycle level of growing great and eventual dissolution, is not separate from the formless; the tiniest particle-like phenomena and even the expansion of space is a process continuously emanating within the absolute transcendental "space". Our mundane spatiotemporal world is not a background 'container' in which matter moves about, rather spatial and temporal relations actualise along with material manifestations. Our measures of Space, Time and Mass are all ultimately based on measurements of *waves in space*[110]. The *Maya* world or illusory appearance of the empirical world also parallels the QM understanding that matter is but a higher-level manifestation of the imperceptible energetic vibrations at a deeper level. As already indicated, the fundamental Planck equation ($e=hf$) relates the scientific notion of **energy** (and hence also **mass** due to $e=mc^2$) of a particle phenomenon to **wave** frequency and de Broglie showed that the Planck Constant (h) divided by the **momentum** of a particle gives the **wave**length (indicating a deeper level wave activity constituting the 'particle')[111, 112, 113, 114]. Thus **matter** is 'insubstantial', it is not some ultimate stuff but rather our cognitive abstraction of spatiotemporal forms from the underlying, continuous wave activity. The Mind/Matter paradox is simply the result of immature Western metaphysics.

In deep, subtle planes of manifesting existence, still transcending normal space and time, the yogi realises that normal spatiotemporal causality arises from a deeper transcendental, holistic causality wherein all phenomena are interconnected without limitations of space or normal temporality. We shall see that Milo Wolff's aforementioned holonomic wave model of the electron ties in with such yogic knowledge in that particle phenomena are actually created by the coalescence of wave-fronts from the entire 'universe' creating 'particle' like wave-centres from which new spherical scalar waves rebound outward to the rest of the universe. Thus all matter is interpenetrating (or 'entangled' in the language of QM) on a 'universal' scale and all true, transcendental causality *holonomic* (operating by relativity to everything else). Such 'holonomy' is found not only in Hindu and Buddhist traditions but also in the NeoPlatonic and Hermetic traditions of the Middle East and Europe. The yogi can also attain mystical realisations of the creative principles of phenomenal manifestation underlying all forms of existence and also subtle information emanating from all created things associated with the yogic notion of *akasa* (space as subtle matter (ether) characterised by vibration).

We saw above that 'stopping the mind' or 'introception' involves purifying the Stream of Consciousness of sensory and mental activity and content. The above-described Gestalt-switch like transformations between Nothingness and Fullness are related to the fact that contentless Pure Consciousness, though free of empirical superimpositions, under careful lucid discernment reveals itself to be totally full of vibratory 'subtle energy' or 'information'. The mystic experience of the subtlest vehicle of Consciousness floating in the flow of Light, welling forth full of subtle 'omniscient' information, a little of which may crystallise into subtle, inspired concepts, is known as the realisation of the dense luminous mass of ***prajna*** (wisdom-consciousness) or the *prajnaghana* in Vedanta. Plotinus said that *Nous* is omniscient, containing all contents of knowledge altogether at once[115]. According to von Franz, Jung described the archetypes as interpenetrating each other in a 'Cloud of Cognition'[116]. This perennial mystical realisation has led to notions of God's Infinite Wisdom and the myth of the Fount of All Wisdom, related to the term *gnosis* or divine knowledge from which we get "Gnosticism".

There is a remarkable quotation from the doxography of Hippolytus concerning the teachings of the Docetist sect of Gnostics (note that the Greek *chaos* here means the same as *hyle* or formless matter). The **Light** (of Intelligible Nature) or ***Sophia*** is described as having within itself *Ideas, infinite in number and this Light is said to endow Form upon the chaos by the action of Ideas*[117]. The Docetists, supposedly founded by a Julius Cassianus, developed a 'docetic Christology' claiming that Jesus's body was actually spiritual and only appeared to be carnal[118]. Thus, *contra* Nicene dogma, the physical human body is not to be saved. This belief was resurrected by the medieval Cathars in Southern France and neighbouring areas. They were not linked directly to the earlier Gnostics although they were influenced by Eastern Christianity. At the core of the Cathar religion, was the idea that the sacrament of the *consolamentum*, the Baptism of the Spirit, meant reunion of the soul with Divine Light (the heavenly spirit)[119]. The Catholic Church responded with the Albigensian Crusade, massacres, Inquisition, hangings and burning at the stake of the 'heretics' who threatened their authority.

Such mystical realisation is also related to the true meaning of the Greek word ***philosophia*** (Love of the "*Sophia*" or Divine Wisdom) which has been largely misunderstood and distorted in the racial fantasies of Classics misrepresenting the Ancient Greeks as non-mystical rationalists and modern Western conceptions of so-called "Philosophy". Most Western philosophers would not realise that, as Lee Bailey[120] points out, for Plato the purpose of Philosophy was to unforget that primal, vision of pure, powerful Light. In 2006, I heard a Professor Anthony O'Hear publicizing his new book *Plato's Children*[121] on BBC Radio. The title refers to contemporary British society. O'Hear gave a completely superficial misrepresentation of Plato's famous allegory of the cave as representing merely our difficulty in facing up to difficult truths about our lifestyles, consumer and celebrity culture etc. Like many Westerners O'Hear imagines Plato and other Ancient Greeks to resemble modern Western European secular rationalists ahead of their times, ignoring the glaring truth that Plato was actually a mystic believing in reincarnation. The term 'unforget' refers to Plato's doctrine of Recollection involving Past Life memories. The greater part of the 'world' of the Ancient Greeks (Hellenes) was in Afro-Asia rather than Europe thus the Hellenes were not even 'European' in the modern sense, let alone 'Westerners', but 'Mediterraneans'.

Similarly, we will later see that the alchemical myths of an Elixir of Life are similar projections of the mystical experience of the Divine Light as the energy that continually sustains our individuated conscious existence, a fact that ties in most beautifully with my identification of the direct physical correlate of the Divine Light of Pure Consciousness in the brain and its relationship with the scientific understanding of brain-death. Campbell tells us that the mythical Serpent sheds its skin, as the Moon sheds its shadow, to be born again. The serpent is also a symbol of Lunar Consciousness, that is to say, of Life Energy and Consciousness[122]. The famous Alchemist Robert Fludd spoke of the 'vivifying Light'. The *Hermetica* refers to God or *Nous* as Light (*phos*) and Life (*zoe*)[123]. The Christian 'Holy Spirit' is also referred to as the 'Giver of Life'[124]. We saw above that Merrell-Wolff also linked the flow of Consciousness to 'Life'. The medieval Persian Sufi Rumi called Mysticism "learning to die before you die"[125]. For Plato the True Philosopher, as with the Buddhist *arahant*, is a practitioner of Death in order to transcend it[126]. Medieval Christian mystics Theresa of Avila and John of the Cross stated that Mysticism was a preparation for death. The likes of Theresa, Julian of Norwich and Catharine of Siena were led to the spiritual path following NDEs[127].

This association of the Divine Light and the processes of Death have led in recent decades to a much wider acceptance in Western popular culture of the factuality of rare mystical experiences of the Divine Light, Transcendental and Universal Consciousness, and experiences of seeming 'omniscience' which have been reported by mystics in all cultures throughout history. This is because modern Medicine has allowed many thousands of people to survive close encounters with death and return to tell tales of their so-called Near Death Experiences (NDEs). Indeed, it was this experience of the Light in such NDEs which led to my breakthrough in 1994 when I realised that this Inner Light was correlated with the brainwaves generated by a well-established brain process known to all medics. This initial correlation has since been reinforced by a considerable amount of further research into authoritative yogic and mystical knowledge of the Light. The overwhelming evidence in favour of this identification of the (direct) physical correlate of the Divine Light of Pure Consciousness is presented throughout this book and the key pieces of evidence are collated in the Appendix.

That Thou Art: The Nondualist Doctrine of *Atman-Brahman*

However, this identification of the (direct) physical correlate of the Divine Light of Pure Consciousness leads to an understanding of the true nature of Consciousness and of Spirituality which turns on its head the Physicalist - Materialist metaphysics of modern Science (which imagines Consciousness to be a latecomer in the evolution of the supposedly insentient universe). It also undermines the dualist doctrines of Theistic religions which instil belief in a personal God (a Divine Personality resembling the human ego as opposed to an impersonal Godhead or Spirit) very different from a supposedly *immortal human soul* which Theism claims can never become one with the Divinity. Such strict dualism of a supposed personal God and a supposedly immortal human soul is found in the Theistic religions, Judaism, Christianity, Islam and Sikhism as well as in Theistic branches of Hinduism which claim that the individuated human consciousness never actually attain union with the Godhead (*Brahman*). The Semitic religions (Judaism, Christianity and Islam) all hold to common set of doctrines derived from Zoroastrian and Hebraic superstitions: Creation *ex nihilo* of the geocentric cosmos (extending to Neptune) by a man-like lawgiver god, some sort of Last Judgement at the End of this World, (i.e., the 'Earth' meaning Jerusalem or Arabia) after a few millennia and the physical resurrection, from the grave, of the dead bodies of the Community of the Faithful. And of course each believes, as did the Zoroastrians, that their own mythological beliefs constitute the 'One True Faith'.

Thus the **Great Secret of Existence** is that there is no God (nor an immortal soul) as the Theists believe but that, co-existing with our everyday waking and dreaming consciousness, there is another Divine Consciousness (the *Atman*) which can be uncovered through meditation and which is one with (or indistinguishable in essence from) the Transcendental Ground of all Being (the *nirguna Brahman*). The individual mind is identical in essence with this impersonal Absolute that can be experienced in this life rather than after death. Furthermore, advanced practise in encountering this Divine Light/ Consciousness can also lead to realisations of the creative principles underlying the entire cosmic manifestation (the *saguna Brahman*), known in the West as the ***archetypes*** from the *Archetypal Light* in the *Corpus Hermeticum* and as "Ideas in the Mind of God" in the writings of Augustine of Hippo. We saw above the Docetist Gnostics who described the Light of Sophia as full of infinite ideas and as informing the chaos (unformed matter or *hyle*). Whiteman interprets what A.A. McDonell in his 1917 translation of *Rig Veda* rendered in English as 'ordinances' (presumably *dharman*) to be equivalent to archetypes; the same 'ordinances' are to be found at work in Man's Spirit and manifest in the world[128]. Von Franz says that the Eastern *bija* (seed-potentialities) are equivalent to archetypes[129]. The Great Secret also involves realisations revealing that the phenomenal (or physical) world of Nature, studied by modern Science, is, like our own minds, a manifestation of this Godhead of Transcendental Pure Consciousness. Consciousness is not the late, complex, 'emergent' (actually meaning "magically appearing") product of Nature's evolution as Physicalism/Materialism asserts; rather the entire universe of Nature is a dynamic manifestation within this infinite Light of Pure Consciousness, the Absolute Plenum beyond all dualities, the Sheer Completeness (*purnam*) which, to our relative consciousness appears as No-thing-ness.

Such knowledge denying the existence of a personal God and asserting our essential identity with an impersonal Godhead is of course heresy to the dogmatic monotheists of the mythological Semitic religions who fear such Truth and thus try to suppress it. We saw above how these religions rose to prominence through coercion and forced-conversion rather than through philosophical interpretations of spiritual facts. Merrell-Wolff says that, before the final moment of transformation, he was aware of an Otherness but this vanished in Identity. Consequently, there was no need for the term God[130]. He also recognises that many Western scholars of Mysticism have fallen into the error of misunderstanding Buddha's (vaguely expressed) term *Nirvana* ('extinction' or 'blowing out' of a flame) in the absolute sense as meaning literal annihilation. The famous works of Pseudo-Dionysius (St Denis) have reinforced such false impressions[131]. Christopher Bache, who attained mystical union using Grof's holotropic breathwork methods, has stated in regard to the overrated notion of ineffability, if you can't represent even to yourself where you've been, you probably got lost[132]; or blanked-out into unconsciousness as Merrell-Wolff would put it. The anonymous medieval English author of *The Cloud of Unknowing* points out that the supposed "Divine Darkness" of Pseudo-Dionysios which illuminates the soul is spiritual Light, not actual 'darkness' as in such misleading negative terminology[133]. The Eastern Christian 'Dionysios the Areopagite' or St Denis is regarded as the Father of Christian Mysticism. In his *Theologia Mystica*, he developed the doctrines of Neoplatonist Proclus and refers to the "superlucent darkness of silence" or the "ray of Divine Darkness, stripped of all and loosed from all"[134]. Cary says that Pseudo-Dionysios, did in fact clarify the meaning of his phrase 'Divine Darkness' as a superabundance of Light[135] but I have found that some, supposedly knowledgeable Westerners, still think that there should literally be Darkness!

Merrell-Wolff says that Church Council theology shows great ingenuity in working out artificial conceptual constructions to give the mystical teachings of Jesus externalised meanings. Bodily self-torture grew out of the literal materialistic interpretation of Jesus's teachings. Indeed, he says that he finds no clear evidence that either Jesus or Buddha entered into the full trance state, (i.e., attained the deepest realisations)[136]. The cyclical Greek notion of time or *Aion* in the Gospels were reinterpreted by the Nicene Church to make punishment in the After-world (for the sinful) last forever and make the supposed incarnation of God in the man Jesus a unique event[137]. Before the Council of Nicaea outlawed mystical exploration as heresy, Augustine of Hippo immersed himself in the writings of Plotinus and wrote of Christ as the Inner Teacher and God as the Light found by the inward turn[138]. We shall see that my physical correlate of the Inner Light of Pure Consciousness (also known in Vedanta as the *saksin* or Witness Consciousness) explains such questions as how (the Inner Light of) Conscience as the Divine Authority within knows all of our thoughts and feelings. It also explains the Christian association between this Conscience and the 'Life-Giving' Holy Spirit which Catholic theologian James P. Hanigan argues are essentially one and the same[139].

The contemporary Christian theologian Phillip Cary was rather disturbed and worried in finding that Augustine himself, the great patriarch of Catholicism, had written such things and dismisses Plotinus's (heretical) view as "ugly, incoherent and false". Cary notes that the pre-Nicene Augustine tried to keep Divinity within the soul yet separate from the soul (to cater to Theistic Church dogma). However, if Divinity were within us, it could not remain an Otherness, (i.e., Theism) but must lead to the "strange identity" or Oneness taught by Plotinus[140]. Cary's "strange identity" is of course Nonduality. The Christian establishment's fear of such spiritual truth is clearly illustrated in the case of the great medieval German theologian and mystic, Meister Eckhart, who had held the same Chair (Professorship) in Paris as had Thomas Aquinas. Eckhart was not condemned as a heretic and put to death mainly because he died during his trial and was not hostile to the Church. But, Eckhart's mystical discoveries, very similar to those of the great seers who wrote the Upanishads over two thousand years earlier, were of course denounced as heresy by the Church.

Here God's ground is my ground and my ground is God's ground.
The knower and the known are one. Simple people imagine that they should see God as if he stood there and they here. This is not so. God and I, we are one in knowledge.

Meister Eckhart[141]

Eckhart also teaches that, from the timeless God flows the "flow of grace" creating an ever-present now so that God is simultaneously stillness and an everlasting flux[142]. Eckhart's references to a 'birth' (*geburt*) of 'the Son in the Soul'[143] reaffirm the true esoteric meaning of the Greek terms *Iesous Christos* and of the 'Virgin Birth' of a 'Son of God' (in the Purified or Virgin Spirit) as referring to well-known, perennial mystical experiences[144].

The dominant form of Brahmanism (*Vedanta*) holds to Nonduality (*Advaita*–prononounced 'adwaita'). I have used the word *nondual* above as referring to the transcendence of the subject/object relation leading to oneness (identity) of the knower and the known as in quotation from Eckhart. *Advaita* is better expressed as Absolute Monism, implying not only transcendence of subject/object duality but also Non-theism (as Theism involves a God/soul distinction or duality as in theistic *Dvaita Vedanta*) and a monism of Spirit and Nature (or Godhead and Creation) as ultimately the same in essence. From this nondual perspective, everything is experienced as Oneness with no real separation of seemingly distinct, individuated beings. Such Oneness is hinted at in the Christian notion of *atonement* (at-one-ment), the reconciliation of man with God. In his Christian Apologetics book *The New Age Movement and the Biblical Worldview*, Harvard scholar John Newport refers repeatedly to St Paul in attacking the essentially Vedantic ('All is One') views of US 'New Agers'[145]. Such reassertions of faith in Christian dogmata to defend Theism against 'New Age' Brahmanic teachings of finding Divinity within us and (Nondual) Monism are infantile philosophically and laughable. They are also disturbing in that Newport himself was actively involved in the New Age Movement and gives a reasonably good discussion of New Age groups and ideas. However a 'split-personality' emerges in such Christians, revealing their doctrinal 'brainwashing', as they proclaim that the supposed 'intellectual' and 'moral' superiority of Christianity is 'proved' by simply asserting superstitious dogmata with which they have been indoctrinated.

Newport defends the belief in 'Resurrection from the Grave' of the (decomposed) physical bodies of the true believers at the Last Judgement (a belief common to all three Semitic religions). He pronounces that Israel alone knew amongst nations that the world was not Divine, (i.e., Spirit/Nature dualism). Becoming a Christian means, says Newport, learning the story of Israel and Jesus and interpreting everything in terms of that story. Christianity, he claims, is rooted in verifiable Christian History[146]! In fact the Old Testament 'history' is largely a self-aggrandising fantasy constructed by the tiny Judaean tribal community. As *The Bible Unearthed* reveals, the stories of Abraham and the migration from Ur, Moses and the Exodus, Joshua and the conquest of Canaan, the great empire of David and Solomon etc. are discredited by the archeological facts and factual histories of the truly great imperial peoples such as the Egyptians and Babylonians. The Old Testament 'history' is largely a self-aggrandising, nationalistic myth concocted by King Josiah's priests known as the Deuteronomist ideology[147]. The only true historian to mention a historical Jesus was Flavius Josephus and then only in a trivial passing reference. This saved Josephus's work from burning by the Church. The Church also interpolated fanciful nonsense, falsely attributed to the Jew Josephus, that Jesus was the one and only Son of God.

The airbrushing and fabrication of history by the Church would make Stalin blush as we have seen with the demonisation of Emperor Julian and suppression of the Gnostics (who wrote their own Gospels). The four Gospels in the New Testament are not History but a mishmash of ethical parables, mystical allegories etc. written to be understood by a cognoscenti familiar with the traditional esoteric symbolism, certainly not meant to be read literally in vulgar English mistranslations. The name Dionysios means 'Son of God' in Phrygian and Dionysos was called the 'God of the Vine' in the Mystery Religions. The Gospels refer to Jesus's secret teaching and John chapter 15 refers to the 'God of the Vine'[148]. Whiteman says that St Paul's references to such traditional mystical terms would have been recognised immediately by his Hellenistic audiences in places such as Antioch and Corinth. That suffering was necessary for 'Redemption' and 'Raising' ('raising-up') was well known in the Ancient Eastern Mediterranean world. This teaching was related to the myth of the Tree of Life (which finds echoes in the symbol of the Wooden Cross). From early Mesopotamian times, the Tree was associated with Tammuz, 'the son who rises' and 'Lord of the faithful tree'. When St Paul spoke of *Christos* (Greek for 'the Annointed') being crucified, his hearers would have recognised the mystical meaning. St Paul was careful to use language that ruled out interpretation in terms of an historical event as found in the Gospel stories current a century later[149].

Joseph Campbell interpreted Saul's conversion on the Road to Damascus as Saul's realisation that the story of Jesus's death on a cross corresponded to the ancient Mystery Religions. Campbell even shows us a cylinder-seal from 300 *c.e.* (not long before the Council of Nicaea) depicting a man crucified on a cross above which is the moon (the 'Death and Resurrection' motif) and the Seven Stars of the Pleiades (known as the Lyre of Orpheus). The character being crucified is identified clearly in capital Greek letters as Orpheus-Bacchus. Orpheus is the Fisher who fishes us out of the Waters of Ignorance. Bacchus is also Dionysos (the Son of God)[150]. The famous 2nd Century *c.e.* Bishop Irenaeus stressed that the Cross symbol is related to the ancient myth of the *Axis Mundi* or Pillar of Light at the centre of the world that connects Earth and the After-world[151]. This imagery clearly reflects Near-Death Experiences of the Divine Light as found in Plato's myth of Er. Er comes back to life on his own funeral pyre and recounts his experience including the Pillar of Light connecting the worlds[152]. Campbell says that it was an accident of history that the Gospels came to be seen as the fruits of predictions (*tempoi*) in the Hebraic Old Testament. They could just as easily have woven together early Christianity with the Greek Tradition[153].

There was a great debate in early Christianity as to whether Christianity had anything to do with Judaism. Some early Christians (Gnostics) called Yahweh 'The Fool' as Yahweh deluded himself that he was God and that there was no higher power than Him. The Son was to carry us past Yahweh; the Son was a revelation of a Higher Light. And so Yahweh was equated with the Platonic demiurge that brought all the Agony, Evil and Sorrow into the world. This, says Campbell, was a very definite thrust in the early Christian tradition. Unlike the deities of older cultures, says Campbell, Yahweh is not the personification of an Energy that precedes his person; Yahweh is not open to receive the transpersonal, transcendent Light shining through[154].[N7] The famous Bishop Marcion of Sinope went as far to reject entirely the message of the Jewish Old Testament and its deity Yahweh as incompatible with the teachings of Jesus although the Council of Nicaea later decided to retain the Jewish Testament.

Newport concludes that Christians do not fear the Truth for, as it says in John; 8:32, it is the Truth that sets us free[155]. I doubt that Newport understood the mystical meaning of John's statement which relates to the freedom from worldly attachments, desire and fear experienced in the Bliss (*ananda*) aspect of mystical union. The Divine Light is the Light of Truth (Reality). The Gospels also say that the Kingdom of Heaven is within us. In regard to Newport's simplistic rejection of Nonduality or Oneness, let me quote St Paul from Galatians (*emphasis mine*)[156]:

> *Every partition has broken down, every restriction and distinction, and division* ***in the sight of God*** *has been abolished. The love of God is as all-embracing as the sky above us...* ***In Christ Jesus*** *there is neither Jew nor Greek, bond nor free, male nor female.*

Although some interpret this passage merely at the level of social differences, note how the phrase 'in Christ Jesus' here is used in a manner equivalent to 'in the Sight of God'. Thus in attaining *Christ Jesus* we attain a 'God's-eye-view', (i.e., Cosmic Consciousness) in which everything is Oneness.

Paul Deussen wrote that the Bible does not explain the meaning of the injunction "Love thy neighbour as yourselves". However, the meaning is found in the Upanishads with the famous *mahavakya* (grand pronouncement), *Tat tuam asi* (That thou art)[157]. This is perhaps not surprising for Guy Sorman, following the famous Orientalist Ernest Renan, asserts that the Christian emphasis on Love and Charity was a total break from earlier Hebraic teachings.[N8] Sorman sees these new teachings of Jesus as derived from the Indian Buddhism of Emperor Asoka's missionaries whose monasteries in Alexandria, Antioch and other Hellenistic capitals were still present, after over 500 years, at the start of the 4th Century *c.e.*[158]. The notion of self-examination in Consciousness (Conscience) also originated in the teachings of the Buddha[159].

From the ultimate perspective, after dissolution of the individuated subtle bliss-vehicle, there is no individual "soul", the *Atman* is taken to be the same in all individuals. This assertion has created confusion as to how each of us has the *Atman* within but which is the same *Atman* as in everyone else as two different types of Consciousness are involved. My identification of the physical correlate of the *Atman* helps resolve this confusion (as well as undermining the previously mentioned Constructivists in Comparative Religion). There is an *Atman* in each of us (as viewed from our everyday Waking or Empirical conscious perspective) but this set of activating brainwaves is simultaneously **universal** in the sense that it is the same in every human; it has no personal differentiation due to our memories or cultural information, (i.e., it is *impersonal*).

The Constructivists deny that there can be a common core mysticism of the Light as they claim that all mental processes are 'constructed' or mediated by our cultures and individual perceptual biases. Such assertions are bandied about as authoritative views by academics in Comparative Religion who possess little, if any, knowledge of the actual scientific facts. Medicine has long recognised a brain process which is the same in everyone, underlying all other gross brain activity; the Reticular Activating System. Medicine even distinguishes this *activating* or **arousal** activity (the prerequisite for any form of Consciousness) from the **content** of Consciousness! But this sense of (common human or 'archetypal') *universality* of the *Atman* due to its lack of differentiation between individuals, its lack of gross cognitive content, is considering it as an objective concept from the empirical perspective of individuated, ego consciousness.

The other sense of (cosmic) *universality* is apparent only if one can attain ego dissolution then there is the actual experience of Oneness with all created entities. *Advaita Vedanta* stresses the essential identity of the *Atman* within each one of us and the macrocosmic Light of Pure Consciousness, the Divine Ground of All Being (*nirguna Brahman*). *Brahman* is **not** God (or like an individual person) but an impersonal Absolute Spirit, the transcendental source and the all-pervading substance of Creation. Merrell-Wolff notes that the generally held (misconceived) view of Western Idealists is that Consciousness is an attribute of Spirit rather than itself being Spirit[160]. The term *Idealism* based on the Greek primacy of Thought/Intellect and Geometric, Idealistic abstractions is not appropriate in regard to the Brahmanic Primacy of Consciousness (a concept that never existed in Ancient Greek philosophy).

It is important to realise here that Christianity, as well as being dualistic in the theistic sense in denying the individual's essential identity with God, is dualistic in another sense. Christianity holds to the doctrine of *Creatio ex nihilo* with a substance dualism of "God" (conceived as like a human person writ large) and Nature. The Christians' 'Nature' is not created out of Godhead as is the case in *Advaita Vedanta* or the more thoroughly monistic Nondual Kashmir Saivism. The Christian 'Nature' is created magically out of absolutely nothing and a personal (human ego-like) God is sovereign over it. This dualism was implicit in Newton's conception of the 'Laws of Nature' designed to keep the Christian God as Prime Mover and maintainer of harmonious order[161]. Descartes' teacher Mersenne, an ardent Catholic, helped eradicate occultist notions of the World Soul (*anima mundi*) implying that Nature was both animate and sentient from Natural Philosophy[162]. Until Descartes made the clockwork image of the universe a soulless automaton or **mechanism**, Christian theologians such as Nicholas of Cusa in his *Vision of God* (1453) used the clock image to represent God's Divine Plan working itself out in human history[163].

This pre-existing Christian Spirit/Nature dualism was reinforced in the West by Galileo's concept of Primary and Secondary Qualities. Galileo considered only the quantifiable properties of an object like weight and length to be real calling these 'primary' qualities whereas colours and other subjective attributes were held to be 'secondary' and not real. This was influenced by Plato's notions of the subjectivity of sensory appearances whereas Geometry was (supposed to be) objective[164]. We still find famous scientists asserting naively that Ultimate Reality is Geometry! This reduction of Nature to quantities clearly indicates Pythagorean influence as well. Pythagoras considered numbers to be the ultimate realities. As stated above, Galileo's supposedly primary qualities actually presuppose a conscious observer to determine them. Even Newton recognised this fallacy[165]. But the point to note here is that, not only Christianity, but Greek-influenced Natural Philosophy also "**de-spiritualised**" Nature. By abstracting only idealised, mathematically quantifiable aspects of Nature, Science de-spiritualises Nature by abstraction. Epistemologically naive Physicalists and Materialists then mistake these idealised, skeletal constructions as depictions of Reality as it actually is.

Although early Buddhism (known as Hinayana or 'the Lesser Vehicle') rejected a theistic personal God and an immortal soul, it also rejected the Brahmanic Ground of all Being. It thus mired itself in self-created paradoxes of an insubstantial world created constantly out of discontinuous moments appearing and disappearing out of *absolutely nothing* or even out of each other. The later Buddhist Mahayana (the 'Greater Vehicle') has in some of its branches, especially the sort of Tibetan Buddhism advocated by the Dalai Lama, reinstated a Transcendental Consciousness as the Ground of all Being. The well-known branch of Mahayana Buddhism known as the Middle Way (*Madhyamaka*), steeped in the, seemingly nihilistic, negative discourse of the Indian Buddhist Nagarjuna rejects a Ground of all Being. This can only be due to dogmatic adherence to Nagarjuna's teachings which, if actually based on his own realisations, imply that he did not attain the deepest and most ultimate realisations. Buddhist scholar and practitioner Herbert Guenther tells us that Nagarjuna was a Logical Reductionist who thought in static terms and failed to gain a holistic understanding of lived reality[166]. Guenther adds[167]:

> *The much vaunted Madhyamaka philosophy, particularly in its Prasangika version is the ultimate in reductionism, and its manifestation as dogmatic intolerance in Tibetan history is well known. This system has much in common with the now-defunct Western school of logical positivism and its anemic revival, "analytical" philosophy. For this reason, the Madhyamaka system has attracted the attention of academics who, because of their tacit presuppositions, unwittingly paint a one-sided picture of Buddhist thought.*

We shall see that father of American psychology, William James' own experiences of the so-called 'Stream of Consciousness' and founder of European phenomenology, Edmund Husserl's experiences of the Flow of the Absolute or Temporal Consciousness are in fact modern rediscoveries of the flow of the Light of Pure Consciousness underlying our minds and that both James and Husserl unwittingly confirm the Hindu position of the ultimate continuity of Consciousness as opposed to the Buddhists' abstraction of discrete 'moments' or 'pulses'. Niels Bohr cited James in regard to Bohr's Principle of Complementarity[168]:

Just as light becomes both wave and particles, consciousness is both substantive and transitive, both a pulsing and a continuous wave.

Bohr's much-hyped Complementarity Principle is basically just epistemological 'Neutral Monism', the view that human concepts can only capture dichotomous aspects of an underlying Reality whose true nature transcends our conceptual constructs of e.g., Mind and Matter, waves and particles etc. But as we have seen, Matter actually reduces to cognitively abstracted forms in Consciousness just as 'particles' reduce to seemingly distinct forms abstracted from more fundamental wave activity.

Merrell-Wolff also recognised that discontinuous 'Momentariness' (the Buddhist *ksanika*) is a product of abstraction by the ego mind from the true underlying continuity of the Transcendental Absolute Consciousness which he asserts is the true *Nirvana*[169]. In O/OM I argued that the Hindu doctrine of *Ekatattva* (the One Principle) is a deeper insight inclusive of more of Reality subsuming the (less inclusive) Buddhist view of Momentariness which results from abstraction of wave-peaks from the underlying 'continuously vibrating energy field' description of the Inner Light given by the Hindu *Yoga Sutra* tradition. It should be noted that a **physical** correlate (in this case brainwaves) is, by definition, a spatiotemporally limited empirical concept. It is of necessity an abstraction and captures only part of the energetic aspect of the Absolute which generates the "illusory" multiplicity of phenomena. The seeming discontinuity, (i.e., separate brainwaves) of my correlate of the Inner Light results from our empirical discrimination of multiplicity at the spatiotemporal level of energetic activity (the *Prana* aspect of the Light) masking the underlying Oneness of Consciousness in itself (the *nirguna Brahman*).

The *Advaita Vedanta* and the *Yoga Sutra* traditions, as with Buddhist schools, give useful insights into the Phenomenology of Perception and the nature of the mind. The Nondual or 'Monistic' form of Kashmir Saivism, the most sophisticated branch of Hinduism in regard to its understanding of creative manifesticn, refers to the Ground of all Being as the Supreme Shiva, the Absolute Consciousness or the Great Light which is explicitly equivalent to the Vedantic *nirguna Brahman*. Shiva is best known as *Siva Nataraj* (Shiva, the Lord of Dance); with Shiva's dance representing the creative, cosmic energy of the Godhead. This energetic *Shakti* aspect of the Absolute is emphasised in Hindu Tantrism therefore this Kashmir Saivism may be referred to as 'Tantric'. Nondual Kashmir Saivism correctly challenges the misinterpretations of the Upanishads by Sankara, the most famous exponent of *Advaita Vedanta*, that the phenomenal (or physical) world is mere illusion (*maya*) and false. The very word *Brahman* comes from the Sanskrit root *brih* meaning "to grow" indicating that *Brahman* ("growing great") becomes the universe[170]. The Vedantic summaries of the Upanishads known as the *Brahmasutras* stress the noton of *parinama* or 'transformation' of Brahman[171]. In contrast to Sankara's supposedly unchanging Ground of all Being the Saivites stress the energetic, creative aspect of the Ground. The Kashmiri Saivites' view of Creation, with its Doctrine of Vibration, actually resembles those of Gaudapada, Sankara's great predecessor in the *Advaita* tradition and also with the modern scientific understanding of the true nature of energy and matter. As stated above, this Doctrine of Vibration is actually rooted in the

Upanishadic doctrine of the *Panch Bhuta* (five 'elements') with the first-created element *Akasa* (space as subtle matter, ether) characterised by **vibration**. Sankara's misleading views have been taken by many Westerners and modern Neo-Hindus (keen to show off Sankara's Scholastic-like Rationalism) to be the authoritative Hindu position although the likes of Ramakrishna and Aurobindo have stressed Tantric views. Unlike *Advaita Vedanta*, monistic Kashmir Saivism also stresses, explicitly, the fact that Pure Consciousness is Divine Light or Luminous Consciousness.

References

1. Lal, B.B. "Aryan Invasion of India: perpetuation of a myth". In Edwin F. Bryant and Laurie L. Patton (Editors) (2005) *The Indo-Aryan Controversy: Evidence and inference in Indian history*. Routledge.
2. Barua, B.P. (1988) *Raja Rammohan Roy and the New Learning*, Sangam Books and Orient Longman.
3. Dirks, Nicholas, B. (2006) *The Scandal of Empire: India and the Creation of Imperial Britain*, The Belknap Press (Harvard University Press).
4. Davis, Mike (2001) *Late Victorian Holocausts: El Niño Famines and the Making of the Third World,* Verso.
5. Polya, Gideon has written various articles on the Bengal Holocaust viewable on the Internet including "UK BBC Holocaust Denial" on www.Countercurrents.org/polya/2400509.htm
6. Mukerjee, Madhushree (2010) *Churchill's Secret War: The British Empire and the Ravaging of India during World War II*, Basic Books.
7. Davis, Mike (2001) *ibid.*
8. Mukerjee, Madhushree (2010) *ibid.*
9. Feuerstein, Georg, Kak, Subhash and Frawley, David (1995) *In Search of the Cradle of Civilisation: New Light on Ancient India*, Quest Books.
10. Bryant, Edwin (2001) *The Quest for the Origins of Vedic Culture: The Indo-Aryan Migration Debate*, Oxford University Press.
11. "Aryan-Dravidian divide a myth: Study" *The Times of India* (Newspaper) 25th September 2009.
12. Lal, B.B. (2005) *ibid.*
13. Daniélou, Alain (1986) "The Caste Institution". Reprinted in Daniélou, Alain (2005) *India – A Civilisation of Differences: The Ancient Tradition of Universal Tolerance*, Inner Traditions.
14. Trautmann, Thomas R. "Introduction". In Thomas R. Trautmann (editor) (2005) *The Aryan Debate*, Oxford University Press.
15. Schwab, Raymond (1950, French) English translation *The Oriental Renaissance: Europe's Rediscovery of India and the East 1680-1880* (1984) Columbia University Press.
16. Bryant, Edwin (2001) *ibid.*
17. Asher, Catherine B. "A Ray from the Sun: Mughal ideology and the Visual Construction of the Divine". In Matthew T. Kapstein (Editor) (2004) *The Presence of Light: Divine Radiance and Religious Experience*, Chicago University Press.

18. Barua, B.P. (1988) *ibid.*
19. Barua, B.P, (1988) *ibid.*
20. Sorman, Guy (2001) *The Genius of India*, McMillan India.
21. Sorman, Guy (2008) *The Empire of Lies: The Truth about China in the 21st Century*, Encounter Books.
22. Davis, Mike (2001) *ibid.*
23. James, William (1902) *The Varieties of Religious Experience*, Longmans, Green, and Co.
24. Curtis, Mark (2010) *Secret Affairs: Britain's Collusion with Radical Islam*, Serpents Tail (Profile Books Ltd).
25. Kirsch, Jonathan (2004) *God Against the Gods: The History of the War between Monotheism and Polytheism*, Viking Compass.
26. Sorman, Guy (2001) *ibid.*
27. Shahak, Israel (1994) *Jewish History, Jewish Religion: The Weight of Three Thousand Years*, Pluto Press.
28. Sand, Shlomo (2009) *The Invention of the Jewish People*, Verso.
29. Rose, John (2004) *The Myths of Zionism*, Pluto Press.
30. Finkelstein, Israel and Silberman, Neil A. (2002) *The Bible Unearthed: Archaeology's New Vision of Ancient Israel and the Origin of its Sacred Texts*, Touchstone (Simon and Schuster).
31. Sand, Shlomo (2009) *ibid.*
32. Kirsch, Jonathan (2004) *ibid.*
33. Versluis, Arthur (1993) *American Transcendentalism and Asian Religions*, Oxford University Press.
34. Yates, Frances (1964) *Giordano Bruno and the Hermetic Tradition*, Routledge and Kegan Paul.
35. Radhakrishnan, Sarvepalli (1940) *Eastern Religions and Western Thought (2nd Edn)*, Oxford University Press.
36. Anderson, William (1996) *The Face of Glory: Creativity, Consciousness and Civilisation*, Bloomsbury.
37. Anderson, William (1996) *ibid.*
38. Anderson, William (1996) *ibid.*
39. Kanigel, Robert (1991) *The Man Who Knew Infinity: A Life of the Genius Ramanujan*, Scribners.
40. Whiteman, J.H. Michael (1967) *Philosophy of Space and Time and the Inner Constitution of Nature: A Phenomenological Study*, Muirhead Library of Philosophy, George Allen and Unwin and the Humanities Press.
41. Kanigel, Robert (1991) *ibid.*
42. Kanigel, Robert (1991) *ibid.*
43. Merrell-Wolff, Franklin (1995) *Transformations in Consciousness: The Metaphysics and Epistemology* (Containing His *Introceptualism*), State University of New York Press.
44. Abraham, Ralph (2008) *Mathematics and the Psychedelic Revolution* (on-line article), www.ralph-abraham.org, MS#124.

45. Tieszen, Richard (2005) *Phenomenology, Logic, and the Philosophy of Mathematics*, Cambridge University Press.
46. d'Espagnat, Bernard (2006) *On Physics and Philosophy*, Princeton University Press.
47. Grof, Stanislaw (1985) *Beyond the Brain: Birth, Death and Transcendence in Psychotherapy*, State University of New York Press.
48. Hass, Lawrence, (2008) *Merleau-Ponty's Philosophy*, Indiana University Press.
49. Tieszen, Richard (2005) *ibid.*
50. Merrell-Wolff, Franklin (1995) *ibid.*
51. Kanigel, Robert (1991) *ibid.*
52. Hammond, Richard on *Richard Hammond and the Holy Grail* (Television Programme), British Broadcasting Corporation, January 2006.
53. Campbell, Joseph (1990) *Transformations of Myth through Time*, Harper and Row.
54. Anderson, William (1996) *ibid.*
55. Whiteman, J.H. Michael (2006) *Universal Theology and Life in the Other Worlds*, Colin Smythe.
56. Campbell, Joseph (1990) *ibid.*
57. Whiteman, J.H. Michael (2006) *ibid.*
58. Campbell, Joseph (1990) *ibid.*
59. Campbell, Joseph (2008) *The Hero with a Thousand Faces (3rd Edn)*, New World Library.
60. Yates, Frances (1964) *ibid.*
61. Anderson, William (1996) *ibid.*
62. Merrell-Wolff, Franklin (1995) *ibid.*
63. Merrell-Wolff, Franklin (1995) *ibid.*
64. Merrell-Wolff, Franklin (1995) *ibid.*
65. Whiteman, J.H. Michael (1967) *ibid.*
66. Bhattacharya, Sutapas (1999) *The Oneness/Otherness Mystery: The Synthesis of Science and Mysticism,* Motilal Banarsidass.
67. Whitehead, Alfred N. (1919) *The Concept of Nature*, Cambridge University Press.
68. Whitehead, Alfred North (1925) *Science and the Modern World*, MacMillan.
69. Malin, Shimon (2001) *Nature Loves to Hide: Quantum Physics and Reality, a Western Perspective*, Oxford University Press.
70. Kealey, Daniel "The Theoria of Nature in Plotinus and the Yoga of the Earth Consciousness in Aurobindo". In Paulos Mar Gregorios (Editor) (2002) *Neoplatonism and Indian Philosophy*, State University of New York Press.
71. von Franz, Marie-Louise (1992), *Psyche and Matter*, Shambhala Publications.
72. Coward, Harold (1985) *Jung and Eastern Thought*, State University of New York Press.
73. Lindorff, David (2004) *Jung and Pauli: The Meeting of Two Great Minds*, Quest Books.
74. Sartre, Jean-Paul (1957; English translation) *Being and Nothingness: An essay on phenomenological ontology*, Methuen and Co.

75. Goonatilake, Susantha (1998) *Toward a Global Science: Mining Civilisational Knowledge*, Indiana University Press.
76. Austin, James H. (1998) *Zen and the Brain: Toward an Understanding of Meditation and Consciousness*, MIT Press.
77. Skrbina, David (2005) *Panpsychism in the West*, MIT Press.
78. Goonatilake, Susantha (1998) *ibid.*
79. Skrbina, David (2005) *ibid.*
80. Skrbina, David (2005) *ibid.*
81. Goonatilake, Susantha (1998) *ibid.*
82. Brown, Daniel P. "The Stages of Meditation in Cross-Cultural Perspective". In Ken Wilber, Jack Engler and Daniel P. Brown (Editors) (1986) *Transformations of Consciousness: Conventional and Contemplative Perspectives on Development*, Shambhala Publications.
83. Brown, Daniel (1986) *ibid.*
84. Indich, William, M. (1980) *Consciousness in Advaita Vedanta*, Motilal Banarsidass.
85. Merrell-Wolff, Franklin (1994) *Franklin Merrell-Wolff's Experience and Philosophy: A Personal Record of Transformation and a Discussion of Transcendental Consciousness*: Containing his *Philosophy of Consciousness without an Object* and *His Pathways through to Space*, State University of New York Press.
86. Merrell-Wolff, Franklin (1994) *ibid.*
87. Grof, Stanislaw (1998) *The Cosmic Game: Explorations of the Frontiers of Human Consciousness*, State University of New York Press.
88. Benedict, Mellen-Thomas "Through the Light and Beyond". In Lee W. Bailey and Jenny Yates (Editors) (1996) *The Near-Death Experience: A Reader*, Routledge.
89. Merrell-Wolff, Franklin (1995) *ibid.*
90. Merrell-Wolff, Franklin (1994) *ibid.*
91. Ghose, Aurobindo (Sri Aurobindo) (1948) *The Synthesis of Yoga*, Sri Aurobindo Ashram Publications.
92. Ghose, Aurobindo (1948) *ibid.*
93. Satprem (1968, English translation) *Sri Aurobindo or the Adventure of Consciousness*, Sri Aurobindo Ashram Publications.
94. Kealey, Daniel (2002) *ibid.*
95. Ghose, Aurobindo (Sri Aurobindo) (1939) *The Life Divine*, Sri Aurobindo Ashram Publications.
96. Merrell-Wolff, Franklin (1995) *ibid.*
97. d'Espagnat, Bernard (2006) *ibid.*
98. Whiteman, J.H. Michael (1967) *ibid.*
99. de Sautoy, Marcus "How Long is A Piece of String". 11th April 2009. Episode in *Horizon* series on BBC Television.
100. Nagel, Thomas. Excerpted in chapter entitled "Thomas Nagel" in D.S. Clarke (2004) *Panpsychism: Past and Recent Selected Readings*, State University of New York Press.

101. Merrell-Wolff, Franklin (1995) *ibid.*
102. Tieszen, Richard (2005) *ibid.*
103. Merrell-Wolff, Franklin (1995) *ibid.*
104. Ghose, Aurobindo (1939) *ibid.*
105. Dyczkowski, Mark S.G. (1987) *The Doctrine of Vibration: An Analysis of the Doctrines and Practises of Kashmir Shaivism*, State University of New York Press.
106. Lott, Eric (1980) *Vedantic Approaches to God*, MacMillan/Harper and Row.
107, Bowes, Pratima "Mysticism in the Upanishads and Sankara's Vedanta". In Karel Werner (Editor) (1989), *The Yogi and the Mystic: Studies in Comparative Mysticism*, Curzon Press.
108. Merrell-Wolff, Franklin (1995) *ibid.*
109. Radhakrishnan, Sarvepalli (1953) *The Principal Upanisads*, (Centenary Edition 1989), Unwin Hyman.
110. Wolff, Milo (1990) *Exploring the Physics of the Unknown Universe*, Technotran Press.
111. Whiteman, J.H. Michael (1967) *ibid.*
112. Schommers, Wolfram (1995) *Symbols, Pictures and Quantum Reality: On the Theoretical Foundations of the Physical Universe*, World Scientific.
113. Wolff, Milo (2008) *Schrödinger's Universe: Einstein, Waves and the Origin of the Natural Laws*, Technotran Press.
114. Arp, Halton (1998) *Seeing Red: Redshifts, Cosmology and Academic Science*, Apeiron.
115. Kealey, Daniel (2002) *ibid.*
116. von Franz, Marie-Louise (1984) "Some Reflections on Synchronicity". English translation in Marie-Louise von Franz (1992) *Psyche And Matter*, Shambhala Publications.
117. Pepin, Jean "Theories of Procession in Plotinus and the Gnostics". In Richard T. Wallis (Editor) and Jay Bregman (Associate Editor) (1992) *Neoplatonism and Gnosticism*, State University of New York Press.
118. Mahé, Jean-Pierre "Gnostic and Hermetic Ethics" and van den Broek, Roelof "The Cathars: Medieval Gnostics?". Both in Roelof van den Broek and Wouter J. Hanegraaff (1998) *Gnosticism and Hermeticism: From Antiquity to Modern Times*, State University of New York Press.
119. van den Broek, Roelof "The Cathars: Medieval Gnostics?". In Roelof van den Broek and Wouter J. Hanegraaff (1998) *Gnosticism and Hermeticism: From Antiquity to Modern Times*, State University of New York Press.
120. Bailey, Lee, W. "Unknown Well-known Near-Death Experiences: Peter Sellers, Eddie Rickenbacker, Plato, and Black Elk." In Lee W. Bailey and Jenny Yates (Editors) (1996) *The Near-Death Experience: A Reader*, Routledge.
121. O'Hear, Anthony. Interview with Simon Mayo on BBC Radio 5, 2006.
122. Campbell, Joseph (1990) *ibid.*
123. Mahé, Jean-Pierre (1998) *ibid.*
124. Hanigan, James P. "Conscience and the Holy Spirit". In Charles E. Curran (Editor) (2004) *Conscience*, (Readings in Moral Theology No.14) Paulist Press.

125. Cressy, Judith "Mysticism and the Near-Death Experience" In Lee W. Bailey and Jenny Yates (Editors) (1996) *The Near-Death Experience: A Reader*, Routledge.
126. Obeyesekere, Gananath (2002) *Imagining Karma: Ethical Transformation in Amerindian, Buddhist and Greek Rebirth*, University of California Press.
127. Cressy, Judith (1996) *ibid.*
128. Whiteman, J.H. Michael (1967) *ibid.*
129. Von Franz, Marie-Louise (1978) "The Psychological Experience of Time". In Marie-Louise Von Franz (1992) *Psyche And Matter*, Shambhala Publications.
130. Merrell-Wolff, Franklin (1995) *ibid.*
131. Merrell-Wolff, Franklin (1995) *ibid.*
132. Bache, Christopher (2000) *Dark Night, Early Dawn: Steps to a Deep Ecology of Mind*, State University of New York Press.
133. Wolters, Clifton (1961) Introduction. In Clifton Wolters (Translator) (1961) *The Cloud of Unknowing and Other Works*, Penguin Books.
134. Radhakrishnan, Sarvepalli (1940) *Eastern Religions and Western Thought (2nd Edn),* Oxford University Press.
135. Cary, Phillip (2000) *Augustine's Invention of the Inner Self: The Legacy of a Christian Platonist*, Oxford University Press.
136. Merrell-Wolff, Franklin (1995) *ibid.*
137. Anderson, William (1996) *ibid.*
138. Cary, Phillip (2000) *ibid.*
139. Hanigan, James P. (2004) *ibid.*
140. Cary, Phillip (2000) *ibid.*
141. Forman, Robert K.C. (1991) *Meister Eckhart: Mystic as Theologian*, Element.
142. Von Franz, Marie-Louise (1978) *Time: Rhythm and Repose*, Thames and Hudson.
143. Forman, Robert K.C. (1991) *ibid.*
144. Whiteman, J.H. Michael (2006) *ibid.*
145. Newport, John P. (1998) *The New Age Movement and the Biblical Worldview: Conflict and Dialogue*, William B. Eerdmans Publishing Company.
146. Newport, John (1998) *ibid.*
147. Finkelstein, Israel and Silberman, Neil Asher (2002) *The Bible Unearthed: Archaeology's New Vision of Ancient Israel and the Origin of its Sacred Texts*, Touchstone (Simon and Schuster).
148. Whiteman, J.H. Michael (2006) *ibid.*
149. Whiteman, J.H. Michael (2006) *ibid.*
150. Campbell, Joseph (1990) *ibid.*
151. Sismanian, Ara Alexandru (1985-6) "Le Nombre et son Ombre (Resumé)". In Richard T. Wallis (Editor) and Jay Bregman (Associate Editor) (1992) *Neoplatonism and Gnosticism*, State University of New York Press.
152. Obeyesekere, Gananath (2002) *ibid.*
153. Campbell, Joseph (1990) *ibid.*
154. Campbell, Joseph (1990) *ibid.*

155. Newport, John (1998) *ibid.*
156. Bhandarkar, D.R. (1925) *Aœoka*, University of Calcutta. Reprinted 2005 by Asian Educational Services.
157. Radhakrishnan, Sarvepalli (1940) *ibid.*
158. Sorman, Guy (2001) *ibid.*
159. Bhandarkar, D.R. (1925) *ibid.*
160. Merrell-Wolff , Franklin (1995) *ibid.*
161. Jacob, Margaret, C. (1976) *The Newtonians and the English Revolution 1689-1720*, Cornell University Press.
162. Yates, Frances (1964) *ibid.*
163. Von Franz, Marie-Louise (1978) *ibid.*
164. Burtt, E.A. (1954) *The Metaphysical Foundations of Modern Physical Science, 2nd Revised Edn*, Doubleday.
165. Burtt, E.A. (1954) *ibid.*
166. Guenther, Herbert V. (1989) *From Reductionism to Creativity: rDzogs-chen and the New Science of Mind,* Shambhala Publications.
167. Guenther, Herbert V. (1989) *ibid.*
168. Hunt, Harry T. (1995) *On the Nature of Consciousness: Cognitive, Phenomenological, and Transpersonal Perspectives*, Yale University Press.
169. Merrell-Wolff, Franklin (1995) *ibid.*
170. Chatterji, J.C. (1931) *India's Outlook on Life: The Wisdom of the Vedas*, (reprinted 1973 as *The Wisdom of the Vedas*) The Theosophical Publishing House.
171. Lott, Eric (1980) *ibid.*

3

The True 'Light of Truth': The Link between Spiritual and Material Realms

Western Rationalist Distortions and Constructivist Denials of True Enlightenment

In his 2007 BBC TV series *The Story of India* British historian Michael Wood depicted the years that Siddharta Gautama spent seeking enlightenment as merely getting away from the crowd, sitting under a tree, clearing his mind and *thinking* things through (*emphasis mine*)! This is as much a travesty as the claim that all Alchemists were trying transmute lead into gold. The Europeans refer to the 18th Century *c.e.* period of Rationalist re-examination of traditional thought as 'The Enlightenment'. As I mentioned in Chapter 1, in episode one of his TV series *Light Fantastic*, Cambridge Historian of Science Simon Schaffer presented Eurocentric and anti-mystical myths. He downplayed the shamanic mysticism of Empedocles (who claimed to be Divine and to be able to save souls from Hades)[1]. He even claimed erroneously that Greek culture dominated India after Alexander's (brief) incursion into (the Persian-occupied part of) India. In fact, as discussed in Chapter 4, the Doctrine of the Elements for which Empedocles became famous was a corrupt form of the Upanishadic *panch bhuta*[2, 3, 4]. The original Upanishadic version parallels 21st Century scientific understanding whereas Empedocle's version is no more than a museum relic. Schaffer's first episode concluded with Schaffer presenting Isaac Newton as just a 'Natural Philosopher'. No mention was made of the fact that Newton spent more time on mystical studies and thought that these were more important than his work in Natural Philosophy. According to Schaffer, Newton's study of the diffraction of Light using a prism disproved the ancient myths of Divine Light and led to the true (Rationalist) "Enlightenment" in Europe. As with Professor Al-Khalili's dismissal of Alchemy, Schaffer dismissed the notion of Divine Light without understanding what he was referring to!

The use of the term 'The Enlightenment' for the 18th Century Rationalist transformation of European high culture is rather apt in regard to mainstream European thought mistaking true (spiritual) enlightenment to be a mere metaphor rather than as a special mode of knowledge acquisition by Divine Illumination. Immanuel Kant famously denied this 'Third Mode of Knowledge' beyond the limitations of Sensation and Conception[5]. In his *The Shape of Ancient Thought*, Thomas McEvilley states that most Western scholars have difficulty with the phrase "destroying the hypotheses", in Plato's *Republic*. Some amend the text to remove this key phrase whilst others reject Plato's obvious meaning out of hand. The mind is drawn by negative dialectic, beyond the realms of Mathematics and Astronomy, which it destroys in passing. The 'wisdom eye' or 'eye of the soul' rises above the false knowledge of the sense-world to the higher realm of Mathematics and Astronomy but these non-sensory 'tools' must, in their turn, also be cleansed. Progressive cleaning of the 'wisdom eye' requires annihilating these tools (these hypotheses) befouling the 'wisdom eye':

> *Now the wisdom eye sees, and the light of knowledge, which, like the sun shining on a shuttered window, has always been right there waiting, shines in.*
>
> Plato[6]

We saw that Merrell-Wolff acknowledged the traditional view that a well-developed intellect is a barrier to enlightenment. Obeyesekere notes that Reason itself is a barrier to *nirvana* or *moksa*[7]. The use of the term *supra-rational* knowledge would thus be appropriate in regard to the Divine Wisdom (*Sophia*) gleaned through the Divine Illumination or *gnosis* attained through true spiritual enlightenment. But I have used a quotation from Plato whose Demiurge (the speculative 'Creator God') in the *Timaeus* is the embodiment of Reason itself[8]. Obeyesekere says that Plato apotheosised Reason. Reason is for Plato the objective faculty that permits one to understand the nature of the world[9]. Wolfgang Pauli wrote that Plato associated the (supposedly) eternal, unchanging Idea with the Rationality of Being[10]. Such *Logocentrism* (the view that human Reason mirrors the supposedly 'real order in Nature' or the *Logos*) permeates Western thought. Francis Bacon endeavoured to show that the 'Laws of Nature' are there in Nature to be discovered by the knowing mind. The reason why our minds are capable of inductive learning and leaping is because there is an orderliness, partly visible and partly invisible, pervading Nature. The Divine Mind informed Nature[11]. Plotinus went beyond Plato's fixation on (human generic) Ideas with his supposedly ineffable One beyond the Ideas or Forms in *Nous* (Plotinus's realm of unity-in-multiplicity which is the first emanation from the One). Plato's supposedly eternal Ideas such as Good and Beauty are actually no more than human constructs, value judgements, projected onto the Light. Echoing Pythagoras, Plato saw Ideas as patterns of Numbers[12]. For Plotinus there is no discursive thought in *Nous*, no passing from one point to another[13]. In *Nous* everything is something primarily and everything else subsidiarily[14]. This is not *Reason* related to *Ratio* and supposedly perfect Rational Numbers; this is holonomic *prajna*, the luminous **Wisdom**-Consciousness which transcends dichotomous human Reason.

As with nearly all great philosophical mystics from all cultures, Plato asserts that the Light of Wisdom is in fact present in everyone but clouded over by concepts and sense perceptions, (i.e., mental activity), a point stressed by Forman *et al.* in *The Innate Capacity: Mysticism, Psychology and Philosophy*[15]. Thus, contrary to the pseudo-scientific myths of Richard Bucke, Aurobindo Ghose and Gopi Krishna (repeated by Sarvepalli Radhakrishnan and many New Agers such as Ken Wilber and Ervin Laszlo), there is no 'Evolution of Consciousness' in the New Age sense (*see Chapter 6*). The enlightened mystic is not more evolved biologically than normal humans nor a progenitor of a new variety of 'Gnostic Being' or 'Superman' as imagined by Western-educated Aurobindo Ghose in his *The Life Divine*. In fact, Aurobindo himself restates the 'Innate Capacity' argument early on in *The Life Divine* referring to enlightenment as *uncovering* (*emphasis mine*) our Innermost Self (the Light or *Atman*). But in the second half he proceeds to speculate inconsistently on unsubstantiated grounds for hundreds of pages about the rise of the new Gnostic 'Supermen'. He makes clear that this is just speculation (it cannot of course be grounded in experience) but many followers mistake such speculation as facts[16]. Rather than such so-called 'Evolution', based on misunderstandings of Biological Evolution both as being teleological and as occurring within an individual's lifetime (*see Chapter 6*), enlightenment involves what Buddhists call 'stopping the mind' to attain a state resembling a Near-Death state (hence the lack of heartbeats during deepest *Samadhi* or 'trance' in Ramakrishna). This 'Innate Capacity' argument again fits perfectly my Reticular Activating System (RAS) brainwave correlate of the Divine Light as the RAS brainwaves generated by the brainstem Reticular Formation constitute the background matrix of gross (brainwave) activity. The RAS brainwaves become 'covered-over' by brainwaves from the rest of the brain correlated with various sorts of mental activity. The RAS spreads out from the Reticular Formation to all other brain centres and so underlies all gross (brainwave) activity. 'Stopping the Mind' thus uncovers this background field (the Yogic *tanmatra*; 'that matrix of previous gross activity') underlying the mind.

Hanegraaff says that such views of Evolution towards Universal Gnosis began with the Romantics fusing the Platonic idea of circular return to the Good with the idea of linear progress. Both A.O. Lovejoy and M.H. Abrams wrote that Romantics transformed Plotinus's Emanation into an Evolution. Whereas Plotinus saw this material world as devoid of Good, the Romantics transferred ultimate value to *this world*. The process of self-education was seen as leading to a progressive 'Evolution of Consciousness' culminating in a 'Universal Gnosis' when Humanity will repossess everything which in earlier stages of partial knowledge it had been alienated from[17]. This repossession of everything from which Humanity has been alienated is in fact a false projection onto collective human history of Plato's doctrine of Recollection. The individual philosopher-mystic progressing toward enlightenment 'unforgets' progressively the 'omniscient knowledge' of all things in the universe, (i.e., attains gnosis) which is latent within us but which we forget when the soul is reincarnated into Matter. Similarly, says Hanegraaff, the Theosophy and New Age movements have turned Reincarnation into a positive process of Spiritual Evolution. In Hinduism and Buddhism Reincarnation was negative and Enlightenment freed one from the Wheel of Rebirth. Such Romantic Evolutionism has led to New Age conceptions of world history culminating in the 'Age of Aquarius'[18].

In his 1943 essay "Religion and Time" (in the journal *Vedanta and the West*) Aldous Huxley wrote that the Humanistic 'pseudo-religions' (Nationalism, Fascism, Communism) resemble the Apocalyptic perversions of true religion. Apocalypticism leads to preoccupation with an extraordinary cosmic event which will occur in the future and this guarantees the Apocalypticist against the possibility of a timeless realisation of the eternal Reality. Religious believers in a temporal God seek temporal values associated with the 'psychical' rather than the spiritual. They make use of petitionary prayer for concrete, material benefits and seek to enter an everlasting (rather than Eternal or Atemporal) heaven[19]. In "Some Reflections on Time" (1946) Huxley wrote that Death is only transcended when Time is transcended, as Time destroys all that it creates. In all traditional philosophies and religions Time (the Temporal) is the enemy, the deceiver. But under the influence of evolutionary theories, Western philosophers of recent generations had raised Time, imagining it to be the creator of the highest values, so that *even God is emergent* (*emphasis mine*). Bergson claimed 'duration' (temporality) was the primary, Ultimate Reality. Hegel and Marx imagined History with a capital 'H' as a temporal providence leading to the Kingdom of Heaven on Earth. Such views assume that the Divine, History, *Geist* or Cosmic Process is concerned with humanity in the collective and not with humanity at any given moment. However, all the evidence points to the fact that it is the *individual soul which alone can contact the Divine* (*emphasis mine*)[20].

In the introduction to *The Presence of Light: Divine Radiance and Religious Experience*,[21] the editor Matthew Kapstein (a scholar of Buddhism at Chicago) refers to Light being a near-universal factor in mystical experiences and to the fascinating role of Light as a bridge between the physical and spiritual realms. In mysticism East and West, says Kapstein, not only is the Light ubiquitous, but there exist strikingly precise similarities between traditions. Light cannot be dismissed as a culturally-constructed concept limited only to one culture and thus inadmissible as a common element of all Mysticism. At the beginning of the book, Kapstein presents a quote stating that God is Light. However, Kapstein and most of the Western religious studies and art historian contributors to this book are heavily influenced by the prevailing Constructivist dogma of contemporary Comparative Religion. Constructivism stands opposed to the 'Perennial Philosophy' or Universalist view (advocated by Forman *et al.* in *The Innate Capacity*) that, beneath the superficial diversity, there is a deep, common core Mysticism based on the Pure Consciousness experience, reflecting universal human transformations of Consciousness. Constructivism asserts that all mystical experiences are hallucinatory, arising as a consequence of the mystic's indoctrination and prior expectations.

Even the Inner Light is often treated by naïve Constructivist academics as being merely a metaphor! Even some non-Constructivist scholars who try to link Buddhist meditation to Cognitive Science make this error. In the recent *The Cambridge Handbook of Consciousness* there is one chapter on non-Western knowledge entitled "Asian Perspectives: Indian Theories of Mind", focusing mainly on Buddhist Abhidhamma, written by Buddhologist Georges Dreyfus and Buddhophile Philosopher-of-Mind, Evan Thompson (who is also a co-editor of the book). These authors state that in the Indian philosophical system called Sankhya, the non-material self is described metaphorically as a light as it passively illuminates objects[22]. The dualist Sankhya philosophy, is commonly associated with Patanjali's *Yoga Sutras* although Sankhya actually first appeared 600 years after Patanjali[23]. The Self (*Purusa*) in the Sankhya/Yoga tradition is quite clearly equivalent to the Vedantic *Atman* and contemporary yogis in the *Yoga Sutra* tradition quite clearly refer to experiencing the flow of the Light underlying gross cognitions as a phenomenological fact[24]. The Inner Light is not a metaphor!

One must question the motivation of such academics given, for instance, that Thompson's mentor Francisco Varela co-wrote a book with the Dalai Lama in which the Dalai Lama spoke quite literally of the Clear Light! The underlying assumption seems to be that the phenomenological assertions of non-Europeans are not trustworthy even though Dreyfus and Thompson themselves state that Cognitive Science should utilise such Buddhist phenomenological knowledge. Varela ignored the Dalai Lama's views in his so-called 'Neurophenomenology', relying exclusively on the phenomenology of Edmund Husserl. Even then Varela ignored Husserl's distinction between the Flow of the Absolute or Time-Consciousness and the ego-consciousness to try to make Husserl's facts fit his Emergent Materialist assumptions[25, 26]. Note that the European Husserl *did not experience the Light*. As we shall see in Chapter 8, Husserl's Flow of the Absolute- (or the Time-) Consciousness is in fact the flow of the Inner Light but not experienced as such as Husserl remained limited to studying predominantly object-perception in the Waking state. Thus the Pure Light remained 'clouded-over' for him.

In his concluding chapter to *The Presence of Light*, Kapstein shies away from the glaring conclusion of an underlying, universal, core Mysticism involving the Light or Pure Consciousness, common to spiritual traditions (also known as the 'Perennialist' or 'Perennial Philosophy' view) even though it stares him in the face! Instead he reassures readers, assumed to be fellow Constructivist believers, that he shall not "pull the perennialist rabbit out of the hat"[27]. Such 'selective blindness' to the obvious facts that contradict one's own ideological stance is not confined to the Constructivists in Western Comparative Religion but found in numerous academic disciplines which pretend to produce unbiased, 'value free' knowledge. In regard to the brazen suppression of facts contradicting their theories by the orthodox Astrophysics establishment, Halton Arp tells us that the educated see *theory* not facts (*emphasis mine*)[28].

The Constructivist argument is a simplistic, unscientific and downright false argument based largely on the absurd premise that the naive assertions of the European Immanuel Kant are infallible truths and must be taken on authority. The corollary of this is that for millennia Eastern philosophers must either have been fabricating claims, or else mistaking mere hallucinations as real, and are thus not to be taken seriously. This is in spite of the fact that reports of Eastern yogic experiences and Eastern philosophical ideas are nonetheless included in the comparisons. This asymmetric approach reveals a tacit patronising attitude on the part of mainstream Western academia toward non-Western thought. This attitude is most apparent in works such as *Culture and Modernity: East West Philosophic Perspectives*[29]. In this Hawaii Conference aiming supposedly to bring about greater understanding between Eastern and Western philosophies, the first chapter, (i.e., pride of place) was given to US Eliminative Materialist Richard Rorty[30]. Rorty dismissed the claims of mystics to supposedly 'penetrate the veil of appearances', (i.e., perceive the transcendent Reality beyond phenomena) using the totally discredited pseudo-scientific 'psychoanalysis' of Sigmund Freud's and Skinnerian Behaviorism. The latter reduces human mentality in the most simplistic manner to being mere stimulus-response behaviour based solely on pleasure and pain. No attempt was made by the editor to refute Rorty's view. Thus the conference proceedings opened with a self-deluding Westerner (Rorty) claiming to dismiss the very basis of most Eastern Philosophy, (i.e., mystical apprehension of the Transcendental) as self-delusion or fraud utilising pseudo-scientific, modern Western mythologies which he assumed to be scientific! We shall see in Chapter 9 that Freud's 'Psychoanalysis' was based on fraudulent claims to having cured patients and supposedly scientific studies. It has no scientific basis whatsoever!

Kant was unremittingly hostile to the claims of mystics to have experienced the Divine in this life and his (speculative) ideas actually preclude the possibility of any such Divine or mystical insights[31]! Kant's famous epistemological distinction between things as they are apprehended by us (*phenomena*) in perception and things as they actually are in themselves (*noumena*) assumes that the latter (noumenal reality) can never be apprehended. Thus Kant denied Plato's 'Third Mode of Knowledge', beyond Senses and Conception, which reveals metaphysical, (i.e., noumenal) reality. We have seen that Kant revealed very little about his so-called 'Transcendental Method' upon which he based his claims and yet there has been remarkably little actual debate about Kant's method[32], even though Kant's conclusions are widely treated as if they are undisputed facts in mainstream Western philosophy. We have also seen that Kenneth Westphal argues in his *Kant's Transcendental Proof of Realism* that Kant's method of 'thought-experiments' to supposedly ascertain the prerequisites of sensory perception actually fail to support Kant's Idealism but actually support Realism[33]. We have seen that Cognitive Science has rendered epistemological Realism untenable. Whether or not Westphal's argument is correct does not concern us.

The contributors to the *Blackwell Guide to Hegel's Phenomenology of Spirit* (2009)[34] edited by the same Kenneth Westphal are either ignorant of or suppress the mystical background to Hegel's work, in spite of its suggestive title, reducing all explanations to socio-political projections. I suspected that there was more to it and sure enough discovered Glenn Magee's *Hegel and the Hermetic Tradition* (2001)[35] which reveals the Hermetic and Christian-Kabbalist occult roots of Hegel's absurd superstitions which the naive, spiritually-ignorant Marxians find so fascinating. Once again Western academics are caught out revising historical facts to suit modern Materialist cultural expectations. Many of the facts undermining the superstitions of Freudian 'Psychoanalysis', which supporters pretend is 'scientific', are debunked in Chapter 9. Psychoanalysis was also derived partly from (Jewish) Kabbalism[36].

Wilhelm and Rawlinson stated that Kant's doctrine is essentially that of the Upanishads, that the phenomenal world is illusory (*Maya*)[37]. However there is a crucial difference. Transcending our perceptual and cognitive constructions in supra-sensory perception, (i.e., 'penetrating the veil of appearances') and eventually reaching Reality-as-it-is-in-itself is precisely what yogic mysticism claims to attain. I showed in Chapter 1 how my Brain Deactivation/Retreat-to-the-Brainstem interpretation of Enlightenment, grounded on my identification of the physical correlate of the Inner Light, finally kills off the Kantian superstition that there is no ***Third Mode of Knowledge*** *that reveals metaphysical truths*. We saw in Chapter 2 that my physical correlation of the Inner Light with the activating brainwaves from the brainstem Reticular Formation also undermines the scientifically-ignorant and dogmatic Constructivist claim that there can be no ***unconditioned*** *mental processes*.

This Constructivist denial of mystical transcendence is just one example of Western *pretensions to universality*. This is the false belief that mainstream, modern Western rationalist thought applies to all human activities and that such all human activities can be reduced to supposedly 'scientific' Western understanding. The facile Eurocentric appeal to Kant's naive belief, that mystical realisations cannot be true, has been misused by self-serving academic apologists for the exclusivity and uniqueness of Semitic monotheisms such as Catholicism, (e.g., R.C. Zaehner[38, 39]) and Judaism, (e.g., Stephen Katz[40]) in an attempt to counter the perceived threat of a true Universal Spirituality underlying the diverse religious mythologies superimposed on spiritual experiences by various cultural traditions. As indicated in the previous chapter Judaism, unlike Hinduism, Buddhism, Christianity and Islam, is not based on the Inner Light. Nonetheless, the vengeful, bloodthirsty tribal deity Yahweh is based on the same, universal human brain structures underlying tribal war-gods found in other cultures.

Kapstein's 'scholarly' book jumbles together diverse references to supposedly spiritual light although some are clearly not truly *mystical* phenomena such as lights reportedly seen on the top of some sacred mountain in China. Astoundingly, Kapstein makes no effort to address why mystics in different cultures might have taken different interpretative perspectives on what may indeed be the same basic mystical phenomena. Such Constructivist arguments against a universal common core to mystical experience involve 'explaining away' on ideological grounds the glaringly obvious similarities between traditions in descriptions of enlightenment (*see Chapter 7*). Such dogmatic, superficial sophistry passes for scholarly analysis in academic Religious Studies to the bemusement of those, like me, who were trained in Natural Sciences. At my selective-intake secondary school in London (with a strong academic reputation) the bright boys usually went into Science through peer pressure, the less able into Humanities. Seeking a degree in the Humanities was seen as a fall-back for the less able not intelligent enough to study Natural Sciences or Mathematics. I had wanted to take study 'Religious Education' at Ordinary Level (age 15-16) hoping that it would be a 'World Religions' syllabus. But the teacher chose to teach a strict Christian syllabus for the benefit of a boy (who had been a child actor on a BBC children's TV drama) and whose parents insisted he study Christianity. Only four of us started attending lessons (held during lunch-hours) but all except the child actor stayed beyond the first one or two lessons given the absurdity of what was being taught. We were supposed to just accept what the teacher spewed out, including the theological superiority of the supposedly Hebrew invention of Monotheism' without discussion. Christian theologians tend to write so-called Apologetic tracts, attempting to defend mythological beliefs which clearly cannot be defended, either rationally or on evidential grounds. Christian scholars such as John Newport[41] and Philip Cary[42] give eloquent and informative discussions of the beliefs of other traditions. But, in their conclusions, they revert to their dogmatic indoctrinations and simply reassert the superiority of Christian beliefs and ideas without justification.

The afore-mentioned Persian mystic Suhrawardi was put to death in Palestine during the Crusades by Saladin who obviously felt that Suhrawardi's teachings threatened the Mohammedan faith. One contributor to Kapstein's book, Paul Muller-Ortega (whose discussions with Kapstein prompted the *Presence of Light* project), has actually experienced the Inner Light himself[43]. But this was not mentioned in the book as Western academia frowns upon such personal testimonies as 'subjective'[44, 45]. Muller-Ortega was the only one of the contributors who responded to my email criticising the anti-Perennialist *The Presence of Light* and showing my evidence confirming that a well-established brain process was correlated directly with the Inner Light. Seeing the overwhelming evidence from all spiritual traditions and scientific research supporting my identification for the physical correlate of the Inner Light, Muller-Ortega[46] wrote:

> *...much of the scientific research on mysticism has had either of two purposes: either to support and confirm a particular group's claims for the superiority of their method (witness the work on TM in the seventies, and the revival of such scientific investigations in the recent investigation of Buddhist meditation; or alternatively to be used as a tool for reductive explanations that explain away mystical experience and meditative practice as reducible merely, to brain chemistry, brain electricity and so on. I am pleased to see that your work appears to take neither of these tacks and seeks rather an intelligent adjustment between these two modalities of knowledge...*

In his chapter in *The Presence of Light*, Muller-Ortega notes that the Indian philosopher Abhinavagupta, living in Kashmir about one thousand years ago (before the Mohammedan invasions of this now-divided Indian kingdom) had access to thousands of years' worth of Hindu and Buddhist yogic knowledge going back to the *Rig Veda*. The Kashmir Saivites' Doctrine of Vibration is itself rooted in the Upanishads' Doctrine of the 'Elements' (*panch bhuta;* five spirits). As we saw, the first created element is *akasa* which means Space conceived as subtle matter (ether) characterised by vibration. Maurice Bloomfield wrote in his *The Religion of the Veda* (1908), "There is no important form of Hindu thought, 'heterodox' Buddhism included, which is not rooted in the Upanishads."[47]. Those familiar with the story of Siddhartha Gautama, the Shakya prince known as the 'Buddha' (Awakened One), will know that, although he challenged the Brahmanical Orthodoxy, he travelled far and wide across India debating with Brahmins and other traditions and lived to the age of eighty, and died peacefully.

We have seen that Buddha denied a Ground of all Being and also put forward the central Buddhist doctrine of Doctrine of *Anatta* (Pali for *Anatman;* meaning 'no *Atman*'). Thus if we took Buddha literally, he asserts that there is no Inner Light either. The Kerala-born philosopher-mystic Sankara (*fl.* 8th Century *c.e.*), was the most famous proponent of *Advaita Vedanta* which replaced Buddhist supremacy across India, following famous debates with leading Buddhist scholars. The point at issue here is that mystics living in Christian and Mohammedan societies were generally isolated individuals often persecuted, if not killed, for revealing their experiences. They also lacked access to the vast knowledge of yogic methodology and philosophical interpretation that existed in India and to a lesser extent in China. We have seen that the early French Indologists even called the Indian spiritual tradition 'Tolerationism'[48].

In fact Mohammedans, especially the Shia of (Aryan) Persia/Iran have been far more open to mystical revelation and persecuted mystics far less than the heretic-burning Christianity of the West[49]. Thus, as with many such books, Kapstein's opens with profound statements about Light as the intriguing bridge between the physical and the spiritual etc. but falls far short of even beginning to elucidate these questions in any insightful way. Kapstein just tells readers, assumed to be fellow Constructivist believers, what they want to hear. Academics seem interested only in getting papers published, regardless of how vacuous their arguments. As we shall see below, scholars of Religion are not alone in appeasing the orthodox 'powers that be'.

Physics-appeasement in Western Academic Philosophy

Astrophysicist Arthur Eddington asserted that Time was the bridge between Matter and Mind[50]. Physicist David Peat claims that Carl Jung's concept of Synchronicity is the bridge between Matter and Mind through Jung's notion of a 'Psychoid realm' where Matter and Mind are indistinguishable[51]. Jung's Synchronicity (which was actually a special case of his 'Acausal Orderedness') is related to the Hindu *akasa* (and its transcendental, vibrational resonances of form) found in the *Yoga Sutras*. Synchronicity is also related to the nonlocality of QM highlighted by the ongoing 'entanglement' (interconnectedness) of particle-like phenomena which have interacted in the past even though they may be separated by vast distances (in theory this could be many Light Years). Clearly the experience of the Inner Light is much easier to grasp and thus Light is a much better candidate than such vague, inchoate notions of Time and Synchronicity which Eddington and Jung did not clarify.

I should add that, given the *Prana/Atman* identity (the Vedantic version of the perennial correlation between the Inner Light and 'Life Energy'), and the association of feelings of energy in various spiritual phenomena, *energy* is thus another link between the Material and the Spiritual. Indeed, the scientific concept of *energy* arose during the 19th Century Romantic era of reaction against the increasingly dominant Mechanistic and Rational world-view. The Newtonian system used the concepts of *work* and *force*. Prior to the use of *energy* in relation to the new scientific studies of heat by the likes of Joule, *energy* was used in a personal context referring to feelings of vitality and freedom[52]. In fact many scientific concepts, including *force, acceleration, work, attraction, heat* and *pressure* are, like *energy*, are animistic projections of human feelings onto Nature just as the ancients used notions such as Love and Sympathy for Synchronicity-like resonant effects. The notion of the Conservation of Energy actually came as an insight to the physician (not a physicist) Robert Meyer in a sort of mystical realisation he experienced whilst suffering from a fever in the East Indies. As Jung noted, it is in fact an archetypal idea, prefigured by many traditional spiritual views of a power or energy that underlies the various manifestations of Nature[53].

In their book *The Non-Local Universe: The New Physics and Matters of the Mind*,[54] historian of science Robert Nadeau and physicist Menas Kafatos (N and K) state:

> *It is also interesting that light was the primary object of study in new theories that would displace classical physics. Light in Western literature, theology, and philosophy appears rather consistently as the symbol for transcendent, immaterial, and immutable forms separate from the realm of sensible objects and movements. Attempts to describe occasions during which those forms and ideas appear known or revealed also consistently invoke light as that aspect of nature most closely associated with ultimate truths.*

Although these authors limit themselves to Western thought; refer to Eurocentrism; mention Husserl's efforts to ground mathematical physics in human consciousness; disclose some of the hidden Platonist assumptions underlying Natural Science; depict matter as a (holonomic) web of relations, and even state that it is not unreasonable to conclude that the universe is conscious, they nevertheless still exhibit a naïve understanding of the relationship between the New Physics and actual matters concerning the Mind. In the quotation above, the authors themselves seem to imply that the simplistic Platonic notions of static, unchanging forms or abstract, generic ideas are the ultimate truths. They also assert that they find it totally unacceptable to imply that Metaphysics is prior to Physics, claiming that they practice epistemological Realism and refuse to make metaphysical leaps! This is absurd. How *Metaphysics* (Aristotle's term meaning "above" or "beyond" Physics) could not be epistemologically prior to Physics as Physics, like any human conceptual system, is based on numerous unproven metaphysical assumptions is not explained.

Such "lip service" assertions of *Physics-appeasement* are typical of many Western academics afraid of facing the ridicule of their peers if they appear to be dabbling in Metaphysics. Most physicists are not that sophisticated, philosophically, to base their rejection of Metaphysics on Kant's denial of the Third Mode of Knowledge. Rather their hostility tends to be based on the naive Positivist Reductionism that underlies mainstream Science which asserts that, if something cannot be measured, it does not exist. Thus Western academics such as the well-known US Philosophy professor John Searle, make statements about Consciousness which, if followed through consistently, contradict the Physicalist-Materialist metaphysical assumptions of Science.

However, if pressed publicly on these implications, Searle quickly backtracks and denies that his view contradicts Materialism in regard to 'causal closure' etc.[55] The afore-mentioned Evan Thompson also displays such Physics-appeasement in his recent work *Mind and Life: Biology, Phenomenology and the Sciences of Mind*, reassuring readers that he has not strayed beyond Physics, (i.e., into Metaphysics)[56]. We shall see that the founding fathers of the New Physics (whose work the likes of Kafatos, Nadeau, Searle and Thompson bow to) frowned upon such naive Positivist rejection of Metaphysics. Not surprisingly, having refused to challenge the Physicalist orthodoxy, Thompson then exclaims that the so-called "Hard Problem", a fashionable new label for the age-old problem of the Ontological Status of Consciousness (misleadingly called the 'Mind/Body problem') seems impossible[57]. Thompson, like N and K, follows the Western tradition in conflating Mind (individuated or ego consciousness) with Consciousness *per se* (primarily Awareness).

Emergent Materialism (such as Thompson's), which dominates contemporary Western 'Philosophy of Mind' is actually tacit Substance Dualism. It is not really consistent with (monistic) Physicalism-Materialism as it is tacitly introducing a new ontological 'substance' with properties which were not present (even potentially) in the Physicalist ontology. Given Galileo's preclusion of Subjectivity and Physicalism's assumption of insentient energy as the only 'substance', Sentience (Awareness) cannot possibly arise within the scientific conception of the 'Physical Universe' except by Magic. A more logically-consistent (though still erroneous) form of Emergentism is tacitly implied by the views which Skrbina has labelled Pluralist Panpsychism (as opposed to *Idealist* ('Monist Panpsychism') views which admit an all-pervading Universal Consciousness)[58]. Pluralist Panpsychism includes Whitehead's *Process and Reality* which acknowledges the fact that emergent processes (or Whitehead's 'organisms') appear throughout Nature at all levels of order from electrons upwards, not just in the brains of higher animals.

But Western academics largely steer clear of such supposedly 'Panpsychist' speculations as Panpsychism (actually the true Monistic Universal Consciousness type) is tainted by its traditional association with Mysticism! Thus the likes of the well-known academic philosopher Thomas Nagel[59] presents arguments supporting Panpsychism but ultimately shies away from the logical conclusions. I presume this self-censorship serves to stop the raising of hackles of their Materialism-indoctrinated, Scientism-ridden peers. Nagel does point out correctly that the concept of 'Emergence' is epistemological, referring only to the limitations of human theoretical constructs to predict higher-level phenomena. It is not actually an ontological concept[60]. As Hermann Weyl pointed out, paradoxes exist only in the human mind[61]. Reality transcends the contradictions forced upon the human mind by conceptual abstractions and the unwillingness to question dogmatically-held assumptions.

The arguments put forward by N and K for concluding that the whole universe may be conscious (clearly a metaphysical assertion – their earlier book was entitled *The Conscious Universe*) are vacuous. They appeal to pseudo-arguments about complexity and the whole being more than the sum of its parts and suggest that Consciousness is an Emergent property of the whole[62]. Even those writers far more amenable to Mysticism such as physicist Fritjof Capra, anthropologist Charles Laughlin and neurologist James Austin reduce mystical knowledge in a facile manner to Emergent Materialist nonsense. As with most science academics, N and K exhibit next to no knowledge of the actual processes of Mind and Consciousness and fill nearly the whole book with the paradoxes of the New Physics. Roger Penrose's misleadingly-titled book *Shadows of the Mind: A Search for the Missing Science of Consciousness* actually says nothing about Mind and Consciousness save a few vague speculations in the final chapter rehashing the naive 'Quantum Mind' conflation of two separate mysteries. All the previous chapters are filled discussing his specialist work in Mathematical Physics which really has no bearing upon the title[63]. The only concern of N and K seems to be harmonising the so-called "two cultures" (a phrase coined by C.P. Snow) of Science and Humanities scholars in Western academia. They nonetheless refer also to the 'European Enlightenment' ideal of unifying human knowledge in the service of the common good. However, as they have next to no knowledge of altered states of Consciousness or of non-European human knowledge, remaining ignorant of their own Eurocentric blinkers, N and K come nowhere near to advancing this ideal.

Divine Light in Popular Culture, Conscience and the True Resurrection

Most of us are not familiar with mystical knowledge of the Divine Light although nearly all of us in the English-speaking world have heard the phrase "seen the Light" referring to someone who has realised the truth about some issue. In the musical, comedy film *The Blues Brothers* (1980) we hear singer James Brown, playing a preacher in an Afro-American Gospel Choir church, asking the congregation repeatedly, "Have you seen the Light?" But the mystical meaning is reduced to simply a 'bright idea' coming to John Belushi's character as the sun breaks through the clouds in the sky and a ray of sunlight enters the Church. It is true that flashes of intuition may come in periods of relaxation when the thoughts clouding over the 'Mystical Sun' (the Inner Light) are stilled but this is not *enlightenment* (or gnosis). In his Best Actor Oscar acceptance speech in 2007, Forest Whitaker said that he believed that there was a Light within each of us. The Afro-Americans with their charismatic practises relating to possession by the 'Holy Spirit', derived from traditional West African religiosity, are closer to true Spirituality than the White Christians in the 'Bible Belt' with their Bible-bashing literalism and apocalyptic 'fire and brimstone' sermons. Christianity itself began as a faith for the poor and oppressed subjects of the Roman Empire and its success was linked to its socialistic, collectivist ethics and communal welfare practises. Afro-American music was rooted in Black Gospel music of the oppressed and the term *Soul* music reflected such deep spiritual inspiration in one's singing. It is highly likely that the suffering, depression and suppression of (egoic) free will of the Afro-American slaves were factors conducive to their inward spiritual development. Their harsh conditions constituted a sort of involuntary world-renunciation resembling the voluntary asceticism, including performance of menial tasks, practised by certain monastic orders. Tarnas tells us that the original pre-Nicene Christian communities included numerous *enthusiasts*, those filled with the Holy Spirit, speaking in tongues and performing acts of prophecy, healing and pronouncing new mystical revelations[64].The majority of the early Christian Gospels, the Gnostic Gospels rediscovered at Nag Hammadi in 1946, were of course suppressed by the Nicene Creed.

The 1958 film version of Norman Mailer's famous war novel *The Naked and the Dead*, though not referring to Divine Light as such, ends with an American soldier stating, "The Spirit in Man is godlike, eternal, indestructible." This statement, referring to the heroic self-sacrifice of ordinary privates, is aimed at the army general who, rather like Alexander of Macedon or a Christian primate, has attempted to present a 'godlike' image, superior to and worthy of worship by the rank and file. David Edwards and David Cromwell, the leftwing writers of the media-bias scrutinising *Newspeak in the 21st Century* (2009) also quote Norman Mailer as saying that the only way Socialism[N1] can work is if there is some larger sense of things, otherwise it just becomes a play of egos. I was surprised to find that this book ended with a chapter on 'Compassion, Awareness, Honest Journalism' discussing yogic knowledge of the Witness Consciousness that observes our thoughts[65]. This Witness Consciousness (*saksin*) is another term for *cit* (Pure Consciousness) or the *Atman*.

In January 2014 British newspapers, including the left-wing Marxian-leaning *Guardian* (which regularly promotes the Materialist views of Richard Dawkins, Daniel Dennett, Jim Al-Khalili etc.) were waxing lyrical about the scientifically-proven medical benefits of Mindfulness Meditation practises taught by Western professors as 'Mindfulness-based Cognitive Therapy' (MBCT). This was developed from Ancient Indian Buddhist Mindfulness techniques. The method involves focusing on our breath and identifying with our Deeper Self (the Witness) to observe the endless 'chatter' of thoughts rising and passing away and not identifying with these thoughts. Although Western Materialist science and philosophy rejects the possibility of Pure Consciousness, the main practical guide-book for MBCT refers in Chapter 1 to our "inner self... no longer drowned out by the noise of the mind". Chapter 2 even refers to "pure awareness" that "transcends thinking" and is "unclouded by your thoughts, feelings and emotions"[66].

Aurobindo's *The Life Divine* begins with quotations from *Rig Veda* including the following attributed to the ancient sage Vamadeva, "That which is immortal in mortals and possessed of the truth, is a god and established inwardly as an energy working out in our divine powers..."[67]. We have seen that Self-examination in Consciousness (Conscience) was part of the Buddha's teachings[68]. The Vedantic Deeper Self or *saksin* parallels the Christian understanding of Conscience as a Second Self, and as a Witness to all of our Thoughts. Conscience is the Divine Authority dwelling in our heart, God's herald and witness within. It is where we meet God's Spirit and where God speaks to us[69]. In ancient Rome the likes of Cicero linked Conscience to Spirit. Julius Caesar referred to the *anima conscientia*[70]. We also saw that contemporary Catholic theologian James P. Hanigan identified the authority of Conscience with the presence of the Holy Spirit within us. He states[71]:

I would argue, precisely in the absolute and authoritative character of these judgments, or in the quest of conscience for this absolute authority, that we meet the presence and work of the Holy Spirit in us.

Having suppressed Gnosticism as heresy and outlawed mystical explorations outside the Church's supervision, the Catholic Church asserts that it, the Church, is the dwelling place of the Holy Spirit and that the Catholic Church is the *Lumen Gentium* (God's Light to the World's People)[72]. The Second Vatican Council (1962-5) did acknowledge the presence of the Holy Spirit in Non-Catholic individuals and institutions[73].

In fact, the Christian admission of Conscience or the Holy Spirit as a Divine presence within us compromises the Theistic claim that God is completely separate from created Nature. Christianity and the other Semitic Monotheisms are not troubled by such philosophical inconsistencies as they insist upon unquestioning faith in myths rather than metaphysical consistency. Such troublesome questions are usually dismissed as unanswerable 'mysteries'. In referring to Conscience as God's herald, Christianity is echoing the Hermetic mythology in which *Hermes*, the Spirit within, is the Herald or messenger linking the worlds of Spirit and Nature. Martin Luther described Conscience as a lightning bolt of intuition from the Holy Spirit[74]. From John's Gospel onwards, the Christians' Conscience is repeatedly linked to the Inner Light[75]. In *Humanae Vitae* Pope Paul VI referred to the Light of the Holy Spirit[76]. The early Protestant sects, including the Quakers, placed great emphasis on the Inner Light of Conscience. This led John Locke to denounce the unregulated enthusiasm of Evangelical true believers responding to a Light in his or her own mind, thinking it from God[77].

I recall from primary school that in the Christmas Carol "Oh Little Town of Bethlehem", there was a verse about the Everlasting Light shining in the dark streets at the supposed time of the birth of Jesus. In fact the celebration of December 25th originated long before the birth of Jesus. It was the supposed 'Virgin-Birth-day' of Mithra (Mithras), the Persian god (related to the Vedic Mitra) worshipped by some of the great Roman emperors. Mithraism was the official religion of Rome for 300 years with his temple at the Vatican.[N2] Mithra was known as 'The Light of the World' and as the Sun god *Sol Invictus*. The appearance of the Magi (wise men or sometimes warriors) to witness the birth of a son under the Sun or a bright star (representing Divine Light) is an ancient symbolic image for mystical transfiguration of the soul long preceding the time of Governor Herod[78]. We also sang a hymn which began with the line (sung twice), "Now are we the Sons of God". Whiteman tells us in his *Universal Theology* that terms like 'Son of God' (the meaning of the name Dionysos in Phrygian), Firstborn son, and the 'Earthly incarnation of the Divine' also refer to such mystical 'rebirth' of the soul in enlightenment. Indeed, the ancient Hindu *Rig Veda* has a hymn to the 'Son of the Waters'[79]. Philo Judaeus wrote of the Divine *Logos* (a non-standard use of the Greek Rationalist term *Logos*) as the 'firstborn son', the 'image of God' or 'archetypal man'[80]. We saw in Chapter 2 that the Cathars' Gnostic-like *Consolamentum* or Spiritual Baptism involved the soul reuniting with Divine Light (the Heavenly Spirit)[81].

Another primary school hymn had the lines: "I've seen the Light, I've seen the Light, I know what I have seen/I know the joy, I know the joy, of what loving Jesus means". At age seven or eight I could not possibly appreciate the mystical "Union with Christ" alluded to in this hymn, which is related to the Gnostics' Love of *Sophia* (the Light of Divine Wisdom) as indicated in St Augustine of Hippo's assertion that, "The true *philosopher* is a lover of God". Before the Nicene Creed outlawed mystical exploration, Augustine, the most influential father of Catholicism, had been immersed in Plotinus and had written of the inward turn that leads to the Light or God and of Christ as the Inner Teacher[82]. This parallels the Hindu knowledge of the *Atman* as the Inner Teacher or Hidden Guide (it is also the Hidden Observer of hypnosis). The "joy" is of course the same as Schiller's Divine Joy. At assemblies in my second primary school, along with secular 'hymns' like 'Blowing in the Wind', The Ink is Black, the Page is White, we sang a Negro spiritual called "This Little Light of Mine". Again at age ten or eleven, I had no idea what it was actually about; I liked the unconventional Afro-American use of "Oh Lordy" for "Oh Lord" in the song. Now I know that it was based on Gospel teachings about not hiding our Light under a bushel but letting our Light shine so that *our* Father might be glorified.

The Gospel is clearly stating that everyone has this Light and that the "Father" is everyone's Father, in contrast to the later dogmatic Christian claptrap about Jesus alone, in the entire universe, being the "Son of God" or Divine Incarnation (remember that the Semitic God is totally separate from material Nature)! Christianity childishly maintains its claim to exclusive revelation asserting that the dubious historical figure Jesus alone is the "True Light" and that others can only attain salvation "through Jesus". In fact the supposedly unique divine status of Jesus and his supposed redemption of the entire 'world', as with the Christian appropriation of Mithraic traditions, reflects earlier examples of man worship in the Helleno-Roman world. Jesus appropriated much of the iconography of the supposedly divine, godlike Alexander[N3], whose hyped-up mythology continues to be peddled by academics in the West today.[N4] The Divine status of the man Jesus in Christianity reflects more the emperor worship cult of the Roman Caesars. The Church transferred divinity from the supposed "world-conquerors" to this "world-renouncing" Hebrew heretic whose non-tribal brand of monotheism served the political purposes of Constantine.

Merrell-Wolff says that the mystical understanding of the Gospels implies that Jesus was not a unique Son of God, in a sense unattainable by anyone else, simply an exemplar[83]. Merrell-Wolff, himself the son of a Methodist minister, only "understood the true Jesus" after a period of atheism and then learning from Buddhism. He notes that Mahatma Gandhi said that Jesus played a vital part in bringing the Light to him even though Gandhi came from India, the very Fount of Spiritual Wisdom. Gandhi could treat Jesus on his own terms without needing to clear away the theological rubbish or overlying superstition (of Christian tradition). Christian theology, he says, makes Jesus a symbol of bondage. Divinity for the superstitious is an object to be feared or in which to place irrational confidence. He also agreed with the great Indian Vedantin Sankara, contrary to Christian doctrine, there is no such thing as essential (ontological) evil[84]. Indeed, many foreigners staying in Indian ashrams claim that they began to understand the true meaning of the religious traditions they were brought up in properly only after learning from Indian Yoga. After Bengali Swami Yogananda's sell-out speech at the Los Angeles Philharmonic in 1925, the *LA Times* described him as[85]:

...a Hindu invading the United States to bring God in the midst of a Christian community, preaching the essence of the Christian doctrine.

Whiteman's rather arcane descriptions of the true esoteric meaning of the Greek ***Iesous Christos*** (Annointed Saviour) as the 'Son of God'[86] correspond to the well-established Vedantic *anandamayakosa* (Bliss Sheath or Causal Body) which is a 'Rebirth' or an Incarnation of the 'Soul' (ego) in the Divine Light. Vedanta also calls this, the most subtilised or purified (of worldly attachments) form of individuated consciousness, the Causal Body as it is the First Cause of *Avidya* (Ignorance; mistaking the sense world for Reality) thus it is the 'firstborn' form of the Egoistic and hence Earthly existence. Whiteman describes the Spiritual Body as the inmost motivational character that is *causally first* (*emphasis mine*). This mystical rebirth (or resurrection) of the soul in the Divine Light (after ego 'death' or dissolution) has been 'transmogrified' by the Semitic religions. The mystical 'Ending of Time' and 'Life Review' experiences associated with the process of dying have also been corrupted into absurd Materialistic myths. As in the parent Judaic superstition, Christianity and Mohammedanism teach that, on the Day of Last Judgement at the End of Time, the 'Dead (bodies) of the Faithful' shall literally rise from the grave to be resurrected physically! This is why they bury their dead. In text IX of the *Nag Hammadi* Gnostic texts, the Valentinian author refutes those who expect a *carnal resurrection on the Last Day*. Rather **True Resurrection** involves gaining spiritual **gnosis** (*emphases mine*)[87]. The 17th Century Hermetic Rosicrucians referred to *Corpus Hermeticum* XIII in which it states that the *regenerated man* becomes a **son of God** and can sin no longer (*emphasis mine*)[88]. This parallels the Hindu *jivanmukta* (one who attains Liberation in life) who no longer deposits *karma* (associated with egoic acts).

Catholic Luke Coppen tells us that Gandhi's favourite hymn was John Henry Newmans' "Lead, kindly Light" which he had sung to him after being beaten up by a racist gang in Johannesburg in 1908. Gandhi later even made 'Lead, kindly Light' as his motto for the Indian Independence Movement, quoting it often, as he felt that it contained the "quintessence of all philosophy"[89]. In her 2010 BBC TV series on Gandhi, Mischal Husain told of what actually happened after the racist Europeans threw Gandhi off the train at Pietermaritzburg for refusing to leave the First Class compartment for which he had bought a ticket. Whilst waiting in the station Gandhi had a conversion experience in which his Inner Voice (his Conscience) spoke to him. Husain also told us how Gandhi's Indian Muslim merchant clients in Durban taught him of the true spiritual meaning of the Koranic *Jihad* as an inner struggle related to his own Hindu *Satyagraha*.

Ashis Nandy, in a famous essay on the Psychology of Colonialism, saw Gandhi's nonviolent, turn-the-other-cheek approach as completely outwitting the cynical British (with their Divide and Rule etc.). Gandhi showed that Indians could be more Christian than the Christians whilst the British rule was based on primitive brute force[90]. British historiography has largely suppressed the fact that Britain grew to be the richest country in the world through economic parasitism of India, de-industrialising and pauperising India and killing tens of millions of Indians in artificial famines. On his Christmas Day 2007 TV programme, black Christian scholar Robert Beckford, after showing the countless borrowings from older traditions in the Jesus myths, presented the Indian leader known as the 'Mahatma' as the modern day equivalent of the true, non-mythological Jesus who stood up for the oppressed masses. Beckford thus ended his programme standing amongst the Palestinians *fellahin* (the true descendants of the Biblical Israelites[N5]) whose farms were being dispossessed by the Zionist Settler-Colonialists in Palestine[90].

References

1. Kingsley, Peter (1995) *Ancient Philosophy, Mystery, and Magic: Empedocles and Pythagorean Tradition,* Clarendon Press (Oxford University Press).
2. Whiteman, J.H. Michael (1967) *Philosophy of Space and Time and the Inner Constitution of Nature: A Phenomenological Study*, Muirhead Library of Philosophy, George Allen and Unwin and the Humanities Press.
3. McEvilley, Thomas (2002) *The Shape of Ancient Thought: Comparative Studies in Greek and Indian Philosophies*, Allworth Press.
4. Goonatilake, Susantha (1998) *Toward a Global Science: Mining Civilisational Knowledge*, Indiana University Press.
5. Leonard, Ron (1999) *The Transcendental Philosophy of Franklin Merrell-Wolff*, State University of New York Press.
6. McEvilley, Thomas (2002) *ibid.*
7. Obeyesekere, Gananath (2002) *Imagining Karma: Ethical Transformation in Amerindian, Buddhist and Greek Rebirth*, University of California Press.
8. Obeyesekere, Gananath (2002) *ibid.*
9. Obeyesekere, Gananath (2002) *ibid.*
10. Lindorff, David (2004) *Jung and Pauli: The Meeting of Two Great Minds*, Quest Books.
11. Chattopadhyaya, D.P. "Plato, Neoplatonism, and Their Parallel Indian Ideas". In Paulos Mar Gregorios (Editor) (2002) *Neoplatonism and Indian Philosophy,* State University of New York Press.
12. Chattopadhyaya, D.P. (2002) *ibid.*
13. Obeyesekere, Gananath (2002) *ibid.*
14. Chattopadhyaya, D.P. (2002) *ibid.*
15. Forman, Robert K.C. (1998) (Editor) *The Innate Capacity: Mysticism, Psychology and Philosophy*, Oxford University Press.
16. Ghose, Aurobindo (Sri Aurobindo) (1939) *The Life Divine*, Sri Aurobindo Ashram Publications.
17. Hanegraaff, Wouter "Romanticism and the Esoteric Connection. In Roelof van den Broek and Wouter J. Hanegraaf (Editors) (1998) *Gnosis and Hermeticism: From Antiquity to Modern Times*, State University of New York Press.

18. Hanegraaf, Wouter "The New Age Movement and the Esoteric Tradition". In Roelof van den Broek and Wouter J. Hanegraaf (Editors) (1998) *Gnosis and Hermeticism: From Antiquity to Modern Times*, State University of New York Press.
19. Huxley, Aldous (1943) "Religion and Time". Reprinted in Jacqueline H. Bridgeman (Editor) (1992) *Huxley and God: Essays*, Harper Collins.
20. Huxley, Aldous (1946) "Some Reflections on Time". Reprinted in Jacqueline H. Bridgeman (Editor) (1992) *Huxley and God: Essays*, Harper Collins.
21. Kapstein, Matthew T. "The Divine Presence of Light". In Matthew T. Kapstein (Editor) (2004) *The Presence of Light: Divine Radiance and Religious Experience*, University of Chicago Press.
22. Dreyfus, George and Thompson, Evan "Asian Perspectives: Indian Theories of Mind". In Philip D. Zelazo, Morris Moscovitch and Evan Thompson (Editors) (2007) *The Cambridge Handbook of Consciousness*, Cambridge University Press.
23. Whiteman, J.H. Michael (1993) *Aphorisms on Spiritual Method: the "Yoga Sutras of Patanjali" in the light of mystical experience*, Colin Smythe.
24. Brown, Daniel P. "The Stages of Meditation in Cross-Cultural Perspective". In Ken Wilber, Jack Engler and Daniel P. Brown (Editors) (1986) *Transformations of Consciousness: Conventional and Contemplative Perspectives on Development*, Shambhala Publications.
25. Varela, Francisco J. "Present-Time Consciousness". In Francisco J. Varela and Jonathan Shear (Editors) (1999) *The View from Within: First-person approaches to the study of consciousness*, Imprint Academic.
26. Varela, Francisco J. "The Specious Present: A Neurophenomenology of Time Consciousness". In Jean Petitot, Francisco J. Varela, Bernard Pachoud and Jean-Michel Roy (Editors) (1999) *Naturalising Phenomenology: Issues in Contem-porary Phenomenology and Cognitive Science*, Stanford University Press.
27. Kapstein, Matthew T. "Rethinking Religious Experience: Seeing the Light in the History of Religions". In Matthew T. Kapstein (Editor) (2004) *The Presence of Light: Divine Radiance and Religious Experience*, University of Chicago Press.
28. Arp, Halton (1998) *Seeing Red: Redshifts, Cosmology and Academic Science*, Apeiron.
29. Deutsch, Elliot (Editor) (1991) *Culture and Modernity: East-West Philosophic Perspectives*, University of Hawaii Press.
30. Rorty, Richard L. "Philosophers, Novelists and Intercultural Comparisons: Heidegger, Kundera and Dickens." In Elliot Deutsch (Editor) (1991) *Culture and Modernity: East-West Philosophic Perspectives*, University of Hawaii Press.
31. Perovich Jr, Anthony, N. "Does the Philosophy of Mysticism Rest on a Mistake?". In *The Problem of Pure Consciousness: Mysticism and Philosophy* (1990) edited by Robert K.C. Forman, Oxford University Press.
32. Westphal, Kenneth R. (2004) *Kant's Transcendental Proof of Realism*, Cambridge University Press.
33. Westphal, Kenneth R. (2004) *ibid.*

34. Westphal, Kenneth R. (Editor) (2009) *The Blackwell Guide to Hegel's Phenomenology of Spirit*, Wiley-Blackwell.
35. Magee, Glen A. (2001) *Hegel and the Hermetic Tradition*, Cornell University Press.
36. Bakan, David (1958) *Sigmund Freud and the Jewish Mystical Tradition*, D. Van Nostrand Company.
37. Wilhelm, Friedrich and Rawlinson, H. G. "India and the Modern West." In *A Cultural History of India* (1975) edited by A.L. Basham, Clarendon Press (Oxford University Press).
38. King, Richard (1999) *Orientalism and Religion: Postcolonial Theory, India and 'The Mystic East'*, Routledge.
39. Smith, Huston (2000) *Cleansing the Doors of Perception: The Religious Significance of Entheogenic Plants and Chemicals*, Tarcher Putnam.
40. Forman, Robert K.C. (1999) *Mysticism, Mind, Consciousness*, State University of New York Press.
41. Newport, John P. (1998) *The New Age Movement and the Biblical Worldview: Conflict and Dialogue*, William B. Eerdmans Publishing Company.
42. Cary, Phillip (2000) *Augustine's Invention of the Inner Self: The Legacy of a Christian Platonist*, Oxford University Press.
43. Muller-Ortega, Paul. Personal Communication 7th April 2006.
44. Forman, Robert K.C. (1999) *ibid.*
45. Barnard, G. William (1997) *Exploring Unseen Worlds: William James and the Philosophy of Mysticism*, State University of New York Press.
46. Muller-Ortega, Paul. Personal Communication 7th April 2006.
47. Bloomfield, Maurice (1908) quoted in Radhakrishnan, Sarvepalli (1953) *The Principal Upanisads*, (Centenary Edition 1989), Unwin Hyman.
48. Sorman, Guy (2001) *The Genius of India*, McMillan India.
49. See for instance Tim Winter (Editor) (2008) *The Cambridge Companion to Classical Islamic Theology*, Cambridge University Press and Watt, W. Montgomery (1962) *Islamic Philosophy and Theology*, (2009 Reprint) Aldine Transaction (Rutgers University).
50. Eddington, Arthur, S. (1928) *The Nature of the Physical World*, J.M. Dent and Sons.
51. Peat, David (1987) *Synchronicity: The Bridge Between Matter and Mind*, Bantam Books.
52. Sirag, Saul-Paul "Hyperspace Reflections". In Beverley Kane, Jean Millay and Dean Brown (Editors) (1993) *Silver Threads: 25 Years of Parapsychology Research*, Praeger.
53. Jung, Carl G. (1917, 1926, 1943) "On the Psychology of the Unconscious". Excerpted in Anthony Storr (Editor) (1983) *Jung: Selected Writings*, Fontana.
54. Nadeau, Robert and Kafatos, Menas (1999) *The Non-local Universe: The New Physics and Matters of the Mind*, Oxford University Press.
55. Schwartz, Jeffrey M. And Begley, Sharon (2002) *The Mind and The Brain: Neuroplasticity and the Power of Mental Force*, Regan Books (Harper Collins).

56. Thompson, Evan (2007) *Mind in Life: Biology, Phenomenology, and the Sciences of Mind*, Belknap Press (Harvard University Press).
57. Thompson, Evan (2007) *ibid.*
58. Skrbina, David (2005) *Panpsychism in the West*, MIT Press.
59. Nagel, Thomas. Excerpted in chapter entitled "Thomas Nagel" in D.S. Clarke (2004) *Panpsychism:Past and Recent Selected Readings*, State University of New York Press.
60. Nagel, Thomas (2004) *ibid.*
61. Tieszen, Richard (2005) *Phenomenology, Logic, and the Philosophy of Mathematics*, Cambridge University Press.
62. Nadeau, Robert and Kafatos, Menas (1999) *ibid.*
63. Penrose, Roger (1995) *Shadows of the Mind: A Search for the Missing Science of Consciousness*, Vintage.
64. Tarnas, Richard (1991) *The Passion of the Western Mind: Understanding the Ideas that have Shaped Our Worldview*, Ballantyne Books.
65. Edwards. David and Cromwell, David (2009) *Newspeak in the 21st Century*, Pluto Press.
66. Williams, David and Penman, Danny (2011) *Mindfulness: A practical guide to finding peace in a frantic world*, Piatkus.
67. Ghose, Aurobindo (Sri Aurobindo) (1939) *ibid.*
68. Bhandarkar, D.R. (1925) *AĐoka*, University of Calcutta. Reprinted 2005 by Asian Educational Services.
69. Strohm, Paul (2011) *Conscience: A Very Short Introduction*, Oxford University Press.
70. Strohm, Paul (2011) *ibid.*
71. Hanigan, James P. "Conscience and the Holy Spirit". In Charles E. Curran (Editor) (2004) *Conscience*, (Readings in Moral Theology No.14), Paulist Press.
72. May, William E. "Vatican II, Church Teaching, and Conscience". In Charles E. Curran (Editor) (2004) *Conscience,* (Readings in Moral Theology No.14), Paulist Press.
73. Hogan, Linda "Conscience in the Documents of Vatican II". In Charles E. Curran (Editor) (2004) *Conscience,* (Readings in Moral Theology No.14), Paulist Press.
74. Strohm, Paul (2011) *ibid.*
75. Anderson, William (1996) *The Face of Glory: Creativity, Consciousness and Civilisation*, Bloomsbury.
76. McCormick, Richard, A. "Hierarchical Chucrh Teaching and Conscience". In Charles E. Curran (Editor) (2004) *Conscience,* (Readings in Moral Theology No.14), Paulist Press.
77. Strohm, Paul (2011) *ibid.*
78. Whiteman, J.H. Michael (2006) *Universal Theology and Life in the Other Worlds*, Colin Smythe.
79. Whiteman, J.H. Michael (2006) *ibid.*

80. Radhakrishnan, Sarvepalli (1953) *The Principal Upanisads*, (Centenary Edition 1989), Unwin Hyman.
81. van den Broek, Roelof "The Cathars: Medieval Gnostics?". In Roelof van den Broek and Wouter J. Hanegraaff (1998) *Gnosticism and Hermeticism: From Antiquity to Modern Times*, State University of New York Press.
82. Cary, Phillip (2000) *ibid.*
83. Merrell-Wolff, Franklin (1995) *Transformations in Consciousness: The Metaphysics and Epistemology* (Containing His *Introceptualism*), State University of New York Press.
84. Merrell-Wolff, Franklin (1994) *Franklin Merrell-Wolff's Experience and Philosophy: A Personal Record of Transformation and a Discussion of Transcendental Consciousness*: Containing his *Philosophy of Consciousness without an Object* and *His Pathways through to Space*, State University of New York Press.
85. Goldberg, Philip (2010) *American Veda: From Emerson and the Beatles to Yoga and Meditation – How Indian Spirituality Changed the West*, Harmony Books, Random House.
86. Whiteman, J.H. Michael (2006) *ibid.*
87. Mahé, Jean-Pierre "Gnostic and Hermetic Ethics" In Roelof van den Broek and Wouter J. Hanegraaff (1998) *Gnosticism and Hermeticism: From Antiquity to Modern Times*, State University of New York Press.
88. Edighoffer, Roland "Hermeticism in Early Rosicrucianism". In Roelof van den Broek and Wouter J. Hanegraaff (1998) *Gnosticism and Hermeticism: From Antiquity to Modern Times*, State University of New York Press.
89. Coppen, Luke. *The Guardian* (Newspaper, London) 18th May 2010.
90. Nandy, Ashis "The Psychology of Colonialism: Sex, Age and Ideology in British India". In Ashis Nandy (1983) *The Intimate Enemy: Loss and Recovery of Self under Colonialism*, Oxford University Press (India).
91. Beckford, Robert (2007) *The Hidden Story of Jesus* (Television programme), Channel 4 (UK).

4

Modern Physicists' Understanding of Mysticism and the Transcendental

Philosopher-Physicists: Contemplative 'Big Fish' of New Physics

Ernst Mach: Buddhistic Godfather of the New Physics and the even newer "Machian physics"

The Austrian physicist and philosopher Ernst Mach (1838-1916) is largely remembered due to his influence on the development of Logical Positivism. But in fact, through his major influence on the work of Albert Einstein, Werner Heisenberg and his godson Wolfgang Pauli, as well as his influence on Erwin Schrödinger, Mach can be considered the 'Godfather of the New Physics'. In Chapter 2 we saw that Mach had a largely Nature Mystical experience of ego dissolution. This experience made him abandon his earlier Kantianism and develop a Panpsychist view called Pan-Sensism which held that the world consists of various sensations. In his *Toward a Global Science*, Susantha Goonatilake reveals the Buddhist influences upon Mach. Mach was interested in Indian literature and science, including Indian mathematics. His friends included Buddhists like the famous Paul Carus whose Monism was closely related to Mach's philosophical positions. Mach contributed to the journals founded by Carus, *The Monist* and *Open Court*[1]. Mach's Principle, which relates the *inertia,* (i.e., resistance to acceleration due to the *mass*) of an object to its interaction with the rest of the universe, bears similarities to the Buddhist holonomic notion of Dependent Co-origination.

Mach's *Analysis of Sensations* included Buddhistic views of the ego as nothing (permanent) at all, resolving itself into a transitory connection of changing elements[2]. In some autobiographical writing from 1913 Mach wrote[3]:

> *After I recognised that Kant's thing-in-itself was nonsense, I also had to acknowledge that the unchanging ego was a deception. ...how happy I felt, on thus becoming free from every tormenting, foolish notion of personal immortality, and seeing myself introduced into the understanding of Buddhism, a good fortune the European is rarely able to share.*

The first references to the parallels between Mach's views and Buddhism appeared in 1903. In the year of his death a number of articles referred to Mach's advocacy of Buddhist doctrine on the 'self' and the 'ego'. Anton Lampa wrote in his 1918 biography of the remarkable agreement between Mach's thought and that of the Buddha in regard to the exclusion of metaphysical speculation and the concept of substance. Einstein, who had tried to make his General Theory of Relativity (GTR) conform to Mach's Principle[4], later rejected adherence to what he called "Mach-Buddhist reductionism"[5].

Thus it appears that Mach's Pan-Sensism was based on the experience of discontinuous sensory mind moments and, as did Buddha, he abstracted the discontinuities from the underlying substantial unity of Consciousness. The exclusion of metaphysical speculation refers to Mach's Empiro-criticism. The Eurocentric Shimon Malin tells us that Mach's contributions to Philosophy are all but forgotten. His Empiro-criticism was a reaction to 19th Century German philosophy which he dismissed as a verbose morass of world-views lacking empirical evidence and clarity of thought. Mach's insistence on operational definitions of scientific concepts led to re-examination of basic concepts of Space, Time and Energy by the likes of Einstein and Heisenberg leading to Einstein's Relativity and the new QM[6]. Mach also played a significant role in the intellectual development of his godson Wolfgang Pauli whose famous Exclusion Principle underlies Quantum Chemistry and who predicted the existence of the Neutrino[7].

The Kantian physicist Wolfram Schommers tells us that Mach demanded the elimination of all metaphysical, (i.e., speculative) elements including *absolute* space and *absolute* time because they are, in principle, not accessible to empirical tests. We can only speak about *distances* in regard to (separate) masses and about *times* in regard to physical processes[8]. Schommers ignores the fact that Mach was a Panpsychist! Einstein's belief that Matter and Space-Time are so deeply interrelated that neither should be able to exist without the other was derived from Mach. Einstein's Special Theory of Relativity does not fulfil Mach's Principle as it simply changes Newton's absolute Space to absolute Space-Time (Minkowski's space). Even GTR failed to fulfil its initial goal of removing the absolute Space-Time as De Sitter's 1917 solution of GTR contradicted Mach's Principle as it could result in an empty Space-Time without Matter[9]. In his *Symbols, Pictures and Quantum Reality* (1995) Schommers reformulated QM in order to satisfy Mach's Principle by eliminating vestiges of Classical Physics such as the particle notion and the Time-operator. In mainstream QM Schrödinger's Equation is assumed to be fundamental without itself being derived from deeper principles[10]. The results of Schommer's reformulation are discussed below in regard to Wolfgang Pauli.

Halton Arp tells us that in 1964 Fred Hoyle and Jayant Narlikar proposed a Theory of Gravitation (Arp prefers to say a 'Theory of Mass') based on Mach's Principle in which every particle derives its inertia from interaction with the rest of the particles in the universe. When a particle is created it has zero mass but as time passes it receives information from a volume of space that increases with the speed of light. Younger electrons, having *lower mass*, will emit weaker (more red-shifted) photons[11]. In 1977 Narlikar generalised the 'sacred' equations of GTR showing that $m=at^2$ where a is constant. This means that particle masses vary in relation to their age squared. In 1993 Arp himself co-authored a paper with Narlikar on such time-dependence of elementary mass. Arp concludes that Mass is related to Frequency (which of course it is as Energy is directly related to Frequency in QM and Mass is interchangeable with Energy). Arp says that electron mass as expressed in units of Time is attainablc by using the Compton frequency, the Planck constant and the velocity of light. He also relates Spin to temporal processes and speculates that Time itself may be quantised. Perhaps the materialising and dematerialising (virtual) matter in QM would be related to steps in Time[12].

Arp refers to 'Machian Physics' because the particle "feels" the mass with which it communicates inside its light-horizon. It stays in contact (with the rest of the particles in its light-horizon) through an electromagnetic wave whose particle aspect materialises and dematerialises like a quantum[13]. By Machian Physics Arp is rcally referring to Nonlocal, Particle-free Physics as is also found in the work of Schommers. Indeed Arp says that his ideas are consistent with the Space Resonance model proposed by Milo Wolff[14]. The point I want to stress is that such generalisations of QM and GTR, such as by Schommers and Narlikar, all point to a deeper, nonlocal Wave Structure of Matter (WSM).

Parallels for Atman, Brahman and Tantra in writings of "Acharya" Arthur Eddington

The famous astrophysicist Arthur Eddington, helped confirm Einstein's GTR by taking measurements of stars during a solar eclipse in 1919 to show the effects of the sun's gravity on starlight. He also predicted correctly that the sun (and stars) shone due to conversion of mass into energy in the interior of stars before the advent of QM and the theory of nuclear fusion. Eddington, who was also the mentor of the great Indian astrophysicist Subramaniam Chandrasekhar, came from a Quaker background. The Quakers place emphasis on the Inner Light of Conscience. The English word "consciousness" comes from the Latin *conscience* also known as the Inner Voice[15]. Albert Einstein lauded Eddington as one of the few men in the entire world who truly understood his theory. But, although the media and establishment scientists hype up Albert Einstein, Eddington's understanding of metaphysics and his insight into Reality was deeper and more profound than that of Einstein. In his *The Mathematical Theory of Relativity* Eddington wrote that the Space-Time frame of GTR is overlaid by the observer on the external world; "We must endeavour not to lose sight of its fictitious and arbitrary nature."[16].

Eddington proposed the existence of two time dimensions; ordinary Directed-Time and another Arrowless-Time so that micro-events could occur as if 'backward' and 'forward' in Time in the latter. This dimension would be 'imaginary', (i.e., its values should be multiplied by the "-1). Similar ideas were proposed by Wheeler and Feynman (the time-reversed 'Advanced Waves' mentioned below)[17]. Von Franz says that Eddington's efforts stem from an effort to grasp that double aspect of reality which Jung called 'Acausal Orderedness' and 'Synchronicity', (i.e., the holonomic Transcendental Realm underlying the Empirical Realm of Space/Time/Causality). Thus Eddington's micro-events occurring in the Imaginary Time dimension could sometimes have micro-effects on events in the ordinary Time dimension. This parallels Jung's Synchronistic events sporadically interrupting and interfering with the normal flow of events observed in our normal state of Consciousness[18]. Jung's anthropomorphic term 'meaningful coincidences' for such Synchronicities, as repeated by von Franz, is in itself misleading. A more developed understanding of such interactions with the Transcendental based on the Brahmanic/Yogic notion of the *Akasa* was given in my 1999 book *The Oneness/Otherness Mystery* (O/OM) and is summarised later in this chapter.

In his *The Nature of the Physical World*, Eddington[19] states:

In the mystic sense of the creation around us, in the expression of art, in a yearning towards God, the soul grows upward and finds the fulfilment of something implanted in its nature. The sanction for this development within us, a striving born with our consciousness or an Inner Light proceeding from a greater power than ours. Science can scarcely question this sanction,... Whether in the intellectual pursuits of science or the mystical pursuits of the spirit, the light beckons ahead and the purpose surging in our nature responds.

This passage reminds me of my own assertions in O/OM regarding my own sense of destiny, driven on or compelled against my personal will by my Deeper Self which spoke through the Inner Voice and which seemed to know in advance my future, somehow sensing my potential (or 'scanning my brain') from the depths of my being. Aurobindo tells us that the secret part of ourselves, the impersonal Inner being (the Light) is capable of direct communication with the universal forces, movements, objects of the cosmos[20]. Frederick Myers called it the Subliminal Self and it is known as the Hidden Observer in hypnosis. As a Quaker, Eddington obviously knew of the Inner Light and wrote extensively in defence of Mysticism and the epistemological primacy of Consciousness over scientific knowledge[21].

Rather like Petitot's claim that Galilean ontology avoided the intrinsic nature or substance of Reality, in *The Nature of the Physical World*, Eddington described the network of self-referential concepts constructed by Physics as "the house that Jack built", empty on the inside. If one searches for an insight into the intrinsic nature of these physical entities, one is sent around in circles as they are all defined in relation to each other. The only true (ontological) insight into the background reality we have, if we assume metaphysical Monism, is that the inaccessible reality underlying physical phenomena is the same as that background reality that manifest as our thoughts; i.e., it must be like Consciousness[22]. The stuff of the world is mind-stuff, something more general than our individual conscious minds but not altogether foreign to the feelings in our consciousness. The matter and fields of force in Physics are imaginings that the mind-stuff has itself spun. Our bodies are more mysterious than our minds. The mind-stuff is not spread in space and time, (i.e., it is transcendental)[23]. For Eddington, 'matter' was the metrical description of aspects of the activity of mind. A universe without conscious mind would have no more status than Utopia. The *potentiality* of being known to mind, he added, was a fundamental objective property of matter, giving it actuality whether individual consciousness is taking note or not[24]. In *Science and the Unseen World*, Eddington presents a Neo-Brahmanic (Universal Consciousness as Ground of Being) and Tantric (matter as manifestation of energetic activity of Consciousness) picture that any advocate of Vedanta or Kashmir Saivism would immediately recognise as almost identical to the dominant Indian metaphysics of the Ocean of Consciousness/Light and its waves of phenomenal manifestation[25]:

> *Similarly, I assert that the nature of all reality is spiritual, not material nor a dualism of matter and spirit. ...Interpreting the term material (or more strictly, physical) in the broadest sense as that which we can become acquainted through sensory experience of the external world, we recognise now that it corresponds to the waves, not to the ocean of reality.*

Hence I have given him the Sanskrit title *Acharya* (the Master) as when Sankara is referred to as Sankaracharya or Johannes Eckhart as the Meister.

The fifth element, photons, matter waves and Einstein's confused 'cosmic religious feeling'

As I first typed this section, the Sci-Fi Channel kept showing Luc Besson's delightful Science Fiction comedy film, *The Fifth Element*. This was a 'meaningful coincidence' as Jung would say. The climax of this film utilises mythological interpretations of the production of the so-called Fifth Element or of "Divine Light" through secret rituals involving the four elements Earth, Fire, Wind and Water. This is a classic case of the false projection by non-mystics of mystical qualities onto the realm of Nature. Whiteman[26] says:

> *In this process of dissemination, moreover, true insights became rapidly coloured over by fanciful speculation or altogether transformed by people who did not understand the form in which they were expressed. The doctrine of the four (or five) elements, which in the Upanishads is presented as purely mystical, becomes in Empedocles a semi-mystical or philosophical doctrine, and in Aristotle a theory of natural phenomena.*

McEvilley showed that the notion of the elements can be traced through a long development period in the much older *Rig Veda* hymns whereas Empedocles' version suddenly appears fully fledged[27]. Whiteman is referring to the aforementioned Upanishadic Theory of the Elements (*panch bhuta* means Five Elements) in which the first created element is *Akasa* (Space as subtle matter or Ether) characterised by vibration. This condenses progressively into the other four elements which constitute gross matter; *vayu* (Air), *tejas* (of which heat and light are manifestations; equivalent to 'Fire'), *ap* (water) and *prithvi* (Earth)[28,29].

Although Luc Besson's film refers to the Fifth Element as Divine Light, Aristotle's Fifth Element (also known as *Quintessence*) was Aether or Starstuff. The Divine Light (or Pure Consciousness), as we have seen, is in its *prajna* (Luminous Wisdom) aspect a sort of Ether (*akasa*) full of subtle vibratory energy or information. Magee tells us that Aristotle connected *pneuma* (Air/Breath or Life Force) and *aether*. *Pneuma* as Life Force was found in semen causing semen to be productive. The foam-like and natural principle of in the *pneuma* is like the element in stars, (i.e., *aether*). Insofar as we humans are knowers, (i.e., receivers of form) we contain something of this astral substance or *aether.* Plotinus took the doctrine further claiming that we possess an Astral or Aetherial Body (a concept prominent in Renaissance Hermetica and later Spiritualism and New Age thought). Thus Man's Life Force is identical with the substance of heavenly bodies[30]. Cicero wrote that Aristotle, having accepted the Four Elements (of Empedocles), added a fifth *Quintessence* in order to explain the basis of Mind which he thought was not present in the Four Elements. Cicero based his argument for the immortality of the soul on the basis that the soul is Quintessence with the power of Memory, Mind and Thought[31] Ancient Materialists such as the Stoics still believed in God and the immortality of the soul as the soul was made of the same material as the gods. The soul contains Living Divine Fire as do the stars which are celestial gods[32]. The Aether as Life Force and the immortal soul as Living Divine Fire both clearly parallel the *prana/atman* (Life Energy/Inner Light of Pure Consciousness) identity of the earlier Upanishads.

Note a couple of things in regard to *The Fifth Element* and the notions of the four or five elements. Along with projection of the mystical onto the mundane, Luc Besson's film also highlights another tendency in contemporary Western mythology, that of projecting mystical secrets onto the new mythology of UFOs and alien beings from outer space as well as onto Egyptian pyramids. This includes the non-sensical Science-Fiction stories such as some of the 1960s *Star Trek* episodes which suggested that perhaps the supposedly miraculous Ancient Greek civilisation was actually due to the Olympian gods being advanced aliens from outer space as in *Who Mourns for Adonais*, alien visitors copying Plato in *Plato's Stepchildren*, and that great human geniuses were actually superhuman or alien beings as in *Requiem for Methuselah*. Such UFO mythology is still superimposed upon spirituality by some, who imagine extraterrestrials performing the (supposedly factual) supernatural acts of the Old Testament myths. These ideas resemble Erik von Daniken's *Chariots of the Gods* and more recent nonsense about extraterrestrial knowledge encoded in Egyptian pyramids which appeal to the childish fantasies of the uneducated. As Martin Bernal highlighted in his *Black Athena: Afro-Asiatic Roots of Classical Civilisation. (Volume 1: The Fabrication of Ancient Greece 1785–1985* [33], the real aliens, who introduced advanced knowledge such as writing to the primitive Ancient Greeks, were in fact Phoenicians and Egyptians. Ancient sources repeatedly state that famous Greek thinkers learnt and copied doctrines from the Orientals including the Babylonians, Persians and Indian Brahmins, Buddhists and Jains.

Interestingly, in these Five Elements, we seem to find an ancient rendering of the five states of matter known to modern science (Earth as solids, Water as liquids, Air as gases, Fire as plasma and Light as radiation) although this was not what the elements were actually supposed to represent. The Indian *panch bhuta*, based on mystical experience of material manifestation, shows an appreciation of the progressive 'condensation' of matter from the energetic vibrations of Absolute Transcendental Consciousness through gases and liquids to solids. In fact, there is another known state of matter which only occurs at temperatures almost identical to absolute zero thus this state was first observed in the laboratory in 1995 using laser technology. This state is known as the Bose-Einstein condensate named after the Bengali physicist Satyendra Nath Bose and Albert Einstein. Particulate matter approaching absolute zero temperature becomes more and more wave-like and, eventually, macroscopically visible matter behaves like one gigantic Schrödinger wave function collectively incorporating all the atoms in the sample. Thus **matter waves** are not merely an idea. Einstein broke off from his own work to translate Bose's paper and to develop the new Bose-Einstein statistics from which we get the term *boson* for the class of quantum particles that carry force.

In fact, the concept of the particle of light was only given the name *Photon* (by Lewis in 1926) after S.N. Bose put the Quantum Theory of Light on a secure footing. Max Planck[N1] had never suggested the actual existence of electromagnetic quanta (particle-like packets of energy), Planck said in 1931 that quantisation was a purely formal assumption. He like others thought of light as really being waves and the quantum as a mathematical trick to account for interactions of light and matter (a view to which physics is returning in regard to the Wave Structure of Matter (WSM)). However, in India astrophysicist Meghnad Saha took the light quantum seriously to describe radiation pressure in 1919. This led Bose to seek to put Planck's law of black-body radiation on a consistent footing. This involved treating light quanta as behaving like gas particles, removing all vestiges of Maxwell's wave theory, thus allowing application of statistical laws to light[34]. In fact Saha and Bose had produced one of the first English translations of Einstein's 1915 General Theory of Relativity in 1919 thus helping to publicise Einstein's major work. Einstein was so impressed by Bose's paper on the statistical treatment of light quanta that he translated it into German himself hence ensuring its publication in a top German journal[35].

Ironically, Schrödinger said that Einstein's 1924 work on developing Bose-Einstein statistics, which Einstein interpreted in terms of de Broglie's new concept of **matter waves**, inspired him to create his own wave mechanical Schrödinger Equation in 1925, the centrepiece of QM, soon after Heisenberg invented the highly abstract Matrix Mechanics[36]. Matrix Mechanics was merely a way to calculate results of experiments without a conceptual model behind it. Schrödinger's Equation was based on an existing wave equation used in Optics and the Phase Space mechanics introduced by William Hamilton in the 1830s. Thus Schrödinger converted De Broglie's idea of matter waves into a full-fledged theory. For Schrödinger, the waves in his Wave Mechanics were as real as water waves, they were Matter Waves[37]. But mainstream Physics followed the Probabilistic Interpretation of Max Born much to Schrödinger's frustration. Such ideas leading to the manmade Wave/Particle dichotomy were enshrined in Niels Bohr's Copenhagen Interpretation with his aforementioned epistemological Neutral Monism[N2] of the 'Complementarity Principle' leaving the underlying Ontological Reality beyond the scope of human conceptualisation, (i.e., ineffable). Heisenberg described the attitude of the (half-Jewish) Bohr in his meeting with Schrödinger as that of a remorseless fanatic. Bohr was not prepared to make the least concession or grant that he could ever be wrong[38].

Even more ironic is the fact that Einstein was an admirer of another Bengali physicist Jagadish Chandra Bose in regard to Bose's aspirations to create a new Indian holistic science inspired by Brahmanic Monism[39]. J.C. Bose, a pioneer of microwave research was also the second man to send a wireless signal after British physicist Oliver Lodge. Lodge was a founder of the UK

Society for Psychical Research. Thus it seems that Wireless Communication was invented by men with interests in the psychical aether and the closely related yogic *akasa* (Space as subtle matter with its vibratory resonances), which also involves such wave-like communication. In fact most of the electrical components utilised by Marconi for the transmission of his pioneering transatlantic radio signal were patented by the Serbian-born genius Nikola Tesla, inventor of the Alternating Current. The inventive genius of Marconi was hyped-up, largely by Marconi himself, and much of the real credit for Radio communication should go to the great Tesla.[N3] Tesla claimed to have had a telepathic Crisis Vision notifying him of his mother's death. He also discussed telepathy with the famous physicist and mystical spiritualist Sir William Crookes. Crookes, whose work on cathode rays and vacuum tubes helped give us television, thought that telepathy was mediated by high-frequency brainwaves[40]. Tesla, who befriended Swami Vivekananda in the 1890s was also deeply interested in Indian metaphysics[41].

Therefore Meghnad Saha and S.N. Bose's role in developing the notion of the photon actually went against the traditional Indian monistic view which is incompatible with discrete particles! Note also that mainstream Western histories of Physics present the photon concept as appearing with Planck and Einstein at the turn of the 20th Century with no mention of this Indian role. Einstein, and, as we shall see, Heisenberg, the inventors of GTR and QM both felt it worthwhile to debate philosophical issues with the Bengali poet Tagore who was like a living *avatar* of Indian civilisation. Tagore was the first Non-European person to whom the Europeans gave their Nobel Prize for Literature. The first Non-European to receive this European prize in Physics was C.V. Raman in 1930 for his work in Calcutta on the scattering of light and discovery of the Raman Effect. Raman Spectroscopy detects subtle vibratory changes[42]. Perhaps Raman too was subconsciously influenced by Brahmanic ideas of subtle vibrations in the *Akasa*. In 1932 Raman and Bhagavantam provided experimental proof that the light photon possesses the quantum property known as 'spin' (not to be confused with macroscopic rotations of spheres). Raman also researched acoustic vibration in musical strings related to harmonics and developed the Raman-Nath theory of the acousto-optic effect (light scattering by sound waves) used in laser-optic communications.

Einstein wrote in his *The Meaning of Relativity* that, prior to the development of Relativity, the question as to whether the world was non-Euclidean had been discussed extensively[43]. He also wrote the foreword to *Concepts of Space* by the physicist and historian of Science Max Jammer. In this book, Jammer wrote that P.D. Ouspensky's *Tertium Organum* had been important in sensitising people to the new perspectives on space and that Ouspensky's *The Fourth Dimension* had put him amongst the first rank of writers on Mathematics[44]. The Russian Ouspensky made famous the mystical doctrines of the Caucasian mystic Gurdjieff who studied various Oriental practises. Both Ouspensky and Flaude Boyden, who wrote on Hyperspace notions, got interested in the 4th Dimension (notion) through their interests in Theosophy. Russian Helena Blavatsky's *The Secret Doctrine*, the Bible of the Theosophists who eventually made their headquarters in Madras, inspired interest in extra spatial dimensions. Although Blavatsky herself did not believe in a 4th Dimension, the famous Theosophist C.W. Leadbeater (*see below on Isotope discovery*) linked 'astral vision' to the notion of 4-D vision[45]. Psychical extension of perception is not really equivalent tc the naive notion of a 4th Dimension as our Euclidean space-dimensions refer to the possible translations or motions (degrees of freedom) of material objects. Metaphysical speculations that Consciousness may like another dimension or a 5th Dimension are vacuous given what a dimension actually represents. Even Einstein's representation of Time as a 4th Dimension, the 'Block Universe' is fraught with misleading implications. However, LSD subjects, well-versed in Maths do refer to experiencing non-Euclidean geometries in altered states of Consciousness[46].

Interestingly, Einstein's holistic Monist sympathies presumably came from Spinoza's Panpsychist metaphysics (which was almost certainly derived from mystical Cabbala[47]). Einstein famously asserted that his god was the god of Spinoza, the impersonal pantheistic conception of Nature which we have seen is similar to the Nature Mysticism of Mach and James. Einstein was aware of Mach's personal experience of Nature Mysticism with its parallels to Buddhism[48]. However, Einstein, whilst adhering to Spinoza's Determinism did not seem to accept Spinoza's Panpsychism, remaining a Physicalist[49]. Malin says that, although deeply influenced by Mach early on, Einstein became a Realist. He accepted the Kantian *noumenon/phenomenon* distinction but, like d'Espagnat went beyond Kant in believing that we could discover characteristics of noumenal reality through Science and that this is our only mode of access to reality[50]. It seems however from Abraham Pais story about Einstein asking Pais if he thought that the moon only exists if one looks at it[51] that Einstein mistook Idealism naively to mean the solipsistic 'Subjective Idealism'. Thus many of the quotations from Einstein used by pop philosophers, who imagine Einstein to be a modern prophet with some unique mystical communion, are misleading. Einstein's philosophical beliefs above are not consistent with an understanding of real mystical experience and its metaphysical implications.

The pro-mystical psychiatrist Arthur Deikman quotes both Isaac Newton and Albert Einstein in support of Mysticism with Einstein writing[52]:

> *The most beautiful and profound emotion we can experience is the sensation of the mystical. It is the source of all true science. ...To know that what is impenetrable to us really exists, manifesting itself as the highest wisdom and the most radiant beauty, which our dull faculties can comprehend only in their primitive forms—this knowledge, this feeling, is at the center of true religion.*

However, Einstein with his idealised, artificial Space-Time continuum, as also in the case of Spinoza with his geometric, abstract, conceptual psycho-physical parallelism, did not understand true transcendental spirituality. Einstein's inability to accept the Nonlocal Entanglement and Indeterminacy of QM reflects this ignorance of Transcendental Reality transcending Space/Time/Causality. Radhakrishnan commented that the (Platonism-influenced) Spinoza treats God, understanding and human passions as though they were circles and triangles[53]. Note how Einstein conflates mystical experience with emotions and sensations which transcendent experiences certainly are not. Thus

Einstein's vague talk of "cosmic religious experience" conflates Spinoza's Pantheism and Machian Nature Mysticism with Cosmic Consciousness and shows no knowledge of the Plenum/Void where Time itself is transcended by 'Eternity'.

In his writings on cosmic religious feeling, Einstein claims that the religions of all civilised people, especially Oriental ones, are primarily moral religions with anthropomorphic conceptions of God. But Einstein does talk of a more advanced third stage of religious experience or cosmic religious feeling which knows no dogma and no God conceived in man's image so there can be no church whose central teachings are based on it[54]. In fact this statement by Einstein seems identical to the views of his friend the French Nobel laureate writer, mystic and fellow pacifist Romain Rolland.[N4] The latter, like Einstein himself, was a friend of Rabindranath Tagore and the man who regarded Tagore as his guru, Mohandas Gandhi. Deeply into Vedanta, Rolland had told Sigmund Freud (whose absurd reductions of spirituality to sex etc. we shall examine later), "religious sensation... is entirely different from religions and much more durable". Religious experience, Rolland asserted, referring to the Bengali mystic Ramakrishna and his apostle Vivekananda, was, "independent of all dogma... of all organisation of the church, of every holy book"[55]. Einstein, however, jumbles together naively the Psalms of David, Buddhism, Francis of Assisi and Spinoza. He misunderstood Idealism to mean solipsistic, Subjective Idealism in which the observer's mind literally creates the observed rather than simply abstracting a phenomenal aspect of it. Einstein said that we learnt from Schopenhauer that Buddhism contains a much stronger element of cosmic religious feeling than the Psalms[56]. Schopenhauer's primary association with Eastern spirituality was with the Upanishads which he described as the solace of his life and stated that they would be the solace of his death[57]. He even kept the Upanishads (in Latin) on his bedside table and performed devotions from them before going to bed[58]. As stated in Chapter 1, it is clear that, in spite of his celebrity 'icon' status in the popular media, encouraged by books like Schilpp's *Albert Einstein: Philosopher-Scientist*, Einstein was actually a lesser philosopher than Eddington, Heisenberg, Schrödinger and Pauli.

David Bohm: Taking Physics into the Transcendental and Holy

Besides Heisenberg's original Matrix Mechanics and Schrödinger's dominant Wave Mechanics, the third best known formulation of QM is the 1951 Causal Interpretation put forward by David Bohm which gives exactly the same experimental predictions. Bohm developed Louis de Broglie's earlier Pilot Wave ideas and treated the Schrödinger Wave Function as a real 'quasi-physical' field-like entity or Quantum Potential (when previously it had been viewed as merely a mathematical tool; *see* Heisenberg's naive criticism below). Bernard d'Espagnat makes many references to Bohm's Causal Interpretation in *On Physics and Philosophy* as it reintroduced particle trajectories but achieved this seeming return to normality at the expense of introducing **non-locality,** (i.e., independence of normal spatiality, or of 'simple location', apparently existing everywhere at once) in the underlying Quantum Potential guiding the particle. Although Bohm himself stressed this distinctly non-Classical nonlocality of the Quantum Potential, implying monistic holism, Bohm's model drew attention mainly because it restored Determinism (*emphasis mine*)[59].

Albert Einstein befriended the young Bohm at Princeton, treating Bohm as if he were his 'intellectual son' before Bohm was forced to leave the USA by the McCarthyite, anti-communist witch hunt[60]. Bohm, who eventually settled in London, befriended the famous Indian mystic Jiddu Krishnamurti whom the Theosophists had aggrandised whilst still a boy. Indian philosophic influence is seen in Bohm's later metaphysical ideas stressing Perception (rather like Eddington's depiction of the 'particle' phenomenon in Chapter 1), a Space-Time transcending, monistic, holonomic (each seeming 'entity' exists in relativistic relation to all others – i.e., is inseparable from the Whole) underlying reality (his 'Holomovement') which Talbot[61] and Rosen[62] both say shows Brahmanic influences). Bohm's notion of nonlocal Active Information in the Quantum Potential or in his later, metaphysical 'Implicate Order' resembles the vibratory resonances of form in the *Akasa* of the *Yoga Sutras*. Bohm also befriended neurologist Karl Pribram who had himself put forward Mysticism-inspired views of the underlying reality of the 'holographic Frequency Domain' (a realm of 'frequencies' (a rather tangential term for *waves* or *energetic vibrations*)) which is transformed through Fourier transform-like operations in our perceptual system into our mundane Space-Time world. Pribram noted the parallels with the Hindu *Maya*[63]. The 'Frequency Domain' is really a modern reformulation of the *Akasa*. Interestingly, Pribram, in his later work on so-called 'Holonomic Quantum Field Neurodynamics' points out that the Nobel laureate physicist Denis Gabor, who invented Holography, had already recognised the parallels between the formalism of Quantum Theory and the process of perception[64]. Clearly the confusing mumbo-jumbo introduced by John von Neumann about the role of an unspecified, so-called 'Consciousness' in the so-called 'collapse' of the Schrödinger Wave Function is related to the appearance of the perceptual phenomenon in the mind of the observer.

Although moving toward Panpsychist views in his late works, Bohm's view of Consciousness, like those of his friend David Peat, resembled Jung's vague notions of a deeper Psychoid realm, where Matter and Mind were, in some unspecified sense, indistinguishable. In his last book,[N5] Bohm (and Hiley) say that, "it is convenient to introduce the notion that Consciousness shows or manifests on two sides which may be called the physical and the mental. Active Information can serve as a kind of link or 'bridge' between these two sides"[65]. They also state that there is no real division between Mind and Matter. They add that, unlike Wigner, Everett and Squires, our position is that Quantum Theory can be understood without bringing in Consciousness. However, the intuition that Consciousness and Quantum Theory are somehow related seems good[66]. Finally, they ask, if the subtle levels, (i.e., implicate orders) are carried to infinity[67] which strikes me as resembling Spinoza's idea of God having an infinite number of attributes of which we apprehend only two, Mind and Matter. Ericson says that Bohm suggests that quality is at least as important as quantity and talks of the *qualitative infinity of nature*[68]. Von Franz says that Bohm's Holomovement was supposed to be indefinable, unmeasurable and unknowable[69]. Rosen aptly criticizes Bohm's approach[70]:

Rather than facing the problem of undifferentiability head on – in classical Cartesian language, facing the problem of mind – this problem is put off interminably by an endless series of abstractions upon the differentiable or physical.

Rosen acknowledges that Bohm, in his 'Vedantist' moods recognised that mathematical abstractions such as 'implicate orders' do not approach undifferentiable, Ultimate Reality or the 'infinite totality'[71].

Bohm's oft-repeated description of the particle phenomenon as being like a an extremely rapid sequence of flashes parallels the Buddhist yogic description of the 'Interface of Mind and Cosmos' where, during Insight Meditation, the yogi realises that the principles underlying the manifestation of mental phenomena also underlie the phenomena of the wider Cosmos. The Buddhists also describe phenomena as flashing in and out of existence in a rapid sequence of pulses[72]. Bohm's used the terms Enfolding and Unfolding to allude to the fact that the materialising, localised particle phenomenon is interconnected to the Cosmos as a whole and is a holonomic precipitation of the entire Holomovement. I used the Buddhist term 'Dependent Co-Origination', which expresses clearly the interdependence of all phenomena, for such holistic causation in my O/OM.[N6]

Bohm does however go beyond Einstein's limitation to the totally abstract, mathematical 'Space-Time continuum' which presents a completely misleading picture of Time as a pre-existing Space-like dimension in the 'Block Universe'. Bohm realised that Quantum Theory is less about the motion of particles than with how the Space-Time order emerges from a 'pre-space'[73]. This insight ties in with Schrödinger's emphasis on the fact that there are no individual particles moving with distinct trajectories in QM, only localised manifestations of 'particle-like' phenomena from the underlying (nonlocal) wave activity[74]. Space-Time is thus intimately associated with the emergence of localised, mutually exclusive material phenomena. Hiley and Peat state[75]:

One important feature concerning the holomovement is that it is not described in space-time but from it space-time is to be abstracted. Thus we no longer start with an a priori space-time manifold in order to discuss physics; rather we construct space-time from the underlying process.

The 1995 reformulation of QM by German physicist Wolfram Schommers, which incorporates Mach's holonomic Principle of Inertia involves just such a nonlocal, particle-free, 'prespace' of fundamental energy and momentum process from which empirical Space-Time appears through our perception[76]. Kantian Schommers does not specify further his underlying processes but, as both Schommers himself and Whiteman[77] note, QM relates energy to wave frequency and momentum to wave-length so Schommer's work is pointing to the deeper holonomic, Wave Structure of Matter.

Thus Bohm recognised the 'transcendental' realm with its nonlocality and holonomy. He also rejected static Platonic Forms for the dynamic Akashic view with his Active Information fields. Hiley and Peat describe how Bohm wanted to abandon the traditional notion of separate particles and fields in order to incorporate the holistic properties of Reality indicated by QM. Inspiration in such matters came from the study of Perception where the eye is found to detect not what actually exists outside but only those features that remain invariant for sufficient time to be perceived[78]. Bohm would point out that the word "Holy" actually referred to such transcendental Wholeness (Holiness) or Oneness. This profound sense of Wholeness is conflated by the likes of Nobel laureate Roger Sperry with the trivial formation of 'wholes' or self-maintaining systems in his absurd Emergent Materialist 'holism' which he boasted preposterously accounts for transcendental moral issues etc.[79]. As stated above, in the last chapter of his last book Bohm and Hiley[80] suggested a 'particle-free' holonomic model of QM similar to the holonomic Huygens construction wavefront model put forward by Milo Wolff[81].

However, although Bohm's work is hyped-up as revolutionary by his admirers, there is little that is really that new if one knows about the history of Mysticism. J.H.M. Whiteman's 1967 book *The Philosophy of Space and Time and the Inner Constitution of Nature* (in the Muirhead Library of Philosophy) preceded the mass market writings of Capra and Bohm with a far more scholarly analysis by a real mystic but went unnoticed, as he lamented to me in 1999[82]. According to von Franz[83], Bohm asserted that the transcendental Reality was **unknowable** although his metaphysics was inchoate and sometimes he said some pseudo-mystical things about Consciousness which suggested the opposite, often presupposing the existence of Consciousness in electrons etc. Information is not the same as Consciousness. Actual mystic and broad-ranging scholar Whiteman wrote correctly that the transcendental substructure was known indirectly through the interpretation of QM and knowable directly through mystical contemplation[84].

Heisenberg's Hindu influences and epistemological uncertainties in approaching the One

Heisenberg stated that he was well aware of the parallels between QM and Eastern mysticism long before they reached the popular psyche in the 1970s. He stated that he had himself been subconsciously influenced by Indian mystical philosophy in his invention of QM. It also came as a great comfort to him, after discussions with Tagore on a lecture tour to Calcutta, to find that an entire civilisation (the Indian) held a view of the world resembling in some ways that of the new QM which had so shocked the Western Mind[85, 86]. These talks with Tagore helped him a lot with his work on Physics[87]. Heisenberg, who stressed that the human mind could neither visualise nor conceive the radical Otherness of Quantum Reality described by the abstract language of Mathematics, no doubt recognised the parallels with the Vedantic doctrine of *vyavahara*, that *Brahman*, paradoxically transcending conceptual dichotomies, cannot be characterised in normal human thought.

In contrast mainstream Western scientific culture remains totally perplexed by the supposedly paradoxical, 'weird' and supposedly incomprehensible world revealed by QM. Popular science books and TV documentaries lapped up the glib remarks of the hyped-up, bongo-playing, supposedly 'charismatic' physicist Richard Feynman about nobody understanding QM. However 'cool' they try to appear on TV, physicists who believe Physicalism-Materialism to be the true ontology must be narrow-minded (rejecting contradictory facts), and generally nerdy navel-gazing geeks do not possess real *charisma* (Divine gratuity) related to *enthusiasm* (being filled with Divinity). Rather they have blind faith in Scientism. *Star Trek Voyager* scriptwriters project magical qualities onto QM, imagining future starship engineers as having advanced degrees in it. This allows for fictional storylines allowing false extrapolations of Heisenberg's Uncertainty Principle etc. to permit time travel etc. Such modern fairy tales about wormholes, warping the fabric of Space-Time etc. are little different from medieval wizards performing magical spells. In fact, Feynman was prominent in establishing the "shut-up-and-calculate" orthodoxy in Theoretical Physics (although he might not have coined the phrase) as its centre of gravity shifted from (metaphysical) Germany to the (Mammonite) USA during the 1940s. Lee Smolin, like other would-be philosopher-physicists, laments that many young physicists become depressed entering the profession as it has become taboo to ask deep questions and discuss the philosophical foundations of QM[88].

d'Espagnat refers to the 'sham ontology' associated with the Feynman diagram tools-for-thought, in which a force is described by an exchange of virtual particles, ascribed to by many physicists[89]. In fact, Feynman's 'Sum over Histories' (Path Integral) method implying that particles travel infinite paths and Wheeler and Feynman's 'advanced waves' travelling backward in time from the Universe at large are mathematical abstractions reflecting the underlying holonomic, ethereal existence of particle-like phenomena[90]. Susskind expresses his amazement that in String Theory (derived from QM), the extended structure of the electron spreads out to the ends of the universe or to infinity[91]. This pseudo-mystical status of QM in popular culture recently hit the headlines in 2008 with England's rugby world-cup winning hero Johnny Wilkinson telling the press about his interests in Buddhism, living-in-the-moment and QM. The Buddhist 'living in-the-moment' has long been conflated with true enlightenment, (i.e., receiving divine wisdom) by naive Buddhists and Western Buddhophiles. This is seen in the comments of American Buddhophile poets on the 2010 Public Broadcasting Service TV documentary *The Buddha*, who seem to think that *nirvana* is paying careful attention to the here and now.

Heisenberg was disdainful of the Positivists of the Vienna Circle (trying to emulate the supposed 'exactness' of the 'big boys' in Physics). Positivism dismissed most of Metaphysics as 'pre-scientific' and 'animistic' but, as Bohr had pointed out, such a dismissal would prevent our understanding QM[92]. We have seen that fundamental concepts of modern science (e.g. *acceleration, force, heat, energy, attraction, mass*) are themselves animistic projections onto Nature. In his 1958 *Physics and Philosophy*[93], Heisenberg states:

> ...[T]*he great difficulty which even eminent scientists like Einstein had in understanding and accepting the Copenhagen Interpretation of quantum theory, one can trace the roots of this difficulty to the Cartesian partition,* [i.e., Mind/Body dualism]. ... *We" objectivate" a statement if we claim that its content does not depend on the conditions under which it can be verified,* [i.e., not merely intersubjective empirical consensus]. ...*Dogmatic realism claims that there are no statements concerning the material world that cannot be objectivated. ... When Einstein has criticised quantum theory he has done so from the basis of dogmatic realism.*

Thus Einstein naively mistook the explanation of Nature by simple mathematical laws for the genuine objective reality rather than something we humans have constructed[94]. We saw that Einstein misunderstood Idealism to be solipsistic. We have also seen that Bohr's own Complementarity Principle is a form of epistemological Neutral Monism and his Copenhagen Interpretation similarly avoids Ontology. This is equivalent to the Ineffability doctrine in Mysticism and Bohr's *via negativa* prevents progress toward a deeper. nonlocal WSM understanding which dissolves the manmade paradoxes based on false assumptions such as point particles and externally-related local causality.

In Whiteman's 1967 book *The Philosophy of Space and Time*, for which Heisenberg checked the manuscript of the chapter on QM, Whiteman quotes Heisenberg stating that we cannot return to the ontology of Materialism. However, taking Heisenberg's *Physics and Philosophy* as a guide, it would seem that, rather like Einstein but unlike the explicitly Brahmanic Schrödinger, Heisenberg's rejection of the ultimate reality of elementary particles seems no more than a rejection of what d'Espagnat calls Multitudinism in favour of a Physicalist monistic Holism. Heisenberg places an emphasis on *Energy* as the new metaphysical substance in modern Physics and presents a notion of energy as the potential reality which actualises into material forms, influenced by Bohm's earlier (1951) notion of *tendencies*. In spite of his criticism of Descartes' Mind/Body dualism, the Niels Bohr type epistemological critique of Einstein's naive Realism only heals the Mind/Body dualism within the context of the Western conflation of Mind (as ego) and Consciousness (as Awareness). In spite of his associations with Tagore, his close friend C.F. Weizsäcker's association with mystic Gopi Krishna, Indian philosophy, Pauli, and Whiteman's book which argues for a Universal Consciousness, Heisenberg himself is not an Idealist in the sense of postulating Universal Consciousness as the One. His emphasis is on epistemological limitations and Platonic mathematical forms. Mathematics for Plato meant largely Geometry.

Indeed, in spite of references to Platonism and his later rejection of Multitudinism, Heisenberg's criticisms of Bohm's and Schrödinger's views reveals the limitations of his own understanding of Transcendentalism. Shimon Malin mentions Heisenberg's role in the 1919 suppression of the Munich Soviet. He tells us that Heisenberg was the son of a Classics scholar and had read Plato's *Timaeus* and wrote of a (Platonic) Central Order, (i.e., the realm of Ideas) in language, music, philosophy and religion. Plato wrote of two kinds of knowledge of the Intelligible. The first kind, exemplified by Geometry starts with hypotheses or axioms and proceeds to investigate the consequences. The second type or Contemplation treats assumptions, not as absolute, but literally as hypotheses which it rises above to that knowledge which requires no assumptions at all but involves moving in a (metaphysical) realm of Pure Ideas. Heisenberg wrote of knowing the inherent nature of the actual through contemplation or in a moment of insight in which the subject/object mode is transcended[95]. Unlike many Western scholars, he understood Plato as a mystic stating in regard to Plato's simile of the cave[96]:

The real philosopher is the prisoner who has escaped into the light of truth or, we may in the Christian sense say, with God is the new reality that has begun to be perceived that has begun to become stronger than the reality of the world as perceived by our senses. The immediate connection with God happens within the human soul, not in the world, and this was the problem that occupied human thought ...in the two thousand years following Plato.

In another work, he says that if we wish to approach the "One" in terms of a precise scientific language, we must turn our attention to Plato's centre of Science, that realm of being which can be understood mathematically. Heisenberg recognised that Plato himself was not content with this restriction and evoked poetic images of an altogether different kind of understanding (as in Chapter 3). Probably influenced by his friend Wolfgang Pauli (*see below*), Heisenberg adds that these images are probably connected with unconscious mental patterns that (Jungian) psychologists call archetypes which in some way reflect the internal structures of the world . Whatever the explanation for these other forms of understanding; the language of images and metaphors is probably the only way of approaching the "One"[97]. Ancient Greeks, even Egypt-based Plotinus, in the 3rd Century *c.e.*, spoke of the Light and of the One but did not develop a concept of *Consciousness*. Plotinus presupposes Consciousness in that the One is known or experienced.This leads to the focus on Plato's geometric forms, symmetry, and the emphasis on physical forms and their dynamic inter-relations. Similarly, as Rosen indicated, Bohm sees only the differentiable abstractions (his supposedly infinite subtle orders) but is oblivious of the formless Ground of all Being.

Heisenberg discusses Kant's *a priori* concepts or 'pure intuitions' of Euclidean Space and Time and of Causality and Substance. He says that we now have non-Euclidean geometry in GTR, QM no longer applies the law of Causality and the law of Conservation of Matter (the Kantian substance; *energy* was a 19th Century scientific concept) no longer holds in the annihilation of elementary particles. Thus, at first sight it seems as if Kant's central concept of 'synthetic judgments *a priori*' has been annihilated. Kant could not have foreseen that these *a priori* concepts can be the conditions for Science yet only have a limited range of application; they are relative truths. Heisenberg asserts that such a reinterpretation of *a priori* means that we need not consider only the perception rather than the things as given. In contrast to Kant's view that from the perception we cannot conclude anything about the thing-in-itself, Heisenberg cites his friend astrophysicist Carl von Weizsäcker. Weizsäcker says that for the atomic physicist, if he uses the concept of thing-in-itself at all (Bohr's Copenhagen Interpretation of course does not touch it), it applies to a mathematical structure but this structure is, contrary to Kant, indirectly deduced from experience[98]. We have seen that, as with Einstein, Bernard d'Espagnat goes beyond the (supposedly) "sublime Kant" in arguing that, insofar as human mind-independent "Veiled Reality" conforms to our logical reasoning, the amazing success of mathematics in predicting phenomena implies that mathematical physics is revealing some aspect of the structure of Veiled Reality[99].

Heisenberg also concurs with ethologist Konrad Lorenz's view that our Euclidean *a priori* concepts are the product of our evolution corresponding to innate schemes in other species. Physicist Wolfram Schommers also places much emphasis on the biological basis of our Euclidean perception of Space and Time, claiming that they are uniquely human (as compared to say the world as perceived by a turkey)[100]. I doubt that the world as it appears to turkeys is as radically different from ours as Schommers imagines; the echolocation world of bats may be. Schommers remains a strict Kantian assuming that transcendental perception of noumenal Reality beyond our Euclidean perceptual constructs is impossible (although he cites the New Age books of Michael Talbot, *Mysticism and the New Physics* and *The Holographic Universe* in his references). Whiteman, himself primarily a Platonist, stresses that the transcendental substructure is a realm of potentialities which actualise upon occasion. Whiteman stresses a point related to Heisenberg's comment about Kantian *a priori* concepts and Jungian archetypes reflecting in some way the innate structures of the world. Whiteman says that given the intersubjective nature of scientific knowledge, Western philosophy cannot account for the Paradox of Communal Objectivity. Why do different independent subjects construct the world in a similar manner allowing intersubjective consensus. The answer, says Whiteman, is that we all have access to a Universalised Pure Consciousness[101]. By this he must mean the holonomic Akashic or Noetic information in the Inner Light, which is the same in all, informing our innate, basic ('archetypal') cognitive structures thus ensuring cognitive coherence between individual subjects. This is related to notions that our mental archetypal patterns are inherited (karmically) from the 'Akashic Records' rather than being inherited via DNA.

Heisenberg discusses Bohm's 1951 Causal Interpretation. In this model, Bohm considered particles to be 'objectively real' point masses. The waves in the configuration space (the positional component) are also considered 'objectively real', like electric fields, (i.e., the Quantum Potential). Heisenberg challenges this objective Quantum Potential etymologically, saying that the word "real" goes back to the Latin *res* (thing) but things exist in ordinary 3-D space not in abstract configuration space. One may call them 'objective' in the sense of not being dependent on an observer but one can't call them "real", says Heisenberg, unless one changes the meaning of the word[102]. Hence I used the term 'quasi-physical' above. Heisenberg adds that Pauli emphasised that Bohm's Causal Interpretation also implies that electrons in atomic ground states should not be performing any orbital motion. But Bohm can counter-argue that the measurement can no longer be evaluated by the ordinary laws unlike a normal evaluation which would lead to a velocity distribution. But due to strange Quantum Potentials introduced *ad hoc* by Bohm then the statement is inadmissible that the electrons 'really' are at rest. Thus Bohm rejects the ordinary interpretation for velocity measurements. Heisenberg calls Bohm's objective description an "ideological structure" which has little to do with immediate physical reality. Bohm's hidden parameters, he says, are of such a kind that they can never occur in the description of real processes, if Quantum Theory remains unchanged[103]. Later, in discussing Language and Reality, Heisenberg says that physicists have become accustomed to considering the electronic orbits not as reality but as "potentia" (objective tendencies or possibilities)[104].

Of Schrödinger's opposition to the Copenhagen Interpretation, Heisenberg says that Schrödinger has taken an exceptional position inasmuch as he would ascribe "objective reality" not to the particles but to the waves and he won't accept the interpretation of waves as 'probability waves only'. In his discussion of Schrödinger's denial of the existence of (discontinuous) 'quantum jumps' Heisenberg replaces this provocative term with 'discontinuity'. Heisenberg says that Schrödinger overlooks the fact that only the waves in configuration space (or 'transformation matrices') are probability waves in the usual view, whereas the 3D matter waves or radiation waves are not. These 3D waves have just as much "reality" as the particles; they have no direct connection to the probability waves but have a continuous density of energy and momentum, like an electromagnetic field. Although he says that Schrödinger rightly emphasises that these processes can be conceived as more continuous than they usually are, Heisenberg adds that this interpretation cannot remove the element of discontinuity that is found everywhere in atomic physics as demonstrated by any scintillation screen or Geiger counter[105]. However by 1967, as seen above, Heisenberg seems to have changed his mind and rejected such Multitudinist views. I have already shown above that this aspect of seeming discontinuity, or the existence of light photons or 'particles' of matter is becoming resolved with views resembling the 'particle-free physics' of Schrödinger and the later Bohm. Mathematical physicist Richard Thompson[106] and d'Espagnat[107] both explain why the continuous tracks in cloud chambers do not prove the existence of individual particle trajectories, as Eddington also indicated[108]. Thompson says that the word "particle" is used metaphorically in QM. Physical descriptions are actually given in terms of waves, or more generally in terms of 'state vectors' (wave functions) in Hilbert space. As d'Espagnat says, Multitudinism (the ultimate, indestructible particle view) is no longer tenable[109].

Heisenberg's arguments against Bohm's Quantum Potential once again touch upon the questions of Space-Time transcendence as he grants the status of "reality" only to "things" in 3D space. He does not specify what distinguishes a thing in 3D space from objective entities existing beyond 3D space. This strikes me as self-contradictory given his Platonic assertions as Plato held the 3D world to be mere phenomena or temporal shadows! The Pauli Exclusion Principle, excluding particles from each other's energy space[110] (*see below*), suggests to me that Heisenberg's 3D 'reality' implies spatial exclusivity, extensiveness or impenetrability for matter as opposed to the mutual superposition or interpenetration of potential forms as found in the wave function and in mystical descriptions of transcendental realms. One also detects a hostility given the fame of Heisenberg's Uncertainty Principle limiting our simultaneous knowledge of 'conjoined' pairs of particle attributes (position and momentum; energy and time (duration)). As mentioned above, Bohm's Causal Interpretation reintroduced trajectories and Determinism at the cost of the underlying nonlocal Quantum Potential. Peter Ericson in an essay entitled *Indeterminism and the Bohm Interpretation of Quantum Mechanics* focuses on Bohm and Hiley's 1993 development of the Causal Interpretation called the Ontological Interpretation. Ericson has difficulty with the "weird" features such as nonlocality and active information (presumably being attracted to Bohm's model by the familiar old particles with trajectories). He says one reason why many people prefer an interpretation other than Bohm's is because of the Indeterminism that is, in one way or another, implied. But such opponents of Bohm fail to understand his broader ideas about Nature and Reality such that it is possible to support Bohm's interpretation without giving up Indeterminism. He adds[111]:

The Bohm interpretation being an ontological interpretation, does not agree that the [Heisenberg] *uncertainty principle sets an ontological limit on knowledge. It says that particles do have all attributes simultaneously. On this view the uncertainty principle is purely epistemological. Furthermore, contrary to what is believed when the uncertainty principle is taken to set an ontological limit, the uncertainty is due to disturbances introduced by measurements:*

Of course the Copenhagen Interpretation restricts itself to epistemology and what humans can perceive (communicable intersubjective phenomena). Heisenberg's overall approach is one of epistemological limitations of human understanding with an antipathy toward granting "reality" to entities whose behavioural patterns do not conform to empirical, three-dimensional Space-Time-Causality. Although he recognises Plato's higher mystical mode of nondual knowledge, Heisenberg thinks it can only be described in poetic symbolism. Given his discussions with Tagore, I presume that–being a product of the 19th Century Bengal Renaissance and Neo-Hinduism–Tagore was familiar with the negative discourse of the ineffable Reality in Vedanta. The notion of Matter as the vibratory densification of *Akasa* was in the Upanishads, the original Vedanta, but only elaborated by non-mainstream Schools like the Grammarians with their *Sabdabrahman* where *Sabda* (Sound) represents Vibration[112]. The positive descriptions of transcendental vibrations in Tantric traditions like Kashmir Saivism is not that well known to my own Bengali *bhadralok* community of which Tagore was the most famous representative. However modern Bengali mystics Ramakrishna and Aurobindo both stressed Tantric views of Creation. Similarly Whiteman (1967) claims that Plotinus provides the most developed form of such mystical philosophy. The Kashmir Saivite Doctrine of Vibration was not well known until the 1980s (I shall look at the failings of Plotinus's and Plato's doctrines in Chapter 10). Heisenberg even refers to Carl Jung's reformulation of Hermetic archetypes but, unlike Pauli, does not know too much about such notions. Heisenberg's friend C.F. von Weizsäcker was deeply into Indian Philosophy.[N7] In fact, we shall see that, like the 'blind men' and the elephant, Bohm, Heisenberg, Schrödinger and Pauli are all abstracting limited aspects of the same underlying "Bigger, Deeper Picture" of the Transcendental Realm and that the notions of Non-locality, Active Information, Potentia, particles as epiphenomena of underlying waves, and archetypes are all inter-related.

Erwin Schrödinger: Quantum wave mechanics reflects the unity and continuity of Advaita Vedanta

When QM first appeared, says d'Espagnat, neither physicists nor philosophers apprehended clearly its implications of a Wholeness, radically foreign to Classical Physics; the one exception being Erwin Schrödinger. He adds that the views of Schrödinger are hardly known, even amongst the experts[113]. Some Western commentators familiar with his views suppress the fact that in his *My View of the World* and in appendices to other works, Schrödinger stressed that he advocated Nondual Brahmanism (*Advaita Vedanta*), that Ultimate Reality is Consciousness which is One (*Brahman*) although he was also well-versed in Greek philosophy. D'Espagnat does mention Schrödinger's Vedantism. He also refers to the French Schrödinger scholar, neurophenomenologist and Buddophile admirer of Nagarjuna, Michel Bitbol who has discussed d'Espagnat's 'Veiled Reality' views in his own works. Recently, I purchased Schrödinger's monographs *My View of the World* and *The Interpretation of Quantum Mechanics*, both reprinted by Oxbow Press[114, 115]. The former had an orange cover with a Hindu style eye (Inner Eye) on the front as Schrödinger openly stressed his advocacy of *Advaita Vedanta*. However, the second monograph had an introduction by Bitbol which claimed that Schrödinger's Idealism was inspired by Ernst Mach's Pansensism. Bitbol even gave the Oxbow Press *My View of the World* as a reference for this claim[116]. However, having just read the latter, I could not recall Schrödinger mentioning Mach although he repeatedly referred to Vedanta as he also did in the appendices to *What is Life* and *Mind* and *Matter*.[N8]

Biographer Walter Moore tells us that Schrödinger had read everything written by Schopenhauer who rejected Kant's thesis of the unknowable noumenal reality. Schopenahuer was himself deeply influenced by Vedanta and Buddhism and called his dog Atman and kept the Upanishads on his bedside desk[117]. He also read devotions from the Upanishads before going to bed[118]. Schrödinger thought deeply about the Hindu teachings and ultimately came to believe them. Both Schopenhauer and Schrödinger rejected the personal God of the Theists and called themselves 'atheists' although Schopenhauer thought that Pantheism was only a euphemism for Atheism. Moore, like others, conflates Nature Mystical Pantheism with Transcendental Monist or 'Panentheist' Brahmanism. Perhaps Schrödinger's own famished state at the end of the 1914-18 war was conducive to spiritual experience. In July 1918 he wrote[119]:

> *Nirvana is a state of pure blissful knowledge... it has nothing to do with the individual. The ego or its separation is an illusion. ...The goal of man is to preserve his Karma and to develop it further. ...When a man dies, his Karma lives and creates for itself another carrier.*

This view ties in with my interpretation of Past Life Memories in O/OM as originating from the Karmic Resonances in the *Akasa* where they exist without individuation and my rejection of the myths of personal transmigration (as there is no permanent individuated consciousness).

At this time Schrödinger was also deeply influenced by Irish-Greek Lafcadio Hearn who went to Japan and was immersed in Buddhism. In his "The Diamond Cutter", Hearn wrote (*emphasis mine*)[120]:

> *The ego is only an aggregate of countless illusions...a bubble sure to break. It is Karma. Acts and thoughts are forces integrating themselves into material and mental phenomena...Even swords and things of metal are manifestations of spirit. ...There is one reality but there is no permanent individual.*

> *...And even as the storming of a sea is a motion of undulation, not of translation,—**even as it is the form of the wave only, not the wave itself, that travels** – so in the passing of lives **there is only the rising and vanishing of forms – forms mental, forms material.***

Moore writes that perhaps these thoughts recurred to Erwin when he made his great discovery of Wave Mechanics and found the reality of Physics in wave motions which he based on an underlying Unity of Mind (Consciousness). Unlike the Eurocentric Bitbol and Malin who have suppressed the fact that Schrödinger was a Vedantin, Moore adds that **throughout his life Schrödinger expressed** in graceful essays **his belief in Vedanta.** But he remained what the *Chandogya Upanisad* calls a *Mahavit,* a Knower of the Word, not an *Atmavit* or a Knower of Atman (*emphasis mine*) [121].

Schrödinger saw QM as perfectly consistent with *Advaita Vedanta*. He viewed the unity and continuity of QM, with 'particles' being merely epiphenomena generated by underlying wave activity, reflecting the All in One and One in All (holonomy) of Vedanta[122]. Hence the opposition to (Multitudinism) and discontinuous quantum jumps. He also held the Upanishadic doctrine of the *Atman-Brahman* (that the impersonal 'Self' within us is one with the Universal 'Self') to be the grandest thought ever put forward by Humankind[123]. The *Atman-Brahman* doctrine is in fact not a 'thought' (or a product of conceptual speculation) but a mystical realisation; Knowledge by Identity ('becoming one with). Schrödinger also says[124]:

> *We know, when God is experienced, this is an event as real as an immediate sense perception or as one's own personality. Like them, he must be missing in the space-time picture. I do not find God anywhere in space and time—that is what the honest naturalist tells you. For this, he incurs blame from him in whose catechism is written: God is spirit.*

I would point out that most mystics actually claim that the experience of Divinity within actually has a greater sense of reality than our experience of the sensory world. In Heisenberg's reference to Plato's cave, the real philosopher perceives the Light of Truth as more real than the sense world. It has a sense of being the Real or True Reality. In Islamic Sufi mysticism, which al-Biruni says is etymologically derived from the Greek *Sofia* (Divine Wisdom), the Light (*nur*) is called *al haqq* (the Real)[125].

My critique of Varela's neurophenomenology (*see Note 7*) which reduced Consciousness to Materialist myths of (magical) emergence in self-organising, living cell-like 'autopoietic' processes included the following:

> *Surely, said Schrödinger, the singularity of consciousness is more intuitively convincing than the western plurality of consciousnesses which leads inevitably to the invention of souls.*

Having quoted this and some other Vedantic assertions of Schrödinger on the nature of Consciousness from *What is Life*, Benjamin Libet (famous for his EEG 'Readiness Potential') and co-editors of *The Volitional Brain* stated that they find Schrödinger's conclusions "outrageous"[126]. His co-editors, Anthony Freeman and Keith Sutherland, are the editors of the *Journal of Consciousness Studies*. Freeman is actually also a Christian priest. Christianity of course holds that immortal souls are forever distinct from God, (i.e., Theism). Libet *et al.* add in a footnote, referring to "the *observed* multiplicity of conscious minds", that "we may feel that it is hardly scientific to call *observable* facts illusory in favour of a universal entity whose existence is not testable" (*emphasis mine*)[127].

These comments of Libet, Freeman and Sutherland are in fact the truly outrageous verbal and epistemological 'sleights of hand' so typical of Materialist sophistry, falsely posing as "scientific" to rubbish views which challenge their beliefs. They are ones invoking magic with their mumbo jumbo of 'Emergence' which is in fact magical *creation ex nihilo*. Schrödinger himself wrote of ***objectivation***; Science starts by removing the subject of cognizance, (i.e., Galileo's secondary qualities) and treats its subject matter as lifeless (and insentient) objects[128]. Consciousness cannot possibly 'emerge' out of the insentient matter imagined to be real by Materialists. Increasing evolution of complexity of spatiotemporal forms (matter) only creates more complex and larger-scale stable forms. Even if given infinite time, evolution could not possibly create Consciousness if energy-matter was truly insentient. Libet *et al.* ignore the fact that conscious 'Other Minds' cannot be seen nor even proven to exist logically. We can only infer the existence of conscious minds in other humans by analogy with our own experience of our own seemingly individuated consciousness. Yet Libet *et al.* state that this analogical imputation of the multiplicity of conscious minds is an "***observable*** fact[s]" (*emphasis mine*). Could Libet *et al.* describe for us what these "observable" conscious minds look like and how they managed to observe them! Perhaps they secretly possess extrasensory perception granting them some sort of X-ray vision into living heads. Even if it was possible to observe individual minds (egos) this would not disprove Schrödinger's assertion that Consciousness is unitary.

In regard to testing the *Brahman* doctrine, have Libet *et al.* ever practised Yoga and actually experienced their own conscious minds dissolving into Universal Consciousness or *Brahman*. The multiplicity of our egos or individuated conscious minds does not necessarily imply a plurality of consciousnesses as the non-egoic processes, as Husserl and Sartre noted, are themselves forms of Consciousness and not actually insentient. Thus the individuation of ego minds does not mean that Consciousness *per se* is not an underlying unitary existence. Furthermore, Merrell-Wolff did test the *Brahman* doctrine and, having eventually (after 24 years) found it to be true, came to appreciate his earlier subtle error that *Brahman* cannot be observed as Universal Consciousness is not an *object* but the universal *subject* or Self in nondual mystical realisation[129]. d'Espagnat says that Schrödinger argues that the reason our sentient ego is nowhere found in the scientific world picture is that it itself is that world picture. Although there appears to be a great multitude of these conscious egos, the World however is only one. Schrodinger's solution to this "Arithmetical paradox" is that of the Upanishads, the thesis of the Unity of Consciousness which shines in each of us. The multiplicity of Consciousness is only appearance[130]. Schrödinger did not believe that it was possible to demonstrate the Unity of Consciousness by logical argument,[N9] one had to make an imaginative leap guided by mystical communion and analogies[131].

Wolfgang Pauli's Bombay dream of dance: Atoms, archetypes and Shiva's dance

The views of Wolfgang Pauli, another of the founding fathers of QM have also been largely ignored by historians of the New Physics as he was deeply interested in mystical and psychic phenomena[132]. Pauli was the godson of

Ernst Mach who was influential in Pauli's intellectual development. Pauli claimed to be a mystic and spoke of both Inner and Outer ways of connecting to Reality. He asserted that Christianity would be replaced by something else but refused to say what. His father Wolfgang Pascheles was born a Jew in Prague but converted to Christianity to enhance his academic career. As with Schrödinger, Pauli's view of religion was based on (the Indian-influenced) Schopenhauer and he was drawn strongly toward Indian mysticism. He was also drawn to Lao-Tzu and Taoism. Like Schrödinger, he detested the (Theistic) word *soul* as an intellectual obscenity and he also recognised the Inner Voice as an expression of the (impersonal) Self. Refusal to conform to the intent of the Inner Voice could be very disturbing as his neurotic condition immediately returned if he ever tried to be disloyal or to deny his Inner Voice[N10 133].

Pauli wrote that the 'unquenchable fire' revealed a reality deep within himself that was beyond rational understanding and which brought light to the dark centre. He knew that the centre, as an attribute of the Self, was associated in mystical traditions with the Divine. Like his friend Carl Jung, Pauli shared the need to develop a sense of the 'god within' which he thought was dark as well as light. He found Jung's focus on the Christian God without regard for the influence of the pre-Christian doctrines distasteful[134]. This interesting information comes from a recent book on Pauli and Jung by the Jungian David Lindorff. As is quite typical of such books, Lindorff ends up dishing out the usual Jungian Dream Interpretation mumbo jumbo that the Cult of Jung degenerated into rather than trying to develop further insights into the scientific understanding of mysticism. Jung said that God is a symbol of the Self and the Self is a superordinate *personality*[135]. The goal of Jung's transformative practise is so-called *individuation* which, as with Roger Sperry's Emergent Materialist holism nonsense, confuses the trivial sense of 'wholeness' with the profound meaning of **Holiness** which results from mystical experience of Oneness in Transcendental Cosmic Consciousness.

The collection of essays entitled *Psyche and Matter* by the Jungian scholar Marie-Louise von Franz displays a much clearer understanding of the scientific meaning of Archetypes, Synchronicity and Acausal Orderedness. She also mentions that Pauli challenged the view that gene mutations underlying biological evolution were purely random. Pauli argued that the time period was too short for random selection[136]. Similar ideas related to Platonic Forms, archetypes and biological morphogenesis were put forward by D'Arcy Thompson in his *On Growth and Form*[137] and later by the likes of Rupert Sheldrake[138] and Brian Goodwin[139]. However, von Franz clarifies things that remained totally vague and inchoate in Jung's own writings (perhaps Jungians like ancient Pythagoreans credit their patriarch with their own newer ideas). Lindorff himself notes that Pauli moaned to von Franz, who was Pauli's therapist and perhaps also his lover, of the lack of education in Maths and Natural Sciences of the whole of Jung's inner circle. Unlike Heisenberg, Pauli understood the Fire of Heraclitus as a symbol of the Psycho-Physical Unity[140]. But in spite of his interest in Eastern mysticism, familiarity with Plato, Plotinus, Gnosticism etc., Pauli remained ignorant of transcendental experience claiming that metaphysical reality was only describable by mathematical symbolism.

Instead he, like Jung, seemed obsessed with Alchemical symbols and Pythagorean Numerology[141].

Pauli became convinced that a new conception of Reality had to include Matter and Spirit as complementary aspects. In discussing the 17th Century dispute between Kepler and the alchemist Robert Fludd, who took Kepler to task over his quantitative view of the world, Pauli stated that he identified with both Kepler and Fludd[142]. Pauli wrote that, in the new science, the World-Soul (*anima mundi*; the NeoPlatonic 'Cosmic Consciousness') was replaced by the abstract mathematical Law of Nature. Against this one-sidedness, Alchemistical philosophy represented a counterpoise; "there dwells in matter a spirit awaiting release" [143]. Pauli attempted to create a neutral language to unify the concepts of Physics, Psychology and Parapsychology, speculating that imaginary numbers may have a role to play [144]. As Pauli himself stated, this was an attempt at a "Psychophysical Monism" relating to deeper invisible reality[145]:

> *We should then have found a mode of expression for the unity of all being, transcending the causality of classical physics as a form of correspondence (Bohr); a unity of which the psychophysical interrelation, and the coincidence of a priori instinctive forms of ideation with external perceptions,* [i.e., synchronicities], *are special cases. On such a view, traditional,* [i.e., Western] *ontology and metaphysics become the sacrifice, but the choice falls on the unity of being.*

In 1947 Pauli was an enthusiastic founding member of the Jung Institute. He kept up a correspondence with Jung for 26 years until Jung's death in 1958. The letters were published in English in 2001 under the title *Archetype and Atom*[146]. I was given a review copy by a colleague in the Journals department of the publishing company where I worked. Although it was the world's largest publisher of scientific journals, such books on unorthodox topics were not going to be reviewed. Pauli wrote to Jung in 1952 about a dream he had in Bombay containing the motif of dance. He interpreted such dance motifs, or rhythmic sensations as based on an inner perception of "*archetypal sequences*" and linked it to the Indian symbolism of the Dance of Shiva (which represents the creative energy of manifestation of the Absolute), the rhythmic movement of the transmigration of souls and the World Age (*yuga*)[147]. Pauli argued that at the Quantum level all of Nature engages in an abstract dance[148]. We shall discuss the notions of Synchronicity and Acausal Orderedness which Jung developed through his correspondence with Paul below including remarkable new scientific support for such ideas from the work of physicist Wolfram Schommers.

Pauli was reputed to have psychokinetic influences on sensitive physical instruments which friends referred to jokingly as the "Pauli Effect" as distinct from the famous Pauli Exclusion Principle[149]. This principle, prohibiting two electrons with the same energy from occupying the same atomic orbital, underlies modern Quantum Chemistry and the stability of matter. Without it there could be no regular atoms and Periodic Table of elements and hence no stable cosmic evolution. It is also involved in the Quantum Coherence phenomena of laser light and superconduction[150]. Physicist David Peat says Pauli recognised that his famous Exclusion Principle, this *exclusion* of particles from each other's energy space, cannot be reduced to an act of normal causality explicable in conventional physical terms such as a force, a field or mechanical connection. Rather it was an *acausal connecting principle*, related both to his concept of the abstract dance of energies constituting Quantum Reality and to Jung's notion of Acausal Orderedness. The underlying pattern of the *whole dance* has a profound effect on the behaviour of the individual particle[151]. This sounds very much like Bohm's Quantum Potential ideas with nonlocal Active Information connecting each particle to the whole universe. In fact, David Peat, himself a co-author with the late David Bohm, supported me when a Professor Chris Clarke, challenged my assertion that the Pauli Exclusion Principle was an example of transcendental resonance in the *Akasa* (equivalent to Bohm's nonlocal Active Information). In regard to Pauli's speculation about imaginary numbers (another Indian mathematical invention), Eddington had already noted that although these seem rather mystical, 19th Century physicists and engineers knew that the presence of the (imaginary) square root of minus one in their equations was a signal to look out for waves or oscillations[152].

The description of Quantum Reality as an 'abstract dance' needs clarification. 'Dance' implies a dynamic, rhythmic pattern of activity. As discussed later, I realised as a teenager that Physics only describes the regular (quantifiable) spatiotemporal patterns of energetic activity and thus precludes Consciousness *per se* (or Awareness) from the scientific world-picture. The word *abstract*, usually refers to extraction of limited or partial aspects of the total information. In *abstract dance* it means hard-to-conceive, hard-to-imagine or imperceptible, (i.e., non-empirical). This is equivalent to being non-spatiotemporal in the mundane (sense perception) sense and hence *abstract dance* symbolises transcendental rhythmic patterns of activity. The rhythmic nature of such activity is itself suggestive of waveforms. Similarly Heisenberg's difficulty with the reality of 'configuration waves', taken as real by Bohm and Schrödinger, was that they were 'abstract' and not 3D like 'matter waves'. Pauli's transcendental dance of energies or 'archetypal sequences' tie in with Eddington's waves and oscillations symbolised by imaginary numbers for, as physicist Nick Herbert notes in his *Quantum Reality,* all the dynamic attributes of Matter (there are no static attributes) are represented in Quantum Theory by waveform families [153]. There is no underlying particle which is vibrating to create these waveforms. Rather the 'particle' is but the phenomenon that we abstract from the localised concentration of these universal waveform-fields constituting, charge, spin etc. The influence of the underlying pattern of the whole dance on the individual 'particle' phenomenon is thus a roundabout reference to holonomy; the relativistic dependence of each entity on every other entity, as in Bohm's enfolding and unfolding from the underlying Holomovement.

Culture-bound Cavemen: Contemptuous Dismissal of Mysticism by Metaphysical Minnows of Modern Science

Hyped-up Hawking's hubristic hogwash and hostility to Mysticism

In fact, Nick Herbert told me that his own metaphysical view is known as Quantum Tantra as he recognises the convergence between the Indian view of matter as the manifestation of the energetic activity of the underlying Absolute Consciousness and the world-picture presented by QM[154]. We shall see below that Heisenberg's view of energy as *potentia* is consistent with such views when we distinguish Transcendental Reality from his Empirical "reality" based on the Latin *res.* Whereas the great founding fathers of the New Physics were open to Indian influences, most much lesser scientists recoil from any mention of Indian concepts in regard to Physics or even in regard to Psychology due to their Eurocentric cultural indoctrination that Spirituality (and Mysticism) has nothing to do with Science. It is also due to racist distortions of History and due to mainstream Western science viewing Indian philosophy as nothing more than superstition. Back in the 1990s, a British physics graduate work colleague Jim, who worked as a lowly copyeditor on science journals, said, on hearing of the book I was then writing, (i.e., O/OM), Physics is true, Eastern mysticism is nonsense! Admittedly, he was something of a pariah in our workplace due to his right-wing, Conservative Party supporting views making him even more Eurocentric (though ironically Europhobic as a 'little Englander') and narrow-minded than most.

When I worked in another scientific publishing company in 1990, a young Northern English woman fresh out of college with a degree in Mathematics, found it extremely ridiculous that I thought that Physics doesn't actually deal with reality. She proclaimed it out loud so other members of the office could hear. Admittedly, most of the people in the office were older and wiser than her. But such immature views that Physics gives direct access to Reality are held zealously and dogmatically by most scientists. Indeed Nobel laureate Harvard physicist Sheldon Glashow proposed an 'article of faith' shared by scientists that our sense-organs can discern the one full and unique true theory of the world and that Science will lead to this one correct theory which will rule out all alternative views[155]. We could call this faith 'Monotheorism'! In 2000 I was told by the man who invited me to speak at the Society for Psychical Research (SPR) in London, Professor John Poynton (a friend of J.H.M. Whiteman) that use of Sanskrit terms put off many members. The primary aim of most members of the SPR was to try to disprove claims of psychical phenomena. They assume that all Spirituality resembles the blind faith and literalist dogma characteristic of the Semitic religions and thus all Spirituality must be hostile to scientific notions such as Evolution.[N11] Not only are most scientists unworthy of the title 'philosopher', as stated previously, most contemporary so-called 'scientists' are in fact 'glorified technicians' unable to think beyond the narrow tram-lines of their specialities, projecting their limited range of concepts and pet theories onto the whole of Reality.

The contemporary "celebrity" scientist so loved by the media, Stephen Hawking says that all attempts to integrate Science and Mysticism are Pure Rubbish[156]. Hawking seems more famous for his remarkable life story, afflicted with a degenerative disease, than his actual contributions to Science. My criticism below is of Hawking's ideas not the man himself to whom the human-interest obsessed media is drawn. Astrophysicist Peter Coles in his book *Hawking and the Mind of God* refers to the Hawking Cult, the pseudo-religious notions in Hawking's themes and the fact that Hawking, contrary to the popular myth, is not one of the "greats" of physics[157]. In fact, those who know point out that, the aforementioned, Paul Dirac who held the same Lucasian Chair of Mathematics at Cambridge from 1932-1969 is considered the second greatest English physicist after Newton (James Clerk Maxwell was a Scot). Dirac's father was in fact French and made him speak French at home[158]. Dirac is largely is unknown to the pseudo-intellectual "chattering classes" (literary type, novel-reading "intelligentsia" of the sort who think that Sigmund Freud was a great thinker!) and the media although, historically, Dirac is a much greater figure in the history of Physics than Hawking.

The Bishop Road Primary School in Bristol attended by both Dirac and Archibald Leach (Cary Grant) had a blue plaque commemorating the Hollywood star but not one for Dirac who is historically a far more significant figure than a mere actor. The vulgar obsession with vacuous celebrities of the moronic masses is reminiscent of the medieval peasants' belief that they could be healed (made 'whole') by touching royalty. However, having said that, Cary Grant was deeply interested in Mysticism (including Self-hypnosis) and played a key role in preaching the benefits of LSD use in the USA in the 1950s and referred to his psychiatrist Mortimer Hartmann as "My wise Mahatma"[159].[N12] Thus Cary Grant did play a minor historical part in the rise of the beatniks, psychedelia and the US Baby Boomers' counterculture.

Dirac, a founder of Quantum Electrodynamics, made the remarkable prediction of the existence of antimatter. He was also open-minded enough to invite mathematical physicist and mystic Michael Whiteman to Cambridge to discuss with him the draft of Whiteman's aforementioned 1967 book which argued for a transcendental Universal Consciousness, that the metaphysical interpretation of QM implied a deeper Wave Structure underlying Matter, and that this transcendental substructure underlying Nature could be apprehended directly through mystical contemplation[160]. Indeed, Dirac's description of his notion of "antimatter" involved the creation of matter out of an imperceptible form of substratum leaving a "hole" in the latter which is a peculiarly material form of Nothingness[161]. d'Espagnat says that Dirac's conceptual aid of the 'Sea' of invisible and nonlocalised fermions preserved the everlasting existence of each individual fermion but at an exorbitant conceptual price. Thus it was soon replaced by Quantum Field Theory which applies to both fermions and bosons (force carriers) and readily accounts for the lack of individuality of each particle[162]. Merrell-Wolff, who attained enlightenment in 1936, found Dirac's notion of matter and antimatter coming together and annihilating into radiant energy as a particularly good metaphor for the absolute plenum of Pure Consciousness transcending all dualities which polarise out of the Oneness of this plenum[163].

In 2010 Discovery Channel was promoting its TV programme about Hawking by hyping him up as the "greatest living physicist". In September 2010, he was again in the news for saying that there is no need for a God in Creation, the Laws of Physics are sufficient. The Hawking-worshipping mass media does not however tell you the following story from Leonard Susskind's 2008 mass market book *The Black Hole War: My Battle with Stephen Hawking to make the World Safe for Quantum Mechanics*. Susskind refers to Relativity theorist Hawking's "conservative views of space-time". We saw that the truly great Eddington, who helped confirm GTR, nonetheless dismissed the Space-Time continuum of GTR as a fictitious and arbitrary human construct. Susskind tells us that the rubber sheet and ball analogy for Space-Time curvature in GTR is "all wrong". It has no Time curvature and, worse still, it uses the Earth's gravity (tautologically) to model Gravity[164]! At the end of his 2006 book *The Trouble with Physics*, Lee Smolin speculates that the fundamental flaw in modern Physics is the treatment of Time as equivalent to another Space-like dimension which originated with Cartesian Coordinates in Descartes' Analytical Geometry[165].

In 1981 at a seminar in San Francisco Hawking claimed that the Quantum vacuum was full of virtual black holes erasing Information even if there were no 'real' black holes in the vicinity. Susskind and the Nobel laureate Gerard 't Hooft both intuited that Hawking must obviously be wrong although they could not immediately locate a flaw in Hawking's reasoning. *Information conservation* (also called *Reversibility*) may be more fundamental than *Energy conservation*. The mathematical reversibility (*Unitarity*) of QM is critical to its consistency. Thus Hawking's claim threatened the very basis of QM! Hawking, rather like Bohr in his meeting with Schrödinger, was smug and self assured as if he could never be wrong! Hawking said, "*You* may not understand what I'm saying, but *I* do, and I am right". Susskind states wryly that Cosmologists are often in error but never in doubt! In fact it transpired that, if Hawking were correct, the virtual black holes in empty space would generate entropy or heat. Thus if Hawking was right, as he boasted vainly, *empty space would heat up to 10^{30} degrees in a tiny fraction of a second* (emphasis mine)[166].

Hawking's view, expressed in his bestselling *A Brief History of Time* (a hyped-up book which many bought but few actually read!), that we can ignore the fundamental differences between Space and Time and treat Time as just another dimension of Space is considered wrong by most theoretical physicists working on such problems as Quantum Gravity[167]. I bought a copy of Hawking's book as a present for a physicist relative then undertaking research at the University of Nevada in Las Vegas who put me up on holiday in 1989, so I did peruse the book myself and found it contained just more of the same mediocre, mainstream mass-market fodder as in countless pop science books. The *Daily Express* newspaper published a two page spread about Stephen Hawking on June 15th 2006, after he called for humans to colonise Mars, with the huge headline: "Vain truth about the Professor of Publicity". Whilst rubbishing Science-Mysticism integration possibilities, Hawking, at the end of *A Brief History of Time* says that if we had the final Theory of Everything we would know the "Mind of God".

In a sense, this resembles the views of the greatest Lucasian Professor, Isaac Newton, who thought that the Laws of Nature had to be found by experimentation rather than mystic communion with spirits[168]. But, contrary to the hubris of Hawking, Newton thought that his mystical studies were more important than his scientific work, and actually spent more time on mystical studies although this included Kabbalistic nonsense seeking hidden codes in the Bible as well as Alchemy. We saw in Chapter 1 that Natural Philosophy was originally viewed as a mystical pursuit seeking God's hidden order behind

Nature. In his biography of Newton, economist John Maynard Keynes famously described Newton as being better understood as the **last of the great magicians** [Renaissance magi] rather than the first great scientist. It is well known that Newton was a secret supporter of the Arian heresy that denied the Christian dogma of the Trinity (ironically Newton was a fellow of Trinity College)[169]. Newton recognised the logical error in Galileo's Doctrine of Primary Qualities which presupposed subjective Secondary Qualities. Influenced by Neoplatonist Henry More, he also held privately some mystical views such as considering all of Space to be the Divine Sensorium (like a Universal Consciousness)[170].

> *...if there be an universal life and all space be the sensorium of a thinking being who by immediate presence perceives all things in it, as that which thinks in us, perceives all their pictures in the brain; these laws of motion arising from life or will may be of universal extent.*
>
> Isaac Newton[171]

It is well known that Copernicus' heliocentrism was influenced by the mystical symbolism of the Sun (representing the Inner Light as in the quote from Plato above) at the centre, if not also by the heliocentrism of the *Aryabhatiya*. Pauli mentions Johannes Kepler's Platonist writings of Ideas, pre-existent in the mind of God and imprinted in the soul as the image of God. These primal images, Kepler calls archetypes (a Hermetic term)[172]. Kepler's work had been inspired by his lifelong belief in Astrology and Pythagorean Numerology hence his great work was entitled *Harmonice Mundi*[173]. Michael Faraday was inspired by his spiritual belief in the underlying unity of all phenomena to try to demonstrate the underlying unity of Electricity and Gravity back in the Victorian era. Stephen Hawking, like many contemporary cosmologists and other scientists, seems happy to utilise profound, pseudo-mystical assertions for his own naive views whilst, simultaneously dismissing actual Mysticism as rubbish. Thus, keeping to Plato's simile, Hawking and the loudmouthed Mysticism-bashing, defenders of Materialist orthodoxy such as Richard Dawkins and Lewis Wolpert may be considered culture-bound 'cavemen'.

Epistemologically, the very notion of a "Theory of Everything" is puerile and a contradiction in terms. A scientific theory can never be more than a set of idealised abstractions or formalised representations. As with scientific concepts, these skeletal abstractions of regular features of phenomena omit the flesh or the qualitative, intrinsic substance of Reality and are merely human mental constructions. Though by far the most successful scientific theory yet created QM, as we have just noted, has at least three different versions, each of which make exactly the same predictions and so cannot be tested against each other even though they are based on different intuitive pictures of what exists. Even the greatest conceivable mathematical model or "theory" is as close to conveying the "real thing", the experienced world, as a romantic novel in some difficult-to-learn foreign language is to the actual experience of making love.

Popular expositions of the arcane maths are little better than impressionistic, black and white pencil sketches of two lovers. The map is not the territory; you cannot taste the food in a restaurant by licking the menu. A mathematical model is a predictive tool for studying the regular behaviour of phenomena or predictable spatiotemporal patterns of energetic activity. As Pauli and Jung recognised, scientific models can only predict repeated patterns of events, they cannot predict synchronicities which, like psychic phenomena are one-off anomalous interactions, although special instances of a deeper all-pervading 'Acausal Orderedness'[174]. Like a novel, a scientific model can describe the 'mechanics' of the attraction and intercourse between two 'bodies' but the scientist, like the reader doesn't experience the 'real thing'! Furthermore, as physicist Schommers states, all theories contain metaphysical elements as no theory can ever have a one-to-one correspondence with actual events[175]. Thus a puerile belief in reaching a final "Theory of Everything" is little different from blind faith in the "one true faith" or the "one true God". All of these are but human mental constructions, not Reality.

It also takes a huge leap of blind faith to believe that a mathematical model of supposed 'particles' and supposed 'forces' could also explain "everything", all the emergent spatiotemporal complexity of Nature, let alone conscious experiences which can only be sneaked in to such pictures by 'magic'. The mathematical models of Physics deal with extremely simplified, isolated systems and usually lose their predictive utility when more than merely two 'particles' are considered. Statistical models of large numbers of 'particles' deal with only averaged-out general behaviour patterns, losing sight of the particulars. This is a problem even before we recognise that no individual particle trajectories exist in QM. Isolated atoms still display interference patterns in two-slit experiments[176]. This indicates the deeper level, nonlocal Wave Structure of Matter. Then, if we are true "scientists", we have to consider paranormal psychic phenomena which don't obey these theories of regular phenomenal behaviour. One the other hand, mystical communion with the *archetypes* (to which Pauli related the Dance of Shiva as a Jungian 'archetypal image'), and which Augustine of Hippo anthropomorphised as the 'Ideas in the Mind of God' (to which Hawking alludes indirectly) is something we shall begin to understand as rational and factual rather than fantasy.

These *archetypes* are not the supposed 'Laws of Nature' sought by Newton through experiment rather than mystic communion. Newton's laws actually invoked an imaginary force of 'Gravity' acting-at-a-distance, (i.e., paranormally) and are only mathematical tools allowing us to predict the behaviour of various dynamical systems. Physicist Shimon Malin makes the naive assertion that the (static) Platonic Ideas are the Laws of Nature[177]. By Laws we tend to mean regularities in the spatiotemporal behaviour of phenomena. The archetypes are deeper vibratory patterns of energy or 'principles of manifestation' or self-limitation of the Absolute (as found in Tantric Kashmir Saivism) underlying material phenomena. It may be that some Constants determined by the New Physics relating to the manifestation of 'particle' phenomena are precise constraining limits emerging out of the interaction of the various energy fields underlying particle-like phenomena. We have seen that all the attributes of Matter are described by QM as waveform families[178]. The standard Jungian view stated by Odajnyk and in most of von Franz's essays is that archetypes in themselves are not knowable, only their spatiotemporal actualisations as images. But late in life Jung began to recognise archetypes in their deeper sense as dynamic psychophysical patterns of energy[179] equivalent to the Indian *samskara* (reverberating memory impressions linked to Karma)[180]. Von Franz says that archetypes are like the Indian *bija* (seeds) and that they are (holonomically) present at every point in the 'Collective Unconscious'[181]. Whiteman says that the so-called 'ordinances' in McDonnel's translation of the *Rg Veda,* (i.e., *dharman*) are equivalent to the later (Mediterranean) notion of 'archetypes'[182]. Such views conform to Pauli's understanding of his own Exclusion Principle underlying the stability of atoms as a case of holonomic Acausal Orderedness created by the 'rhythmic dance' of underlying energetic vibrations. Pauli speculated about archetypes as primary probabilities and mathematical *a priori* intuitions belonging to a class of archetypal representations whose roots must be found outside maths[183]. As in knowing what it is like to make love, so to truly know the "mind of God" you must become a true *philosopher*, a mystical lover of *Sofia* (the Cosmic Light of Wisdom), attaining Knowledge by Identity through becoming one with the "mind of God". Only then may one claim, as did Meister Eckhart, "God and I, we are one in knowledge".

Christian 'demons', hidden human potentialities, psychical phenomena and Quantum potentialities

The *Yoga Sutras* assert that the deeper, transcendental realms of Consciousness are intrinsically associated with *Siddhis* or supernatural phenomena not limited by empirical Space-Time-Causality and related to the aforementioned *Akasa.* In *The Medium, The Mystic and the Physicist,* Lawrence LeShan described the parallels between the Transcendental Reality of mystics, QM, and the extrasensory perception of the so-called "clairvoyant reality" described by psychics, not limited by normal Space and Time relations[184]. Materialists will argue that it is only delusional primitives and ancients living in pre-scientific cultures who misinterpret hallucinations induced by schizophrenia, temporal lobe epilepsy, drugs or sensory deprivation in primitive psychical and mystical terms. In regard to the extraordinary perceptual capabilities of 'primitive' peoples, I noted that in her 2009 BBC TV Series, *The Incredible Human Journey*, Alice Roberts travelled with Polynesian sailors on raft-like boats which their ancestors used to settle the remote islands of the South Pacific and 'New Zealand'. As with his ancestors, the contemporary navigator could 'read' the complex wave-forms on the ocean surface and from this information (which looks like random noise to you or I) he could tell in which direction they would find land.

Using space-age telemetry equipment, Dr Valerie Hunt has shown that the high-frequency fields surrounding the human body, which mainstream scientists dismissed as random noise, are associated with information fields including correlations with the yogic and psychic knowledge of the so-called human aura and *chakras*[185]. We have seen that the Nicene Creed suppressed mystical exploration in the Christian world though the original Christians had been like charismatics possessed by the Holy Spirit and performing supernatural acts. Rather like Emmanuel Swedenborg, J.H.M. Whiteman in his final book *Universal Theology* focuses on mystical encounters with 'Co-

Minds', semi-autonomous elements of the complex nexus making up our individual psyches. Many Biblical references to groups, tribes, angels etc. actually refer to such perennial mystical realisations as in the Fathers (*pitara*) and Ancestors/Relatives (*bhratrivyah*) of the Vedas and Upanishads[186]. These Co-Minds (Sanskrit *nirmana-cittani*) correspond to Jung's autonomous 'complexes' which were called 'demons' by the early Church[187].

Origen, the first major Christian thinker studied under the same Ammonias Saccas who taught the great Plotinus[188]. Von Franz tells us that Origen wrote that each of us is not One but Many. As long as we are sinners we have in us 'herds of sheep' and 'birds of heaven'. These need to be integrated through the influence of Christ. She claims that the Monotheism of the Old Testament and the idea of Christ being the One Man required believers to confront the inner demons and animal souls and become ethical. They also alienated the West from Nature as the animal souls were seen as existing partly in Man and partly externally[189]. She adds that Zosimus of Panopolis (the 4th Century *c.e.* Graeco-Egyptian father of Alchemy) distinguished between 'demonic' synchronistic events (occult sympathies associated with such autonomous complexes) and synchronistic transformations connected with the Divine Spirit or the Self[190].

Along with very useful insights, von Franz does rehash Eurocentric myths about Greeks and other anachronistic and uncritical views along with exaggerating the originality of Jung. The primary god of the Old Testament, Yahweh[N13], does not represent Divine Light as does the Christ and the Father of the Gospels but one of these 'demonic' complexes linked to aggression, fear and sex instincts. Jung himself recognised that his old teacher Sigmund Freud replaced one jealous god Yahweh with another, Sexuality[191]. Freud actually secularised Kabbala mysticism, stripping it of supernatural elements in his totally absurd but highly influential 'Psychoanalysis'[192] which posed fraudulently as a scientific psychology. Yahweh may be 'ethical' but his actions are those of a tribal war-god advocating genocide, hatred of outsiders, misogyny and countless acts of jealousy and violent rage[193] In the Gospel of John, Chapter 8 Jesus is said to have told his fellow Jews[194]:

> *You are of your father the devil ...He was a murderer from the beginning...and there is no truth in him.*

In his essay, *What India can Teach Us*, Jung wrote that unlike the West, India had followed the other way of civilising Man, the way without suppression, without violence. *India embraced the whole man from top to bottom* (*emphasis mine*)[195].

We have seen that Positivistic, Materialist 'cavemen' overlook the animistic basis of the concepts of Physics, projecting human feelings onto Nature. There is also a subliminal racism in such arguments as the prevalence of such mystical philosophy in the East thus indicates the primitive, mythological worldviews of the Eastern cultures. Eurocentric 'Classics' and 'History of Science' still misrepresent Ancient Greek mystics as supposed 'scientists', suppressing facts such as (self-proclaimed god-man and shamanic healer) Empedocles' supposedly "scientific" poem *On Nature* makes magical claims regarding powers such as controlling the wind and weather and leading the life-force of a dead man out of Hades[196, 197]. Similarly the fact that modern

Science arose more out of Magic, (Alchemy, Astrology etc.) which observed phenomena and sought principles rather than Aristotelian logic is suppressed[198, 199]. The argument goes that intelligent scientists and rationalists can see through such mystical delusions as mere hallucinations.

Albert Einstein was open-minded enough to write a foreword for Upton Sinclair's book on telepathy entitled *Mental Radio*[200] and was even open-minded in regard to Carl Jung's notion of Synchronicity[201] which is a modern reformulation of the ancient mystical Doctrine of Sympathies found in the likes of Empedocles, Hippocrates, Alchemy, Renaissance Hermetica and German Idealism. The Greek idea of an *oulomeliē* (all-harmony) or a 'Sympathy' of all things is found in Hippocrates, Philo and Theophrastus. The Latin *Sapientia Dei* (Divine Wisdom) represents the *sympnoia* or Psychic Total Interconnectedness of the Universe through the Spirit of Love[202]. One can find precursors of Jung's notions in various mysticism-inspired German philosophers including Hegel[203] and Schopenhauer. Even the first great achievement of modern Science, Newton's model of Gravity was not actually Mechanistic but interconnected mysteriously all material bodies without explanation. Leibniz pointed out that Newton's 'force', acting-at-a-distance, "introduced occult qualities and miracles" into Science. Galileo had dismissed Kepler's notion of the moon affecting the tides (which Newton later 'explained' using as his 'Gravity) "occult properties and such like fancies"[204].

As stated above, Jung realised that *archetypes* were in fact the same as Yogic *samskara*, the impressions bringing about fruition of Karma[205]. We have also seen above Schrödinger's own views on transmigration of Karma and Buddhist Hearn's quotation about Karma integrating mental and material manifestations. In my O/OM, I surveyed the variety of paranormal psychic phenomena and discerned the common underlying principle. This was the Space-Time transcending 'Karmic' vibratory-resonances in the *Akasa*. This was based on the Yoga Sutra's theory of the *Akasa*. Sutra IV.10 states, "There is a relation of cause and effect because memory and impressions (*samskara*) are the same in form"[206]. When I wrote the final part of O/OM in 1997, I had not connected this with Jung's vague talk of 'Meaningful Coincidences'. To me this implied anthropocentrism as 'meaning' exists in relation to human understanding and implied a magical predetermination of events! Stephen E. Braude had already raised such objections to Jung's confusing and inchoate presentation of Synchronicity[207].

However in 1998, after checking first proofs for O/OM, I read David Peat's book on Synchronicity which clarified things as does *Psyche and Matter*. Peat's book also reminded me of David Bohm's Active Information which I had read of in Bohm and Peat's book *Science, Order and Creativity*[208] but forgotten. I realised that Jung's famous but misleading quadrant diagram was actually meant to distinguish Space-Time and Causality from a general "Acausal Orderedness" (including the special cases of Synchronicity) although this is not clear from the diagram. A quadrant is clearly the wrong symbol for this bipartite distinction! Jung's views, I recognised, were a modern rediscovery of the undivided wholeness of the Transcendental Realm realised by the yogi after transcending the Time/Space Matrix of perception. Here all the potentialities for the manifestation of gross phenomena are interconnected and exist relative to everything else (holonomy)[209]. In O/OM, I told of how I was surrounded by synchronicities, especially in the period leading up to my identification of the physical correlate of the Divine Light. This had led me to look again, after eleven years, at a book containing excerpts from Jung's writings.

I had also recognised that psychic phenomena were special cases of the more general Transcendental Causation by vibratory resonance underlying the appearance of empirical Space-Time-Causality. This deeper True Causation (for which I had used the Buddhist term 'Dependent Co-Origination') would explain the emergent stabilities of the cosmos through 'phase-locking' of resonances. Such views are being confirmed by the aforementioned work of Milo Wolff which I discovered in 2008. That such vibratory resonance is the central principle underlying paranormal psychic phenomena is a view gaining proponents as claimed in the uncritical pop-science paperback *The Resonance Key*[210]. Furthermore, German physicist Wolfram Schommers has reformulated QM incorporating Mach's Principle (treating *inertia* as relative to the whole universe). This reveals that unlike the Space-Time-Causality of the empirical world of our senses, the deeper Quantum Reality is 'particle-free', nonlocal and relativistic in its operations. Schommers calls this deeper transcendental causality "Synchronicity"[211]. The correct Jungian equivalent would be 'Acausal Orderedness', the general holonomic order interconnecting all things, which accounts for phenomena Science cannot truly explain. These include Pauli's Exclusion Principle and the individual order of Radioactive Decay which, as with Newton's 'Gravity', remain mysterious as well as paranormal psychic phenomena. This, like Bohm's nonlocal 'Active Information' (where a subtle energy, too small to detect, informs the larger energetic systems forming matter), is related to the *Yoga Sutras* notion of the *Akasa* and its Space-Time transcending resonances of form.

The British Nobel laureate physicist Brian Josephson told a Bombay Conference in 1986 that, in order to experience Quantum Reality and the deeper planes, scientists might have to practise meditation. He also linked Quantum Reality to the dream state as both seemed to involve possibilities or potentialities[212]. At the same conference, the Nobel laureate neurobiologist George Wald told of how he had received an insight into the fundamental nature of Consciousness which had eluded him in spite of decades of scientific knowledge and enquiry. He soon found that this enquiry placed him in great company, alongside Eastern philosophy and great physicists such as Schrödinger, Eddington and Pauli[213]:

> *Let me say that it is not only easier to say these things to physicists than to my fellow biologists, but easier to say them in India than in the West. For when I speak of mind pervading the universe, of mind as a creative principle perhaps primary to matter, any Hindu will acquiesce, will think, yes, of course, he is speaking of Brahman. The Judaeo-Christian-Islamic God constructed as universe and just once. Brahman thinks a universe and does so in cycles, time without end.*

I would add that the so-called 'universe' of the Semitic religions was merely the Earth, Sun and the six visible planets with stars as tiny lights. Augustine and Eckhart refer to Creation lasting one or a few thousand years. Kepler and

Newton both believed the Biblical myth that the Earth was created six thousand years ago. The Hindu universe was infinite, at least in regard to its formless background or *nirguna Brahman* with countless worlds and the Hindu time scales for Creation of billions of years resembling modern cosmological time scales. As we have seen, modern cosmology is paralleling Hindu views of cyclic Creation, multiverses and that ¾ of the Creation may be non-manifest Plenum/Void (like the Vacuum Energy).

On the other hand, the British media always seems to wheel out the same old polytechnic psychologists to rebuff any claims of Near-Death Experiences and paranormal psychic phenomena on the grounds that they contradict the "Laws of Physics". Polytechnics were the second class education establishments in the UK which since 1992 have been allowed to use the title "university". In spite of the tenuous status of academic Psychology, even as a soft "science", plus the pseudoscientific superstitions propounded by the likes of Sigmund Freud, such polytechnic psychologists present themselves as authoritative spokespeople for "Science" and the "Laws of Physics", defenders of Reason over superstition. This need amongst psychologists to stress their 'scientific credentials' seems to arise from insecurity linked in part to 'Physics Envy'. Yet rather than being defenders of Reason, they come across more like defenders of the 'blind faith' in a 'bright schoolgirl' type conception of Science, regurgitating simplistic school textbook type clichés about the nature of scientific enquiry.

They are merely noisy "cheerleaders" appealing to established authority in comparison to the heavyweight 'giants' of Physics such as Einstein and Pauli who remained open-minded and critical of established opinion. We have seen that the idea of immutable 'Laws of Nature' is based on Christian anthropomorphic mythology of a god like a Roman Emperor laying down laws for the universe He created miraculously out of nothing and that Classical Physics was centred around Newton's *occult* force of 'Gravity'. Contemporary physics is increasingly realising that the regularities and stabilities of Nature must now be viewed, not as immutable "laws" and constants transcendent to Nature, but as emergent behavioural patterns and stabilities arising within Nature; perhaps there are other universes which evolved differently. We also noted that Milo Wolff has begun to show how such regularities and stabilities (or seeming 'Laws of Nature' and fundamental constants) can emerge from the underlying holonomic, Wave Structure of Matter (WSM)[N14, 214].

We have already seen various references from Brahmanic, Hermetic and NeoPlatonic mysticism to the transcendental realm as one of *potentialities* (or possible manifestations). The *field* concept in modern Physics represents potentialities for a type of spatiotemporal phenomenon to occur or a type of 'particle' to manifest. Milo Wolff's WSM model allows us to begin to visualise such holonomic potentialities and begin to understand how we are connected to the future by incoming waves from all distant events in the entire universe (which in Feynman's Path Integral model were treated as 'advanced waves' travelling backwards in Time). This helps us get some idea as to how precognitive influences as well as telepathy probably operate. The potentialities for possible future manifestations are co-mingled in the holonomic flux of the present.[N15] Nobel laureate physicists Brian Josephson and Eugene

Wigner endorsed mathematical physicist (and Hindu convert) Richard Thompson's book *Mechanistic and Nonmechanistic Science* on its back cover. One of Thompson's arguments was that the Laws of Physics are limiting constraints within which the Wave Function of QM is allowed a certain limited degree of freedom. This would help account for the experimental data on Psychokinesis gathered by Professor Robert Jahn (who had been Dean of the School of Aeronautical Engineering at Princeton) where the statistically combined data conformed to the Laws but individual results could deviate considerably beyond statistical norms[215]. I myself have performed successfully in such psychokinetic set-ups at Jahn's lab using display systems based on random radioactive decay which I had to try and steer off a random path.

Sexing Up Physics and suppression of psychical phenomena by Western media

When one of Britain's two living Nobel laureates in Physics (as of 2001), wrote the following in the Royal Mail's 2001 Nobel Prize Centenary stamp set:

> *Quantum theory is now being fruitfully combined with theories of information and computation. These developments may lead to an explanation of processes still not understood within conventional science such as telepathy, an area where Britain is at the forefront of research.*
>
> — Brian D. Josephson[216]

Robin McKie, the Science correspondent of the left-wing *Observer* newspaper depicted the Nobel laureate Trinity College, Cambridge don as if he was an oddball heretic using his Nobel laureate status to give publicity to some absurd magical notion rejected by all sensible scientists. McKie quoted with approval the Oxford physicist David Deutsch who said, "It is utter rubbish; telepathy simply does not exist"[217]. Yet it was not mentioned that Deutsch openly advocates the so-called "Many Worlds interpretation" of QM, an attempt to show that "God doesn't play dice" that is actually far more preposterous than a belief in telepathy. Occurrences of seeming telepathy have been reported in all human societies throughout history. I had such an experience in 1995. Proven aspects of QM such as Entanglement immediately bring to mind Space-Time transcending influences operating through the deeper interconnectedness of all phenomenal manifestations.

We have seen that the EEG was invented after Berger's telepathic Crisis Experience. Tesla had a Crisis Vision[N16] of his dying mother. Wireless Communication was invented by Oliver Lodge and J.C. Bose who were interested in the Psychical Aether or the *Akasa*. In his *Entangled Minds* Radin elaborates on the discovery of isotopes story which I told in O/OM. J.J. Thomson, who discovered the electron, speculated that electromagnetic fields were carriers for telepathy. His student Francis Aston read the 1908 book *Occult Chemistry* by Theosophists Annie Besant and Charles Leadbeater who described their clairvoyant vision[218]. Actually they used the Yogic *Anudhristi Siddi* – supernormal power to see small things (or 'atoms') – to see into atomic structure to study the known elements provided to them by Sir William Crookes[219]. They claimed that the element Neon existed in another form which they called Meta-neon with atomic weight of 22.33. Aston discovered a substance of the same atomic weight and called it Meta-neon, the first known isotope. But by the time he got the Nobel Prize in 1922 he did not mention how he came to discover this[220]. Wolfgang Pauli had psychokinetic influences upon instruments and I have personally had successful psychokinetic results upon a radioactivity based device at the famous PEAR laboratory at Princeton.

The Many Worlds interpretation holds that, rather than quantum particles mysteriously assuming one of a number of possible alternative states as observed, the particle magically becomes all possible alternatives. We only see one state as the alternative states appear magically in a near-infinite number of parallel universes which are constantly splitting off from ours so that all possible alternatives are realised in countless parallel universes, each varying slightly from adjacent ones! This view also requires our conscious minds to be constantly splitting as well with no real free will. Richard Thompson notes that it is ironic how scientists dismiss spiritual ideas as (supposedly) unverifiable whilst simultaneously advocating (actually) unverifiable views like the Many Worlds view[221]. Many TV physicists peddle 'worm holes' as tunnels to other regions of the universe. Susskind tells us that J.A. Wheeler's 'wormhole' can stay open for such a short time that it is impossible for anything, even light to pass through! There is no evidence that QM might somehow stabilise (hypothetical) wormholes. When the Einstein equations are applied to the formation of a Black Hole they simply do not have 'worm holes' attached[222].

BBC Radio 4 (supposedly the intellectual channel) marked the switch-on of the Large Hadron Collider at CERN on September 10th 2008 as "Big Bang Day" claiming "Physics Rocks" with celebrities, including comedian Dara O'Briain and the baby-faced pop-musician turned TV presenter-physicist Brian Cox, presenting 'Particle Physics' as the new 'Rock 'n' Roll'. The phrase "Rock 'n' Roll" comes from the negro slang for having sex. Like the British GCSE examinations which are harder to fail than get to an A-grade in, this reflects the 'Dumbing Down' of culture or the cultural 'tyranny of the majority'. I recall attending a Science Journalism day course in 2002' as part of our redundancy package given by the world's largest Science publishers Elsevier who had bought out Harcourt Brace. Journalists from UK broadsheets basically taught would-be science journalists to pick out the most 'sexy' snippet in the report and turn it into an eye-catching, sensationalist headline. The Science journalism mantra seems to be "MAKE IT SEXY". It is not just Science journalists of course, as in 2003, Tony Blair's sidekicks produced the infamous "dodgy dossier", partly copied off the Internet from a Ph.D. thesis, which deliberately "sexed up" the NeoCon propaganda deception that Iraq possessed WMD.[N17]

In December 2008 Irish comedian Dara O'Briain, who studied Mathematical Physics at University College Dublin, was peddling his DVD on TV advertisements. Like British comedian Stephen Fry, O'Briain presents himself as a sceptical scientific 'clever-clogs' making fun disdainfully of New Age type ideas. On the advert he mocked herbal remedies saying that such remedies had indeed been tested for thousands of years and the ones that work we call "medicines". This is Eurocentric arrogance as it is well known that countless herbal remedies cures from India, South America etc., which have beneficial effects remained unknown to the medical establishment until recently and some have yet to be tested in the laboratory. In November 2008 I chanced upon O'Briain speaking on BBC Radio 5. His radio host admittedly, was rather wary of guest physicists who seem normal suddenly 'going off' into wild and wacky pet theories little removed from Science Fiction. What was most amusing was that O'Briain defended his belief in the literal truth of the Many Worlds interpretation claiming naively that his belief was confirmed by the maths! In England, Irishmen and the Irish accent used to be the butt of racist jokes with the Irish being stereotyped as stupid. Thus an Irish comedian defending his mythological view of countless, slightly different parallel universes imperceptibly splitting off from our world at every moment came across as amusing as more typical Irish comedians who parody the Catholic obsession with Sin.

As with Martin Rees' view of the universe as a computer simulation played by some Cosmic Geek, the Many Worlds' view assumes that we cannot transcend Empirical Reality and attain supra-sensory perception of the deeper transcendental reality underlying the manifestation of phenomena. As I stated above, perennial mystical knowledge of yogis and Western esoteric traditions refers to the transcendental as a realm of potentialities containing possibilities which are not all actualised or manifested as phenomena. Werner Heisenberg wrote in *Physics and Philosophy*[223]:

> *All the elementary particles are made of the same substance, which we may call energy or universal matter; they are just different forms in which matter can appear.*
>
> *...we can say that the matter of Aristotle, which is mere "potentia," should be compared to our concept of energy, which gets into "actuality" by means of the form, when the elementary particle is created.*

Nick Herbert says in his *Quantum Reality*, Quantum Theory treats objects as "vibratory possibilities", oscillating opportunities for something real to happen[224]. In fact by 'real' here, Herbert means the manifestation of empirical phenomena from a supramundane Deeper Reality resembling Heisenberg's *potentia*. Thus even if the so-called 'collapse of the Wave Function' is not actually an outdated epistemological (existing only in the human mind) pseudo-problem done away with by new notions of decoherence, it is outrageous and infantile to postulate countless parallel universes constantly being created in order to resolve an epistemological paradox.

Fred Hoyle raised the philosophical objection against the "Big Bang" (a derogatory phrase coined by Hoyle) hypothesis that it pushes the problem of origins beyond our possible experience. Hence supporters of the Big Bang hypothesis, claim that we can say nothing whatsoever about or that it is even meaningful to talk about what happened before this miraculous modern version of the Christian *Creatio ex nihilo* myth. Evidence which seems to contradict the Big Bang idea is suppressed by the orthodoxy such as the visible links between high red-shift quasars and nearby Seyfert galaxies[225, 226]. Ashmore has shown in his 'Ashmore's paradox', that the Hubble Constant is a measure of the amount of electron in a unit volume of space. The actually measured red-shifts of light photons are ultimately due to activities of electrons creating the photons. Thus, as the *galactic red-shift*, supposedly due to the Big Bang expansion is based on properties of electrons, the Big Bang proponents are actually measuring a property of the electron in a tautological manner[N18, 227]. Ashmore's argument supports indirectly Wolff's holonomic WSM model of the electron phenomenon in which the Hubble 'Light Horizon' represents a limit to the holonomic interrelationship of nonlocal wave phenomena[N19, 228]. Teresi says that the history of the Big Bang hypothesis has been one of unproven *ad hoc* add-ons like Inflation, still undetected Dark Matter[N20] and Dark Energy to make the existing theory fit the facts[229]. In O/OM I had noted, prior to the 1998 discovery of the accelerating expansion of the universe linked to so-called 'Dark Energy', Bohm's view based on the method utilised in QM known as Renormalisation. Bohm stressed that Physics assumed a vast ocean of energy (virtual particles in the so-called 'quantum vacuum') which it cannot deal with practically and thus 'magics away' using mathematical simplification procedures, (i.e., Renormalisation). If Dark Energy does actually constitute nearly three quarters of the known universe and, if it is indeed a by-product of the Zero-Point Energy of the quantum vacuum, then this would parallel the assertion of the *Chandogya Upanishad* that three fourths of the Formless *Brahman* remains non-manifest in the heavens. Steinhardt and Turok also use Dark Energy as the basis for a cyclic universe and multiverse model paralleling Hindu views and Hindu timescales[230].

In fact, in recent years the emphasis in Big Bang cosmology has shifted from study of the galaxies through radio-astronomy to trying to recreate near-Big Bang conditions in accelerators such as the multibillion dollar LHC at CERN which uses more power than the city of Geneva. Many have commented that the vast sums of money spent on such High Energy Physics or Particle Physics research using accelerators was just a ploy to maintain a pool of scientists capable of working on nuclear weapons. Similarly, Artificial Intelligence (AI) research was not originally meant to model the human mind but to help create AI-guided cruise missiles. Far from being 'Rock-gods' or philosopher-kings, the hyped-up Materialist exponents of Particle Physics are actually better described as *Plato's cavemen* or *Physics' Flintstones*. These metaphysical vulgarians project the rocks and stones of the sense world onto transcendental reality. Far from exclaiming "Particle Physics Rocks", the wise should be saying "Particle Physics Sucks" for, as we have seen, as d'Espaganat stresses in *On Physics and Philosophy* and Schrödinger in *The Interpretation of Quantum Mechanics*, particle-like phenomena only manifest in physical experiments through artificial human interaction, there are no moving elementary particles. No one has observed an electron in isolation. What instruments actually register is a quantised transfer of energy not a 'particle'[231]. Similarly solid-state physicist and IT pioneer Carver Mead, who was a colleague of Richard Feynman, says in his *Collective Electrodynamics* (published in 2000), as does Milo Wolff, that the metaphysical problems faced by 20th Century physics arose from refusal to abandon the myth of fundamental particles. Mead says that the last seventy years will be remembered as the Dark Ages of Theoretical Physics[232].

References

1. Goonatilake, Susantha (1998) *Toward a Global Science: Mining Civilisational Knowledge*, Indiana University Press.
2. Goonatilake, Susantha (1998) *ibid.*
3. Goonatilake, Susantha (1998) *ibid.*
4. Schommers, Wolfram (1995) *Symbols, Pictures and Quantum Reality: On the Theoretical Foundations of the Physical Universe*, World Scientific.
5. Goonatilake, Susantha (1998) *ibid.*
6. Malin, Shimon (2001) *Nature Loves to Hide: Quantum Physics and Reality, a Western Perspective*, Oxford University Press.
7. Lindorff, David (2004) *Jung and Pauli: The Meeting of Two Great Minds*, Quest Books.
8. Schommers, Wolfram (1994) *Space and Time, Matter and Mind: The Relationship between Reality and Space-Time*, World Scientific.
9. Schommers, Wolfram (1994) *ibid.*
10. Schommers, Wolfram (1995) *ibid.*
11. Arp, Halton (1998) *Seeing Red: Redshifts, Cosmology and Academic Science*, Apeiron.
12. Arp, Halton (1998) *ibid.*
13. Arp, Halton (1998) *ibid.*
14. Halton, Arp (1998) *ibid.*
15. Gupta, Bina (2003) *Cit Consciousness*, Oxford University Press India.
16. Whiteman, J.H. Michael (1967) *Philosophy of Space and Time and the Inner Constitution of Nature: A Phenomenological Study*, Muirhead Library of Philosophy, George Allen and Unwin and the Humanities Press.
17. von Franz, Marie-Louise (1968) "Symbols of the *Unus Mundus*". Revised English translation in Marie-Louise von Franz (1992) *Psyche and Matter*, Shambhala Publications.
18. Von Franz, Marie-Louise (1968/1992) *ibid*.
19. Eddington, Arthur, S. (1928) *The Nature of the Physical World*, J.M. Dent and Sons.
20. Ghose, Aurobindo (Sri Aurobindo) (1939) *The Life Divine*, Sri Aurobindo Ashram Publications.
21. Wilber, Ken "Eddington". Selected excerpts from Eddington in Ken Wilber (Editor) (1984) *Quantum Questions: Mystical Writings of the World's Great Physicists*, Shambhala Publications.
22. Eddington, Arthur, S (1928) *ibid.*
23. Eddington, Arthur (1935) *New Pathways in Science*, The MacMillan Company.
24. Eddington, Arthur (1928) *ibid.*
25. Eddington, Arthur (1929) *Science and the Unseen World*, The MacMillan Company.
26. Whiteman, J.H. Michael (1967) *ibid.*
27. McEvilley, Thomas (2002) *The Shape of Ancient Thought: Comparative Studies in Greek and Indian Philosophies*, Allworth Press.

28. Radhakrishnan, Sarvepalli (1953) *The Principal Upanisads*, (Centenary Edition 1989), Unwin Hyman.
29. Goonatilake, Susantha (1998) *ibid.*
30. Magee, Glen A. (2001) *Hegel and the Hermetic Tradition,* Cornell University Press.
31. Cary, Phillip (2000) *Augustine's Invention of the Inner Self: The Legacy of a Christian Platonist, Oxford University Press.*
32. Cary, Philip (2001) *ibid.*
33. Bernal, Martin (1987) *Black Athena: The Afroasiatic Roots of Classical Civilisation. Volume 1. The Fabrication of Ancient Greece 1785-1985.* Free Association Books.
34. Gribbin, John (1995) *Schrödinger's Kittens and the Search for Reality*, Weidenfield and Nicolson.
35. Gribbin, John (1995) *ibid.*
36. Moore, Walter (1994) *A Life of Erwin Schrödinger*, Cambridge University Press.
37. Malin, Shimon (2001) *Nature Loves to Hide: Quantum Physics and Reality, a Western Perspective*, Oxford University Press.
38. Malin, Shimon (2001) *ibid.*
39. Nandy, Ashis (1995) *Alternative Sciences: Creativity and Authenticity in Two Indian Scientists (2nd Edn)*, Oxford University Press India.
40. "Tesla, Master of Lightning" (2000) Public Broadcasting Service (Television, USA).
41. See www.teslasociety.com/tesla_and_swami.htm (Tesla Memorial Society of New York).
42. Tiller, William A. (1997) *Science and Human Transformation: Subtle Energies, Intentionality and Consciousness*, Pavior Publishing.
43. Goonatilake, Susantha (1998) *ibid.*
44. Goonatilake, Susantha (1998) *ibid.*
45. Goonatilake, Susantha (1998) *ibid.*
46. Grof, Stanislaw (1985) *Beyond the Brian: Birth, Death and Transcendence in Psychotherapy*, State University of New York Press.
47. Franks, Paul W. "Jewish Philosophy after Kant: The Legacy of Salomon Maimon". In Michael L. Morgan and Peter Eli Gordon (Editors) (2007) *The Cambridge Companion to Modern Jewish Philosophy*, Cambridge University Press.
48. Goonatilake, Susantha (1998) *ibid.*
49. Dutta, K. And Robinson, A. (1995) *Rabindranath Tagore: The Myriad-Minded Man,* Bloomsbury.
50. Malin, Shimon (2001) *ibid.*
51. Malin, Shimon (2001) *ibid.*
52. Deikman, Arthur "A Functional Approach to Mysticism". In Jensine Andresen and Robert K.C. Forman (Editors) (2002) *Cognitive Models and Spiritual Maps*, Imprint Academic.

53. Radhakrishnan, Sarvepalli (1940) *Eastern Religions and Western Thought (2nd Edn),* Oxford University Press.
54. Wilber, Ken "Einstein". Selected excerpts from Einstein in Ken Wilber (Editor) (1984) *Quantum Questions: Mystical Writings of the World's Great Physicists*, Shambhala Publications.
55. Forman, Robert K.C. (1991) *Meister Eckhart: Mystic as Theologian*, Element.
56. Wilber, Ken (1984) *ibid.*
57. Radhakrishnan, Sarvepalli (1953) *ibid.*
58. Halbfass, Wilhelm (1988) *India and Europe: An Essay in Understanding*, State University of New York Press.
59. d'Espagnat, Bernard (2006) *On Physics and Philosophy*, Princeton University Press.
60. Peat, F. David (1997) *Infinite Potential: The Life and Times of David Bohm*, Addison Wesley.
61. Talbot, Michael (1991) *The Holographic Universe*, Harper Collins.
62. Rosen, Steven M. "Time and Higher-Order Wholeness: A Response to David Bohm." In David R. Griffin (Editor) (1986) *Physics and the Ultimate Significance of Time*, State University of New York Press.
63. Ferguson, Marilyn "Karl Pribram's Changing Reality". In Ken Wilber (Editor) (1982) *The Holographic Paradigm and Other Paradoxes: Exploring the Leading Edge of Science*, Shambhala Publications.
64. Pribram, Karl, H. (1991) *Brain and Perception: Holonomy and Structure in Figural Processing*, Lawrence Erlbaum Associates.
65. Bohm, David and Hiley, Basil J. (1993) *The Undivided Universe: An Ontological Interpretation of Quantum Theory,* Routledge.
66. Bohm, David and Hiley, Basil J. (1993) *ibid*.
67. Bohm, David and Hiley, Basil J. (1993) *ibid*.
68. Ericson, Peter (2004) "Indeterminism and the Bohm Interpretation of Quantum Mechanics". Unpublished essay appearing on www.http:pericson.com/writings/
69. von Franz, Marie-Louise "Some Reflections on Synchronicity" (1984). English translation in Marie-Louise von Franz (1992) *Psyche and Matter*, Shambhala Publications.
70. Rosen, Stephen M. (1986) *ibid.*
71. Rosen, Stephen M. (1986) *ibid.*
72. Brown, Daniel P. "The Stages of Meditation in Cross-Cultural Perspective". In Ken Wilber, Jack Engler and Daniel P. Brown (Editors) (1986) *Transformations of Consciousness: Conventional and Contemplative Perspectives on Development*, Shambhala Publications.
73. Hiley, B.J. and Peat, F. David "General introduction: The development of David Bohm's ideas from the plasma to implicate order". In Basil J. Hiley and F. David Peat (1987) *Quantum Implications: Essays in Honour of David Bohm*, Routledge and Kegan Paul.
74. Schrödinger, Erwin (1995) *The Interpretation of Quantum Mechanics: Dublin seminars (1949-55) and other unpublished essays*, Ox Bow Press.

75. Hiley, B.J. and Peat, F. David (1987) *ibid.*
76. Schommers, Wolfram (1995) *ibid.*
77. Whiteman, J.H. Michael (1967) *ibid.*
78. Hiley, B.J. and Peat, F. David (1987) *ibid.*
79. Sperry, Roger "Holding Course Amid Shifting Paradigms". In Willis Harman with Jane Clark (Editors) (1994) *New Metaphysical Foundations of Modern Science*, Institute of Noetic Sciences.
80. Bohm, David and Hiley, Basil (1993) *The Undivided Universe:An Ontological Interpretation of Quantum Theory*, Routledge.
81. Wolff, Milo (2008) *Schrödinger's Universe: Einstein, Waves and the Origin of the Natural Laws*, Technotran Press.
82. Whiteman, J. H. Michael(1999) Personal communication.
83. Von Franz, Marie-Louise (1984) *ibid.*
84. Whiteman, J.H. Michael (1967) *ibid.*
85. Capra, Fritjof (1988) *Uncommon Wisdom: Conversations with remarkable people*, Century Hutchison.
86. Weber, Renée "The Tao *of Physics* Revisited: A conversation with Fritjof Capra". In Ken Wilber (Editor) (1982) *The Holographic Paradigm and Other Paradoxes: Exploring the Leading Edge of Science*, Shambhala Publications.
87. Weber, Renée (1982) *ibid.*
88. Smolin, Lee (2006) *The Trouble with Physics: The Rise of String Theory, the Fall of a Science, and What Comes Next*, Houghton Mifflin.
89. d'Espagnat, Bernard (2006) *ibid.*
90. Wolff, Milo (2008) *ibid.*
91. Susskind, Leonard (2008) *The Black Hole War: My battle with Stephen Hawking to Make the World a Safe Place for Quantum Mechanics*, Back Bay Books, Little Brown and Co.
92. Wilber, Ken "Heisenberg". Selected excerpts from Heisenberg in Ken Wilber (Editor) (1984) *Quantum Questions: Mystical Writings of the World's Great Physicists*, Shambhala Publications.
93. Heisenberg, Werner (1958) *Physics and Philosophy: The Revolution in Modern Science,* (US Edition 1962), Harper and Row.
94. Heisenberg, Werner (1958) *ibid.*
95. Malin, Shimon (2001) *ibid.*
96. Heisenberg, Werner (1958) *ibid.*
97. Wilber, Ken (1984) *ibid.*
98. Heisenberg, Werner (1958) *ibid.*
99. d'Espagnat, Bernard (2006) *ibid.*
100. Schommers, Wolfram (1994) *ibid.*
101. Whiteman, J.H. Michael (1967) *ibid.*
102. Heisenberg, Werner (1958) *ibid.*
103. Heisenberg, Werner (1958) *ibid.*
104. Heisenberg, Werner (1958) *ibid.*
105. Heisenberg, Werner (1958) *ibid.*

106. Thompson, Richard, L. (1981) *Mechanistic and Nonmechanistic Science: An Investigation into the Nature of Consciousness and Form,* The Bhaktivedanta Book Trust.
107. d'Espagnat (2006) *ibid.*
108. Eddington, Arthur (1928) *ibid.*
109. d'Espagnat (2006) *ibid.*
110. Peat, David (1987) *Synchronicity: The Bridge between Matter and Mind*, Bantam Books.
111. Ericson, Peter (2004) *ibid.*
112. Beck, Guy L. (1993) *Sonic Theology: Hinduism and Sacred Sound*, University of South Carolina Press.
113. d'Espagnat (2006) *ibid.*
114. Schrödinger, Erwin (1961) *My View of the World*, English translation 1964 Cambridge U.P. Reprinted 1983, Ox Bow Press.
115. Schrödinger, Erwin (1995) *The Interpretation of Quantum Mechanics: Dublin Seminars (1949-55) and other Unpublished Essays*, Ox Bow Press.
116. Bitbol, Michel (1995) "Introduction". In Schrödinger, Erwin *The Interpretation of Quantum Mechanics:Dublin Seminars (1949-55) and other Unpublished Essays*, Ox Bow Press.
117. Moore, Walter (1994) *ibid.*
118. Radhakrishnan, Sarvepalli (1953) *ibid.*
119. Moore, Walter (1994) *ibid.*
120. Moore, Walter (1994) *ibid.*
121. Moore, Walter (1994) *ibid.*
122. Moore, Walter (1994) *ibid.*
123. Moore, Walter (1994) *ibid.*
124. Wilber, Ken "Schrödinger". Selected excerpts from Schrödinger in Ken Wilber (Editor) (1984) *Quantum Questions: Mystical Writings of the World's Great Physicists*, Shambhala Publications.
125. Chittick, William C. "Between the Yes and the No: Ibn al-'Arabi on *Wujûd* and the Innate Capacity". In Robert K.C. Forman (Editor) (1998) *The Innate Capacity: Mysticism, Psychology, and Philosophy*, State University of New York Press.
126. Libet, Benjamin, Freeman, Anthony and Sutherland, Keith "Editors' Introduction" in B. Libet, A. Freeman and K. Sutherland (Editors) (1999) *The Volitional Brain: Towards a Neuroscience of Free Will*, Imprint Academic.
127. Libet, Benjamin *et al.* (1999) *ibid.*
128. Malin, Shimon (2001) *ibid.*
129. Merrell-Wolff, Franklin (1994) *Franklin Merrell-Wolff's Experience and Philosophy: A Personal Record of Transformation and a Discussion of Transcendental Consciousness*: Containing his *Philosophy of Consciousness without an Object* and *His Pathways through to Space*, State University of New York Press.
130. d'Espagnat (2006) *ibid.*
131. Moore, Walter (1994) *ibid.*

132. Wolf, Fred. A. (1994) *The Dreaming Universe*, Simon and Schuster.
133. Lindorff, David (2004) *Jung and Pauli: The Meeting of Two Great Minds*, Quest Books.
134. Lindorff, David (2004) *ibid.*
135. Lindorff, David (2004) *ibid.*
136. von Franz, Marie-Louise (1983) "A Contribution to the Discussion of C.G. Jung's Synchronicity Hypothesis". English translation in Marie-Louise von Franz (1992) *Psyche and Matter*, Shambhala Publications.
137. Thompson, D'Arcy – *See* Ball, Philip (1999) *The Self-Made tapestry: Pattern Formation in Nature*, Oxford University Press.
138. Sheldrake, Rupert (1988) *The Presence of the Past: Morphic Resonance and the Habits of Nature*, Harper Collins.
139. Goodwin, Brian C. (1994) *How the Leopard Changed its Spots: The Evolution of Complexity*, Charles Scribner.
140. Lindorff, David (2004) *ibid.*
141. Lindorff, David (2004) *ibid.*
142. Wolf, Fred. A. (1994) *ibid.*
143. Wilber, Ken "Pauli". Selected excerpts from Pauli in Ken Wilber (Editor) (1984) *Quantum Questions: Mystical Writings of the World's Great Physicists*, Shambhala Publications.
144. Wolf, Fred. A. (1994) *ibid.*
145. Wilber, Ken (1984) *ibid.*
146. Meier, C.A. (Editor) (2001) *Atom and Archetype: The Pauli/Jung Letters 1932-1958*, Princeton University Press (USA) and Routledge (UK).
147. Meier, C. A. (2001) *ibid.*
148. Peat, David (1987) *ibid.*
149. Wolf, Fred. A. (1994) *ibid.*
150. Peat, David (1987) *ibid.*
151. Peat, David (1987) *ibid.*
152. Eddington, Arthur (1928) *ibid.*
153. Herbert, Nick (1985) *Quantum Reality: Beyond the New Physics*, Anchor Books.
154. Herbert, Nick (2006) Personal Communication.
155. Glashow, Sheldon "Positivism lives". In *New York Times* (Newspaper) 22nd October 1989.
156. Hawking, Stephen. Interview with Renée Weber in Weber, Renée (1986) *Dialogues with Scientists and Sages: The Search for Unity*, Arkana (Penguin Group).
157. Coles, Peter (2000) *Stephen Hawking and the Mind of God*, Icon.
158. Malin, Shimon (2006) *ibid.*
159. *See for instance*: Cary Beauchamp and Judy Balaban "Cary in the Sky with Diamonds" *Vanity Fair* (Monthly Magazine) August 2010.
160. Poynton, John. On-line biography of J.H.M. Whiteman (www.colinsmythe.co.uk/authors/whiteman.htm).
161. *See for instance* "The Infinite Sea" chapter in Close, Frank (2007) *The Void*, Oxford University Press or "Being and Nothingness" chapter in Pagels, Heinz

R. (1982) *The Cosmic Code: Quantum Physics as the Language of Nature*, Simon and Schuster.

162. d'Espagnat (2006) *ibid.*
163. Merrell-Wolff, Franklin (1994) *ibid.*
164. Susskind, Leonard (2008) *ibid.*
165. Smolin, Lee (2006) *ibid.*
166. Susskind, Leonard (2008) *ibid.*
167. Smolin, Lee (2006) *ibid.*
168. Hesse, Mary "Hermeticism and History: An apology for the internal history of science" in *Historical and Philosophical Perspectives of Science* (1970) edited by R.H. Steuer, University of Minnesota Press.
169. White, Michael (1997) *Isaac Newton: The Last Sorceror*, Fourth Estate (Harper Collins).
170. Burtt, E.A. (1954) *The Metaphysical Foundations of Modern Physical Science, 2nd Revised Edn*, Doubleday.
171. Jacob, Margaret, C. (1976) *The Newtonians and the English Revolution 1689-1720*, Cornell University Press.
172. Wilber, Ken (1984) "Pauli" *ibid.*
173. Yates, Frances (1964) *Giordano Bruno and the Hermetic Tradition*, Routledge and Kegan Paul.
174. Von Franz, Marie-Louise (1992) *Psyche and Matter*, Shambhala Publications.
175. Schommers, Wolfram (1998) *The Visible and the Invisible: Matter and Mind in Physics*, World Scientific.
176. Gribbin, John (1995) *ibid.*
177. Malin, Shimon (2001) *ibid.*
178. Herbert, Nick (1985) *ibid.*
179. Von Franz, Marie-Louise (1992) *ibid.*
180. Coward, Harold (1985) *Jung and Eastern Thought*, State University of New York Press.
181. Von Franz, Marie-Louise (1978) "The Psychological Experience of Time" and von Franz (1974) "Matter and Psyche from the Point of View of the Psychology of C.G. Jung". English translations in Marie-Louise von Franz (1992) *Psyche And Matter*, Shambhala Publications.
182. Whiteman, J.H. Michael (1967) *ibid.*
183. Von Franz, Marie-Louise (1978) *ibid.*
184. LeShan, Lawrence (1974) *The Medium, The Mystic and the Physicist*, Viking Press.
185. Hunt, Valerie V. (1989) *Infinite Mind, The Science of Human Vibrations*, Malibu Publishing Company.
186. Whiteman, J.H. Michael (2006) *Universal Theology and Life in the Other Worlds*, Colin Smythe.
187. Von Franz, Marie-Louise (1975) "Psyche and Matter in Alchemy and Modern Science". Reprinted in Marie-Louise Von Franz (1992) *Psyche and Matter* (1992) Shambhala Publications.

188. Coward, Harold (1985) *ibid.*
189. Von Franz, Marie-Louise (1975) *ibid.*
190. Von Franz, Marie-Louise (1975) *ibid.*
191. May, Robert M. (1991) *Cosmic Consciousness Revisited: The Modern Origins and Development of a Western Spiritual Psychology*, Element.
192. May, Robert M. (1991) *ibid.*
193. Joseph, Rhawn "Sex, Violence and Religious Experience". In Rhawn Joseph (Editor) (2002) *NeuroTheology: Brain, Science, Spirituality, Religious Experience*, University Press, California.
194. Whiteman, J.H. Michael (2006) *ibid.*
195. Jung, Carl. Quoted in Clarke, John J. (1995) *Jung on the East*, Routledge.
196. Obeyesekere, Gananath (2002) *Imagining Karma: Ethical Transformation in Amerindian, Buddhist and Greek Rebirth*, University of California Press.
197. Kingsley, Peter (1995) *Ancient Philosophy, Mystery, and Magic: Empedocles and Pythagorean Tradition,* Clarendon Press (Oxford University Press).
198. Hesse, Mary (1970) *ibid.*
199. Kingsley, Peter (1995) *ibid.*
200. Sinclair, Upton (1930) *Mental Radio*, Albert and Charles Boni.
201. Von Franz, Marie-Louise (1998) *On Dreams and Death: A Jungian Interpretation*, Open Court.
202. Von Franz, "Some Historical Aspects of C.G. Jung's Synchronicity Hypothesis" (No date given). English Translation in Von Franz, Marie-Louise (1992) *Psyche and Matter*, Shambhala Publications.
203. Magee, Glen A. (2001) *ibid.*
204. Lord, Eric (2006) *Science, Mind and Paranormal Experience*, lulu.com.
205. Coward, Harold (1985) *ibid.*
206. Taimni, I.K. (1961) *The Science of Yoga:The Yoga Sutras of Patanjali in Sanskrit with transliteration in Roman, translation in English and commentary*, The Theosophical Publishing House.
207. Braude, Stephen E. "The Synchronicity Confusion". In William G. Roll (Editor) (1979) *Research in Parapsychology*, Scarecrow Press.
208. Bohm, David and Peat, F. David (1987) *Science, Order and Creativity*, Bantam Books.
209. Brown, Daniel P. (1986) *ibid.*
210. Jones, Marie D. and Flaxman, Larry (2009) *The Resonance Key: Exploring the Links between Vibration, Consciousness and the Zero Point Grid*, New Page Books.
211. Schommers, Wolfram (1995) *ibid.*
212. Josephson, Brian, D. (1982) "Science and Religion: Can the Two be Synthesised?" delivered as part of *1982-3 Isthmus Foundation Lectures on Science and Religion*, The Isthmus Institute. Revised as "Science and Religion: How to Make the Synthesis". In T.D. Singh (Editor) (1988) *Synthesis of Science and Religion: Critical Dialogues and Essays*, The Bhaktivedanta Institute.

213. Wald, George "The Cosmology of Life and Mind". In T.D. Singh (Editor) (1988) *Synthesis of Science and Religion: Critical Dialogues and Essays*, The Bhaktivedanta Institute.
214. Wolf, Milo (2008) *ibid.*
215. Thompson, Richard, L. (1981) *ibid.*
216. Josephson, Brian, D. (2001) Quoted in Steven, H, Strogatz (2003) *Sync: The Emerging Science of Spontaneous Order*, Hyperion.
217. McKie, Robin "Royal Mail's Nobel guru in telepathy row". *The Observer* (Weekly Newspaper, UK) 30th September 2001.
218. Radin, Dean (2006) *Entangled Minds: Extrasensory Experiences in a Quantum Reality*, Paraview and Pocket Books (Simon and Schuster).
219. Murphy, Michael (1992) *The Future of the Body: Exploration into the Further Evolution of Human Nature*, Jeremy P. Tarcher.
220. Radin, Dean (2006) *ibid.*
221. Thompson, Richard, L. (1981) *ibid.*
222. Susskind, Leonard (2008) *ibid.*
223. Heisenberg, Werner (1958) *ibid.*
224. Herbert, Nick (1985) *ibid.*
225. Arp, Halton (1998) *ibid.*
226. Ashmore, Lyndon (2006) *Big Bang Blasted: The Story of the Expanding Universe and how it was shown to be wrong*, BookSurge LLC.
227. Ashmore, Lyndon (2006) *ibid.*
228. Wolf, Milo (2008) *ibid.*
229. Teresi, Dick (2002) *Lost Discoveries: The Ancient Roots of Modern Science – from the Babylonians to the Maya*, Simon and Schuster.
230. Steinhardt, Paul J. and Turok, Neil (2007) *Endless Universe: Beyond the Big Bang – Rewriting Cosmic History*, Broadway Books.
231. Wolf, Milo (2008) *ibid.*
232. Mead, Carver (2000) *Collective Electrodynamics: Quantum Foundations of Electromagnetism*, MIT Press.

5

Metaphysical Roots of Cognitive Science and its Confounded Neo-Darwinist Misconceptions of Consciousness

Metaphysical Foundations of Cognitive Science

Physicalist science is inherently Behaviorist, precluding Sentience and hence wrong

I first examined the problem of Consciousness at the age of 18. Very quickly I realised that Consciousness could not be included in the current scientific world-picture (its metaphysics). The Physicalist ontology underlying Science was 'inherently Behaviorist' in that it is intrinsically limited to the description of regular patterns of spatiotemporal, energetic activity (or *behaviour*) which can be modelled mathematically. This ontology evolved out of the old Mechanistic Materialism of Classical Physics which focused primarily on the *motion* of objects (Dynamics, Kinematics and Kinetics) as well as on Statics. All the 'phenomena' described by Science are such behavioural patterns of energetic activity; as seen in Chapter 4 QM describes all attributes of Matter in terms of (dynamic) waveforms. This includes forces, particles, atoms, molecules, and all manner of dynamic systems such as the solar system and weather patterns. Even the analysis of static material structures in Chemistry and Mechanics is based on dynamic *processes* (the motion or lack of it in chemical bonding) of electrons, atoms and molecules and the effects of such processes (forces) on larger-scale structures.

The scientific conception of Life as an 'emergent phenomenon' remains essentially such a 'behavioural' concept. An *emergent* phenomenon or process is the higher-level pattern of spatio-temporal activity arising from the collective activity of smaller-scale (e.g., subatomic, atomic, molecular and, in multicellular life, cellular) processes. In striking contrast to the presence of Life, the presence of Awareness cannot be determined by monitoring the behaviour of a system.[N1] Yet the notion of 'Emergent Materialism', in a variety of forms, is the most widely held view amongst scientists as to the nature of Consciousness;

i.e., that it is a novel property emerging from complex physical activity occurring in the brain of humans and perhaps other higher animals. Strictly speaking, an *emergent phenomenon* is one that *cannot be predicted* by the established scientific models describing the behaviour of the smaller-scale substructures constituting the phenomenon. 'Emergence' thus refers to the limitations of human knowledge and scientific models, (i.e., it is an *epistemological* concept). However it is assumed that such complex, collective behaviour (or emergent, large-scale phenomena), such as living systems, are *in principle* **reducible** to smaller-scale, physico-chemical processes involving molecules and atoms.

In his introduction to *Neural Correlates of Consciousness: Empirical and Conceptual Questions*, the editor Thomas Metzinger asserts (*emphasis mine* {*e.m.*}), "what we are lacking is *not a new metaphysics*, but a new variant of practical rationality"[1]. Finnish Cognitive Science philosopher Antii Revonsuo states confidently that Consciousness is but the phenomenal level of organisation of the brain, the brain's real-time virtual reality simulation of the world[2]. Alan Wallace says that, according to the official scientific interpretation of Evolution taught in US college textbooks, there are utterly compelling grounds for concluding that Consciousness is an emergent property of Matter. Physics graduate and practising Buddhist Wallace asserts that, if we were limited to using the theoretical and empirical tools of Science, we would not know that Consciousness exists in the universe[3]. Wallace's argument, though essentially correct, is phrased rather badly as we already know *intuitively* that we are conscious regardless of the fact that scientific methods cannot demonstrate the existence of Consciousness. This *intuitive background of Consciousness* has been taken for granted by most Western thinkers. Gordon Globus argues that the whole notion of "Mind", (i.e., Consciousness) emerging only in high complexity structures is human chauvinism at its worst[4]. Metzinger does state correctly that "reduction" (as in Reductionism) is a relation between *theories,* (i.e., abstract conceptions) and not between *phenomena* (by which he means the actualities)[5]. Thus, as we have seen, 'emergence' is an *epistemological* concept, referring to the limitations of manmade theories to predict higher-level phenomenal manifestations. In spite of its widespread usage as an 'explanation' for how Consciousness arises, 'emergence' cannot actually be applied *ontologically* to Consciousness. Galileo excluded subjective experiences as 'non-real' *secondary qualities.* Scientific ontology describes an **insentient** universe of primary (measurable) qualities which are taken to be all that really exists.

The 20th Century shift from the old Materialism (Matter as Primary) to Physicalism (Energy as Primary) does not change this fact; according to the New Physics energy is multi-dimensional (non-Euclidean) vibratory patterns of spatiotemporal activity.[N2] Energy is *insentient*. Radically different properties such as Awareness (Sentience) which are not present, even in potentiality, in the Physicalist ontology at 'lower levels' (smaller scales) cannot suddenly appear *ex nihilo* at 'higher levels' of complexity. Given the assumption of insentient energy, all that can possibly emerge is more complex insentient patterns of spatiotemporal activity or more complex behaviour! Physicist Tony Rothman makes a point which is of relevance to this debate when he states that *complex systems* ought really to be renamed 'ordinary' and that the systems of interest to physicists should be labelled '*simple* systems'[6]. Just as real Nature is full of thermodynamically *open* systems in contrast to the artificial *closed* test tube systems of chemists; real Nature is full of complex systems and *complexity* cannot be evoked, pseudo-ontologically, to differentiate (as yet unspecified) brain processes from the rest of Nature. To do so, as Cognitive Science does, is surreptitious ontological Dualism. A radically different property such as Awareness, irreducible to patterns of (insentient) energy, cannot be part of the 'Physical World'!

This is why we have to use Direct **'Physical Correlate'** in regard to my brainstem brainwave correlate of the Inner Light of Pure Consciousness. I have *not reduced* Consciousness to energy; the Reticular Activating System (RAS) brainwave energy correlates directly with the Inner Light or the phenomenal aspect of the Pure Consciousness within us (*see Appendix*). The Physicalist ontology is incorrect. The universe is not created out of insentient energy and Consciousness is not a late-comer to cosmic evolution associated only with complex brains. Simple epistemological analysis (*see* Ch. 9) shows that the 'Physical World' is simply a human conceptual abstraction from our conscious experience and cannot exist independently of Universal Consciousness! Thus Metzinger is completely wrong when he claims that *a new metaphysics* is not required. Physicalist ontology is incapable of accounting for the existence of Consciousness as Consciousness is not complex behavioural patterns created by energy. If Consciousness was physical, scientific instruments would be able to detect its presence!

Behaviorist roots of Functionalism

In his introduction to *Neural Correlates of Consciousness* Metzinger claims that revolutionary developments are resulting in subjective experience becoming technologically accessible in a way it has never been in the history of mankind[7]. Given that the title includes "neural correlates" it is revealing to note this immediate misleading slip by the editor, claiming that new technology allows us to access "subjective experience" rather than (hypothetical) neural correlates associated with subjective experience. We have seen already (Ch. 4) similar misleading verbal and epistemological 'sleights of hand' practised by Benjamin Libet and the editors of *Journal of Consciousness Studies* rubbishing Schrödinger's assertion that Consciousness was One, (i.e., singular and all-embracing). Metzinger comments sneeringly that more than eighty percent of people on this planet, in their personal lives, do not accept the most general standards of rationality[8]. Given the context of his discussion, not only is he attacking popular beliefs amongst laypeople but he also seems to be perpetuating Eurocentric myths that equate non-Western cultures with irrationality. Metzinger refers to Cicero's conception of philosophy as *cultura animi* or taking care of and cultivating the soul. Metzinger even suggests that the classical motif of defining the Love of Wisdom as cultivating the soul could inspire us but he leaves it as an open question as to whether a new interpretation of this classical view of *Philosophia* could actually be achieved in the light of contemporary neurobiological discoveries[9]. I would point out that such a new interpretation of *Philosophia* is indeed possible but not within the old Materialist metaphysics which Metzinger clings onto in the vain belief that he is more rational than non-Materialists. True *philosophia* (Love of Divine Wisdom) transcends Rationality, reconciling the conceptual opposites created by dichotomous reasoning. I would challenge anyone to demonstrate the irrationality of my arguments undermining the false claims made by the likes of Metzinger, Libet, Crick and others.

In contrast, French philosopher Jean-Pierre Dupuy gives a more realistic assessment of the philosophical underpinnings of Cognitive Science. He says that what gives coherence to many different research programmes that go under the name of "Cognitive Science" is the associated "cognitive" philosophy. Such Cognitive philosophers (rather than the psychologists, neurologists, computer scientists and linguists) have reflected upon and systematised the basic attitude shared by workers in the various specialities that constitute so-called Cognitive Science[10]. Such 'Cognitive Philosophy' has brought undeserved prestige to a number of well-known academics in the Western study of Philosophy-of-Mind. Their works tend to be filled with currently fashionable jargon from Cognitive Science and culturally-limited concepts steeped in Eurocentric and Christocentric assumptions. Such jargon-laden gibberish appeals tautologically to the geeky specialists in Cognitive Science research as it simply restates their own dogmatic beliefs with more literary gusto than the geeks themselves can muster. The egos of such academic pop philosophers get inflated given the praise from the geeky scientists, who, being clueless about real Metaphysics, hype up their cheerleaders as distinguished philosophers! It is just self-aggrandizing mutual back-scratching. This resembles the Indian intellectual *sepoys* who win Booker Prizes and other Western awards and receive acclaim as supposedly great writers by writing what their White masters want to hear.[N3]

Dupuy adds that Cognitive Science represents itself as having reclaimed for Science all the ancient questions posed by Philosophy about the Mind. But the true character of this self-proclaimed 'Science of Mind' remains deeply philosophical; the 'science' that provides these scientists with the spirit (or mind) which otherwise would be absent is in reality a philosophy. It is a peculiar philosophy which has crept in like the Trojan horse into these sciences and which claims dominion over the realm of Mind, chasing out rival philosophies such as Phenomenology and Existentialism, rival psychologies such as Behaviorism and Psychoanalysis and rival sciences such as Structural Anthropology[11]. I would take serious issue with this Frenchman's choice of examples of rival viewpoints. In regard to 'Behaviorism', Dupuy is referring to the discredited notions of Watson and Skinner. Skinner's ludicrous approach regarded the Mind as a 'Black Box' to be ignored. But the editors of the book in which Dupuy writes (*see next paragraph*) acknowledge that Cognitive Science is 'Behaviorist' as of course I am stressing here[N4] The French have lagged behind the Anglo-Americans in recognizing Freud as a fraud. The French intelligentsia have a penchant for pretentious linguistic, pseudo-philosophical poseurs and ponces[N5]. But Dupuy's general point about the dogmatism of Cognitive Science is correct. When Cognitive Science actually comes face to face with the Ontological question of Consciousness, (i.e., subjective experience or the 'hard problem'[N6]) it immediately falls back upon naive and erroneous philosophical conjectures, based upon appeals to the authority of Physics, to disguise its own abject failure.

As the editors of *Naturalizing Phenomenology: Issues in Contemporary Phenomenology and Cognitive Science* (in which Dupuy's paper appears) state, "Cognitive Science *remains faithful to behaviorism*" {*e.m.*}. It focuses on behaviour and rejects any non-behavioural evidence such as introspective and phenomenological data[12]. Cognitive Science, they add, claims to have discovered a non-controversial Materialist solution to the Mind/Body problem. The Computational-Symbolic view (rooted in Anglo-American Analytical myths) gave rise to Functionalism which viewed Biology as irrelevant as it was conceived as merely 'hardware'. Mental entities, as they are (supposedly) purely 'functional', do not have to be viewed as ontologically different from biological entities at lower-levels. Cognitive Science *claims Functional 'explanations'* {*e.m.*}[13]. Lakoff and Johnson state that early Cognitive Science was Functionalist, rooted in Anglo-American Analytical assumptions of a disembodied mind, symbolic manipulations etc. The Functionalists viewed the mind as an abstract computer program which could be run on any appropriate hardware. Thus the brain itself was viewed as largely irrelevant[14]. I would add that Cognitive Science also has social roots in the Cold War. The reports of Chinese brainwashing of prisoners in the Korean War played a role in stimulating Cognitive Science research. Furthermore, much of the early Artificial Intelligence (AI) research was motivated by the goal of producing cybernetic control systems for weaponry such as computer-guided cruise missiles based on the German V1 'doodlebugs'. Thus, although AI researchers made ludicrous claims about how they would recreate minds in machines and how computers would soon be keeping us as pets, etc., often their research was not actually investigating issues related to biological processes in the brain but top secret control and guidance systems for the Pentagon.

Functionalism claims to explain what is done but not what composes the 'doer'[15]. 'Functionalism' is a subtle retention of Behaviorism, with minor adjustments. Biological functions, as with other Physicalist explanations involve describing spatiotemporal patterns of energetic activity or behaviour. If something performs a certain *biological function*, then it does something within a larger context, or plays some role. Its actions, activity or 'behaviour' results in the change of state, activity or 'behaviour' of other interacting elements. The concept of *function* is similar to that of 'meaning' in that it refers to the role played by an element which contributes to the overall normal activity of a larger system of interconnected elements. It refers to how the operations or *behaviours* of things are inter-related. If its behaviour becomes abnormal it becomes *dysfunctional*. Such activity or performing a function involves, in this cognitive context, the internal *behaviour* of the brain (e.g. the activity of neurons). All biological organs and systems perform various functions but scientists do not suggest that the extremely complex functions of the liver, kidneys or immune system are associated with subjective experiences! Thus talk about 'functions' does not truly bring us any closer to Consciousness (the Ontological 'hard problem') although it has some value in elucidating aspects of the 'soft problems' of Mentation.

I have stressed that the Western tradition conflates Mind (Mentation[N7]) and Consciousness mistaking Consciousness as a property associated only with the Waking ego (mind) and Dream Sleep. Three thousand years ago the Upanishads recognised that the Light of Pure Consciousness persists through Dreamless Sleep. This seems paradoxical from the Western point of view but my physical correlate of the Light of Pure Consciousness confirms the Upanishadic knowledge as the RAS remains active (at lower frequency) throughout Dreamless Sleep. Varela and Shear state that Behaviorism and most Cognitive Scientists make a distinction between behaviour and subjectivity. Most Cognitive Scientists assume explicitly that this behaviour comes from a cognitive subject or agent without elaboration. Thus they insinuate (assume tacitly) the existence of the subject's position (point-of-view) and concerns whilst claiming to maintain a third-person stance[16]. Hardin says that merely schematic specifications, (i.e., thought experiments) plague both sides of the Functionalism/anti-Functionalism debate[17]. Note that such so-called 'thought experiments' as with scientific notions of 'measurement' and 'observation', presuppose tacitly an underlying Consciousness in which such thoughts are manifest. Thus, as with the Philosophy of Mathematics (presupposing Conscious Intuition of axioms) and the Epistemology of Physics (tacitly presupposing conscious observations of measurements), Cognitive Science cannot escape the *epistemological fact of the Primacy of Consciousness.*

Connectionism and Embodied-Enactive models

The second generation of Cognitive Scientists questioned Analytical philosophy and its disembodied, symbolic notion of Mind. The new view included notions that Reason is imaginative in that bodily forms are mapped onto abstract modes of inference by metaphor. This is the primary focus of Lakoff and Johnson in their critique of such Analytic, Symbolic philosophy[18]. Dupuy says that there are two Cognitive Science paradigms, Classical Cognitivism and Connectionism[19]. Roy *et al.* say that the main divisions of Cognitive Science's information processing models are the Symbolic-Computational and the Connectionist[20]. Connectionism, or Parallel Distributed Processing, which came into fashion in the 1980s involved simulating the behaviour of the brain's biological neural networks. Such ideas had already been proposed by Canadian psychologist Donald Hebb in 1949 with his *cell assembly* model of continuously reorganizing neural connections in perceptions and learning. The new Connectionism was supplemented by mathematics to represent this interconnectivity, based on probabilistic calculus to represent the fluidic processes of thermodynamics in terms of multiple attractors, repellors, limit cycles etc. Unlike the serial computations of old Artificial Intelligence, computation in Parallel Distributive Processing is based on waves of excitation and inhibition which move across neuron-like elements that compete and cooperate, amplifying and suppressing patterns of connectivity[21]. This picture of waves of excitation and inhibition at the macro-level brings to mind of course the gross electrical activity detected by the EEG based upon so-called 'brainwave' activity.

Roy *et al.* say that Connectionism challenged the Computationalist orthodoxy of discrete symbols and rule manipulation positing instead a new language of Nonlinear Dynamical Systems. In this sense it ceased to be 'information-processing' in the strictest sense. They also claim that it was Connectionism which introduced to Cognitive Science the radically new and important idea of the *emergence* of high-level structures from the interaction of lower-level terms. They say that the notion of emergence is intrinsic to dynamical formulation and that it is derived from the idea of self-organisation and it has recently become a hot topic in the new fields associated with the study of complexity[22]. I do not agree. Emergent Materialism clearly has older roots including the old Gestalt Field Theory of 1930s Germany[N8] with its famous notion of the *Whole* being more than the *sum of its parts*. Emergent Materialism has also, especially in Anglo-American circles, been championed by neurologist Roger Sperry (*see below*) who is not associated with AI Connectionism. The first-generation Cognitive Science with its notion of Mind as a higher-level function of lower-level brain substrates was itself a form of (epistemological) *emergence* given that how the assumed 'higher level' *function* is actually generated is not elaborated.

Roy *et al.* also assert that both Connectionism (in its dominant form at least) and Computationalism share an unquestioned assumption of *Representationalism* which holds to a semantic-like correspondence between mental entities and external events giving mental processes their behavioural efficacy. Petitot *et al.* subscribe to what they call the *Embodied-Enactive* view which, although it shares with Connectionism a belief in the importance of dynamical processes and emergence, questions the relevance of representations in regard to cognitive processes. According to this view, such processes emerge or are enacted by 'situated agents', the actions of which drive the establishment of meaningful couplings of regular interdependencies with their surroundings. Meaning becomes inseparable from such interdependencies. Roy *et al.* say that, as with Connectionism, these ideas have their roots in the work of thinkers such as J.J. Gibson[23]. In fact, Gibson's 'ecological' view of Mind and Environment appealed to Western pseudo-radical Philosophers-of-Mind of the sort who try to reduce Eastern spirituality to Materialism (e.g. Harry Hunt *see below*). Gibson's central notion of Unmediated Perception by Resonance between Mind and the animal's life-world is completely untenable as sensory perception is unquestionably mediated by nervous systems.

The Embodied-Enactive view stresses the embodied, situated nature of cognition[24]. Roy *et al.* do not elaborate as to what they actually mean by 'situated agents' and how such agents operate in regard to physical causality etc. Note the overlap here with my own 1980s ideas on *meaningful organisation* in that 'meaning' arises from regular interdependencies between the organism and its environment (*see Ch. 11*). The phenomenological investigations of William James contradict the Analytic fantasies of fixed symbols and rules, (i.e., Representationalism)[25] and such phenomenological knowledge ties in with the recent work of the likes of Walter Freeman on cortical field dynamics in the rabbit which suggests that the brain-dynamical correlates of external stimuli are non-static patterns of electrical activity which transform subtly over periods of time[26].

Lakoff and Johnson locate the origins of such embodied approaches to Perception and Cognition in Merleau-Ponty's *Phenomenology of Perception*. Although they expose the groundlessness of Anglo-American Philosophy and the first-generation Cognitive Science that is firmly rooted in such Symbolic-Computational approaches, Lakoff and Johnson themselves display the same sort of pseudo-radicalism as displayed by Roger Sperry (*see below*) in believing that their minor revisions to scientific orthodoxy are sufficient to resolve the problems of Mind and Consciousness which have plagued Philosophy for thousands of years. They are obsessed with the notion of 'metaphor' and similar ideas derived from Linguistics, Lakoff's own speciality. They tell us that there are hundreds of primary metaphors which "provide subjective experience with extremely rich inferential structure, imagery, and qualitative 'feel,' when the networks for subjective experience and the sensorimotor networks neurally connected to them are co-activated"[27]. This vague waffle suggests a Dualistic notion of special *networks for subjective experience* and even perhaps implying that the *qualitative 'feel'*, (i.e., the raw feels or 'qualia' that we actually experience) in themselves, not just the differentiation of such experiences, are somehow generated by these metaphors!

They also state that the central scientific metaphor of "neural computation" is so robust and stable that "it has gained the status of embodied truth". They stress that this is not a literal truth but an indispensible metaphor for Neuroscience. For them, concepts are neural structures[28]. Although I agree that concepts are neural structures, I find Lakoff and Johnson, not only obsessed with metaphors, but also wedded to the myth of Neuronal Man (*see below*) which fails to see beyond the 'trees' (neurons) to the 'forest' (field dynamics). Petitot *et al.'s* critique of Representationalism and my points above about William James', Walter Freeman's and related work questioning the fixed neuronal basis of mental phenomena also apply here. Lakoff and Johnson also believe, on doctrinaire grounds, that the yogic Pure Consciousness Experience or non-conceptual, uncategorised experience is impossible. We have seen that Maurice Merleau-Ponty tried to rid Phenomenology of what he took naively to be the 'Transcendental Illusion' found in traditional philosophy, and the likes of Kant and Husserl[29]. Merleau-Ponty is another one of the hyped-up heroes of Western pseudo-radical, tacit Reductionism.

Crude Cognitive Conceptions of Consciousness Concocted by Nobel Laureates

We see from this brief discussion of the philosophical basis of Cognitive Science, that both Functionalism and the more recent Connectivist and Brain Dynamics models tend to evoke views of mind as emergent phenomena arising at the higher spatiotemporal levels of order from lower-level brain processes. We have already seen that such Emergent Materialism is untenable in regard to Consciousness *per se* (i.e., Awareness) although *emergence* does have some relevance in regard to the nature of Mentation or physical processes correlated with mental activity. Emergence resembles superficially my theory of Consciousness from the 1980s (*see Ch. 11*) in that my notion of the subjective closure of self-organising substructures leaves only the higher-level electric field processes of the brain correlated with mental events. However, my ideas were based on Panpsychist ontological notions and thus avoided the ludicrous flaw in Emergent Materialism in that emergence of higher-level phenomena occurs everywhere throughout the natural world. Emergent Materialists give no adequate explanation whatsoever as to how the emergence of higher-level processes in the brain could somehow create Awareness unless they sneak-in new ontological properties precluded by Physicalist/Materialist metaphysics. Few, if any, seem to even understand this contradiction with the Galilean presuppositions of Science. Even if they do understand, we saw in Chapter 3 that 'Physics appeasement' related to fear of ridicule and to the 'Physics Envy' (*see Ch. 4*) of biologists, psychologists and academic philosophers leads them to shy away from challenging the Physicalist/Materialist orthodoxy. This sneaking-in of Consciousness *ex nihilo* into Physicalist ontology is, as stated previously, a tacit recourse to Magic! The sorts of arguments put forward by Cognitive Scientists for the supposed 'emergence of Consciousness' are actually arguments related to the emergence of 'mind-like' physical processes (*See Ch. 11*) and not ontologically adequate accounts for the existence of subjective experience correlated with these mind-like processes. Some of the contributors to Metzinger's book even think that world-model-like process or 'virtual reality' simulations in the brain are all that is required to solve the so-called 'Mind/Body problem' (by which they mean the 'hard' ontological problem of Consciousness).

Sperry's tacit Dualist 'Emergent Mentalism'

Nobel laureate neurologist Roger Sperry, famous for his so-called 'split-brain' research, has been perhaps the leading advocate of Emergent Materialism as the solution to the 'mind/body problem'. In fact, Sperry actually called his view "Emergent Mentalism". Sperry touted his approach as more than a mere shift in our perceptual and conceptual frames of reference from the Reductionist focus of old-fashioned Skinnerian Behaviorists on components such as neurons to more holistic, 'higher-level', complex physical phenomena. Sperry went so far as to claim that his view was not just the key to understanding Consciousness but that it constituted a *new cosmology* that *makes possible the derivation of transcendent moral guidelines* {*e.m.*}[30]. By such statements, we are presumably supposed to believe that the simple notion of Downward Causation from 'higher-level' emergent physical processes influencing the behaviour of neurons etc. is sufficient to form the basis of our understanding of Free Will.

In fact, recent neurobiological studies of the role of focused attention on neuroplasticity reveal what clearly appear to be Downward Causation effects reorganizing neural patterns[31]. But such Downward Causation is really just a long overdue correction to the naive Reductionist presumption of Upward Causation in traditional scientific thought, (i.e., as with *emergence*, Downward Causation has to do with limitations of manmade conceptions and theories). It does not necessarily challenge the (supposed) *causal closure* of the 'physical world', an unproven belief which is so dear to Materialists. Downward Causation in itself does not necessarily entail any true *freedom* from the causal nexus of the physical world. The unproven belief of Physicalists in the 'causal closure' of the physical world, if true, would mean that subjective experiences are no more than *epiphenomena* (or byproducts devoid of causal efficacy) of the physical processes constituting mentation. Now, if this were true, this would contradict NeoDarwinist arguments that Consciousness somehow emerged in higher animal brains. *Natural Selection could obtain no purchase on Epiphenomena that have no physical effects!*

Indeed, as I typed this chapter, the *Daily Mail* reports on new scientific research using MRI brain-scanners by J-D Haynes at the Max Planck Institute in Germany which suggests that free will in humans seems little more than an illusion. The 'unconscious' mind seems to have chosen a course of action seconds before the volunteers thought they had made up their minds[32]. In fact the results resemble the well-known work of Benjamin Libet on the so-called Readiness Potential detected by the EEG before the subject appears to consciously make a decision[33]. Such results will be pertinent in considering the Cognitive Science myth that Consciousness (Awareness) emerged in evolution as it provides a selective advantage. Journalist Michael Hanlon states correctly that it is still completely unknown how the brain gives rise to Consciousness.

> *Few modern people believe that the brain is pervaded by some sort of mysterious "soul"; but how the neurones and synapses of the mind can generate subjective experiences of colour, smell, hate, fear and love is an utter mystery.* ***In fact, many scientists believe it is the greatest mystery of all.***
>
> — Michael Hanlon {*e.m.*}[34]

Pascal Engel says that the supposedly "non-Reductionist" Materialist theories (e.g. Emergentism) flirt with disguised forms of Dualism. The more "successful" the Materialist reduction appears, the less the supposedly "Mental" concepts seem correct[35]. D.S. Clarke points out that Karl Popper's argument that "solidity" arising from the crystallisation of a liquid is an emergent property is false. In fact it is a *resultant property* that can be deduced from the liquid's constituents[36]. Similarly, Alan Wallace dismisses Emergent Materialist arguments along the lines that Consciousness is to the brain as water is to the molecule H_2O. It is easy to show how H_2O crystallises into ice. An imaginary microscope with sufficient power would show H_2O molecules in water but you can't imagine seeing Consciousness[37]. Although such debates get rather heated, to use a bad pun, they are all redundant arguments given that *emergence* actually refers to our epistemological ignorance, our inability to predict higher-level phenomena from lower-level ones; there cannot in fact be any truly ontological emergence of radically new properties irreducible to physico-chemical behaviour. Given that Emergent Materialists accept that Consciousness does indeed exist (unlike 'Eliminative Materialists'; *see below*) this failure implies that the Physicalist ontology must be wrong. As shown in my 'creating Life *de novo*' argument, an emergent property such as the presence of Life in a manmade 'living system' could be detected as Life is a *behavioural phenomenon*. Consciousness is non-detectable physically (or 'behaviourally') so it is not comparable to the emergence of Life. The simple thought experiment based on extrapolation of evolving complexity of insentient energy-matter, historical understanding of Science's roots in Christian Spirit/Nature Dualism and Galileo's de-spiritualisation of Nature and Phenomenological knowledge prove that Consciousness is not an emergent phenomenon.

Sperry even stated that "there is growing reason to suspect that the secret trick for generating consciousness could turn out to be some relatively simple form of network processing or programming, something that computer-cognitive science may already be close to discovering"[38]. Rather than making such extremely vague statements invoking the fashionable contemporary jargon, the onus is on advocates of views such as Sperry's to specify in detail how such emergence creating Free Will and even Awareness could possibly arise out of *insentient* energy-matter. Certainly simple network processing and programming cannot possibly create such novel properties. In Physicalist ontology all 'emergent' physical properties, whether or not they are unpredictable, can be nothing more than just complex behavioural patterns of (supposedly) insentient matter/energy. Such emergent physical activity may constitute higher-level collective-activity forces such as 'pressures', which cannot be attributed to individual molecules. According to Physicalism, forces, as with matter, are just forms of energy and have no sentience. Similarly the collective systemic property of 'temperature' is merely an averaged measurement of the kinetic energy of the particles in a system. Note also that warmth and coldness are subjective experiences existing in conscious minds and not actually present in the environment; a hypnotised subject may feel cold in conditions where everyone else feels warm.

Furthermore, Sperry asserted naively that, because Science tests its "truths" against "outside reality", Science is lifted beyond culture, tradition, metaphysics etc. and is grounded directly in the interactions of Reality itself. As with Nadeau and Kafatos in Chapter 4, we frequently find scientists exclaiming unabashedly that Physicalist science or 'Physics' somehow transcends its own root assumptions (or *metaphysics*) which is really a statement of blind faith as it is obviously irrational and self-contradictory. Sperry considered his 'Emergent *Mentalism*' to be monistic and "mentalist" and took objection with philosopher of science Mario Bunge's naming of this view as "Emergent *Materialism*" and his classification of Sperry as a Dualist. Sperry, believing that Consciousness is merely an emergent phenomenon, spoke of "subjective emergents"[39]. Thus Sperry imagined that his view went beyond mere Physicalism whilst somehow deluding himself that it remained a Monist view although Bunge was, of course, correct. True or 'ontological' emergence of Consciousness would imply a complete transcendence of the possibilities inherent in the 'Physical World' and thus must be Dualist, as both Bunge and Engel recognise, as *sentience* bears no relation to what supposedly existed previously (i.e., *insentient* energy and matter).

Of course, the Physicalist Ontology or supposedly insentient energy/matter exists only in the imagination of those who believe this myth; in reality the Physical Universe is no more than a human idea. Sperry's reference to testing 'truths' against 'outside reality' is a false assumption of epistemological Realism which is untenable.[N9] Contrary to popular misconceptions, the fact that a scientist possesses a Nobel Prize does not make him a philosophically sophisticated thinker or even a creative one. People have won Nobel Prizes sometimes simply because the molecule that their team isolated is important biologically and the key creative step in isolating it was to try a new detergent! Outside the comfort zone of their very limited technical specialities, most scientists reveal themselves to be little more than 'glorified technicians', unable to think beyond the conceptually 'blinkered' tramlines of their narrowly-focused paradigms. Yet, rather like the Postmodernist Humanities academics who pontificate on grand philosophical questions amongst their equally deluded 'fellow travellers', most scientists remain largely oblivious of the embarrassing puerility of their thought.

Changeaux's 'Neuronal Man'

Sperry is not the only Nobel laureate scientist displaying glaring inadequacies of philosophical analysis when it comes to tackling the problem of Consciousness. We saw in Chapter 1 that Nobel laureate biophysicist turned neuroscientist Francis Crick held a crude Behaviorist view asserting that our subjective experiences, personal identity and free will are nothing more than the behaviour of a vast assembly of nerve cells and their associated molecules[40]. I referred to Crick's crude view as the 'Neuronal Man' myth after the eponymous book written in the early 1980s by the French Nobel laureate neurobiologist Jean-Pierre Changeaux. As the back cover promotional copy on the English translation stated, Changeaux's "radical and controversial hypothesis" was "that there is no 'mind' in man, nothing psychic, but rather only neurones, synapses, electricity, and chemistry"[41]. The Indian fable of the blind man and the elephant springs to mind when discussing these scientific technicians unable to think beyond the limited phenomena detectable using their micro-electrodes. Changeaux discusses regulatory loops in the brain with re-entries at several levels of organisation which he says could lead to high amplitude oscillations. Changeaux continues[42]:

> *These linkages and relationships, these "spider's webs", this regulatory system would function as a whole. Can one say that consciousness emerges from all this? Yes, if one takes the word "emerge" literally, as an iceberg emerges from the water. But it is sufficient to say that consciousness is the functioning of this regulatory system. Man no longer has a need for the "Spirit"; it is enough for him to be Neuronal Man.*

Along with the subtilised Behaviorism of Functionalism, the reader will notice the confusing metaphor of 'literal *emergence*' such that consciousness emerges out of these neural feedback loops and regulatory circuits "as an iceberg emerges from the water". This is not the conventional usage of *emergence* as an unpredictable, higher-level phenomenon. The *submerged* bulk of the iceberg is constituted of exactly the same type of frozen crystalline water molecules as the part protruding above the water. The 'subconscious' or supposedly 'unconscious' processes underlying attention have often been compared to the submerged bulk of the iceberg. But this metaphor gives us no clue whatsoever as to what is the difference between the (supposedly) 'unconscious' and the conscious mind that makes the latter so radically different. If we take Changeaux "literally" as he suggests, this metaphor simply suggests that Consciousness is the functioning of the uppermost regions of the regulatory loops in the brain. This is absurd! Changeaux remains clueless as to what Consciousness actually is and, as with Gallic Postmodern philosophical *poseurs*, he simply befuddles the uncritical reader with such misleading images and words in a vain attempt to appear profound; So much for scientific precision. Natalie Depraz, a French scholar of Phenomenology, says that J.P. Changeaux's *Neuronal Man* is a crude, caricature-like form of Reductionism as opposed to subtle forms which are more *deceptive* and hence more "dangerous" {*e.m.*}[43]. Such crude metaphors are in fact the stock-in-trade of most Cognitive Science 'explanations' of Consciousness.

Crick's crude Behaviorism

Crick's own book *The Astonishing Hypothesis: The Scientific Search for the Soul*[44] is equally crude and totally devoid of philosophical sophistication. His preface begins with the statement, "This book is about the mystery of consciousness—how to explain it in scientific terms". The aim of Science, Crick tells us, is to explain *all* aspects of the behaviour of our brains, *including those of mystics* {*e.m.*}. The behaviour of the brain, Crick tells us is "emergent". Behaviour does not exist in separate parts, such as individual neurons, rather it is the intricate interaction of many of them that can do such marvellous things. However, Crick cautions, there are two meanings of 'emergent'. The first has mystical overtones in its implication that emergent behaviour cannot, even in principle, be understood in terms of its component interactions. Crick rejects this view saying that the scientific meaning of emergent, or at least his usage of 'emergent', assumes that whilst the whole may not be the simple sum of its parts, its behaviour remains, in principle, understandable from the nature and interactions of its components[45].

Crick seems to recognise that *emergence* can be nothing more than a behavioural concept in stating that, "the *behaviour* of the brain is emergent" {*e.m.*}; i.e., it simply refers to complex, higher-level patterns of physical activity (or 'behaviour') which is all that is actually permitted within the ontology of Physicalist science. But this same fact undermines his own arguments! It is true that by 'emergence', Science means theoretically-unpredictable complex, collective behaviour still conforming to underlying physico-chemical principles, (i.e., it is *epistemological* as there is no *ontological* break with Physicalism). Thus, strictly speaking, 'emergence' cannot mean *completely irreducible* as in Crick's former case (with 'mystical overtones'). However, some writers including Fritjof Capra (*see Ch. 6*), have used the term 'emergence' incorrectly in this *more overtly dualistic* sense (as 'irreducible') whilst still claiming to espouse Physicalism. If some property is irreducible *even in principle*, it cannot be part of the Physical World. But, as we have seen, the Ontological Status of Consciousness (as Awareness) actually is **irreducible** to *inherently Behaviorist* physico-chemical principles! Thus, even when used correctly, 'emergence' remains **disguised-Dualism.** My point here is that even those explicit Dualists who believe Consciousness is irreducible to Physics, yet somehow only appears in egoic mentation (e.g. Karl Popper and John Eccles) are also incorrect. In truth, it is the entire Physical Universe including Space-Time that emerges through the vibratory, energetic activity arising within the all-pervading Distinctionless, Transcendental Consciousness (*nirguna*

Brahman). Nondual Consciousness is Being in itself, it does not emerge out of anything.

As is typical of most scientists, once Crick moves beyond the technical details he is familiar with, his arguments in regard to Spirituality, etc., are little more than naive clichés. Like many Westerners, Crick projects the characteristics of Western religions with their ridiculous myths and superstitions onto Eastern mystical philosophies assuming that the latter are just like the former and thus that they do not give any evidence or logical arguments in support of their views. As stated previously, faced with the glaring anomaly that, unlike Judaeo-Christian cosmology, Hinduism viewed the cosmos as vastly greater than the Earth and its locality, Crick's crude explanation for this anomaly is that Hindus inflated times and distances for the "sheer joy of it". His second chapter, entitled 'The General Nature of Consciousness' opens with a quote from physicist John Archibald Wheeler, "In any field find the strangest thing and then explore it"[46]. Ironically, Crick immediately ignores Wheeler's dictum in considering only normal states of Consciousness and ignoring the mystical states which are clearly the strangest aspect of Consciousness. Use of such quotes serves subliminally to suggest to the reader that Crick was a maverick (i.e., a person of independent or unorthodox views), a 'cool dude' operating at the boundaries of Science, where no man has gone before, when in fact he was blinkered by and hidebound to orthodox Materialist dogma.

His second chapter's contents have little if anything to do with 'The General Nature of Consciousness' as Crick ignores altered states of Consciousness and talks only about normal Wakeful consciousness[47]. It is a well established scientific method that, to understand some phenomenon, one should try to see how the phenomenon manifests under varying conditions to see if it exhibits different states. Furthermore, scientific methodology considers it best, if possible, to start with the simplest form of the phenomenon, in its purest form, uncontaminated by other factors. However, Crick and his fellow Western scientists, largely on doctrinaire grounds, deny the possibility of a simple state of Pure Consciousness. This denial is also partly based on the fact that they themselves only have experience of non-mystical states of Consciousness and are not open-minded enough to even consider the possibility that yogic descriptions of a Pure Consciousness may actually be valid. Similarly, the existence of truly strange paranormal psychic phenomena is denied. This orthodox scientific mindset parallels that of Edwin Abbot's allegorical 'Flatlanders' who refuse to believe in the existence of a Third Dimension as they have never experienced it.

Crick grants that there might be some aspects of Consciousness such as qualia that science will not be able to explain but, in Crick's opinion, as with the limitations of Quantum Mechanics (QM), we learn to live with these[48]. The term *qualia* is employed by Western academic philosophers as a fancy new version of the older 'raw feel'; perhaps using Latin gives it a veneer of scientific authority. But, as the term 'qualia' denotes the qualitative content of experiences (the actual 'raw feels' of subjective experience such as redness or warmth rather than the measurable, quantitative aspects) which are the crux of the so-called 'Mind/Body problem', it is thus apparent that Crick has largely abandoned the hope that Science can actually resolve the Mind/Body problem. This "mystery of consciousness" was what his book was supposed to tackle! Crick's "astonishing hypothesis" is that *qualia* or subjective experiences such as "joys and sorrows", and free will, are **nothing more** than the *behaviour* of vast assemblies of neurons and molecules {*e.m.*}. What is actually truly 'astonishing' about such crude Materialist pronouncements is that no attempt whatsoever is made to explain why it is that the higher-level behaviour of neuronal networks in the human brain should thus differ from the higher-level behaviour of other natural systems and, as this cannot be explained, why one should not logically assume Panpsychism. But this is typical of the confidence tricks and verbal 'sleights of hand' practised by apologists for Materialism, who deride non-Materialists and Eastern mystics, etc., as irrational fools presenting fantasies as facts. Crick claims that Hindu cosmology exaggerated scales for sheer fun, yet scientists regularly present as a serious scientific hypothesis, the Many Worlds interpretation of QM put forward by J.A. Wheeler's student Hugh Everett III; Talk about exaggerating things! As we saw in Chapter 4, the Many World's view postulates a near-infinite number of universes constantly splitting off from each other. This scientific mythology presupposes that transcendental knowledge is impossible but as I stated, and Richard Thompson also hinted[49], the Many Worlds myth can be proven false in spiritual experience.

Ironically, in asserting that we should learn to live with the paradoxical aspects of QM (which lead to views like Everett's), Crick is himself adopting hypocritically the safe, secure, unquestioning belief of received-wisdom approach which he chastises in religious believers and thus Crick's blinkered approach runs contrary to the open-minded, questioning spirit of scientific enquiry. By refusing to accept the possibility that yogis might be correct in referring to Pure Consciousness, Cognitive Scientists are being non-scientific, as an open-minded humility to phenomenal facts, however contradictory to one's own assumptions, is supposed to be the way of Science. Crick, who was a British 'boffin' during the 1939-45 war, had a message for his fellow scientists working in Human Vision Research. Crick suggested that every *Human* {*e.m.*} Vision Research laboratory (N.B. the tacit anthropocentric connotations about Consciousness) should stick up a poster on its walls. Upon this poster is written in large block capitals the words 'CONSCIOUSNESS NOW' along with the shadow of the huge outline letters spelling now[50]. Clearly, the boys in Human Vision Research may find out quite a lot of interesting things about the behaviour of human brains. But when it comes to the real question of the mystery of Consciousness (the so-called 'Mind/Body problem') which Crick states that he wishes to address, it is quite obvious that the poster that they should be putting up, which is more honest in its assessment of the limitations of Behaviorist, Physicalist science, would say 'CONSCIOUSNESS NEVER'.

Edelman's evasive, Evolutionary Emergent Materialism

Another Nobel laureate biologist who has switched his attention to Neurobiology and the problems of Mind and Consciousness is ex-immunologist Gerald Edelman. Like Crick, Edelman shows a lack of philosophical *nous* when faced with the ontological problem. However, he is somewhat more sophisticated in articulating his own assumptions and more mature in recognising that it is better to focus on fundamental, general features of Consciousness rather than higher-order forms of Consciousness as found in normal human consciousness. Edelman and Tononi (E and T) say, that to avoid confusion one must clearly state one's assumptions in regard to investigating Consciousness as a scientific *object* {*e.m.*}[51]. E and T seem oblivious of the fact that Consciousness *per se* is the *subjective* 'givenness' of experience, the taken-for-granted background in which *objective* phenomena (appearances) manifest. When Science studies external *objects* it brings information about such entities into the subjective consciousness of scientists. Thus treating Subjectivity as an object is a 'category error' and bound to be problematic. E and T propose three assumptions: (1) the Physics assumption; (2) the Evolutionary assumption; (3) the Qualia assumption. The first assumption states that only conventional physical processes are required for a satisfactory explanation of Consciousness – no Dualism is allowed[52]. Note here the erroneous assumption that the only alternative to Physicalism (Materialism) is Mind/Body Dualism. As E and T allow only conventional physical processes, they must obviously, as does Crick, reject *ontological emergence* (which is less tacit in disguising Dualism) so this is consistent. However, they completely ignore the possibility of Panpsychism. No argument whatsoever is offered as to why we must assume that nothing other than conventional physical processes can possibly exist. This is either a statement of faith or a tacit presumption of scientific 'omniscience'.

Thus they actually start with the (disguised Dualist) assumption that Consciousness emerges, saying that they assume that Consciousness is a process which arises in the structure and dynamics of certain brains. Their second (Evolutionary) assumption states that Consciousness evolved during Natural Selection in the animal kingdom, implying that it is associated with certain biological structures and that it depends on *dynamic processes* {*e.m.*} generated by a certain morphology which itself is the product of Natural Selection. Thus Consciousness is efficacious, Consciousness is not only such a product but also influences various behaviours that are subject both to Natural Selection and to selective processes within an individual's lifetime. This assumption also implies that Consciousness is the product of recent morphological developments and is not a process shared by all animal species. They say that such an assumption helps avoid fruitless speculations such as treating Consciousness as a by-product of computation or introducing bizarre notions such as Quantum Gravity whilst avoiding Neurobiology[53]. As indicated previously, I agree wholeheartedly with E and T's dismissal of the misguided and rather amusing attempts by Oxford Mathematical Physicist Roger Penrose to link Consciousness to his theories of Quantum Gravity. As with The Emperor's New Clothes fable, anyone not in thrall to Penrose's academic standing can see through his arguments.

E and T also advocate focusing on fundamental features of Consciousness common to *all conscious species* rather than the higher-order forms as in humans {*e.m.*}[54]. As stated above in regard to US college textbooks, the idea that Consciousness evolved as an advantageous adaptation in certain animals is widely held amongst scientists but the fact is that the 'automaton' thought experiment seems to show, no actual subjective experience seems necessary to fulfil such adaptational functions. We saw above that very recent brain-scanning experiments seem to indicate that 'free will' is an illusion and our behaviour seems to actually be like that of an 'unconscious' automaton. If conscious experiences are *epiphenomenal* (as Causal Closure implies) then Natural Selection can have no purchase on them. What the **selective advantage** of subjective experience actually is never specified by proponents of such evolutionary views. Even more fundamentally, as we have seen, Science cannot actually prove the existence of Consciousness in anything, not even humans. We only infer the existence of Consciousness in others by *analogy* with our own private experience! E and T give no explanation as to how we can define the set of 'all conscious species' so as to focus upon them!

E and T state that recent advances in Neurobiology and Cognitive Psychology have made it possible to address a series of questions, the answers to which should help resolve some of the mysteries associated with Consciousness. They themselves focus on two such questions. The first question is, what are the neural mechanisms that can account for the emergence of Consciousness? Their second question is, how can such neural processes account for key properties of conscious experience? They qualify this by stating that each conscious state is an indivisible whole and, simultaneously, each person can choose among a vast number of such states[55]. Note the quiet implication of Free Will in the word *choose*. Of course, if we were Materialist automata as Science implies, the whole Western system of Law based on a person's *intent* would be meaningless. They say that conscious experience, "as a physical process", is integrated, conscious states cannot be subdivided into independent components. Based on studies with 'split-brain' patients, they also assert that Consciousness does not tolerate breaks in coherence and abhors holes or discontinuities[56]. Although such observations are quite interesting in regard to the *Gestalt* wholeness and field-like properties of the ego consciousness, E and T display an ignorance of phenomenological knowledge of egoic constitution such as Husserl's description of 'acts' of object-perception in which the 'noematic' unity is constituted from component processes. The existence of so-called 'Multiple Personality Disorder' (nowadays called Dissociative Identity Disorder), although its existence is questioned by orthodox psychiatrists, also suggests that the integrated wholeness of personhood can be subdivided into subpersonalities (in a manner resembling cell division in that each sub-personality is itself a whole).

In regard to subjective experience, E and T say that their "Qualia assumption" says that, qualitative aspects of Consciousness are private and incommunicable through scientific theory which is intersubjective and hence public. But this does not mean that the necessary and sufficient conditions for Consciousness cannot be described. It only implies, they say, that describing them is not the same as generating and experiencing them. Furthermore, they continue, qualia can be considered scientifically as forms of multidimensional discrimination carried out by a complex brain. We can analyse qualia and prescribe how they emerge although this presupposes the existence of appropriate brain structures in a living body. This assumption helps avoid the notion that a scientific theory can act as a surrogate for conscious experience itself or can allow one to grasp the *experience* on the basis of scientific descriptions {*e.m.*}[57]. Thus although E and T have asserted their Materialist belief that Consciousness is a process which arises in the structure and dynamics of certain brains, like Crick they start backtracking quietly when facing up to the ontological paradox. They seem to recognise that describing scientifically accessible conditions for Consciousness are not the same as qualia (types of experience); i.e., what they actually aspire towards is finding neural *correlates* of qualia. They then add that qualia may be considered *scientifically* as "forms of multidimensional discrimination". The term *discrimination* is their *functional* term (*forms* are obviously spatiotemporal patterns and a *function* is a subtilised *behavioural* concept). Their phrase "forms of multidimensional discrimination" taken in conjunction with their view that Consciousness depends upon *dynamic processes* implies that they view qualia as the products of complex information processing (or more simplistically 'computations') in complex brain-dynamical processes as in Connectionism.

Edelman and Tononi are clearly more sophisticated philosophically than Crick in using the qualifier *scientifically* for their view of qualia. What they actually seem to be saying is that Science can only consider the behavioural correlates of qualia which they believe are multidimensional dynamic patterns of activity associated with information processing in complex brains. The Physicalist world picture is simply constituted by multidimensional dynamic patterns of energetic activity making up forces, atoms, molecules etc. We have seen that this ontology is incapable of accounting for Awareness. As E and T assume without question that only conventional physical processes are allowed for a "satisfactory explanation of Consciousness", their view of qualia is little more than a reflection of their underlying Physicalist world-view. They are at least consistent with its limitations. One obvious flaw is their failure to distinguish Consciousness *per se* or Awareness from conscious *mentation*. In spite of treading cautiously around qualia, they nonetheless exclaim that "*conscious experience is a physical proces*" which is integrated {*e.m.*}. If conscious experience really is a physical process why then are we faced with this subjective/objective distinction which does not apply to other physical processes described by Science! How can it possibly be that "forms of multidimensional discrimination" (i.e., complex patterns of information processing) in brains differ so radically from the rest of the physical world! This is by no means a *satisfactory or adequate explanation of Conscio*although it might be of some value in regard to the physical correlates of egoic *mentation*.

Of course there are deeper metaphysical questions here relating to questions of being the thing-in-itself and to Science and Perception as descriptions of phenomenal aspects of things other than oneself. We have seen already that, to be logically consistent, the question must be asked, could other physical processes not associated with what we normally call 'Consciousness' also have subjective aspects. After all, Science cannot even prove the existence of Consciousness in humans and only humans can communicate the fact that they have experiences. The logical answers to such questions reveal the tacit dualism of all non-eliminative forms of Physicalism. These pretend to accept the existence subjective experience which cannot actually exist within the insentient Physicalist world-picture. Logic also implies that the only consistent position is Panpsychism, a position which E and T do not even contemplate the possibility of.

Thus we see that both Crick and Edelman acknowledge tacitly the inadequacy of Physicalist scientific explanation when faced with subjective experience. Crick says that Science might have to live with such paradoxes whereas Edelman sneaks around the problem simultaneously recognizing that Science can only describe behavioural correlates of Consciousness. Yet Edelman still proclaims his faith that Physicalism is correct and that conscious experience is a physical process! This inability to see beyond the fundamental framework of Physicalism is not surprising. Orthodox scientists are no less indoctrinated into dogmatically upheld metaphysical orthodoxy than medieval Scholastic theologians. Thus the glaringly obvious fact that Physicalist science simply cannot come to terms with the Ontological Problem of Consciousness is glossed over, swept under the rugs woven from impressive-sounding jargon (e.g. emergence, complexity, multidimensional discrimination etc.) or even accepted as supposedly irresolvable paradoxes which should be ignored rather than problems which undermine the validity of the entire Physicalist ontology. At the turn of the 20th Century many physicists were convinced that Physics was almost complete with only a few outstanding trivial problems left to resolve such as black-body radiation and the ether-drift. Yet, as is well known, such seemingly trivial problems led, respectively, to the revolutionary new Quantum and Relativity theories. Although transforming radically much of the metaphysical assumptions of Classical physics, the ontological impact of these new theories resulted more in a subtle shift to energy-based 'Physicalism' from the older Materialism based on immutable atoms.[N10]

Can Natural Selection Create Consciousness: Nicholas Humphrey's Darwinian Fables

Back in the early 1980s when I first started to think about the problem of Consciousness, I recall reading in *New Scientist* magazine a little piece by the English Psychologist Nicholas Humphrey entitled "Consciousness: A Just-So Story". The gist of such Neo-Darwinian 'just-so' stories (named after Rudyard Kipling's children's fables) is that, if we ask how did some strange biological structure, function, or behaviour arise, then all one needs to argue is that it arose because it provided some selective advantage to the organism. Such Neo-Darwinian 'armchair explanations' simply assume that all biological *form* and *function* came into being by Natural Selection and concoct some hypothetical ancient scenario in which environmental pressures stimulate the evolution of the unusual structure or behaviour in question. In essence, everything biological is the way it is as it was at some period in the past advantageous in terms of Natural Selection for it to be this way. We have seen that Consciousness (Awareness) cannot be reduced to *form* or *function*, structure or behaviour, as even the distinguished Nobel laureate biologists like Crick and Edelman tacitly acknowledge. But then we have seen that in Psychology, the creation of outrageous fantasy myths like those concocted by Sigmund Freud have fooled countless uncritical followers into thinking that they were 'scientific'. Thus it is not surprising that Psychologist Humphrey should think that the facile concoction of Darwinian 'just-so' stories are a valuable contribution to Science and Philosophy faced with the mystery of Consciousness.

However, Mathematical Biologist Brian Goodwin has shown, even for simple biological structures (with no ontological mystery associated with them), this simple NeoDarwinian catch-all argument can be proven to be false. Using mathematical models run on computer simulations of the morphogenesis of the green alga *Acetabularia acetabularium,* Goodwin has shown that the distinctive whorl-like cap structure (like an inverted umbrella) of this particular species arises simply due to the complex physico-chemical processes operating in the developing organism. Combinations of positive and negative feedback processes involving the concentration of calcium, which affects the mechanical properties of the cytoplasm, generate the unusual whorl-like cap structure. The point that Goodwin stresses is that, according to Neo-Darwinism, this highly unusual structure should be an unlikely possibility arrived at through aeons of chance mutations in the genome. On the contrary, Goodwin's model shows that the form seems to be a simple, natural consequence of the physical forces acting within the developing alga. The genes only define the parameters of the forces acting on the developmental field in morphogenesis[58].

I was amused to find that in the 1999 publication of the third Tucson Conference, entitled *Toward a Science of Consciousness III*, Nicholas Humphrey was still peddling such philosophically-puerile NeoDarwinian 'just-so' stories in the vain belief that he was resolving the Mind/Body problem. In his paper entitled 'The Privatisation of Sensation', he states:

> *And equally, I'd say, unexplained subjective experience arouses an irritation in me. It is the irritation of someone who is an unabashed Darwinian: one who holds that the theory of evolution by natural selection has given us the licence to ask "why" questions about almost every aspect of the design of living nature, and, what's more, to expect that these "whys" will nearly always translate into scientifically accredited "wherefores."*
>
> *Our default assumption, I believe, can and should be that living things are designed the way they are because this kind of design is—or has been in the past—biologically advantageous. And this will be so across the whole of nature, ...**and even when what's at issue are the central facts of consciousness**.*
>
> — Nicholas Humphrey {*e.m.*}[59]

Humphrey then begins his attempt to give his Darwinian explanation to raw feels (or qualia), with the following sentence, "Why is it like *this* to have red light fall on our eyes"[60]. Note immediately that 'redness', (i.e., colour) is a subjective experience and is not simply correlated with particular wavelengths of electromagnetic radiation (*see below*). Humphrey says that we should first ask as about the biological function of having sensations at all and, once we have answered this, proceed to the trickier question as to the *function* {*e.m.*} of our sensations having this special qualia character. In response to the first question, he goes on to distinguish *sensations* from *perceptions*, quoting an 18th Century philosopher Thomas Reid that 'sensation' implies no conception of external objects, it supposes a *sentient* {*e.m.*} being and a manner in which that being is affected. In contrast, 'perception' implies a conception of something external, something different from the perceiving mind and the act of perception. But, says Humphrey, Reid never asked why do humans need both sensation and perception; why not make do with perception on its own[61]. Humphrey continues that, only in recent years, have psychologists started addressing the question of why we have sensations at all. The view that Humphrey endorses is that the main role of sensations is to "flag the present" or to help keep perception honest. Whereas sensation represents the stimulation more or less as it is given, perception combines the evidence of stimulation with contextual information, memory and rules to construct a hypothetical model of the external world. The danger with this is that, without being continually tied in to present-tense reality, this model might go off on its own losing correspondence with the external world. Sensation provides a reality check for the perceiver, giving a here-ness, now-ness and a me-ness to the experience of the world. But, Humphrey notes correctly, this does nothing to explain why sensations exist in the particular qualitative *form* they do[62]. I have emphasised 'form' here as its use here instead of 'type' connotes *spatiotemporal* or physical differentiation of experiential qualities. But experienced sensations, pain, colours, smells, sounds, tastes etc. are **not** spatiotemporal (or Material) forms.

Humphrey then raises the old philosophical conundrum about raw feels such as redness being subjective and private and, as far as we know, one person's experience of redness may be what another person experiences as greenness[N11], but such differences in the actual qualities of subjective experience would make no difference in terms of our behaviour. Any 'quality' (type of raw feel) could serve as well as another to represent external features. The important point that Humphrey does manage to raise in his paper is that, if it is true that qualia (or raw feels) are private, inaccessible, individual experiences then we may as well give up hope of a Darwinian explanation because nothing evolves by Natural Selection unless it has some major 'public' effect; i.e., a measurable positive selective advantage[63]. I would note that disadvantageous variations would also 'evolve' in that they would gradually disappear but this not important here. If qualia are 'private', then Natural Selection could have got no purchase on them. Even if this privacy argument is partially correct, says Humphrey, Darwinians might as well give up trying to explain how Natural Selection gave rise to sensory qualities[64]. Humphrey is correct to recognise that subjective experience constitutes a problem for Darwinian explanation. However, the actual issues relating Natural Selection to subjective experience are not nearly as simplistic as in Humphrey's presentation of 'public' and 'private' effects but let us not spoil the ending of this Darwinian story. It is a veritable minefield of conceptual distortions, conflations, tautologies, *ad hoc* reasoning etc. utilised by true believers in Materialist, Darwinian orthodoxy resulting in verbal 'sleights-of-hand' or confidence tricks based on inferring illegitimate conclusions to pull the 'rabbit of Consciousness' out of the Physicalist hat.

Although acknowledging the 'privacy' of subjective experience is a commonsense fact, being an "unabashed Darwinist", Humphrey refuses to accept defeat and concocts a Darwinian 'just-so' story to explain both how qualia originally evolved through Natural Selection and also why they now appear as private and inaccessible. The story goes that in the distant past the specific quality of an experience was selectively important for primitive animals and the 'privacy' came about later in evolution after the selection of these distinct qualities (such as redness, for sensations of (supposedly) 'red' light) had occurred. The analogy is made with other areas of biology where *function* of an organ or *behaviour* {*e.m.*} has shifted over evolutionary time but obsolete aspects of original design have remained unchanged. For instance, the salt content of human blood resembles sea water as blood originated in sea fishes 400 million years ago. Such persisting remnants of ancestral history are also found in the evolution of Language, manners, dress etc. "I think we have struck gold", exclaims Humphrey, imagining that this analogy can explain the mystery of what sensations are and how they evolved. The "remarkable truth", Humphrey believes, is "that a person has sensations by *acting* in a certain way" and that, "each sensory action has its own inherited style", e.g. "a red style, redly"[65].

Humphrey's story continues with recourse once again to Thomas Reid who argued that the expression "I feel pain" is misleading as it implies that the feeling is something distinct from the pain. According to Reid, "feeling a pain" signifies no more than *being pained*. The same would hold for all other sensations. Humphrey himself goes further, asserting that the correct expression should not be "being pained" but "paining" because sensing is not a passive state but a form of active engagement with the stimulus occurring at the body surface. He even states, "when I have a red sensation at my eye, I am in effect reaching out to the site of stimulation with a kind of evaluative response"[66]. *Feeling* is a general term quite obviously distinct from the *type of feeling* such as pain. The phrase "being pained" is mere wordplay, in that the word 'being' actually means 'being conscious of' or 'having a feeling of', hence the actuality of conscious awareness is tacitly being brushed under the carpet of deceptive words. A *colour* is not correlated unequivocally with a certain range of wavelengths of electromagnetic radiation impacting the rods and cones in our retina (*see also Note 11*). Colour constancy is subjective, depending on neuronal organisation. Sensations do not simply occur at bodily surfaces and do not depend upon an evaluative response or act as in the case of automatic reflex responses!

The Darwinian fable proceeds with Humphrey transmuting (conscious) *feelings* tacitly into supposed 'sensory responses' (or *behaviours*). He states that, although sensory responses are largely internal and private, he believes that their evolutionary origin was in fully-fledged bodily behaviours (no evidence is given for this belief). Instead Humphrey 'sketches' the "evolutionary story in cartoon form". When 'red light' {*inverted commas* mine} fell on an ancient amoeba-like organism, it wriggled in a particular way, it wriggled 'redly'. In response to sugar, it wriggled 'sugarly' and in response to salt it, wriggled 'saltly'. These responses are nothing other than responses, he says, the animal is not "mentally aware". He continues by imagining that as the animal's life becomes more complex, the time comes when it is advantageous for it to have "inner knowledge" or "mental representation" of the sensory stimuli at its surface and how it *feels* {*e.m.*} about it. Thus he asserts, sensations do indeed originate as corollaries of the animal's *public* bodily activity, determined by selection[67]. Note how his confident assertion "*do indeed*" {*e.m.*} is based on his imaginary scenario rather than empirical facts. It thus follows, he says, that its mental representation, its sensory "experience" or proto-experience, is "determined *in all its aspects* by selection"[68]. Humphrey then concludes his 'just-so' story saying that the whole sensory activity gets "privatised", sensory responses get short-circuited before they reach the body surface etc. until "the whole process process becomes closed off from the outside world in an internal loop within the brain". The sensory responses have lost their original biological importance and have *disappeared from view* {*e.m.*}. Thus, claims Harvey, Darwinists can explain sensory *quality* as a product of selection and also accept the common sense idea that *sensations* are as private as they seem to be. Humphrey does not wish to end his story here. The rewards of this Darwinian approach, he believes are greater still, allowing him to explain how sensing becomes self-sustaining and partly self-creating, etc., with talk of 'time-loops' and the "*what it's like of consciousness*"[69].

Note that Humphrey claims to redeem Darwinian 'explanation' showing that it can explain sensory qualities (raw feels) as products of selection and the 'privacy' of sensations. Both underlined terms imply the existence of conscious awareness. Thomas Reid himself acknowledged that 'sensation' like 'perception' "*supposes a* ***sentient*** *being*" {*e.m.*}. Humphrey's cartoon-sketch evolutionary story is the most puerile Materialist sophistry ridden with tacit assumptions, conflations, and verbal confidence tricks trying repeatedly to 'pull a fast one' on uncritical readers. A *sensation* implies that a person is consciously sensing something as opposed to the constant barrage of sensory input or information, much of which remains unconscious (habituated) unless attention is paid. Note how Humphrey transmutes *sensations* into *behaviours* ('actions', 'sensory responses') so that Natural Selection can get a purchase on them. Numerous *ad hoc* assumptions about sensations are made which contradict biological facts. He ignores reflex actions, proprioception, kinaesthesia etc. and twists sentient sensation into supposed evaluative responses to stimuli at the body surface! He assumes sensory information is never passively received but always results from the organism's actions or behaviours. It is true that vision depends upon rapid eye movements (oculomotor saccade) but this is not an evaluative response but an automatic process. By conflating sentient sensations with behaviours he ends up with comical tautologies of 'wriggling redly', 'wriggling sugarly' etc.

Humphrey tries to show that *redness* and such raw-feels are the same in everyone as such qualities of consciousness evolved through selection of particular behavioural responses in primitive organisms (*see Note 10*). This *ancestral history* analogy implies that all of us have evolved from these same origins and thus supposedly have the same experience. However, as we have seen above, in regard to the views of Nobel laureate scientists Crick and Edelman (rather than psychologist and story-teller Humphrey), Physicalist science (of which Darwinian thought is a small part) can only deal with behavioural or neural *correlates* and not with qualitative experience *per se*. Humphrey naively tries to explain **the existence of the raw feel itself,** (i.e., ontology) and not just the physical correlate. Being a Materialist true believer he does not even seem to appreciate the distinction between a raw feel and a physical correlate. All that the Physicalist, Darwinist picture can allow is a description of how a physical structure or process possibly evolved; there are no raw feels (or qualia) in the insentient Physicalist ontology.

Even if we let this pass and restrict ourselves to physical correlates of raw feels, we must question the usefulness of amoebic 'wriggling' as precursors of neural correlates of Consciousness. It is easy to understand why human blood retains the evolutionary history in terms of salt content and why languages retain ancient terms. Note that his cited examples of such persisting ancestral vestiges, such as salt content of blood, linguistic terms, and clock dials, involve persistence of ancestral *forms* or in the case of blood, simple chemical *composition* (an easily discernible physical feature based on chemical *structures*). Not only are these spatiotemporal or behavioural concepts but it is easy to see the evolutionary commonality in structure or form. If we follow this analogy, letting pass the absurdly tautological sugarly, saltly and redly styles, we would expect to find similar structures or forms of cellular behaviour in mammalian brains. No Neurobiologist worth his salt thinks that mental processes or representations involve neurons wriggling in different modes. Neurons are not amoeba (although white blood cells or leukocytes may have evolved from amoeba). Nor are neurons wiggling cilia. Neuroscience suggests that the physical correlates of Consciousness are complex patterns of electrical activity generated by neurons in the central nervous system and not in peripheral motor nerves associated with direct responses to stimuli. An amoeba doesn't even have a nervous system. Furthermore, it is extremely unlikely that an amoeba-like organism exhibits specific modes of behavioural response to specific stimuli such as various wavelengths of light. An amoeba's simple repertoire of basic responses seem to be limited to 'can I eat this or can this eat me' and a few others. It might possess Phototaxis or a response to the presence of light in general (rather than specific wavelengths). Thus Humphrey's ancestral history analogy, with which he thinks he has "struck gold", is of course nothing more than "fool's gold".

Even before 'mental awareness' or 'experience' supposedly arises as the 'amoeba' evolves, Humphrey is assuming tacitly the existence of *feelings* which presuppose awareness. Thus, as a Monist, he is presupposing tacitly Panpsychism! No explanation is then offered as to what is meant by 'mental' (perhaps he means perceptual world-modelling) and how inner *representation* of external stimuli creates *experience*. Although the notion of sensations 'flagging the present' or a reality-check for internal world-modelling is interesting, it is extremely simplistic in regard to the actually complex interactions of senses and perception. The primary function of senses obviously cannot be to maintain a reality-check on the evolutionarily more recent perceptual models of the world. Most of the sensory input that we receive does not enter our consciousness and powerful sensory reflexes operate that bypass conscious control totally. We also have internal senses, proprioception and kinaesthesia, etc., which can also manifest in our consciousness.

Note also the absurd, infantile explanation of Subjectivity (or Humphrey's 'privatisation') of experience as the creation by short-circuiting of closed neuronal loops. He appears to be saying that Natural Selection cannot operate inside an organism's body which is of course nonsense. Somehow, Humphrey's already miraculously appearing experiences in internal representations become inaccessible to Natural Selection because they 'short-circuit' into closed neuronal loops. This is 'loopy'! The electrical activity inside a neural circuit or loop is no more inaccessible to the outside world than any other nervous activity inside an animal. What appears at the bodily surface is not internal neuronal activity but transducer activity in sensory receptors receiving stimuli and effector organs mediating behavioural responses. Furthermore, if truly closed loops appeared possessing no connections to other bodily systems, they would degenerate very quickly as they would not be integrated with other bodily systems. They would be totally *dysfunctional*! Thus, in reality, evolution would not result in completely closed circuits! Humphrey's ideas also imply that electrical activity within nerves, if closed in a loop magically change their ontological properties and create subjective experience.

The deep metaphysical questions relating to subjectivity of experience are reduced to facile metaphors of inner/outer relations at the bodily surface when of course the subjective 'I' or ego sense is not of a simple body/other distinction but includes a sense of a 'conscious mind' or controlling agency presiding over the body! As with his explanation of qualia involving crass reductionism of deep ontological and epistemological questions to simplistic, incoherent and downright incorrect, biological speculations, he fails completely to understand the true ontological and epistemological significance of the subjectivity of experience. The true significance of the inaccessible subjectivity of experience is related to metaphysical questions of being the *thing-in-itself* and perceiving other things as *phenomena*. The fact of the matter is that we, as individuals, cannot truly know anything directly beyond our subjective experience which includes external entities as phenomenal constituents of our internal, subjective experience. It is not a simple matter of physical or spatial inner/outer relations which privatises experience. Humphrey fails to recognise the basic epistemological fact that our public knowledge of the external 'physical world' is not '*objective*' as common sense would have it but is *intersubjective*; a point which, to their credit, E and T recognised. It is Humphrey who needs a reality-check on his unabashed armchair-fantasising about deriving scientific explanations from dreaming up imaginative stories which ignore *empirical* (derived through sensory perception) facts and twist the meanings of terms (e.g. *sensation, feeling*) illegitimately to fit preconceived Behaviorist frameworks.

Humphrey also overlooks the fact that Natural Selection can only operate on heritable variation; i.e., differences in phenotype (physical manifestation of the species) which can be transmitted to offspring via the genome. The standard biological criterion determining whether or not Natural Selection can act is heritability of the traits. Thus the manifestation of varying types of subjective raw-feels in individuals would have to be related to transmissible genetic factors if Natural Selection was to have an influence upon the differences between them. If we assume that specific raw-feels do indeed have specific physical, neural correlates then it is quite feasible that Natural Selection has influenced their *differentiation* (N.B. not their actual *existence*). Obviously individuals with colour blindness or with lack of colour vision due to defective rods and cones in the retina etc. are selectively at a disadvantage. The philosophical conundrum to which Humphrey refers posits the hypothetical interchangeability of specific raw-feels as they would be functionally equivalent in that the behavioural responses of individuals would remain unchanged if say one person's experience of 'red'-wavelength-light was how another person experienced 'yellow'-wavelength-light. What in fact is being selected are not qualia or raw feels but the behavioural responses depending upon the perceptual processes, such as world-modelling and anticipatory behaviour which gives a huge selective advantage in pre-empting life-threatening dangers. In the case of the sense of Smell it is the existence of specific receptor molecules that are selected and not specific raw feels of smells.

The Non-Representational view of 'Embodied-Enactive' models of Cognition in which meaning is inseparable from couplings of regular interdependencies with their surroundings actually lends weight to this old philosophical conundrum. All that is necessary is that internal models maintain regular, meaningful, interdependencies with the environment rather than identical representations within all individuals. As stated above, the work of Walter Freeman suggests that the, seemingly symbolic, dynamic electrical potential attractor patterns formed in the rabbit cortex slowly transform over time[70]. Again, if this were correct, Natural Selection cannot act on subjective experiences themselves but on the heritable factors underlying physical *correlates* of perceptual 'world-modelling'. In neither case does Natural Selection create or generate raw-feels, it can only operate upon heritable *physical correlates*. D.C. Clarke rubbishes the evolutionary view of consciousness proposed by Cognitivist 'cheerleader' D.C. Dennett who is listed as a co-author with Humphrey in Metzinger's paper discussed below. Dennett has proposed that random genetic mutations generated organisms with primitive mental capacities. Clarke asks, what evolutionary advantage could the postulated first mutation confer? If one postulates a 'sensitivity' then why should it not be insentient like a photosensor[71]. I would add that a random gene mutation (implying usually a change in a DNA base-pair) should only result in a minor amino acid change in a protein. The onus is on Dennett to explain how such simple changes in a protein structure, resulting in the sort of protein polymorphism variability associated with, for instance, variable immune responses (a type of 'sensitivity' completely unrelated to egoic consciousness), could magically result in the appearance of 'mental capacities'. Antibody genes mutate rapidly to create an immense variety of antibody proteins but biologists do not think of them as sentient! Thus the US college textbooks' claim that there is utterly compelling evidence that Consciousness evolved as an emergent phenomenon is fundamentally wrong on two counts. First in regard to its 'how' notion of *emergence* and second in regard to it its 'why' notion of Consciousness *per se* or Awareness 'emerging' or appearing out of insentient Material Nature due to its adaptive evolutionary benefits. What can arise through evolution of nervous systems in the Physicalist world-picture is 'meaningfully-organised' 'mindlike' processes such as perceptual world-modelling (*see Ch.11*), not Awareness and its differentiated raw feels or qualia.

Metzinger's Misrepresentation of Subjective Experience as World-Modelling and the Book of Daniel

We saw above that Cognitive Science philosopher Thomas Metzinger, asserts in his editorial introduction to *Neural Correlates of Consciousness*[72] that we do not need a new (non-Physicalist) metaphysics to explain Consciousness, but a new variant of practical rationality. In his own chapter in this same volume, Metzinger acknowledges the likes of Francis Crick, Crick's neuroscientist collaborator Christof Koch, and academic philosopher Patricia Churchland for helpful comments and critical discussions. Canadian-American Patricia Churchland's 'claim to fame' (or notoriety) stems from her staunch advocacy of Eliminative Materialism, the radical viewpoint associated with Richard Rorty. Although the crudest and most simplistic form of Materialism, denying the reality of Consciousness as just a 'Folk Psychology' myth, Eliminative Materialism is at least 'honest' to Materialist and Physicalist ontologies as these preclude the possibility of any sort of Awareness. Metzinger's chapter also includes a reference to a paper co-written by the aforementioned Daniel C. Dennett and our modern-day Aesops, Nicholas Humphrey. Thus Metzinger's view, which, in contrast to Humphrey's, appears quite sophisticated philosophically, can very much be considered as representative of contemporary Cognitive Science thinking. We saw in Chapter 4 that Nobel laureate Neurobiologist George Wald stated that it was easier to discuss his insight that Consciousness was all-pervasive and perhaps even primary to Matter with Physicists rather than amongst his fellow Biologists. The reason for this is that Theoretical Physicists are often appreciative of the problematic status of the ontological and epistemological foundations of Physical Science. Perhaps also, Mathematicians and Mathematical Physicists, such as mystics Merrell-Wolff and Whiteman, can see the simple fact that mathematical description is intrinsically limited to the behaviour of phenomena. Contrary to naive Materialist hopes of future 'breakthroughs', there cannot possibly be some genius coming forward in future to explain Awareness in physical terms. In contrast most practising Biologists (and Cognitive philosophers), partly due to the Physics Envy of other academic disciplines, tend to take the Physicalist ontology unquestioningly on authority as if it is indisputable, or even sacrosanct.

Metzinger's Representational Analysis of the subject-object 'perspective'

Metzinger's chapter is entitled 'The *Subjectivity* of Subjective Experience: A Representationalist Analysis of the First-Person Perspective'. His first assumption, he says, is a weak version of Brentano's Intentionalism, (i.e., that all Consciousness is 'consciousness of something') which he calls the 'hegemony of representation'. This essentially holds that the explanatory base for *all* mental properties is formed by functional and representational properties of the class of systems under investigation[73]. This general statement implies the existence of mental properties in non-biological systems. More specifically, Metzinger points to human brains in Waking and Dream states[74]. Note that, once again, the focus is on human consciousness as limited to just Waking and Dream states. His use of "*all* mental properties" tacitly implies that Awareness and Volition must be functional, (i.e., behavioural), representational properties. Mentation and Consciousness are, as we have seen, conflated by Westerners who remain ignorant of the distinct, underlying flow of the Light of Pure Consciousness. Consciousness is viewed as a property associated with Wakefulness and Dreaming in normal functioning. Forman points out the fact that were Consciousness not distinguishable from its *content* we could not even conceive the thesis of *intentionality*. As Sartre said, 'intentionality' is the notion that we are confronted with a concrete presence which is *not-Consciousness*[75]. Thus the assumption of 'Intentionality', denying the possibility even of Pure (Objectless) Consciousness is self-contradictory. Note that the Cognitivists' assumption of Intentionality implies that an insentient physical 'subject' must encounter an insentient physical 'object' (regardless of what these might actually be neurologically) and hey presto, Consciousness or Sentience magically appears through their coming together.

My direct correlation of the Pure Consciousness with the RAS brainwaves elucidates this question of Intentionality, as it did with the Constructivists' claim that there are no unmediated mental processes. Modern Medicine distinguishes the *Arousal* component of Consciousness (associated with RAS activity; the RAS activity is the prerequisite for any form of Consciousness) from the *Content* of Consciousness (assumed by Medicine to be generated by the cerebral cortex). Thus we can see that the modern Western philosophical dogma of Intentionality, denying Pure Consciousness, is clearly a myth as Bio-Medical knowledge of Consciousness indicates a generalised 'Arousal' component (the RAS) which becomes superimposed with content from the cerebral cortex. Metzinger refers correctly to "physical correlates of phenomenal states". Interestingly , in his table of his seven most important theoretical problems connected with conscious experience, the first phenomenological property he lists is 'ultra-smoothness' or lack of granularity of qualia. The conjectured neural correlate listed by Metzinger is "Synchronicity [*sic*] of feature detectors contributing to perceptual object, read out by higher-order mechanism?"[76]. Once again, electric fields as the possible physical correlates accounting for the psychophysical non-granularity of conscious experience are overlooked given Cognitivists' fixations upon neurons and the computer 'wiring' analogy.

Metzinger says that, if it turns out that there are principled reasons why important features of subjective experience are impossible to grasp epistemically through interdisciplinary (Cognitive Science) approaches, a philosopher attempting a reductive explanation of consciousness will be quite happy. A reductive explanation of Consciousness is never an ideology or an emotional substitute for religion, he claims[77]. It is hard to envisage Eliminative Materialists and Behaviorists who have ridiculed Mysticism, Spirituality and Panpsychism as primitive, irrational and nonsensical truly being 'happy' once the general public begins to appreciate that Materialist Reductionists were completely and utterly wrong in clinging dogmatically to their false beliefs. Such are the delusions of Materialists, pretending to be fair and open-minded when they are actually narrow-minded dogmatists disguising their tacit recourse to the magical power of creation *ex nihilo*. Surely, dramatic loss of public prestige and subjection to ridicule as blinkered, dogmatic 'dinosaurs' is not conducive to happiness? They deserve ridicule for their derisory slandering of critics as amateurish, irrational, unscientific believers in Folk Psychology etc. It is Materialists like Metzinger who behave, metaphorically, like the Pot that calls the Kettle black. Notice below how supposedly fair-minded Metzinger acts as a 'Mudslinger' slurring those who refuse to believe in his dogmatic faith.

Metzinger's own words 'emotional substitute' reveals his simplistic understanding of all Spirituality as simply fulfilling an emotional need. The goal in the first place, says Metzinger, was always epistemic progress, a growth of knowledge[78]. In fact the scientific establishment tends to stifle the growth of knowledge through its refusal to contemplate the existence of evidence contradicting its own metaphysical assumptions which it holds dogmatically to be proven beyond question. Science, says Metzinger, is reliant upon reductionist methodology and objective, third-person criteria[79]. In fact Science actually deals with intersubjective, consensual and conventional first-person criteria as objective phenomena remain part of our subjective experience. Scientific 'third-person' evidence cannot exist without the first-person subjectivity of each individual. Thus intersubjective, consensually agreed facts of Yoga and Phenomenology, as utilised by myself as evidence in support of my RAS brainwave correlation are epistemologically equivalent to so-called 'scientific', 'objective' knowledge. Thus there are fundamental epistemological errors in Metzinger's simple distinction between subjective and 'objective' or third-person perspectives.

Metzinger continues, how then can (Reductionist) hard Science do justice to the first-person character of subjective phenomena. This can only happen if the concept of a 'first-person perspective' is clarified in a manner that makes the corresponding phenomenon empirically tractable[80]. By 'empirically tractable', Metzinger implies here accessibility to neuro-scientific instrumentality, describable in behavioural or dynamical terms. However, in *The View from Within: First person approaches to the study of consciousness*[81], Pierre Vermersch tells us that Husserl's method of suspension of the Natural Attitude (our normal involvement in the perceptual spectacle) is aimed at grasping the actual unfolding (or 'dynamics') of the perceptual spectacle[82]. Natalie Depraz says that Husserl, in his *Cartesian Meditations*, argues that the Transcendental-ego is an apodictic repository of a radicalised scientificity [*sic*] whose unique 'object' is precisely the subject. Subjectivity however appears only when we pull away from prejudices rooted in the taken-for-granted character of the world (or Natural Attitude)[83]. Given Metzinger's conception of the Self as the centre of a world-modelling process (*see below*), it is interesting to note, as Claire Petitmengin-Peugeot tells us, that the original meaning of the word *meditation* (medi-tation) is 'return to the centre'[84]. However, we have seen that it is the Light of Pure Consciousness that is at the 'centre'. Thus Husserl's introspective (first-person) methodology, similar to certain Buddhist yogic practises, makes the actual mental processes constituting the subject-object 'perspective, as opposed to Metzinger's speculations, empirically accessible as *phenomena* or objects of enquiry. However, such introspective 'first-person' approaches are considered taboo by Cognitive Science as they are supposedly irredeemably *subjective*.

However, Metzinger says that 'folk-psychological' {*inverted commas mine*} talk of subjectivity is based on a soft visuo-grammatical metaphor. Our visual space possesses a perspectival geometrical structure, the visual part of the folk metaphor. To understand subjectivity on the logical, epistemic or *metaphysical* {*e.m.*} level, Metzinger says that one has to understand what the *phenomenal* first-person perspective is. Metzinger is really asserting arrogantly that those who can think rationally must share his own Materialist metaphysical assumptions and thus can understand 'subjectivity' logically. We have seen that Metzinger dismisses 80 per cent of human beings as being irrational. One should note here that phenomenologist Edmund Husserl started off as a mathematical logician, mystic Franklin Merrel-Wolff was a mathematician and mystic Michael Whiteman a mathematical physicist! Of course, Metzinger's logical analysis is just speculation based on computational analogies (or metaphors) and not based on observed facts. His essay only deals with one aspect of phenomenal experience, its *perspectivalness*. According to his analysis, the "phenomenal first-person perspective", the essence of being a person consists of three phenomenological target properties; *Mineness, Selfhood* (or 'prereflexive self-intimacy') and *Perspectivalness*. Mineness is a 'higher order' property of *particular* forms of phenomenal content. In folk psychological terms it is a sense of ownership of the content. Selfhood is described in terms of the sense of Personal Identity through time and that the contents of self-consciousness form a coherent whole. It endows our mental space with centredness and perspectivalness, (i.e., the Self/other or subject/object distinction). Prereflexive self-intimacy means the immediate sense of being a coherent unity. Perspectivalness is a global, structural property of phenomenal space, with the phenomenal Self as the immovable centre around which the overall dynamics of experience is organised around a supramodal point-of-view. This centredness of the world model around the phenomenal Self gives the first-person perspective[85].

Note that Metzinger assumes that 'visual space' possesses a 'geometrical structure' and conceives the Self metaphorically as the geometric 'centre' around which experience is organised. Such assumptions are not that obvious at all, the Self seems a polar locus rather than central as my psychophysical 'visual space' extends forwards from my body and not behind me! Rather than being 'clear-cut', it is 'fuzzy' and indistinct at the periphery. Idealised or geometrical structures, easily described by Mathematics, are of course exactly the 'targets' so-called 'hard science' likes to impose on Nature in order to create its idealised models. In his 1936 book *Crisis of the European Sciences and Transcendental Phenomenology* Husserl wrote that Galilean science 'mathematises' or 'geometrises' Nature into idealised limit-shapes. Metzinger's extremely dubious Self as centre metaphor smacks of Copernicus' heliocentrism (inspired by the mystical Light at the centre) around which we find the dynamical trajectories of planets.

What constitutes the philosophical puzzle, according to Metzinger, is that I am this centre *myself*; to be phenomenally aware means to possess an inward perspective and to take this perspective in the subjective experience of the world and one's own mental states. Thus phenomenal subjectivity, as opposed to epistemological and ontological subjectivity, is simply the fact that the dynamics of conscious experience unfold in a space that is centred on a singular, temporally-extended experiential Self. The key question is to identify the minimal set of functional and representational properties that an information processing system must possess in order to exemplify these *phenomenal* properties. Metzinger asks, "What could be a more *complex* phenomenon than conscious experience?" {*e.m.*}[86]. Note the assumption here that *conscious experience,* (i.e., implying *Awareness* rather than the dynamics of perceptual phenomena) is necessarily **complex**, linked to the assumption that Consciousness exists only as content-filled Wakefulness and Dreaming rather than in a simple state of Pure Consciousness. For Metzinger, conscious experience is the activation of a stable, integrated model of reality. A phenomenal first-person perspective, he says, involves functionally "the capacity to open and employ centred representational spaces, to operate under egocentric world models". The latter is the "central necessary (but not sufficient) condition in ascribing subjectivity to a given system". Phenomenal subjectivity, a subsymbolic, nonconceptual first-person perspective is a property only *instantiated* {*e.m.*} if the system activates a coherent self-model embedded in its global world model [87].

I have emphasised 'instantiated' here as Metzinger refers to phenomenal subjectivity as a property that arises with activation of a self-model in a world model. Although Metzinger might argue that he is only describing hypothetically how a perspectivalness arises within a world-model, there is a again a tacit reliance on *ontological dualism* here when his other statements are taken into account. He states *there is no need for a new metaphysics* and that *conscious experience is a complex phenomenon* or the activation of an integrated model. This implies magical 'emergence' or disguised Dualism. Metzinger tells us that the 'self-model' possesses a true neurobiological description. It is a complex neural activation pattern with a certain temporal fine structure or a complex functional state[88]. It is extremely logical to counter-argue against Metzinger that the non-self part of the world model must also be a complex neural activation pattern or a complex functional state so why should the 'self-model' alone have conscious experience? What functional property, Metzinger asks, marks out the self-model's special role in the informational architecture and exactly how does it become the stable centre of both phenomenal and behavioural space. The answer is that the self-model is the representational structure that is anchored in the brain by a continuous source of *internally* generated input. The body is the only coherent perceptual object that *constantly* generates input[89]. Thus the self-reference frame of the world model arises from the constant proprioceptive input as distinct from sensory input from external stimuli. In the human case, Metzinger thinks that it is plausible that the self-model is "based on an innate and *'hardwired'* {*e.m.*} model" of the spatial properties of the system, for example, a long-term body-image[90]. Metzinger cites some interesting research such as distortions in the sense of the top-bottom body axis in astronauts living in zero gravity and phantom body limbs in regard to body image models. Such information suggests that the neural correlate of the spatial model of the self is partly immune to neuroplasticity[91]. In fact, more recent research on neuroplasticity indicates the plasticity of the cortical body maps especially following damage to the related body structures[92]. Although such information is interesting in regard to world-modelling, it still fails to address the ontological question of how the experience of self arises.

Metzinger's 'Semantic Transparency' of the Self-model and Ontological Subterfuge through Semantic Sophistry

Recall that Metzinger also refers to a basic form of primitive self-awareness, 'phenomenal selfhood' or prereflexive self-intimacy, a fundamental form of non-conceptual self-knowledge preceding higher cognitive self-consciousness and which makes possible conceptually mediated forms of self-consciousness[93]. At first glance, his sounds more promising in regard to the ontological question. But from Metzinger's Representationalist perspective this "basic form of primitive self-awareness" must clearly be the result of subsymbolic *dynamics* {*e.m.*}. It implies "the existence of a single, coherent, and temporally extended self-representation forming the centre of the global representational state"[94]. Thus all that this Representationalism can manage is to reduce all forms of *awareness* to 'dynamics' or *behaviour*, the stock in trade of Materialist Behaviorism. Similarly, the volitional (intentional) aspect of Consciousness is reduced to 'dynamics'. In addition to his 'transparent self-model' he postulates another speculative entity, "the 'phenomenal model of the intentionality-relation'; i.e., an ongoing, dynamical representation of the system *as currently interacting with an object-component*"[95]. The 'hegemony of representation' means reducing everything to representations! We have seen that the assumption of Representationalism is itself questioned by Embodied-Enactivists influenced by the Phenomenology of Husserl and Merleau-Ponty. Metzinger warns against indulging in any "amateurish speculation" which presumably refers to Non-Representationalist, supposedly 'non-scientific', ideas which take 'folk-psychological' descriptions seriously. Here Metzinger reverts to 'Mudslinger' tactics, slurring anyone who criticizes the all-knowing Cognitivist priesthood as amateurish, non-scientific believers in folk traditions!

Nonetheless, Metzinger does recognise the Anti-Reductionist response to his theoretical model, although like E and T, he claims falsely that such objections would come only from a Property-Dualist (as with E and T Metzinger remains oblivious that his own view is in fact disguised Dualism). *Panpsychist challenges are not even considered possible.* He notes that an Anti-Reductionist might argue that everything he has just described could happen without the instantiation of the phenomenal, (i.e., experiential) properties of Mineness, Selfhood and Perspectivalness. He asserts that the cardinal philosophical question is: What is needed, by *conceptual* {*e.m.*} necessity to make a phenomenal first-person perspective *emerge* {*e.m.*} from a functionally centred representational space?[96]. Note that when Metzinger finally addresses the ontological question, his framing of the philosophical question still clings tacitly to presuppositions that such matters must be addressed *conceptually* (as opposed to direct *empirical* evidence gleaned by introspective, first-person phenomenological investigation) although the answers to such fundamental ontological questions may be beyond simple logical analysis. He also assumes that the phenomenal or experiential property *emerges* from a centred world-model rather than considering the possibility of an all-pervading experiential property pre-existing throughout Nature and 'individuating' due to some self-limiting character as with my subjective 'closure' (*see Ch.11*). Introspective phenomenological knowledge of altered states of Consciousness indicate that Metzinger's 'hardwired' cortical body-image, although perhaps partially relevant in regard to the so-called yogic *subtle body* of intermediate planes or states is not involved in deeper states where no sense of the physical body exists yet there still remains a sense of Self and Self-agency.

Metzinger does briefly allude to mystical states and religious experiences such as 'oceanic boundary loss' and to psychiatric depersonalisation, 'dreadful ego-dissolution' in regard to his Perspectivalness. But his reference to non-centred global states indicates that these are viewed simply as dysfunctional self-models. He acknowledges that a comprehensive theory of Mind will have to deal with the full range of phenomenal states undergone by human beings but thinks that the major epistemological obstacle in neuro-scientific consideration of such pathological or spiritual states is "the logical contradiction inherent in all reports from a purportedly *auto*biographical type of memory". The self-contradictory nature of such reports, he says, makes such information very dubious[97]. As stated above, this is a very facile view of Yogic or Phenomenological knowledge given that highly consistent intersubjective consensus about the transformations of human consciousness lead to notions of 'Perennial Phenomenology', describing universal structures of human consciousness as we have seen. I have shown that authoritative descriptions of the dynamical flow, momentariness and other features of the Light of Pure Consciousness can indeed be correlated with well-established neuroscientific knowledge (in contrast to Metzinger's highly tenuous speculations). Mystical ego-dissolution is not of course limited to Nature Mysticism in which the 'physical' world remains. Religious and mystical experience is more commonly associated with states where normal physical phenomena have disappeared and even normal Space and Time are absent once the Time/Space Matrix of perception is transcended. Yogic ego-dissolution and reconstitution of 'vehicles of consciousness' in deeper states, nondual States of Consciousness where the once-objective phenomena are perceived as Self, and Pure ('objectless') Consciousness simply cannot be reduced to self-representation within a model of the sensory environment.

Returning to Anti-Reductionist, ontological objections about how a phenomenal first-person perspective could possibly arise from a (Physicalist conception of a) functionally centred representational space (that could hypothetically be created in a computer rather just than in the human brain), Metzinger offers the following 'explanation'. Supposedly it is due to the "semantic transparency" of the data structures used by the system. The basic idea is that the representational vehicles employed by the system are 'transparent' in the sense that they do not contain the information that they are models on the level of their content. He adds that "transparency" means that we are systems which are unable to "*recognise*" their representational instruments as representational instruments and we thus "*look* through" those representations in a naive Realistic manner as if we were in direct contact with their content[98]. (I have italicised Metzinger's unacknowledged, tacit presuppositions of Consciousness). This transparency seems a conceptual necessity on the representational level of analysis and, Metzinger adds, is a highly plausible as an empirical assumption about the way our brain actually works. A prereflexive phenomenal Self, therefore, emerges if a system operates under a model of reality centred by a transparent self model[99]. However, his assumptions about how our brain actually works are challenged by facts such as Husserl's reflexive reduction whereby this naive-Realism or Natural Attitude is suspended and the constitutive process of perception is apprehended by ego-consciousness. Metzinger concludes that we are physical systems which were configured by Evolution in such a way that they constantly *confuse* themselves with the content of their phenomenal self-model. We know ourselves only under a representation. The evolutionary advantage of this constant confusing of self with self-representation is, according to Metzinger, obvious. It makes a selfless biological system *egotistic* by generating a strong self-illusion[100].

Note how Metzinger appeals to the evolutionary selection of Consciousness argument of which Materialists are so fond, presenting the supposed adaptive 'advantage' as that of making the organism egotistic! We have seen that such appeals to the authoritative status of Darwinian Natural Selection, as with appeals to Physics, are themselves fraught with insurmountable problems. There does indeed seem to be differences between egoistic consciousness and the seeming non-egoic consciousness of newborn infants, and perhaps primitive human hunter-gatherers and animals with less complex central nervous systems such that ego consciousness can perhaps be viewed as an adaptive advantage related primarily to the foresight given by such self-representational world-modelling simulations as I myself realised in 1983. In fact, I find some of what Metzinger has to say about possible self-representation and world-modelling is quite useful in regard to the question of how Mentation operates in physical terms. But even as a teenager, I could see that evolutionary selection of a meaningfully-organised world-model process cannot supply an ontological explanation of Consciousness! Metzinger says that "we *know* ourselves only under a representation" {*e.m.*}. Once again the Materialist uses of language serve only to obfuscate. What '*we know ourselves*' actually means is: we are aware of (or conscious of) ourselves. Metzinger is in fact aware of the obvious logical mistake in his argument, related to the Western philosophical conundrum of the homunculus which leads to the *reductio ad absurdam* or infinite regress of sentient observers. The existence of the self-model generates an *illusion*! But an illusion implies that a sentient or conscious being is experiencing the illusion[101].

Metzinger attempts to overcome this logical problem with the following argument[102]:

It makes sense to speak of truth and falsity, of knowledge and illusion,

> *only if you already have an epistemic agent in the sense of a system possessing conceptualised knowledge in a strong conceptual sense. But this is not the case: We have just solved the homunculus problem; there is nobody in there who could be wrong about anything. All you have is a functionally grounded self-modeling system under the condition of a naive-realistic self-misunderstanding {e.m.}. ...what I have been saying in this paper is that the conscious self is an illusion which is no one's illusion.*

Metzinger, of course is fooling no one (except perhaps deluding himself and his fellow 'true believers') that he has solved the homunculus problem! His argument is mere Materialist sophistry, yet another subterfuge strategy to sneakily avoid the ontological abyss which Subjectivity opens up for Materialism. He tells us that *knowledge* and *illusion* can only occur in a thinking being capable of manipulating abstract concepts. This is of course utter nonsense. As indicated above, to 'know' actually means in such cases to 'be aware'. I am aware of something or I can become aware of it potentially by information retrieval from my memory. Faced with the failings of his Materialist faith, the real question that Metzinger is evading is of course, how can there be *Awareness*.

Even, if doctrinaire (Anglo-American) Analytic Philosophy denies consciousness to a bee or a bird, it cannot deny non-conceptualising animals the possession of representations or *knowledge* of the territory etc. as utilised for navigation. When a non-conceptual animal mistakes a reflection of itself for another individual it is experiencing an illusion. A creature like a frog can easily be deceived by experimenters into ejecting its tongue towards a prey-like form wiggled in its field of vision. Nobody can seriously maintain that conceptualisation is a necessary prerequisite for experiencing an illusion. We have seen that recent research shows how the study of illusions helps explain the illusory tricks which constitute the world-modelling of our normal perception, filling in familiar patterns when the sense data is partially obscured. The true prerequisite for experiencing illusion or knowing something is possession of *Awareness*. Yet having practised verbal *illusionism* to sweep the homunculus paradox under his magic carpet of conjuror's, confidence tricks and conceptualist, computationalist contortions of conventional semantics, Metzinger states astoundingly in the very next sentence that all that exists is a system under a naive-realistic self-misunderstanding {*e.m.*}! Not only does the same logical error apply to *understanding* as it did with *knowledge* and *illusion*, but self-proclaimed member of Humanity's 'rational elite' Metzinger digs an even deeper hole for himself as understanding is *obviously far more dependent on the pre-existence of conceptuality than either knowledge or illusion!*

Notice that Metzinger refers to *conceptual* necessity, *semantic* transparency in information processing, representations, *hardwired,* complex computational states etc. indicating his entrapment in the language, logic, and computational symbolist mindset of Analytic philosophy that dominated first-generation Cognitive Science. Although written from a Eurocentric, Hegelian-Constructivist stance that denies Universalism, Joseph Margolis's

2003 book *The Unravelling of Scientism: American Philosophy at the End of the Twentieth Century* remains a useful critique of the dogmatically held Scientism and Materialism underlying (American) Analytic Philosophy. Margolis exposes the zealotry and absurdities spouted by some of the most famous exponents such as Willard Quine, Daniel Dennett, Paul Churchland and Donald Davidson. Margolis states correctly in his introduction that there is no compelling evidence that Scientism is inching closer to its goal. Rather, we are learning more and more about our puzzlement gripped by the profoundest stalemate of the entire (Western) philosophical undertaking. The grand systems of Analytic Philosophy have all long faded away. The Logicism of Russell and Frege, the Atomisms and Extensionalist Materialism of Russell, the Positivists, the Unity of Science program all simply collapsed due to internal weakness that could not be papered over. These systems were, he says, "precocious in vision but deficient in resources" and "*damned by basic errors that all who cared could see*" {*e.m.*}[103].

Such Analytic philosophy type arguments are also anthropocentric in presenting knowledge and 'thinking' as a purely abstract, conceptual operations as if nonconceptual animals are incapable of possessing any sort of knowledge or 'thought'. Such Analytic mythology is also discredited for as Lakoff and Johnson stress in *Philosophy in the Flesh: The Embodied Mind and its Challenge to Western Thought*, conceptualisation is itself based upon figurative and motor operations; Conceptualisation piggybacks upon Perception[104]. Furthermore, ironically, the evolutionary argument in favour of a *World-Model* or 'virtual reality' *simulation* process itself contradicts Metzinger's verbal sophistry. The main supposed selective advantage of such a simulation process has to be *foresight*, the ability for the organism to predict 'virtually' the likely outcome of pursuing a particular course of action rather than risk life and limb in conventional 'trial and error' behaviours. Even in us humans, such anticipation usually actually involves *visual reasoning*, 'seeing what will happen' in our imagination rather than some abstract conceptual process as is imagined in Analytical fantasies of how minds operate. The followers of William James have long mocked the fantasy views of human cognitive operations expounded by Analytics[105].

Notice also that, although Metzinger's use of notion's like *instantiation* suggest a tacit ontological Dualism, which he then tries to counter with pseudo-arguments, there always remains in such Materialist arguments, a tacit use of sentences implying *ontological Panpsychism*. This is of course clear in Metzinger's talk of systems not knowing themselves as representations, prereflexive self-intimacy as a primitive form of self-awareness etc. which are magically wished away as system's misunderstanding themselves and 'subsymbolic dynamics'. Another tacit suggestion in the phrase 'subsymbolic dynamics' is that somehow 'information processing' magically creates new properties out of physical, dynamical complexity etc. But of course this is tacit Dualism and if Dualism is denied, as in Metzinger's case, then it must be tacit Panpsychism as Awareness cannot arise from physical dynamics describing spatiotemporal forms. Awareness is known through Yoga as the formless ground of spatiotemporal forms. Let us remember that new developments in Theoretical Physics involve integrating Information Theory such that physical theories and physical entities are understood more in terms of *information*. Not only is there nothing ontologically special about information processing, but most of the Natural World, which Materialism pictures as insentient, can be represented just as much in terms of informational states as any sort of hypothetical world-modelling in brains or computers! Scott Kelso, himself an expert in Synergetics and self-organisation in brain dynamics rubbishes the orthodox Cognitivists' Computational view of the brain. The use of terms such as 'motor programs' by scientists, he says, is like attributing thunder to the Norse god Thor. The same applies when attributes like 'alcoholic' and 'depressive' are ascribed to genes[106].

Thus, in spite of Metzinger referring disdainfully to rival philosophies as irrational and amateurish speculation we see that, faced with the intractable homunculus paradox which undermines Materialism, he reacts like a Flat-Earther unable to abandon his cherished beliefs when its untenable assumptions are exposed. His supposed solution to the homunculus paradox is both irrational and amateurish! It is no better than Scholastic sophistry claiming to prove logically the existence of a theistic God! Remember that Metzinger asserted that Reductionist Materialists like himself are not beholden to an ideology and that they would be happy to accept principled reasons why it is impossible for interdisciplinary Cognitive Science to grasp subjective experience. Supposedly their true goal is simply the growth of knowledge although Metzinger as we just saw distorts the meaning of 'knowledge' to suit his Analytic prejudices. The problem with interdisciplinary Cognitive Science is that it is not really the 'broad church' that it pretends to be. It rejects approaches like Introspectionism and Phenomenology on rather 'unprincipled' grounds. As we saw above, the various disciplines included are those steeped in Behaviorism and Analytical thought. Cognitivist philosophers, like Metzinger, simply pronounce upon received wisdom and, faced with glaring ontological contradictions, fall back upon absurd conceptual subterfuge to defend their faith. Like the narrow-minded Christian believers in the 'One True Faith' who slurred non-believers as 'pagans' (village idiots), these Cognitivists spew out verbal slurry in the direction of their critics. Yet they never turn introspective to find out why they themselves are so (metaphorically) 'full of crap', or realise that they create such crap because their blinkered, pseudo-philosophical minds have (metaphorically) got their 'knickers in a twist'.

The Book of Daniel: 'High Priest' of Cognitivist sect sticks steadfastly to his Scientism faith

Evan Thompson *et al.* state that, in his (modestly titled) 1991 book *Consciousness Explained*, Daniel C. Dennett advised Cognitive Scientists to construct a preliminary description of human experience from the third-person perspective, and then to evaluate this description in relation to an account of the brain[107]. Metzinger's paper discussed above was presumably a product of this pronouncement from the 'High Priest' of Cognitivism. Thompson *et al.* add that Dennett's proposal precluded a place in this program for the autonomous investigation of human experience as it is lived, independent of scientific accounts. Proposals such as Dennett's, they say, rest on a misconception of the relation between the person or experiencing subject and the person's brain, treating the brain rather than the person as if it were the proper subject of experience. Due to this misconception, Dennett and like-minded others not only describe falsely the character of perceptual experience, but also evaluate incorrectly the conceptual and empirical significance of issues about perceptual completion in Vision Research. Dennett's view implies that perceptual content is entirely constituted by neural content. According to Dennett, there is nothing over and above sub-processes as a unitary person or agent. Furthermore, these errors were long ago identified within the phenomenological tradition, which of course Dennett rejects[108].

I recall watching a British television science documentary back in the 1990s in which Dennett rehashed the old Behaviorist myth of the Turing Test as a test for the existence of Consciousness in a computer. Dennett failed to mention that Alan Turing himself argued that the strongest argument against a computer passing the test was that, unlike a human being, it would not have paranormal psychic experiences such as Extra-sensory Perception and Telepathy[109]. Dennett displayed some maps of the British Empire in an effort to relate communication problems between London and Calcutta to the Philosophy of Mind. Thompson *et al.* explain that for Dennett, the person or animal is no more than a logical construct of sub-personal brain states and processes, just as the British Empire at the time of the 1812 War was a logical construct of its component institutions, the monarchy, parliament, bureaucracy and subjects etc.[110] Thus no actual higher-level entity is supposed to exist, only a concept in the mind of the beholder! Thus Dennett says that there can be no specific answer to the question as to when the British Empire was informed of the truce in the 1812 War (Napoleon in Russia) as different constituents received the information at different times. Similarly says Dennett, conscious experience is a succession of states *constituted* by various processes and not some higher-level entity above these processes that is *caused* by them [111]. Not only Phenomenology with its various levels of ego contradicts this but similar knowledge in Yoga of the individuated mind and its transformation into various individuated vehicles of consciousness in deeper states. Furthermore, such yogic and phenomenological descriptions, which Dennett excludes from scientific consideration, indicate that mental activity is associated with field processes caused by the underlying activity of the countless neurons. The actual temporal succession of states is due neither to the sub-processes or the higher-level ego. Rather the Now moments of our experience are constituted by the Background Flow of the Light of Pure Consciousness.

Harry Hunt says that the rejection of the importance of Consciousness by the likes of Daniel Dennett is central to the AI movement. This is because, if sentient awareness should prove necessary for understanding symbolic cognition, especially in its recombinatory and novel aspects, then computer simulations of cognition must be limited to those functions that can become completely automatised[112]. William Seager rubbishes Dennett's view of neural representations in Dennett's *Consciousness Explained* which Seager tells us is "fixated on debunking the generation problem", (i.e., the ontological problem as to how sentience arises from insentient material bodies). There can be no question of eliminating the distinction between conscious and unconscious representations which "modulate behavior", given the undeniable fact that some unconscious representations modulate behaviour. Thus there exists a very stark form of the 'generation problem' located in Dennett's theory which was supposed to banish it[113]. In fact the phenomenon of Blindsight has revealed two distinct streams of visual information in humans, one of which is linked to motor control and is not associated with (ego-) consciousness! We saw above D.C. Clarke's and my own scathing counter-arguments to Dennett's naive view of random gene mutations generating 'primitive mental capacities'. Overall, we may view Daniel Dennett's cheerleading efforts for Cognitive Science as a classic example of Scientism. Scientism was described by Jacques Barzun as "the fallacy of believing that the method of Science must be used on all forms of experience and, given time, will settle every issue."[114]. Back in 1944 sociologist Wellmuth recognised 'Scientism' as a widespread and institutionalised form of behaviour in which current science and Materialism are treated as the final and absolute truth[115]. Jeffrey Schwartz M.D., a research professor of Psychiatry who is interested in Buddhism and attentional influence on neuroplasticity, tells an interesting story in this regard. When Schwartz said to an ex-President of the American Society of Neuroscience that there is more to mental life than action potentials, the curt retort he received was, "You're not a scientist!"[116].

A Look at some other Cognitive Conceptual Confabulations of Normal and Mystical Consciousness

Wolf Singer: Awareness as an organisational rather than ontological question

Nicholas Humphrey is not alone in putting forward absurd Cognitive Science explanations of Consciousness based on the most puerile grasp of the metaphysical issues. Neurophysiologist Wolf Singer is the author of a chapter entitled 'Phenomenal Awareness and Consciousness from a Neurobiological Perspective' in Metzinger's *Neural Correlates of Consciousness*. He notes that the term *consciousness* has a number of connotations ranging from awareness of one's perceptions and sensations to self-awareness and the perception of oneself as an agent endowed with intentionality and free will[117]. Note that he is using 'intentionality' in its normal sense of volition rather than Brentano's Scholastic sense. In contrast to the more circumspect Edelman and Toni, Singer says that his view is that phenomenal awareness should in principle be tractable within neurobiological description systems. Singer thinks it is tractable as the problem of its relation to neuronal processes can probably be reduced to the question of how neuronal representations are *organised* {*e.m*}. Rather surprisingly, Singer thinks that the other connotations of 'consciousness' transcend purely neurobiological descriptions due to their social, cultural and historical dimensions[118]. Materialists often conflate the *meaningful organisation* aspect of conscious *mentation* in 'mindlike' systems with Consciousness *per se* or Awareness (*see Ch.11*).

According to Singer, brains that have consciousness possess a representational metalevel which explicitly represents internal states. This supposedly constitutes an "inner eye" *function* {*e.m.*}. This 'inner eye' function could be realised by a reflexive iteration of self-similar cortical functions. Phenomenal awareness results from an iteration of the same cognitive operations that support primary sensory processing. The 'Explanatory Gap', (i.e., Mind/Body Problem) "reduces itself to the question of how the cerebral cortex processes signals and generates representations". Singer thinks that if this question were answered in regard to primary sensory functions, the strategies should be 'generaliseable' to the formation of metarepresentations[119]. This is of course just straightforward Functionalist conflation of subjective experiences to higher-level representational processes with the fashionable but vacuous notions of self-similar iterations thrown in. *Self-similarity* is a fashionable item of jargon from Chaotic Dynamics and refers to repetition of forms at different scales of spatial order usually exemplified by the irregular nature of coastlines which exhibit self-similarity at different orders of scale. The Rabbinical, writing-obsessed Jacques Derrida tried to reduce self-consciousness to similar notions of *iterations* in his absurd language-based models of mind[120]. Such facile notions of iterations or repetitive processes usually embellished with related mumbo-jumbo of self-referential loops, etc., simply raise the Ghost in the Machine problems or homunculus paradoxes so beloved of Western 'philosophers' indulging in mere speculation. Such hypothetical, thought experiment scenarios such as infinite regressions of 'observers' are nonsensical as self-representation or formal self-similarity etc. are far removed from Awareness. Reflexive iterations of self-similar cortical functions representing internal states, whatever this actually means in the flesh, is nothing more than just repetitive behaviour. If self-similarity applies throughout Nature to things like the form of coastlines, why are such widespread iterative and similar natural phenomena not also considered as conscious!

Singer's use of the metaphor '*inner eye*' function is itself fraught with philosophical confusion. The implication is that just as the outer eye generates visual consciousness (the dominant sensory mode) so some equivalent *function* is performed by iteration of self-similar whatnots. But the eye does not generate visual consciousness; it simply receives stimuli in certain wavelengths of light and transmits nervous signals to the brain. Furthermore, as stated above, there exist two streams of visual information processing in humans. One, associated with motor functions is not associated with (ego-) consciousness whereas the other, associated with perception is. Singer adds that other aspects of Consciousness, such as self-awareness and the experience of individuality require explanations transcending neurobiological reductionism. It is his view that such phenomena, unlike the question of the *qualia* of phenomenal awareness, are the real ontological or 'hard' problems of Consciousness which give rise to Dualistic views. As stated above, Singer cites social, cultural and historical dimensions as reasons why these other connotations of Consciousness transcend neurobiological description. The implication here seems to be that all manner of 'Folk Psychological' notions of Self, ego, Free Will, etc., make such (linguistic) terms, socio-cultural constructions or concepts, irreducible to neurobiological terms. His use of 'term' indicates an Analytical emphasis on linguistic usage. The exact reasons behind Singer's perverse interpretation of what actually constitutes the ontological problem of Consciousness need not bother us as his views are so obviously wrong.

As with Crick, Singer is taking *Consciousness* to mean erroneously just normal Waking consciousness and ignoring altered states which bear no resemblance to his simplistic notions of phenomenal awareness arising from self-similar iterative functions involving metarepresentations of internal states. The fact that Pure Consciousness exists completely contradicts this view. The fact that patients Near-to-Death have heightened conscious experiences when their cerebral cortices are deactivated also contradicts Singer's speculations. Nondual mystical experiences and the dissolution of the 'naked ego' or basic individuated vehicle of Consciousness in mystical union and phenomenological knowledge of subject-object polarisation etc. in the constitutive processes of object perception and similar knowledge shows, as I have argued that the fundamental ontological problem of Consciousness is the existence of Awareness. The question of Free Will, as we have seen is a tricky one, and does pose serious ontological problems given the limitations of the Physicalist world-picture but, given mystical knowledge of all-pervading Awareness, it is a secondary question. The individuation question has ontological aspects as to how an all-pervading singular Universal Consciousness becomes plural but this is obviously not what Singer has in mind. Knowledge of ego constitution and dissolution indicate that the full answer to this problem also involves conventional physical, neurological descriptions as with the question of so-called 'Self-awareness'.

Cognitive caricatures of the mystical (Divine) Light

Psychologist Harry Hunt's attempt to give a Cognitive Science based interpretation of the Light experienced by mystics involves reducing the Light to J.J. Gibson's notions of the Optic Flow and imagining it as the background of the flowing visual sensory field created by the organism's movement[121]. Hunt completely misunderstands the fact that the Divine Light is not a sensory phenomenon but only revealed when sensory processes are held in abeyance. The flow of the Divine Light has nothing whatsoever to do with the motion of the organism in the light envelope of the visual environment! Yogis and mystics are famously rather motionless creatures when absorbed in enlightened states of Consciousness! So too are Near-Death patients who 'see the Light'. Hunt naively conflates Gibson's (external, sensory) dynamic flow notion of Optic Flow of the visual field with Heidegger's (internal, cognitive, and 'welling upward') dynamical flow notions (*ereignis* dynamics)[122]. Yet aforementioned psychologist John Pickering, himself familiar with Hindu spiritual training, lauds Hunt's "innovative integration of cognitive, phenomenological and transpersonal perspectives"[123]. This resembles the Reductionism of Charles Laughlin who sings the praises Eastern mystical knowledge before immediately reducing it Eurocentrically to Emergent Materialism[124].

Numerous scientists commenting on Near-Death Experiences (NDEs) dismiss reports of seeing the Light and other related experiences with facile Reductionist nonsense posing as explanations such as release of opiates or oxygen depletion. Such appeals to the indisputability of Scientism and simple pronouncements by scientists about chemicals or oxygen depletion do not of course account in any way for such NDEs, they are just another Materialist subterfuge strategy to evade the real questions which Behaviorist Science cannot answer. Such physiological factors may indeed be associated with NDEs (as 'indirect' correlates) but oxygen depletion in itself is nothing more than one small part of the complex processes correlated with the experiences and hardly comes near to a sufficient explanation as to why NDEs occur. In fact the only published study in which blood oxygen was measured during an NDE found no effects of anoxia or hypercapnia[125]. Oxygen depletion and opiate release etc. also occur in numerous situations which have nothing to do with NDEs and so scientists touting such simplistic pseudo-explanations resemble Witch Doctors uttering magical formulae or performing confidence tricks on uneducated laymen to pretend that they are in possession of higher knowledge.

The sort of amazingly crude argument put forward by many scientists was exemplified by a Harvard Neurobiology professor, David Potter. Addressing the Dalai Lama of Tibet, who had made reference to yogic experience of the Clear Light at a Mind-Brain symposium at Harvard, Potter responded {*e.m.*}[126]:

> *I am a cellular scientist and a notorious radical materialist. I have a question that may be shared by other scientists or neuroscientists, as to whether one should invoke a non-material mind in order to understand brain science, or increase our understanding of human behaviour... the particular* ***nerve cells*** *upon which cocaine is known to act* ***are neither clear nor formless****; they are amazingly intricate in shape and they occur in collections of nerve cells whose form is wonderfully intricate. They are not clear, they contain a pigment... though no one knows whether it is related in any way to these phenomena [referring to cocaine-induced euphoria].*

Potter's capabilities as a philosopher are clearly lightweight. His simplistic 'Neuronal Man' style argument as to how one can experience a 'clear light' when nerve cells are not clear is clearly absurd. If our experience was limited by the structure and pigmentation of nerve cells, then we certainly would not be able to experience the forms and colours of everyday perception which we nonetheless do. We do not experience tangles of dendritic-synaptic connections or sub-cellular pigments. How do we perceive the clear blue sky without grey neurons in the way! On the contrary, the question as to why the neuronal structure of physical brain does not appear in our conscious experience is one that needs to be carefully addressed. My 1980s model of a nested hierarchy of fields and the notion of 'subjective closure' attempted to account for this (*see Ch. 11*). However, it remains a tricky question needing much clarification. The slowly dissipating after-images left by bright objects like light bulbs appear to be constellations of neural patterns which remain in an excited state, breaching an energetic threshold of attention, after egoic attention has shifted elsewhere. In *Principles of Psychology* William James said that Attention and Volition were essentially the same[127]. This suggests that our willing results from a focus of egoic energy. In fact, some information the Dalai Lama of Tibet has presented in recently published books regarding highest Tibetan Buddhist *Vajrayana* knowledge of the Clear Light as a continuous series of moments[127] and that the notion of the Clear Light as like the background state of the cerebral cortex[128] fit perfectly with my RAS brainwave interpretation of the physical correlate of the Divine Light.

Persinger's philosophically puerile purview on the neuropsychology of religious experience

Michael Persinger is a professor of Psychology and head of the Neuroscience Research Group at Laurentian University in Canada whose specialism is in the clinical and experimental correlates of stimulation within the temporal lobes of the mammalian brain. This information is provided in his book *Neuropsychological Bases of God Beliefs*[130], a title which presents a sense of scientific certainty and supposed authority. But, as with other scientific specialist researchers such as Francis Crick, Persinger exhibits the most superficial knowledge and no understanding whatsoever of the subtleties of the Philosophy of Religion, Mysticism or Spirituality in general but this does not stop him from reducing the whole gamut of human spiritual experience to a supposedly singular so-called "God Experience" which he correlates with electrical instabilities such as epilepsy in the Temporal lobe of the cerebral cortex! He does however refer in his preface to both the (singular) God Experience as well as the (plural) experiences of religious believers. Right from the start he refers simply to 'God' with no distinction made between deities such as Allah, Yahweh, Great Spirit or the 'Great Cosmic Whole'. Showing true faith in Scientism, Persinger tells us that God Experiences appear to have emerged in human evolution as a means of coping with our ability to anticipate aversive events. He states that, "*All* {*e.m.*} religious arguments are based on word games and appeal to simplistic, emotionally loaded concepts..."[131]. His purportedly all-encompassing analysis of human religious experience and religious or spiritual philosophy is, we are told, "the synthesis of several years of clinical and academic investigation". Initially, Persinger began by investigating the neural basis of paranormal experiences but it soon became clear to him that a more fundamental and pervasive phenomenon, (i.e., the 'God Experience') was being 'tested'[132].

Persinger tells us that he extrapolates systematically from the concepts presented in the text and that these will surprise the reader as much as they surprised him. There is no attempt, he adds, to embarrass any particular group of believers. His basic premise is that, if something is true, then no amount of challenge will ever change it[133]. However, the true believers in Scientism should be embarrassed by such crude, simplistic, philosophically puerile attestations of their faith. But like any zealots, as witnessed by their supportive reviews on Amazon.com, rather than being embarrassed by Persinger's lack of substance and sophistication, the true believers are reaffirmed in their Scientism by Persinger's exhortations. In a time when the semi-literate Western underclasses feel no shame in exposing their startling ignorance to the public in Reality TV shows, it seems as if highly specialised scientists are equally unabashed to abase themselves intellectually in their publications. In spite of his purported several years of academic investigation, Persinger displays no understanding of the distinction between *Theism* and *Non-Theism* (let alone the difference between the tribal Yahweh and the Christian deity), henotheism, the meaning of *transcendental,* the exoteric/esoteric distinction, Perennialism or any other aspect of the Philosophy of Religion or Mysticism. The attitude of most founding fathers of modern Science was that some of the alchemical and religious mythologies may be allegories for some hidden existential secrets and it was unwise to throw out the 'baby with the bathwater'[134]. But no such open-mindedness and insight is found in psychologist Persinger. His understanding is at a crude, puerile level which views all forms of Spirituality as equivalent to the most literalist forms of Semitic Theistic Fundamentalism. I wasted my money on this overpriced book as I had come across Persinger's name in regard to his earlier work on paranormal phenomena and electric fields on television and in books. I thus assumed, incorrectly, that, as he had bothered to investigate the paranormal, he would be open-minded and perhaps give useful information on electric field phenomena and mystical states.

On page 1 Persinger refers to union with (supposedly) the symbolic form of Space-Time. Elsewhere he says that the religious experience implies that God is all of Space-Time[135]. No reference is made to Space-Time *transcendence* which is a crucial characteristic of most spirituality. His references to 'Space-Time' indicate that he holds Einstein's conception based on a mathematical convenience of treating Time as a Space-like dimension as if it is undisputed Reality. In Chapter 4 we saw that Eddington, who helped confirm Einstein's GTR, dismissed the 'Space-Time frame' as a fictional and arbitrary human construct and that QM points to a deeper nonlocal reality transcending Space-Time. We saw above that Persinger's conception of Truth is simplistic to say the least (no amount of challenge will change something that is true)! He thinks that nonphysical things can never exist except as words and that it would be impossible to ever prove the God argument[136]. We have seen that even the likes of Edelman and Crick acknowledge that 'qualia' might be irreducible to physical terms. On page 2 and 3 in referring to the supposed 'God Concept' Persinger lumps together Non-Theistic Buddhists with Christians and Muslims. Even Atheists are accused of substituting the conventional God Concept for abstract forms of mysticism such as the 'Great Nothingness'.

Persinger trivializes Perennialist Universalism stating that sometimes maverick peacemakers attempt to show that all religions are different experiences of the same thing but that, deep down, the feelings of uniqueness remain[137]. We are not told how Persinger attained this knowledge. He is implying that he has psychic abilities including clairvoyancy which allowed him to read the minds and deeper feelings of such supposed 'peacemakers', including deceased ones! Of course, we have seen that such facile generalisations of all spiritual traditions as being dogmatic and Exclusivist as with Semitic Religion is completely contradicted by Indian history. Interestingly, Persinger castigates Western missionaries and systematic destruction of non-Western cultures in the name of profit and zeal and refers to black South Africans shot by the white police. Such politically commendable views however indicate Marxian leanings and hence also indicate that a simplistic Marxian view of Religion as the 'opium of the masses' tacitly complements Persinger's crude Behaviorist analysis. Persinger goes on to treat Biblical Literalists as equivalent to Tibetan Buddhists and asserts that ancient texts are universally treated as sacred and necessarily true[138]. Although doctrinaire scholasticism indeed infects popular Buddhism, elite Buddhist philosophy is based on Empiricism and Logic over textual authority and the Dalai Lama has even accepted that old doctrines may need to be abandoned if Science can provide incontrovertible evidence to the contrary[139].

Persinger adds that religious believers have a contempt for the *science* {*e.m.*} of Psychology which he goes on to describe as "the analysis of human behaviour" or as "behavioural science"[140]. His own text makes evident his own unreconstructed Behaviorism, reducing religious experience to mere conditioning associations with expectations of food (and presumably other) rewards as with Skinner's laboratory pigeons. Such emotional cravings to be acclaimed as *scientists* is common amongst practitioners of 'soft' Psychology including the aforementioned Polytechnic Psychologist 'cheerleaders' who appear on British television to deny the possibility of paranormal psychic phenomena on supposedly scientific grounds. Not surprisingly one such 'witchfinder' visited Persinger's labs in one of her television programmes. In 2004 Granqvist *et al.* published a paper in the prestigious science journal *Nature* reporting on their attempts (in Sweden) to repeat Persinger's reported results. In stark contrast to Persinger's claims, they found that *magnetic stimulation had no effect*. They conducted Double-Blind experiments, with 43 students exposed to magnetic fields and 46 in the control group not actually exposed. Yet over half of those reporting 'spiritual' experiences[N12] belonged to the control group {*e.m.*}[141].

Persinger's view of religious experience is basically as follows. As with Nicholas Humphrey he concocts a ridiculous 'Just-So Story' and takes this fantasy to constitute reliable evidence. The benefits gained by humans in their ability to plan and anticipate also had their downside with their concomitant anxiety and apprehension of suffering and the fear of death and its unknown consequences for the individual. The God Experience is assumed to be critical for the survival of the species in order to balance the terror of personal extinction. Persinger betrays his Anglo-American Analytic leanings in his assumption that the (supposedly) sudden development of the capacity to speak, (i.e., Language) being closely correlated with the ability for Thought[142]. Such Analytical dogmas are myths based on glaring ignorance of biological evolution's conservatism and the true nature of Language and Cognition. Yet Persinger does not stop here, he then asserts that, by processes not yet elucidated technically, these properties, (i.e., Speech and Thought) were preconditions for the appearance of phenomena known as Awareness and Experience[143]. Note the logical contradiction and anthropocentrism here in that Persinger admits that Science does not understand, yet, the 'processes' by which Awareness 'appeared' but, nonetheless, these could not have arisen before humans possessed Speech and Language! On this analysis, no other species has Awareness or experiences! Persinger remains blissfully oblivious of the Christian mythological roots of his own anthropocentrism (Man alone amongst God's creatures has a soul becomes Man alone has Consciousness), and his Materialism (from Christian *Creatio ex nihilo*).

Furthermore, he says that along with such developments, the hippocampus and amygdala began to migrate deep within the human brain until they both rested in the Temporal lobe of the cerebral cortex. Apparently, the appearance of these two structures in the Temporal lobe contributed to 'the experience of' *remembering* and *evaluation*[144]. Note that these structures are bilateral and thus we possess pairs of hippocampi and amygdalae. Persinger says that the hippocampus became a gateway to the experience of images from our memories, its stimulation can unleash vivid images and fantasies. The amygdala became a display centre for the experience of emotions and moods. Because of links to the frontal lobes results in such emotions becoming mixed with experiences of the self; the ability to anticipate and the ability to inhibit being the two key capacities of the human frontal lobes. If such inhibition is lost due to alcohol or drugs, images of hate, impulses of revenge and sexual desires emerge into Awareness[145]. Thus it seems that Awareness exists only in humans as they posses Language and Thought and that the neural location of Awareness is the frontal lobes which occupy about half the human cerebral capacity.

Persinger says that he is not arguing that the God Experience is localised in the Temporal lobe but that the God Experience is a phenomenon associated with the construction of the temporal lobe. He claims that spiritual transfiguration is due to single bursts of Temporal lobe seizures resulting in people finding personal conviction of truth and meaning. Seizures in the temporal lobe lead to perception of nonhuman entities, such as little men, glowing forms or bright, shining sources[146]. Persinger's Temporal lobe epilepsy (TLE) related effects or 'God Experience' is also associated with a sense of 'cosmic consent' to kill and manipulate others and a conviction that one is *absolutely right*. Uncontrolled aggressive outbursts are also associated with such TLE and Persinger links this to the Old Testament genocide of native inhabitants associated with prophetic experiences of the aggressive Jehovah (Yahweh). The Mohammedan Allah running Yahweh a close second in regard to aggression[147]. Neurologist Rhawn Joseph has linked the amygdala to the mystical experience of the vengeful, bloodthirsty, jealous, sex- and violence-obsessed tribal war god Yahweh (as have other writers), and its counterparts like Wotan[148]. Sigmund Freud secularised Jewish mysticism[149], and Jung stated that Freud replaced the jealous god Yahweh with the jealous god Sexuality[150]. Such facts indicate a neurological link between the two. But Yahweh is clearly not the same deity as the Christian god of Love and Light, which is equivalent to the Light in Hinduism, Buddhism, the Light known as *al haqq* (Reality) of Sufi mysticism, or the Love-filled Light of NDEs. Persinger's simplistic interpretation of the phrase "God is love" is that the powerful associations of the word 'love' can be easily passed onto unseen and unproven things so that the word 'God' becomes associated with the security and quiescence of early parental relationships[151].

Similarly, Persinger says that God Experiences cannot be verified, they are part of the language process. Unwaveringly faithful to Analytic belief, Persinger stresses that God words are embedded in metaphors which invoke rich imagery. Metaphors or parables are so general, he adds, that they can be meaningful to anyone[152]. As an example, he chooses, "God's goodness flows into the soul of man", and links the effect to free association with the notion of a river that can both give and take away life[153]. We have seen that all concepts including scientific concepts are based on metaphors (and in fact from animistic projections onto Nature such as Force from human Volition). Of course, most Westerners who remain ignorant of the mystical Flow of the Light and its Life-sustaining role as the *Prana* (which ties in beautifully with my RAS brainwave interpretation) including contributors to Kapstein's *The Presence of Light* imagine that such metaphors of *flowing* Light or goodness are no more than fancy metaphors without any factual basis!

The 'Hindu-Buddhist' concept of *Nirvana* is also equated by Persinger with this same TLE-based 'God Experience' resulting from the first human brain [*sic*] contemplating death[154]. Note this amusing and completely unscientific utilisation of a 'first human brain'; a modern reformulation of the Adam or First Man myth! It implies that human characteristics (including supposedly Consciousness as uniquely human) magically appeared fully formed in one individual mutant when previously they did not exist! As the first human brain contemplated death, Persinger continues, the first experience may have been a 'cosmic serenity' without fear, anxiety, only the sensation of becoming a part of everything. This quiescence has survival value in allowing humans to cope with the anticipation of self-annihilation! In periods of helplessness, such as when a person lies dying, ludicrous magical thinking re-emerges in the otherwise rational human. Any kind of severe psychological helplessness can elicit God Experiences. The *Tibetan Book of the Dead* is dismissed as merely an anxiety-reducing, psychological balm for the dying and thus it makes no difference as to whether it contains facts or complete fantasies. The fact that similar Near-Death reports exist in many human cultures *may only reflect the similar construction of the human brain*[155].

Although some of Persinger's arguments such as the common structure of human brains underlying cross-cultural commonalities of experience, the role of the amygdala in religious fundamentalist aggression and paranoia (from fear), the fact that much religious mythology is merely comforting fairy tales, etc., holds partial truths cannot disguise the overall preposterous philosophical puerility of Persinger's approach. Like an immature schoolboy, he rubbishes all spiritual belief and philosophical thought as ludicrous, magical, simplistic nonsense, whilst failing to appreciate any of the glaring absurdities in his own zealous Scientism, steeped in Analytic and Behaviorist mythology. His crude dismissal of, for instance, Tibetan Buddhism is just as Eurocentric, ignorant and arrogant as the demonisation of Buddhism by Christian Missionaries. Just as he accuses universalist 'peacemakers' of harbouring secret feelings of the uniqueness of their own traditions, perhaps Persinger secretly approves of the brutal repression, genocide and 'cultural genocide' of the supposedly primitive Buddhist culture in Tibet by the (Scientific Materialist) Chinese Communists. After all Marxist dictatorships function like an organised Semitic creed but without a traditional god. Stalin, Mao or some other dictator becomes the object of Communist personality cults and the secret police search out the heretical dissidents[N13]. He refers to the contradiction between the scientific training and the personal beliefs of a professor of Biology who is also an ardent member of a Pentecostal church[156]. In spite of

Persinger's naive inability to really come to terms with such seemingly contradictory facts of life, the flagship journal of British Science, *Nature* conducted a survey in the mid-1990s showing that forty per cent of US scientists believed in a personal god and an immortal soul. This percentage had remained much the same over the course of the 20th Century in spite of the amazing advances in scientific knowledge. Although I do not concur with such beliefs in a personal god and immortal soul, I do however concur with such 'believer' scientists (presumably believing in Christianity and Judaism rather than Scientism and Marxism) in recognising that Science is limited, not omnipotent, and cannot explain all the mysteries of existence.

References

1. Metzinger, Thomas, "Introduction: Consciousness Research at the End of the Twentieth Century". In Thomas Metzinger (Editor) (2000) *Neural Correlates of Consciousness: Empirical and Conceptual Questions*, MIT Press.
2. Revonsuo, Antii "Prospects for a Scientific Research Program on Consciousness". In Thomas Metzinger (Editor) (2000) *Neural Correlates of Consciousness: Empirical and Conceptual Questions*, MIT Press.
3. Wallace, B. Alan (2000) *The Taboo of Subjectivity: Toward a New Science of Consciousness*, Oxford University Press.
4. Skrbina, David (2005) *Panpsychism in the West*, MIT Press.
5. Metzinger, Thomas (2000) [1] *ibid.*
6. Rothman, Tony and Sudarshan, George (1998) *Doubt and Certainty: The Celebrated Academy Debates on Science, Mysticism, Reality, In General on... ...To Name a Few,* Helix Books (Perseus Books).

7-9. Metzinger, Thomas (2000) [1] *ibid.*

10. Dupuy, Jean-Pierre "Philosophy and Cognition: Historical Roots". In Jean Petitot, Francisco J. Varela, Bernard Pachoud and Jean-Michel Roy (Editors) (1999) *Naturalising Phenomenology: Issues in Contemporary Phenomenology and Cognitive Science*, Stanford University Press.
11. Dupuy, Jean-Pierre (1999) *ibid.*
12. Roy, Jean-Michel, Petitot, Jean, Pachoud, Bernard and Varela, Francisco J. "Beyond the Gap: An Introduction to Naturalising Phenomenology." In Jean Petitot, Francisco J. Varela, Bernard Pachoud and Jean-Michel Roy (Editors) (1999) *Naturalising Phenomenology: Issues in Contemporary Phenomenology and Cognitive Science*, Stanford University Press.
13. Roy, Jean-Michel, Petitot, Jean, Pachoud, Bernard and Varela, Francisco J. (1999) *ibid.*
14. Lakoff, George and Johnson, Mark (1999) *Philosophy in the Flesh: The Embodied Mind and its Challenge to Western Thought,* Basic Books.
15. Roy, Jean-Michel, Petitot, Jean, Pachoud, Bernard and Varela, Francisco J. (1999) *ibid.*
16. Varela, Francisco J. and Shear, Jonathan "First-person Methodologies: What, Why, How?" In Francisco, J. Varela and Jonathan Shear (Editors) (1999) *The View From Within: First-person approaches to the study of consciousness,* Imprint Academic.

17. Hardin, Larry C. "Color Quality and Color Structure". In Stuart R. Hameroff, Alfred W. Kaszniak, and David J. Chalmers (Editors) (1999) *Toward a Science of Consciousness III: The Third Tucson Discussions and Debates.* MIT Press.
18. Lakoff, George and Johnson, Mark (1999) *ibid.*
19. Dupuy, Jean-Pierre (1999) *ibid.*
20. Roy, Jean-Michel, Petitot, Jean, Pachoud, Bernard and Varela, Francisco J. (1999) *ibid.*
21. Hunt, Harry T. (1995) *On the Nature of Consciousness: Cognitive, Phenomenological, and Transpersonal Perspectives*, Yale University Press.
22. Roy, Jean-Michel, Petitot, Jean, Pachoud, Bernard and Varela, Francisco J. (1999) *ibid.*
23. Roy, Jean-Michel, Petitot, Jean, Pachoud, Bernard and Varela, Francisco J. (1999) *ibid.*
24. Roy, Jean-Michel, Petitot, Jean, Pachoud, Bernard and Varela, Francisco J. (1999) *ibid.*
25. Bailey, Andrew R, "Beyond the Fringe: William James on the Transitional Parts of the Stream of Consciousness". In Francisco, J. Varela and Jonathan Shear (Editors) (1999) *The View From Within: First-person approaches to the study of consciousness,* Imprint Academic.
26. Freeman, Walter J. (1999) *How Brains Make up their Minds*, Wiedenfeld and Nicolson.
27. Lakoff, George and Johnson, Mark (1999) *ibid.*
28. Lakoff, George and Johnson, Mark (1999) *ibid.*
29. Hass, Lawrence (2008) *Merleau-Ponty's Philosophy*, Indiana University Press.
30. Sperry, Roger "Holding Course Amid Shifting Paradigms". In Willis Harman with Jane Clark (Editors) (1994) *New Metaphysical Foundations of Modern Science,* Institute of Noetic Sciences.
31. Begley, Sharon (2007) *Train Your Mind, Change Your Brain: How a New Science Reveals Our Extraordinary Potential to Transform Ourselves,* Ballantine Books.
32. Haynes, J-D. Research reported by Michael Hanlon in *Daily Mail* (Newspaper, UK) 17th April 2008.
33. Libet, Benjamin. *See for instance* Libet, Benjamin, Freeman, Anthony and Sutherland, Keith (Editors) (1999) *The Volitional Brain: Towards a Neuroscience of Free Will*, Imprint Academic.
34. Hanlon, Michael in *Daily Mail* (Newspaper, UK) 17th April 2008.
35. Engel, Pascal (1994). Quoted in Dupuy, Jean-Pierre (1999) *ibid.*
36. Clarke, D.S. (Editor) (2004) *Panpsychism: past and Recent Selected Readings*, State University of New York Press.
37. Wallace, B. Alan (2000) *ibid.*
38. Sperry, Roger (1994) *ibid.*
39. Sperry, Roger (1994) *ibid.*
40. Crick, Francis (1994) *The Astonisihing Hypothesis: The Scientific Search for the Soul*, Simon and Schuster.

41. Changeaux, Jean-Pierre (1986) *Neuronal Man*, English Translation, Oxford University Press.

42. Depraz, Natalie "When Transcendental Genesis Encounters the Naturalisation Project". In Jean Petitot, Francisco J. Varela, Bernard Pachoud and Jean-Michel Roy (Editors) (1999) *Naturalising Phenomenology: Issues in Contemporary Phenomenology and Cognitive Science*, Stanford University Press.

43-48. Crick, Francis (1994) *ibid.*

49. Thompson, Richard, L. (1981) *Mechanistic and Nonmechanistic Science: An Investigation into the Nature of Consciousness and Form,* The Bhaktivedanta Book Trust.

50. Crick, Francis (1994) *ibid.*

51. Edelman, Gerald M. and Tononi, Giulio "Reentry and the Dynamic Core: Neural Correlates of Conscious Experience". In Thomas Metzinger (Editor) (2000) *Neural Correlates of Consciousness: Empirical and Conceptual Questions*, MIT Press.

52-57. Edelman, Gerald M. and Tononi, Giulio (2000) *ibid.*

58. Goodwin, Brian C. (1994) *How the Leopard Changed its Spots: The Evolution of Complexity*, Charles Scribner.

59. Humphrey, Nicholas "The Privatisation of Sensation". In Stuart R. Hameroff, Alfred W. Kaszniak, and David J. Chalmers (Editors) (1999) *Toward a Science of Consciousness III: The Third Tucson Discussions and Debates.* MIT Press.

60-9. Humphrey, Nicholas (1999) *ibid.*

70. Freeman, Walter J. (1999) *ibid.*

71. Clarke, D.S. (Editor) (2004) *ibid.*

72. Metzinger, Thomas [1] (2000) *ibid.*

73. Metzinger, Thomas [2] "The *Subjectivity* of Subjective Experience: A Representative Analysis of the First- Person Perspective". In Thomas Metzinger (Editor) (2000) *Neural Correlates of Consciousness: Empirical and Conceptual Questions*, MIT Press.

74. Metzinger, Thomas [2] (2000) *ibid.*

75. Forman, Robert, K.C. (1999) *Mysticism, Mind, Consciousness*, State University of New York Press.

76-80. Metzinger, Thomas [2] (2000) *ibid.*

81. Varela, Francisco J. and Shear, Jonathan (Editors) (1999) *The View From Within: First-person approaches to the study of consciousness,* Imprint Academic.

82. Vermersch, Pierre "Introspection as Practice". In Francisco, J. Varela and Jonathan Shear (Editors) (1999) *The View From Within: First-person approaches to the study of consciousness,* Imprint Academic.

83. Depraz, Natalie "The Phenomenological Reduction as *Praxis*". In Francisco, J. Varela and Jonathan Shear (Editors) (1999) *The View From Within: First-person approaches to the study of consciousness,* Imprint Academic.

84. Petitmengin-Peugeot, Claire "The Intuitive Experience". In Francisco J. Varela and Jonathan Shear (Editors) (1999) *The View From Within: First-person approaches to the study of consciousness,* Imprint Academic.

85-91. Metzinger, Thomas [2] (2000) *ibid.*
92. Begley, Sharon (2007) *ibid.*
93-102. Metzinger, Thomas [2] (2000) *ibid.*
103. Margolis, Joseph (2003) *The Unravelling of Scientism: American Philosophy at the End of the Twentieth Century*, Cornell University Press.
104. Lakoff, George and Johnson, Mark (1999) *ibid.*
105. Bailey, Andrew R. (1999) *ibid.*
106. Kelso, J.A. Scott (1999) *Dynamic Patterns: The Self-Organisation of Brain and Behavior*, MIT Press.
107. Thompson, E., Noe, Alva and Pessoa, Luiz "Perceptual Completion: A case Study in Phenomenology and Cognitive Science." In Jean Petitot, Francisco J. Varela, Bernard Pachoud and Jean-Michel Roy (Editors) (1999) *Naturalising Phenomenology: Issues in Contemporary Phenomenology and Cognitive Science*, Stanford University Press.
108. Thompson, E., Noe, Alva and Pessoa, Luiz (1999) *ibid.*
109. Herbert, Nick (1993) *Elemental Mind: Human Consciousness and the New Physics*, Dutton.
110. Thompson, E., Noe, Alva and Pessoa, Luiz (1999) *ibid.*
111. Thompson, E., Noe, Alva and Pessoa, Luiz (1999) *ibid.*
112. Hunt, Harry T. (1995) *ibid.*
113. Seager, William "Consciousness, Information and Panpsychism". In Jonathan Shear (Editor) (1997) *Explaining Consciousness*, MIT Press.
114. Schwartz, Jeffrey M. and Begley, Sharon (2002) *The Mind and the Brain: Neuroplasticity and the Power of Mental Force*, Regan Books (Harper Collins).
115. Tart, Charles, T. "Transpersonal Psychology and Methodologies for a Comprehensive Science of Consciousness". In Stuart R. Hameroff, Alfred W. Kaszniak, and Alwyn C. Scott (Editors) (1998) *Toward a Science of Consciousness II: The Second Tucson Discussions and Debates*, MIT Press.
116. Schwartz, Jeffrey M. and Begley, Sharon (2002) *ibid.*
117. Singer, Wolf "Phenomenal Awareness and Consciousness from a Neurobiological Perspective". In Thomas Metzinger (Editor) (2000) *Neural Correlates of Consciousness: Empirical and Conceptual Questions*, MIT Press.
118. Singer, Wolf (2000) *ibid.*
119. Singer, Wolf (2000) *ibid.*
120. *See for instance* Globus, Gordon "Derrida and the Quantum Brain". In Gordon Globus (2003) *Quantum Closure and Disclosures: Thinking-together postphenomenology and quantum brain dynamics*, John Benjamins.
121. Hunt, Harry T. (1995) *ibid.*
122. Hunt, Harry T. (1995) *ibid.*
123. Pickering, John "Words and Silence". In Francisco J. Varela and Jonathan Shear (Editors) (1999) *The View From Within: First-person approaches to the study of consciousness,* Imprint Academic.
124. Laughlin, Charles D. "Biogenetic Structural Theory and the Neurophenomenology of Consciousness". In Stuart R. Hameroff, Alfred W. Kaszniak,

and David J. Chalmers (Editors) (1999) *Toward a Science of Consciousness III: The Third Tucson Discussions and Debates.* MIT Press.

125. Greyson, Bruce "Near-Death Experiences". In Etzel Cardeña, Steven Jay Lynn, and Stanley Krippner (Editors) (2000) *Varieties of Anomalous Experience: Examining the Scientific Evidence*, American Psychological Association.

126. Potter David, Dalai Lama *et al.* "Dialogue". In Daniel Goleman and Robert A.F. Thurman (Editors) (1991) *Mind Science: An East-West Dialogue (The Harvard Mind Science Symposium)*, Wisdom Books.

127. James, William (1890) *The Principles of Psychology: Authorised Edition (Two Volumes)*, Dover.

128. Dalai Lama "Understanding and Transforming the Mind". In B. Alan Wallace (Editor) (2003) *Buddhism and Science: Breaking New Ground*, Columbia University Press.

129. Varela, Francisco J. (Editor) (1997) *Sleeping, Dreaming and Dying: An Exploration of Consciousness with The Dalai Lama*, Wisdom Publications.

130. Persinger, Michael (1987) *Neuropsychological Bases of God Beliefs*, Praeger.

131-33. Persinger, Michael (1987) *ibid.*

134. Hesse, Mary "Hermeticism and History: An apology for the internal history of science" in *Historical and Philosophical Perspectives of Science* (1970) edited by R.H. Steuer, University of Minnesota Press.

135-38. Persinger, Michael (1987) *ibid.*

139. Dalai Lama (2003) *ibid.*

140. Persinger, Michael (1987) *ibid.*

141. Radin, Dean (2006) *Entangled Minds: Extrasensory Experiences in a Quantum Reality*, Paraview and Pocket Books (Simon and Schuster).

142-47. Persinger, Michael (1987) *ibid.*

148. Joseph, Rhawn "Sex, Violence and Religious Experience". In Rhawn Joseph (Editor) (2002) *NeuroTheology: Brain, Science, Spirituality, Religious Experience*, University Press, California.

149. Bakan, David (1958) *Sigmund Freud and the Jewish Mystical Tradition*, D. Van Nostrand Company.

150. Stevens, Anthony (2002) *Archetype Revisited: An Updated Natural History of the Self* (2nd Edn), Brunner-Routledge (Taylor and Francis).

151-56. Persinger, Michael (1987) *ibid.*

6

New Age Misunderstandings of the Science-Mysticism Inter-relationship

Gopi Krishna, Fritjof Capra, M-L. Von Franz and Richard Jones on Science and Mysticism

The 'Evolution of Consciousness' myth: separating grain from chaff

Heisenberg's close friend and colleague, Carl von Weizsäcker was an eminent astrophysicist who worked on nuclear fusion in stars and was the brother of German President Richard von Weizsäcker. Weizsäcker expressed his view that the Indian concept of *Prana* or Life Energy was compatible with Physics. He was a friend of Indian Kundalini Yoga exponent Gopi Krishna, writing a lengthy foreword containing Weizsäcker's own views, for Krishna's little book *The Biological Basis of Religion and Genius* (1971) which was of about equal length to Krishna's own 64 pp. text. Heisenberg also met with Gopi Krishna[1]. Unfortunately the copy of Krishna's book I bought for research does not contain the foreword. As with Heisenberg, Weizsäcker's focus was on energy rather than Consciousness, seeing Oneness in a homogeneous sea of energy as the source of all physical phenomena[2]. I would comment that energy actually has more to do with the differentiation of the underlying Oneness of Formless Pure Consciousness. The authoritative understanding of *Prana* is that it is a correlate of the *Atman*; i.e., so-called 'Life Energy' is in fact the energy aspect of the Inner Light. Weizsäcker became head of a new organisation in Starnberg called "Eastern Wisdom and Western Science"[3].

However in *The Biological Basis of Religion and Genius*, Krishna peddles primarily the self-aggrandising myth of the 'Evolution of Consciousness' claiming that, as the human brain is still evolving, the revelations of prophets and sages are "not the product of a normal mind, but of a consciousness still far beyond the capacity of the normal human brain". He also interprets the experience of the so-called 'rising of the Kundalini energy' up the spine as semen travelling up the spine to nourish the brain cells[4]. These claims are totally unscientific gibberish and, not surprisingly, no attempt was made to validate them! We saw in Chapter 3 the "Innate Capacity" argument which is based on the testimony of the more intellectual, philosophically-sophisticated mystics which contradicts this Evolution of Consciousness myth. New Agers who peddle this Evolution of Consciousness myth assume falsely that Evolution is teleological, (i.e., reaching towards a final goal or purpose). They also do not understand the meaning of biological evolution. They claim that enlightened individuals are more evolved than others and the frequency of such enlightened people in the population increases as mankind evolves. This is utter nonsense. Evolution does not occur in individuals within their own lifetimes but in populations across generations through biological reproduction. Evolution of a new subspecies usually occurs amongst isolated breeding groups of a species who transmit their peculiarities to their offspring. Even socio-cultural transmission of meditative techniques for attaining enlightenment to an increasing number of people does not constitute creation of a new subspecies of human. Enlightenment does not entail some sort of brain-mind evolution, quite the opposite in fact; it actually involves a sort of regression to a simpler, more primitive form of Consciousness.

We have also seen that, the far more scholarly, Aurobindo Ghose also peddled a version of the Evolution of Consciousness myth with his Gnostic Supermen as the progenitors of the future evolution of humanity. The notion of Supermen is most closely associated with Friedrich Nietzsche[N1] who ended up insane and whose ideas influenced Nazism. Nietzsche reinterpreted ancient philosophical notions using Spencerian views of 'survival of the fittest' and declared that a man of science declares his independence from philosophy. Although not denying the possibility that a *metaphysical world* did exist, he thought that Metaphysics originated in dreams which were mistaken to be a second real world. The notion of the Transcendental was a worthless self-deception as all that one could say about it was that it was an inaccessible, incomprehensible other being[5]. Nietzsche admired the elitism of Hindu caste ideology as reflecting the natural order as opposed to the Christian imposition of false egalitarian morality myths. Christian morality fables inverted the true character of Spirit and its Will to Power within us. His view remained naively teleological in that everything was moving toward a *goal*. In *Daybreak* (1881) Nietzsche wrote (*emphasis mine* {*e.m.*})[6]:

> *Formerly one sought the feeling of the grandeur of man by pointing to his divine origin: this has now become a forbidden way, for at its portal stands the ape... One therefore now tries the opposite direction:* ***the way mankind is going shall serve as proof of its*** *grandeur and* ***kinship with God.***

Aurobindo's view was also influenced by the European Romantics' temporalisation of the NeoPlatonic levels of Being culminating in an Universal Gnosis for all Mankind; a reinterpretation of Judaeo-Christian Historicism with its End of the World mythology[7]. The Theosophists *superimposed Evolution upon Reincarnation* mythology which was transformed from a Karmic punishment for those failing to attain 'Release' from the 'Cycle of Rebirths' into a positive process of spiritual advancement[8]. Aurobindo studied Western Classics and his understanding of Science left much to be desired.

Many people, including Karl Marx, misinterpreted biological evolution as being teleological (goal-directed). However, Aurobindo's understanding of Divine Inspiration linked to the *Akasa* was useful for those interested in establishing the facts. Western parapsychologists do not mention that their Ganzfield (sensory deprivation) techniques used to induce such phenomena were actually inspired by Indian yogic knowledge that mental activity must be stilled to reveal Akashic information.

The Evolution of Consciousness myth is also found in Richard Bucke's 1901 *Cosmic Consciousness* (a 'New Age classic'). Bucke argued absurdly that the Ancient Greeks could only perceive three or four colours because ancient texts such as those of Xenophanes knew of only three colours of the rainbow (purple, red and yellow) and Democritus only mentioned four colours (black, white, red and yellow). According to Bucke, even Aristotle spoke of the tricolored rainbow[9]. Bucke believed human consciousness had evolved dramatically in but three millennia! Nonetheless such pseudo-scientific nonsense has had a big influence on the US New Age movement as is reflected in Philip Goldberg's recent *American Veda* in which a number of prominent Americans, influenced by 'Vedanta-Yoga', profess their belief in one form or another of the Evolution of Consciousness[10]. In 2007 Gopi Krishna's original US publisher Gene Keiffer, whilst correctly rubbishing recent works like the reductionist "Neurotheology" of Andrew Newberg, peddled hyperbole to me about how nobody understood the true relationship between Science and Mysticism as well as Gopi Krishna had done. He seemed to be implying that I myself could not possibly have a better understanding than his old friend Gopi had without knowing anything about me[11].

Such exaggerated claims are not uncommon amongst New Agers in their 'incestuous' circles. The Evolution of Consciousness views of Aurobindo, Bucke and Ken Wilber are cited approvingly in the 2004 book *Science and the Akashic Field: An Integral Theory of Everything* by New Ager Ervin Laszlo. Laszlo includes a picture depicting his name alongside Newton, Darwin (whom Laszlo mistakenly associates with Herbert Spencer's notion of "Survival of the Fittest"), Einstein and (Sigmund) Freud (whom Laszlo mistakes for a great scientific mind – *see Ch. 9*). Beneath the name 'LASZLO' is written "coherent fine-tuned interconnected whole", implying that Ervin Laszlo first revealed this aspect of the universe to humanity[12]. What actual achievements justify this incredible claim remains unspecified! Laszlo says that he is a philosopher and 'Systems Theorist'. But as Fritjof Capra asserted correctly, 'Systems Theory' is a misnomer as it is not a scientific theory but a point of view or a framework[13]. Systems Theory is a fancy name for wishy-washy holistic speculation which usually involves confusing vaguely defined abstract concepts such as ecosystems and societies as being equivalent to actual unitary 'wholes' such as cells and organisms. Thus one finds Systems thinkers speculating that an ecosystem constitutes a sentient whole even though an 'ecosystem' is merely a conceptual superimposition overlaid on Nature. If you asked different ecologists to define the boundaries of a particular ecosystem, it is unlikely that any two of them would concur as; like a 'country', an 'ecosystem' is a human construct.

In fact the central integrating idea in Laszlo's book is the same idea as the so-called 'Morphic Resonance' notion used by Rupert Sheldrake (who is not mentioned) which, as Arthur Ellison[14] and Suzanne Padfield[15] have pointed out is actually Patanjali's notion of vibratory resonance in the *Akasa*. Yoga *Sutra* IV.9 states[16]:

There is a relation of cause and effect even though separated by class, locality and time because memory and impressions are the same in form.

In regard to teaching the world about universal interconnectedness, a non-Eurocentric and impartial jury would surely list Siddharta Gautama and the Indian Buddhists who developed the notion of Dependent Co-Origination (*pratitya samutpadha*) as the great geniuses. Furthermore, Laszlo gives an erroneous interpretation of the status of the Vedantic Akasha, presenting it as ontologically prior to Consciousness. Laszlo states[17]:

In Indian philosophy the ultimate end of the physical world is a return to Akasha, its original subtle-energy womb. ...In Akasha, all attributes of the manifest world merge into a state that is beyond attributes: the state of Brahman.

Akasha or 'subtle energy' is not the Ultimate Reality in Vedanta from which the universe arises. The Ultimate Reality is Pure Formless Consciousness (*nirguna Brahman*) and Akasha is the 'first created element' (corresponding to the Neoplatonic *Nous*). Consciousness is primary. Yet on the front cover of this self-aggrandising and misleading pop philosophy book we have a quote from Indo-American New Ager Deepak Chopra, M.D.[18]:

The most brilliant, comprehensive, and intellectually satisfying integral theory of everything that I have ever read.... transcends the vision of Darwin, Newton, Einstein, the quantum pioneers, and many other scientific giants of history.

The traditional association of enlightenment with dying was not alluring to Western New Agers with their Evolution of Consciousness mythology and their focus on material profit. The Transcendental Meditation organisation completely misinterpreted the EEG slow wave coherence they found associated with enlightenment to mean that this indicated global integration of brain functions. Peter Fenwick has discussed the claims of TM-sponsored EEG researchers that EEG Coherence implied increased ordering of brain areas, pointing out that such EEG Coherence occurs in schizophrenia, epileptic seizure, delta coma and even during death[19]. EEG Coherence is simply the degree to which the frequency profiles of scalp electrodes are similar[20]. Of course, a deep understanding of perennial mystical knowledge of Enlightenment totally contradicts such global brain integration myths. As the Buddhists state, enlightenment is attained by 'Stopping the Mind' not by integrating mental functions[21]. On 8th October 2012 *Newsweek* told the story of a Harvard neurosurgeon Dr Eben Alexander who supposedly experienced 'Heaven' after his cerebral cortex had stopped functioning due to bacterial meningitis. NDEs certainly do not involve global integration of brain function! The Light is consistently described as the background field underlying mental phenomena. We have seen that certain Gnostics described Sophia (the Cosmic Light of Wisdom) as full of infinite ideas [NP&G]. The Divine Wisdom is inherent in the Light of Pure Consciousness in its *Prajna* aspect as 'Luminous Wisdom Consciousness'. These facts once again underline the total inconsistency of New Age pop philosophy which peddles such obvious errors whilst heaping totally undeserved praise on many of its hyped-up 'leading lights' who are, in fact, neither true 'pioneers' nor 'great philosopher-scientists'.

Haanegraaf says that the New Age movement is a trivialised and commercialised travesty of real esotericism[23]. There is much truth in this assertion although there is also some grain hidden amidst the New Age chaff. The rapid advances in Molecular Biology after the 1939-45 war were partly due to more 'hard-nosed' investigators from Physics entering Biology and developing more powerful investigative tools. These ex-physicists were partly put off Physics by the horrors of Hiroshima and Nagasaki. They were also inspired to study living organisms by Erwin Schrödinger's little book *What is Life* (1944) in which he wrote that the understanding of Life might require new 'Laws of Physics'[24]. This influx of talent from the 'hard sciences' revolutionised Biology although this also led to a totally Reductionist misrepresentation of Life as merely molecular interactions. Only a few bio-physicists such as Mae-Wan Ho have dared to pursue an unorthodox 'Quantum-Biological' research programme in which the organism is understood as a coherent spatiotemporal manifestation from deeper-level activities of vibratory, field-like coherent excitations co-ordinating the activity of vast numbers of semi-autonomous biomolecules, organelles and organs[25]. As discussed in my O/OM, a true understanding of *Life,* (i.e., being *alive*) has more to do with *energy* as was recognised in traditional philosophies in both East and West. *A dead cell and a dead body still contain DNA*! What differentiates a dead organism from a living one is not the presence of DNA, nor simply the normal functioning of macromolecules, but flows of energy which both sustain such activities and help co-ordinate them through subtle field processes.

Physicist Wolfgang Pauli, trying to make sense of his personal experiences, complained about the *lack of scientific education amongst Carl Jung's inner circle* {*e.m.*}[26]. Jungian analyst David Lindorff's 2004 book on Pauli and Jung[27], from which this information is taken, culminates in highly tenuous Jungian Dream Analysis and numerological speculations concerning Pauli's dreams which are of no real scientific interest. However, even hard scientists such as William Tiller, a Stanford Materials Science professor gets carried away in sometimes rather wild flights of fantasy in his New Age book *Science and Human Transformation: Subtle Energies, Intentionality and Consciousness*[28]. Similar flights of fantasy are common in New Age writings by scientists, medics and academic philosophers as in the Atlantis and Lemuria myths in *Vibrational Medicine* by Richard Gerber, M.D.[29] and the ludicrous Galactic Destiny final chapter in academic philosopher Mark Woodhouse's *Paradigm Wars*[30]. Historian of Science, Mary Hesse tells us that, contrary to the sterilised historiography of the Democritan-Archimedean tradition, most of the founding fathers of modern Science were actually dabbling in the occult[31]. Contrary to the Logocentric and Eurocentric Classics and Scientific History, modern Science arose more from 'Magic' (Occultism) with its observations, experiment and seeking underlying principles than from Logic[32]. The first modern scientific work, William Gilbert's *De magnete* expresses the view that the magnetic force is animate and like a soul[33]. Thus whereas the likes of British biologists Lewis Wolpert and Richard Dawkins rubbish New Age ideas in an uncritical knee-jerk manner, we need to learn from history and understand that scientific understanding of Consciousness and Spirituality needs careful separation of the 'baby from the bathwater'.

Emergentist caricatures of Eastern mysticism by Capra and Buddhophiles

Heisenberg revealed his subconscious Indian mystic influence and discussions with Tagore in an interview with physicist Fritjof Capra, famous for his 1975 pop philosophy bestseller *The Tao of Physics: An exploration of the parallels between modern physics and Eastern mysticism*. Capra had difficulty finding a publisher. It was first published by a small start-up UK publisher Wildwood House after 12 publishers rejected it[34]. It was not the first book to explore such parallels as Talbot's aforementioned *Mysticism and the New Physics* had been delayed by its publishers. In fact, as we have seen Whiteman had published his highly scholarly *Philosophy of Space and Time and the Inner Constitution of Nature* in 1967. Whiteman had already gone beyond Capra's mere finding of parallels to asserting, on the basis of personal experience of transcendental realms, that meditation actually revealed the 'Transcendental Substructure of Nature' which Quantum Mechanics indicated. Whereas, Capra denied the Primacy of Consciousness (whilst presupposing it tacitly), Whiteman recognised the fact of an Universal Consciousness transcending appearances in Space and Time which was also the real core of our consciousness, (i.e., confirming the Vedantic notion of the *Atman-Brahman*)[35]. The Vedanta Society of the USA had published a small monograph exploring such parallels in the 1950s in *Vedanta and the West*, the magazine founded by Aldous Huxley, Christopher Isherwood and Gerald Heard (*see below*)[36]. J.P. McKinney in 1953 had published an article in *Philosophy East and West* arguing that Quantum Mechanics (QM) brings the West closer to the Eastern view. J.J. Clarke states that such ideas go back, further, to the 1930s to Jung's collaboration with Pauli[37]. We have seen that Schrödinger and Heisenberg were themselves aware of such parallels back in the 1920s. In fact the 19th Century Theosophists also sought to integrate Indian spirituality with Science and Philosophy with supporters including Thomas Edison. The famous inventor of the alternating current (and radio technology) Nikola Tesla was deeply interested in Vedic and Vedantic knowledge and even used terms like *akasa* and *prana* in his descriptions of natural phenomena. Dobson says that Tesla, influenced by Vivekananda and the Tantric understanding of matter as energetic manifestations, wanted to demonstrate the energetic basis of matter before Einstein's 1905 mass-energy equivalence[38,39].

Capra used to gripe about how his own university library, the radical UC Berkeley, refused to stock his book as it was not scholarly. To be fair to Berkeley library, for all Capra's praiseworthy efforts in publicising the parallels between the New Physics and Eastern mysticism, *The Tao of Physics* was an unscholarly pop philosophy book. No explanation was given as to what Yoga actually entailed in scientific or phenomenological terms. Having no acquaintance with Yoga myself, when I read it in 1990 I could not understand where Eastern philosophy was coming from. How was it actually derived? In regard to his choice of title, the Chinese concept of *Tao* as the ineffable One, the unchanging essence of all things, does not seem to include Consciousness.[N2] In fact, in his chapter on Vedanta Capra did not mention once that *Brahman* is described primarily as Pure Consciousness! This omission is misleading and important even though Capra is seeking thc parallels between Physics and Mysticism rather than the differences. Rather Capra stuck to his Taoist focus on Energy as the underlying Oneness in which every 'material' thing is actually just a dynamic web of relations such that everything is inseparable from the whole universe[40]. Capra's view resembled Weizsäcker's Physicalist 'ocean of energy' view. As with Plotinus, Capra tacitly presupposes the existence of Awareness as one cannot *know* or *experience* the One or the *Tao* without Awareness.

In the 1975 epilogue to *Tao of Physics*, Capra states that he thinks that any question of the possibility of mutual influence between Science and Mysticism, or even a synthesis, have to be answered in the negative. He saw Science and Mysticism as two complementary manifestations of the human mind, extreme manifestations of its rational and intuitive faculties[41]. Capra's 1982 epilogue to *Tao of Physics* ends with a clear statement of his Physicalist presuppositions and hence his failure to come to terms with Consciousness which is the primary stuff or Ground of all Being in many, if not most, systems of Eastern mystical philosophy. Capra states {*e.m.*}[42]:

> *Finally, both approaches recognise that* ***consciousness*** *may be an essential aspect of the universe that will have to be included* ***in a future theory of physical phenomena****. Such a future theory may well arise from the merging of theories of Bohm and Chew, which represent two of the most imaginative and philosophically profound approaches to* ***physical reality****.*

Capra is asserting that Consciousness is a physical phenomenon (both 'physical' and 'phenomenon' are incorrect labels for Consciousness (Awareness)).

Capra is not a 'Materialist, as he stresses that all things, physical forces and matter, are mutually inter-related forms of energy, forming a sort of 'web of relations'. In a 1982 interview entitled *The Tao of Physics Revisited* he stressed that in his (then) new book *The Turning Point* he presented his Systems Theory view and stressed the strong influence of Ken Wilber on his own ideas[43]. However, in response to notions of a Universal Consciousness, Capra stated[44]:

> *I think the awareness starts with living organisms, biological organisms. At a very high level of complexity, we have self-awareness, we have consciousness, organisms being aware of themselves as thinking, feeling beings.*

A quick search on the Internet shows that, in Capra's 1996 book *The Web of Life*[45], Capra presents a naive 'Systems Theory' Emergence view in which he claims that the Whole contains new 'Emergent Properties' *irreducible* to its parts. Strictly speaking, this is a *misuse of the term 'emergence'*. We have seen in Chapter 5 Francis Crick's differentiation of two different usages of 'emergence'. Strict 'emergence' implies that the higher-level 'emergent' property remains *reducible in principle* to established Physics but our theories are not sophisticated enough to predict them. Capra's use is a philosophically naive conflation of such ***epistemological* unpredictability** with ***ontology*** (a new irreducible property suddenly appears with no connection to what was assumed to exist previously). Thus Capra presents himself as an 'Emergent Physicalist' imagining Consciousness to appear (magically or *ex nihilo*) within an (insentient) Physical universe. In truth his position is actually a not very subtle appeal to Dualism (whereas mainstream 'reducible emergence' uses a thicker blanket, (i.e., supposed reducibility to Physics) to disguise its magical Dualism.

More recently Buddhophile Western writers such as anthropologist Charles Laughlin[46], neurologist James Austin (*Zen and the Brain*[47]) and 'neuro-phenomenologist' and friend of the Dalai Lama, Francisco Varela[48, 49], have made grand statements referring to profound Eastern transcendental knowledge such as the interconnectedness of all things. But in the next breath, these very same Westerners reduce such Eastern transcendental knowledge to facile and (tacitly Eurocentric) Emergent Materialist and Emergent Physicalist travesties and caricatures, invoking fashionable notions of systems theory etc. I say 'tacitly Eurocentric' as these Westerners are assuming that the actual metaphysics developed by the Easterners such as the Brahmanic Primacy of Consciousness cannot be correct! But, as I show in this book, the Primacy of Consciousness is the correct ontology, the only one that can actually account for Consciousness. This tacit Eurocentrism is related to the notion of 'Institutional Racism' which sociologists in Britain say arises due to the whole nexus of cultural assumptions including the Eurocentric presentations of world history. Even liberals imbibe such prejudices and pander unwittingly to such racist preconceptions. Western academia often conflates 'European' erroneously with 'scientific' as in the case of the myths peddled by the likes of Max Muller and Sigmund Freud (*see Ch. 9*). Yet the New Age movement, as obsessed with celebrity as any pop cultural movement, lionised Capra and his 1975 book.[N3]

Richard Jones' scholarly superficialities of spacetime, spiritual substance and scientific structures

The 'Capra-style' juxtaposition of seemingly parallel descriptions of Physics and Eastern traditions and the much more 'wild' speculations that typified the vast majority of New Age writings can easily be dismissed as uncritical 'pop philosophy'. There were a few more scholarly attempts to address such questions. For instance, in 1986 the Canadian academic philosopher, Richard H. Jones published a scholarly book entitled *Science and Mysticism: A Comparative Study of Western Natural Science, Theravada Buddhism and Advaita Vedanta*[50]. As with Capra's book, I basically overlooked this book when it came to writing up my Science-Mysticism integration ideas in the 1990s as it had nothing useful to say. The author's misunderstanding of the ontology of Physics precluded any possibility of Transcendentalism as he mistook Einstein's highly idealised mathematical model of a Space-Time continuum for the ultimate stuff of reality in Physics and as the primary reality. Jones asserts that matter and energy are just concentration vortices in it. In fact, as we have seen, our mundane Space and Time emerge in conjunction with the appearance of material phenomena from the deeper nonlocal, holonomic vibratory energetic activity of the transcendental realm. As Capra noted correctly, *energy* is the ultimate stuff of Reality in Physics. The Space-Time continuum is merely a manmade construct, misrepresenting Time as a Space-like dimension, superimposed on Nature for mathematical convenience. Jones' is guilty of what Whitehead labelled the Fallacy of Misplaced Concreteness, mistaking a conceptual abstraction for Reality.

In regard to the aforementioned, Holographic metaphor of Pribram and Bohm, Thompson concludes that it may be a 20th Century version of the analogy that the world is the wave-phenomena of an ocean of Pure Awareness and no more and no less explanatory[51]. Contrary to the ontological naivety and lack of insight exhibited by Jones, we have seen already that such holonomic models can in fact begin to explain the self-organisational emergence of the so-called Laws of Nature! Furthermore, I would challenge anyone to put forward an ontological explanation that can truly account for Consciousness, not based on this picture. Time and space does not permit me providing an *argument by elimination* of all rival viewpoints. But, we saw in the last chapter that most seemingly diverse Physicalist hypotheses can be reduced to deeper 'Inherent Behaviorism' with a tacit Dualist recourse to Magic labelled as 'Emergence'. Even the supposedly 'Panpsychist' views of Whitehead and others, which deny an underlying Ground of Pure Awareness, are actually forms of Pan-Emergentism where the magical creation of Awareness occurs with every individuated phenomenon from an electron upwards (*see Ch.10*). That leaves overt Substance Dualism as the only alternative (*see Ch.11*). In fact, as Willis Harman pointed out correctly, although the holographic theories appear to make more plausible the Space-Time transcending psychic and mystical phenomena, they still interpret the primary datum, Consciousness, in terms of something ultimately quantifiable. Harman looked forward to a new science in which Consciousness is more nearly cause than effect stating that the holographic theories remain part of the old science which attempts to explain away Consciousness rather than understand it[52].

Jones's principal conclusion is as follows[53]:

> *...even the more modest claim that "modern physics lends some support" to the "mystical vision" cannot be accepted. As was concluded under the previous topics, scientific theories about the subatomic realms cannot justify mystical mindfulness in principle either;*

Jones' view is simply the consequence of his own misunderstanding of both Physics and Mysticism; we have seen that actual mathematical physicist and mystic J.H. M. Whiteman recognised that that the metaphysical interpretation of QM (indicating a Wave Structure underlying Matter) gives indirect knowledge of the Transcendental Substructure of Nature which can be known directly through meditation[54]. Nonetheless, in a manner resembling Petitot's distinction between the *substance* of reality and the (dynamical) *law-like structure* of phenomena, Jones suggests a way of reconciling Science and Mysticism. The unstructured, non-objectifiable depth-reality is the "substance" or "being" of the realm of structures, both material and mental.

He adds that Mysticism does not abolish the diversity of structures, but sees objects in relation to 'beingness'[55].

Von Franz on the Hindu God-image of Modern Physics

Marie-Louise von Franz, a famous student of Jung, was also associated with Wolfgang Pauli. Pauli went to Princeton in 1940 and later became a US citizen before returning to Switzerland. In her collection of essays entitled *Psyche and Matter* she, like Bohm and Peat, focuses on Synchronicity and the Psychoid realm as the bridge between Mind and Matter[56]. Von Franz mentions the 1974 book by French philosopher of science Raymond Ruyer entitled *La Gnose de Princeton* (The Gnostics of Princeton). I see that the Wikipedia entry for Ruyer claims that *La Gnose*, Ruyer's most popular book, was a hoax as it (supposedly) presented Ruyer's own Panpsychist philosophy under the guise of being the view of some unnamed Princeton physicists. Ruyer wrote that some physicists at Princeton held metaphysical views resembling the Hindu concept of *Maya*. Matter is an external image created by sense perception whereas our direct perception of ourselves or 'inwardness' reveals our true nature[57]. This is similar to (Cambridge astrophysicist) Eddington's argument in *The Nature of the Physical World* discussed in Chapter 9. According to Ruyer's 'Gnostic physicists' our corporeal existence is only an illusion created by sense perception or observation. We also possess another faculty for acquiring knowledge consisting of participating in trans-spatial themes. Ruyer calls such trans-spatial themes 'superindividual domains' which are part of a Universal Consciousness. Science reveals the world of participation but Science can only see it from its observable side, (i.e., empirical reality)[58].

This may indeed be Raymond Ruyer's personal philosophy but we should not dismiss the claims that similar views are also held by distinguished physicists (regardless of whether they are at Princeton or not). The Scientific and Medical Network is an international network of open-minded scientists, engineers, medical doctors, philosophers and others who share an interest in such 'New Age' style questions about the relationship between Science and Mysticism or Spirituality. When I was a member in 1998 to 2001 it had a few Nobel laureate members. The membership list needs to be kept secret as the Western academic establishment still retains its Christian Scholastic character weeding out 'heretics' who refuse to abide by the dogma. A public expression of interest in Mysticism can be damaging to a scientist's or a medic's career[N4] hence it tends to be retired professors or those with Nobel laureates who speak openly on such matters in the West (as we saw with Nobel laureate George Wald's comments at the 1986 Bombay conference). We have seen that the "Shut-up-and-calculate" taboo on questioning orthodox assumptions holds sway in academic research in Physics. Similarly, Ramanujan's atheistic patron at Cambridge G.H. Hardy, could not understand the claims of the great mathematical genius from India that his insights came to him through Yoga and so Ramanujan kept silent on these matters in England[59].

Marie-Louise von Franz, says[60]:

The God of modern physicists resembles more the God-image of Hinduism, or generally of the Far East, and has been, as Ruyer points out, actually influenced by it.

Robert Oppenheimer was Director of the Institute of Advanced Study at Princeton, the USA's premier centre for Physics, where during the McCarthy witch-hunt he was suspected of being a Communist sympathiser and David Bohm was forced to resign. Previously he had been the Director of the Manhattan Project which led to the building of the first atomic bomb. His interest in Indian Philosophy was clear from his writing that ancient Indian Buddhist logic was too sophisticated for the Europeans of the 17th and 18th Centuries to comprehend[N5 61]. Oppenheimer had studied Sanskrit at Berkeley and called the *Bhagavad Gita* the most beautiful song existing in any known tongue. He said that the *Gita* was one of the books that shaped his philosophy of life and read from it at the memorial for Franklin D. Roosevelt[62]. On witnessing the explosion of the first atomic bomb in New Mexico, Jewish Oppenheimer famously cited lines from the *Gita:*

If the radiance of a thousand suns were to burst at once into the sky, that would be like the splendour of the mighty one.
Now I am become Death, the destroyer of worlds.

False Arguments against Science-Mysticism Integration from Ken Wilber

Wilber's epicyclic model-making and false view of enlightenment as evolution

The afore-mentioned American New Age guru Ken Wilber has been hyped-up in certain New Age circles as the "Einstein of Consciousness". There are no seminal achievements recognised by impartial critical scholars to justify this wild hyperbole. Such ludicrous accolades resemble the vast array of medals paraded by Britain's Prince Charles on his military costumes although he has never actually seen any combat. Wilber is the ex-biochemist turned meditator and prolific writer of paperback pop philosophy mainly under the American Buddhist imprint Shambhala. In the mid-1990s Shambhala were already preparing 'The Collected Works' even though his first book was published in 1977! I recall attending a Scientific and Medical Network meeting in 2000 where a prominent British Wilber acolyte (an ex-banker rather than an actual scientist) who had just returned from the inauguration of Wilber's 'Integral Institute' gave a talk. We were told that just by being in Wilber's presence our speaker could literally sense that he was in the presence of one of the greatest minds in the world. We were then 'privileged' to be shown the latest insightful creation of this 'great mind', a rather simple-looking quadrant diagram. We were supposed to believe that this diagram, looking little different from countless such diagrams displayed at seminars, was actually something remarkably original and profound.

Wilber's quadrant diagram is reproduced in the chapter "The Promise of Integralism: A Critical Appreciation" by Wilber-admirer Christian de Quincey (CdQ) in the book *Cognitive Models and Spiritual Maps* published in 2000. CdQ tells us that it is in fact an ontological mandala[63]. Thus Wilber has based his 'model' on the mandala diagrams created for thousands of years in India and the East. The quadrant mandala has four quarters representing Subjectivity, Objectivity, Inter-Subjectivity and Inter-Objectivity. CdQ points out that Wilber claims repeatedly in his books that unmediated, direct experience of 'the other', (i.e., non-self) is impossible. Wilber stressed that there is only 'Inter-

Subjectivity' which is subject-to-subject connection mediated by language and interpretation, which is the standard Western Physicalist-Materialist view[64]. We have seen that Kant claimed, on false grounds, that unmediated, direct perception was impossible. As CdQ himself indicates, Wilber's view (embodied in his quadrant mandala) *precludes the possibility of unmediated, non-egoic Consciousness* such as true transpersonal empathy and telepathy {*e.m.*}[65]. I would stress that it also precludes Nature Mystical 'oneness' (ego dissolution) with the external world (reported by the likes of Tennyson, Rousseau, Mach, William James and James Austin) and the deeper non-egoic Cosmic Consciousness where one experiences oneness with the universe! CdQ points out that Wilber's orthodox, mediated view of Inter-Subjectivity is *inconsistent with his simultaneous espousal of (Vedantic) Nondualism* as the latter implies that Spirit (Universal Consciousness) would permeate all the quadrants (in an unmediated manner) and make the Inter-Subjectivity quadrant redundant {*e.m.*}[66].

In fact, CdQ goes on to show that *Wilber's models do not even begin to offer a solution to the Mind/Body Problem* and this omission seriously undermines the rational integrity of his 4 quadrant system {*e.m.*}[67]. Wilber's 'solution' to the Mind/Body Problem is to claim that this is solved only by an individual evolving into a Nondual Awakening which transcends the rational mind and includes all the quadrants[68]. In exposing the numerous inconsistencies and failings of Wilber's treatment of this ontological 'hard problem', CdQ says that Wilber's discussion only adds more tangles to the problem rather than helping to unravel it. Wilber's claim to have resolved the Mind/body Problem is, he adds, at best naive and at worst a case of hubris[69]. He also mentions in a footnote that, in *Integral Psychology* Wilber displays a lack of familiarity with issues in (Western) Philosophy of Mind. In a list of influential Philosophers-of-Mind over the previous decade Wilber lists (Radical Darwinian) Nicholas Humphrey (*see Ch. 5*) first[70].

He adds that Wilber seems to be confused about what the 'Mind/Body Problem' actually means, given Wilber's use of the 'felt body' (body as experienced by the mind) resulting in Wilber saying that the 'Body' is in the Mind[71]. Although partially correct here, CdQ's argument is Eurocentric. If we were not bound by Western Physicalist assumptions, a consistent epistemology of what we actually experience would concur with Wilber that the body we know directly is the 'felt body' not an objective physical body (that is only an abstract conception). Wilber's talk of various forms of mind supported by various forms of body implies Mind/Body 'Dualism'. CdQ even refers to Wilber's 'Now you see it, now you don't Mind/Body shuffle' whereby, although claiming that there is no sub-mystical solution Wilber refers to himself as an 'Interactionist' but is explicit that he will not attempt to explain how Mind and Body interact[72]. He also points out that (supposedly Nondualist) Wilber tends to conflate Consciousness with 'Interiority' rather like Non-Idealist Panpsychists (such as Whitehead) who reject a Universal Consciousness[N6 73]. I have labelled this Non-Idealist version of 'Panpsychism' "*Pan-Emergentism*" (*see Ch. 10*) as it is in fact a more logical form of Emergent Physicalism spreading what is actually a Dualist vision of miraculous *ex nihilo* appearance of Awareness across the whole of Nature as emergent processes occur throughout Nature, not just in brains.

In the concluding chapter entitled "Toward a Science of Wholeness" in his *New Metaphysical Foundations of Modern Science* published by the main US New Age organisation (Institute of Noetic Sciences (IONS)), IONS President Willis Harman had urged would-be Consciousness researchers and Holistic scientists to learn from the Indians[74]:

> *India appears to have specialised on inner exploration for longer than any other society. The classical writings go back thousands of years, and modern summaries are available in the writings of Sri Aurobindo, Rabindranath Tagore, Swami Vivekananda and others.*

A little further down he added:

> *The Western concept of scientific causality is easily included in the Indian cosmology as a special case. The reverse is not true;*

As indicated above, New Age hyperbole reflects the tacit Eurocentrism of the Western New Age movement which, whilst paying 'lip service' to Eastern thought, seeks to present themselves as the pioneering geniuses of so-called "Consciousness Studies" or "Transpersonal Psychology" by reformulating in Western terminology mainly Indian ideas first developed in Sanskrit or Pali amongst ancient Indian yogic pioneers. This is related to the so-called 'Elvis syndrome'. Most White people tend to listen to non-European music or ideas if it is 'fronted' by a White face, as in the rise of Elvis Presley who copied Afro-American Rhythm and Blues styles. White America ignored the Black American Blues music until White British Blues imitators such as the Rolling Stones came to the USA and spoke about their Black American idols. Berlinerblau tells us that certain Afro-Americans called Martin Bernal the 'Academic Elvis' as his famous book *Black Athena* included pre-Colonial era knowledge of Afro-Asiatic influences on the Greeks that Black scholars had been emphasising for 100 years. But White academia ignored these facts, exposing the racist myths of 'Classics', until a White man publicised them[75].

In 2000 I was invited to join the Infinity Foundation's 'YogaPsychology' web discussion forum which included most of the top professors of Hinduism and Buddhism in the USA. I recall that they had a discussion 'thread' on Wilber and the general consensus amongst members of the forum was that Wilber's so-called 'Integral Psychology' was largely copied from Aurobindo's Integral Yoga. We have seen that Wilber shies away from any serious attempt to explain the ('hard') Mind/Body Problem claiming that the solution can only be realised in Nondual states of Consciousness. In fact, Ram Shankar Misra in his *Integral Advaitism of Sri Aurobindo* uses repeatedly this same inadequate and unsatisfactory argument that certain assertions of Aurobindo about higher states of Consciousness cannot be explained in any other way, you just have to experience them[76]. Such arguments are unacceptable as someone experiencing such states cannot be relied upon to give an accurate phenomenological description let alone a philosophically and scientifically valid interpretation of it. We have seen the wild flights of fantasy that are published in New Age books. My work undermines such facile fallbacks on the overused excuse of 'ineffability' showing how even authoritative, collectively corroborated, ontological interpretations of Altered State experiences must be cross-corroborated with other lines of evidence which converge on the same conclusions.

In fact, Stanislaw Grof has provided descriptions of experiences in higher states of consciousness in which what was once perceived as Material or 'Matter' dissolves into vibratory patterns of energy and ultimately everything is realised to be manifestations of the One Consciousness[77]. Grof says that he favours the metaphysics of Indian NonDual Kashmir Saivism[78]. Given Tantric Kashmir Saivism's emphasis on the vibratory energy inherent in the ultimate Light of Consciousness, this avoids the tacit dualism of Sankara's *Mayavada* (Doctrine of Illusion). Grof's interpretation is consistent with my own in that 'Matter' is but our perception of stable energetic forms arising out of Universal Nondual Consciousness and this resolves the basic 'Mind/Body Problem' (the relationship between Consciousness and Matter) although more detailed problems are left to be resolved in regard to individuation, etc., CdQ refers to the 'Promissory Idealism' of the likes of Wilber and other 'Idealists' who hold to a view of Spirit, without any trace of Matter, as ultimately real but claim that Matter is created out of it without satisfactory explanation. He recognises that is no better than the Miracle of Emergence in 'Promissory Materialism' which claims that Consciousness appears out of Matter which has no trace of Consciousness in it[79].

In his *Integral Psychology*, CdQ says that Wilber follows the Vedanta (in fact the famous 4 states AUM model of the states of Consciousness from the Mandukya Upanishad) in his use of three 'bodies' each correlated with a type of 'mind'. These are the Gross Body (Waking State), Subtle Body (of Dream States) and the Causal Body (Deep Sleep) state[80]. In the AUM model the Fourth State (*turiya)* is that of mystical union or *moksa* (Liberation). CdQ claims that Wilber's great contribution is to have made a provocative case for extending modern science, a model of Evolution reaching beyond rational creatures all the way to Spirit. CdQ says this also makes a case for integrating modern science with "premodern spiritual wisdom"[81]. As we have seen, this 'Evolution of Consciousness' idea is neither *premodern* nor *spiritual wisdom*; it was a myth invented by the modern Romantics and Theosophists[82]. In discussing Wilber's rehashing of the Evolution of Consciousness, CdQ cites Aurobindo from 1939 and a Gebser from 1985 [83]. CdQ himself is a follower of Whitehead's Process Philosophy. He agrees with Wilber that Whitehead's metaphysics omits the 'Great Chain of Being', (i.e., the Planes of Being/ Consciousness as in Plotinus' Emanationism). In order to incorporate this into Whitehead's metaphysics, CdQ says that we need to augment it with Aurobindo[84]. Note that de Quincey, the self-proclaimed admirer of Wilber's work, turns to the seminal source Aurobindo *not to Wilber*!

Wilber's old-friend turned critic Michel Bauwens states in his web article *The Cult of Ken Wilber* that Wilber's work is essentially based, not on the whole of Spirituality, but on a particular Hindu-Buddhist Nondualist tradition ignoring other forms of mystical philosophies[85]. However, I would disagree very strongly with Bauwens that Wilber has produced a 'masterly synthesis' of this Hindu-Buddhist Nondualism. Aurobindo Ghose produced a masterly work *The Synthesis of Yoga* integrating various Hindu schools in his 'Integral Yoga' based on his own phenomenological disclosures on the path to Enlightenment[86]. However, as stated above, Aurobindo's *Life Divine* wasted its second half on unsubstantiated speculative drivel about the evolutionary rise of the Supermen[87]. We have seen that Wilber basically appeals to the authority of the Mandukya Upanishad's famous AUM model, Aurobindo and other Hindu-Buddhist Nondualist masters but even then his understanding leaves a lot to be desired, as demonstrated below. Where he argues correctly, as in regard to Whitehead's lack of Planes of Being, Wilber is neither profound nor original. J.H.M. Whiteman had pointed out this and other failings of Whitehead's metaphysics in his 1967 book (*see Ch.10*) [88].

Where Wilber attempts to be original as in his Quadrant mandala and other 'models' he has just created a false 'House of Cards' which even his admirer de Quincey has suggested may resemble Ptolemaic epicycles attempting desperately to salvage a false basic viewpoint. In 2000 CdQ noted that Wilber's system included 31 streams, 17 levels and 4 quadrants resulting in at least 2,108 'consciousness variables' [89]. As we have seen above, CdQ does not realise that Wilber's Evolution of Consciousness (supposedly beyond rational creatures to Spirit) is a pseudoscientific myth which contradicts the perennial understanding of Enlightenment as uncovering the Divine Light that is always present within us. Note that Wilber is not claiming some sort of cultural evolution but actual biological changes in brains. This Evolution myth led to Wilber's other supposedly great original idea, the 'Pre/Trans Fallacy', which Michael Washburn has argued is itself a fallacy[90]. My work corroborates this as Wilber's 'Pre/Trans Fallacy' and 'Height Psychology' is basically a rejection of the traditional view of Enlightenment as a return to a simpler, original state of being as also indicated in the 'Depth Psychology' of Jung and various Perennialist thinkers. In his early works Wilber stuck to this traditional understanding. Wilber's later supposed insight of the 'Pre/Trans Fallacy' was that spiritual progress toward Enlightenment was not a regression or return to a less-developed state, but an evolutionary development beyond the normal, rational egoic consciousness. Thus Wilber claims that the solution to the Mind/Body Problem can only be experienced by an individual *evolving* into a Nondual Awakening {*e.m.*}[91].

As I have stressed, this is pseudoscience. Evolution does not occur in individuals within their lifetime but across generations through biological reproduction. The 'Innate Capacity' argument[92] and of course my RAS brainwave correlate of the Inner Light (backed up by overwhelming authoritative evidence; *see Appendix*) both contradict and undermine these Evolution of Consciousness myths. Wilber's speculative philosophy even takes seriously the discredited Kabbalistic myths of Sigmund Freud (*see Ch. 9*) alongside other tenuous psychological speculations which scientists would dismiss quite rightly as 'psychobabble'. In stark contrast to Wilber's fundamentally flawed, ludicrously complex, error-laden quadrants, spirals, etc., which are of no value to real scientific investigation of Consciousness, my RAS brainwaves tie in with established scientific knowledge. Biomedical science knows that the brainstem Reticular Formation which underlies these RAS brainwaves is the one brain centre whose normal functioning is a prerequisite for *any form of consciousness* in humans (*see Note 7 for Ch. 1*). Of course, by 'any form of Consciousness' modern Medical Science means only Waking, Dreaming and abnormal states of mind rather than the more general non-mental forms of Consciousness not associated with mental activities known to Mysticism.

My RAS brainwave correlation along with my Retreat-to-the Brainstem interpretation of the yogic path to Enlightenment is also extremely simple compared to Wilber's ludicrously complicated so-called 'models' (with over 2,000 variables!) with which he keeps tinkering. As my interpretation is a factually grounded understanding it was able to accommodate easily new facts that I was not aware of when I first discovered it in 1994. This includes elucidation of the Buddhist-Christian notion of self-examination in the (Light of) Conscience explaining why Conscience has been understood in the West as a 'Second-self' that knows all of our thoughts. It also elucidates the perennial mythology of Enlightenment linked to the 'Fount of Youth' wherein, by stripping the ego of its attachments or the accreted habit-patterns of a lifetime, one is 'rejuvenated' or 'reborn' in a pure, original state. Enlightened Gnosis resembles Dying; it is a return or regression to a more simple, less-evolved, state of a purified, 'naked ego' floating in the Pure Light (with mental superimpositions held in abeyance) and perhaps dissolving into the Light in Mystical Union.

In her book *On Dreams and Death* von Franz discusses spiritual transfiguration as described in the Egyptian, Mithraic and Christian traditions leading to the attainment of a 'Garment of Light'. This parallels Near-Death experiences of 'Ego Purification'[93]. This Garment of Light is also paralleled in Neoplatonism where the theurgist dons Divine Light[94]. Theurgic rites purify the soul leading to the ethereal and luminous vehicle of the soul or *ochēma*[95]. Von Franz quotes an NDE report[96]:

> *My new ego was no longer the old familiar ego but a sublimate of it ... like something I had always known but had been deeply buried under a superstructure of fears, hopes, wishes and desire. This ego had nothing to do with the ego of this world... It was a spirit...*

She also quotes Carl Jung's report from his own NDE which occurred late in his life leading to a new form of ego that Jung called the '*objective ego*' {*e.m.*}[97]:

> *I had the feeling that everything was being sloughed away...the whole phantasmoagoria of earthly existence, fell away or was stripped from me...*

In his *Universal Theology* Whiteman describes essentially the same process in arcane language including 'leaving aside our habits' to reveal the *individual core identity* (a 'unique I AM') which in normal individuals is habitually identifying with a body and desires {*e.m.*}[98]. He notes that[99]:

> *The higher states, as anyone who knows separation must believe, are logically prior to the physical state and consequently not to be interpreted in terms of physical phenomena posterior to them.*

This contradicts Wilber's Pre/Trans Fallacy as Whiteman is saying that 'Higher States' precede physical phenomena in terms of the manifestation process (Wilber uses A.O. Lovejoy's phrase 'Great Chain of Being'); they are not some more developed evolution of the physical. It is physical embodiment and physical phenomena that arises out of deeper, more primitive 'Higher States'.

In my O/OM, I presented my Brain Deactivation/Retreat-to-the-Brainstem interpretation of Enlightenment in which new lower energy state dissipative structures (the correlates of new forms of the ego) are stabilised in deeper brain structures as the cortex is deactivated. This leads to the penultimate state prior to Mystical Union known as the Causal Body or *anandamayakosa* (Bliss Sheath) in the Mandukya's AUM model. In Vedanta this is known to be equivalent to *susupti* or Lucid Deep Sleep. Normally in Deep Sleep only the Pure Consciousness is present without being superimposed by any objective content (as stated in Chapter 1, this famous Vedantic fact becomes easy to understand given my RAS brainwave correlation). Such 'awakened' Deep Sleep indicates clearly a more simple state that underlies the normal activity of the mind rather than a more complex state. It is the creation of a translucent, 'naked' ego or individuated consciousness which floats almost at one with the Inner Light of Pure Consciousness resulting in *vijnana* (gnosis). Dissolution of this Causal Body into the Light is Mystical Union (*moksa, Liberation* or *turiya*, the 4th State). Wilber refers to the Causal Body corresponding to the Deep Sleep state as we have seen above but misunderstands it as an evolutionary development. This purification of the ego into a 'naked ego' stripped of worldly attachments is interpreted as the individuated ego consciousness being deactivated in the world-modelling patterns of neural connections in the cerebral cortex and reconstituting in more subtle forms in deeper brain structures. As Rumi stated, Mysticism is learning to die before you die[100].

Bauwens does note that after Wilber received considerable donations from an Internet millionaire fan Joe Firmage to set up his Integral Institute, a number of Wilber's erstwhile critics became his admirers. Wilber himself had disdained UFO believers[101]. Firmage had been pushed out of his position as CEO of USWeb due to his publicly expressed views on UFOs and extraterrestrials intervening in human history (performing Biblical miracles, etc.,) leading to him being known as the 'UFO-CEO' or the 'Fox Mulder of Silicon Valley'. Bauwens also mentions that Wilber's stock response to criticism is that the critic 'does not understand'[102]. De Quincey mentions that others in the 'Transpersonal Psychology' movement have suggested that Wilber's vitriolic and emotional style of criticising his opponents, with *ad hominem* attacks, is incompatible with someone who claims to have stabilised 'Higher States of Consciousness' (which are supposed to be characterised by Love and Compassion)[103]. Bauwens also raises this argument in regard to Wilber's aggressiveness and Wilber privately denouncing rival institutes like the California Institute of Integral Studies (founded in honour of Aurobindo) and the (Buddhist) Naropa Institute as being "cesspools"[104]. Both de Quincey and Bauwens state that Wilber's books 'set up' (misrepresent) his opponents views as 'Straw men' in order for Wilber to claim to have 'shot them down'[105,106]. Indeed, Wilber's style leads to aggressive counter-attacks from critics leading to what wags refer to as 'Wilber's Great Chain of Being Nasty'[107]. This claim that he is not really an enlightened master makes much sense given both his 'nasty' style of writing and his glaring misunderstandings of the metaphysical implications of Mystical Union. A truly enlightened guru displays Grace, a generosity of spirit, not spitefulness.

Wilber's Misconceptions Regarding Planes and the Synthesis of Science and Mysticism

I have only read three of Wilber's twenty or so books. These three books were only edited by Wilber and the valuable information which helped me develop my own ideas actually came from the other contributors in these books such as Willis Harman and David Bohm in *The Holographic Paradigm*[108], the 'Fathers' of the New Physics in *Quantum Questions*[109] and especially Daniel Brown in *Transformations of Consciousness*[110]. I recognised from Wilber's own contributions to these three books that he really was nowhere near as insightful as his New Age acolytes presented him to be and thus I never bothered to buy any of his own (single author) books. Indeed, I wrote in O/OM, with direct reference to Wilber, that my previous lack of familiarity with 'New Age' type subject matter had been fortuitous as it meant that I had not been conditioned by the gurus of the Western 'New Age' counterculture into thinking that even a linkage of Science and Mysticism, let alone a synthesis, was impossible[111].

In the 1982 collection of articles on Pribram and Bohm's holographic metaphor ideas entitled *The Holographic Paradigm*, editor Wilber quoted approvingly the views of physicist Jeremy Bernstein that it is a "wild over-generalisation" to say that the world views of Physics and Mysticism are similar based "on the use of accidental similarities of language as if these were somehow evidence of deeply rooted connections"[112]. Wilber added himself[113]:

> *Further, physics and mysticism are not two different approaches to the same reality. They are different approaches to two quite different levels of reality, the latter of which transcends but includes the former. ...Bohr's complementarity principle ....means two mutually exclusive aspects of ....one interaction. ...Physics and mysticism are no more two mutually exclusive approaches to one reality than are, say, botany and mathematics.*

Capra agreed but added that ultimately these two levels (of Physics and Mysticism) are the same, only different aspects of the same worlds[114]. We have looked at Capra's (Wilber-influenced) view above. In my crucial 1990s rereading of this book (*see Ch. 13*), I found that Bohm seemed to be in favour of integration of Science and Mysticism, but Wilber concluded against this[115].

Christian de Quincey claims that in *Quantum Questions*, Wilber showed that "subatomic physics could no more enlighten us about consciousness and mysticism than the physics of Newton"[116]. In *Quantum Questions* (1985), Wilber asserted that *any linkage*, let alone a future synthesis *of Science and Mysticism is impossible*. The 'higher levels', (i.e., spiritual planes), said Wilber are emergent, creative, novel and transcendent {*e.m.*}[117]. He adds {*e.m.*}[118]:

...if we emphasise solely the transcendental nature of spirit, ***then religion (and spirit)*** *are obviously "out of this world" and* ***have absolutely nothing in common with earth-bound science****. Any attempt to identify spirit with the manifest world of nature is, in this truncated view, charged with the ugly epithet of "featureless pantheism".*

In fact, as has already been indicated in the previous two chapters, it is the 'lower levels', (i.e., the material planes) which in fact *emerge* out of the transcendent planes and not *vice versa.* But, as Professor of Religion Frederick Streng pointed out in his essay "The Transcendental in a Comparative Context"[119], the "transcendental" is not simply the 'hidden' or 'beyond' outside conventional experiences but is a factor in the experiencing processes themselves. We saw that Plotinus stated that the transcendental realm of Ideas/Forms or *Nous* is not another place, it *is this* very *world of appearances seen with complete penetration* {*e.m.*}[120]. Physicist and advocate of *Advaita Vedanta* Amit Goswami[N7] picked up on Wilber's tacit Dualism between the Material and the Spiritual realms hiding behind Wilber's assertions of Monism ('one reality')[121]. I had already noted this glaring misunderstanding of Wilber's in the manuscript of my *The Oneness/Otherness Mystery* (O/OM; completed 1997). Basically Wilber conflated the use of word *material* in mysticism with the *matter* of Physics. When mystics talk of the "material plane" they do not mean the entire world of *matter* dealt with by Physics. The mystics' material plane refers to the gross perception of everyday macroscopic forms such as animals, trees and rocks in waking perception. They do not mean, nor do we ever actually perceive, without the aid of scientific instruments, the matter described by Physics. Recent advances in microscopic techniques allow visualisation of atoms, under highly artificial conditions[122]. As Aurobindo Ghose stated in his *Synthesis of Yoga*[123]:

For to the supramentalised seeing the material world and space and material objects cease to be material in the sense in which we know, on the strength of the sole evidence of our limited physical organs and of the physical consciousness that looks through them, receives as our gross perception and understands as our conception of matter.

Wilber was also an editor of the 1986 book *Transformations of Consciousness* which proved crucial to my identification of the physical correlate of the (Inner) Divine Light (the Spirit within) a few days after reading a chapter in this book in 1994 (*see Ch.13*). However, it was not the latest versions of Wilber's epicyclic mandalas or 'models' that interested me. In *The Holographic Paradigm,* our 'scientific' man of 'models' Ken assumes that children have Oedipal complexes (*see Ch. 9*). Wilber's "Height Psychology" model again seems like a facile conflation of mere words (*higher* states as emergently 'higher'). Ironic, given his quoting Bernstein on "accidental similarities of language" as evidence of deep connections! As we shall see later, the crucial chapter in *Transformations of Consciousness* was Harvard psychologist Daniel Brown's scholarly cross-cultural phenomenological comparison of states of Consciousness in three Hindu and Buddhist yogic traditions[124]. Brown's description of the yogic processes of 'stopping the mind' as a '*deconstruction of perception*', along with the Jungian notions of

Perception as a filter restricting information helped me to understand the 'higher planes' of Consciousness as '*broadening of perception*', letting in more of the information that sense perception filters out. Brown's chapter also mentioned the yogic discrimination of the underlying flow of the Light generating the Time/Space Matrix of Perception which I have already indicated was unwittingly paralleled in the speculative thought of Eugen Fink on Husserl's Time Consciousness. I have already indicated in Chapter 1 my new science-based interpretation of how perception of transcendental realms is attained in mysticism.

In fact, Capra in *The Holographic Paradigm* argues against Wilber in a response to Renée Weber's question that mystics have never seen the subatomic realm, that nobody, not even physicists have seen the subatomic realm. Thus, Capra states correctly, "*the perception of physicists is also* **extraordinary because the machines are an extension of the senses**" {*e.m.*}[125]. Thus Capra was on the right track here in spite of his Emergent Physicalist reductionism. In fact, as stated in Chapter 4, the use of a yogic *anudrishti siddhi* (supranormal perception technique for perceiving extremely small things) by Theosophists led to the prediction of the existence of isotopes of atoms before they were discovered by Science[126]. Given his puerile errors and consistent display of lack of true insight in regard to the scientific understanding of Consciousness, and given his constantly changing 'epicyclic' models, Wilber is better likened to Claudius Ptolemy than Albert Einstein in analogy to scientific cosmologists. Even his self-proclaimed admirer Christian de Quincey compared Wilber's constantly changing models to 'epicycles'. De Quincey asks questions including; Is this bewilderingly complex edifice leading metaphorically to a 'Taj Mahal' or a 'House of Cards' and is such a complex typology more likely to overwhelm than enlighten us.[127]. The deferential de Quincey 'sits on the fence' in regard to these questions. I too had thought of Wilber's tinkering as being like epicycles after reading his chapters in *Transformations of Consciousness*[128] back in 1994. Comparing Wilber to Ptolemy is rather unkind to the great Ptolemy as his models actually worked reasonably and Copernicus did not eliminate epicycles, he only reduced the number required.

Independence of Nonlocality and my Correlate of Pure Consciousness from Particular Paradigms

We saw above that Jeremy Bernstein claimed that Physics-Mysticism parallels were merely "accidental similarities of language" not implying any deep connections. This argument simply doesn't hold up given the views of greats like Eddington, Bohm, Heisenberg, Schrödinger and Pauli given in Chapter 4. Bernstein had also warned New Agers not to hitch Mysticism to contemporary QM as the latter will one day be superceded[129]. Bernstein's warning came before the first successful test of the Einstein-Podolsky-Rosen thought experiment by Aspect *et al.* in 1982 confirming that Bell's Inequalities are indeed violated as QM predicted. Einstein's arguments based on dogmatic realism were defeated. I started learning about these questions back in 1982, following the Aspect experiment, when I started buying a popular Science magazine. Within the core of contemporary physics, says d'Espagnat is a

Monism, a sense of Wholeness, a singular Reality (Oneness) radically foreign to the Multitudinism of Classical Physics, nowadays referred to as *nonseparability*. In fact, due to experimental confirmation of the violation of Bell's Inequalities (Bell was inspired by Bohm's work[130]) the **nonlocality** aspect of nonseparability will certainly remain true even if quantum formalism is superseded in future[131]. Nonlocality, the transcendence of 'simple location' and normal spatiotemporal causality related to so-called quantum 'entanglement' which seems to contradict Einstein's injunction against superluminal interaction, is a key parallel with mystical ontology. Physicist Paul Davies says[132];

> *In 1965 John Bell extended the EPR [Einstein-Podolsky-Rosen] argument and proved that, roughly speaking, any theory based on 'objective reality', and for which faster-than-light signalling is forbidden, must satisfy certain mathematical inequalities. Quantum mechanics should, according to the standard theory [Copenhagen Interpretation], fail to satisfy them, so one is obliged to relinquish either objective reality (with Bohr and Heisenberg) or the special theory of relativity. Few physicists are willing to follow the latter course.*

d'Espaganat clarifies matters by adding that nonlocality was defined, hence superluminal influences suspected only within the realm of objective realism, i.e., assuming that things actually lie within a really existing Space-Time continuum. If the objective reality standpoint is given up it becomes meaningless to talk of either locality or nonlocality although the nonseparability notion remains valid[133]. He also says that the notion of *influence* [i.e., experimentally confirmed seemingly 'superluminal influences' in the violation of Bell's inequalities] is closely related to that of *cause* and that it is almost impossible not to interpret such violations as revealing the existence of superluminal influences of some sort. Given the unwillingness to relinquish Special Relativity, a supplementary theorem was established independently by Ebehard in 1978 and Ghirardi *et al.* in 1980 which basically states that, in any such interpretation involving superluminal influences, these influences carry neither matter, nor energy, nor any usable signal[134]. D'Espagnat says that the notion of (immediate) influence-at-a-distance without the possibility of sending a signal is difficult to define but if Relativity theory is understood in an instrumental (rather than a realist) sense, (i.e., as simply predictive tools of our experimental set-ups) this supplementary theorem enables us to reconcile the most basic principle of Relativity with QM. The recent so-called "teleportation" experiments do not transfer anything akin to a material object but does imply some transfer of information although not at superluminal speed[135].

As we saw in Chapter 4, unique amongst the philosophers and physicists in the first half of the 20th Century, the one person to recognise these implications was Erwin Schrödinger[136]. Bell's theorem in itself does not say anything about either the features or even the meaningfulness of a human-independent reality[137]. d'Espagnat thinks that Mysticism cannot help us appreciate human mind-independent Reality as he assumes naively that all mystics speak of an ineffable Reality and, as with Heisenberg, he talks naively about poetic symbolism etc. He ventures a little beyond Kantianism and says that the success of Mathematics in predicting phenomena implies that it reflects something of the structure of this noumenal Reality[138]. The detailed implications for superluminal signalling are not really important to the main point however which is that, *nonlocality* (this transcendental notion which even a Western Bohm supporter like Ericson finds 'weird') is here to stay even if QM doesn't survive. As with nonlocality, my brainwave correlation between Pure Consciousness and electrical energy is not dependent on any particular paradigm. As Heisenberg indicated *energy* is the 'substance' of scientific reality and actually serves as an ontological Ground, independent of particular theories or paradigms.

Two Views of 'Brainwaves' and Bohm's Unanswered Question to Krishnamurti

Indeed, in 2000 the man who ran the Temenos Academy whose patron was Prince Charles, told me that my identification of the scientific basis of this most fundamental mystical phenomenon, the Divine Light, would no doubt provoke hostility from others as it undermined their views. A Greco-British participant at a 1999 Scientific and Medical Network seminar whispered to me that their Chairman neuropsychiatrist Professor Peter Fenwick, in the past had rejected suggestions from laypeople that the Inner Light could be a brain process. I can understand the concern here that such a correlation was false Reductionism eliminating Spirituality. The aforementioned Professor Willis Harman, a Stanford Electrical Engineer and Head of Stanford Research Institute had later become President of the New Age Institute of Noetic Sciences in Sausalito, California founded by physicist-turned Apollo 14 astronaut (the 6th man on the moon) Dr Edgar Mitchell. Harman predicted that the new Science of the future will be based on Indian Metaphysics with its Primacy of Consciousness[139]. In 1995, not long before Harman died, he wrote that he was 'not sure' about my Reticular Activating System (RAS) brainwaves correlation[140]. Of course, at first sight it seems so reductionistic.

This negative reaction was also the initial response of a Buddhophile neo-hippy work colleague upon hearing of my correlation in 1994. But later, when he understood via others at work that my explanation of Science fits into the 'Bigger, Deeper Picture' ideas actually preserve grand spiritual claims, he became positive about it. The science graduates and postgraduates at work, not steeped in ideologically motivated dogmas, were far more open to my science-based ideas. I wrote back to Harman along the lines that we had to understand the different perspectives; the *view from outside* using scientific instruments is not the same as the *view from within*. Nothing in our scientific conceptions of brain processes appears immediately like any of our inner experiences. In fact my brainstem brainwave correlation, even in its popular scientific conception does resemble strikingly the yogic knowledge of the Light in Hindu (waves of energy) and Buddhist (pulses) traditions as well as the moment by moment Flow of the Absolute Consciousness in Husserlian phenomenology or William James' Stream of Consciousness (*see Ch. 8*).

In 2000 when I emailed Robert Forman, the Perennialist professor of the Philosophy of Religion, who has defended mystical claims against Constructivists, he responded to me but, surprisingly, did not really seem to appreciate what I had done, in spite of his 'Perennial Psychology' (that mysticism reveals universal deep structures of human consciousness) and 'Innate Capacity' (*see Ch. 3*) arguments. Canadian professor Harold Coward, one of the editors of the *Encyclopaedia of Indian Philosophies* series (co-published by Princeton U.P. and Motilal Banarsidass) and the author of *Jung and Eastern Thought*, responded prior to publication that he could not really recommend any further reading to me like his book on Jung as nobody had done anything like my work before. He did not comment after receiving a copy. In contrast, Professor Peter Stewart DSc, a physicist and engineer (who had been Head of Rolls Royce Aero-engines when Concorde was built) and also a psychic and dowser, kept stressing that my brainstem brainwaves must be full of subtle information. I responded yes, my 'subtle energetic vibrations' are equivalent your (abstract notion of) 'information', or like Bohm's nonlocal Active Information (of the QM Wave Function) creating holonomy etc. Note that *information* is an abstract concept relating to human purposes; what actually exists in space is not information but subtle waveforms or vibrations of electromagnetic and other energetic fields. As Valerie Hunt states in regard to the detection of human energy fields, what science dismisses as random noise may actually be complex information, (i.e., it is labelled 'noise' as humans cannot decipher its organisational relevance)[141]. In 1999 the rumbustuous Stewart, was most pleased when I showed him my notebooks containing 'mind maps' planning the structure of my chapters on Science-Mysticism. The very first ringed piece of information in my very first 'mind map' was the fact that Buddhists claimed that each mind moment contains the information of the entire universe. "YES", exclaimed Stewart punching the air. We have seen that Hippolytus, in *Refutation of all Heresies*, quoted a sect of Docetist Gnostics who wrote of the Light of Sophia being full of infinite ideas and the Light informing matter out of the chaos (formless matter or *hyle*)[142].

In the early 1990s I had a strong compulsion to buy a little Krishnamurti, Bohm dialogue paperback entitled *The Ending of Time*[143], which I had seen in a central London bookshop but not bought at first. But when I first read it, it appeared like meaningless gobbledook as I was only beginning to learn about Indian Philosophy. Later in the 1990s, as I worked things out and then re-read it, it made perfect sense. In this book Bohm asks {*e.m.*}[144]:

> ***Is there a function in the brain*** *which is independent of the content? Which is* ***not conditioned by the content****, but that might still be a physical function?* [Krishnamurti]: *I understand. Is this the question? Apart from the consciousness with its content, is there in the brain an activity which is not touched by consciousness?* [Bohm]: *By the content; yes.* [Krishnamurti]: *Content is the consciousness.*

Note that the *RAS brainwaves* that I identified as the physical correlate of the Inner Light of Pure Consciousness in 1994 *constitute just such an unconditioned brain process* known in modern Medicine as the 'Arousal' component of and necessary prerequisite for any Consciousness and distinguished from the varying 'Contents' of Consciousness which Medicine assumes are generated by the cerebral cortex. My correlation thus undermines the dogmatic argument of Constructivists such as those in Comparative

Religion who claim that there is no unconditioned human mental (i.e., brain) process. Note also the staggering ignorance of the much-hyped Krishnamurti in his assertion that Content is Consciousness which is directly contradictory to the mainstream Indian understanding of the distinction between the Pure Consciousness and objective contents! In fact it is called Pure Consciousness as it is free of sensory superimpositions (so-called *avidya* or 'ignorance' in Vedanta) but advanced yogis can discriminate the subtle, (holonomic) Akashic vibrations or subtle energy constituting 'information' in the seeming 'emptiness' as Peter Stewart stressed. No wonder then that Bohm, unlike Schrödinger, never understood Pure Consciousness as the Ground of Being. Krishnamurti's ignorance validates Merrell-Wolff's lament at the lack of intellectual capabilities of most mystics!

References

1. Krishna, Gopi "Carl Friedrich von Weizsacker as a Thinker of the Future". In Klaus M. Meyer-Abich (Editor) (1982) *Physik, Philosophie und Politik: Festschrift für Carl Friedrich von Weizsäcker zum 70. Geburtstag*. Hanser.
2. Krishna, Gopi (1982) *ibid.*
3. Krishna, Gopi (1982) *ibid.*
4. Krishna, Gopi (1971) *The Biological Basis of Religion and Genius*, NC Press.
5. Hollingdale, R.J. (Translator) (1977) *A Nietzsche Reader*, Penguin.
6. Hollingdale, R.J. (1977) *ibid.*
7. Hanegraaff, Wouter, J. "The New Age Movement and the Esoteric Tradition". In Roelof van den Broek and Wouter J. Hanegraaff (Editors) (1998) *Gnosis and Hermeticism: From Antiquity to Modern Times*, State University of New York Press.
8. Hanegraaff, Wouter, J. (1998) *ibid.*
9. Bucke, Richard, M. (1901) *Cosmic Consciousness: A Study in the Evolution of the Human Mind*, Innes and Sons.
10. Goldberg, Philip (2010) *American Veda: From Emerson and the Beatles to Yoga and Meditation – How Indian Spirituality Changed the West*, Harmony Books, Random House.
11. Keiffer, Gene (2007). Personal Communication.
12. Laszlo, Ervin (2004) *Science and the Akashic Field: An Integral Theory of Everything*, Inner Traditions.
13. Weber, Renée "*The Tao of Physics* Revisited: A Conversation with Fritjof Capra". In Ken Wilber (Editor) (1982) *The Holographic Paradigm and Other Paradoxes: Exploring the Leading Edge of Science*, Shambhala Publications.
14. Ellison, Arthur J. "Western Science and Religious Experience". In T.D. Singh (Editor) (1987) *Synthesis of Science and Religion: Critical Essays and Dialogues*, The Bhaktvedanta Institute.
15. Padfield, Suzanne. Cited in Combs, Allan and Holland, Mark (1990) *Synchronicity: Science, Myth, and the Trickster*, Paragon House.
16. Taimni, I.K. (1961) *The Science of Yoga; The Yoga-Sutras of Patanjali in Sanskrit with transliteration in Roman, translation in English and commentary.* The Theosophical Publishing House.

17. Laszlo, Ervin (2004) *ibid.*
18. Chopra, Deepak. Quoted on front cover of Laszlo, Ervin (2004) *ibid.*
19. Fenwick, Peter "Meditation and the EEG". In Michael A. West (Editor) (1987) *The Psychology of Meditation*, Oxford University Press.
20. Fenwick, Peter (1987) *ibid.*
21. Brown, Daniel P. "The Stages of Meditation in Cross-Cultural Perspective". In Ken Wilber, Jack Engler and Daniel P. Brown (Editors) (1986) *Transformations of Consciousness: Conventional and Contemplative Perspectives on Development*, Shambhala Publications.
22. Pépin, Jean "Theories of Procession in Plotinus and the Gnostics". In Richard T. Wallis (Editor) and Jay Bregman (Associate Editor) (1992) *Neoplatonism and Gnosticism*, State University of New York Press.
23. Hanegraaff, Wouter, J. (1998) *ibid.*
24. Schrödinger, Erwin (1944) *What is Life,* Cambridge University Press.
25. Ho, Mae-Wan (1993) *The Rainbow and the Worm: The Physics of Organisms*, World Scientific.
26. Lindorff, David (2004) *Jung and Pauli: The Meeting of Two Great Minds*, Quest Books.
27. Lindorff, David (2004) *ibid.*
28. Tiller, William A. (1997) *Science and Human Transformation: Subtle Energies, Intentionality and Consciousness*, Pavior Publishing.
29. Gerber, Richard (1996) *Vibrational Medicine:New Choices for Healing Ourselves*, Bear and Co.
30. Woodhouse, Mark, B. (1996) *Paradigm Wars: Worldviews for a New Age*, Frog Ltd.
31. Hesse, Mary "Hermeticism and History: An apology for the internal history of science" in *Historical and Philosophical Perspectives of Science* (1970) edited by R.H. Steuer, University of Minnesota Press.
32. Kingsley, Peter (1995) *Ancient Philosophy, Mystery, and Magic: Empedocles and Pythagorean Tradition,* Clarendon Press (Oxford University Press).
33. Skrbina, David (2005) *Panpsychism in the West*, MIT Press.
34. Weber, Renée (1982) *ibid.*
35. Whiteman, J.H. Michael (1967) *Philosophy of Space and Time and the Inner Constitution of Nature: A Phenomenological Study*, Muirhead Library of Philosophy, George Allen and Unwin and the Humanities Press.
36. Clarke, John, J. (1997) *Oriental Enlightenment: the Encounter Between Asian and Western Thought*, Routledge.
37. Clarke, John, J. (1997) *ibid.*
38. Dobson, John (1995) *Cosmic Beginnings and Human Ends: Where Science and Religion Meet*, Open Court.
39. Goldberg, Philip (2010) *ibid.*
40. Capra, Fritjof (1975) *The Tao of Physics: An exploration of the parallels between modern physics and Eastern mysticism*, Wildwood House.
41. Capra, Fritjof (1975) *ibid.*

42. Capra, Fritjof "The New Physics Revisited: Afterword to the Second Edition". In Fritjof Capra (1983) *The Tao of Physics* (with revisions and new Afterword), Flamingo (Fontana Paperbacks).
43. Weber, Renée (1982) *ibid*.
44. Weber, Renée (1982) *ibid*.
45. Capra, Fritjof (1996) *The Web of Life*, Anchor.
46. Laughlin, Charles, D. "Biogenetic Structural Theory and the Neurophenomenology of Consciousness". In Stuart R. Hameroff, Alfred W. Kaszniak, and David J. Chalmers (Editors) (1999) *Toward a Science of Consciousness:The Third Tucson Discussions and Debates*, MIT Press.
47. Austin, James H. (1998) *Zen and the Brain: Toward an Understanding of Meditation and Consciousness*, MIT Press.
48. Varela, Francisco J. (Editor) (1997) *Sleeping, Dreaming and Dying: An Exploration of Consciousness with The Dalai Lama*, Wisdom Publications.
49. Varela, Francisco J. "Present-Time Consciousness". In Francisco J. Varela and Jonathan Shear (Editors) (1999) *The View from Within: First-person approaches to the study of consciousness*, Imprint Academic.
50. Jones, Richard, H. (1986) *Science and Mysticism: A Comparative Study of Western Natural Science, Theravada Buddhism, and Advaita Vedanta*, Bucknell Univesity Press (Associated University Presses).
51. Jones, Richard, H. (1986) *ibid*.
52. Harman, Willis "The New Science and Holonomy". In Ken Wilber (Editor) (1982) *The Holographic Paradigm and Other Paradoxes: Exploring the Leading Edge of Science*, Shambhala Publications.
53. Jones, Richard, H. (1986) *ibid*.
54. Whiteman, J.H. Michael (1967) *ibid*.
55. Jones, Richard, H. (1986) *ibid*.
56. Von Franz, Marie-Louise (1992) *Psyche and Matter*, Shambhala Publications.
57. von Franz, Marie-Louise (1991) "Meaning and Order". Reprinted in Marie-Louise von Franz (1992) *Psyche and Matter*, Shambhala Publications.
58. von Franz, Marie-Louise (1991) *ibid*.
59. Kanigel, Robert (1991) *The Man Who Knew Infinity: A Life of the Genius Ramanujan*, Scribners.
60. Franz, Marie-Louise (1991) *ibid*.
61. Goonatilake, Susantha (1998) *Toward a Global Science: Mining Civilisational Knowledge*, Indiana University Press.
62. Goldberg, Philip (2010) *ibid*.
63. De Quincey, Christian "The Promise of Integralism: A Critical Appreciation of Ken Wilber's *Integral Psychology*". In Jensine Andresen and Robert K.C. Forman (Editors) (2000) *Cognitive Models and Spiritual Maps*, Imprint Academic.
64. De Quincey, Christian (2000) *ibid*.
65. *Ibid*.
66. *Ibid*.
67. *Ibid*.

68. *Ibid.*
69. *Ibid.*
70. *Ibid.*
71. *Ibid.*
72. *Ibid.*
73. *Ibid.*
74. Harman, Willis "Toward a Science of Wholeness". In Willis Harman with Jane Clark (Editors) (1994) *New Metaphysical Foundations of Modern Science*, Institute of Noetic Sciences.
75. Berlinerblau, Jacques (1999) *Heresy in the University: The* Black Athena *Controversy and the Responsibilities of American Intellectuals*, Rutgers University Press.
76. Mishra, Ram Shankar (1998) *The Integral Advaitism of Sri Aurobindo*, Motilal Banarsidass.
77. Grof, Stanislaw (1985) *Beyond the Brain: Birth, Death and Transcendence in Psychotherapy*, State University of New York Press.
78. Grof, Stanislaw (1998) *The Cosmic Game:Explorations of the Frontiers of Human Consciousness*, State University of New York Press.
79. de Quincey, Christian (2000) *ibid*.
80. *Ibid.*
81. *Ibid.*
82. Hanegraaff, Wouter, J. (1998) *ibid*.
83. de Quincey, Christian (2000) *ibid*.
84. de Quincey, Christian (2000) *ibid*.
85. Bauwens, Michel (No date) "The Cult of Ken Wilber" (Web article: www.kheper.net/topics/Cult_of_Ken_Wilber.html).
86. Ghose, Aurobindo (Sri Aurobindo) (1948) *The Synthesis of Yoga*, Sri Aurobindo Ashram Publications.
87. Ghose, Aurobindo (Sri Aurobindo) (1939) *The Life Divine*, Sri Aurobindo Ashram Publications.
88. Whiteman, J.H. Michael (1967) *ibid*.
89. de Quincey, Christian (2000) *ibid*.
90. *Ibid.*
91. *Ibid.*
92. Forman, Robert K.C. (1998) (Editor) *The Innate Capacity: Mysticism, Psychology and Philosophy*, Oxford University Press.
93. Von Franz, Marie-Louise (1998) *On Dreams and Death: A Jungian Interpretation*, Open Court.
94. Johnston, Sarah Iles "*Fiat Lux, Fiat Ritus*: Divine Light and the Late Antique Defense of Ritual". In Matthew T. Kapstein (Editor) (2004) *The Presence of Light: Divine Radiance and Religious Experience*, Chicago University Press.
95. Berchman, Robert M. "Rationality and Ritual in Neoplatonism". In Paulos Mar Gregorios (2002) (Editor) *Neoplatonism and Indian Philosophy*, State University of New York Press.

96. von Franz, Marie-Louise (1998) *ibid.*
97. von Franz, Marie-Louise (1998) *ibid.*
98. Whiteman, J.H. Michael (2006) *Universal Theology and Life in the Other Worlds*, Colin Smythe.
99. Whiteman, J.H. Michael (2006) *ibid.*
100. Cressy, Judith "Mysticism and the Near-Death Experienc" In Lee W. Bailey and Jenny Yates (Editors) (1996) *The Near-Death Experience: A Reader*, Routledge.
101. Bauwens, Michel (No Date) *ibid.*
102. Bauwens, Michel (No Date) *ibid.*
103. de Quincey, Christian (2000) *ibid.*
104. Bauwens, Michel (No Date) *ibid.*
105. Bauwens, Michel (No Date) *ibid.*
106. de Quincey, Christian (2000) *ibid.*
107. de Quincey, Christian (2000) *ibid.*
108. Wilber, Ken (Editor) (1982) *The Holographic Paradigm and Other Paradoxes: Exploring the Leading Edge of Science*, Shambhala Publications.
109. Wilber, Ken (Editor) (1985) *Quantum Questions:Mystical Writings of the World's Great Physicists*, Shambhala Publications.
110. Wilber, Ken, Engler, Jack and Brown, Daniel, P. (Editors) (1986) *Transformations of Consciousness: Conventional and Contemplative Perspectives on Development*, Shambhala Publications.
111. Bhattacharya, Sutapas (1999) *The Oneness/Otherness Mystery: The Synthesis of Science and Mysticism,* Motilal Banarsidass.
112. Wilber, Ken "Physics, Mysticism, and the New Holographic Paradigm: A Critical Appraisal". In Ken Wilber (Editor) (1982) *The Holographic Paradigm and Other Paradoxes: Exploring the Leading Edge of Science*, Shambhala Publications.
113. Wilber, Ken (1982) *ibid.*
114. Weber, Renée (1982) *ibid.*
115. Wilber, Ken (1982) *ibid.*
116. de Quincey, Christian (2000) *ibid.*
117. Wilber, Ken "Introduction: Of Shadows and Symbols". In Ken Wilber (Editor) (1985) *Quantum Questions: Mystical Writings of the World's Great Physicists*, Shambhala Publications.
118. Wilber, Ken (1985) *ibid.*
119. Streng, Frederick "The Transcendental in a Comparative Context". In Elliot Deutsch (Editor) (1991) *Culture and Modernity: East-West Philosophic Perspectives*, University of Hawaii Press.
120. Kealey, Daniel "The Theoria of Nature in Plotinus and the Yoga of the Earth Consciousness in Aurobindo". In Paulos Mar Gregorios (Editor) (2002) *Neoplatonism and Indian Philosophy*, State University of New York Press.
121. Goswami, Amit (1994) *Science within Consciousness: Developing a Science based on the Primacy of Consciousness*, Institute of Noetic Sciences.

122. d'Espagnat, Bernard (2006) *On Physics and Philosophy*, Princeton University Press.
123. Ghose, Aurobindo (Sri Aurobindo) (1948) *ibid.*
124. Brown, Daniel P. "The Stages of Meditation in Cross-Cultural Perspective". In Ken Wilber, Jack Engler and Daniel P. Brown (Editors) (1986) *Transformations of Consciousness: Conventional and Contemplative Perspectives on Development*, Shambhala Publications.
125. Weber, Renée (1982) *ibid.*
126. Radin, Dean (2006) *Entangled Minds: Extrasensory Experiences in a Quantum Reality*, Paraview and Pocket Books (Simon and Schuster).
127. de Quincey, Christian (2000) *ibid.*
128. Wilber, Ken "The Spectrum of Development" and "The Spectrum of Psychopathology". In Ken Wilber, Jack Engler and Daniel P. Brown (Editors) (1986) *Transformations of Consciousness: Conventional and Contemplative Perspectives on Development*, Shambhala Publications.
129. Wilber, Ken (1982) *ibid.*
130. Hiley, Basil, J. and Peat, F. David (Editors) (1987) *Quantum Implications: Essays in Honour of David Bohm*, Routledge.
131. d'Espagnat, Bernard (2006) *ibid.*
132. Davies, Paul (1989) "Introduction" to Heisenberg, Werner (1958) *Physics and Philosophy*, Harper and Row.
133. d'Espagnat, Bernard (2006) *ibid.*
134. *Ibid.*
135. *Ibid.*
136. *Ibid.*
137. *Ibid.*
138. *Ibid.*
139. Harman, Willis "Scientific Positivism, The New Dualism and the Perennial Wisdom". In T.D. Singh (Editor) (1987) *Synthesis of Science and Religion: Critical essays and Dialogues*, The Bhaktivedanta Institute.
140. Harman, Willis. Personal Communication 27th October 1995.
141. Hunt, Valerie V. (1989) *Infinite Mind, The Science of Human Vibrations*, Malibu Publishing Company.
142. Pepin, Jean "Theories of Procession in Plotinus and the Gnostics". In Richard T. Wallis (Editor) and Jay Bregman (Associate Editor) (1992) *Neoplatonism and Gnosticism*, State University of New York Press.
143. Krishnamurti, J. and Bohm, David (1985) *The Ending of Time*, Harper and Row.
144. Krishnamurti, J. and Bohm, David (1985) *ibid.*

7

Vedic Knowledge of Spiritual Light Distorted in Diffusion across Eurasia

...and in the knowledge of the being and nature of God they [the Hindus] were already in possession of a light which was but faintly perceived, even by the loftiest intellects in the best days of Athens.

Mountstuart Elphinstone[1]

The Divine Light in the *Rig Veda* and the *Upanisads*

Doniger's Freudian Mistranslations and the True Mystical Meaning of Rig Veda

Although Homeric gods shone with light, notions that Divinity was Fire or Light and notions that mere mortals might interact with or receive it were uncommon in the ancient Mediterranean[2]. These notions however were central to the ancient North Indians known as the Vedic Aryans. It was they who created the first Indo-European literature in the form of the roughly one thousand (predominantly) spiritual poems gathered together at a later date in the collection known as the *Rig Veda Samhita.* In his misleading 2007 BBC TV series *The Story of India*, Michael Wood supported the Aryan Invasion myth which presented the Vedic Aryans as nomadic invaders of India in the 2nd M *b.c.e.* He also voiced views echoing the Colonial myth that advances in Indian history were due to waves of lighter-skinned invaders from the North-West as if Indians themselves lacked historical agency[3]. We saw in Chapter 2 that archaeological and DNA studies have discredited the White Supremacist myth of the Aryan Invasion of India. The facts support the traditional Brahmanical claim that the *Rig Veda* was written in an Ancient Indian civilisation which would be what is now known as the Saraswati-Sindhu (or Indus-Saraswati) civilisation. The now extinct Saraswati river remains a sacred river for Hindus and, in Hindu myth, it is said to join the Ganges and Jamuna at *Prayaga.* Joseph Campbell wrote that the idea of a Sacred River symbolised the Grace of the Divine flowing inexhaustibly out of some (unknown) source[4].

Chicago University's Wendy Doniger (*a.k.a.* Wendy Doniger O'Flaherty) has been labelled the 'Queen of Hinduism' studies in the USA. Her Penguin translations of *Rig Veda* are the best known in the West. Yet they present a travesty of the true meaning of *Rig Veda*. Harvard Indologist Michael Witzel has asserted that Doniger misunderstands First Year Sanskrit. In her translation of one Rig Vedic hymn of just 18 stanzas, Doniger made 43 errors or questionable translations. Witzel stated that Doniger would have done better by using old translations and then adding her Freudian interpretation, (i.e., it's all about sex). Witzel wrote that "Doniger's rendering of even the first two *paadas*" of the *Rig Veda* "is more of a paraphrase than a translation", and her style "is rather a stream of unconnected George Bush-like anacoluthas"[5]. Harvard would not have accepted her work. But Witzel was privately reprimanded by Harvard for posting his criticisms of Doniger on the internet[6]. After all US academia had heaped praise and awards upon her 'scholarship'[7]. European Indologist Nicholas Kazanas examined Doniger's obsession with sexual connotations and wrote that she overlooks spiritual connotations of sexual metaphors as are also found in Christianity. She is obsessed, he says, with one meaning, the most sexual imaginable[8]. In Christian mysticism, enlightenment is often depicted using sexual metaphors of 'passion' or 'marriage' with Christ' for the penetration of the 'soul' by Divine Light.

Vedic scholar Professor Antonio de Nicolas noted that Doniger even uses Hebrew translation in the *Rig Veda*. The 'jewel' of her mistranslations is that of '*aja eka pada*' (literally meaning *aja*= unborn, unmanifest; *eka*=one; *pada*=foot, measure). De Nicolas says it is the unmanifest one foot measure of music present in the geometries of the 'Asat' meaning the Rig Vedic world of possibilities where only geometries live without forms[9]. This is a rather Platonic interpretation given his use of 'geometries', (i.e., idealised forms). Doniger translated it as "the one-footed goat" because 'aja' in Hebrew means goat[10]. Hugh Urban has shown that in the 19th Century USA, Hindu *Tantra* was appropriated and misrepresented as simply sexual practises by conservative, white Christian society starved of erotica[11]. Doniger avoids criticism of Buddhism whilst demonising Hindu Tantra given the Shangri-La image of Buddhism amongst US liberals, especially Tibetan Buddhism. Ironically, Tibetan Buddhism is based on the same Tantra which Doniger demonises selectively in its Hindu forms[12]. Doniger's *Purana Perennis* was criticised by Hans Bakker as poorly researched but heavily promoted as the book's racy, sensationalist style attracts attention and sales although devoid of authenticity[13].

Rajiv Malhotra pointed out that Doniger intentionally destroys any shades of meaning in deference to her preferred one[14]. I pointed out to De Nicolas and Malhotra that Adam Curtis showed in his award-winning BBC documentary series *The Century of the Self* how Sigmund Freud's ideas caught on in the USA, not due to any scientific authenticity, but due to their sexually titillating content attracting attention. Curtis also pointed out the role played by Freud's nephew Edward Bernays, the pioneer of Public Relations (PR). Bernay's used Freud's 'wish fulfillment' (an idea already known and better understood by *Advaita Vedanta*[N1]) to associate products in advertisements with sexual fantasies, etc., rather than the intrinsic merits of the product[15]. Even, the notion of the 'Unconscious', familiar in one form or another to all mystical traditions, was developed and publicised in modern Europe by Eduard von

Hartmann, and Buddhism-inspired Paul Carus (friend of Ernst Mach) before Freud. J.J. Clarke says that both Hartmann and Carus were influenced by Hindu Vedanta[16]. Scientific facts debunking Freud's Psychoanalytic superstitions are to be found in Chapter 9.

Michael Wood also claimed ludicrously in his TV series that the essence of Hinduism was ritual[17]. Professor Sarvepalli Radhakrishnan, who later became President of India, had written[18]:

If there is one doctrine more than any other which is characteristic of Hindu thought, it is the belief that there is an interior depth to the human soul, which, in its essence, is uncreated and deathless and absolutely real. The spirit in man is different from the individual ego...It is the core of all being,...

The term 'Divine' is used here to mean the *Uncreated Source* of the created, phenomenal world. The Vedic *aja* (Unborn) above is an archaic, metaphoric way of referring to the Uncreated or the Divine. The ancient hymns of the *Rig Veda* refer to an intoxicating drink, made from a plant, called *Soma*. *Soma* was offered to the gods and drunk by the priests. As Huston Smith states, *Soma* may have been the basis of all Vedic spirituality[19]. Hymns of the *Rig Veda* say that by drinking *Soma*, one becomes immortal, arrives at the Light and finds the gods[20]. Whiteman points out that many of the references to *Soma* in *Rig Veda* are mystical allegories referring to experiencing the flowing *Spirit* rather than drinking the plant juice. Plato uses the term *drinking* in the same manner in his *Laws* and the Gospels refer to turning 'water' (egoic mind) into 'wine' (Spirit)[21].

J.L. Mehta, chastises the Western scholars who have distorted the interpretation of the Vedas by imagining that the Vedic seers were talking about Nature in the modern sense. It is often stated that the Vedic Aryans worshipped the elements of Nature as deities. Western scholars have projected European preconceptions onto the most important word in the Veda *Rita* (Truth) and translate it repeatedly as Order. The Vedic seers never personified or deified *Rita* as it stood for the Ultimate Source of all beings, including gods, above Being and Nonbeing. In *Soma*, says Mehta, we have a more substantial symbol and embodied form of transcendent *Rita* than Light. Both are footholds for the **shining forth of Truth** as the ultimate, sacred reality (*emphasis mine* {*e.m.*})[22].

In a letter, Whiteman told me that even Radhakrishnan has misinterpreted the *Rig Veda* as Nature worship when in fact these hymns contain deep and profound mystical knowledge[23]. We have seen in Chapters 2 and 4 that Whiteman interpreted the Vedic term *dharman* (McDonnel's 'ordinances') as being the same as so-called 'archetypes'. In default of such deep mystical knowledge, dismissive characterisations have been imputed to *Rig Vedic* hymns[24, 25]. In fact Aurobindo Ghose had recognised the true esoteric meaning of *Rig Veda* in his *The Secret of the Veda* (1914-16) and he, like other Hindus, questioned the validity of the (now discredited but still widely believed) Aryan Invasion Theory (AIT). The proper enunciation of each syllable was critical in the oral transmission of these (mantra-like) hymns. When the Veda was finally written down in a later age by the grammarians they had to write another text, the *Padapatha*, to allow recovery of the euphonic combinations and harmonics[26]. Antonio de Nicolas also stresses the importance of the musicality and of chanting the hymns for the proper understanding in his *Meditations through the Rig Veda*[27]. Aurobindo says that the main medieval interpreter Sayana was obsessed with ritualistic formulae and spiritual interpretation is a rare element in Sayana. The European translators seized upon the historical element admitted by Sayana and even more so on Sayana's naturalistic interpretations. Thus Aurobindo blamed Sayana for the modern view of the Vedas as crude and primitive[28].

The Vedic hymns, says Aurobindo, point to a spiritual culture. The distinguishing sign of the *Aryan* is a *worship of Light* and the powers of *Light*, and of a self-discipline based on the culture of Truth (*Ritam*) and the aspiration to Immortality (*Amritam* the Nectar of Immortality, the Water of Eternal Life) {*e.m.*}[29]. Mehta says that Rig Vedic man was not only aware of a **Light within** him but also of a Light that comes from beyond. The *arya* (the Sanskrit for "noble") of the *Rig Veda* is one who pursues the Light and is open to transcendence, hospitable to the **Light from beyond** {*e.m.*}[30]. The *Brahmana* (the Sanskrit term nowadays used for the elite Hindu priestly caste, the Brahmans or Brahmins) is dedicated to his creative vocation of "wording the world" (through divine inspiration) and has one all-consuming passion, the *unceasing pursuit of* ***Light*** {*e.m.*}[31]. Unlike this "wording the world" linked to Divine Light, Existentialist Maurice Merleau-Ponty's *chanter le monde* or "singing the world", the effort to illuminate the world by creatively expressing it[32], is a superficial modern notion of creative illumination as Merleau-Ponty rejected notions of transcendental or supernatural realms and thus remained totally ignorant of true Illumination or Divine Inspiration.

Aurobindo tells us that the repeated references in the Vedic hymns to cows and horses actually refers to Light (or Consciousness) and Energy. The word *go* (*gow*) means both cow and *light*[33]. Indeed, some scholars have suggested that the English word 'God' is derived from the Sanskrit *gow*. Aurobindo says that the cows and horses are constantly associated in the Veda with Dawn (*Ushas*; which Whiteman tells us refers to Divine Illumination[34]). The Cows of the Dawn bring rays of light as an image of the dawn of Illumination. This parallels the Homeric kine (cattle) of Helios. The *wealth* of cows and horses in the Veda thus refers to richness of Divine Illumination. The gods are Children of Light, sons of *Aditi* (Infinity) bringing to Man Light, pouring on him the Fullness of the Waters (the repeated reference to 'floods'), the abundance of the Heavens[35]. Mehta says that **Light** is the **keyword of** the ***Rig Veda***, *the central concept* that illumines and holds it together. *Deva*, the Rig Vedic word for a god or deity literally means "the Shining One" and these deities constitute a differentiated structure of the one Light {*e.m.*}[36].

The *deva* closest to Man is *Agni* (fire), present in Man's heart as the Light by which Man sees and knows and as the immortal within the mortal[37]. Joseph Campbell states that the *Upanisads*, in which philosophising began, date from around 1000 *b.c.e.* The two large Upanishads are the *Brihad-Aranyaka Upanisad* and the *Chandogya*. The Upanishads teach that the fire within you is *Agni*, the fire of the sacrificial flame. Why do you need to go to the **Brahmans** when the sacrificial flame is actually within you? All those gods that you are invited to worship in the public rituals are in fact projections of the fire of your own (sacred) energy within. The Chandogya Upanishad asserts that the source of the gods is in your own heart. If you return to that centre you will know that you are that of which the gods are born[38].

The perennial fountainhead of truth or the Godhead

The *Rig Veda* says that this immortal Light in our hearts is the one source of all thought, the **fountainhead of Truth** {*e.m.*}[39]. This 'fountainhead' metaphor for the Inner Light or God-head, the fountain of Divinity, is repeated throughout history, along with related notions of water-like flowing, and echoes of it are found in the *Ereignis* dynamics of Heidegger with its welling-up flow of Being and Time. Giordano Bruno dedicated his collection of poems *De gli eroici furore* (*The Heroic Enthusiasts*) of 1585 *c.e.* to Philip Sidney writing of a religion of 'natural contemplation' by which the Divine Light, which shines in all things, possesses the soul, raising it and converting it to God. Bruno's poetry mentions the **Fountain of Light** as the **Truth of Truths**, the *God of gods* {*e.m.*}[40]. Historians of science continue to misrepresent the mystic Bruno as a martyr for Science when he was not a scientist and mathematician but an Occultist whose maths was Mathesis or esoteric Astrological Numerology [N2 41].

William Blake wrote of the "Fountains of Living Waters flowing from the Humanity Divine" and that, "There is no other God than that God who is the intellectual fountain of humanity". Blake's Divine Humanity is the Light or Spirit within all humans[42]. His use of 'intellectual' here does not mean 'rational'; Blake chastised those who saw only the Ratio. For Meister Eckhart 'Pure Intellect' meant the Spirit or Light[43]. This reflects the older Platonic notion of intelligibility or intellectual vision[44]. All things are apprehended in their Eternal Forms in the Divine Body of Jesus Christ the Imagination (meaning the Divine Core or Essence, the Divine Image in Man)[45]. This Divine Image (*imago dei*) is the *Inner Man* of St Paul, our innermost being and the Universal within our hearts. The Living Water is clearly a metaphor for the *Prana* or Life energy aspect of the Inner Light.

The Alchemical Fountain is also the Source of Life[46]. The 'philosophical mercury'(*Aqua Permanens*) (Mercury is the Latin version of Hermes) is the Water of Life (*Aqua Vitae*) and it is the source of the soul (ego) The Life-giving drink from the Water of Life (Mercurial Water or Hermes' Fountain) leads to Rebirth, *enthusiasm* (being filled with Divinity) and omnipresence[47]. Mercurious was often identified with Wisdom (*Sapientia*) or the Holy Ghost. Hermes as a symbol of the means of Grace guides the Alchemist to the **philosophical gold** of God. The *Chemical Wedding* is an experience of a 'rebirth' by means of the Mercurial Water which corresponds to the teaching of Jesus in John: "Unless a man be born again, he cannot see the kingdom of God" {*e.m.*}[48]. The transmutation of the Alchemist involves radical alterations in the experience of the subject/object relation, causality and time[49].

We saw in Chapter 2 that Joseph Campbell wrote that the Holy Grail represented the God in your own hearts. The Holy Grail is that fountain in the centre of the universe from which pour forth the energies of Eternity into the temporal world. That same energy is in each of our hearts[50]. The Virgin Mary stood near the fountain where the Light from Heaven impregnates her resulting in the Virgin Birth[51]. This is the rebirth of the soul in the Spiritual realm[52]. This myth of the Virgin Birth (which long predates the Gospels) is found all over the world. In the Fountain of Youth myth, a man becomes young again as his ego is stripped of all the habits (attachments) accrued throughout his life (he is reborn)[53]. "Thou art the living fountain of hope", says Dante after his perilous passage through the Three Worlds in *Paradiso*[54]. In this perennial knowledge of the Inner Light as a welling-up of 'Life' (and new moments of Time) lies the true meaning of Alexander Pope's, "Hope springs eternal in the human breast" from his *Essay on Man*.

In *Varieties of Religious Experience*, William James quotes an unnamed scientific man who refers to that 'indefinite consciousness' as the Absolute Reality behind phenomena or this fundamental Cosmical *It*. The unnamed man continues, "It was an unfailing fountain of living justice, truth..."[55]. In fact, the fountainhead metaphor is a rather apt phenomenological description for the flow of the brainwaves from the brainstem which constitute the direct physical correlate of the Inner Light. It is of course related to the metaphor of the Fount of all Wisdom referring to mystical realisation of holonomic (mutually interpenetrating) or Akashic (of the vibratory subtle matter that is Space) information (or subtle energy) from the whole universe permeating each spatially limited portion of existence.

Max Muller's Christian, Colonialist Caricature of Vedic Aryans as Northern Nomadic Invaders

As with the Hinduism-demonising historian of India James Mill[N3], who was second in command of the East India Company (EIC), political considerations were never far from the surface of the work of British Colonial Indology. Like Scottish-born Mill, German born Oxford Professor of Comparative Philology Max Muller was associated with the mafia-like EIC which had looted India's wealth, extorted her resources and killed many millions of the poorest Indians through its economic plunder resulting in numerous famines. After this state-chartered corporation was finally dissolved in 1857, the direct 'Raj' (rule) of the British state continued such Crimes against Humanity in India. Nearly all of Britain's leading families had stakes in the EIC through shares or lucrative jobs for their sons. Thus, in spite of Parliament's occasional shedding of 'crocodile tears', British profit always outweighed the socio-economic devastation of India and the murder of tens of millions forced into starvation. As with the vast compensation given to the British slave-owners after 1833 (*see Note 6 to Ch. 1*), in spite of the devastating effects on India, the British shareholders in the EIC were richly compensated after 1857. Like Mill, Muller never visited India. Muller was the famous English translator of the *Rig Veda* who concocted the White Supremacist Aryan Invasion Theory (AIT) myth that has completely distorted Western (and Western-educated Indian) understanding of Ancient Indian history. He justified his fabricated historical interpretation of the Veda involving White Aryan invaders conquering Black Indian natives on the basis of one ambiguous word found in only one of the over one thousand hymns of the *Rig Veda*. Muller made up the supposed dates for the *Rig Veda* on equally flimsy grounds allowing only a couple of centuries each for major periods based on ancient Indian literary genres which almost certainly did not transform so rapidly[56, 57]. Although his dating was immediately criticised by other Indologists and he quickly backtracked on the veridicality of his dubious dating, these false dates were taken as 'scientific facts' by other Western academics and continue to be peddled by most of them to this day. We have already seen above the criticism by the likes of J.L. Mehta, J.H.M. Whiteman and Aurobindo Ghose of the false interpretations of *Rig Veda* as worship of the forces of Nature, etc., concocted by such Colonial Indologists.

Muller wrote that Indians were a people never destined to act a prominent part in the history of the world[58]. This racist view, first expounded by the likes of James Mill, is still echoed tacitly in the subtext of British historians as we have seen above. Muller described the *Rig Veda* as crude, childish and unscientific, reflecting the characteristic of an ancient and simple minded race[59]. Muller rejected possible connections between Greek and the (older) Indian philosophies out of hand[60]. Yet, as with William Jones and other Indologists before him, Muller's 'scientific' European mind assumed the time frame of the Bible myths as the overarching guide to supposed World History. He even made a fervent effort to absolve Robert de Nobili of forgery of the so-called Jesus Veda (*Ezour Vedam*) by trying to place the blame on de Nobili's Indian servant[61]. Such forgeries and fabricated history were aimed at claiming Christian origins for the Vedas and Upanishads. Western-funded Christian Evangelists continue to peddle false myths about the Tamils, St Thomas in India and the supposed Christian origins of Bhakti[62].

B.B. Lal, Retired Director General of the Archaeological Survey of India, says that, even as late as 1920 (just before the rediscovery of the Indus cities), Western scholars denied India any iota of civilisation prior to the incursion of the (White Man) Alexander[63]. It was Dugald Stewart, another Scottish mythmaker, who replaced Alexander of Macedon with St Thomas as the supposed White Man who introduced all knowledge to the Indian darkies[64]. Elaine Pagels, an expert on the Gnostic Gospels, tells us that the exact opposite was the case. Thomas, who never actually visited India, was the apostle who most represented Indian spirituality (especially Buddhism) in influencing early Christianity[65]. We saw in Chapter 2 that Guy Sorman argues that the notions of Love and Charity in Christianity were derived from Buddhism via Asoka's missionaries[66]. Self-examination in Consciousness (Conscience)[67] and rosary beads are also of Buddhist origin. Indeed, the medieval Catholic Church canonised the Buddha unwittingly as they mistook the story of Barlam and Josaphat to be Christian when in fact it was a story about Buddha (*Bodhisat* had become Josaphat via Persian translation)[68]. Sorman points out that Catholic missionaries were indignant when they found Indian religious ceremonies used bell-ringing and incense and Indians worshipped relics. They assumed that Indians copied such practices from Christianity when in fact Christians had copied these practises from Indian traditions[69]. Numerous famous Western historians of philosophy, maths, science, society and art have acted in a similar manner, twisting facts to give precedence to the European Greeks when the evidence actually suggested Indian origins.

The Boden Chair of Sanskrit at Oxford (which Muller originally applied for) was created by Colonel Joseph Boden in order to translate the Bible so as to convert (heathen) Indians to Christianity (the 'one true faith')[70]. Muller's contemporary, the second Boden Professor, Monier Williams wrote[71]:

When the mighty walls of Brahmanism are encircled, undermined and finally stormed by the soldiers of the cross, the victory of Christianity must be signal and complete.

The Scientific Racism of late 19th and early 20th Century Western academia attempted to show that all ancient civilisations were created by White Men, primarily Northern European Germanics. Famous US Anthropologist Samuel G. Morton claimed that Ancient Egyptians were White. The woolly African-style hair depicted in Egyptian pictures was reduced to wigs[72]. For G.W.F. Hegel, the Aryans, Alexander, Caesar, and Charlemagne were, "Always us"; that is Germanics[73].

Max Muller picked out one ambiguous word *anasa* (noseless) in one hymn, from over one thousand hymns, and used it to justify his racial conquest of aboriginal Blacks by White men fantasy. According to Muller, *anasa* referred to the flat-nosed (African-like) dark-skinned Indian aborigines[74]. Ronald Inden has pointed out Muller's hypocrisy in warning against the conflation of Language and Race. 'Scientific Racist' Raj official Herbert Risley based his pseudo-scientific Nasal Index on Muller's (noseless) 'speculation' to depict the dynamic and fluid contemporary Indian *jatis* (occupational castes) as Classical 'Hindu' *varnas* or rigid castes based on racial differences in the British Censuses. The British emphasis on rigid castes and sectarian religious communities in censuses and official dealings reinforced and exacerbated such divisions and thus was integral to their 'Divide and Rule' policies[75]. EIC men were prominent in preaching Human Inequality, against French Republican Egalitarianism, both in Britain and in India where they encouraged caste hierarchy. In Britain they were involved with founding the Royal Institute. The famous Christmas lectures on Science were partly motivated by a desire to inculcate a belief in social hierarchy amongst lower class Britons[76]. In 1931, the 1920 *Oxford Student History of India* by Vincent Smith was reprinted, telling of beautiful, tall, fair-skinned Nordic Aryans conquering dark-skinned, flat-nosed, ugly aborigines in 2nd Millennium *b.c.e* India[77]. Anthropologist Edmund Leach wrote that the discovery of the Indus Civilisation in 1922 should have led scholars to dispense with the Aryan Invasion myth and start again from scratch but too many academic reputations were at stake[78]. Professor Colin Renfrew pointed out in his *Archaeology and Language* that archaeologists took literally the myths of (pseudoscientific) 19th Century Linguists about Aryan migrations. The Linguists in turn took the archaeological interpretations built upon these Linguistic myths as hard facts and so each built upon each other's unsubstantiated myths[79].

After the discovery of the cities of Mohenjo-Daro and Harappa in the Indus Valley by R.D. Banerjee and D. Sahni in1922, Western scholars tried to demote this ancient Indian civilisation, predating anything in Europe, to merely a peripheral offshoot of Mesopotamia[80]. The self-hating, anti-Indian writer, beloved of his conservative British patrons, Nirad C. Chaudhuri repeated this myth[81]. To salvage the AIT myth, the Western scholars promoted the so-called 'Dravidians'[N4] (i.e., South Indian Tamils etc.) from savage aborigines to the builders of this ancient civilisation. This fantasy appeals to Tamil separatists.[N5] But even the historian Romila Thapar, lauded by her Western patrons given her secularist stance opposing 'Hindu Revisionism', says that Tamil poetry was first written down by Aryan migrants to the South. There was no script in South India until the coming of Brahmi, an early form of Sanskrit[82]. How could the Tamils lose all knowledge of city-building and high culture after the supposed Aryan invasion(s) displaced them South. We saw in Chapter 2 that recent DNA studies show that the North Indian peoples possessing Ancestral North Indian genetic markers (closely related to European genetic markers) indicate that the ancestors of the so-called 'Indo-Aryans' were present in Northern India from at least 40,000 years ago[83].

In fact, long before Muller's translation of *Rig Veda*, two late 18th Century Western astronomers had shown, independently, that the ancient Brahmanic Astronomy suggested that the Brahmans or their ancestors must have been in Northern India around 3,102 *b.c.e.* French astronomer Bailly and Scottish astronomer Playfair found that, for all practical purposes, the ancient Brahmanic astronomy was just as good at predicting eclipses, etc., as the contemporary Western astronomy of Meyer and Cassini. The position of the sun in a 3,102 *b.c.e.* eclipse matched that determined by Newtonian theory along with knowledge of the Precession of Equinoxes. However, the Indians could not have back-calculated this fact as the margin of error would have grown significantly over such long periods using the Brahmanic system. The only conclusion was that the Brahmins or their ancestors observed the position of the sun from India in 3,102 *b.c.e.* before the Precession of the Equinoxes led to changes of the solar trajectory relative to the Indian Zodiac[84].

We have seen that the geography of the *Rig Veda* coincides with the vast territorial extent of the Saraswati-Sindhu (Indus-Saraswati) civilisation which extend way beyond the Indus Valley. The Veda even states that the great river Saraswati once flowed between the Yamuna and the Sutlej (where its ancient course has been rediscovered using LANDSAT satellite imagery) dotted with ancient cities[85]. *Rig Veda* even mentions a place called *Hariyupia* which sounds like Harappa[86]. The river names of the Punjab are all Aryan. American and European rivers retain names given by original settlers[87]. London's Thames retains its Celtic name (related to the Sanskrit *Tamas*) even though the Romans built London. There is no evidence for any Aryan invasion or indeed any major cultural discontinuity between the Saraswati-Sindhu civilisation and the later, supposedly the first Aryan civilisation in the Gangetic plain of Northern India beginning in the 2nd M *b.c.e.*[88].

Thus the spread of the Vedic Aryans into the Gangetic plain of North India seems to have followed the drying up of the once-great Saraswati around 1900 *b.c.e.* after earthquakes diverted tributaries into the Indus and Yamuna turning the once great river into a seasonal river flowing through the recently formed desert of modern Rajahstan[89]. The Vedic term which refers both to Man and Spirit is *Purusa* as still used today. Feuerstein *et al.* note that *Pur* in Sanskrit means city and say that *Purusa* was derived from *Pur-vasu* meaning city-dweller. Thus *contra* Muller's nomadic hordes, Rig Vedic Man called himself **city-dweller** {*e.m.*}[90]. Radhakrishnan had pointed out long ago, without reference to the AIT controversies, that *Purusa* was used as a term for Spirit as Spirit was that which dwells in the citadel (of the Heart) {*e.m.*}[91]; the central citadel being a metaphor for the heart as the centre of the body. Again, in stark contrast to Muller's presentation of Vedic Aryans as nomadic invaders, *Rig Veda* refers to one hundred-oar boats (ships)[92]. The Saraswati-Sindhu civilisation traded by sea in the 3rd M *b.c.e.* with the Sumerians who called the Indians *Meluha*. The world' first dockyard was built by these Northern Indians in Lothal, Gujarat in the mid-3rd M *b.c.e.*

Central Rig Vedic theme of Atman-Brahman *Conceptualised in Upanishads*

We find in J.L. Mehta's phenomenological analysis of the *Rig Veda* (above) that the concept of *Atman* (the microscosmic, inner Light of Pure Consciousness) which is one with *Brahman*, the macrocosmic Light, that this, the central theme of the later Upanishads, was already present in inchoate form in these hymns, the oldest Indo-European literature. Western scholarship still treats Muller's original view that the *Rig Veda* was composed in the 2nd M *b.c.e.* as 'written in stone' even though he largely retracted these claims. Western academia treats this imaginary dating as 'authoritative' facts due to its tacit racism in conflating the assertions of famous 'European' scholars with 'scientifically' determined facts. However, as we have seen, based on the Biblical mythology that the Earth is only around 6,000 years old! This false Western dating leaves it open that some of the older hymns may date back much further to the dawn of human civilisation. The most famous hymn in the *Rig Veda* is *Nasadiya Sukta* (The Hymn of Nonbeing) which, speaks of a paradoxical Void-like state referred to as 'That One' from which the Creation (also called 'That One') arises. The paradox of the Void which is simultaneously *purnam* (plenum or fullness) has become a key element of perennial mystical insight and the dual use of 'That One' involves the paradox of the Creation arising out of an indescribable, infinite source which remains undiminished.

Nasadiya Sukta, although older than most of the religious mythologies of the Bible[N6] actually ends with a remarkable open-minded scepticism asking, who truly knows whence came this cosmos? Perhaps, it asserts, that He who surveys everything from the highest of realms, even He may not know the answer. In another *Rig Veda* hymn (RV I.164.46) we find the famous basis of the *Sanatana Dharma* (Eternal Truth), underlying various relative paths. "To what is one, the seers give many a name. They call it Agni, Yama, Matarisva"[93]. This overarching Monistic emphasis of so-called 'Hinduism' (*Sanatana Dharma*) is nowadays restated as the aphorism, "**Truth is One** though sages call it by many names".[N7] Later texts would stress the impersonality of the highest, or the most fundamental, realm of *nirguna Brahman*, beyond all dualities, although the poetic use of "He" was not abandoned. British comedian Bill Bailey comments about this remarkable open-mindedness of Hinduism, in contrast to the Judaeo-Christian threats of 'fire and brimstone' in Hell, in his *Part Troll* stand-up show. The joke is of course on primitive Judaeo-Christian superstition resembling the 'monsters will get you' warning to errant toddlers. Oxford physicist Professor Frank Close ends his *The Void* with a quote from *Nasadiya Sukta* preceded by Close's comments including[94]:

In Genesis some God said, 'let there be light,' but for the Rigveda, gods are creations of human imagination, invoked to explain what lay beyond understanding: 'the Gods came afterwards...who then knows whence all has arisen?'

The *Rig Veda* contains the famous Hindu imagery of the two birds dwelling in one body which distinguish the unborn Spirit or *atma* as the passive spectator from the *jiva* (individual soul) which enjoys the fruits of one's actions. The Upanishads, mystical *sutras* (aphoristic poetry summarising the key knowledge) were composed over a number of centuries starting around three thousand years ago. They are known as the *Vedanta* (the end of the Vedas) as they are supposed to represent the culmination of the Vedic mystical tradition with the transition from the numerous shining deities of the *Rig Veda* to the realisation of the Ultimate Reality in the doctrine of the *Atman-Brahman*. They contain the famous grand pronouncements such as *Tat tuam asi* (That thou art), *ayam atma Brahman* (this *atman* is *Brahman*), and *aham brahmasmi* (I am Brahman) which refer to the identity of the impersonal *Atman* (not the personal or individuated ego) with *Brahman*. Radhakrishnan notes that Yajnavalkya, the sage accredited with the famous *Brihadaranyaka Upanisad* refers to the Light of the Self [95], the Self (*Atman*) indeed is his light[96]. The Deeper Self, says Radhakrishnan, be it called a ghost, a soul or a spirit, is a Light which dwells in each being, a Light which no power can extinguish, (i.e., it is uncreated and eternal), an immortal spirit, the silent witness in the heart. The Upanishads assert that the Light of Absolute Truth is refracted as it passes through the distorting medium of human nature[97]. The *Chandogya Upanisad* asserts that the unchangeable essence of the empirical Self is immortal. It is the highest Light (*parama jyotih*), the Light of lights[98]. The *Maitri Upanisad* asserts, "That is the realm of Brahman. That is the ocean of Light" [99].

Of course, as Radhakrishnan points out, these aphoristic mystical insights leave us with many questions as to how the primal Reality in which the Divine Light shines everlastingly can yet be the source and fount of all empirical being, (i.e., all that we experience)[100]. Yajnavalkya describes the Self (*Atman*) as its own light, self-effulgent, self-luminous[101]. He also describes different states of Self Consciousness, Waking, Dreaming and Deep Sleep. In Deep Sleep, though the eyes are inactive, the Self is still the *seer* as the Self sees by its own Light, its intrinsic nature is to see. In Deep Sleep, the True Self is experienced because consciousness (*cit;* Pure Consciousness) alone is present without an object[102]. The Hindu AUM (Om) symbol represents primarily the famous 4-state model of the States of Consciousness (Waking, Dream, Deep Sleep & the Fourth State or *Turiya*) from the Mandukya Upanishad. We have seen that the Upanishad's contained the *panch bhuta* (Five Elements) theory with *Akasa* as the first element (Space as subtle matter characterised by Vibration). The AUM symbol represents secondarily the concept of *Sabdabrahman* (Sound Brahman) or the Vibratory Creation. These questions about the exact nature of the relationship between the individual consciousness and impersonal, Absolute Consciousness, and of the relationship between transcendental Absolute Consciousness, the phenomenal universe (the Creation), states of Consciousness, etc., have occupied the great Indian philosophers for thousands of years.

The Vedic Roots of the Buddhist Heterodoxy and the Mahayanists' Tacit Return to the *Atman* and *Brahman* in Tibetan Buddhism

The Popular Images of Hinduism and Buddhism in the West

French Orientalist writer Guy Sorman tells us in his *The Genius of India* {*e.m.*}[103]:

> *The way Westerners have interpreted Hinduism and Tibetan Buddhism is more indicative of their fantasies than any real adhesion to a theology* [sic] *that has been properly understood. ...the Hinduism meant for foreign consumption which is often no more than a series of exercises that passes off as yoga....the adoration of the Dalai Lama tells us more about the West than about Buddhism.*

We saw above that Wendy Doniger carefully avoids criticising Tibetan Buddhism whilst demonising tantric Hinduism. The fact is that Tibetan Buddhism was largely derived from Indian Tantric Buddhism which has a lot in common with Tantric Hinduism. Doniger's circumspection in regard to Buddhism is because it is not Politically Correct to attack Buddhism in Western Liberal intellectual circles given the obsession with Tibetan Buddhism and the Dalai Lama. The anti-Tamil warmongering Buddhist priests of Sri Lanka who urged on the Sri Lankan army in its recent massacres of Tamils and the Buddhist dictatorship in Burma are quietly overlooked along with all the theocratic aspects of Tibetan Buddhism.

The Western Liberal antipathy toward so-called 'Hinduism' is obviously related to the discriminatory practises associated with the Caste System which are indeed despicable. But such Western demonisation of Hindu Caste practises is somewhat hypocritical given the massive inequalities that existed, and still remain, within Western society associated with African slave-trading, looting and genocide in the Americas, Africa and Asia, along with the Colonial apartheid-like societies and laws. Social progress in much of the Western world was funded by the economic prosperity gained through exploitation of African slaves, looting the wealth of other civilisations and economic parasitisation of the colonised world. Christian missionaries and their Indian converts like Vishal Mangalwadi[104] and even pro-Hindu Frenchman Guy Sorman[105] regurgitate the British-created myths of India as the land of Eternal Poverty and Famine. In reality, India was known throughout most of Eurasia's civilised history for its great wealth. It was Britain which grew rich by pauperising India and inflicting dozens of manmade famines, looting and extorting India's wealth and resources and confiscating much of India's food-grains to benefit Britain, providing Food Security for Britons and helping to feed other Europeans. The poorest Indians were deliberately left to starve and even killed off deliberately through the policies of Churchill[106] and Disraeli[107] in numerous holocausts covered up by mainstream British history. I quoted Alain Daniélou in Chapter 2 in regard to how the Caste system allowed the co-existence of different communities and the preservation of ancient stone age tribes without their extermination and forced assimilation.

Sorman points out that, contrary to mainstream Western misrepresentations, the Hindu Nationalist (BJP) notion of *Hindutva* is not a call for a return to the Past but an Indian way of combining the 'Eternal' Dharma with Modernity. *Hindutva* represents *cultural authenticity*[N8] and not either 'Fundamentalism' or 'Fascism' as outsiders portray it falsely {*e.m.*}[108]. In fact, the Dalai Lama has been welcomed at Hindu Nationalist BJP gatherings as he represents an indigenous Indian tradition, Buddhism. The BJP opposes those religions which look to foreigners in the Vatican, Arabia, the UK or the USA for leadership as these often urge converts to act in a socially disruptive manner against India's national interests.[N9] Gandhian Sorman quotes the Mahatma himself on how independence was worthless if all it meant was *aping blindly the coloniser* {*e.m.*}[109]. This is what the Western-educated, self-hating Indian middle class are best at whilst denouncing anything associated with the native 'Hindu' tradition as superstitious nonsense that needs to be eradicated[N10]. They are just living up to the pejorative epithet *bandor lok* (Monkey People) with which Rudyard Kipling mocked them metaphorically in his racist fable *The Jungle Book*. Frenchman Daniélou also noted how European colonial empires created native elites to serve the colonial empires and it is through the prism of these (self-hatred filled) Western-educated elites that the West gleans most of its information about the once-dominated cultures[N11 110]. Richard Crasta, brought up in the Sin-obsessed, guilt-ridden, sex-fearing, White Man worshipping world of Indian Christianity which he has abandoned, writes {*e.m.*}[111]:

> *What a yogic feat, what a giant leap for one of the world's oldest, greatest, and philosophically exalted cultures:* ***from becoming one with Brahman...*** ***...to impressing the whites...*** *we have surrendered our souls to white* worship... *and self-hatred... Inside our heads, Indian civilisation has been defeated by Western values and materialism.*

Eurocentric Western mainstream History also tends to misrepresent Western history as if it was rooted in (the actually non-Western) Classical Athens and always a form of incipient democracy and individual liberty[112]. In fact, the Ancient Greeks never proclaimed Individual Freedom[113]. The word *idiot* has its roots in Aristotle's mocking of men who put the individual's good before that of the collective good. Siddharta Gautama (the so-called 'Buddha') used the Sanskrit term *Sangha* for his following as this was the term for the popular assemblies in the many *Kshatriya* (Warrior caste) republican cities that existed in the Northern India of his time[114, 115]. Certain European Colonial Indologists tried to reduce the true antiquity of the Buddha in order to make the so-called 'Democracy' in Classical Athens look more exceptional than it was[116, 117]. Athens was a slave-holding imperial city and the Parthenon, far from being a symbol of Democracy (as it is presented in the modern West) was built to store the loot which Athens extorted from fellow Hellenic states under it 'protection racket' known as the Delian League. Athens also led the way in suppressing and veiling women[118]. Women were far more independent in ancient Babylon and Egypt than in later Graeco-Roman Classical civilisation. Sorman stresses the 'Democratic spirit' of native Indian tradition, with its pluralism, freedom of expression and decentralised power, which was present long before the British conquered India[119].

Western Liberal Buddhophilia is also due to the Naturalistic (Materialist) predispositions of many Western Buddhophiles who imagine falsely that, in supposedly rejecting gods and souls as well as focusing on individual psychology rather than grand Cosmology, Buddhism is more 'scientific' than Brahmanism which rejects Physicalist ontology. Alongside Vivekananda at the 1893 Chicago World Parliament of Religions, Sri Lankan Buddhist delegate Anagarika Dharmapala promoted Buddhism as the religion for the Scientific Age. Prior to Stalin's terror against all religions, early Bolsheviks had promoted Buddhism as Atheistic and Rationalistic[120]. As Professor Muller-Ortega pointed out (*see Ch. 3*) there has been a recent trend amongst Western Buddhophile scientist friends of the Dalai Lama to claim that their methods are superior to those of other traditions. Yet ironically, as we saw in Chapter 3, the Dalai Lama's friend Francisco Varela ignored the Tibetan's actually very helpful comments about the nature of the Inner Light, in order to reduce Buddhist phenomenological knowledge to Varela's Emergent Materialist mythology[121, 122].

Naive Western Buddhophiles sometimes seem to imagine that Siddharta Gautama, who came to be known as Buddha (Awakened One), was the first man to attain enlightenment when, as the likes of enlightened mystics Whiteman and Merrell-Wolff recognised, that Siddharta was only reformulating the much older knowledge of the *Rig Veda* and Upanishads (the secret knowledge of the Brahmans) which he clearly did not realise fully given his vague, inconsistent and often misleading teachings. As Sri Lankan Obeyesekere notes, Buddhist texts recognise that some Buddhas of the past were Brahmans. Depending on the text, Siddharta is viewed as the 7th, 24th or 28th in the line of Buddhas. Obeyesekere says texts say that Nirvana is achievable in this very existence. This truth has always been there and the Buddha, following the example of previous Buddhas (including Brahmans) rediscovered and did not invent it[123].

We saw in Chapter 3 that Maurice Bloomfield wrote in his *The Religion of the Veda* (1908), "There is no important form of Hindu thought, 'heterodox' Buddhism included, which is not rooted in the Upanishads."[124]. Famous Anglo-Ceylonese scholar Ananda Coomaraswamy stated in his *Hinduism and Buddhism*[125]:

> *The more superficially one studies Buddhism, the more it seems to differ from the Brahmanism in which it originated; the more profound our study, the more difficult it becomes to distinguish Buddhism from Brahmanism or to say in what respects, if any, Buddhism is really unorthodox.*

It seems as if the doctrine of transmigration that is now associated with both Buddhism and Hinduism originated in Jainism and Buddhism. Such a doctrine of transmigration is not really found in the Upanishads (the 'Vedanta' or End of the Vedas) but, during the Classical Period in India such popular notions were projected backwards in time onto the Vedanta. They reflected the Jain and Buddhist focus on the social world and in particular on Ethics. The credits and deficits of the mercantilist accountant's ledger were projected onto the notion of *samsara* (literally 'ceaseless'; meaning the ceaseless flux of the phenomenal world)[126]. This is not to say that Past-Life memories do not exist but rather that they must be interpreted in more subtle and sophisticated ways than simplistic transmigration of souls or even transmigrating 'Streams of Consciousness'!

The Lack of Light and Clarity in Buddhism

Siddharta Gautama, the so-called "Buddha", created great confusion amongst his followers, with a number of ill-defined doctrines, especially that of *Anatta* (Pali form of Sanskrit *Anatman*). As with the Jains, Buddhism's main patrons were uneducated merchants who became increasingly wealthy in the early part of the Classical Period in India (*c.*600 *b.c.e.* to *c.*500 *c.e.*). The rather vulgar Pali expression *anatta* literally means "no *Atman*" although this need not correspond exactly to the Vedantic *Atman* (impersonal Spirit or the 'Higher Self') and Buddha, almost certainly, meant that there is no immortal ego (or personal Self). Whiteman says that the persistent rendering of *Atman* as "Self" rather than universal (impersonal) Spirit has created such confusion[127]. I noticed by chance that my Collins Concise English Dictionary, published in the 1980s, includes the term 'atman' and translates it incorrectly as the *personal* soul or self in Hinduism. No doubt many unsophisticated Hindus view it as such, including the priest at my mother's funeral. Modern scholars such as Mrs C.A.F. Rhys-Davids, A.K. Coomaraswamy, George Grimm, K.C. Bhattacharya, J. Pérez-Remón and famous translators including I.B. Horner and Edward Conze have asserted that early Buddhism implicitly, or even explicitly, asserted existence of an (*Atman*-resembling) Self [128]. Scholars cognizant of actual mystical experience have argued that Buddha was actually denying the immortality of the ego rather than an impersonal *Atman* but, due to the vague teachings of Buddha, many Buddhists still believe that there is no inner core or essence to the "soul" resembling the Vedantic *Atman*.

American Transcendentalist Ralph Waldo Emerson disliked the over-rationality of Buddhism[129]. I recall reading neuroscientist Cristopher deCharms' *Two Views of Mind: Abhidharma and Brain Science*[130] which was largely a dialogue with a Tibetan Buddhist teacher. I felt sorry for the Buddhist who could only come out repeatedly with one simplistic pseudo-logical stock answer like a medieval Scholastic. Emerson was also repelled by the Buddhist concept of *nibbana* (Sanskrit: *nirvana*) which he took to mean complete annihilation[131]. The word *nibbano* in my native Bengali (which developing directly from Middle-Indic is closer to Sanskrit than Hindi) means to extinguish a light! Merrell-Wolff says that vast groups of Buddhists have misunderstood Nirvana as meaning literal annihilation, (i.e., 'blacking out' into 'unconsciousness') and many Western scholars and mystics such as Pseudo-Dionysius (with his 'Divine Darkness') have fortified this impression[132]. Although starting off as a Buddhist, Merrell-Wolff's own realisations led to him reconfirming the Brahmanic understanding. Whereas Buddha denied an underlying Substance or Ground of Being, Merrell-Wolff says that Voidness (*Sunyata*) in its inherent nature is the one and only self-existent substance[133]. Similarly, Whiteman, though heaping praise on Buddha, stresses Buddha's confused teachings[134]. He says that the Classical Hindu texts actually describe all the phenomena correctly [135].

McEvilley notes the confusion as to the nature of Enlightenment in many important Buddhist texts which say that simply living in the present moment without conceptualising is Enlightenment[136]. This Living-in-the-Moment notion is prominent in Western New Age Buddhist pop psychology. But such sensory phenomena should not be confused with Enlightenment (Gnosis)! We have seen that non-Indian traditions such as Neoplatonism, Gnosticism, Sufism, Western and Orthodox Christianity, etc., all declare the presence of an Inner Light or Divine Spark which parallels the Vedantic *Atman*. My identification of the direct physical correlate of this Inner Light undermines naïve Buddhist denials of this inner core or universal essence to the human mind. However, such knowledge also supports Buddhism in its denial of any permanent "soul" or Self as in the Hindu *jiva* as the individuated conscious mind is merely a self-organising, fluctuating process with no permanent essence as the Buddha also maintained.

Peter Harvey mentions one of Buddha's own descriptions of *nibbana* as Consciousness, non-manifestive, shining in every respect[137]. In the earlier Hinayana (Lesser Vehicle) Buddhist *suttas* (Pali form of *sutras* or aphoristic verses), the Buddha's awakening is often compared to radiant light. However, strong currents in the early tradition resisted positive images of Enlightenment, preferring negative terminology and reducing (the Inner) Light to the status of a metaphor. Later Mahayana (Greater Vehicle) Buddhism kept this *via negativa* approach (which is associated mainly with Nagarjuna's Middle Way) but images of Light still proliferate in the Mahayana *sutras*. The names of Buddhas (enlightened ones) in Mahayana include *Amitabha* (Limitless Light) and *Vairocana* (Radiant Splendour). In Mahayana, the Buddha's teaching (the *Dharma*) is, itself, regarded metaphorically as Light and important *sutras* (aphoristic texts) have names like *Supreme Golden Light*, and the nature of Mind is Clear Light. Although the later Tibetans do support a concept of luminous spiritual substance, some earlier commentators (presumably bookmen and not mystics) such as the Indian Buddhist Haribhadra took such references to Light as a metaphor[138]. Luminous gnosis is the core soteriological (relating to 'salvation') concept in the Indo-Tibetan tantric text *Ratnamala* (Garland of Gems)[139]. Tantrism is the Hindu spiritual tradition, associated primarily with Bengal, which stresses the *shakti* (energetic) aspect of the Absolute. Tantric Buddhism has a strong emphasis on Yoga leading to intense experiences of Light and a tendency to pronounced positive affirmations of Light[140].

In the Tantric Yoga of Tibetan Buddhism, the Clear Light plays a central role and is considered the Ground of all Being[141]. In Tibetan Buddhism, says Michael Grosso, the Divine Light is the Self[142]. Thus, in the Tantric Tibetan Buddhism known as *Dzogschen* (Supercompleteness; implying the final complete formulation) advocated by the Dalai Lama, we find emphasis on an inner Clear Light and the Clear Light of the Void as the Ground of All Being. Neither of these conform to the original teachings of Siddharta Gautama with its *Anatta*, *Ksanika* (Momentariness) and denial of an Absolute Ground, *nibbana* meaning extinction etc. Both represent a tacit return by these Buddhists to the central Vedic and Vedantic elements of the Inner Light (*atman*) and the macrocosmic Light from beyond (*Brahman*). As Ananda Coomaraswamy stated in *Hinduism and Buddhism*, the deeper our understanding of Buddhism the more difficult it becomes to distinguish from the Brahmanism in which it originated [143].

How the Spiritual Light from India Conquered Eastern Asia

The Western Myth that Chinese Ideas will Increasingly Dominate the Globe in the 21st Century

There is a tendency in the West to imagine that China has historically been the dominant culture in the East and that the forthcoming rise of East Asia will be dominated by China. When we look beneath the distorted historical presentations which denied historical agency to India, we find that India has in fact played the leading role in the cultural history of East Asia. In some respects, modern India and China may be compared to Athens and Sparta respectively. One is a chaotic, pluralistic, open democratic society (though Athenian 'democracy' was restricted to, autochthonous male citizens). Behind the 'smoke and mirrors' of the public spectacles, the other is an aggressive, totalitarian dictatorship. In his *Empire of Lies:The Truth about China in the 21st Century*, Sorman points out that it is Westerners, regurgitating the false propaganda of the Communist Party of China (CPC), who prophesise that China will dominate the 21st Century. Most actual Chinese people don't think this. Sorman tells us how, after the brutal humiliations of the two Opium Wars and the Boxer Rebellion, the self-hatred filled Chinese elite set about eradicating all of traditional China's heritage long before the Maoists finished the job. Beijing once had more temples than any European city. Now only one fake Confucian temple (actually an exam hall) remains as a museum. The so-called 'Neo-Confucianism' peddled by the Communist Party is itself a Western Jesuit invention stripped of true Confucian religiosity including rites, sacrifices and ceremonies. The real Chinese tradition, the religions of the masses rather than the elite Mandarins, was Daoist (Taoist) and Buddhist with a vast pantheon of deities like that in Hinduism. China apes the 'West' (including Communist ideology) far more than India where native traditions have been preserved[144].

Note also the savage brutality of the first Chin (Qin) Emperor (221-210 *b.c.e.*) of all China, working to death one million peasants to build the first Great Wall (using their bones for mortar[145]) and all the slaves who built his vast, vain mausoleum as well as burning books to hide the past history from the people. Mao Zedong killed countless intellectuals and boasted in doing so that he resembled an ancient Empress who did the same. Compare such behaviour with Asoka's public welfare schemes, Mughal Akbar's debates with scholars of all religions and Mahatma Gandhi. China occupies East Turkestan, Tibet, Aksai Chin, part of Vietnam, threatening all its neighbours. It props up the brutal North Korean and Burmese dictatorships, cynically gave Pakistan the nuclear blueprint and, via N. Korea missiles, whilst suppressing the freedoms of its servile masses. In January 2014 the global media reported on the vast and unaccountable fortunes, sometimes billions of dollars, stashed away by the top leaders of the CPC dictatorship. Beyond military prowess on land, Sparta is little remembered. In his *The Genius of India*, Sorman wrote that, in truth, China is a civilisation that has been devoured by the West and

China has nothing new to offer. **India is the only great civilisation not devoured by the West** {*e.m.*}[146].

Sorman says that, even today, as in the 19th Century India remains a 'Voyage of Discovery' and a counterpoint to Western civilisation[147]. Mark Twain wrote[148]:

> *So far as I am able to judge, nothing has been left undone, either by man or nature, to make India the most extraordinary country that the sun visits on his rounds. Nothing seems to have been forgotten, nothing overlooked.*

In his *What India Can Teach Us*, Carl Jung wrote that, if the White Man does not to destroy himself with his scientific inventions, he will have to settle down to a desperately serious course of self-education. The White Man would do well to learn from Indian civilisation the other way of civilising man, the way without suppression and violence, the way which embraced the whole man[149]. Sorman does not think that the 21st Century will be dominated by Indian mystical thought as some, mistakenly, think that André Malraux prophesied. Rather, he thinks that the 21st Century's most innovative ideas in regard to how mankind lives together with each other and with Nature will probably come from Indian thought. He links both the Feminism (in the broader 'Feminine side of all Humans' sense) and the Ecology-Sustainable Development ideas to Gandhi's inspiration[150].

In my *The Oneness/Otherness Mystery* (O/OM), I had written about how Bankim Chandra Chattopadhya, the so-called 'Father of Indian Nationalism', had written in his *Dharmatattva* of fusing European Science with Indian Spirituality and self-control (or mastery over the negative aspects of our psyche). This would put Science to much better use. Indeed, the scientific basis of Hinduism became a powerful idea in the early Indian (elite) Nationalists' discourse[151]. We have seen that, at the turn of the 20th Century, J.C. Bose and the first generation of modern Indian scientists had wanted to challenge Western Materialist science with a New Indian (holistic) Science based on Vedanta[152]. Sorman himself is a follower of the great French Nobel laureate poet Romain Rolland whom we have seen was a friend of Albert Einstein. Rolland, whose biographies introduced M.K. Gandhi, Ramakrishna and Vivekananda to Continental Europeans in the 1920s, saw the 'Marriage of the Genius of India with the Genius of Europe' as the great hope for the future salvation of mankind. "The Great Soul of India will topple our world", said Rolland[153].

The Old Harrovian, Cambridge Natural Sciences graduate and London-trained barrister Jawarharlal Nehru is usually presented as a Westernizer.[N12] The nepotistic and corrupt Nehruvian 'dynasty' has indeed tried to turn India into a poor imitation of the West, a path destined to fail. But in his *Another Reason*: *Science and the Imagination of Modern India*, Gyan Prakash tells of Nehru's desire that modern India should seek an Indian path of synthesising 'Science and Humanism'. Although Nehru recognised that India had to decrease its religiosity and turn to Science, he recognised that the real explanation for India's lack of development was not Religiosity but British colonial exploitation with its 'deindustrialisation' of India. But Science could not solve all of our problems as it lacked the larger outlook that takes everything into perspective. For Nehru, the struggle for national freedom was inseparable from this ambition to see *Science extend its horizons to embrace the totality of Being* {*e.m.*}[154]. The West's technological successes, wrote Nehru, had not solved the basic problems of life. Conflict and self-destruction appeared inherent in the West. Nehru looked for an urge driving the Indian people in a direction not wholly realised. He wrote that India first stirred with the composition of the Vedas and Upanishads. Science must bring *Spirit and Flesh into harmony* {*e.m.*}[155]. In spite of modern Science's progress, we know very little about the soul. Science had shrunk the sphere of Religion and had little to say about the Purpose of Life. The Indian ethos was actually more scientific than that of the West[156]. As stated above, Hinduism was seen as being naturalistic and 'scientific' (evidence-based) unlike Western Christianity. Thus for Nehru, Modern India should not imitate the West but unlock the Indian Nation's own creative energy[157].

British historian Arnold Toynbee stated in the 1950s, in the 21st Century, India will conquer her conquerors, not politically but with her ideas[158]. However, Toynbee naively thought that Indian Buddhism would play the key role in India's philosophical dominance of the globe. In 1986 Willis Harman told the Bombay conference on the Synthesis of Science and Religion that the New Science of the future would replace the old Materialist metaphysics with Indian-style metaphysics based on the **Primacy of Consciousness** {*e.m.*} [159]. Siddharta Gautama denied that there was a Ground of all Being. The Indian metaphysics, said Harman, can include the Western concept of Causality within it as a limited case (of the deeper, transcendental, holonomic true causation). The reverse is not the case[160]. After receiving a copy of my O/OM in 1999, Japanese physicist Shiuji Inomata wrote a letter to thank me. He mentioned that ten million Japanese TV viewers heard him repeating Harman's conclusions in his inaugural speech to the 1998 Tokyo conference of Eastern Philosophy and Science[161].

As I started showing in O/OM, contrary to the universalist pretensions of the West, the Indian metaphysics of Brahmanism and Tantrism supplies the ontological base for a truly 'Universal Science' which can account for so-called 'anomalous phenomena' precluded by Western science. Physicalist science is not wrong but is limited and not truly all-encompassing. It represents the abstraction of stable phenomenal forms and their mathematically-predictable patterns of regular behaviour from the bigger, deeper Transcendentalist picture of Indian cosmology.

Indian knowledge also undermines all Western (and non-Western) Theistic religion. Werner Heisenberg had told Tagore that Indian civilisation already subscribed to a view resembling that of the new QM that had shocked the Western Mind [162]. In his novel *A Passage to India*, E.M. Forster's modern 'parable of the cave', which so disorients the Western visitor with its resounding echoes, is said to stand as a metaphor for India civilisation herself. It was a metaphor for the fact that **India undermines the Westerner's deepest beliefs** {*e.m.*}[163].

The Nonviolent Conquest of China, Tibet and South-East Asia by Indian Spiritual Culture

Westerners brought up with Eurocentric, Orientalist myths about Eurasian history know little of India's massive cultural influence on China as well as on Europe. The system of geomancy known as *Feng Shui* originated in the Indian system of *Vastu* and the martial art of *Kung Fu* originated with an Indian Buddhist monk known as Boddhisattva who brought the Keralan martial art of Kariyappa to the Shaolin monastery in China. As the famous Chinese scholar and Chinese Nationalist Ambassador to the USA, Hu Shih[164] stated:

> *India conquered and dominated China culturally for twenty centuries without ever having to send a single soldier across her border. This cultural conquest was never imposed by India on her neighbours. It was the result of voluntary searching, voluntary learning, voluntary pilgrimage and voluntary acceptance on the part of China.*

Hu Shih adds that the gifts of India learnt by the Chinese were both philosophical and practical. As S.N. Chopra, once an Indian Ambassador to China elaborates, Buddhism dominated China for six centuries, calming China down after centuries of war and allowing for constructive creativity. Sanskrit and Pali added 35,000 words to the Chinese vocabulary. Carved wood printing entered China with the Buddhists who used it to spread their message. The first extant book printed by carved wood block-printing was the Buddhist text *Vajracohedika-prajna-paramita-sutra* (a form of the *Diamond Sutra*) in 868 *c.e.* discovered in Chinese-occupied Turkestan[165]. The 16 foot long scroll contains a version of the famous Indian Buddhist Kumarajiva's (*see below*) translation into Chinese of the Sanskrit Diamond Sutra. It was found in 1900 by an Abbot Wang in the secret library in Cave 17 near the Silk Road outpost of Sogdian (Dunhuang) along with over 10,000 manuscripts and silk paintings. In 1907 Sir Aurel Stein took away 24 cases of manuscripts and 5 boxes of art for just £130 [166].

The Chinese claim to have invented printing rests on this Buddhist text from Central Asia translated into Chinese from the Sanskrit. But this is only the oldest *extant* printed book. In fact, as Hu Shih (not an apparatchik of the CPC 'Empire of Lies') admitted, printing was brought to China by Buddhist missionaries from India. The Buddhist idea of printing books was probably derived from the printing of patterns onto textiles in India. Furthermore, medieval Sogdian was not part of China or even part of its empire. The native Turkic Uighurs in Chinese-occupied East Turkestan are Muslims who certainly do not see themselves as 'Chinese'. Rule over the region known as Sogdiana has changed hands on many occasions over the centuries. Achaemenid Persians, Seleucid Macedonians, Bactrian Greeks, Parthians, Kushans, White Huns and Sassanid Persians ruled there until the Arab conquest in the late 7th Century *c.e.* In 1127 *c.e.* Sogdian was invaded by Northern nomads known to the Chinese as Hsi-hsia. The caves remained an important Buddhist site for several more centuries before falling into neglect and lost beneath the sands of the desert[167]. Of most significance was the Kushana Empire which linked this region to Northern India and it was during this period that Buddhism was transmitted from India to China. The chauvinist Chinese try to hide these facts about Indian origins of printing and Kung Fu, out of a Sinocentric (Han-centric) sense of superiority over Indians. Chinese racism towards Indians and Africans in Hong Kong and China remains a problem.

Much of China's heritage in painting, sculpture, printing, poetry and grammar owes a great deal to Indian influence. The first known Chinese 'opera' *Pu-tow* was based on a South Indian story and Indian classics added to Chinese literature[168]. Even the Chinese word *Mandarin* comes from the Sanskrit *mantrin* meaning a Brahmin advisor to a king. Kautilya (*a.k.a.* Chanakya) was the most famous *mantrin*, advising the great Indo-Aryan *ksatriya* emperor Chandragupta Maurya and writing the famous *Arthasastra* (Treatise on Statecraft). The famous Chinese writer and inventor Lin Yutang stated that India was China's teacher in trigonometry, quadratic equations, grammar, phonetics and so forth[169]. Goody notes the influence of Indian logic on China, Korea and Japan via Buddhism. Hu Shih himself wrote *The Development of the Logical Method in Ancient China* noting that China lacked adequate logical methods[170]. Japanese philosopher Nakamura said that India differed from China and Japan where he found little by way of logical thinking. Japanese scholars visited China to study under Hsuan-Tsang who had travelled in India in 629-645 *c.e.* translating 74 Buddhist works[171]. Thus Buddhism was not simply India's spiritual gift to East Asia. Numerous Chinese scholar-pilgrims travelled to India with a view to taking back to China the '**true light**' of knowledge or the '**original light**' {*e.m.*}[172]. Such references indicate a spiritual search for methods of accessing Divine Light, alongside intellectual knowledge, in India.

Tibet, which communist China under the mass-murdering maniac and tyrant Mao Zedong invaded in 1950 and continues to occupy with brutality, had a similar historical experience in regard to India. As the USA's leading Buddhist scholar Robert Thurman, father of Hollywood actress Uma (named after a Hindu goddess), states[173]:

> *Over a period of millennia, the Indian Buddhist civilisation profoundly influenced all the other civilisations of Asia. ... in the seventh century* c.e., *the Tibetan civilisation opened itself in a unique way to receive the great treasures of Indian Buddhism...*

In fact the Tibetans were once warlike barbarians who invaded North-Eastern India, ruled by the Pala Dynasty, around 1,350 years ago. The Buddhist Palas drove the Tibetans back up the Himalayas but the Tibetans took back with them Indian Buddhism and invited Indian Buddhist masters to Tibet. As in China, this Buddhist influence pacified their warlike instincts. Sixteen centuries earlier the great Mauryan emperor, Asoka, who completed the Indo-Aryan conquest of virtually the entire Indian subcontinent (bar the Southern tip whose rulers nonetheless became vassals of the Mauryans) started by his grandfather Chandragupta Maurya, is said to have converted to Buddhism and renounced bloodshed. The doctrine of *ahimsa* (noninjury to all living things) actually originated with Mahavira's Jainism. Many Western Neo-Buddhists, steeped in Christian and Buddhist anti-Hindu myths make ridiculously exaggerated claims for Tibetan Buddhism ignoring the fact that more or less all of these Tibetan notions, bar some of the mythology of reincarnation such as the *Bardo* myth and Tibetan deities, can be traced back to either Indian masters or to precursors in Indian philosophy.

The influence of India is more prominent throughout South-East Asia, where Indians, often becoming Hindu kings, brought in person the advanced civilisation of the Indo-Aryans to the tribal peoples of the Indo-Chinese jungles and the islands of Indonesia. Thus British Indologist A.L. Basham wrote in his famous *The Wonder that was India,* "The whole of South-East Asia received most of its culture from India"[174]. Contrast these facts, including the debunking of the AIT, to the absurd claims of Karl Marx that India had no history at all except for that of its invaders[175]! Marx was repeating the myths of his teacher Hegel (who claimed that all ancient civilisations had been created by White Germanic 'Aryans') and the self-serving British historians linked to the EIC who denied Indians any historical agency. Thus we have the Hindu temples of Angkor Wat in Cambodia, Buddhist Burma, Buddhist kings and Hindu-influenced culture in Thailand. One of the airports in Bangkok besieged by anti-government activists in 2008 had the Sanskrit name *Suvarnabhumi* (Golden Land). The Chinese-majority city state in Malaysia is known as Singapore from the Sanskrit for Lion City. From the great Rig Vedic god Varuna, through the local corruptions of the Sanskrit to Barunai, we get the name of the oil-rich, now Mohammedan, kingdom of Brunei. The liberal Hindu culture still survives on the island of Bali in Indonesia, now a mainly Muslim country, making it a target for Jihadi terrorists. Indonesia's oldest cities still bear their Sanskrit names like Yogjakarta and the leaders still bear Sanskritic names like Sukarnoputri (daughter of Sukarno) as found in India with the Brahmaputra (son of Brahma) river.

In October 2007 the President of the Philippines, Gloria Arroyo, sought to revive the ancient ties with India. India played an important role in Filipino culture through trade with the two Indo-Malayan empires before Spanish colonisation. The Srivijaya Empire (7th to 13th Century *c.e.*) based in Palembang, Sumatra was a mix of Buddhism and Hinduism. The Majapahit Empire (1293 to 1527 *c.e.*) was Hindu and centred in Java. Scholars believe that Indian influence on Filipino culture has been underestimated given the Sanskrit roots of the pre-Hispanic script, epic folk literature, traditional dress, social customs, arts, crafts and Sanskritic roots of words all indicate massive Indian influence[176]. Even as far away as South Korea, prominent Koreans still claim ancestry from an Indian princess, known in Korea as Queen Huh, who came almost two thousand years ago from Ayodhya to marry King Suro, founder of the Kara kingdom.

Dallmayr says that Kumarajiva and Bodhidharma were probably the two most celebrated Indian Buddhists travelling to China. Kumarajiva (4th Century *c.e.*) translated into Chinese the *Mahaprajnaparamita Sutra* (Sutra of Perfect Wisdom) traditionally ascribed to Nagarjuna. Through Kumarajiva's efforts Nagarjuna's Madhyamika became ascendant in Chinese Buddhism. The 6th Century *c.e.* Bodhidharma is said to have been born a Brahman in South India before converting to Buddhism in his youth. In China he is said to have met and debated with Emperor Wu who founded the Liang Dynasty. Bodhidharma's unconventional teaching and yoga methods were controversial at the time and included his paradoxical verbal exchanges (*koans*). He became the founder of *Ch'an* Buddhism[177]. The word *Zen,* which nowadays has such mystique in Western 'pop culture' is the Japanese form of *Ch'an*, itself derived from the Sanskrit *dhyana* (meditation). The Zen that D.T. Suzuki popularised in the West was actually a highly Vedanticised interpretation[178].

For Japanese tourists, the "Holy Land"[N13] is not Palestine but Bihar in Northern India, the region once known as *Aryavarta* (the Aryans' country) with its capital Patna built above ancient Pataliputra, capital of the Mauryan Empire. It was here in Bihar that Siddharta Gautama is said to have attained enlightenment at Gaya and started teaching his *Arya Dharma* (Noble Truths). We have seen that, depending on the texts, he was seen by Buddhists as the seventh, twenty fourth, or twenty eighth in a long line of previous Buddhas (awakened ones) including a number of Brahmans[179]. Such facts highlight the supreme prestige of the great and ancient Indian civilisation amongst the nascent civilisations of the Far East. It was at Chandragupta's court in Pataliputra that Seleucus Nikator's [N14] envoy Megasthenes marvelled at the vast wealth and wonders of the "slaveless" society of Mauryan India and wrote his *Indika*.

Ex Orient Lux: The Influence of Indian Philosophies in the Ancient Mediterranean

The Divine Light in Plato, 'Pimander' and Plotinus

We saw above that notions that Divinity was Fire or Light and that mortals might interact with it were uncommon in the Ancient Mediterranean[180]. My RAS brainwave correlate of the Divine Light confirms the view that such notions can arise independently in various places given that the Light is not mere speculation but an archetypal or universal experience of human transformations of consciousness. We saw that roots of Vedic spirituality in the use of the entheogenic drug known as Soma. Anthropology graduate Jomo Kenyatta, first leader of independent Kenya, wrote about his apprenticeship with his Witch Doctor grandfather. His arguments about the scientific basis of telepathy and other occult practises in vibrations parallel both ancient Indian and Greek philosophical knowledge[181]. Athenian philosophers would have been familiar with the secret Mystery rites practised at Eleusis some 15 miles along the Sacred Way from Athens[182].

As Peter Kingsley stresses in his *Ancient Philosophy, Mystery and Magic: Empedocles and the Pythagorean Tradition*, many of the early Greek philosophers were actually Shamanic healers whose mystical practises and beliefs have been suppressed by Eurocentric and Athenocentric Classics. Ancient Greek Philosophy was really part of a much broader Eastern Mediterranean tradition and non-European texts in the same tradition elaborated the secretive occult practises alluded to by Greeks[183]. Archaeological excavations near Naples in the 1950s showed that the great philosopher Parmenides (whose Monistic Being was also Thought) was the founder of a shamanic healing sect[184]. Pythagoras and Empedocles (whose Doctrine of Elements seems to have been derived from the Upanishadic *panch bhuta*[185, 186, 187]) were both clearly shamanic occultists[188]. Heraclitus claimed he searched within himself to derive his philosophy[189]. For Western Classics and History of Science, ancient White shamanic mystics and magicians are presented as 'scientists' well ahead of their time, whereas non-Europeans are presented as superstitious mystics! Peter Kingsley states[190]:

> *To ignore these* [non-European] *connections, or try to banish the word 'shaman' from discussion of Greek religion...is simply to perpetuate the myth that ancient Greeks were magically sealed off from external influences.*

In glorifying Plato, Classics asserted that Pythagoreanism had died out by his time when in fact Plato's contemporaries accused him of plagiarising the Pythagoreans who were still very active during Plato's lifetime[191]. That Pythagoras copied many ideas is well known and Herodotus had Pythagoras in mind when he wrote of Greeks making their names by copying Oriental ideas (much like New Agers today)[192]. Numerous scholars have noted the Pythagorean roots of Platonism. The later Neoplatonists stated that they were returning to the same Oriental sources from which Pythagoras drew his inspiration[193]. Kingsley points out numerous Oriental roots of Ancient Greek Philosophy. He mentions Central Asian Shamanism transmitted through Thrace, and influences from Anatolia, Babylon, Persia and Egypt. But his overlooking the possibility of Indian influence is especially glaring given his focus on Empedocles[194]. In fact, Diogenes Laertius (and the much later Church father Eusebius) had ascribed to Aristoxenus, a pupil of Aristotle, the famous story of Socrates' meeting with Indians in Athens[195]:

> *Aristoxenus the musician tells the following story about the Indians. One of these men met Socrates at Athens, and asked him what was the scope of his philosophy. "An inquiry into human phenomena," replied Socrates. At this the Indian burst out laughing. "How can we inquire into human phenomena," he exclaimed, "when we are ignorant of divine ones?"*

I have mentioned the Afro-Asiatic roots of Classical Grecian civilisation which Martin Bernal's *Black Athena* restored from under the whitewash of Colonial Era 'Classics'[196]. These Oriental roots were well known prior to the rise of racist 'Classics' in the Colonial Era which abstracted Greece and Rome from their Afro-Asiatic Mediterranean context. For instance, Isaac Newton's Platonist friends Henry More and Ralph Cudworth both claimed that it was well known that Greek culture actually came from Egypt. Henry More wrote of the mysteries that Pythagoras and Plato brought out of Egypt and parts of Asia into Europe. He added that the doctrine of the pre-existence of the soul was taught by the Gymnosophists and other wise men of Egypt but also by the Brahmans of India and the Magi of Babylon and Persia. Seventeenth Century Jesuit Athanasius Kircher, basing himself largely on the famous 2nd Century *c.e.* Clement of Alexandria, claimed that the Platonic doctrine of Ideas originated with the Egyptians[197]. Alexander Polyhistor (1st Century *c.e.*), Apuleius (2nd Century *c.e.*) and Philostratus (*c.* 200 *c.e.*) stated that Pythagoras learned many things from the Brahmins[198]. Iamblichus, the biographer of Pythagoras tells us that he travelled widely and studied the teachings of the Egyptians, Assyrians and the Brahmins[199]. Lucianus (2nd Century *c.e.*) wrote (correctly) that Indians cultivated Philosophy before it came to the Greeks and Clement of Alexandria wrote that the Greeks stole their philosophy from the Orientals[200]. Clement also named the Brahmins as amongst the teachers of Pythagoras. Eusebius wrote of Numenius (who had a deep influence on Plotinus) seeking to synthesise Pythagoras and Plato whilst seeking a confirmation of their doctrines in the doctrines of the Brahmins, Magi and Egyptians[201].

Given Plato's roots in Pythagoreanism, there seems to be some truth in Kircher's claims as Pythagoreanism is a continuation of older Oriental traditions. This link is clearer when, unlike racist Classics, one accepts the mystical basis of Platonism. Plato's Forms/Ideas may be derived from Egyptian deities just as Empedocle's Elements were primarily deities. Jung said that ancient deities were archetypal forces in the 'Collective Unconscious' paralleling Aurobindo's assertion that the Vedic deities were in fact powers of his 'Supermind' (equivalent to *Nous* or *Akasa*). Yates refers to the magi manipulating the (archetypal) images in the intermediary realm corresponding to the Platonic realm of Ideas[202]. In the same way, the deities of the *Rig Veda* became philosophical concepts in the Upanishads. It is interesting that More thought Gymnosophists were Egyptian as they were actually Indian yogis but itinerant Indian yogis and Asoka's Buddhists were famously present in Alexandria.

Greek Monism arose in Lydian and Persian-ruled Ionia when previously the Greeks had no such philosophy, only anthropomorphic myths of Olympian gods etc. Athenians were themselves Ionians unlike the Northern Dorian Spartans. The Sanskrit term for Greek *Yavana* (Ionian) was coined before Macedonian Alexander's brief and unsuccessful incursion into the Indus Valley from which the Greeks were soon expelled by Chandragupta Maurya. The two Greeks who wrote pre-Alexandrian texts on India, Skylax and Ctesias, were both employed by Persians. Around 519 *b.c.e.* Darius I sent seafaring Skylax to reconnoitre the Indus prior to Darius's conquest in 515*b.c.e*[203] Darius frequently called Greeks and Indians together for counsel[204]. McEvilley demonstrates the Yoga-like nature of Plato's *philosophia* which he argues was brought to Greece by Indian Jains as Jainism, unlike Vedic spirituality, had a missionary ethic[205].

All the metaphysical elements of Milesian Monism were present in Indian thought considerably earlier than their appearance in Greece[206]. Western scholars' refusal to consider non-European evidence makes Heraclitus appear enigmatic and idiosyncratic. In 1971 M.L. West gave a rigorous and scholarly proof of connection between Heraclitus and an Upanisadic doctrine demonstrating that ideas were travelling between India and Greece in the pre-Socratic period. But West erroneously saw Persia not as the intermediary but as the common source of both Indian and Greek ideas[207]. West pointed out that the *Brihadaranyaka Upanisad* alone throws more light on what Heraclitus was talking about than all the remains of the Pre-Socratic Greeks put together[208]. In fact Heraclitus's single work is extinct; we only have fragments attributed to him in the works of others. Even the commonplace view that Heraclitus asserted that 'All is Flux' is disputed. In fact Heraclitus's epigrammatic and cryptic style earned him the epithet 'the obscure'[209]. He claimed that his philosophy was derived (mystically) by searching or investigating himself and his *Fire represented the Soul* {*e.m.*}[210]. This mystical basis is generally suppressed by Western Historians of Science.

We saw above that Divine Light was the central concept of the *Rig Veda* the sacred hymns of the Vedic Aryans largely written before the Mycenaean Greeks invaded and looted Hittite outposts in what was later to become Ionia. These conflicts laid down the ancestral memories for the anthropomorphic god-filled *Iliad* which attained its final form around 700 *b.c.e.*[211]. Whereas Indian literature fully absorbed the philosophical monism of the Upanishads, Greek literature continued the polytheism of Homer, ignoring the new Monist philosophy[212]. In Greece, the Monism which followed from mystical realisation of the Light remained a small cult, as noted above. Merrell-Wolff points out that Plato and (Egypt-based) Plotinus were not typical of ancient Greek culture as a whole[213]. Psychoanalyst Sudhir Kakar says that the notion of *moksa* ('moksha': liberation, meaning mystical union with *Brahman*), the direct experience of the fundamental unity of human being with the Infinite, is central to the Hindu world image[214].

In Fifth Century *b.c.e.* Athens, Plato's "meditation" involved being flooded with Light, opening the inner eye and becoming wedded to *Sophia* (Divine Wisdom)[215]. We saw in Chapter 3 Plato's famous "destroying the hypotheses" passage from *Republic*, indicating that the sense world and the tools of the intellect must be transcended. For pure knowledge of anything, Plato claimed, we must quit the body. The soul in herself must behold things in themselves, attaining the Wisdom (*Sophia*) of which we say we are lovers (philosophers)[216]. Plato's famous allegory of the cave, as Bailey states, reflects the centrality of the Cosmic Light of Wisdom[217]. Here we see **medi-**tation as the Return to the Centre, not merely *meditare* or reflection but a return to the Light at the Centre. This ties in well with my brainstem brainwave correlation. My Brain-Deactivation/Retreat-to-the-Brainstem interpretation of Enlightenment explains the feeling of 'quitting the body' as the ego is purified, stripping it of attachments to bodily representations in the cortex. Meyer tells us that Plato's philosophy, although inspired somewhat by Monism, cannot be considered as consistently monistic. Traditional Platonism involved a two-tier system with priority given to the permanent and unchanging perfect realm of Forms, under the primacy of the Form of the Good, the True and the Beautiful. Time, the moving shadow of Eternity, characterises a lesser, chaotic, unformed domain[218]. Plato failed to go beyond static forms, projecting human generic ideas logocentrically onto the Transcendental, and failed to truly grasp the formless Pure Consciousness beyond his supposedly Ideal Forms (*see Ch. 11*).

The *Corpus Hermeticum* which purports to be of Ancient Egyptian origin was actually written in Greek in 2nd Century *c.e.* Roman-occupied Egypt. We have seen that Isaac Casaubon claimed that it must have been a Christian forgery as it pretended to prophesy the end of the old Egyptian religion and the coming of Christianity. The Greeks identified Hermes with the Egyptian God of Wisdom *Thoth*[219]. Book One of the *Hermetica* known as *Pimander*[220] or *Poimandres* says that the Supreme *Nous* (Divine Intellect) is Life (*zoe*) and

Light (*phos*) [221, 222]. In general the God of the Hermetica is **Light** and **Life** {*e.m.*}[223], corresponding to the Upanishad's *Atman* and *Prana*. Book XIII says that the Truth is not polluted, has no limit, no colour, no form, is motionless, naked, shining, incorporeal, is the unalterable Good and can only be apprehended by itself. With the arrival of Truth comes the Good, accompanied by Life and Light[224]. Scott summed up the teaching of the Hermetica as "Blessed are the Pure in Heart as they shall see God"[225]. The Renaissance Alchemist Robert Fludd would refer to the vivifying Light paralleling the Upanishads which state that the Pure Consciousness is not a faculty but that which vivifies (gives life energy to) every faculty[226].

In 3rd Century *c.e.* Alexandria, Plotinus was taught by Ammonias Saccas [N15] (who also taught the first great Christian thinker Origen) and influenced by Numenius. Plotinus became the father of Neoplatonism, which would influence deeply St Augustine of Hippo (in Nortn Africa) and other Christian theologians. For Plotinus gods are entities arising from Light. Plotinus' The One is the infinite and undifferentiated Light above light[227]. Plotinus' One does not know itself but has self-intellection. The One is impersonal and matter is the pure negation of Being[228] Although Plotinus avoided any positive descriptions as these would limit the unlimited One, as his Mind and Soul are the first two emanations, it is hard to consider the One as very different from Spirit or (impersonal) Consciousness[229]. In fact, in having *experienced* the One, Plotinus was assuming the presence of Consciousness so the One was not totally ineffable! In contrast to the Indians, the ancient Greeks did not develop a concept of Consciousness[230]. Even before Plotinus's time, in his *Refutationis Omnium Haeresium* (Refutation of All Heresies (*c.*225 *c.e.*), the aforementioned Christian Hippolytus knows of the Indian Brahmins[231] {*e.m.*}:

> *...among the Indians a heresy of those who philosophise among the* ***Brahmins... They say that God is Light****, not like the light one sees, ...but that of knowledge (*gnosis*) through which the secret mysteries of nature are perceived by the wise.*

McEvilley suggests that Hippolytus, a contemporary of Plotinus, had seen the *Taittiriya* and the *Maitri* Upanishads[232].

As we saw in Chapter 3, before the Council of Nicaea outlawed such mystical views, Augustine of Hippo was deeply immersed in Plotinus and had referred to Christ as the Inner Teacher. The pre-Nicene Augustine described the **Light or God** as the *potential for all knowing*. God is the Light, found by the inward turn that makes intellectual (noetic) vision possible. The inward turn ends with the insight that it is Truth that makes all knowing possible and this insight is a glimpse of the nature of God {*e.m.*}[233]. Again Augustine's phraseology is a circumlocution around the concept of *Consciousness*. Unlike the more Eurocentric Anglophones, I have noticed that French scholars like Sismanian[234] and Schwab point out that Alexandria-born Plotinus himself tried to get to India. Schwab says that in 242 *c.e.* Plotinus dropped everything to follow Emperor Gordian's expedition against Persia (actually under the Scythian Parthians) hoping to make contact with gymnosophists (yogis). He also mentions that the 19th Century vogue for Oriental philosophies exceeded even the Roman world of Plotinus[235]. The *Milindapanha* tells us that Indians frequently travelled to Alexandria[236]. Asoka sent Buddhist missionaries to the capitals of the Hellenitsic kingdoms hundreds of years before Plotinus. Sylvain Levi[237] even asserted:

Plotinus, Porphyry, and the entire school of Neoplatonists reflect the metaphysics of Kapila and Patanjali. Mani and the Gnostics introduced the Brahman and Buddhist spirit into Christianity.

McEvilley asserts that Plotinus was philosophising in an Indianised tradition derived from India almost a thousand years earlier[238].

In later Neoplatonism which moved more toward ritual and occultism (theurgy), the theurgist must prove himself for ascent by donning Divine Light. As 'Like attracts like' the mortal must make himself as much like Divinity as possible. In fact it was the vehicle (*ochēma*) of the theurgist's soul that had to become 'assimilated' to Divine Light (i.e., it had to become like Light). The *pneuma* ("breath" or spirit) descending upon the theurgist is Divine Light[239]. For Iamblichus, theurgic rites purify the soul, cleansing the vehicle of the soul permitting its union with the gods. The ethereal and luminous vehicle of the soul (*ochēma*) is illuminated by an evocation of light resulting in it being impressed with the images of the god. Only the rational soul can be purified by Divine Light to behold the Forms in the noetic realm and ascend to unite with, perhaps, the hypercosmic gods, if not the One[240]. Iamblichus also refers to the Divine Sympathy pullulating throughout the universe manifesting itself universally, particularly in matter[241].

In one of the Gnostic Gospels (*Pistis Sophia*), Jesus tells a follower to come to him in a fine linen garment in order to learn the secret doctrines. A spiritually ignorant female American scholar, who mentions this on a TV documentary, asserts, in a naive Freudian manner, that this suggests Homoeroticism! The fine, see-through garment, as with the Egyptian and Mithraic *garment-of-Light* or Neoplatonic *vehicle* is referring to the subtilised or purified forms of the ego, stripped of its corporeal attachments (habits) resulting ultimately in the translucent 'naked ego' that is equivalent to the yogic innermost sheath known as the *anandamakosa* or Causal Body. We have seen that Whiteman interprets the true meaning of *Iesous Christos* as attainment of such a state; a reborn or resurrected soul (ego) as the Firstborn Son of the Virgin (Pure) Consciousness or an Earthly Incarnation of the Divine. Thus this Gnostic symbol-character 'Jesus' represents the Divine Light, which must be approached by donning the translucent garment of light in order to attain Gnosis or reception of Divine Wisdom.

The Divine Light in Christianity and other Middle Eastern traditions

We have seen that the likes of Guy Sorman, Sylvain Levi and Elaine Pagels have referred to Buddhist and Hindu influences leading to the rise of Christianity. There were numerous other influences such as the Persian myths of angels and the apocalypse, Greek philosophical influences such as the Stoic *Logos* and the *pneuma*. We have also seen that many of the mystical allegories found in the Gospels were already present in the Mediterranean Mystery Religions such as Cult of Dionysos (Bacchus). Joseph Schulz tells us that knowledge of Buddhist and Hindu ideas was prevalent in First Century *c.e.* Palestine. The aforementioned historian Flavius Josephus wrote *The War with Rome*, attributing to Eleazar, commander of the last band of Hasidic Zealots besieged in Masada (73 *c.e.*), the following[242]:

...let us look at those Indians who profess the practise of philosophy. They, brave men that they are, reluctantly endure the period of life, as some necessary service due to nature but hasten to release their souls from their bodies; and though no calamity impels or drives them from the scene, from sheer longing for the immortal state...

Josephus also wrote that the Pharisees of Alexandria copied Reincarnation from the Indians. As late as the 4th Century *c.e.* St Jeremy was raging at the 'false prophets' from India, indicating that the monasteries founded by Asoka's Buddhist Missionaries were still present in the Middle East after over 500 years[243]. A number of scholars have suggested that the so-called *Theraputae* linked to the Essenes was a corruption of the Buddhist *Theravada*[244]. We have seen that in early Christianity there was a great debate as to whether the Old Testament belonged with the Gospels. We have seen that the Yahweh, god of Mount Zion, was a deity in the Canaanite pantheon (whose supreme god was El). The exclusive worship of the monotheistic Cult of Yahweh had been forced upon the polytheistic Judaeans by King Josiah and by the Hasmoneans presumably in the hope of instilling unity at times of war. The Hasmonean Judaeans also forced Yahweh worship onto neighbouring Israelites (such as the Samarians) and other Canaanite tribes whom they conquered. Yahweh was mocked by early Christian Gnostics as The Fool who thought he was the Supreme God[245]. Yahweh, unlike the mystical 'Christ' of the New Testament, is clearly not a personification of Divine Light. Such facts contradict the nonsensical propaganda peddled by Judaeo-Christian theologians and Western historians that the monotheistic Cult of Yahweh represented a major advance in humanity's spiritual development!

Although the Christian Church viewed written doctrines as the essence of *religion*[246], it should be noted that the Greek Orthodox Church did realise the spiritual message encoded in the Gospel myths far better than has occurred in Western Christianity and has maintained a tradition of meditation. The Greek Church makes a differentiation between Theosis and *Henosis* based on the distinction of God's Subjective Essence (*ousia*) and His Activity (*energeia*). The *ousia/energeia* distinction was also found in the teachings of the Hellenized Jew Philo of Alexandria. Note the parallel with the Hindu *Siva* (Supreme Consciousness) and *Sakti* (Energy). Philo claimed that Man could only know God's energies not his subjective essence[247]. This separation influenced the later Christian belief in Creation *ex nihilo* resulting in Spirit/ Nature Dualism. *Henosis* is the term for complete absorption (mystical union in the sense of total dissolution of the core-individuality or 'Naked Ego' (*anandamayakosa*)) into God as is taught by Plotinus and other nondual mystical traditions, implying Oneness with Divine Consciousness (God's subjective essence or *ousia*). The Orthodox Christian Theists stress that *Henosis* is not attainable only *Theosis* which is a loving cooperation (*synergeia*) between Man and God (presumably the maintenance of the *Naked Ego* equivalent to the *Virgin Birth of the Son of God in the (Pure Virgin) Spirit* of the earlier Mystery Religions). Western traditions (originally Catholicism alone) have largely been hostile to the Orthodox *hesychasm* (ascetic prayer or meditation) which leads to *Theosis* (enlightened gnosis).

The emphasis on written texts has often led to infantile literalism in the Christian understanding of the Gospel parables, etc., which are generally intended to be read as mystical allegories as with Plato's famous allegory of the cave which many contemporary Western scholars misunderstand. Nonetheless, in spite of rage-filled war-god Yahweh, foaming at the mouth, and the literally-interpreted myths about Jesus distorting and clouding over the presence of the True Light in Christianity, we have Christian renderings of the Divine Light. However, orthodox doctrine and dogma prohibits open discussion of its true spiritual import as also occurred with the Church's suppression of Gnosticism, which was prominent in early Christian worship. Thus St Paul claims that *the One God*, the Father, is inconceivable and that He *dwells in Light* which no man can approach unto, whom *no man hath seen or can see* {*e.m.*}[248]. Though interpreted by some as a *via negativa* statement of Ineffability (inconceivable), it is clearly also an expression of Theist doctrine quite definitely maintaining the distinction between God and Man.

In spite of this, numerous Christian mystics (as also with Sufi mystics in theistic Mohammedanism) have asserted their own experience of progressing beyond the dualist, theistic experience of separation from the Light and attaining mystical union or Oneness with the Light. However, due to the pressure of Christian orthodoxy and a desire for life, they have often downplayed this great "heresy". As we saw, early on the Nicene Creed outlawed Gnostic Christianity which threatened Church authority as the Gnostic Heresy with brutal suppression as later occurred again with the medieval massacre of the Cathars. Gnosticism, rather like Mohammedan Sufism, taught direct access to Divinity through meditation without the mediation of a priesthood and some Gnostics challenged correctly the special status accorded to Jesus. Though not a return to mystical Gnosticism, the Protestants with their emphasis on Conscience and direct access to Divinity are undoubtedly closer to the True Light or True Spirituality than the Catholic Church. The Vatican's imperialist ambitions resembled both the Nazis as well as the activities of the *Mafiosi*. The massive-scale genocide and enslavement of natives in Central and South America, leading to the death of some 70 million natives, was sanctioned by the Vatican.[N16] So too was the murderous 'protection racket' imposed on the non-Christians by barbaric Vasco de Gama and the Portuguese in the once-peaceful Indian Ocean.[N17] The medieval Church famously sold pieces of paper called Indulgences absolving the purchaser from Sin. The repression of Sex and homosexuality of course went hand in hand with hushed-up sexual malpractice by the priesthood as continues to this day.

Robert May points out that critics have pointed out that true *conscience* has nothing to do with the Freudian so-called 'super-ego' associated with Freud's so-called 'father complex' linked to religious indoctrination. On the contrary, May says that it is likely that the Conscience is a function of the *higher Self* which does not exist in Freud's tripartite model[249]. The Ancient Egyptian *ba* was the innermost centre of being, the basic ground of the soul which reveals itself as the Inner Voice. Transfiguration in the Ancient Egyptian texts was described as the acquisition of a Garment of Light[250]. St Paul, as Saul of Tarsus, during his conversion to Christianity was thrown down by the

Light and heard the Divine Voice in the Light[251]. The English word 'consciousness' comes from the Latin *conscience* or Inner Voice[252]. The concept of *conscience* (which, in French, is one of the words for *consciousness*), is something clearly absent in the genocidal, vindictive hilltop deity Yahweh. Anderson claims that Conscience is introduced by Jesus in the New Testament: "Let he who is without sin among you, let him first cast a stone at her… in their own conscience"[253]. Anderson notes that Conscience is connected by Jesus with the image of Light. In the Gospel of John (the most mystical of the four Gospels) the themes of Conscience as an Inner Voice and of Light are brought together with *Christ* as *"the True Light,* which lighteth every man that cometh into the world". Jesus says, "I am the light of the world…the *light of life*" {*e.m.*}[254].

Anderson's assertion is Christocentric as the idea of conscience was certainly not new. Back in 1925 D.R. Bhandarkar {*e.m.*}[255] wrote:

> *The idea of self-examination is looked upon at present as so essentially Christian both in origin and practice that one is apt to doubt whether Asoka, as a matter of fact, preached the duty of introspection. ...Buddhaghosha in his* Visuddhi-magga *distinguishes between various forms of* pachchavekkhana, *which has been consecrated to the sense of* ***'examination of conscience'****, 'self-examination'. And this idea...he has adopted from Buddha himself, who taught it to Ambalatthika-Rahula.*

Paul Deussen wrote that the Gospels assert, 'Love they neighbour as thyself'. But the Gospels gave no explanation. The true meaning was to be found in the Upanishads written a thousand years earlier[256]. It is the transcendental or transpersonal aspect of the Light that underlies true empathy, conscience and compassion. In Chapter One I pointed out St Paul's association (in Galatians) of 'Christ Jesus' (*Christos Iesous*) with the 'Sight of God' and the All-embracing Love of God.

In Western cathedrals Christ was set in the light-radiant mandorla, holding the book of the *logos* (Divine Reason), or at the centre of the radiating rose windows as the ultimate source of Life and Light[257]. We have seen that the perennial knowledge includes the Divine Light as the Life Energy or as the Eternal Life. In Gnostic Christianity the *Sophia* (Divine Wisdom) pours her Light on Earth[258]. Yates notes the parallels of this Inner Light of Christ, the Holy Spirit or the Light of *Sophia* with the Tibetan Buddhists' Clear Light of Wisdom. *Sophia Zoe* (*Zoe* means Life) is the daughter of *Sophia*[259]. There were parallels in early Buddhism also. The precursor of the Mahayanists' Buddha Nature (Inner Light) was the Brightly Shining *Citta* (Mindstuff) known as the *Bhavanga*. This was also the Life Principle[260]. We have seen that the Christians refer to the Holy Spirit as the *Life-Giver*[261]. We have also noted the perennial references to the Light as the Fount of all Wisdom, the source of Gnosis, superior to knowledge gleaned by the senses and intellect.

St Augustine of Hippo, the North Africa-based "Father" of Catholicism, had a vision of the unchangeable Light of the Lord ending the first stage of his enlightenment[262]. Evelyn Underhill[263] quotes Augustine:

> *It was not the common light which all flesh can see, nor was it greater yet of the same kind, as if the light of day were to grow brighter and brighter and flood all space. It was not like this, but different: altogether different from all such things.*

Given Augustine's conversion to Christianity, belief in the End-of-the-world-is-nigh myths and his anthropomorphic reinterpretation of the NeoPlatonic *archetypes* into his 'Ideas in the Mind of God', we may conclude that Augustine failed to attain mystical union. Thus he projects egoic characteristics onto the impersonal Light! Before converting to Christianity, Augustine had been a Manichaean for nine years. Mani was actually born into the Jewish community of Southern Iraq and not a Persian as was widely thought. Mani claimed that only he, the Final Prophet, possessed the 'Twin' (the Inner Light or Divine Light). The Persian term *grev* referred to the transcendent and true subject of salvation which is not identical to the empirical soul (i.e., ego). A Chinese Manichaean text refers to it as the Luminous Nature or our Original Luminous Nature or Inner Nature. Manichaean hymns call it the Living Self (i.e., the *Prana* or Life Energy aspect) or the Luminous Self[264].

Meister Eckhart referred to the true self as the Spark (*finklein*) or a Light in the soul or the Ground of the soul[265]. Divine Light breaks forth in the soul more and more as spiritual development progresses until in the transformed state the soul is suffused with Divine Light[266]. For Eckhart the Godhead is identical with the Ground or (Nondual) Consciousness with no Subject/Object distinctions. Both God and Man are transcended by Godhead[267]. Eckhart's Divine Light is also Knowledge and Love[268]. Mechtild of Magdeburg refers to the *Flowing Light of the Godhead* (the title of her autobiography) and describes three typical stages of Christian Mysticism: 1. Purgation; 2. Illumination; 3. Union[269]. For the Flemish Christian mystic Ruusbroec (Ruysbroeck), contemplative life is lived in Divine Light, Divine Consciousness itself. The defining characteristic of contemplation is that Divine Light transforms and pervades our spirit[270]. For Ruysbroeck the Divine Light is the Uncreated Essence, the Onefold Ground[271].

Note that, as with Eckhart, Mecthild stresses mystical union which Ruysbroeck also asserts although this poses severe problems for the dogmatic Christian belief in Theism (dualism of God and soul). Woodhouse says that the term "God" normally connotes a Supreme Being among other beings, one among many. The term Godhead, however, implies an infinite ground, the One-without-a-second (a famous monist assertion from *Advaita Vedanta*). Theologians, says Woodhouse, speak of God whilst mystics express the Godhead in their daily lives. Conservative Christians see Oneness of Godhead as counterfeit as it reverses the (supposedly) true relationship between God and Man. It allegedly makes God an extension of an extension of the ego and appears not to take evil seriously[272]. This supposedly true relationship is based on the dogmatic, doctrinaire beliefs of Christian theological bookmen as Woodhouse indicates rather than any phenomenological evidence as gleaned by the great Christian mystics.

The 17th Century English writer Richard Baxter, in his *Reliquiae Baxterianae,* discussed those in England who followed the Inward Light such as the 'Behemenists' (followers of German mystic Jakob Böhme[273]. Carey tells us that the prime purpose of John Locke's (17th Century) philosophy was to require conflicting religious claims to be adjudicated by Reason alone, *ruling out any appeal to an Inner Light of Divine Illumination* such as those made by religious radicals whom Locke and other members of the establishment called "enthusiasts" {*e.m.*}[274]. We have seen that the word *enthusiasm* comes from Greek and originally meant to be filled with God or Divinity. Locke did not deny that God by special miracle could bypass the windows of the senses and illuminate the mind as apparently happened with Biblical prophets long ago. But Locke's purpose was to make the very notion of Inner Vision seem irrational or crazy[275]. In such ways true Enlightenment was replaced with the Logocentrism of the so-called European Enlightenment. Note the absurdly naive Realism of Locke in viewing senses as being like windows.

Jos van Meurs writes of William Blake's religious background amongst the Protestant Dissenters who, following the tradition of the 17th Century Puritans, trusted their own "inner light" and sought the "God within"[276]. Blake's "Divine Humanity" and "Spiritual Essence of the True Man" were both derived from Swedenborg's 'Divine Man' (God is a very Man). Blake later identified this Spirit (Light) of Divine Humanity with Christ in his Universal Humanity[277]. Such references to Universal Humanity tie in with my discussion in Chapter 1 of the *common human Universality* aspect of the *Atman* as the same in all humans (as also with St Paul's 'Inner Man'; *see also* Jung's *Anthropos* notion in Ch. 8). Blake also identifies the 'devils' of religious mythology with the *energies* within us[278]. This is in agreement with Origen's demotion of the autonomous complexes (associated with 'Pagan traditions') to Inner Demons and Animal Souls within us[279]. But for Blake, good and evil are relative and both are necessary. Bibles and sacred moral codes are harmful in suppressing our energies. He stressed the Primacy of Spiritual Energy and asserted that Energy is the only life and is from the body. Reason serves only to keep Spiritual Energy within bounds. The imposition of rational rules, moral codes and the belief that God will torment man in Eternity for following his energies only do harm to oneself and to others. On the contrary, "Energy is eternal delight"[280]. As discussed in O/OM, such Romantic notions of *energy* opposed to the Mechanistic worldview of Natural Science were transformed into the scientific concept of energy.

In the Byzantine monastic tradition of the Greek Orthodox Church, God is the experience of the Uncreated Light of the Godhead. The Hesychasts dominated the monastic tradition in Byzantium. The oldest hymn in Christian Greek is a hymn to Joyful Light sung to this day in Orthodox Christianity. The evening lamps in Greek and Slavic Orthodox monasteries symbolise the Eternal Light of the Godhead[281]. Philo Judaeus, the 1st Century *c.e.* Alexandrian Jew who developed a Platonic and somewhat Gnostic form of Judaism refers to God as the eternal Light[282]. The main text of the medieval Jewish *Kabbala* mysticism, the *Sepher haz Zohar*, means The Book of Splendour ("splendour" implying radiance or Light). Kabbala has roots in 2nd Century *c.e.* Gnosticism and in NeoPlatonism[283]. We have seen the many possible Indic influences upon these mystical traditions largely centred in Alexandria. Charles Seife notes that the medieval appearance of the *Zohar* coincides with the revolutionary influence of the new Indian mathematics (*Hindisat*) into medieval Arabia. The Indian mathematical concepts of Zero and Infinity, based on mystical insights of the Void, shattered the Aristotelian cosmology of the Arabs, Sephardic Jews and later the Christians. Kabbala, with its concepts of *Ayin* (nothing) and *ein sof* (infinity), as scholars have noted, strikingly resembles Hindu notions[284]. Kabbala's *ein sof aur* means the Limitless Light[285]. However, in spite of such elements, Kabbala, in the main, seems obsessed with tribal and parochial issues of reinterpreting Biblical stories, historicism, occultism, etc., rather than true spirituality.

William James wrote that mystical Sufism must have originated in Persia through Hindu influence long before the coming of Mohammedanism to Persia[286]. We saw in Chapter 4 that al-Biruni derived the term *Sufi* from the Greek *Sophia* (Divine Wisdom) but we also know that Greek *philosophia* was derived from Oriental (including Indian) sources, especially the later Alexandrian Neoplatonism which influenced Islamic beliefs. The Sufi saints', *fana'* (annihilation) refers to experiencing God's brilliant Light. The authority for perceiving God as Light is the Koran's chapter on "Light" (*Sura al-Nur)* which begins with the words, God is the Light of the Heavens and Earth[287]. Human beings are near to God through their spirits. The spirit is perfect, luminous', alive, rational, intelligent etc. It possesses all the attributes of God. The soul must be transformed so it becomes fully infused with spiritual light[288]. For Ibn al-Arabi, the closest synonym for God is *al haqq* (the Real). Furthermore, *al haqq* is a Light, forever shining; there is only this One Light. Consciousness is inseparable from Being, when the Light shines, the soul disappears[289]. In the Persian Cult of Mithras, the Light-Glory envelops the soul of the dying and is also the Light of Healing[290]. Suhrawardi, the medieval Persian mystic living under Muslim rule, also refers to the Light of Lights illuminating everything. Its luminosity, essence and power are all one and the same. It is self-emanating but, unlike Plotinus's One, the Light of Lights emanates another Light, though not essentially different[291]. Suhrawardi held that any subject conscious of its own essence is a self-subsisting light. Everyone who perceives his own essence is a Pure Light[292]. The Parsee D.M. Homji says that neither the Hindus nor Parsis worship Fire. We worship Light, the Supreme Being is all Light, the Light of Lights. He also expresses his view that Light as the common element of Religion and this common heritage will provide the basis for our future civilisation with the marriage of Science and Religion[293].

References

1. Elphinstone, Mountstuart (1841) *The History of India* (Volume 1), John Murray.
2. Johnston, Sarah Iles "Fiat Lux, Fiat Ritus*: Divine Light and the Late Antique Defense of Ritual". In Matthew T. Kapstein (Editor) (2004)* The Fresence of Light: Divine Radiance and Religious Experience, *Chicago University Press.*
3. Wood, Michael (2007) *The Story of India* (Television series) British Broadcasting Corporation.
4. Campbell, Joseph (1990) *Transformations of Myth through Time,* Harper and Row.

5-14. Ramaswamy, Krishnan, de Nicolas, Antonio and Banerjee, Aditi (Editors) (2007) *Invading the Sacred: An Analysis of Hinduism Studies in America*, Rupa and Co.

15. Curtis, Adam (2002) *The Century of the Self* (Television series) British Broadcasting Corporation.

16. Clarke, John J. (1997) *Oriental Enlightenment: The Encounter Between Asian and Western Thought*, Routledge.
17. Wood, Michael (2007) *ibid.*
18. Radhakrishnan, Sarvepalli (1940) *Eastern Religions and Western Thought (2nd Edn),* Oxford University Press.
19. Smith, Huston (2000) *Cleansing the Doors of Perception: The Religious Significance of Entheogenic Plants and Chemicals*, Tarcher Putnam.
20. Smith, Huston (2000) *ibid.*
21. Whiteman, J.H. Michael (2006) *Universal Theology and Life in the Other Worlds*, Colin Smythe.
22. Mehta, J.L. "Reading the Rigveda: A Phenomenological Essay". D.P. Chattopadhyaya, Lester Embree and Jitendranath Mohanty (Editors) (1992) *Phenomenology and Indian Philosophy*, State University of New York Press.
23. Whiteman, J.H. Michael. Personal Communication 1999.
24. Whiteman, J.H. Michael (2006) *ibid.*
25. Whiteman, J.H. Michael (1993) *Aphorisms on Spiritual Method: The "Yoga Sutras of Patanjali" in the Light of Mystical Experience*, Colin Smythe.
26. Ghose, Aurobindo (Sri Aurobindo) (1956) *The Secret of the Veda*, Sri Aurobindo Ashram Publications.
27. de Nicolas, Antonio (1976) *Meditations Through the Rig Veda: Four-Dimensional Man*, Nicolas-Hays Ltd.
28. Ghose, Aurobindo (Sri Aurobindo) (1956) *ibid.*
29. Ghose, Aurobindo (Sri Aurobindo) (1956) *ibid.*
30. Mehta, J.L. (1992) *ibid.*
31. Mehta, J.L. (1992) *ibid.*
32. Hass. Lawrence (2008) *Merleau-Ponty's Philosophy*, Indiana University Press.
33. Ghose, Aurobindo (Sri Aurobindo) (1956) *ibid.*
34. Whiteman, J.H. Michael (2006) *ibid.*
35. Ghose, Aurobindo (Sri Aurobindo) (1956) *ibid.*
36. Mehta, J.L. (1992) *ibid.*
37. Mehta, J.L. (1992) *ibid.*
38. Campbell, Joseph (1990) *ibid.*
39. Mehta, J.L. (1992) *ibid.*
40. Yates, Frances (1964) *Giordano Bruno and the Hermetic Tradition*, Routledge and Kegan Paul.
41. Yates, Frances (1964) *ibid.*
42. van Meurs, Jos "William Blake and His Gnostic Myths". In Roelof van den Broek and Wouter J. Hanegraaff (Editors) (1998) *Gnosis and Hermeticism: From Antiquity to Modern Times*, State University of New York Press.
43. Kelley, C.F. (1977) *Meister Eckhart on Divine Knowledge*, Yale University Press.
44. Cary, Phillip (2000) *Augustine's Invention of the Inner Self: The Legacy of a Christian Platonist*, Oxford University Press.
45. van Meurs, Jos (1998) *ibid.*

46. Voss, Karen-Claire "Spiritual Alchemy: Interpreting Representative Texts and Images". In Roelof van den Broek and Wouter J. Hanegraaff (Editors) (1998) *Gnosis and Hermeticism: From Antiquity to Modern Times*, State University of New York Press.
47. Edighoffer, Roland "Hermeticism in Early Rosicrucianism". In Roelof van den Broek and Wouter J.Hanegraaff (Editors) (1998) *Gnosis and Hermeticism: From Antiquity to Modern Times*, State University of New York Press.
48. Edighoffer, Roland ((1998) *ibid.*
49. Voss, Karen-Claire (1998) *ibid.*
50. Campbell, Joseph (1990) *ibid.*
51. Campbell, Joseph (2008) *The Hero with a Thousand Faces (3rd Edn)*, New World Library.
52. Campbell, Joseph (1990) *ibid.*
53. Campbell, Joseph (2008) *ibid.*
54. Campbell, Joseph (2008) *ibid.*
55. James, William (1902) *The Varieties of Religious Experience*, Longmans, Green, and Co.
56. Bryant, Edwin (2001) *The Quest for the Origins of Vedic Culture: The Indo-Aryan Migration Debate*, Oxford University Press.
57. Feuerstein, George, Kak, Subhash and Frawley, David (1995) *In Search of the Cradle of Civilisation: New Light on Ancient India*, Quest Books.
58. McEvilley, Thomas (2002) *The Shape of Ancient Thought: Comparative Studies in Greek and Indian Philosophies*, Allworth Press.
59. Dallmayr, Fred (1996) *Beyond Orientalism: Essays on Cross-Cultural Encounter*, State University of New York Press.
60. McEvilley, Thomas (2002) *ibid.*
61. Malhotra, Rajiv and Neelakandan, Aravindan (2011) *Breaking India: Western Interventions in Dravidian and Dalit Faultlines*, Amaryllis.
62. Malhotra, Rajiv and Neelakandan, Aravindan (2011) *ibid.*
63. Lal, B. B. "Aryan Invasion of India: perpetuation of a myth". In Edwin F. Bryant and Laurie L. Patton (Editors) (2005) *The Indo-Aryan Controversy: Evidence and inference in Indian history*. Routledge.
64. Malhotra, Rajiv and Neelakandan, Aravindan (2011) *ibid.*
65. Pagels, Elaine (1979) *The Gnostic Gospels* (cited in Malhotra and Neelakandan (2011) *ibid.*).
66. Sorman, Guy (2001) *The Genius of India*, McMillan India.
67. Bhandarkar, D.R. (1925) *Aœoka*, University of Calcutta. Reprinted 2005 by Asian Educational Services.
68. Basham, Arthur L. (Editor) (1975) *A Cultural History of India*, Oxford University Press.
69. Sorman, Guy (2001) *ibid.*
70. Dallmayr, Fred (1996) *ibid.*
71. Malhotra, Rajiv and Neelakandan, Aravindan (2011) *ibid.*
72. Painter, Nell I. (2010) *The History of White People,* W.W. Norton and Co.

73. Schwab, Raymond (1950, French) English translation *The Oriental Renaissance: Europe's Rediscovery of India and the East 1680-1880* (1984) Columbia, University Press.
74. Bryant, Edwin (2001) *ibid.*
75. Malhotra, Rajiv and Neelakandan, Aravindan (2011) *ibid.*
76. Raj, Kapil (2007) *Relocating Modern Science: Circulation and the Construction of Knowledge in South Asia and Europe, 1650 6 ᴸ 1900*, Palgrave MacMillan.
77. Bryant, Edwin (2001) *ibid.*
78. Bryant, Edwin (2001) *ibid.*
79. Renfrew, Colin (1987) *Archaeology and Language: The Puzzle of Indo-European Origins*, Jonathan Cape.
80. Lal, B. B. (2005) *ibid.*
81. Chaudhuri, Nirad, C. (1951) *The Autobiography of an Unknown Indian*, McMillan India.
82. Thapar, Romila (1973) *Aœoka and the Decline of the Mauryas*, Oxford University Press.
83. "Aryan-Dravidian divide a myth: Study" *The Times of India* (Newspaper) 25th September 2009.
84. Dharampal (1971) *Indian Science and Technology in the Eighteenth Century*, Impex India.
85. Lal, B. B. (2005) *ibid.*
86. Kenoyer, Jonathan M. "Cultural change during the Late Harappan period at Harappa: new insights on Vedic Aryan issues". In Edwin F. Bryant and Laurie L. Patton (Editors) (2005) *The Indo-Aryan Controversy: Evidence and inference in Indian history*, Routledge.

87-89. Lal, B. B. (2005) *ibid.*

90. Feuerstein, Georg, Kak, Subhash and Frawley, David (1995) *In Search of the Cradle of Civilisation*, Quest.
91. Radhakrishnan, Sarvepalli (1953) *The Principal Upanisads*, (Centenary Edition 1989), Unwin Hyman.
92. Lal, B. B. (2005) *ibid.*
93. Radhakrishnan, Sarvepalli (1953) *ibid.*
94. Close, Frank (2007) *The Void*, Oxford University Press.
95. Radhakrishnan, Sarvepalli (1940) *Eastern Religions and Western Thought (2nd Edn),* Oxford University Press.
96. Indich, William M. (1980) *Consciousness in Advaita Vedânta*, Motilal Banarsidass.
97. Radhakrishnan, Sarvepalli (1940) *ibid.*
98. Gupta, Bina (2003) *Cit Consciousness*, Oxford University Press India.
99. Indich, William M. (1980) *ibid.*
100. Radhakrishnan, Sarvepalli (1953) *ibid.*
101. Gupta, Bina (2003) *ibid.*
102. Gupta, Bina (2003) *ibid.*
103. Sorman, Guy (2001) *ibid.*

104. Mangalwadi, Vishal (1997) *India: The Grand Experiment*, Pippa Rann Books.
105. Sorman, Guy (2001) *ibid.*
106. Mukerjee, Madhusree (2010) *Churchill's Secret War: The British Empire and the Ravaging of India during World War II*, Basic Books.
107. Davis, Mike (2001) *Late Victorian Holocausts: El Niño Famines and the Making of the Third World*, Verso.
108. Sorman, Guy (2001) *ibid.*
109. Sorman, Guy (2001) *ibid.*
110. Daniélou, Alain (1961) "Hinduism and Human Behaviour". In Alain Daniélou (2003) *India–A Civilisation of Differences: The Ancient Tradition of Universal Tolerance*, Inner Traditions.
111. Crasta, Richard (2000) *Impressing the Whites: The New International Slavery*, Invisible Man Books.
112. Hobson, John, M. (2004) *The Eastern Origins of Western Civilisation*, Cambridge University Press.
113. Isaac, Benjamin (2004) *The Invention of Racism in Classical Antiquity*, Princeton University Press.
114. Obeyesekere, Gananath (2002) *Imagining Karma: Ethical Transformation in Amerindian, Buddhist and Greek Rebirth*, University of California Press.
115. Graeber, David (2011) *Debt: The First 5,000 Years*, Melville House.
116. Chakrabarti, Dilip K. (1997) *Colonial Indology: Sociopolitics of the Ancient Indian Past*. Mushiram Manoharlal Publishers.
117. McEvilley, Thomas (2002) *ibid.*
118. Hughes, Bethany (2007) *Athens: The Truth about Democracy* (UK Television programme) Channel 4.
119. Sorman, Guy (2001) *ibid.*
120. Clarke, John J. (1997) *ibid.*
121. Varela, Francisco J. "Present-Time Consciousness". In Francisco Varela and Jonathan Shear (Editors) (1999) *The View From Within: First-person approaches to the study of consciousness*. Imprint Academic.
122. Varela, Francisco J. "The Specious Present: A Neurophenomenology of Time Consciousness". In Jean Petitot, Francisco J. Varela, Bernard Pachoud and Jean-Michel Roy (Editors) (1999) *Naturalising Phenomenology: Issues in Contemporary Phenomenology and Cognitive Science*, Stanford University Press.
123. Obeyesekere, Gananath (2002) *ibid.*
124. Radhakrishnan, Sarvepalli (1953) *ibid.*
125. Coomaraswamy, Ananda, K. (1999) *Hinduism and Buddhism (New Edn)* Manohar.
126. Obeyesekere, Gananath "The Rebirth Eschatology and its Transformations: A Contribution to the Sociology of Early Buddhism." In Wendy Doniger O'Flaherty (Editor) *Karma and Rebirth in the Classical Indian Traditions*. University of California Press.
127. Whiteman, J.H. Michael (1993) *ibid.*

128. Harvey, Peter (1995) *The Selfless Mind: Personality, Consciousness and Nirvana in Early Buddhism*, Curzon Press.
129. Clarke, John J. (1997) *ibid.*
130. deCharms, Cristopher (1998) *Two Views of Mind: Abhidharma and Brain Science*, Snow Lion Publications.
131. Clarke, John J. (1997) *ibid.*
132. Merrell-Wolff, Franklin (1995) *Transformations in Consciousness: The Metaphysics and Epistemology* (Containing His *Introceptualism*), State University of New York Press.
133. Merrell-Wolff, Franklin (1995) *ibid.*
134. Whiteman, J.H. Michael (1993) *ibid.*
135. Whiteman, J.H.M. Uncited work referred to by Ellison, Arthur J. "Western Science and Religious Experience". In T.D. Singh (Editor) (1987) *Synthesis of Science and Religion*, The Bhaktivedanta Institute.
136. McEvilley, Thomas (2002) *ibid.*
137. Harvey, Peter (1995) *ibid.*

138-41. Kapstein, Matthew T. "The Strange Death of Pema the Demon Tamer". In Matthew T. Kapstein (Editor) *The Presence of Light: Divine Radiance and Religious Experience*, Chicago University Press.

142. Grosso, Michael "The Archetype of Enlightenment and Death". In Lee W. Bailey and Jenny Yates (Editors) (1996) *The Near-Death Experience: A Reader*, Routledge.
143. Coomaraswamy, Ananda, K. (1999) *ibid.*
144. Sorman, Guy (2008) *The Empire of Lies: The Truth about China in the 21st Century*, Encounter Books.
145. Sorman, Guy (2008) *ibid.*
146. Sorman, Guy (2001) *ibid.*
147. Sorman, Guy (2001) *ibid.*
148. Twain, Mark (1897) *Following the Equator:A journey around the world*, American Publishing Co.
149. Jung, Carl G. "What India Can Teach Us". Excerpted in John, J. Clarke (Editor) (1994) *Jung on the East*, Routledge.
150. Sorman, Guy (2001) *ibid.*
151. Prakash, Gyan (1999) *Another Reason: Science and the Imagination of Modern India*, Princeton University Press.
152. Nandy, Ashis (1995) *Alternative Sciences: Creativity and Authenticity in Two Indian Scientists (2nd Edn)*, Oxford University Press India.
153. Sorman, Guy (2001) *ibid.*

154-57. Prakash, Gyan (1999) *ibid.*

158. Toynbee, Arnold. Uncited work referred to by Smith, Huston "Foreword" to Swami Prabhavananda (1979) *The Spiritual Heritage of India: A Clear Summary of Indian Philosophy and Religion*, Vedanta Press.
159. Harman, Willis "Scientific Positivism, The New Dualism and the Perennial Wisdom". In T.D. Singh (Editor) (1987) *Synthesis of Science and Religion: Critical Essays and Dialogues*, The Bhaktivedanta Institute.

160. Harman, Willis (1987) *ibid.*

161. Inomata, Shiuji. Personal Communication, 1999.

162. Capra, Fritjof (1988) *Uncommon Wisdom: Conversations with remarkable people*, William Collins.

163. Philip, D.S. (1987) *Perceiving India through the works of Nirad C. Chaudhuri, R.K. Narayan and Ved Mehta,* Oriental University Press.

164. Hu Shih. Quoted in Chopra, S.N. (1997) *India and China: Perspective on the Culture of the Hans and the Hindus*, Vikas Publishing House.

165. Chopra, S.N. (1997) *India and China: Perspective on the Culture of the Hans and the Hindus*, Vikas Publishing House.

166. "The Diamond Sutra" (http:reluctant-messenger.com/diamond_ sutra.htm).

167. *Ibid.*

168. Chopra, S.N. (1997) *ibid.*

169. Yutang, Lin (1942) *The Wisdom of China and India*, Random House.

170. Goody, Jack (1996) *The East in the West*, Cambridge University Press.

171. Goody, Jack (1996) *ibid.*

172. Chopra, S.N. (1997) *ibid.*

173. Thurman, Robert A.F. "A Tibetan Perspective". In The Dalai Lama, Herbert Benson, Robert A.F. Thurman *et al.* (1991) *Mind Science: An East-West Dialogue*, Wisdom Publications.

174. Basham, Arthur L. (1954) *The Wonder that was India,* Sidgwick and Jackson.

175. Marx, Karl "The Future Results of British Rule in India". In *New York Daily Tribune* (Newspaper) 8th August 1853.

176. Ubac, Michael L. "Arroyo cites ancient Philippines-India ties". In *Daily Inquirer* (Newspaper, Manila) 6th October 2007.

177. Dallmayr, Fred (1996) *ibid.*

178. King, Richard (1999) *Orientalism and Religion: Postcolonial Theory, India and 'The Mystic East'*, Routledge.

179. Obeyesekere, Gananath (2002) *ibid.*

180. Johnston, Sarah Iles (2004) *ibid.*

181. Chakrabarty, Dipesh (2000) *Provincialising Europe: Postcolonial Thought and Historical Difference*, Princeton University Press.

182. Anderson, William (1996) *The Face of Glory: Creativity, Consciousness and Civilisation*, Bloomsbury.

183. Kingsley, Peter (1995) *Ancient Philosophy, Mystery, and Magic: Empedocles and Pythagorean Tradition,* Clarendon Press (Oxford University Press).

184. Kingsley, Peter "Parmenides and Empedocles" (Article on www.peterkingsley.org).

185. McEvilley, Thomas (2002) *ibid.*

186. Whiteman, J.H. Michael (1967) *Philosophy of Space and Time and the Inner Constitution of Nature: A Phenomenological Study*, Muirhead Library of Philosophy, George Allen and Unwin and the Humanities Press.

187. Goonatilake, Susantha (1998) *Toward a Global Science: Mining Civilisational Knowledge*, Indiana University Press.

188. Kingsley, Peter (1995) *ibid.*
189. McEvilley, Thomas (2002) *ibid.*
190. Kingsley, Peter (1995) *ibid.*
191. Kingsley, Peter (1995) *ibid.*
192. Hartog, François (1986) "The Greeks as Egyptologists". English translation in Thomas Harrison (Editor) (2002) *Greeks and Barbarians*, Edinburgh University Press.
193. Kingsley, Peter (1995) *ibid.*
194. Kingsley, Peter (1995) *ibid.*
195. Radhakrishnan, Sarvepalli (1940) *ibid.*
196. Bernal, Martin (1987) *Black Athena: The Afroasiatic Roots of Classical Civilisation. Volume 1. The Fabrication of Ancient Greece 1785-1985.* Free Association Books.
197. Yates, Frances (1964) *ibid.*
198. Goonatilake, Susantha (1998) *ibid.*
199. Radhakrishnan, Sarvepalli (1940) *ibid.*
200. Goonatilake, Susantha (1998) *ibid.*
201. Radhakrishnan, Sarvepalli (1940) *ibid.*
202. Yates, Frances (1964) *ibid.*
203. Goonatilake, Susantha (1998) *ibid.*
204. Goonatilake, Susantha (1998) *ibid.*
205-08. McEvilley, Thomas (2002) *ibid.*
209. 'Heraclitus'. Macropaedia entry in *Encyclopaedia Britannica* (1974 Edition).
210-12. McEvilley, Thomas (2002) *ibid.*
213. Merrell-Wolff, Franklin (1995) *ibid.*
214. Kakar, Sudhir (1978) *The Inner World: a psycho-analytic study of childhood and society in India*, Oxford University Press.
215. McEvilley, Thomas (2002) *ibid.*
216. McEvilley, Thomas (2002) *ibid.*
217. Bailey, Lee, W. "Unknown Well-known Near-Death Experiences: Peter Sellers, Eddie Rickenbacker, Plato, and Black Elk." In Lee W. Bailey and Jenny Yates (Editors) (1996) *The Near-Death Experience: A Reader*, Routledge.
218. Mayer, John R.A. "Plotinus' Neoplatonism and the Thought of Sri Aurobindo". In Paulos Mar Gregorios (Editor) (2002) *Neoplatonism and Indian Philosophy*, State University of New York Press.
219-21. Yates, Frances (1964) *ibid.*
222. van den Broek, Roelof "Gnosticism and Hermetism in Antiquity". In Roelof van den Broek and Wouter J. Hannegraaff (Editors) (1998) *Gnosis and Hermeticism from Antiquity to Modern Times*, State University of New York Press.
223. van den Broek, Roelof (1998) *ibid.*
224. Yates, Frances (1964) *ibid.*
225. Radhakrishnan, Sarvepalli (1940) *ibid.*
226. Radhakrishnan, Sarvepalli (1940) *ibid.*

227. Sharma, I.C. "The Four Dimensional Philosophy of Indian Thought and Plotinus". In Paulos Mar Gregorios (Editor) (2002) *Neoplatonism and Indian Philosophy*, State University of New York Press.
228. Basu, Arabinda "The *Sadhana* of Plotinus and Sri Aurobindo". In Paulos Mar Gregorios (Editor) (2002) *Neoplatonism and Indian Philosophy*, State University of New York Press.
229. Mayer, John R.A. (2002) *ibid.*
230. Gupta, Bina (2003) *ibid.*
231. Pagels, Elaine (1979) *The Gnostic Gospels,* Random House.
232. McEvilley, Thomas (2002) *ibid.*
233. Cary, Phillip (2000) *ibid.*
234. Sismanian, Ara A. "Nombre et son Ombre (Resumé)". In Richard T. Wallis (Editor) and Jay Bregman (Associated Editor) (1992) *Neoplatonism and Gnosticism*, State University of New York Press.
235. Schwab, Raymond (1950, French) English translation *The Oriental Renaissance: Europe's Rediscovery of India and the East 168-1880* (1984) Columbia University Press.
236. Radhakrishnan, Sarvepalli (1940) *ibid.*
237. Schwab, Raymond (1950) *ibid.*
238. McEvilley, Thomas (2002) *ibid.*
239. Johnston, Sarah Iles (2004) *ibid.*
240. Berchman, Robert M. "Rationality and Ritual in Neoplatonism". In Paulos Mar Gregorios (Editor) (2002) *Neoplatonism and Indian Philosophy*, State University of New York Press.
241. Berchman, Robert M. (2002) *ibid.*
242. Schultz, Joseph P. (1981) *Judaism and the Gentile Faiths: Comparative Studies in Religion,* Associated Universities Presses.
243. Sorman, Guy (2001) *ibid.*
244. Radhakrishnan, Sarvepalli (1940) *ibid.*
245. Campbell, Joseph (1990) *ibid.*
246. King, Richard (1999) *ibid.*
247. Radhakrishnan, Sarvepalli (1940) *ibid.*
248. Radhakrishnan, Sarvepalli (1940) *ibid.*
249. May, Robert M. (1993) *Cosmic Consciousness Revisited: The Modern Origins and Development of a Western Spiritual Psychology*, Element.
250. Von Franz, Marie-Louise (1998) *On Dreams and Death: A Jungian Interpretation*, Open Court.
251. Bailey, Lee W. And Yates, Jenny "Introduction". In Lee W. Bailey and Jenny Yates (1996) *The Near- Death Experience: A Reader*, Routledge.
252. Gupta, Bina (2003) *ibid.*
253. Anderson, William (1996) *The Face of Glory: Creativity, Consciousness and Civilisation*, Bloomsbury.
254. Anderson, William (1996) *ibid.*
255. Bhandarkar, D.R. (1925) *AĐoka*, University of Calcutta. Reprinted 2005 by Asian Educational Services.

256. Radhakrishnan, Sarvepalli (1940) *ibid.*

257. Anderson, William (1996) *ibid.*

258. Yates, Jenny "Being of Light: Dreaming the Vision Onward". In Lee W. Bailey and Jenny Yates (1996) *The Near-Death Experience: A Reader*, Routledge.

259. Yates, Jenny (1996) *ibid.*

260. Harvey, Peter (1995) *ibid.*

261. Hanigan, James, P. "Conscience and the Holy Spirit". In Charles E. Curran (Editor) (2004) *Conscience* (Readings in Moral Theology No.14), Paulist Press.

262. Whiteman, J.H. Michael (1986) *Old and New Evidence on the Meaning of Life: The Mystical World-View and Inner Contest 6 L An Introduction to Scientific Mysticism*, Colin Smythe.

263. Underhill, Evelyn (1911) *Mysticism: A Study of the Nature and Development of Man's Spiritual Consciousness* (American Edition, 1930 E.P. Dutton).

264. Sweeney, Leo S.J. "Mani's Twin and Plotinus: Questions on 'Self'." In Richard T. Wallis (Editor) and Jay Bregman (Associate Editor) (1992) *Neoplatonism and Gnosticism*, State University of New York Press.

265. Perovich Jr, Anthony N. "Innate Mystical Capacities and the Nature of the Self". In Robert K.C. Forman (Editor) (1998) *The Innate Capacity: Mysticism, Psychology and Philosophy*, Oxford University Press.

266. Forman, Robert, K.C. "Introduction". In Robert K.C. Forman (Editor) (1998) *The Innate Capacity: Mysticism, Psychology and Philosophy*, Oxford University Press.

267. Merrell-Wolff, Franklin (1995) *ibid.*

268. Lorimer, David "The Near-Death Experience and the Perennial Wisdom". In Lee W. Bailey and Jenny Yates (Editors) (1996) *The Near-Death Experience: A Reader"*, Routledge.

269. Cressy, Judith "Mysticism and the Near-Death Experience". In Lee W. Bailey and Jenny Yates (Editors) (1996) *The Near-Death Experience: A Reader"*, Routledge.

270. Price III, James, R. "Mysticism, Meditation and Consciousness: The Innate Capacity in John Ruusbroec". In Robert K. C. Forman (Editor) (1998) *The Innate Capacity: Mysticism, Psychology and Philosophy*, Oxford University Press.

271. Lorimer, David (1996) *ibid.*

272. Woodhouse, Mark, B. (1996) *Paradigm Wars: Worldviews for a New Age*, Frog Ltd.

273. Versluis, Arthur "Christian Theosophic Literature of the Seventeenth and Eighteenth Centuries". In Roelof van den Broek and Wouter J. Hannegraaff (Editors) (1998) *Gnosis and Hermeticism from Antiquity to Modern Times*, State University of New York Press.

274. Cary, Phillip (2000) *ibid.*

275. Cary, Phillip (2000) *ibid.*

276-78. Van Meurs, Jos (1998) *ibid.*

279. von Franz, Marie-Louise (1975) "Psyche and Matter in Alchemy and Modern Science". Reprinted in Marie-Louise von Franz (1992) *Psyche and Matter*, Shambhala Publications.

280. van Meurs, Jos (1998) *ibid.*

281. Louth, Andrew "Light, Vision and Religious Experience in Byzantium". In Matthew T. Kapstein (Editor) (2004) *The Presence of Light: Divine Radiance and Religious Experience,* Chicago University Press.

282. Radhakrishnan, Sarvepalli (1940) *ibid.*

283. Matt, Daniel, C. "*Ayin*: The Concept of Nothingness in Jewish Mysticism". In Robert K. C. Forman (Editor) (1990) *The Problem of Pure Consciousness: Mysticism and Philosophy*, Oxford University Press.

284. Seife, Charles (2000) *Zero: The Biography of a Dangerous Idea*. Souvenir Press.

285. May, Robert M. (1993) *ibid.*

286. James, William (1902) *The Varieties of Religious Experience*, Longmans, Green, and Co.

287. Chittick, William "Between the Yes and the No: Ibn al-'Arabî on *Wujûd* and the Innate Capacity". In Robert K. C. Forman (Editor) (1998) *The Innate Capacity: Mysticism, Psychology and Philosophy*, Oxford University Press.

288. *Ibid.*

289. *Ibid.*

290. Von Franz, Marie-Louise (1998) *ibid.*

291. Ziai, Hossein "Suhrawardî on Knowledge and teh Experience of Light". In Matthew T. Kapstein (Editor) (2004) *The Presence of Light: Divine Radiance and Religious Experience,* Chicago University Press.

292. Ziai, Hossein (2004) *ibid.*

293. Homji, Dastoor M."The Cows are Many Colors, But the Milk is the Same". In Stanislav Grof (Editor) (1984) *Ancient Wisdom and Modern Science*, State University of New York Press.

8

Superficial Insights of Western Phenomenology and Jungian Psychology versus True Depth in Two Scientific Seers

Clouding the Light: James, Husserl, Heidegger and Jung

Phenomenology is the philosophical system founded by Edmund Husserl (1859–1938), born a central European Jew, who saw himself as a new Moses leading his people (the Europeans) into a new territory, Transcendental Subjectivity[1]. Philosophy, according to Husserl, was the 'theory of all theories' but it had not yet begun to be a science. Philosophy as 'self-transparent omniscience' had never been taken to its realisation. It was never undertaken in the only way in which finite Man can reach his infinite goal. Phenomenology was destined to become the '*true* beginning' and Husserl was proud to be 'the *real* beginner'[2]. Schuhmann sums up Husserl's Eurocentric and egotistic view which excluded India from the history of Philosophy[3]:

> *There was no philosophy outside Europe, and in Europe only Plato had conceived its idea, and only Husserl had begun to work it out.*

We have seen that Archaeology has dismissed both Moses and the Exodus as self-aggrandising fiction made up by the Judeans who were actually highland Canaanites all along[4]. As with American New Agers' boasts of being Einstein-like 'pioneers', Husserl's claim to be the pioneer in the new territory of Transcendental Subjectivity is self-aggrandising, Eurocentric nonsense. The followers of the 'new Moses' never reached the 'Promised Land' of self-transparent omniscience or Man's infinite goal. Rather Husserl's followers such as Heidegger, Merleau-Ponty and 'Post-Phenomenologists' like Derrida were left wandering aimlessly for decades in a barren desert. In spite of Husserl's epistemological Idealism, more recent Westerners claiming to follow Husserl such as (the late) Francisco Varela tend to reduce phenomenological knowledge to Emergent Materialism as we have seen.

Schuhmann tells us in his essay "Husserl and Indian Thought", that Husserl thought that all Non-European thought-systems approximating to 'philosophy' (which only existed in Europe), especially Chinese and Indian ones would be abandoned. They were to be superseded by (Husserlian) phenomenology. In his last book *Crisis of the European Sciences and Transcendental Phenomenology* (1936), Husserl claimed that European mankind was the bearer of an absolute idea, whereas India or China represented only 'anthropological types'[5]. We have seen that this attitude permeates tacitly Western academia which continues to conflate 'European' with 'scientific' or 'universal' whereas Non-European thought is relegated to relative, provincial perspectives that are not to be taken seriously. Thus the tacitly racist adherence to the Greek Miracle myth, the clinging to the Aryan Invasion myth concocted by Muller and various attempts to reduce Eastern mysticism to Freudian and Materialist superstitions. J.J. Clarke tells us that Husserl, in his *Crisis of the European Sciences,* went so far as to claim[6]:

> *...that "the Europeanisation of all foreign parts of mankind" is the "destiny of the Earth" and that Western philosophy is a unique spiritual expression which can encompass, but cannot be encompassed by, the thinking of China and India.*

Such are the self-aggrandising delusions of the Europeans. We have seen in Chapter 2 that Husserl, for all his boastful claims to access the 'Transcendental' did not actually know the true, traditional *Transcendental* beyond normal, sensory spatio-temporality. Merleau-Ponty even rejected the notion of the 'Transcendental' as an illusion! I have already indicated, as the likes of Willis Harman also recognised, that a true understanding of Transcendentalism actually leads to an Indianisation of Science based upon Yogic, Transcendental metaphysics, grounded in the Primacy of Consciousness. Thus it is Indian philosophy that is actually all-encompassing and Indian metaphysics that swallows up the Western Natural Science picture and Western philosophy as superficial, anthropocentric abstractions from the bigger, deeper (true) Transcendental Reality unknown to Husserl. Ironically Husserl wrote *Crisis of the European Sciences* in the mid-1930s whilst he himself, having been born an Ashkenazi Jew, was marginalised and the man he had once seen as his successor, Martin Heidegger strutted around as the *Führer* of Freiburg[7]. Until the European Enlightenment traditional European Jewish society had actually been subjected to the totalitarian Rabbinical mind-control (based on Husserl's hero Plato's description of Sparta) of Classical Orthodox Judaism which denied Jews the freedom to think for themselves or even study non-Judaic knowledge.[N1] Thus Husserl's own ancestors had lived the most closed-minded and superstitious society in the civilised world! Whiteman noted that Husserl's account of the method, character and degrees of phenomenological analysis agrees very strikingly in detail and language with classics of Eastern philosophy/psychology. [N2] Without explicit reference, Husserl treads the same ground as Eastern mystical philosophies both in regard to the stages of insight and the path toward the ultimate goal of all possible knowledge[8].

Whilst at Gottingen (1901–16) Husserl befriended the famous Indologist Hermann Oldenberg and Husserl owned a copy of Oldenberg's 1881 book on

Buddha. Husserl's library also included Max Muller's *What India Can Teach Us* (1883) and Paul Deussen's famous work *The System of Vedanta* (1883). But Husserl claimed that the European step up to Rational Philosophy attained by (Socrates and) Plato was as big a leap as from animals to rational Man! European Philosophical Reason was unique and incomparable in the history of mankind[9]. Back in the late 18th Century, Immanuel Kant had spent more time teaching on the (supposed) nature of Man than on epistemology. Kant's hierarchical view of humans was that only Ancient Greeks and modern Western Europeans could be considered full persons and that negroes were only fit for beating severely into servitude[10, 11].

Husserl stated that Buddhism operates at the same level as Husserl's own Phenomenology but Buddhism lacked rational form so it was not really a philosophy[12]. Paulos Mar Gregorios counters Husserl's claims by pointing to the thoroughly secular and rigorously economical methodology of the 5th Century *c.e.* Indian Buddhist logician Dignaga[13]. In fact Dignaga anticipated and solved logical problems related to Truth Functions which were left unresolved by the likes of Bertrand Russell and Ludwig Wittgenstein in 20th Century Europe[14]. We saw in Chapter 6 that Robert Oppenheimer wrote that Indian Buddhist logic was too sophisticated for 18th Century Europeans[15]. Hindu *Nyaya* formal logic was not surpassed in Europe until Boolean algebra in the 19th Century. But Husserl was willing to share the noble predicate 'Transcendendality', usually reserved only for his own phenomenology, with Buddhism. Husserl's meditative 'bracketing' (*epoché*) was clearly influenced by Buddhist and Christian notions of 'overcoming the world', (i.e., spiritual separation from the body)[16].

Schuhmann tells us that Husserl studied under Zollner at Leipzig. Zollner was a staunch supporter of Schopenhauer as were many German intellectuals of the late 19th Century. These followers of Schopenhauer looked down on the parochial Christianity dominating German religiosity with its rituals[17]. Husserl was baptised a Christian in the 1880s. He recognised that (the dominant status of) Christianity in Europe was nothing more than an historical accident. But, with Buddhism particularly in mind, Husserl asserted that Christianity should not be allowed to be superseded by any other religion[18]. Note Husserl's false claim to European philosophic universality was accompanied by his fear of Universal Spirituality from India superseding the parochial, relative, anthropological curiosity of Western Christianity!

Husserl had studied for a while under the Catholic priest turned psychological philosopher, Franz Brentano. Husserl's adoption of Brentano's assumption of the Christian Scholastic notion of "*intentionality*"[N3] (directedness of Consciousness towards an object) has carried over into modern Western Philosophy of Mind. Dogmatic adherence to intentionality, that Consciousness is always 'Consciousness-of-an-object', leads to most Western philosophers denying even the possibility of Pure Objectless Consciousness and Nondual states not limited by the subject/object framework of normal mentation[19]. Merrell-Wolff comments that Bertrand Russell obviously failed to find anything like a 'Self' in his introspection as he no doubt sought an object whereas the Self is pure Subjectivity and Merrell-Wolff himself took twenty four years to realise the Self[20]. I would add that the naïve introspection, reported by Western philosophers like Descartes, Hume and Russell, is certainly not true 'meditation' in the spiritual sense. Although the Latin *meditari* means to reflect upon and Husserlian phenomenology itself is based on reflection, true spiritual meditation, like 'introception', involves a 'Return to the Centre'(middle), back to the Innermost Self or the 'Light at the Centre'. Husserl was greatly disappointed by the failure of his students to develop the requisite skills, (i.e., the meditative 'reduction') [21].

A Harvard colleague of William James wrote that Swami Vivekananda had 'swept Professor James off his feet'. James had brought along many of his friends and colleagues to attend the Swami's lecture to the Graduate Philosophical Club at Harvard in March 1896 [22]. Vivekananda made reference to the Theory of Evolution (perhaps he also believed the Romantic myth of the Evolution of Consciousness) as well as *prana* (energy) and *akasa* (space) as parallels between Vedanta and western science (this was before the rise of the New Physics with its mass/energy equivalence and quantum vacuum). James was deferential toward his new Bengali friend and referred to him as 'Master'[23]. Bardach tells us that, in his seminal work *Varieties of Religious Experience*, James quoted extensively the Swami's *Raja Yoga* including the following: "All the different steps in yoga are intended to bring us scientifically to the superconscious state, or samadhi."[24]. As is usual, most Western academics discussing the ideas of James, the 'Father of American Psychology' make no reference to such non-European influences and parallels. For instance, there is not a single mention of Vivekananda, Vedanta or Yoga in Canadian academic Wesley Cooper's 2002 Vanderbilt University Press published book *The Unity of William James's Thought* [25].

The same cannot be said, however for Jamesian scholar G. William Barnard in his 1997 *Exploring Unseen Worlds: William James and the Philosophy of Mysticism*. Indeed, based on his own experiences of altered states of Consciousness, Barnard advocates that the way forward in resolving the problems inherent in Jamesian thought is to adopt a Nondual Tantric metaphysics with its focus on the vibratory nature of Reality and Consciousness. James' criticism of Monism does not apply to such Nondual Tantric metaphysics which are not simply the products of academic intellectual exercises. Indeed, for many such Eastern traditions the use of the intellect is the primary problem to be overcome[26]. He also suggests developing models based on fields within fields (which resemble my own ideas from the 1980s; *see Ch. 11*)[27]. Barnard comments[28]:

> *These Eastern nondual philosophical traditions are not primarily intended to convince an existentially uninvolved audience. Their basic purpose is not to satisfy professorial egos or to improve the social status of a particular cluster of academics. They are teachings...that are meant to be ...directly realised.*

This resembles Aldous Huxley's chastisement of T.S. Eliot in Huxley's 1956 essay *Knowledge and Understanding* published in *Vedanta and the West*[29]:

> *Turning from the body of the book to the preface, we find an even more striking example of that literally preposterous over-valuation of words and notions to which the cultured and learned are so fatally prone. "I do*

not know," Mr Eliot writes, "whether she [Simone Weil] could read the Upanishads in Sanskrit or, if so, how great was her mastery...of...a way of thought, the difficulties of which become more formidable to a European student the more diligently he applies himself to it." But like all the other great works of Oriental Philosophy, the Upanishads are not systems of pure speculation in which the niceties of language are all important. They...teach a doctrine ...which could be operationally tested...by a direct experience...

James is said to have found the 'Stream of Thought' (Consciousness) using nitrous oxid[30].

> *Contemporary cognitivists love to use William James on the "stream of consciousness", the first phenomenology of immediate awareness, but they usually miss how close James's observations of the flowing moments of awareness are to the states sought in Buddhist meditation. First, he tells us that it is not we who do this streaming but strictly speaking it does it to us – just like more intense mystical experience.*
>
> — Harry Hunt[31]

James himself failed to recognise that the underlying Stream of Consciousness with its temporal moments (each possessing front and rear ends), was the Inner Light of religious experience. This is perhaps because, as stated in Chapter 2, his Pan-Experientialist metaphysics (as with Mach's PanSensism) is based on ego-dissolution in the Waking state leading to Nature Mystical experiences rather than transcendental realisations. We have already seen that *Raja Yoga*, the path to Enlightenment, involves 'stopping the mind' by withdrawing attention from the senses as mental activity clouds over the Inner Light of Pure Consciousness. Most of us as we read this text are ignorant of the Inner Light underlying our visual perceptions (the rare exceptions being advanced yogis who have developed the ability to discriminate the presence of the Light upon returning to Wakefulness or 'Fruition Enlightenment'). Furthermore, as in the case of Aldous Huxley's LSD-induced experience of Enlightenment, a subject using drugs does not develop the capacity for stabilising states of lucidity. Thus there is no 'True Light' in James' own experiences but in *Varieties of Religious Experience*, he quotes a female friend expressing the feeling of continuity with the Infinite Power by which all Mind-Cure (a popular movement in James' time[N4]) disciples are inspired, referring to the Divine Energy we call God. He quotes another woman[32]:

> *...by a constant turning to the very innermost deepest consciousness of our real selves or of God in us, for illumination from within,... When you do this consciously [lucidly], realising that to turn inward to the light within you is to live in the presence of God or your divine self.*

Husserl's phenomenological methods of reflection are similar to the "Mindfulness" practises of Buddhist *Abhidhamma* which results in an expanded conscious discrimination of subliminal mental processes or mind-moments generating *phenomena* (the Greek word for "appearances") referring to our perceptual and cognitive constructions. Mindfulness is thus very different from the *nirbija dhyana* (seedless meditation) with no objective content leading to Enlightenment. Husserl's primary method of "Reduction" (*epoché*) involves dissociation from the so-called "Natural Attitude" of captivation in the world of things. What was once taken for granted as the world outside is now 'seen' as a process of phenomenal manifestation constituted in the Flow of underlying Temporal or Absolute Consciousness. The Rhineland mystical tradition has led to a more accepting attitude in Germanic philosophy towards mystical thought and Indian philosophy. Furthermore, as Schwab elaborated in his *Oriental Renaissance*, the Transcendental Idealist speculations of Post-Kantian 19th Century German Philosophy were unthinkable without knowledge of Indian Philosophy. Unlike the British and French, the German Philosophy curriculum included Indian Philosophy[33].

The Anglo-Americans, unable to understand what is being discussed (partly due to the abstruse language), have tended to ignore, if not dismiss, Continental European phenomenology. Bertrand Russell[N5] thought that Husserl's so-called (intentional) "acts" did not really exist[34]. Husserl's so-called 'acts' are not accessible to simple introspection and thus not obvious. Yet most of us in the English-speaking world are familiar with the tachistoscope studies presenting fleeting data to our senses which somehow we register subliminally even though we are not conscious of their existence. Such 'preconscious' (or pre-egoic) processes can be brought into attention through careful cultivation of attention. Given the elaboration by Aron Gurwitsch[35], who linked Husserl's phenomenology to Gestalt psychology, Husserl's so-called 'acts' with their indivisible wholeness or Gestalt character (James also characterises mental states as indivisible wholes), appear to correspond to Patanjali's *cittavritti* (or the waves of the mindstuff), perceptual Gestalts which cloud over the Self (Inner Light).

Husserl does not refer to Inner (Divine) Light, his method being largely limited to perception of objects in the Waking state where, as we have noted, the Light is clouded over by mental activity. But in his "discovery" of the mysterious deeper, self-sustaining Flow of the Absolute Consciousness (also called the Temporal Consciousness), the ultimate, self-sustaining level of phenomenological constitution producing the "Now" moments, we shall see that he is actually discussing the Pure Consciousness though not in a purified state free of sensory superimpositions. This is most clear in Husserl's late work with Eugen Fink. They refer to the Flow of the Absolute Consciousness as the 'Life Stream'; referring to the 'life' of the ego[36]. This parallels the Vedantic *Prana/Atman* Identity wherein the Light of Pure Consciousness is known also as the Life Energy (*Prana*) as it sustains the life of the individuated consciousness (ego) and cessation of the *Prana* entails death. Husserl's collaborator Eugen Fink did not consider himself a Husserlian. Fink recognised the deficiencies in Husserl's ego-centred and superficial approach limited to Wakeful perception. Husserl had mistakenly given absolute status to the preliminary stages of phenomenology. Fink began to realise that the underlying flow of the Absolute Consciousness lays down the spatiotemporal field horizons, 'world concepts' or the background framework within which the ego and perception operate. Fink had considered the possibility that phenomenology could lead to a 'metaphysics of spirit' linking the notion of Spirit to the ultimate in primordial temporality. He also noted that the pairing of Time and Spirit could equally be a pairing of Time and Life given the ceaseless upwelling and flow of the Life Stream[37].

Hindu and Mahayana traditions have long realised that the underlying flow of the Light of Pure Consciousness (the *Prana* or Life Energy equivalent to the Holy Spirit) constitutes the "Time/Space Matrix of Perception" within which gross perceptions and cognitions arise and dissipate[38]. We saw in Chapter 1 that Marie-Louise von Franz wrote that, in the mythology of all cultures, Time is associated with the image of the supreme Godhead or the image of the Self. She also wrote that, "*Spatialisation seems to be a concept derived from our experience of Time and not* vice versa" (*emphasis mine* {*e.m.*})[39]. Amusingly, in his BBC TV Series *Time*, physicist Michio Kaku tells us that "our fundamental *experience of Time* turns out to be internal, written into our DNA" {*e.m.*}[40]. So now DNA is not only the key to Life, the 'building blocks' of Life as Kaku calls it, but, if we took Kaku seriously, our *experience* of temporality is some molecular mechanism in our DNA! Not only has the genetic code become the (holy) 'Book of Life' it is, for Kaku a least, a substitute Godhead!

I find it interesting that Heidegger's point of departure from Husserl was to do with problems in Husserl's thought relating to the concept of Being. In some ways Husserl's focus on mind moments (though he used other terms like 'Acts') flashing in and out of existence, as with the Buddhists' *ksanika* (Momentariness), distracted his attention from the underlying continuity of Being. A.N. Whitehead's Process Philosophy with its "actual occasions" and temporal movement from subject to object, as with the Buddhists, focused on discontinuous aspects of mind moments. Hence modern Westerners have commented on parallels between Buddhism and Continental European phenomenology. As with Eugen Fink, Jean-Paul Sartre in his *Transcendence of the Ego*[41] argued, contrary to Husserl, that the ego is a process and not an absolute entity as also did Aron Gurwitsch[42]. Husserl actually shifted from an earlier (1900-01) view of the ego as simply a complex of mental acts to a later (1913) adoption of Natorp's Neo-Kantian view of a Pure Ego[43]. This again parallels similar Hindu-Buddhist debates about the existence of a "soul" (*jiva*) with Buddha's famous view that it is merely an impermanent complex of aggregates. More generally, the term 'Phenomenology' may be used in regard to Yoga as a method for uncovering deeper mental processes than those of Husserlian phenomenology.

Marie-Louise von Franz, the aforementioned student of Carl Jung, discusses an interesting aspect of the theology of Thomas Aquinas relating to Divine Light which contributed to the split between the profane sciences and religious belief in the modern West. Aquinas was the 13th Century Scholastic bookman who synthesised Aristotle and Christianity and who was made the official Roman Catholic theologian in 1879 *c.e.* The Aristotelian concept of *Nous poietikos*, developed by the Arabs, had dominated medieval Christian Scholasticism. In Islamic mysticism *Nous poietikos* is the radiant, creative energy of the Divine Spirit, which is comparable to Light. This creative,

Divine Light illuminates and inspires the minds of chosen theologians, prophets and mystics[44]. We saw above, in regard to the Schiller's Ode to Joy and the Vedic concept of *brahmana* as poet, that this role of the Divine Light as the source of Divine Inspiration is an aspect of the so-called 'Perennial Philosophy'; i.e., the same essential notion is found in most cultural traditions throughout history. Aquinas made the decisive step of dividing *nous poietikos* into two. Aquinas identified one part with God or *Sapientia Dei* (a personified, Theistic version of *Sophia* or Divine Wisdom) but made the other a natural light (*lumen naturale*) within the human soul. This division became manifest in the Renaissance when scientists began to develop the theory of information that came from natural light. This led to an open conflict with traditional theological views[45].

This scholastic concept of the *lumen naturale* appears in abstruse writings of Martin Heidegger based on speculation rather than the evidential disclosure of actual constitutive processes by Husserl. Both Mahayana Buddhism and Martin Heidegger, says Harry Hunt, rely fundamentally on terms of shining, glow, radiance, welling forth, and the image of the source of the stream (of Consciousness), ever-present but invisible within its outpouring[46]. Heidegger had been educated in the medieval Christian theology of Thomas Aquinas and Meister Eckhart (the mystic whose teachings were denounced as heresy) and Heidegger's philosophy represented an effort to restate this tradition as phenomenology[47]. Hunt says that Heidegger's focus on *Dasein* (human being in the world) follows the anthropocentric Christian separation of Man and Nature. He would have rejected the Mahayana Buddhist view that all sentient creatures have *bodhichitta* (literally 'awakened consciousness') as a seed[48]. It is clear from perusing Heidegger's *Basic Writings*[49] that he is both highly Eurocentric and ignorant of the true nature of mystical knowledge (McEvilley's comments about Westerners misrepresenting Plato's teachings would be most apt for Heidegger). Ayer states that Heidegger's first step was to query Husserl's assumption that Being was correlative to Consciousness[50].

David Krell says that, in his 1964 essay *The End of Philosophy and the Task of Thinking*, the key words in Heidegger's question of Being shift from "Being and Time" (the title of his 1927 book which was never actually completed) to "Clearing (*Lichtung*; literally "Lighting") and Presence". Influenced by Goethe, Heidegger invites thought on the free or open space where things appear, endure and disappear. *Lichtung* designates that unencumbered place for the 'presencing' (Being) of things. Krell says that Metaphysics, which stresses the "**natural light**" of the thinking subject who casts his beam on "objects" has not attended to the Clearing or Lighting of Being, the opening that precedes all natural and **divine light** {*e.m.*}[51]. Reference here is made to Aristotle's Metaphysics and the ancient theory of the seeing involving the emission of rays from the eyes. In regard to the statement that *Lichtung* precedes all natural and divine light, this is correct epistemologically in regard to human experience of Nature and of the Inner Light within the human experiential world-space. Thus *Lichtung* in itself is not the Inner or Divine Light; although as we have seen in regard to Eugen Fink and the creation of the human 'world concepts', it is the Flow of Husserl's "Absolute Consciousness" (which is in fact the Divine Light but 'veiled' with mental superimpositions) which creates the field horizons of human egoic existence; equivalent to Heidegger's *Lichtung* and also related to his earlier concept of *Dasein* (human being in the world) which the Existentialists seized upon naively. Heidegger himself was not aware of this link to Divine Light; his ideas are mere speculations not based on actual experiences.

Heidegger calls the focus on *Lichtung* "the task of thinking" as it requires a creative return to Greek thinking as the Greeks did not securely establish this clearing for thought[52]. Heidegger seems obsessed with the Greek word *aletheia* (unconcealment) which he had earlier translated as truth[53]. In fact Krell says that the task of thinking at the 'End of Philosophy', for Heidegger, is to deepen meditation "On the Essence of Truth" (the title of an essay written in the early 1940s)[54]. It is quite clear why Anglo-Americans, like the aforementioned Eliminative Materialist and Freudian literary critic Richard Rorty find Heidegger pompous and pretentious, not just because of his Nazi sympathies. In *On the Essence of Truth*, Heidegger states, "The thinking of being from which such questioning primordially originates, has since Plato been understood as 'philosophy' and later received the title 'metaphysics'[55]. Here we find again the false notion that Plato's *philosophia* was just 'Thinking' and thinking of Being! True *philosophia* involved transcending hypotheses (including Thought) to experience mystically the Cosmic Light of Wisdom (*Sophia*). In *The End of Philosophy and the Task of Thinking* (1964), Heidegger says that we cannot ask questions about whence Plato's determination of presence as *idea* and Aristotle's interpretation of presencing as *energeia* have their source. He states[56]:

> *Without the preceding experience of aletheia as the clearing, all talk about committed and noncommitted thinking remains without foundation.... Unconcealment is...the element in which Being and thinking and their belonging together exist. Aletheia is named at the beginning of philosophy, but afterward it is not explicitly thought as such by philosophy. For since Aristotle it has become...as metaphysics to think beings as such ontotheologically.*

We have seen that conceptual Philosophy actually originated with the Upanishads and that they were actually based on phenomenological revelations rather than groundless rational speculation (hence Upanishadic philosophy remains largely valid to this day).

Thus Heidegger is aware that the true grounds and origins of philosophy lie in experience, is some sort of unconcealment (or dis**covering** as in the Perennial Philosophy of unveiling the Light shrouded over by mental activity). He concludes that one thing becomes clear; to raise the question of unconcealment is not the same as raising the question of truth. He also denies that this need to experience unconcealment is unfounded mysticism or irrational and states that we still need an education in thinking[57]. This seems to mark the limit of Heidegger's speculative understanding and we shall leave the question of the 'real meaning of Truth' to a true seer later in this chapter. J.J. Clarke tells us that when Heidegger encountered D.T. Suzuki's writings on Zen, he exclaimed that, "if I have understood Suzuki correctly, this is what I have been trying to say in all my writings"[58]. In fact, as Richard King notes, Suzuki's presentation of Zen for the Western readership was a highly Vedanticised interpetration of Zen[59]. In his *Beyond Orientalism* (a misleading title given the book is full of Eurocentric biases) German-born Heidegger fan Fred Dallmayr has a chapter entitled *Sunyata East and West*. Both (the late) Heidegger and Dallmayr found Dogen Zen with its emphasis on Nagarjuna's Emptiness Doctrine or 'Nonfoundationalism' profound. As with Heidegger, Dogen Zen master Masuo Abe loved to indulge in convoluted word games which numb the mind of the reader. But Dallmayr does state that Nagarjuna never denied the idea of a Supreme Reality, the Brahman of the earlier Upanishadic tradition[60].

Psychologist Gordon Globus in his rather pretentious 2003 book *Quantum Closures and Disclosures* looks at supposed parallels between the (pretentious) so-called 'post-phenomenology' ideas of Heidegger and (Heidegger-influenced) doyen of Deconstruction Jacques Derrida with the (equally pretentious) Quantum Brain Dynamics (or Quantum Thermofield Theory including so-called 'inverse tilde universes' etc.) of the Japanese physicists Jibu, Yasue, Umezawa *et al.* and the related ideas of Italian Vitiello[61]. I stated earlier in regard to Penrose's vacuous 'Quantum Mind' ideas that two separate 'mysteries' (Mind; already conflated with Consciousness and so-called 'Quantum Reality' or the Transcendental Realm) are being conflated by these blinkered physicists. No Light at the end of their 'tunnel vision'! Globus writes of 'thinking together' Quantum Theory and Post-Phenomenology so letting the *lumen naturale* flood in[62]! There is no clear-cut consensus as to what Heidegger actually meant by "being" and related obscure terminology[63]. *Lumen* is light or aperture in Latin. However, Globus does provide some insights into Heidegger's concepts which he elaborates.

In regard to Heidegger's *Lichtung* (clearing), Globus comments that *Dasein* (human being in the world) has a brain that somehow supports the welling up of light, a lighting process, enfiring[64]. Globus tells us that Heidegger's *Ereignis* refers to 'welling-up' or, as Globus prefers, a sense of continuous, dynamic flow. What wells up in *Ereignis* asks Globus. He answers that it is the welling-up of two modes that belong together, *Sein* and *Zeit* (Being and Time)[65]. Heidegger's abstruse Germanic and largely etymological utterances about *Beyng, abgrund,* etc., are just linguistic speculations distorting perennial phenomenology not giving any real new insights. As stated in Chapter 7, Heidegger's *Ereignis* dynamics is a modern restatement of the perennial metaphor of the Fountain representing the welling-up of the flowing Spirit or Divinity. Heidegger's writings constitute Eurocentric and Christocentric circumlocution and metaphors which appeal to the pretentious and superficial Gallic Existentialists and Post-Structuralists or 'Post-Phenomenologists' such as Jacques Derrida obsessed with vacuous word games. These vacuous word games in turn appeal to 'Postmodern' Humanities scholars, especially in English departments, who pretend to undertake philosophical and even 'metaphysical' investigations.

Carl Jung (the son of a Christian clergyman), broke away from the often absurd unscientific, sex-obsessed mythologies of Sigmund Freud and brought into ego consciousness deeper aspects of mind that Freud had considered 'unconscious' and beyond our ego. In fact, both Husserl and Sartre derided Freud's naïve use of 'unconscious for mental processes outside of the ego which phenomenological enquiry revealed, nonetheless, to be 'conscious' or sentient though not in the usual sense. Merrell-Wolff explains that so-called 'unconscious' processes are not devoid of Consciousness but they are not self-conscious like the ego, not aware that they are conscious[66]. The assumption that nonegoic mental processes are actually devoid of Consciousness creates the ontological problem of how turning attention to them magically creates Consciousness *ex nihilo*. Jung's Analytical Psychology thus encroaches upon traditional mystical territory of deeper planes of Consciousness although Jung also used the misnomer "unconscious" for non-ego processes.

In Jung's writings, 'Consciousness' meant only egoic consciousness and he sometimes used other terms like *psyche* for his 'Unconscious' to indicate its non-material, mind-like status. In a 1952 letter to Jung, Wolfgang Pauli wrote that he (Pauli) preferred to restrict "Consciousness" to Ego consciousness in order to avoid paradoxical language such as Consciousness in the Unconscious[67]. In a 1935 letter to Pauli, Jung wrote that Consciousness does not grow out of any activity that is inherent to it. Rather Consciousness is constantly being produced by an energy that comes from the depths of the Unconscious. This centre (source of the ego-consciousness-producing energy) was represented perennially in the form of rays. The Greek Gnostics referred to it as the *Spinther* (the Spark) or the *Phos archetypon* (Archetypal Light)[68]. Note that Jung does not recognise this Perennial (Life) Energy *(Zoe* or *Prana)* as the energetic aspect of the Pure Nondual Consciousness within us. Jung, like Husserl, never progressed beyond the ego to experience egoless Pure Consciousness, as experienced in mystical union with the Divine Light. Husserl, as we saw above, from 1913 onwards held a NeoKantian 'Pure Ego' to be self-evident but his colleague Fink, familiar with Neoplatonism[N6], realised that the ego itself must be constituted by deeper processes rather than existing as an absolute entity. Fink realised that the deeper flow of background matrix constituting Temporal Consciousness was not intentional in the familiar subject/object sense but must have a non-object-oriented ("nonthematic") "performance consciousness" which was aware-of-itself in its very coursing[69]. This resembles the Vedantic *svaprakasa* (self-luminosity) and Fink even used terms like "Transcendental Witness" consciousness[70] resembling the yogic *Saksin* (Witness Consciousness).

Jung's Analytical Psychology is focused largely on intermediate planes (associated with Occultism) between our normal Waking consciousness and the deepest spiritual experiences although his own thought was heavily influenced by Eastern philosophy[71, 72]. Merrell-Wolff says that Jung's Analytical Psychology had not discovered Spirit. In his *The Integration of Personality* Jung briefly considered the idea of a Superconsciousness differentiated from the so-called Unconscious. He did not exclude the possibility but thought that its actuality had not yet been empirically determined[73]. Jungian Walter Odajnyk, in defending Jung against the criticisms of Ken Wilber, unwittingly reveals Jung's lack of experiential depth. He tells us that Plato and Augustine did not use the term *archetype* rather the (Hellenistic) Jew Philo Judaeus of Alexandria living around the time of Jesus used it with reference to the *imago Dei* (God image)[74]. We saw in Chapter 7 that the *imago dei* or St Paul's *Inner*

Man represents our Innermost Being, the Spirit or the Light. In the *Corpus Hermeticum* God is called the Archetypal Light and Jung wrote at length on the image of archetypes as points of light, *scintillae,* Seeds of Light etc. Jung also stressed the link between images of luminosity and Consciousness or quasi-Consciousness. Odajnyk says that the alchemist Paracelsus conceived of the *lumen naturae*, the light of nature inherent in the 'inner man' or subtle body.[N7] But according to Paracelsus this *lumen naturae* is invisible[75].

Philo himself is viewed as reinterpreting Judaic mythology with Platonic and Stoic philosophy, influencing later Judaeo-Christian beliefs. Philo wrote of the Divine *Logos* as the 'firstborn son', 'Archetypal man' or the 'Image of God'[76]. Philo rejected the anthropomorphism of the Old Testament god (Yahweh). For Philo, the Absolute Godhead cannot come into contact with matter but that God generated all things without Himself touching matter. He used incorporeal powers or Ideas which are the archetypal patterns forming an intelligible cosmos which is the Idea of Ideas (Philo's conception of the Greek *Logos*; Reason). God touches matter, not through his essence (*ousia*), but through his powers (*energeia*). The thoughts are in a sense objective to His essential subjectivity but not separate from Him. They are inseparable modes of His energy; their rays are dependent upon His Light. They appear as ideal forms in matter and as thoughts in the human mind. They are independent of space and time due to their divine origin. Thus the perceptible universe has invisible patterns in it, the Thought or the *Logos* which is the pervasive law of the universe[77]. Such views trying to keep God apart from Material Nature reflects the *Creatio ex nihilo* tradition of Judaism (presumably derived from the older Zoroastrianism) later adopted by Christianity.

Odajnyk says, contrary to Wilber's assertions, Jung did refer to the archetypes as the primary patterns upon which all other manifestations are based. He stresses that Jung did distinguish between archetypes *per se* which in their essence are unknowable and purely hypothetical potential fields of energy or consciousness, and archetypal images which take specific form in time and space[78]. Odajnyk says that, according to Wilber, 'true mysticism' is 'formless awareness' and beyond the archetypes and entails 'finding the formless' beyond the light'[79]. But, as we have seen in Chapter 6, Wilber's understanding of mystical terms leaves much to be desired. The formless *nirguna Brahman* **is** the 'Clear Light of the Void' as Aldous Huxley recognised from his own enlightenment. If Jungian Psychology had true spiritual depth then Odajnyk would recognise that so-called archetypes are neither unknowable nor are they purely hypothetical. All this focus on 'points of light' and the invisible 'light of nature', etc., misses the point that Jung does not refer to the Inner (Divine) Light as such. We have seen Docetist Gnostic descriptions of the Light of *Sophia* as full of infinite ideas corresponding to the Vedantic understanding of *prajna* (Luminous Wisdom Consciousness) aspect of the Inner Light. The Eurocentric Jungians such as Jacobi suppressed Jung's references to Eastern Yoga including the fact that Jung stated that archetypes were equivalent to yogic *samskara* (karmic impressions)[80].

Marie-Louise von Franz's *Psyche and Matter* contains essays dating from the early 1970s to late 1980s. Most of the earlier essays assert the Jungian view that archetypes are not knowable ("completely unobservable") in themselves but only through their manifestation as psychical images recognisable as archetypal as they are common to all cultures. The archetype is characterised by the general structure or Form rather than the specific content. She also stresses Jung's naive Pythagorean view of Natural Numbers as archetypes of Order. *Psyche and Matter* also contains essays contradicting Jung's original views.[N8] These contradictory views might be late revisions by Jung himself or perhaps reinterpretations by von Franz which are more in tune with Perennial Philosophy. Having said in some essays that archetypes in themselves were unknowable she later refers to the holonomic omnipresence of Jung's archetypes and says that Jung described the archetypes interpenetrating in a 'Cloud of Cognition'[81]. This corresponds to the Vedantic *prajnaghana* (dense luminous mass of Wisdom-Consciousness) and NeoPlatonic views of noetic forms as intermingled. Aurobindo Ghose's described the so-called 'Beings of Light' (which correspond to such archetypal images) dissolving under sustained yogic discrimination into vibratory patterns of consciousness-energy[82]. This ties in with my elaboration above of Wolfgang Pauli's linkage of 'archetypal sequences' (linked to the archetypal image of the Dance of Siva) to the underlying dance of energetic patterns constituting Quantum Reality.

Jungian psychology and Husserlian phenomenology resemble cults as, due to the difficulty in actual practice of the introspective methods, the followers rely on endless rehashing and debating of the confusing, original writings of their founding 'prophets'. Jungian Psychology has degenerated into speculative Dream Analysis as seen in (Jungian) Lindorff's recent book *Pauli and Jung*[83]. Jung claimed that Indian Philosophy had over-reached itself in making metaphysical and grand cosmological claims on the basis of exploring psychic processes. According to Jung, this made Indian Philosophy 'pre-Kantian'[84]. By this I presume he meant that Indian Philosophy was ignorant of the (imaginary) epistemological limits to human knowledge claimed by Kant which I have dismissed previously. Jung also misinterpreted Gnosticism, translating its metaphysical notions about Divinity and Matter as if they were the same as his psychological terms "unconscious" and "ego" and also misreading medieval Alchemy, (i.e., Hermetica) as the secret, "underground" continuation of the Gnostic heresy[85]. This chastisement of Jung by Gnostic scholar Segal does not tally with Jungian analyst Odajnyk's claim that Jung was familiar with the realm of formlessness and defined it as "the original, non-differentiated unity of the world or of Being". This potential world, says Odajnyk, is the *mundus archetypus* of the medieval Scholastics and defined by (alchemist) Gerard Dorn as the *unus mundus*[86].

It is true that *unus mundus* appears frequently in Jung's writings but his writings are very vague, incoherent and often filled with mythological imagery and symbolism not conducive to clarity. Jung often denied having a metaphysics claiming to be just a psychologist but, as Dourley stresses, there must obviously be a tacit metaphysic underlying Jung's speculations. Jung argues that whatever is known is known through the Psyche and that existence itself is Psychic. Jung dismisses the naive Empiricism of Aristotelians and Thomists who claim that there is nothing in the Intellect that was not first in the senses.

On the contrary, Jung says that the Psyche is full of the god-creating energies of the archetypes, even prior to its creation of (ego) consciousness[87]. Jung gave Psychology the supreme status in Metaphysics arguing that even metaphysical statements are statements of the Psyche and so reflect the dominant complex or complexes in the metaphysician's own psyche[88]. For Jung, all that is significantly knowable, as well as the possibility of (ego) consciousness itself, exists originally in the wholly undifferentiated 'matrix' of the 'Creative Unconscious' the source of all Consciousness[89]. As Dourley himself indicates, Jung's use of the term 'matrix' is problematical as he also claims that the Creative Unconscious is wholly undifferentiated. A 'matrix' suggests a binding substance between elements or a differentiated set of elements. Aldous Huxley stressed that great mystics from all traditions have drawn a sharp distinction between the Psychic and the Spiritual. The Psychic (supernatural) is an extension of the world of Space and Time and not the Timeless, Eternal Ground[90].

Dourley's analysis of Jung's understanding of Perennial Mysticism based on Jung's reading of Alchemy tells us that this leads to the experience of the potential world of the *unus mundus* which Jung believed was the Ground of all Being[91]. Dourley calls Jung's concept the 'Creative Unconscious' or 'Synchronicity' but we have already come across Jung's term 'Psychoid Realm' associated with Synchronicity in which Matter and Mind (Psyche) are indistinguishable. Jung's linkage of Dorn's *Unus Mundus* to Synchronicity parallels the Vedantic *Akasa* rather than the Formless Nothingness from which this potential world arises. This is because, as we have seen, the Yoga Sutras link the vibrations of the *Akasa* with Space-Time transcending resonances based on morphic similarities and Jung's anthropocentric notion of 'meaningful coincidence' touches upon this more general case of vibratory resonances (the Sympathies of Ancient occultism). We have seen that Jung's (mandala-influenced) quadrant diagram for Synchronicity (Acausal Orderedness) is misleading as the real division is bipartite. Jung's anthropocentric presentation of Synchronicity as 'meaningful coincidences' is, as we have seen in Chapter 4, most problematic. It seems to suggest that the universe is predetermined with external events occurring to correspond to (personal) human thoughts[92]. 'Meanings' exist in the individual human mind, not in the external world. Wolfgang Pauli pointed out to Jung in 1949 that Schopenhauer had put forward a notion of meaningful coincidence similar to Jung's in Schopenhauer's essay "On the Apparent Design in the Fate of the Individual". Pauli also added that, like Jung, Schopenhauer had been influenced by Eastern ideas from Asia[93].

Dourley's analysis of Jung's understanding of Perennial Mysticism brings out the parallel with the Historicism of Hegel which Jung himself recognised late in his life[94]. We have seen that Hegel's absurd historical fantasies, which bewitch Marxians, were actually rooted in Christian Kabbalism and other Occult traditions[95]. It is clear that Jung was attempting to interpret the Perennial Philosophy of Enlightenment in that he viewed all collective religions as based on this underlying common mystical experience of archetypes in the 'Unconscious'. Jung reiterated the Empedoclean and Plotinian views of God or the Centre of the Soul being the Centre of the Universe. Jung also approved views espoused by the likes of Philo Judaeus, Plotinus as well as Vedantic and Taoist assertions of the underlying oneness of the personal with the supra-personal *Atman* or the Universal *Tao*. Jung recognised the archetypal symbol of the *Anthropos* or Universal Humanity (associated with the Inner Light as common to all humans) experienced in mystical states and its manifestation in socio-political ideals associated with Humanism and the Brotherhood of Man[96].

Dourley says that Jung's the "Self" gives birth to the ego and exercises a function not unlike the Creator in popular Christian imagination[97]. As such it would correspond to the Vedantic *Prana* (Life Energy) aspect of the *Atman* in that, as we saw above, Jung viewed (egoic) consciousness arising from an 'energy' which arises from the depths of the Unconscious. Indeed, Jordens has shown the parallels between Jung's *libido* (a general psychic energy, not the sexual libido myth of Freud) and the Vedantic *prana*[98]. But Jungian Psychology uses this term 'Self' in two different ways which can be understood better using my RAS brainwave correlate of the *Prana*. Stevens says that Jung's 'Self' is the total archetypal system within which is programmed (or prefigured) the complete scenario for an individual life. The Self bears within it the seeds of the total personality, all the characteristics of a unique individual[99]. Jung wrote that the Self is an *a priori* existent out of which the ego evolves. Although the maturing ego develops a subjectively-experienced independence from the Self, the ego actually remains intimately related to the Self. The Self-ego relation resembles the relationship between (Creator) God and humanity in great world religions[100].

Thus Jungians also use the term 'Self' as the total personality structure or total archetype system suggesting the whole range of brain centres which at some point participate in the egoic activity of the individual, (i.e., the potential field of egoic activity). At any one moment our ego is active only in certain archetypal complexes (brain centres) but this egoic activity is constantly shifting as our attention, moods, emotions and interests change with time. My RAS brainwave correlate of the *prana* or Life Energy aspect of the perennial 'Deeper Self' helps explain this conflation in Jungian Psychology. The brainstem Reticular Formation underlying the RAS brainwaves projects axons into all brain centres (reticular means 'net-like') hence the RAS activating energy underlies all gross brain activity in all the various brain centres at all times. Thus the Self as an underlying energy creating the ego is present in the total personality structure (the entire brain or potential field of egoic activity or Existentialists' 'Lifeworld' filled with the energy of the Self as *libido*). No doubt the Jungian conflation of these two, closely associated, but different entities (the underlying energy of activation aspect (*libido*) and the spatial aspect of the field of egoic activity) is intimately related to the supposed Jungian goal of 'Individuation' as an integration of the personality as a whole or bringing all the archetypal complexes into ego consciousness. Such an integration of the whole brain within a single field of attention seems totally unfeasible to me. We have seen in Chapter 6 that the Transcendental Meditation movement misrepresented EEG Coherence (associated with cortical deactivation and dying) as being such an integration of the whole brain.

Dourley notes that Jungian thought is completely at odds with the Monotheisms' which posit a God ontologically distinct from Creation and wholly Other to Human consciousness. But Dourley limits this non-Theism to Pantheism and repeatedly refers to embodiment in Time and Space[101]. This lack of the Transcendent in Dourley's analysis contradicts the Space-Time transcending character of Synchronicity which Jung called 'Acausal Orderedness' (not mentioned by Dourley). Jung thought that Christian spirituality only extends to the preliminary stage of spiritual development which allows a glimpse of Eternity. Jung also argued that the central figure of Christian myth, Jesus, is not a unifying factor but a dividing sword that sunders spiritual man from the physical (Nature)[102]. For Jung, and also for Dorn according to Jung, (the experience of) un-incarnated spirituality demanded Reincarnation. This refers to Alchemical transformations resulting in (experiences of) 'separation' from the physical body such that the soul is united with the Spirit. This Spiritualised Body or '*caelum*' was symbolised by the 'Glorified body'. Jung suggested that Alchemists may have understood this state to be an experience equivalent to the experience of 'Resurrection'[103]. This aspect of Jung's interpretation is in accord with my own understanding of the 'True Resurrection' (as also argued by Joseph Campbell and Michael Whiteman) as being the attainment of a Pure Ego, stripped of bodily attachments (associated with the Cerebral Cortex) which is translucent to the Inner Light.

Jung's interpretation of the perennial mystical realisation of the Ground or of Divinity was deeply flawed and misleading. Like G.W. Hegel, Jung believed in a teleological view of historical fulfilment of the purpose in Nature resembling also the Romantic myths of the 'Evolution of Consciousness'. His process of 'individuation' was seen by him as a natural goal of the psyche in its maturation. Individuation is not atypical or confined to a privileged few but a universal process in which each psyche participates leading toward universal empathy[104]. Jung argued that 'God' seeks a Unity of Opposites in human consciousness that defied realisation within the Godhead. This is what ultimately demands the creation of (ego) consciousness. For Jung, the creative but unconscious One differentiates into its opposites in historical consciousness and brings the opposites together in the 'Age of Spirit'[105]. Jung claims that this Individuation process is initiated and presided over by the Self which seeks conscious realisation in the individual and in history through first constellating and then re-uniting in human consciousness opposites that remain contaminated or undifferentiated in the Unconscious[106].

In spite of his criticism of Church Christianity it seems that Jung remained unable to shake of his Christian indoctrinations towards a more advanced appreciation of the Perennial Philosophy. The Historicism of the Bible remains in his Hegelian view of the 'Synthesis of Opposites' in an 'Age of Spirit'! He remains ignorant of the fact, stressed in Chapter 6 in regard to Wilber's ignorance of the Immanence of the Transcendental, that the "transcendental" is not simply the 'hidden' or 'beyond' outside conventional experiences but is a factor in the experiencing processes themselves[107]. The Self does not strive to become conscious in the ego, the Self is the underlying Pure Nondual Consciousness that becomes superimposed with objective content in every moment and act of egoic existence. Mystical 'Transcendence of Opposites' does not refer to some goal-directed Eurocentric Hegelian historical myth but to transcendence of conceptual polarisations in the supra-rational Wisdom Consciousness (*prajna*) of the Godhead. Mystical gnosis and enlightenment are not some maturation process inherent in the nature of the individual psyche, they are a deconstructive process resembling the natural process of dying! Huxley emphasised the perennial knowledge that ascetic self-mortification (and also detachment) was indispensable for enlightenment. The more of the ego that remains undiminished, the less the Inner Light shines through. Only the purified soul, (i.e., the 'naked ego') can realise identity with Brahman[108].

I have already mentioned in Chapter 6, Jung's Near-Death Experience (NDE) very late in his life in which he described the ego being shorn of its earthly attachments to create what he labelled an 'objective ego'. Jung's own NDE in 1944 included imagining himself floating in space about a thousand miles above the Indian subcontinent and an image of a meteorite carved out like a Hindu temple representing his life's work[109]. We have seen that a Hindu temple represents the 'subtle body' sheathing the Light at the centre. In spite of considerable Eastern influences upon his own thought which Jung acknowledged, Jung was also naive and condescending towards Indian Philosophy which he claimed was 'pre-Kantian' and merely a description of psychic processes and thus had over-reached itself in its metaphysical pretensions[110]. Jung's Reductionist misinterpretation of Gnostic metaphysics and his dismissal of Indian yogic metaphysics as 'pre-Kantian' give the lie to Odajnyk's defence of Jung. The goal of Jungian practise or 'Individuation', integrating all the aspects of one's personality, runs contrary to the traditional mystical goals of purifying the "soul" of personal content to attain gnosis prior to ego dissolution in mystical union. Rather, Individuation resembles Origen's Christian notion of the 'Whole Man'.

Von Franz states that Jung thought that the archetype is the most fundamental level of our psychic being which we cannot transcend. Archetypes were not like pieces of bread in a soup but they are the whole soup[111]. She also compared the Jungian unconscious to an electromagnetic field with activated archetypes as excited points[112]. This image parallels Bohm's picture of the 'particle' in Quantum Theory as manifesting in Space-Time from the underlying nonlocal Quantum Potential which is omnipresent. It also parallels the Docetist Gnostics' description of the Light of *Sophia* as full of infinite Ideas which inform the formless matter. Bruce Long, describing Hindu notions of *karma* (we saw that Jung said that his 'archetypes' were *samskara*) says that the basal universal energy (*tapas, sakti*) is conceived like a bundle of forces fluctuating in an electromagnetic field (*ksetra*; field)[113]. Von Franz says that the fact that Light is the most frequent image in spirituality and its presence at death led Jung to speculate, very late in his life, that Light was the last transitional phenomenon as the material dematerialises and becomes psychical[114]. We have seen that the shift from the Material Plane to the Spiritual in Dying and Enlightenment is a shift in Consciousness due to the ego being stripped attachment to worldly representations in the cortex. Jung misinterprets such transitions as a literal 'dematerialisation' of Matter rather than a shift in perception due to purification of the ego! Such naive speculations only go to show more clearly that Jung failed to appreciate the Light of Death as the Light of Universal Consciousness.

Certain contemporary 'Jungians' such as British medical psychiatrist Anthony Stevens in his *Archetype Revisited* reject all the mystical, transpersonal aspects of Jungian thought reducing it to archetypal brain centres, inherited instincts and behavioural repertoires. As with others, Stevens talks positively of the spiritual and transcendent but, in the next breath, reduces everything to Materialism! He agrees with Roger Sperry that Consciousness emerges as a property of brain activity working as a whole[115]. Again the 'mystical' is rejected in favour of the 'magical' emergence myth. But Stevens does mention that cortical anaesthesia, ablation or auto-inhibition does not result in abolition of consciousness but only impairs finer aspects. He notes that the brainstem Reticular Activating System (RAS) is the powerhouse driving the whole complex of systems subserving 'consciousness'. Blocking the RAS is the only known way of abolishing 'consciousness' making the RAS (actually the brainstem Reticular Formation) which is the only part of the brain which is indispensible for 'consciousness' (*inverted commas mine*)[116]. I have put Stevens' use of 'consciousness' in inverted commas as this modern Medical knowledge of the RAS is referring of course only to human egoic states. Stevens also concurs with a Dr J.P. Henry of Los Angeles in arguing that the neurological correlates of Jungian archetypes (within the 'personal Unconscious') would be the located in the deeper, subcortical structures. Although it is not possible to locate any precise brain locations for the major archetypes, Stevens agrees with Henry that the core nuclei in the Limbic System and the Brainstem were the likely candidates[117].

Two True Scientific "Seers" : The Light as Seen by Merrell-Wolff and Michael Whiteman

As we have seen, the orthodox dogma of Western Comparative Religion in regard to the interpretation of mystical experiences is Constructivism. All mystical experiences are the products of cultural-mythological indoctrination; what you experience is what you are expected to experience from indoctrination. Space does not permit a detailed debunking of this view which holds partial validity especially for superficial experiences where culture-specific imagery often appears. I pointed out in Chapter 2 that my RAS-brainwave correlate of the Inner Light undermines the unscientific Constructivist dogma that there are no unmediated mental processes; the activating brainwaves from the Reticular Formation *are unconditioned and universal*. But the reader should note here that contemporary Western mystics can confirm in their own experiences the validity of descriptions from other cultural traditions with which they have become acquainted, often in an attempt to understand better their own, often spontaneous experiences. Thus, *contra* Constructivism, an individual's mystical experiences may precede the various cultural interpretations learnt afterwards in order to try to understand them better. Such was the case with Nobel laureate Geneticist Barbara McClintock, of 'jumping genes' fame, who became interested in Buddhism after her own experiences[118]. The same was true of an Englishman Richard who ran a scientific indexing company with whom I worked in 1999 on a scientific encyclopaedia and an English woman with whom I worked in the mid-1990s.

Both of the Western mystics below also have proven themselves in Mathematics and Philosophy at the highest levels whereas the critics of such views tend to be sociologists or historians in Religious Studies. The latter often regard Science in same manner in which they hold their personal faiths, received wisdom to be accepted on the dogmatic authority of the orthodox establishment. This is partly because academics in the Humanities, as with psychologists, generally have a very poor personal grasp of Science. Thus they resort to appeals to authority rather than attempt to interpret the issue of the possibility of mystical experience through personal assessment of scientific knowledge. We have noted the facile, unscientific, arguments of the likes of Matthew Kapstein (Ch. 3). In *The Presence of Light* Kapstein ignored the glaring commonalities in descriptions of Light and stuck *religiously* to his ideological Constructivist standpoint without attempting to account for cross-cultural differences in emphasis. In recent decades, we have witnessed the equally puerile anti-Science movement in the Humanities based on naive Postmodern myths that scientific knowledge is merely a cultural construction without universal (common human) validity. We will see in the next chapter that Richard King adheres faithfully to his own Gadamerian relativist ideology in denying the Neo-Hindu assertions of an underlying Universal Spirituality basically resembling Nondual Brahmanism (*Advaita Vedanta*)[119]. This absolute Relativism mythology peddled by inferiority-complex ridden 'Postmodern' Humanities[N9] academics resembles the egalitarian 'every child is gifted' ideology prevalent in contemporary Leftist pedagogy, dumbing down of TV with 'talent' shows or the Conceptual Art charlatanism of 'Brit Art'.

Franklin Merrell-Wolff (1887–1985), son of a Methodist minister, undertook graduate work in philosophy at Harvard before gaining a position as a Professor of Mathematics at Stanford. However, shortly afterwards he abandoned his academic career in order to pursue his own quest for a 'third way of knowing', not limited by sense perceptions and conceptual cognitions[120]. This corresponds to Plato's 'destroying the hypotheses' and opening the 'wisdom-eye', or true *Philosophia.* Merrell-Wolff wanted to "reach beyond anything contained within the academic circles of the West"[121]. As we have seen, he called his method "Introceptualism" having coined the term *introception* for the faculty of Consciousness to turn back upon itself, away from sense perceptions, a faculty long described in Indian yogic texts. He stressed that Introception is not the grasping of the conceptual fringe but operates in the most intense kind of Light wherein one is more intensely conscious than ever before[122]. Such grasping the Jamesian 'fringe' is the basis of logical abstraction of formal relations, etc., and related to Merleau-Ponty's superficial understanding of creativity where one explores the indeterminacies of the Gestalt background (or Jamesian 'fringe') of attention.

In his scholarly descriptions of his meditations and in the epistemology and ontology that he derived from his experiences, Merrell-Wolff repeatedly refers to Indian philosophy, acknowledging that he has been retracing steps into deeper planes of Consciousness first described in philosophical terms by

Indian mystics thousands of years previously. He was an admirer of his contemporary, the greatest modern Indian mystic-philosopher, Aurobindo Ghose. I have already mentioned the mathematical physicist and mystic, J.H.M. (Michael) Whiteman, mentioning that Werner Heisenberg himself checked the chapter on QM in Whiteman's 1967 book and that Paul Dirac discussed that book with Whiteman. In that book he argued from the basis of personal realisation that the 'transcendental substructure' of Nature indicated indirectly by QM could be known directly through Meditation and that the 'Universalised Consciousness' transcending appearances in Time and Space was also the core of our own consciousness[123]. I have also referred to his last book, *Universal Theology*[124]. Whiteman taught Relativity and Quantum theories at Cape Town University. Professor Arthur Ellison, who put me in touch with Whiteman after seeing the synopsis of my *The Oneness/Otherness Mystery*, spoke of how he began to see the larger picture of reality aided by Indian thought:

> *As I reached this glimmer of an understanding, I was fascinated to read a parallel explanation, amounting perhaps to much the same thing, by Professor J.H.M. Whiteman (a former professor of applied mathematics at Cape Town and also a mystic). He states that everything is described in the classical Eastern (Hindu) literature.*
>
> —A.J. Ellison[125]

Merrell-Wolff describes the being of the Self, which experienced through "introception" is more unequivocal than the being or actuality of perception, (i.e., appears more real), as being like an unsupported Light. It is like the Flame that burns without wick or fuel. It is so pure that it is without the taint of personality. It may be conceived as like a self-supporting Light within a somewhat differentiated lamp; the lamp carrying the individual traits of personality. The Light of the Pure Self has this character of real impersonality. Although it remains highly subjective, it is not a personal subjectivism. Merrell-Wolff stresses that this *impersonality* is a matter of exceptional importance for philosophy as the impersonality of the Self gives it a *universal* value {*e.m.*}[126]. This point resembles closely my discussion in Chapter 2 as to how the *Atman* (the impersonal Light of Pure Consciousness within each individual) can be both the same *Atman* in every individual whilst being present in a plurality of individuals.

> *In the sense of introception, the consciousness related to the I is not a consciousness of the I. It is immediate "knowledge through acquaintance" in the most rigorous sense. ...It is I, together with consciousness that I am, immediately known and not as a mere inference. To be conscious as the pure I is to be conscious of Nothing, which is infinitely more valuable than any thing. I am the pure Light, which by illuminating everything gives to everything existence for me,...*
>
> —Franklin Merrell-Wolff[127]

As well as referring frequently to Indian philosophy, Merrell-Wolff mentions the *Finklein* (Divine Spark) of Meister Eckhart and the *Scintilla* (Divine Spark) of the Franciscan mystic St Bonaventure (who wrote *The Mind's Road to God*). Both Eckhart's and Bonaventure's descriptions resemble closely the original Vedantic descriptions from the Upanishads composed some two thousand years or more before in India. In developing his epistemology (theory of knowledge) from his personal experiences, Merrell-Wolff argues that this Divine Consciousness may serve as the fountainhead of philosophical systems[128]. However, this has already been the case for 3,000 years in Indian philosophy. On the great philosophical questions of Truth and Reality, Merrell-Wolff realises that Truth and Reality mean virtually the same thing. *Truth and Reality are identical with Divinity*, and the Realisation of Truth or Reality is not other than the Realisation of and union with Divinity {*e.m.*}[129].

Merrell-Wolff finally attained mystical union in 1936 after twenty four years effort. He found that the traditional yogic methods involving stopping all mentation were not suitable for his personality and circumstances. Nearer to final attainment he realised that he had made the error of seeking the "Self" or pure subject as an *object* and managed to isolate the subjective moment within the subject-object manifold of perception[130]. I would interpret this 'pure subjective moment' as an activating brainwave of the RAS with the objective consciousness as brainwaves from the cortex and subcortical structures which superimpose the unconditioned, activating brainwaves. The first three of his four critical stages of transformation were linked to insights associated with reading books on Indian sages (we saw that he rated Sankara as the greatest Idealist) and the *Bhagavad Gita*. We saw in Chapter 2 that, at a critical stage, he says, a he realised the I becoming a bare point of light, a zero but this immediately expanded to the whole of space[131]. We also saw that he distinguished clearly the nondual realisation of Cosmic Consciousness from the realisation of the plenum/void of substantive Pure Consciousness (which he calls the High Indifference). He says that the latter is the true *Nirvana* (the *Sunyata*) and that most Eastern texts do not distinguish these. He claims that he goes beyond Vedanta which identifies the Self or the subjective pole as the Ultimate, whereas the plenum of Pure Consciousness transcends all dualities and is neither subject nor object[132].

However, he relied upon the limited available translations and one immediately recognises in his writings of the "High Indifference", with no desires whatsoever, the age old yogic descriptions of the utter completeness with nothing lacking such that all is as it should be, (i.e., indifference). The Vedantic Creation doctrine of *Niskama Karma* (NonDesire Action) asserting that *nirguna Brahman* has no need or goal to create the universe[133]. The Upanishads describe the Pure Consciousness both as *ananda* (Bliss related to freedom from worldly bondage) but also sometimes as *udasina* meaning Total Indifference[134]. The aforementioned Vedantic doctrine of *Vyavahara* (*see Ch. 4*) and the stress on the indicative status of concepts makes clear that all predications fail to capture the Absolute Nonduality of Ultimate Reality transcending all dualities. And of course the distinction between the Cosmic Consciousness and the Plenum/Void is clearly present in the Vedantic *saguna* and *nirguna Brahman*. Given that Merrell-Wolff was familiar with Sankara's teachings, it is surprising that he doesn't mention this, using the Buddhist term *Nirvana* instead which he himself says is misleading as it suggests extinction!

Ron Leonard says that Merrell-Wolff later played down the influence of Sankara on him. Merrell-Wolff also claimed that he himself had brought about a 'Copernican Revolution in Philosophy'[135]. Unfortunately this is an all too familiar scenario whereby Europeans learn from India, then 'Westernise' and/ or 'Christianise' their terminology and claim profound originality for themselves (what Rajiv Malhotra has labelled the 'U-Turn'). Indeed, in 1990 I read J.C. Chatterji's little book *The Wisdom of the Vedas* which was originally published in the USA five years before Merrell-Wolff's enlightenment in 1931 as *India's Outlook on Life*. Chatterji distinguishes the *apparently* two fundamental realities known as "Purusha" (or *Brahman*). First we have the unmanifest, 'spaceless', timeless plenum which is the unchanging Being and second we have the system of ever-changing movements which constitute the universe. In reality the latter is only an aspect of the paradoxically unchanging, unmoving Being[136].

Whiteman (1906-2007), whose book *The Mystical Life* was published in 1961, has experienced the whole range of mystical experiences leading to mystical union (the yogic path known as *Raja Yoga*). He also learnt Sanskrit and Pali so he could read the Hindu and Buddhist texts for himself rather than the distorted renderings of academic "experts" with little understanding of the terms which are often yogic technical terms relating to states of Consciousness, understood only through yogic practise. Both ancient commentators and modern academics, he stated, have misunderstood the true meanings of concepts, such as karmic rebirth, projecting them onto the external world and such distortions are accepted as authoritative interpretations. I shall quote below an extract reprinted in one of his own books which he sent to me in 1999, describing experiences he had in November 1932.

> *Above and in front, yet in me, and around, was the Glory of the Archetypal Light. Nothing can be more truly Light, since that Light makes all other light to be light; nor is it a flat material light, but a creative light of Life itself, streaming forth in Love and Understanding, and forming all other lives out of its substance: a Light become Life not through addition to material light... What can we say of the contemplating soul? Formed by the Life itself, she was yet face to face with its Glory, poised and held aloft as in the air, whilst the Power streamed forth and past...*
>
> — J.H.M. Whiteman[137]

References

1. Moran, Dermot (2002) *Introduction to Phenomenology*, Routledge.
2. Schuhmann, Karl "Husserl and Indian Thought". In D. P. Chattopadhyaya, Lester Embree and Jitendranath Mohanty (Editors) (1992) *Phenomenology and Indian Philosophy*, State University of New York Press.
3. Schuhmann, Karl (1992) *ibid.*
4. Finkelstein, Israel and Silberman, Neil, A. (2001) *The Bible Unearthed: Archaeology's New Vision of Ancient Israel and the Origin of its Sacred Texts*, Simon and Schuster.

5. Schuhmann, Karl (1992) *ibid.*
6. Clarke, John J. (1997) *Oriental Enlightenment: The Encounter Between Asian and Western Thought*, Routledge.
7. Bruzina, Ronald (2004) *Edmund Husserl and Eugen Fink: Beginnings and Ends in Phenomenology 1928-1938*, Yale University Press.
8. Whiteman, J.H. Michael (1967) *Philosophy of Space and Time and the Inner Constitution of Nature: A Phenomenological Study*, Muirhead Library of Philosophy, George Allen and Unwin and the Humanities Press.
9. Schuhmann, Karl (1992) *ibid.*
10. *Racism: A History* (2007) British Broadcasting Corporation (Television Series).
11. Moore, David C. (Editor) (2001) *Black Athena Writes Back: Martin Bernal Responds to his Critics*, Duke University Press.
12. Schuhmann, Karl (1992) *ibid.*
13. Gregorios, Paulos, M. "Phenomenology and the Transcendent: Which Way Does One Transcend?". In D.P. Chattopadhyaya, Lester Embree and Jitendranath Mohanty (Editors) (1992) *Phenomenology and Indian Philosophy*, State University of New York Press.
14. Goonatilake, Susantha (1998) *Toward a Global Science: Mining Civilisational Knowledge*, Indiana University Press.
15. Goldberg, Philip (2010) *American Veda: From Emerson and the Beatles to Yoga and Meditation – How Indian Spirituality Changed the West*, Harmony Books, Random House.
16. Schuhmann, Karl (1992) *ibid.*
17. *Ibid.*
18. *Ibid.*
19. Forman, Robert, K.C. (1999) *Mysticism, Mind, Consciousness*, State University of New York Press.
20. Merrell-Wolff, Franklin (1995) *Transformations in Consciousness: The Metaphysics and Epistemology* (Containing His *Introceptualism*), State University of New York Press.
21. Laughlin, Charles, D. "Biogenetic Structural Theory and the Neurophenomenology of Consciousness". In Stuart R. Hameroff, Alfred W. Kaszniak, and David J. Chalmers (Editors) (1999) *Toward a Science of Consciousness: The Third Tucson Discussions and Debates*, MIT Press.
22. Bardach, A.L. (2012) "What Did J.D. Salinger, Leo Tolstoy, and Sarah Bernhardt Have in Common". *Wall Street Journal* (Online) 30th March.
23. *Ibid.*
24. *Ibid.*
25. Cooper, Wesley (2002) *The Unity of William James's Thought*, Vanderbilt University Press.
26. Barnard, G. William (1997) *Exploring Unseen Worlds: William James and the Philosophy of Mysticism*, State University of New York Press.
27. *Ibid.*
28. *Ibid.*

29. Huxley, Aldous (1956) "Knowledge and Understanding". Reprinted in Jacqueline H. Bridgeman (Editor) (1992) *Huxley and God: Essays*, Harper Collins.
30. Barnard, G. William (1997) *ibid.*
31. Hunt, Harry T. (1995) *On the Nature of Consciousness: Cognitive, Phenomenological, and Transpersonal Perspectives*, Yale University Press.
32. James, William (1902) *The Varieties of Religious Experience*, Longmans, Green, and Co.
33. Schwab, Raymond (1950, French) English translation *The Oriental Renaissance: Europe's Rediscovery of India and the East 1680-1880* (1984) Columbia University Press.
34. Mohanty, J.N. (1994) *Essays on Indian Philosophy*, Oxford University Press India.
35. Gurwitsch, Aron (1966) *Studies in Phenomenology and Psychology*, Northwestern University Press.
36. Bruzina, Ronald (2004) *ibid.*
37. Bruzina, Ronald (2004) *ibid.*
38. Brown, Daniel P. "The Stages of Meditation in Cross-Cultural Perspective". In Ken Wilber, Jack Engler and Daniel P. Brown (Editors) (1986) *Transformations of Consciousness: Conventional and Contemplative Perspectives on Development*, Shambhala Publications.
39. Von Franz, Marie-Louise (1981) "Meaning and Order", *see also* von Franz, Marie-Louise (1978) "The Psychological Experience of Time" both reprinted in von Franz, Marie-Louise (1992) *Psyche and Matter*, Shambhala Publications.
40. Kaku, Michio (2006) *Time*, British Broadcasting Corporation (Television Series).
41. Sartre, Jean-Paul (1957) *The Transcendence of the Ego: An Existentialist Theory of Consciousness* (English Translation 1960), The Noonday Press.
42. Gurwitsch, Aron (1941) "A Non-egological Conception of Consciousness". Reprinted in Gurwitsch, Aron (1966) *Studies in Phenomenology and Psychology*, Northwestern University Press.
43. Gurwitsch, Aron (1929) "Phenomenology of Thematics and of the Pure Ego: Studies of the Relation between Gestalt Theory and Phenomenology". English translation in Gurwitsch, Aron (1966) *Studies in Phenomenology and Psychology*, Northwestern University Press.
44. von Franz, Marie-Louise (Undated) "Some Historical Aspects of C.G. Jung's Synchronicity Hypothesis". English translation in von Franz, Marie-Louise (1992) *Psyche and Matter*, Shambhala Publications.
45. Von Franz, Marie Louise (Undated) *ibid.*
46. Hunt, Harry T. (1995) *ibid.*
47. *Ibid.*
48. *Ibid.*
49. Krell, David, F. (Editor) (1993) *Martin Heidegger: Basic Writings from Being and Time (1927) to The Task Of Thinking (1964)* (Revised Edition), Harper Collins.

50. Ayer, Alfred J. (1982) *Philosophy in the Twentieth Century*, George Wiedenfeld and Nicolson Ltd.
51. Krell, David, F. "General Introduction: The Question of Being". In David F. Krell (Editor) (1993) *Martin Heidegger: Basic Writings from Being and Time (1927) to The Task of Thinking (1964)* Revised Edition, Harper Collins.
52. Heidegger, Martin (1964) "The End of Philosophy and the Task of Thinking". Reprinted in David F. Krell (Editor) (1993) *Martin Heidegger: Basic Writings from Being and Time (1927) to The Task of Thinking (1964)*, Revised Edition, Harper Collins.
53. Heidegger, Martin (1964) *ibid.*
54. Krell, David, F. (1993) *ibid.*
55. Heidegger, Martin (1961) "On the Essence of Truth (Fourth Edition)". English translation in David F. Krell (Editor) (1993) *Martin Heidegger: Basic Writings from Being and Time (1927) to The Task of Thinking (1964)*, Revised Edition, Harper Collins.
56. Heidegger, Martin (1964) *ibid.*
57. Heidegger, Martin (1964) *ibid.*
58. Clarke, John J. (1997) *ibid.*
59. King, Richard (1999) *Orientalism and Religion: Postcolonial Theory, India and 'The Mystic East'*, Routledge.
60. Dallmayr, Fred (1996) *Beyond Orientalism: Essays on Cross-Cultural Encounter*, State University of New York Press.
61. Globus, Gordon, G. (2003) *Quantum Closures and Disclosures: Thinking-together postphenomenology and quantum brain dynamics*, John Benjamins Publishing Co.
62. *Ibid.*
63. *Ibid.*
64. *Ibid.*
65. *Ibid.*
66. Merrell-Wolff, Franklin (1994) *Franklin Merrell-Wolff's Experience and Philosophy: A Personal Record of Transformation and a Discussion of Transcendental Consciousness*: Containing his *Philosophy of Consciousness without an Object* and *His Pathways through to Space*, State University of New York Press.
67. Meier, C.A. (Editor) (2001) *Atom and Archetype: The Pauli/Jung Letters 1932–1958,* Routledge.
68. Meier, C.A. (Editor) (2001) *ibid.*
69. Bruzina, Ronald (2004) *ibid.*
70. Bruzina, Ronald (2004) *ibid.*
71. Coward, Harold *with contributions by* J. Borelli, J.F. T Jordens and J. Henderson (1985) *Jung and Eastern Thought*, State University of New York Press.
72. Clarke, John, J. (1994) *Jung and Eastern Thought: A dialogue with the Orient*, Routledge.
73. Merrell-Wolff, Franklin (1995) *Transformations in Consciousness: The Metaphysics and Epistemology* (Containing His *Introceptualism*), State University of New York Press.

74. Odajnyk, V. Walter (1993) *Gathering the Light: A Psychology of Meditation*, Shambhala Publications.
75. Odajnyk, V. Walter (1993) *ibid.*
76. Radhakrishnan, Sarvepalli (1953) *The Principal Upanisads*, (Centenary Edition 1989), Unwin Hyman.
77. Radhakrishnan, Sarvepalli (1940) *Eastern Religions and Western Thought (2nd Edn),* Oxford University Press.
78. Odajnyk, V. Walter (1993) *ibid.*
79. Odajnyk, V. Walter (1993) *ibid.*
80. Coward, Harold *with contributions by* J. Borelli, J.F. T Jordens and J. Henderson (1985) *ibid.*
81. Von Franz, Marie-Louise (1992) *Psyche and Matter*, Shambhala Publications.
82. Ghose, Aurobindo (Sri Aurobindo) (1948) *The Synthesis of Yoga*, Sri Aurobindo Ashram Publications.
83. Lindorff, David (2004) *Jung and Pauli: The Meeting of Two Great Minds*, Quest Books.
84. Coward, Harold *with contributions by* J. Borelli, J.F. T Jordens and J. Henderson (1985) *ibid.*
85. Segal, Robert A. (1992) *The Gnostic Jung*, Princeton University Press.
86. Odajnyk, V. Walter (1993) *ibid.*
87. Dourley, John "The Innate Capacity: Jung and the Mystical Imperative". In Robert K.C. Forman (Editor) (1998) *The Innate Capacity: Mysticism, Psychology, and Philosophy*, State University of New York Press.
88. *Ibid.*
89. *Ibid.*
90. Huxley, Aldous (1943) "Religion and Time". Reprinted in Jacqueline H. Bridgeman (Editor) (1992) *Huxley and God: Essays*, Harper Collins.
91. Dourley, John (1998) *ibid.*
92. Braude, Stephen E. "The Synchronicity Confusion". In William G. Roll (Editor) (1979) *Research in Parapsychology*, Scarecrow Press.
93. Meier, C.A. (Editor) (2001) *ibid.*
94. Dourley, John (1998) *ibid.*
95. Magee, Glen A. (2001) *Hegel and the Hermetic Tradition*, Cornell University Press.
96. Dourley, John (1998) *ibid.*
97. Dourley, John (1998) *ibid.*
98. Jordens, J.F.T. "Prâna and Libido: Prajñâ and Consciousness". In Harold Coward *with contributions by* J. Borelli, J.F. T Jordens and J. Henderson (1985) *Jung and Eastern Thought*, State University of New York Press.
99. Stevens, Anthony (2002) *Archetype Revisited: An Updated Natural History of the Self* (2nd Edn), Brunner-Routledge (Taylor and Francis).
100. Stevens, Anthony (2002) *ibid.*
101. Dourley, John (1998) *ibid.*
102. *Ibid.*

103. *Ibid.*

104. *Ibid.*

105. *Ibid.*

106. *Ibid.*

107. Streng, Frederick "The Transcendental in a Comparative Context". In Elliot Deutsch (Editor) (1991) *Culture and Modernity: East-West Philosophic Perspectives*, University of Hawaii Press.

108. Huxley, Aldous (1942) "Man and Reality" and (1941) "Distractions –1". Both reprinted in Jacqueline H. Bridgeman (Editor) (1992) *Huxley and God: Essays*, Harper Collins.

109. Jung, Carl G. (1961) "Visions/Life After Death" (From *Memories, Dreams, Reflections*). Reprinted in Lee W. Bailey and Jenny Yates (Editors) (1996) *The Near-Death Experience: A Reader*, Routledge.

110. Coward, Harold *with contributions by* J. Borelli, J.F. T Jordens and J. Henderson (1985) *ibid.*

111. von Franz, Marie-Louise (1974) "Matter and Psyche from the Point of View of Carl Jung". English translation in Marie-Louise von Franz (1992) *Psyche and Matter*, Shambhala Publications.

112. Von Franz, Marie-Louise (1968) "Symbols of the *Unus Mundus*". English translation in Marie-Louise von Franz (1992) *Psyche and Matter*, Shambhala Publications.

113. Long, J. Bruce "The Concepts of Human Action and Rebirth in the *Mahâbhârata*". In Wendy Doniger O'Flaherty (Editor) (1980) *Karma and Rebirth in the Classical Indian Traditions*, University of California Press.

114. von Franz, Marie-Louise (1998) *On Dreams and Death: A Jungian Interpretation*. Open Court.

115. Stevens, Anthony (2002) *ibid.*

116. *Ibid.*

117. *Ibid.*

118. Weber, Renée (1986) *Dialogues with Scientists and Sages: The Search for Unity*, Routledge and Kegan Paul.

119. King, Richard (1999) *Orientalism and Religion: Postcolonial Theory, India and 'The Mystic East'*, Routledge.

120. Merrell-Wolff, Franklin (1994) *ibid.*

121. Leonard, Ron (1999) *The Transcendental Philosophy of Franklin Merrell-Wolff*, State University of New York Press.

122. Merrell-Wolff, Franklin (1995) *ibid.*

123. Whiteman, J.H. Michael (1967) *ibid.*

124. Whiteman, J.H. Michael (2006) *Universal Theology and Life in the Other Worlds*, Colin Smythe.

125. Ellison, Arthur J. "Western Science and Religious Experience". In T.D. Singh (Editor)(1987) *Synthesis of Science and Religion: Critical Essays and Dialogues*, The Bhaktvedanta Institute.

126. Merrell-Wolff, Franklin (1995) *ibid.*

127. *Ibid.*
128. *Ibid.*
129. *Ibid.*
130. Merrell-Wolff, Franklin (1995) *ibid.*
131. Merrell-Wolff, Franklin (1995) *ibid.*
132. Merrell-Wolff, Franklin (1994) *ibid.*
133. Lott, Eric (1980) *Vedantic Approaches to God*, MacMillan/Harper and Row.
134. Gupta, Bina (2003) *Cit Consciousness*, Oxford University Press India.
135. Leonard, Ron (1999) *ibid.*
136. Chatterji, J.C. (1931) *India's Outlook on Life: The Wisdom of the Vedas*, (reprinted 1973 as *The Wisdom of the Vedas*) The Theosophical Publishing House.
137. Whiteman, J.H. Michael (1986) *Old and New Evidence on the Meaning of Life: The Mystical World-View and Inner Contest–An Introduction to Scientific Mysticism*, Colin Smythe.